*When should I travel to get the best*
*Where do I go for answers to*
*What's the best and easiest way to*

# frommers.travelocity.com

**Frommer's**, the travel guide leader, has teamed up with **Travelocity.com**, the leader in online travel, to bring you an in-depth, easy-to-use resource designed to help you plan and book your trip online.

At **frommers.travelocity.com**, you'll find free online updates about your destination from the experts at Frommer's plus the outstanding travel planning and purchasing features of Travelocity.com. Travelocity.com provides reservations capabilities for 95 percent of all airline seats sold, more than 47,000 hotels, and over 50 car rental companies. In addition, Travelocity.com offers more than 2,000 exciting vacation and cruise packages. Travelocity.com puts you in complete control of your travel planning with these and other great features:

**Expert travel guidance from Frommer's** - over 150 writers reporting from around the world!

**Best Fare Finder** - an interactive calendar tells you when to travel to get the best airfare

**Fare Watcher** - we'll track airfare changes to your favorite destinations

**Dream Maps** - a mapping feature that suggests travel opportunities based on your budget

**Shop Safe Guarantee** - 24 hours a day / 7 days a week live customer service, and more!

Whether traveling on a tight budget, looking for a quick weekend getaway, or planning the trip of a lifetime, Frommer's guides and Travelocity.com will make your travel dreams a reality. You've bought the book, now book the trip!

## OTHER GREAT GUIDES FOR YOUR TRIP:

*Frommer's Grand Canyon National Park*

*Frommer's National Parks of the American West*

*Frommer's Rocky Mountain National Park*

*Frommer's Yellowstone & Grand Teton National Parks*

*Frommer's Yosemite & Sequoia/Kings Canyon National Parks*

*Frommer's Zion & Bryce Canyon National Parks*

# Frommer's®

# Family Vacations

## in the

# National Parks

### 2nd Edition

## Charles Wohlforth

## Hungry Minds™

Best-Selling Books • Digital Downloads • e-Books • Answer Networks
e-Newsletters • Branded Web Sites • e-Learning
New York, NY • Cleveland, OH • Indianapolis, IN

## About the Author

**Charles Wohlforth** is a writer of books and magazine articles who lives in Anchorage, Alaska. His other book for Hungry Minds is *Frommer's Alaska*. With his wife, Barbara, an elementary school teacher, and their children, Robin, Julia, Joseph, and Rebecca, Wohlforth spends much of each summer camping, hiking, and boating in Alaska. In the winter the family cross-country skis and ice-skates. He welcomes e-mail from readers with questions, ideas, or criticisms at Wohlforth@gci.net, or check www.wohlforth.net for more writings and answers to others' questions. Postal mail can be sent through the publisher.

Published by:

**HUNGRY MINDS, INC.**
909 Third Ave.
New York, NY 10022

ISBN 0-7645-6363-7
ISSN 1092-6674

Editor: Amy Lyons
Production Editor: M. Faunette Johnston
Cartographer: Roberta Stockwell
Photo Editor: Richard Fox
Production by Hungry Minds Indianapolis Production Services

## Special Sales

For general information on Hungry Minds' products and services, please contact our Customer Care department, within the U.S. at 800/762-2974, outside the U.S. at 317/572-3993 or fax 317/572-4002. For sales inquiries and reseller information, including discounts, bulk sales, customized editions, and premium sales, please contact our Customer Care department at 800/434-3422.

Manufactured in the United States of America

5  4  3  2  1

# C O N T E N T S

## 10 Glen Canyon National Recreation Area 224

## 11 Zion National Park 240

## 12 Bryce Canyon National Park 256

# PART V   THE ROCKIES 273

## 13 The Nature of High Places 275

**Index  532**

# LIST OF MAPS

## An Invitation to the Reader

In researching this book, we discovered many wonderful places — hotels, restaurants, shops, and more. We're sure you'll find others. Please tell us about them so that we can share the information with your fellow travelers in upcoming editions. If you were disappointed with a recommendation, we'd love to know that, too. Please write to:

*Frommer's Family Vacations in the National Parks,* 2nd Edition
Hungry Minds, Inc. • 909 Third Avenue • New York, NY 10022

## An Additional Note

Please be advised that travel information is subject to change at any time — and this is especially true of prices. We therefore suggest that you write or call ahead for confirmation when making your travel plans. The authors, editors, and publisher cannot be held responsible for the experiences of readers while traveling. Your safety is important to us, however, so we encourage you to stay alert and be aware of your surroundings. Keep a close eye on cameras, purses, and wallets, all favorite targets of thieves and pickpockets.

## Acknowledgments

*This book is dedicated to my children, Robin, Julia, Joseph, and Becky, for our wilderness travels together, past and future.*

The members of my family were almost co-authors of this book, for the first and second editions. For the second edition, Don and Barbara Laine took responsibility for updating the chapters on the Southwest parks; they are true professionals, and their Frommer's books on that part of the country are invaluable for travelers. Many generous experts also gave their time for this edition: professors, scientists, and park naturalists who reviewed my natural history chapters and made valuable suggestions for improvement (although the mistakes remain my responsibility, not theirs). Dr. William Forgey, president of the Wilderness Medical Society, helped with the medical and safety information; from the University of Alaska Fairbanks, Dr. Paul Layer reviewed geology information, Dr. Roseann Leiner helped with plant biology, and Richard Steiner reviewed information on West Coast ecology and marine life; Jim Peronto of the National Weather Service reviewed meteorology information; Dr. Robert Christiansen of the U.S. Geological Survey helped with Rockies and Sierra geology; and Donald Collins and Dr. L. Charles Sun of the National Oceanic and Atmospheric Administration assisted with East Coast oceanography and beach morphology. There were many others with the National Park Service who deserve my thanks, including John Quinley, Barbara Maynes, Kris Fister, John A. Dell'Osso, Wanda Moran, Joan Anzelmo, Bob Woody, Kate McCurdy, and Deb Schweizer, as well as others too numerous to mention, including reviewers they coordinated whom I never met. My own researchers were also invaluable, including Wendy Feuer, who worked on the first edition, and, for the second edition, Angela Baily, Tataboline Brant, Lynn Englishbee, Peter Porco, Sarana Schell, Andrea Senn, and Kerry Wilson.

The following abbreviations are used for credit cards:

| AE | American Express | DISC | Discover | V | Visa |
|----|------------------|------|----------|---|------|
| DC | Diners Club | MC | MasterCard | | |

## Frommers.com

Now that you have the guidebook to a great trip, visit our website at **www.frommers.com** for travel information on nearly 2,000 destinations. With features updated regularly, we give you instant access to the most current trip-planning information available. At Frommers.com, you'll also find the best prices on airfares, accommodations, and car rentals — and you can even book travel online through our travel booking partners. At Frommers.com you'll also find the following:

- Daily Newsletter highlighting the best travel deals
- Hot Spot of the Month/Vacation Sweepstakes & Travel Photo Contest
- More than 200 Travel Message Boards
- Outspoken Newsletters and Feature Articles on travel bargains, vacation ideas, tips & resources, and more!

# Taking Kids to the National Parks

*Choosing where to go and when to go, knowing the reservation systems, planning an itinerary, and staying safe and happy on the road. We've boiled down some of our hard-earned lessons from years of traveling and camping with kids, and included sample packing lists, recommended reading, and health and safety tips.*

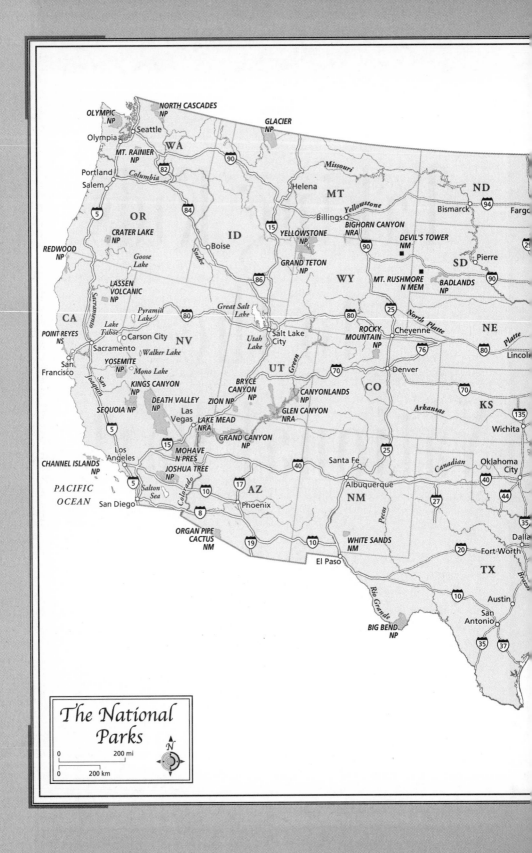

# The National Parks

0    200 mi

0    200 km

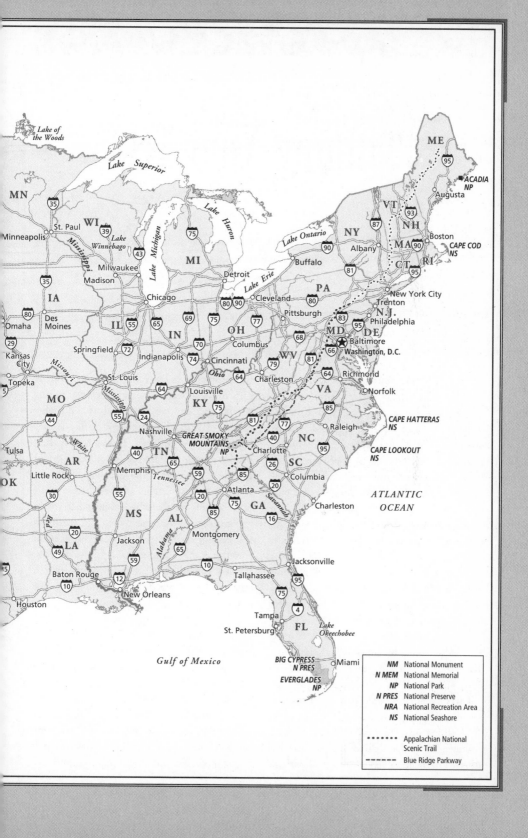

# Planning Your Trip

When our son, Robin, was 5, and our daughter, Julia, was 2, we set off on our first national park odyssey, a 7-week trip from our home in Alaska to California, Massachusetts, North Carolina, Maine, and states in between, researching the first edition of this book. When we returned, my wife, Barbara, and I attended a dinner party with some other parents. Around the table, the conversation came to vacations. Parents told the horror stories all parents tell of miserable flights and restaurant meals with toddlers. What to do with the kids? One dad suggested leaving them behind with family or friends; another couple said they'd stopped traveling until their children were older. When I told everyone that we'd been camping most of the summer and covered thousands of miles by air, train, car, and boat, all with our children, the conversation halted. People stared at us in amazement.

Three years later, we did it again for this second edition, adding to the itinerary parks in Washington, Idaho, Wyoming, and Montana. We also added Joseph, who had just turned 1, to make a party of five. And Barbara was pregnant. As I've told friends, a cliff diver sometimes adds a couple of extra twists during the plunge, and we were ready for a higher degree of difficulty. But, in truth, the trip wasn't scary or difficult. It was a rich, fun, inspiring, unforgettable communion with our children, the most important people in our lives. Their innocent joy and fascination made it so. Again, we shared moments that would become some of our most vivid and meaningful memories. We faced the challenges of travel and the outdoors as a family, and we learned to work together to solve problems in strange places, away from familiar things. We made many campsites into home.

Traveling with children demands extra planning and requires narrower limits than traveling alone. The reward of living your life deeply with your children demands certain sacrifices. Before we had children, Barbara and I would travel by tossing a guidebook and some clothes into a suitcase and flying somewhere. We'd open the book for the first time on the plane to look for a hotel. Now each day is planned, campsites and hotel rooms are reserved months ahead, driving times are carefully calculated to avoid backseat meltdown. The destinations have changed, too. Fewer cities, art museums, and country inns; more open skies, seashores, and forests — places where children have the freedom they crave, and parents can enjoy that freedom with them.

Don't go to the national parks because you think you are supposed to see certain places before you grow up. Be concerned, instead, to make the most of a time when you may be closer to your children, and come to know them better, than at any other in your lives. These natural places make children and adults equals in their wonder. You don't need to know how to read to understand the splendor; in fact, it may be an impediment. Parents can teach their children about natural history; children can teach their parents to see the beauty around them.

The parks can challenge every member of the family both physically and mentally. You can come home with real accomplishments to think back on. And the towns around the parks are accustomed to serving families. You don't have to worry about fitting in, and you'll likely meet other families with children. Many park areas even have educational programs and camps that allow children and parents to spend time apart, learning on their own.

We've taken some trips that no one in their right mind would plan if they weren't writing a book: No one else would skip back and forth across the country to cover the 16 national parks we had to research for each of the two editions. But we wouldn't have missed it.

## WHY THIS BOOK?

This book is unique. It is both a travel book and a read-aloud guide to the natural history and culture of the national parks. The book's definite philosophy can be summed up in five words: Get out of the car. You will find no tips on the best highlights for a 1-day visit, because a 1-day visit to a place like Yellowstone or Cape Cod is simply a waste. Instead, we have set out to include everything you need to know when spending your family's vacation in a park or collection of parks. Your family will come home knowing and understanding that place — its geology, weather, plants, animals, history, people, and controversies.

For the 16 parks we included in this book, we labored to include the kind of details that help to make your visit as easy and pleasant as possible. You can get away from crowds, but often the only way is by possessing information the rest of the crowd doesn't have: certain places they don't know about, tricks of the reservation systems for scarce campsites and backcountry permits, and times when the trails are clear. No other book I'm aware of provides the kind of extensive campground reviews we've included, covering every campground in the parks and many in nearby national forests, state parks, and towns. Park chapters also have hotel reviews and exact prices for almost everything. The restaurant reviews cover places where you can relax with children and those where the kids are welcome but need to be on their best behavior.

*Family Vacations in the National Parks* also covers the nature and culture of the parks at a level accessible to children (depending on their age and the subject matter). We've included science activities and campfire read-aloud stories for fun and learning. Our children went on most of these trips, and their observations helped determine what we recommend. Robin and I invented and tested the experiments to map river eddies and built a baby-bottle altimeter. I have consumed a library of science and nature literature to attain the level of understanding that would allow me to explain it at a level they could understand. For this second edition, university and government scientists have checked all this material for accuracy as well. We went back to the basics: What are tides? Why are some rocks red? Why does it rain? Why do plants grow? How does a glacier work? How do mountains become mountains? Together, these chapters answer many of the questions a curious child will ask about nature.

## HOW TO USE THIS BOOK

The book consists of six regional sections. Some material, such as the travel-planning information, is written for adults. The educational and fun stuff and descriptions of places are written to be read aloud to kids or read by older children.

Each section starts with a chapter on the natural history and culture of the parks in that region. These chapters are written for families to read together, but some material will require explanation for younger children. At 8, Robin had few problems with it; Julia, 5, needed us to stop more often to explain the terms. Rather than reading aloud in the car, consider reading the chapters to yourself before you go, then explaining what you see in the park when the topic comes up.

The first part of the chapter introduces the region and talks about why you might want to visit it. Next is a natural-history essay to help you understand the area. There's a different natural history theme for each region, so you may find chapters of interest and relevance for regions you don't plan to visit. Next is "The Little Field Guide," a selection of plants and animals that you may see, with drawings of some. I've primarily included easy-to-find species so that children can have some success in searching around the campground. Next is a history and culture essay, touching on Native American history and conservation values and issues, intended for the entire family to share and discuss.

Next comes a detailed chapter for each park in the region, with all the travel information you need for a week's vacation. Each park chapter starts with a directory of contact information, the "Address Book," followed by a quick sketch of the park to help you decide if you want to go there, then a park history you can read aloud. The travel-planning information is divided into two parts. "Making the Arrangements" has what you need to know before you go, including weather, getting there, lodgings and campgrounds, packing and reservation tips, and so on. "When You Arrive" includes information you'll need once you're at the park: a handy reference for local stores, hospitals, gear rental, and the like; locations and hours of visitor centers; and regulations, safety tips, and the like. The section called "Enjoying the Park" describes the places to go and things to do in detail, with some tour-guide information to share with the group. Finally, the section on where to eat gives details on places and prices, including whether children can relax or need to mind their manners.

Within the chapters, you'll find fun pieces to read aloud and activities to try with your children, all related to the parks where they are found. Most apply to other places too, so you can use the table of contents and flip through the book to find topics and activities that interest you.

## DECISIONS: WHERE, WHEN & HOW TO GO

The first step in planning a trip is to decide where and when you want to go. Next, make the related, balancing decisions of how to travel and how much time and money to spend when you get there.

### CHOOSING YOUR DESTINATION

Besides your interests, two factors should lead your considerations in narrowing down your choices: when you can travel, and what your kids can handle.

## Advance Planning Time

For most of us, work and school requirements determine vacation dates. Once you get your vacation dates, you should decide if they are far enough in the future to plan a trip to the place you want to go to. For some of the best choices in this book, you have to send in deposits by October for the following summer; most often, February or March is a cut-off for midsummer. But at some parks, you need only a couple of weeks for advance planning. Crowding and reservation complications depend on the season, with different factors at each park. Each park chapter includes these details under "How Far to Plan Ahead" in the "Before You Go" section. Break the offered guidelines to go where you really want to go, but be ready to accept second-best choices, such as lodgings and campgrounds outside the park.

## Travel Seasons

Here are considerations on finding good weather and avoiding crowds.

### CROWDING

Most families can go on vacation only when school is out: during summer vacation, spring break, or the winter holidays. For that reason, these are the busiest times at the national parks. Within these times, however, are considerable variations. For some parks, avoiding weekends gets you away from crowds, although that is less true distant from major cities. In other parks, earlier in the summer is better than later. Spring break is almost always less crowded than summer, and can be the best time to visit the hot Southwest parks. (I've covered the details under "When to Go" in the "Making the Arrangements" section of each park chapter.)

At any time of year, crowding is as bad as you let it be. Crowds are enough to spoil the experience only at busy times at famous places. If you feel you have to see all the famous places, expect to be crowded. But you can get away from people at every park — it's just a question of how hard you try. The best way to do it is to use your feet, a horse, or a canoe to get off the road. Planning well ahead and using the reservation systems to your advantage also help get the best the parks have to offer even at the busiest times. Most park campgrounds don't feel crowded even when they're full — but you have to have a reservation months ahead. I'll show you how to do that later in this chapter, and I'll give specifics under "Making the Arrangements" in each park chapter.

If you don't have to go during school breaks, or if your breaks are different from most, crowds won't be a major consideration. I've often found parks deserted in the shoulder seasons, which are the months adjacent to the most popular visiting periods at the park. (For example, if the high season at a park is June–Sept, then the shoulder-season months are May and Oct.) On some of our shoulder-season trips, prices were lower and the weather was as good or better as in the high season. September is the best month at many mountain parks and national seashores. The dead off-season months offer lots of open country and very low prices, but facilities often operate shorter hours or close altogether, and the weather can shut down activities.

### CLIMATE

Summer weather is the best at most of the parks, and for most families with children in school, summer is the only practical time to visit the mountain parks and national seashores. Aiming for the best weather within the summer probably won't be a productive effort: The variations are too small to give you more than a small chance of better weather in, say, July than in August. On the other hand, it may be worth a few more bugs or colder ocean water to go in a less-crowded June. Summertime generally is too hot for hiking in the Southwest, except at high elevations.

Spring break is a good time to visit some parks, especially in the Southwest, even if the weather isn't the best — often you don't need the very best weather to enjoy a park, anyway. Winter-break trips mostly are for skiing, snowshoeing, or sightseeing. Snowy parks are an entirely different experience, but a rewarding one in their own right. On the other hand, some parks are simply impossible at off-season times. I've included weather statistics and seasonal climate descriptions in each park chapter, under "When to Go" in the "Making the Arrangements" section.

The chart on the next page summarizes the best seasons for each park in terms of crowding, weather, and key activities.

## The Right Age?

The age and capabilities of your children should guide your trip planning. Here are some of our ideas.

### KINDS OF PARKS

We have never found a park that we and our children did not enjoy, but some age-related choices have to be made. The national seashores, Acadia National Park and Glen Canyon National Recreation Area, lack long hiking trails, but have lots of recreation opportunities for children under 10, at the beach, in the marsh, biking, swimming, and boating. Families with strong hikers may prefer to challenge themselves with overnights and long day hikes in the big wilderness parks, such as Grand Canyon, Grand Teton, Great Smoky, Olympic, Rocky Mountain, Sequoia/Kings Canyon, Yellowstone, and Yosemite. Of these, all except Grand Canyon are also great for younger children. Nonhikers should plan to visit the Grand Canyon in a tour that also includes Zion, Bryce Canyon, and possibly Glen Canyon, because there's not as much to do there for younger children.

### TRAVEL DISTANCES

How far can you haul your kids? Long drives and flights with small children can be torture. (For tips on how to keep them busy, see "Practicalities: Our Favorite Car Entertainment," in chapter 13, "The Nature

of High Places.") Also, we've observed a strange physical principle, the law of the inverse relation of child size and luggage quantity. It states that the younger the child, the more luggage involved. If you've ever traveled with an infant, you know what I mean: diaper bag, bottle paraphernalia, portable crib, stroller, special bedding, and so on. Add your camping gear to the pile, and you feel as if you need a caravan of camels to move around. (I've included some tips on how to reduce the load under "Packing to Fly & Camp," on p. 21.)

Thought and planning overcome many of the drawbacks of going a long way with children. If a drive would be too hard, for instance, take a plane or a train and rent a car when you get there. If you've whittled down your luggage and you still can't manage it, buy or rent gear when you get there (see the "For Handy Reference" section in each park chapter for rental information). We use the post office to send back extra gear or things we pick up on the way. Renting an RV can make it all easier, too (that's covered under "Practicalities: The RV Advantage," in chapter 8, "Layers upon Layers").

### APPROPRIATE CHALLENGES

Know what your children are capable of, and plan a trip that's within those limits. Adults can challenge themselves physically, but if you try that with kids, you make everyone unhappy and teach your children to hate the outdoors. That goes for both young children and teens — any physical test has to be self-inflicted.

How much is too much? Many books give guidelines on how old children should be for certain activities or how far they can hike at certain ages. The guidelines aren't accurate or helpful because every child is dramatically different in physical ability and attitude. The only good solution is to know your child's personal best (see "Practicalities: Tracking Your Child's Personal Best," on p. 15), and then plan trips that stay within or just barely push that limit.

An important part of this philosophy is not to get hung up on destinations. Having your mind set on climbing a certain peak or focusing on a certain activity the kids haven't done before can lead to trouble and disappointment. Don't make extended time on horseback or in a sea kayak a major part of your vacation unless you already know that your kids enjoy doing those things and are ready for the challenge. (The parks *are* a great place to try these activities for the first time on short outings.)

The families who have the most fun outdoors, and who grow the toughest, most enthusiastic children, are those who spend a lot of relaxed time together doing things that they all enjoy. The adults I know who hate the outdoors had parents who made them go on long hikes with the drill-sergeant attitude that they had to toughen up and learn to enjoy it. They learned the opposite.

# How to Travel

Choosing how you travel depends on how you value your time, money, and comfort, and how much luggage you need to bring.

## Getting There

How far can you go without ruining the day for everyone? Depending on age and personality, children have different levels of travel tolerance, but anyone can stand to be strapped in for only so long before turning into a monster. My experience tells me that tolerance levels are shortest on airplanes, followed by cars, trains, and boats. Our kids could be happy on a boat indefinitely. I only wish boats went more places.

Of course, planes get the misery over fast. You may be able to put up with one bad day traveling, but not with the pain of spending a large percentage of your vacation driving with kids saying, "Are we there yet?" hour after hour. On the other hand, flying and renting a car is expensive, and creates problems with moving your stuff around.

## By Car

Going by car is the classic and most popular way to visit the national parks, and that's the approach I've covered in greatest depth. At most parks, having a family car is a virtual necessity. The question is, should you bring your own from home or rent one there? Driving your own car offers simplicity,

familiarity, and low cost. There's almost no limit to how much **luggage** you can take if you put on a roof rack, bike rack, or trailer. That means you don't have to rent gear at the park, and can take along bulky extras — even your canoe or kayak.

On the other hand, if you look no further than the parks you can drive to from home, you will be missing out on a lot of wonderful places. And driving all the way across the country is expensive as well as tiring. The driving time from New York to San Francisco is about 60 hours, without stops. Counting the cost of food, rooms, and gas, the round-trip cost for a family of four is roughly the same to fly or drive (about $2,400, by my rough calculation), and that's driving 10 hours a day. As the distances get shorter, the savings of driving increase, but don't forget to count the cost of your time sitting in the car rather than having fun.

## By Air
### Coping

Short flights can be easy and fun, a wise alternative to a day or two of driving. But an airplane's advantage of novelty and excitement wears off long before the end of a long flight, and soon the kid realizes she's strapped into a seat in a noisy metal tube. That's when life gets difficult. The solution is to plan the trip the way a circus ringmaster prepares a show, with

| | BEST ACTIVITIES | SPRING BREAK |
|---|---|---|
| **Acadia** <br> *Bar Harbor, ME* <br> *Chapter 3* | Bicycling, canoeing, day hiking, tide pooling, sea kayaking, whale watching. | Cool, foggy, not much open until May. |
| **Bryce Canyon** <br> *Southern Utah* <br> *Chapter 12* | Day hiking, backpacking, horseback riding, cross-country skiing; mountain biking nearby. | Cold at night, with some snow left, but quiet and especially beautiful. |
| **Cape Cod** <br> *Eastham, MA* <br> *Chapter 4* | Swimming, beach and nature walks, boating, bird- and whale watching, historic sites. | Cool, quiet; water too cold for swimming. Not much open. |
| **Cape Hatteras** <br> *Manteo, NC* <br> *Chapter 5* | Swimming, beach and nature walks, boating, fishing, historic sites. | Comfortable weather, quiet, with off-season prices. Water cold for swimming. |
| **Glen Canyon** <br> *Page, AZ* <br> *Chapter 10* | Boating, swimming, day hikes. | Comfortable temperatures, water too cold for swimming, good hiking, low prices, no crowds. |
| **Grand Canyon** <br> *Northern Arizona* <br> *Chapter 9* | Sightseeing, hiking, backpacking. | Snow possible in early spring, comfortable in canyon. Best time for hiking and backpacking. Crowds. |
| **Grand Teton** <br> *Jackson, WY* <br> *Chapter 15* | Hiking, backpacking, horseback riding, mountain biking, canoeing, river rafting, fishing. | Cold and snowy. |
| **Great Smoky Mountains** <br> *Gatlinburg, TN* <br> *Chapter 7* | Hiking, backpacking, historic sites, horseback riding, inner-tubing, swimming; river rafting, mountain biking near park. | Comfortable daytime temperatures, cool evenings, weather changeable in March, few crowds. Best flowers. |
| **Olympic** <br> *Port Angeles, WA* <br> *Chapter 22* | Hiking, backpacking, wildlife watching, tide pooling, sea kayaking, river rafting, skiing. | Cool and damp; whale watching, no crowds, skiing through March. |
| **Point Reyes** <br> *Marin County, CA* <br> *Chapter 21* | Beach walking, hiking, limited backpacking, whale and bird-watching, sea kayaking, mountain biking. | Foggy and windy, whale watching, no crowds. Best flowers. |
| **Rocky Mountain** <br> *Estes Park, CO* <br> *Chapter 16* | Hiking, backpacking, wildlife watching, climbing, snowshoeing. | Snow still on ground, major routes not open. |
| **Sequoia/Kings Canyon** <br> *Three Rivers, CA* <br> *Chapter 19* | Hiking, backpacking, horseback riding, river swimming, giant trees, cross-country skiing. | Snow still in campgrounds, some routes closed. Foothills area comfortable. |
| **Yellowstone** <br> *Northwest Wyoming* <br> *Chapter 14* | Hiking, backpacking, sightseeing, horseback riding, boating, fishing, cross-country skiing. | Roads still closed by snow, sometimes bike season in April. |

| SUMMER VACATION | FALL | WINTER |
|---|---|---|
| Peak season. June has bugs, but fewer crowds than July and August. Whale season ends mid-August. | Cool and quiet. Things start closing in September. | Not practical. Some skiing, but snow not reliable. Most tourist facilities closed. |
| Peak season. Comfortable temperatures, lots of people. | Cool and quiet. Wintry weather starting in October. | Cross-country skiing and snowshoeing. Park hotel closed. |
| Peak season. Quieter in June, but water still cold. July and August warm and busy. | Quiet, with good weather into October. Whales gone. | Cold and deserted. |
| Peak season. Hot in July and August with warm water, cooler in June with ocean water still cool. | Temperatures and swimming perfect into October. Hurricane season peaks mid-August through October. | Cold and deserted. |
| Too hot for hiking, good swimming, reservations needed many months in advance, Lake Powell busy. | Best time to visit. Cooler air, water still warm, reservations easier to get. | Weather unpredictable, can be chilly. Low prices; many facilities closed. |
| Busiest season, with heavy crowding. Temperatures comfortable on rim, too hot in canyon for much hiking. | Comfortable temperature on rim and in canyon, fewer crowds. | Snowy on the rim, comfortable in the canyon. Unpredictable weather, few visitors. |
| Busiest season and best weather in July and August, with June also good at lower elevations. | September good, quiet. Everything shuts down mid-October. | Skiing at Jackson, but park largely snowed in. |
| Warm and humid at lower elevations, comfortable in mountains. Popular areas crowded, especially on weekends. | October foliage season brings peak crowding on roads and high prices. Weather comfortable, drier than rest of year. | Snow in the mountains, rain below. Cool weather, few visitors. |
| Peak season. Drier weather July and August, marine mammal watching, room reservations needed. | Cool and damp. Few visitors. | Heavy snow at higher elevations, extremely wet at lower elevations. |
| Foggy and windy on coast, warmer and clearer inland, no rain, busy on weekends. | Dry, clear, comfortable weather, little fog, no crowds. | Peak whale watching. Rainstorms, cooler weather. |
| Peak season July and August. Snow still in high country in June. Warm, thunderstorms. Crowded weekends. | September weather excellent, few crowds. Snow closes high country in later fall. | Best winter sports January and February. |
| Peak season. Comfortable temperatures in most of park, crowding on weekends. | Perfect weather with few visitors; snow in late fall. | Cross-country skiing. Much of park snowed in. |
| Peak season. Comfortable temperatures, thunderstorms, heavy crowding, reservations essential. | September days comfortable, cool at night, no crowds, most facilities close in October. | Excellent cross-country skiing late December to early March; deep snow. |

| | BEST ACTIVITIES | SPRING BREAK |
|---|---|---|
| **Yosemite**<br>*El Portal, CA*<br>*Chapter 18* | Hiking, backpacking, sightseeing, climbing, rafting, horseback riding, river swimming, skiing. | Still snowy in high country, Yosemite Valley open, cold in March, cool in April. |
| **Zion**<br>*Springdale, UT*<br>*Chapter 11* | Hiking, backpacking, sightseeing; nearby mountain biking and inner-tubing. | Comfortable temperatures in canyon, still snowy or muddy above the rim. Manageable crowds. |

new sources of entertainment always ready to pull out. Regardless of your preparations, however, toddlers can't stand long flights, and will administer a unique and humiliating form of torture for the last couple of hours (this may be God's punishment for original sin now that we have pain drugs for childbirth). Don't forget a full medicine kit in case of stomachaches, earaches, airsickness, diarrhea (the stories I could tell), and general misery.

If your kid falls asleep on an airplane, you feel like you've won the lottery. Can you bring this about intentionally? You can fly at night, with a cranky, tired child who will probably sleep, or fly during the day, with a cheerful child who will probably stay awake. The night flight is only for gamblers. If the kid sleeps, great, but if he or she doesn't, you're in for a night with a tired, unhappy kid strapped into a seat with 300 trying-to-sleep strangers — a nightmare for you and everyone else.

## TICKET PRICES

Flying with a family is expensive, and time spent shopping for a good deal is well worth the effort. Start well ahead, watching for fare sales, which crop up at certain times of year for different destinations. A good travel agent can help you here, more than earning any added commission you have to pay. He or she will know what a good deal is, and will know how to find children's companion fares, which vary by airline and route and can save as much as 50%; that's tough to do shopping on the

Internet. If you want to go it alone, sign up for e-mail notification of fare sales at any of many websites, including Fare Watcher at travelocity.com. The cheapest tickets are simple round-trips between two large cities; avoid flying in triangles or using small commuter airports (see "Gateways," below). You can carry infants on your lap, saving the cost of a ticket, if you think you can stand it. We always buy a ticket for the baby and bring an FAA-approved car seat along, for the same reason we wouldn't carry a baby in our laps in the car.

## LUGGAGE & THE RENTAL CAR

Flying makes moving your luggage more complicated. The problem arises in the rental car itself, not the plane or transfers. After all, each passenger is allowed two bags, which can be huge duffel bags or, our favorite, hockey goalie bags: You can fit an awful lot of stuff in these things. When you arrive, you can rent a cart or hire a Skycap to get the luggage to the car. If you have to take a van to the car, bring the car back to the ramp to get the luggage. The problem arises when you try to fit the stuff into the car. Even a so-called full-sized car (a Taurus, Impala, or Intrepid) doesn't have enough cargo space for all the stuff a family needs for a camping vacation. It's difficult to tie stuff onto modern cars without a luggage rack, which rentals generally don't have. Renting a minivan, which *will* fit all your gear, is quite expensive. While prices range widely by market and season, minivans generally command

| SUMMER VACATION | FALL | WINTER |
| --- | --- | --- |
| Comfortable temperatures. Extreme crowds in Yosemite Valley. High country opens late June. | Comfortable, growing cooler and damper in October, crowds into September. | Heavy snow above, with downhill and cross-country skiing; snow spotty in Yosemite Valley. |
| Hot in canyon, comfortable on high country trails. Heavy crowds in canyon. Thunderstorms. | Best time. Warm temperatures, few crowds, foliage peaks in October in canyon. | Snowy above, cool and changeable in the canyon. |

double the going rate of an economy car, and at least 50% more than a full-size car. Renting an RV costs 5 to 10 times as much as renting a car: around $1,200 a week, plus mileage, for a smaller unit (see "The RV Advantage," in chapter 8, for details; advice on how to pack for a flying-camping vacation is on p. 21).

## GATEWAYS

If you plan to fly and rent a vehicle, you often have choices about where to land. Airfares and car-rental rates can vary widely among different towns that are within a day's drive of a park. I've listed the reasonable options for each park under "Getting There" in the "Making the Arrangements" section of each park chapter. Starting with that list, use either a good travel agent or the Internet to shop the airfare and car-rental rates to each town, and then figure out which one will save most overall. (Don't forget to ask about car-rental taxes and airport fees, which in some communities are 30% or more — enough to erase any savings you think you're getting.) Often, there's a small airport right at the park, served by propeller-driven planes and usually one or two small car-rental agencies. These generally are the most expensive choices; the largest cities are the cheapest. If you plan to rent an RV, it's especially important to shop around for prices and cities.

## By Rail

Trains let you cover a lot of ground without having to strap the kids into their seats. To some extent, they can range up and down through the train, and seats allow much more room to spread out than a plane or car. We sometimes take the train to avoid a long drive, but not often. Although I love train travel, it is impractical for a family national park trip. Amtrak service is often unreliable, with trains sometimes hours late on long runs, and food service poor. Many trains and stations are dirty. **Luggage** is a major problem; few trains have baggage-checking service, and even if they do, you end up at a depot that's usually far from any car-rental agency. **Rail fares** don't save much on routes with significant airline competition. While rail travel can save time over driving and allow you to go much farther in a day, you have to balance that with the hassles at each end of the trip. For these reasons, I haven't included rail options for visiting the parks in the book; you can get **Amtrak** information directly at ☎ **800/USA-RAIL** or www.amtrak.com.

## WAYS OF VISITING

A national park vacation can be either one of the cheapest or one of the most expensive you can choose. Tenting and hiking with a map as your guide costs next to nothing; renting a beach house or a luxury resort and taking guided outings costs more than most of us have. Often, cheaper is better. We usually prefer to camp, because it's more fun. Here are some of the considerations in deciding how you want to visit.

## Tent Camping

When you camp, you spend more relaxed time together, less time in restaurants or in the car or in the proximity of diversions like the TV that tend to draw the family apart. A campground is an infinite playground for children, one where you don't have to tell them not to run or jump on the bed. Our kids often make friends in camp, too. For the grown-ups, the best park campgrounds put you in glorious places where you can experience nature by touch and smell, as well as sight (some others are crowded and stark; each is reviewed in the park listings). Superb campgrounds are waiting at almost every park in the book, and absolutely amazing ones at Great Smoky Mountains, Grand Teton, Sequoia/Kings Canyon, and Olympic national parks.

Camping wins on price too. Driving to a national park in the family car with the family tent may be the least-expensive vacation you can take besides a trip to Grandma's house. Typical park campground fees are around $15 a night, and groceries cost little more than you'd spend at home anyway.

The downside is that you won't be as clean at a campground as you're used to being at home — trying to get a shower every day is inconvenient and wastes a lot of time, and washing young children in public showers is downright difficult. You're also at the mercy of the weather. This is how we like to travel best, but if the going gets tough, we give up. We check into a motel for the night, clean up, dry out our gear, eat in a restaurant, and watch TV. Don't forget, a vacation is supposed to be fun.

**Camping with an RV** is another subject, which I've covered in detail under "The RV Advantage," in chapter 8.

## Hotels

You can vacation in the parks by staying in hotels every night, but it takes more planning and money than camping and allows less freedom. The attractive hotels in the parks generally have to be reserved far in advance for the summer season. They typically don't have telephones, TVs, or swimming pools, although there are some significant exceptions to that rule. Some unique and wonderful places can make your vacation: The Sol Duc Hot Springs at Olympic, the Jackson Lake Lodge at Grand Teton, and the LeConte Lodge at Great Smoky come to mind. More often, park lodgings offer no better than average, out-of-date rooms, and some are truly terrible (see the park listings for details). Usually, it's much easier to get a room with a pool and other amenities outside the park in one of the gateway communities, although these too tend to book up in the high season. If possible, choose a place where you can cook, at least for part of your trip. Eating out for all your meals can get tiresome and expensive.

## Cottages & Houseboats

Renting your own home at the park combines the comfort of hotel stays with the independence and relaxation of camping. Cottages with cooking facilities are available at or near Acadia, Cape Cod, Cape Hatteras, Great Smoky, Point Reyes, and Olympic (limited choices are available at other parks). At the national seashores and Acadia, a summer cottage tradition makes it the best way to visit. At Glen Canyon, you can rent a houseboat that is a full home on pontoons, taking your kitchen and bedrooms right into the wilderness. Generally, cottage rentals require that you commit to a full week, reserve many months in advance, and put down a big deposit. By the night, they tend to be more expensive than hotels, but you offset some of that price difference by cooking your own meals rather than eating out.

## Summer Camps & Field Institutes

All the parks have ranger programs for children and adults, and some will even take the kids off your hands for an hour or two; but for an in-depth learning vacation, consider joining a field institute or camp. Park educational

I learned my lesson when we took Robin hiking at age 3 on a one-way trail. We didn't turn around to come back until he was already tired, and soon he was exhausted. Most of the way back he was miserable, and he made us miserable, too. On later hikes, I started letting him set the pace and choose rest stops, and I set the turnaround point based on how far he had hiked the last time. He was growing fast, so he made it farther every time. When he did beat his old record, that was a new personal best, and we made a big deal of the accomplishment. Soon, Robin wanted to hike farther every time. It helped us plan our hikes because we always knew what we could manage without getting too tired. We never wrote the records down, but I wish we had, with the names of the trail, miles covered, elapsed time, and date. It would be fun to look back on his progress and our times together.

The same strategy helped us plan itineraries for driving trips. We learned to find the limit on driving days to avoid major risk of meltdown. We would push it only a little farther at a time. The summer when Robin was 5 and Julia 2, our official limit was 5 hours a day, not including stops. If we needed to cover more than 5 hours' distance, we planned to spend the night on the way or to take another mode of travel, such as a plane or train. The only times we have had trouble were when we pushed or broke the rule, and that wasn't often.

institutes offer outdoor seminars and multiday programs for adults or families on subjects such as art, science, and outdoor skills. You'll find these in-depth educational programs at Cape Cod, Great Smoky, Grand Canyon, Yellowstone, Rocky Mountain, Yosemite, Sequoia, Point Reyes, and Olympic (see "Programs" under "Enjoying the Park" in each chapter for details). You can also split up by entering the children in an education program or a summer camp while you visit the park. I've also included summer camps with sessions of a week or less, including day camps and residential camps, at Acadia, Cape Cod, Cape Hatteras, Grand Teton, Great Smoky, and Rocky Mountain. At Sequoia/Kings Canyon, there's even a camp (Montecito–Sequoia Lodge, in chapter 19, "Sequoia & Kings Canyon National Parks") that children and parents attend together: While the kids join in structured outdoor activities, parents enjoy the park or otherwise amuse themselves, and then the family reunites for meals and evenings in family dorms. For any of these opportunities you must plan well ahead.

# Getting Ready to Go: Planning a Visit to a National Park

## Camping and Hotel Reservations

More people want to sleep in the national parks in the summer than the parks can accommodate. To ration the campground sites and backcountry permits, the National Park Service has reservation systems that reward those who know the rules and know when to call. You can't buy your way around these systems or get an agent to reserve for you; the race goes to the prepared.

## National Park Campground Reservations

The parks in this book that are handled by the national reservation system are Acadia, Cape Hatteras, Grand Canyon, Great Smoky, Rocky Mountain, Sequoia and Kings Canyon,

Yosemite, and Zion. At Yellowstone, the park concessionaire handles reservations through a system described under "Where to Spend the Night," in chapter 14, "Yellowstone National Park." Other parks do not take reservations, offering sites on a first-come, first-served basis, usually where you choose your own site and self-register. Some reservation campgrounds, including the campgrounds at Yosemite Valley, allow you to request a particular site when you reserve. Even if they don't, rangers at the campground may give you your choice anyway if you arrive early enough.

## When to Reserve

Timing is everything. At all parks other than Yosemite and Yellowstone, reservations become available on the 5th of the month for the following 5 months. For example, starting on January 5, you can reserve January 6 through June 4. For the next 30 days, no additional days become available. Then, starting February 5, you can reserve the period through July 4. Popular campgrounds on popular dates fill as soon as they become available, so you need to make your move on the 5th day of the month 5 months before your trip. One trick: If your stay begins in the time for which reservations are open, but extends beyond it, you can still reserve enough days to finish your stay — during a time available to no one else. Of course, the phones are tied up on the 5th of each month, so you'll need patience. The system is the same for **Yosemite,** except the magic date is the 15th of the month. Yellowstone's system is entirely separate, as I mentioned in the previous paragraph.

## Whom to Contact

A company called Spherix operates the **National Parks Service Reservations Center** by phone, by mail, or through the Internet. The phone number for reservations is ☎ **800/365-CAMP** (2267) or, for Yosemite National Park only, ☎ **800/436-PARK** (7275). From outside the U.S., call ☎ **301/722-1257.** The

TDD number is ☎ **888/530-9796.** The line is open from 10am to 10pm Eastern time every day except January 1 and December 25. The same hours apply to making online reservations, but you can still use the website to check availability and get much other useful information at any time, at **reservations.nps.gov.** The site also has details on each campground, online listings of how many sites are available for each date, and a way to make reservations. I've used the phone and online systems, and both work well.

## How to Pay

You pay for your campsite when you reserve. The reservation fee is included in the camping fee, which is typically a few dollars more than at a first-come, first-served campground. You can charge it on Discover, MasterCard, or Visa, or, if reserving at least 21 days in advance, send a check or money order. If the money isn't received within 7 days of your call, the reservation is automatically canceled. You can reserve by mail too, but there is no advantage to doing so: You can't get ahead of the phone callers this way, and if your letter arrives before the reservation window for your dates, it is returned. A form for mail reservations is on the Spherix website (above), which you can fill out and send to **NPRS,** P.O. Box 1600, Cumberland, MD 21502.

## Using a Reservation

Once you pay for your reservation, you'll receive a voucher to present at the campground. If you lose the voucher, or if you arrive after the campground office closes, your site is posted on a bulletin board. Come back to the office to check in by 8am the next day, however, or your reservation for your entire stay is canceled. If you need to cancel, the fee amounts to most of the camping fee, but that's not a catastrophe, since campsites cost under $20. We always reserve and pay for as many nights as we think we might use; the insurance is worth it at busy parks.

## BACKCOUNTRY PERMITS

You almost never need a permit for a day hike, but you usually do for overnight camping in national park backcountry, whether you get there by backpacking, canoeing, horseback riding, or other means. Sometimes you need a backcountry permit in national forests as well. Getting a permit is different at every park; sometimes it's as simple as filling out a form at a trailhead, and sometimes you have to do it many months ahead at just the right time. I've covered those details in each park chapter in the "Camping" section under "Where to Spend the Night." If you plan a backpacking trip to the Grand Canyon or the high country camps at Yosemite, the permit should be your first priority, with other arrangements revolving around the dates you're able to get. If your dates are flexible, you improve your chances of going where you want to go.

## National Park Hotel Reservations

The systems to reserve hotel rooms are different at each park. Generally, reserving rooms is similar to booking any hotel room, except that you need to call early to get one. The best places can book up a year early, whereas less desirable lodgings may be open a few months out. Sometimes, calling on a certain day makes all the difference. Details are in each park chapter in "How Far to Plan Ahead" under "Making the Arrangements" and under "Where to Spend the Night."

## Other Campground Reservations

Many thousands of national forest, Corps of Engineers, and state campsites can be reserved through a system separate from the Park Service system, run by ReserveAmerica. Only the most popular and developed national forest campgrounds accept reservations, and they often have sites for people without reservations, too. Reservation rules vary for the states on the system. You can reserve family national forest sites up to 240 days ahead. I've listed

Forest Service campgrounds near many of the parks in this book, but there are hundreds more. ReserveAmerica's National Recreation Reservation Service website lists all the national forest campsites you can reserve in advance, at **http://reserveusa.com**. There are descriptions of each campground and usually of each site, along with availability and often an opportunity to select the particular site you want. Unfortunately, there's no simple, central place to get information on campgrounds you can't reserve — you have to contact each national forest at the addresses listed at the top of each chapter under the "Address Book" section. ReserveAmerica has a separate site for state campgrounds, at **www.ReserveAmerica. com**, with a great wealth of information and a booking system. Phone numbers are different for each state.

For the forests, The **National Recreation Reservation Center** is at ☎ **877/444-6777**; the TDD number is ☎ **877/833-6777**; international callers use ☎ **518/885-3639**. Hours vary for the phone lines depending on the time of year, but they usually are open. To reserve online, you need an American Express, Discover, MasterCard, or Visa card. If you reserve by phone, you can pay by credit card, check, or money order; the postal address depends on where you reserve, and they'll give it to you when you call. The reservation fee is added to the camping fee, and at this writing it was $8.65 per site, no matter how many nights you reserve. The cancellation fee is the same, but you may get some or all of the camping fee back. If you don't show up by the morning after the first night of the reservation, the rest of your nights are canceled automatically.

## PASSES & FEES

After many years of underfunding, Congress let the national parks charge higher fees and keep the money for improvements. The program is making a visible difference in the parks, and the fees still amount to an insignificant percentage of the cost of a vacation, topping out at $20 per car for 7 days at Yosemite, Grand Canyon and Zion, or Yellowstone and Grand Teton. Most other fees are $10 or less. The fee at each park is listed in the relevant chapter under "When You Arrive." It covers everyone in the car.

You may be able to save on park fees by getting a pass. With a pass, people over 62 or with a disability get in virtually free, along with anyone else in the car with them. If you are over 62, get a **Golden Age Passport,** which costs only $10 and never has to be renewed. The **Golden Access Passport** is free to anyone with medical proof of blindness or disability and eligibility for federal benefits, and is also good for a lifetime. Either one also gives 50% off on campsites and some other park fees. For everyone else, the **National Park Pass** costs $50 and is good for 1 year; it covers only park entrance fees. If you plan to visit many parks, on a Southwest tour, perhaps, or to visit one park many times over a single year, the pass may be worth the price; we've saved a little with ours on our extensive travels. The pass also makes it quicker to get through the gate. You can get all three passes at any park fee station or visitor center, or get the National Park Pass by calling ☎ **888/GO-PARKS** or online at www.nationalparks.org.

## ROUTE PLANNING

Any car trip demands a road atlas and detailed maps of the areas you plan to visit. Computerized maps from the Internet or CD-ROM also help in planning your route by providing detailed drive times and directions between points. Click "Maps" on Yahoo.com, or try any of many other similar products, which all work about the same: You type in two places, and the computer returns maps, directions, times, and mileage. This helps us set up each leg of the trip within the endurance limit of our children.

## READING UP

The most important book you can take along is a first-aid or medical guide; I've listed a good one under "Dealing with Hazards," (p. 26). Each chapter lists good books for both kids and grown-ups that relate to the subject at hand, under the heading "Reading Up."

## Outdoors Skills

Unless you're anxious or have spent little time in the outdoors, you don't need a book about how to camp with children, a fact underlined by the painfully obvious advice most of these books include. But if it will make you feel better, or if gaps in your knowledge exist, here are the best we've found.

*Parents' Guide to Hiking & Camping,* by Alice Cary (Norton), is a fun, readable book full of photos, boxes, quotations, and tidbits of advice from real parents that make it easy to browse for ideas. The book is durable, with a plastic cover and thick, shiny paper, and has an index. The emphasis is on beginners setting out with small children and it's somewhat superficial.

*Camping and Backpacking with Children,* by Steven Boga (Stackpole Books), contains more information and has some value for more experienced backpackers, with its detailed sections on health and safety and on survival. Unfortunately, there is no index, and finding a particular piece of information is difficult. The book is cheaply made, with poor layout and gray photos.

## Children's Nature Study

*The Kids' Wildlife Book,* by Warner Shedd (Williamson Publishing), is an ingenious field guide and activity book that has loads of information in little snippets and doesn't talk down to kids. It's a funny book with cartoons and line drawings that will occupy many hours.

*Natural Treasures,* by Elizabeth Biesiot (Denver Museum of Natural History), takes a different approach. It's a serious children's field guide, lushly illustrated with the author's watercolors.

Our children's favorite natural history books are from the "Let's-Read-and-Find-Out Science" series (HarperCollins). These

With a few tools and tips you can fix problems that would otherwise sidetrack your camping trip. Pack a tiny toolkit with pliers, flat and Phillips screwdrivers, pocket knife, small roll of duct tape, sewing needle, thread, dental floss, spare car keys, and nails. Buy a hatchet that can also act as a hammer and nail puller.

**Broken zippers:** Tent zippers or other zippers with metal pulls usually fail because the pull does not engage the teeth tightly enough. Squeeze the zipper pull runners with pliers as an effective temporary fix.

**Ripped fabric:** Packs and soft luggage can easily get ripped by the airlines or other rough handling. Dental floss works well for repairs in this heavy fabric. Duct tape can temporarily stop rips in tent fabric and the like; apply it on both sides so that the sticky part touches through the hole.

**Wind storms:** Nails driven in a wooden platform or large trees make effective tie-downs for tents or rain tarps. Be sure to pull the nails when you leave.

inexpensive paperback picture books take on serious subjects like evolution, the water cycle, or oil spills at a level kids in primary grades can read and understand, without dumbing down the material.

There is a lack of the same kind of book for older children; publishers have focused on books to help with science-fair projects to the detriment of good reading just for curiosity's sake. One good exception is Janice VanCleave's *Ecology for Every Kid* (John Wiley & Sons), which includes activities but also good, clear, concise explanations of concepts. Not all of the books in VanCleave's series follow this pattern; some are just lists of projects.

## Field Guides

The National Audubon Society field-guide series (Knopf) is an extraordinary collection, with color plates and loads of interesting facts on every species, as well as plenty of help in identification. One volume or another covers just about anything you might be interested in: trees, birds, and wildflowers of the East or West; seashore creatures; rocks and minerals; and even the weather, stars, or fossils. The disadvantage is that they are so heavy that you can't pack more than one or two in your luggage. Also, Audubon's own *Sibley Guide to*

*Birds* (Random House), with David Sibley's painted plates rather than photos, is easier to use (published in 2000, it was an instant classic). An alternative are regional field guides, which Audubon publishes for the Pacific Northwest, New England, California, and so on. You carry one book on each trip, but they're not as easy to use. Smaller field guides also solve the weight problem, but can be frustrating: There's a very good chance that the plant or animal you are looking at isn't in the book.

## GEAR

Lots of magazines and websites (www.gorp. com in particular), and the Steve Boca book above, offer more advice for buying stuff. Here are a few of our family discoveries:

• **A high-quality baby-carrying backpack is worth the money.** The less expensive models (under $100) tire you and the child more quickly and wear out fast. With a heavy-duty pack you can carry much larger children and carry them farther, greatly extending your freedom in the toddler years. We have a Kelty Elite, which I can recommend.

- **Bring an inexpensive umbrella stroller** for trips to town and while traveling; baby backpacks don't belong in crowds, shops, or airports. We also have a jogger stroller which we use close to home to carry babies and as a backcountry cart for carrying gear, but it takes up too much space and weighs too much for longer trips.
- **A portable crib enhances safety** for toddlers. This is a dangerous age when they can wander into trouble. When we're car or boat camping, the portable crib is the "baby jail" to keep Joseph out of trouble.
- **A reliable camp stove is not optional.** You need to be able to heat drinks and meals fast in damp weather when hypothermia or fatigue threaten. See "Practicalities: Traveling with Camp Stoves," in chapter 22, "Olympic National Park," for advice on stoves.
- **Sleeping pads are more important than bags.** Everyone in the family needs a good pad. The ground can sap a child's body heat at night. In the summer you can get by with thin, compact bags (we use L.L. Bean's fleece sleeping bag liners) if you have good pads and one large bag to spread over all of you on cold nights.
- **A car-camping tent** should be big enough to be your home, where you can comfortably change clothes or take a sponge bath. It also needs a fly to keep you dry and should be strong enough to withstand windstorms. It doesn't need to be light; you can save a lot of money buying a sturdy car-camping tent that's not light.
- **A backpacking tent** *does* need to be light, but it need only be large enough to lie down in. In the backcountry, you don't have to worry about privacy: You can change or bathe outside. Strength and a waterproof fly are still important.
- **A screen tent** protects your picnic-table area from bugs and rain. We have taken ours into the Alaska wilderness by boat and across the country by car and air on long national park trips. It is our living and

dining room, a place to write journals and play cards.
- **Waterproof your tents** before you set out. Use seam sealer, available from any sporting-goods store, and then spray the whole fly and tent bottom with Scotchgard. Bring a plastic ground cloth to go under the tent, but make sure it doesn't extend beyond the floor area.
- **Get wide, long aluminum tent stakes** designed for snow. The inch-wide, spade-like blades hold in sand and loose soil and don't break. You can purchase them at mountaineering stores such as REI (www.REI.com).
- **Bring a nylon tarp and lots of cord.** If you can, create a shelter outside the tent.
- **A cellular phone is reassuring to have,** in the unlikely event of an emergency or even a minor crisis (especially when boating or hiking), but don't count on coverage in the backcountry; most big western parks don't have good coverage.
- **A collapsible fabric cooler** works almost as well as a hard-sided cooler and takes up much less space.
- **For water in the backcountry** the best solution is a pump water filter, a fabric bucket to gather the water, and plastic water bottles to store clean water. A filter will handle bacteria such as E. coli and protozoan cysts such as giardia. A more expensive purifier also uses a chemical to kill viruses, such as hepatitis A, which are much less common in water because they don't reproduce there. Boiling works, too, but you end up with hot water and you have to carry a lot of fuel. Iodine tablets produce odd-tasting water and are not recommended for use with children. See "Giardia in Water" (p. 29) for information on the risk of drinking untreated water and water treatment.
- **Synthetic thermal underwear is like magic.** It keeps you warm even when you're wet. And, for the amount of warmth it provides, it is far more compact and less

expensive than equivalent outer layers. You can sleep in it, too. We take it along whenever cool, damp weather is possible.

- **Cover your butt.** If you don't bring rain pants, bring a rain coat that will keep you dry when you sit down.
- **Light is important.** When you're car camping, a propane lantern extends the day. Battery-powered headlamps should go car camping or backpacking; they allow you to work with both hands and to read without holding the light.
- **Don't buy** until you know what you need and like. Everyone has different tastes in gear. If you're just starting out, rent or borrow the gear you need to get an idea of what you like and what kind of stuff you should buy later.

## COLD WEATHER PREPARATIONS

We're active outdoors in Alaska winter and summer, but preparing for cold is just as important at any high-elevation park in the Sierra Nevada or Rocky Mountains. It's simple to prepare for inactive time in the cold: You just need heavy parkas, snow pants, boots, and so on. The real challenge is staying warm while active and potentially wet and in situations with changing temperatures. Perspiration is your biggest enemy, so you must choose layers that stay warm when wet: synthetics and wool, and never cotton. Quickly change layers whenever you start to get sweaty or chilled. Our everyday inventory includes synthetic thermal long underwear; wool socks, hats, and mittens; fleece pants and coats; breathable wind-resistant outer jackets and pants; and warm boots. You can cross-country ski well below zero in that outfit. Adding a wool sweater adds even more warmth. For summer in the mountains, add shorts and T-shirts, swap the wind layer for a rain layer, and leave the fleece pants, wool mittens, and warm boots behind. The underwear layer is the most important, great for sleeping on cold nights.

## PACKING TO FLY & CAMP

When you're camping far from home, especially if you get there by air or in a car that's too small, you try to do without anything that's heavy, bulky, or hard to carry. At the same time, you may need to be ready for weather that could be hot, frosty, wet, or buggy. Here is some of what we learned about balancing those two needs on many flying-camping trips:

- **Start with a list.** Sample packing lists are included below. A list keeps you from forgetting things, and makes it easier to decide what *not* to take.
- **Figure out your limits.** Will you need to be able to move everything by hand all at once, to get on a train or boat, for example? If so, assign bags to each person in the family. If you fly and then drive, you don't have to carry everything at once, but it does have to fit in the trunk of the rental car.
- **Start packing early.** You won't believe how much space all your stuff takes until you see it all together. If you start early enough, you'll have time for alternatives, such as buying smaller gear, mailing some of it ahead, or arranging to rent gear at your destination.
- **Use big, flexible bags.** Duffel bags and hockey goalie bags are inexpensive, hold a lot, and get smaller when there is less in them.
- **Bring an extra collapsible bag** for items you pick up on the way, for dirty clothes, or for mailing items back home that you don't need to carry with you.
- **Folding, waffle-pattern sleeping pads,** called Them-A-Rest Z-Rest pads ($20 at REI), take much less packing space than pads that roll up.
- **Bring mailing supplies** so that you can send home any souvenirs you buy or items you aren't using.

- **Don't bring what you can buy cheaply.**
  For example, skip the water bottles—
  they're sold everywhere now with drinking
  water. Use a bottle for a few days while
  you're in camp, then throw it away and buy
  another one at the next stop.
- **Prepare for temperature changes with
  layering.** This works for clothing and bedding. You can deal with the quite cold
  weather with layers of thermal long underwear, a shirt, a sweater, a raincoat, and a
  hat; the total bulk is less than one heavy
  coat. On temperate nights, sleep in light,
  summer-weight bags or fleece bag liners,
  then deal with cold weather by putting on
  your thermal long underwear or warm
  pajamas, hats, and a single large winter-
  weight bag that you can unzip and spread
  over all of you while you snuggle up.
- **Bring only a few toys,** those you need for
  the first leg of the trip, then send them
  back or give them away and buy more.
  This saves space, and new toys are a lot
  more fun to play with and make good
  remembrances of the trip.

## PACKING CHECKLISTS

We keep a packing list that we photocopy
before each trip, marking off the items as we
pack them. During the trip, we edit the master copy, adding or deleting items as we find
out whether we need them. Another good idea
is to keep the master on your computer,
amending and printing it before each trip.

## Car Camping

This packing list probably has more than you
need; it's a starting point to whittle down.
I've left off food, clothing, rain gear, footwear,
toiletries, diapering supplies, and other
givens. Our list of children's entertainment
items is in "Practicalities: Our Favorite Car
Entertainment," in chapter 13. Items for the
first-aid kit are listed on p. 25.

### Kitchen Supplies

| | |
|---|---|
| baby bottles and | paper towels |
|   formula | plates, cups, and |
| bottle brush |   bowls |
| bottle opener | pot holder |
| camp stove | pots, pans, and kettle |
| can opener | salt and pepper |
| cooler and ice packs | sharp cooking knife |
| corkscrew | silverware |
| cutting board | spatula |
| dish soap | sponge with scrubber |
| dish towel | stove fuel |
| fish knife | strainer |
| garbage bags | tablecloth (plastic) |
| large spoon | Tupperware tub |
| lighter |   (for washing and |
| matches |   storage) |
| measuring cup | water jug |
| paper cups | Ziploc plastic bags |

### Camping Supplies

| | |
|---|---|
| bath towel | pliers |
| blanket | propane lantern |
| bungee cords | nylon tarp |
| camping knife | safety pins |
| campsite reservations | saw |
| clothespins | screen tent |
| cord | screwdriver |
| extra tent stakes | sewing kit |
| fire starters | sleeping bags |
| flashlights or | sleeping pads |
|   headlamps | sleeping tent |
| flashlight batteries | soap |
| ground cloth (plastic) | soap box |
| hatchet | super glue |
| nails | toilet paper |
| newspaper | travel alarm clock |
| pillowcases | |

### People Needs

| | |
|---|---|
| art and writing | field guides |
|   supplies | first-aid kit (see |
| baby carrier |   "Health & Safety," |
| binoculars |   below, for tips on |
| camera |   what to include) |
| cell phone | fishing gear |
| day packs | grown-up books |

| guidebooks | sunglasses |
|---|---|
| insect repellent | sun hats |
| Kleenex | sunscreen |
| portable crib | toys and kids' books |
| stroller | water bottles |

## Backpacking

The most common mistake made by beginning backpackers is to take too much. It's hard to have fun when you're carrying an uncomfortably heavy pack. After you're comfortable with your car camping skills and have your own list of essentials, pare it down to the bare necessities, then add items you may need from this list.

| backcountry permit | mirror for signaling |
|---|---|
| backpack | trail maps |
| bear mace | trowel |
| compass | water bottles |
| fabric bucket | water filter pump |
| Global Positioning System receiver | waterproof bags |

# STAYING HAPPY & HEALTHY ON THE ROAD

Our children seem to be happy anywhere as long as they're healthy, rested, fed, feel secure, and have challenges for their minds and bodies. As parents, it's our responsibility to provide those things. With practice, it's not hard, even on the road. Here are a few ideas that work for us. You'll find more tips throughout the book, including "Practicalities: Our Favorite Car Entertainment," in chapter 13 (p. 296), and, in each park chapter, the "Keeping Safe & Healthy" section.

## FEELING SECURE

Children feel secure when their parents are relaxed and they have a reliable place to retreat and find their favorite things. If you're camping or renting a cottage, it's easy to establish such a home base for children. We try to set up camp or get into rooms early in the day so that no one worries about where we're sleeping that night. If you're moving around a lot, your car becomes that reassuring home base. The problem with that is: Sometimes kids and adults don't want to get out of the car to see the places they are visiting. We avoid staying anywhere less than 2 nights; 3 or 4 is much better, a week best. Anything less, and you can get that uncomfortable, nomadic feeling of never really being anywhere, and the pictures passing by in the car's windows can become as hypnotic as a TV screen.

## EATING

Food can be the toughest issue when traveling with children. Here are ways to make it easier.

## Consistent Mealtimes

Anyone who has traveled with children knows the value of regular mealtimes. I know of no more important rule for keeping a family on an even keel. Letting lunch slip just an hour gets everyone tense, leading to whining, snapping, and temper tantrums. As everyone's mood gets worse, stopping for lunch gets harder — you can't agree on a restaurant or picnic area, and the kids' behavior deteriorates to the point that you don't want to take them into a restaurant. After many hard lessons, we've made strict rules about stopping for meals at certain times, even if lunchtime comes at a bad time for whatever else we are doing. We also keep emergency provisions so that we can quickly slap together peanut butter and jelly sandwiches or some other simple, non-snack food at the appointed hour. Snacks and junk food don't cut it; they make you feel worse a little while later.

## Restaurants & Kids

Many travelers, not just families, get tired of eating out for every meal on a trip. There's the stress of keeping your kids in line at the restaurant; the queasy feeling of never getting simple, low-fat foods; the expense; and the time wasted, which can amount to much of your day. If you're camping or have a cottage with cooking facilities, the problem is solved. Otherwise, keep a stocked cooler and picnic basket so that you can have breakfast in your room and frequent picnics for lunch or dinner.

We have to eat in a lot of restaurants to review them for the book, including long, expensive meals with white tablecloths. We've found that the children's behavior, even the babies', gets better through the course of a trip as they learn what's expected of them. The key is to set clear rules at the start and enforce them without exception. For example, our children never, ever get out of their chairs during a meal; otherwise, we've found, they're soon under the table or walking around the dining room. When bad behavior hits, we're always ready to haul a kid out to the parking lot; other times, a threat of that embarrassing march is enough. (This starts at home: If you have no discipline there, you can't expect to start when you go on vacation.) Positive conditioning is important, too: Always bring small toys and crayons to the table, and offer treats after a successful meal.

Of course, if you eat only at McDonald's and the like, you don't have to worry so much about behavior. But fast food is poor nutritionally and often makes us feel ill afterward. Children may think they want to eat at their favorite burger joint every day, but our family ends up happier after picnics and sit-down meals.

## EXERCISE & REST

A national park trip should be physically exhausting but mentally relaxing. This is a chance to find out how much you can do and feel the satisfying weariness in your muscles afterward. Nothing makes sleep come faster. If you spend all your time in the car, on the other hand, the kids drive you crazy with pent-up energy, and bedtime becomes a struggle. Bedtime rituals can be difficult to maintain when you're traveling. When we're camping, darkness settles everything down (in

Alaska, where the sun doesn't set in the summer, children stay up very late). If you're staying in hotels, it's more important to enforce a set bedtime, avoiding the seductions of the TV, which, for some reason, seem more attractive away from home.

## PACING & FLEXIBILITY

People who know how to slow down and enjoy themselves don't need to be told, and people who don't know aren't likely to learn by reading about it here. Still, we have made some practical discoveries that are worth sharing.

An obvious piece of advice that's often ignored is to spend adequate time in each place in a park rather than rushing around to see everything. The times we remember from our trips aren't the 20-minute sightseeing stops; they're the happy, daylong periods of relaxing when memorable things happen all by themselves. When planning your trip, be sure to set aside unstructured time when you can unwind and make your own discoveries — time to play in a stream, check out a newly found trail, or look at shells on a beach. Instead of trying to "do" a park in a few days, try to really know one manageable part of it in the time you have.

Children need time to do nothing. I've listed places for relaxed play in each park chapter, including playgrounds, but a campsite or grassy lawn is all you really need for downtime. Adults need time to do nothing, too, although sometimes we read a magazine or putter around while doing it. On the other hand, there's no reason for the most active and ambitious member of your family to be limited by what the least able or energetic can do. Barbara and I split up — I like to take long, fast hikes; she likes to explore little towns, shop, and go to museums. Sometimes we break into two groups, taking the kids to different activities that fit their ages. They are happy to have one parent at a time, just to play, go to a nature center, or romp down an easy nature trail, while the other parent is off doing something grown-up. As long as you're fair about who gets to go off alone and you still spend plenty of time together, the system works well.

## KEEPING CLEAN

Unless you stay only in commercial campgrounds, showering every day when you're camping at the national parks is a time-consuming and difficult proposition. But keeping clean is important to enjoying yourself. Usually, one spouse doesn't like camping as well as the other does, and being dirty is often a big part of the dislike; if the more enthusiastic member of the team wants to go camping again, it's wise to attend to this issue.

You can easily wash your hair and face every morning in camp with a pot of warm water poured over the head. Nothing does more to make you feel clean. A quick sponge bath and change of clothes in the tent also works wonders. Keeping hands clean is important for your health, especially at campgrounds without running water in the bathroom. We keep soap and water always out and handy in camp. Diaper wipes work well for cleansing sticky little hands and faces when water isn't handy. (There's a box in each park chapter listing the location of showers and coin-op laundries.)

## HEALTH & SAFETY

I'm no expert on health care, but I've culled advice from various sources to repeat here and in the park chapters, on the theory that some information is better than none. We've also listed advice on avoiding outdoor hazards.

## Preparing for Problems
### KNOWLEDGE

On our trips, I have the comfort of knowing that my wife, Barbara, an elementary school teacher, has first-aid and pediatric CPR training. If you're taking your kids into the wilderness, many hours from help, you need to know what to do in an emergency with help hours away. Taking a course is best, reading a book on first aid perhaps the least you should

do. (I've recommended two good ones under "Reading Up," p. 18). I always try to know in the back of my mind how I would get help from wherever we are.

You can avoid most emergencies by using your common sense. Many of the people who have bad things happen to them in the national parks are doing something stupid. That's why there are signs at the top of the huge waterfalls at Yosemite telling you not to swim there. Rangers call it "the Disneyland effect." Our society protects us so carefully from hazards that some people unconsciously believe that this is the normal state of nature. In fact, in the natural environment, survival of the fittest still prevails, even for our species, which is the only explanation for some national park accidents. For example, at the Grand Canyon, which the *Wall Street Journal* rated the third-most-dangerous park, a man posing for a picture in 1999 climbed over a guardrail and then walked backward over the rim, falling to his death.

### MEDICAL KIT

We have split our medical kit into two parts, each in its own zippered pouch. The large kit is for overnight trips away from potential help, in the wilderness or on a boat, or for long vacations. The smaller kit is supplied out of the larger kit with whatever emergency supplies we need for a particular day hike or short outing, and goes with us everywhere.

You can buy premade first-aid kits that contain most or all of the items you need, but they tend to be very expensive compared to just going to the pharmacy and buying the items individually. What's listed here covers most contingencies.

| | |
|---|---|
| adhesive tape | blister pads |
| antihistamine | Calamine lotion |
| (Benadryl) | children's chewable |
| antiseptic wipes | Dramamine |
| Band-Aids | children's Tylenol |
| bandage assortment | diarrhea medicine |
| benzocaine burn | elastic bandages |
| spray | eyewash |

first-aid book
gauze pads
instant ice pack
  (chemical pouch)
iodine
ipecac syrup
latex gloves
laxative
magnifying glass
measuring spoons
antibiotic salve
  (Neosporin)

Pepto-Bismol
petroleum jelly
rubbing alcohol
scissors
splint
thermometer
toenail clippers
Tums
tweezers
waterless hand
  sanitizer

Also:

- Add prescription medications to the kit, even those you don't use at the moment but might need on a long trip; filling out-of-state prescriptions can be difficult.
- A snake-bite kit may be a good idea if you will be in snake country, but you must follow the directions because improper use can cause serious infections.
- We bring a prescription epinephrine injector called EpiPen Jr. for allergic emergencies like the near-fatal bee-sting reaction I had as a child. We don't know if any of our kids is sensitive to stings, but it's best to be ready.

## DEALING WITH HAZARDS

Here are some tips on avoiding and dealing with some common outdoors hazards. Each park chapter also lists hazards particular to that area under "Keeping Safe & Healthy." Don't look to this book for advice for injuries and illnesses you're just as likely to encounter at home, such as cuts, broken bones, and the like.

I recommend taking a good first-aid book or medical guide in your first-aid kit. Many are available, but I like two books by Dr. William W. Forgey, who is president of the Wilderness Medical Society and devotes much of his time to perfecting outdoor medicine. His 64-page *Basic Essentials: Wilderness First Aid, 2nd Edition* (Basic Essentials) is all most

people need. But his *Wilderness Medicine, Beyond First Aid, 5th Edition* (Globe Pequot) is an extraordinary book, designed for people far from medical help, that goes deeply into diagnosis and treatment for a huge range of problems in clear, nontechnical language.

## Altitude Sickness

Altitude sickness is common at elevations above 10,000 feet, where the body needs time to adjust to getting less oxygen in each breath. Spending a few days in the mountains before high-elevation hikes helps, as does drinking lots of water. Symptoms include headache, nausea, fuzzy thinking, and fatigue. Watch children, especially those being carried in backpacks, for lethargy, which could indicate a problem. Dizziness and poor judgment, leading to accidents, may be the main dangers at elevations family hikers are likely to attain. The cure is to return below 8,000 feet.

A life-threatening buildup of liquid in the lungs or brain caused by high elevation normally occurs only above 14,000 feet, but can happen at lower elevations in people who are especially susceptible. Symptoms include coughing, breathing trouble, and poor coordination. Serious altitude sickness can kill fast, so you should get down as soon as possible.

## Burns

In a campsite, sources of burns aren't as well isolated from children as they are at home. Kids can fall into the campfire, tip the camp stove, or spill hot drinks on themselves. Be conscious of this risk and set up camp to be as safe as possible, establishing clear rules about how to behave around the fire. In case of a burn, cool the skin as quickly as possible with cold water, then check your first-aid reference for treatment, which depends on the severity of the burn.

## Crime

The parks are busy, open places, and serious crimes sometimes happen there. A survey by the *Wall Street Journal* in 2000 showed that at many parks there were more serious crimes in a year than search-and-rescue operations, and the pattern wasn't what you would expect: Cape Cod National Seashore had 155 search-and-rescue incidents and only 13 serious crimes, whereas Yellowstone had 35 searches and 119 crimes. Do the same things to protect yourselves as you would do at home: Keep your children with you, lock the car, and so on. You can't avoid all exposure to theft while camping, but you can make it more difficult so that criminals will go after someone else. For example, when you have to leave stuff in camp, don't leave it in plain sight.

## Dangerous Wildlife

All wild animals are potentially dangerous, even little squirrels. Don't ever approach or try to touch a wild animal of any kind. They can carry anything from rabies to bubonic plague, and even a minor bite is serious business.

### BEARS

Black bears are common in many parts of the U.S. Grizzly or brown bears (two names for the same species) are found only in the Rockies, from Yellowstone north, and in Alaska. Either species can be dangerous, but advice about how dangerous black bears are varies in different parts of the country. They are smaller, reaching a few hundred pounds, and in natural conditions live primarily on plants. Unfortunately, many black bears in the national parks, especially in California, have come to rely on food and garbage from human beings (see "Read Aloud: How to Save a Bear," in chapter 18, "Yosemite National Park"). A black bear killed a hiker in Great Smoky National Park in 2000, the first such fatality in the history of the National Park Service.

The most important precaution is to store food securely. Never, ever take food, dirty clothing that smells like food, or even pungent soap or lotion into your tent. Follow Park Service instructions at the campground. At some parks, storing food in the trunk of the car is sufficient, but black bears in California's Sierra Nevada know how to tear cars open to get to the food, and even which models are the easiest to open. Don't even leave loose papers in your car there, because a bear may mistake them for food wrappers. If there's a food storage locker at your campsite, keep all food you aren't eating at the moment in the locker, with the latch closed. Don't leave food unattended for any amount of time. In California, rangers advise that if a bear comes while you're eating you should try to scare it off, but don't try to take food away from a bear. In the Rockies, where black bears are wilder, that doesn't happen as much, and you should steer clear of them at all times.

Before heading into the backcountry for a backpacking trip, you'll receive plenty of advice about bears from the Park Service. Follow it. In some areas, hanging your food and pungent items from a long tree branch is sufficient, but anywhere in the Sierra and above the tree line in the Rockies, only bear-proof containers will do. California bears have learned to get food out of the trees, and can destroy the tree in the attempt. You can inexpensively rent canisters at the parks where they are required (they cost around $80 each to buy), but be sure to plan your rations and toiletries so that everything fits. A typical canister is a cylinder a foot long and 8 inches in diameter that weighs about 3 pounds. Where food hanging is the recommended technique, such as at Yellowstone, be prepared with plenty of cord and a sack. At Great Smoky, food-hanging cables are set up at many campsites. Whatever the storage method, always set up your tent away from your cooking and food storage area.

When hiking, make plenty of noise to avoid startling a bear, especially in brush or thick trees; wearing a bell, singing, or carrying on a lively conversation helps. Keep children nearby, because their small size makes them vulnerable. If you meet a bear in the woods, make a lot of noise, wave your arms, and keep your group together in a knot to look like a larger animal. The bear usually will walk away.

Don't walk or run away, because that may make the bear interested in following, but do retreat slowly, keeping your face to the animal.

In Alaska, where we camp with our children in deep wilderness amid some of the world's thickest bear populations, we carry bear mace, a spray made of capsaicin pepper. If a bear is aggressive, a fog of the burning spray is supposed to deter it (except in wind or rain). We've met bears here and all over the country, but we've never had to use the spray. One can costs about $50. **Counter Assault** brand (☎ **800/695-3394** or 406/257-GRIZ; www.counterassault.com) comes with a handy holster. This stuff is dangerous and must be kept away from children. Unlike a gun, it is legal in the national parks.

### MOUNTAIN LIONS

These great cats live in small numbers in several western states. Sightings are rare, and attacks even rarer; however, a child was killed on a hike at Rocky Mountain National Park a few years ago. Attacks happen near brush, where a lion can hide and pounce, and are unlikely if your group is together and noisy. The boy who was killed had run ahead of his family and was the size of a lion's normal game.

### BISON, MOOSE & DEER

Large mammals are dangerous even if they aren't predators. These animals can move lightning fast and kick and trample a person who approaches too close and appears to be a threat. Each of these species has killed people. Always watch from a distance. Don't try to get closer for a picture. Even gentle-looking deer can be dangerous if you don't respect their space.

## Dehydration & Heat Exhaustion

The body normally uses 2 or 3 quarts of water a day, and in the desert you need four times as much. If you lose just 2% of the water in your body, you can suffer weakness, headaches, and nausea, and you may stop thinking clearly or become irritable. This can happen in any climate, and it's dangerous. If your urine isn't light-colored, you're probably not drinking enough water. The cure is to drink, even if you aren't thirsty. Also make your kids drink, especially when you are hiking. Beverages with caffeine or alcohol are counterproductive. Juice is okay, but when children drink enough for good hydration they also get a lot of sugar, which can spoil their appetite for nutritious food.

In sunny conditions, especially in the desert, eating and sun protection are very important. Caps with cloth flaps that hang down work well for kids, as do broad-brimmed caps. Wear light, loose clothing. If you drink a lot of water but don't eat, your body leaches out nutrients, contributing to dangerous conditions, including heat exhaustion and heat stroke. Both conditions happen when your body loses its ability to get rid of heat because of dehydration, not enough nutrition, or overexertion in the sun.

Symptoms of heat exhaustion include weakness, cramps, dizziness, or nausea; the skin becomes pale and damp. Give the victim food, water, and rest, and apply a wet cloth until the feeling passes. Heat stroke is the same condition, but much worse. Now the victim has similar symptoms, plus an elevated temperature; fast pulse and breathing; hot, dry skin; and mental symptoms such as confusion and passing out. The person's life is at risk, and he or she needs shade, cooling damp cloths applied directly on the skin, water, food, and quick medical attention.

## Drowning

These tragedies happen incredibly fast, so you need to keep a sharp eye on your kids whenever you're near water. You should hold onto toddlers or have them on a leash. Swim in pairs, and make sure someone on shore in your party is keeping track of you. I've included some information on ocean swimming in "Practicalities: Swimming Safely in

Surf," in chapter 5, "Cape Hatteras National Seashore." River swimming and inner-tubing are a highlight of visits to some parks, but do ask a ranger first if water conditions are right, and have a grown-up go in before the kids to get a feel for the current. It doesn't take much to carry away a little person.

## Falls

A considerable number of people are killed or injured in the parks when they fall into canyons or off mountains. They're often young adults attempting dangerous sports without proper training or safety gear, but people have also simply gotten dizzy at the edge of the Grand Canyon and fallen in. Keep a hand on your children, and don't hike where a fall could lead to disaster. Enroll teenagers who want to climb in programs where they can learn to do it safely. With luck, such a class will teach respect for the dangers of climbing, and contempt for those who take risks without knowing what they're doing.

## Giardia in Water

In the past 20 years, streams all over the North American wilderness have become polluted with a protozoan cyst from feces called *giardia lamblia,* which causes chronic diarrhea. In places you can also pick up various nasty bacteria and, less frequently, viruses. Drinking untreated water from any water body is a risk not worth taking. (How to treat your water is covered under "Gear," on p. 19.) Giardia is difficult to diagnose and can last for years if untreated. Symptoms usually show up a week to 10 days after exposure and last 1 to 3 weeks, but can return for repeated bouts. If you come down with diarrhea within a month or so of an outdoors trip, ask your doctor for a giardiasis stool test.

## Hypothermia

Dangerous loss of body heat, also called *exposure,* is a common killer in the outdoors. It happens when your body gets too cold to warm itself. You must be especially vigilant with children because their smaller bodies cool faster, and they may not notice how cold they're getting. Hypothermia can occur on a 50°F summer day if you get damp and it's windy, especially if you are physically exhausted. Avoid hypothermia by eating well, being aware of how everyone is feeling, avoiding getting wet or sweaty, and wearing wool or synthetics that stay warm when wet.

Watch out for shivering, sluggishness, lack of communication, and irrational actions. If a person shows symptoms of hypothermia, get him or her indoors, out of damp clothes, and warm as soon as possible. Shivering is a key symptom. If the victim can still shiver, the body should be able to warm itself with warm, dry clothes and shelter. If the victim is too cold or physically exhausted to shiver, that is a sign that heat must be added from outside the body. Putting on more clothing won't help at this point. In the field, get the victim undressed and into a sleeping bag, skin-on-skin, with one or two warm people. Unless the victim is showing signs of shock, give plenty of warm liquids.

## Insects
### Sting Allergies

Extreme allergic reactions to bee and wasp stings can be life-threatening. Watch children carefully, and head for emergency help at any sign of breathing trouble, fainting, stomach pain, or hives. If you suspect that one of you has a sting allergy, or if it runs in the family and the kids have never been stung, it's wise to prepare with a prescription epinephrine injector kit such as EpiPen Jr. Benadryl helps with swelling from mild bug bites.

### Poisonous Spiders

Bites by poisonous spiders are rare but require an immediate trip to the doctor. Symptoms of a black widow spider bite include severe abdominal pain and hardness, and difficulty breathing.

## DEET

The most effective insect repellents, which contain high percentages of the active ingredient DEET, are not safe for children. Concentrations over 30% readily absorb toxicity into the body of children or adults. Reactions are extremely rare, but children have died from heavy overuse of DEET. We've tried the citronella-based repellents and found they just don't work well enough. We compromise by using a children's repellent with about 5% DEET. To be on the safe side, most doctors recommend using nothing over 10% DEET on children, and none at all on children under age 2. On the other hand, DEET under 30% doesn't work on black flies, and it won't always do the job on thick mosquitoes under 5% concentration. If flies are a concern, research the repellents that combine ingredients to work best on what you will face; Sawyer Products carries a line of concoctions (www.sawyerproducts.com). In any event, read the directions carefully for special warnings and application instructions about children. If possible, use it only on clothing, not on skin, and never on or near the eyes, mouth, or fingers the child might put in his or her mouth.

### MOSQUITOES

At this writing, mosquito bites are not dangerous in North America except in areas with local problems, such as the West Nile virus outbreak around New York City. But mosquitoes can ruin your day. They prefer places with standing water among brush or trees where they have protection from the wind. Breezes keep them away. Dusk is the worst time. Teach children not to scratch bites. If you can resist for 30 minutes to an hour, they stop itching; if not, they get worse and can even become infected. See "DEET," above, for advice on repellent.

### TICKS & LYME DISEASE

Ticks can carry Lyme disease, especially in the Northeast and northern California (cases have turned up in 48 states). It starts with flulike symptoms, and can affect the neurological system and heart if not treated with antibiotics. Ticks in the Rocky Mountains, the Southwest, and the Carolinas and neighboring states can also carry Rocky Mountain spotted fever, which causes fever, vomiting, and a measles-like rash, among other symptoms, and is fatal in 30% of cases.

Ticks attach to people by brushing off grass or undergrowth we walk through. Stay on the trail. Wear light-colored, long-sleeved shirts and pants tucked into your socks for hikes.

Apply DEET-based insect repellent (see above). After a hike, at bed or bath time, check everyone for ticks, especially on the scalp. Ticks are black and roughly the size of a pinhead. It takes about 48 hours for the tick to pass on the disease. Pull it out with pointed tweezers, taking a little of the skin at the insertion point, and apply alcohol and Neosporin antibiotic ointment to the wound. If a bullseye rash or flulike symptoms arise, see a physician. Rocky Mountain spotted fever shows up in about 6 days and progresses quickly. If you suspect something, see the doctor as soon as possible.

## Lightning

About 100 people a year die from lightning strikes in the United States, and many more are injured, making lightning a leading outdoors danger. In mountain areas where afternoon thunderstorms are common, especially the Rockies, plan hikes or boating for the morning so that you can get below the tree line and off the water by afternoon, when the storms usually hit. Storms move faster than you do, so you can't count on getting to shelter once a storm appears. If you can, get inside a building; if you're already inside, stay there until the storm passes.

Lightning doesn't have to hit you directly to kill; an area around a strike becomes electrified. The most dangerous place to be is near a lone tree or another upright object. Standing on top or on the side of a mountain of alpine tundra is also dangerous. A thick forest is a good place to be, but not near the tallest tree.

If you're stuck above the tree line in a storm, squat with your hands on your knees and your feet on the ground in a depression in the ground, and keep your head down. Don't lie down. Stay away from tall rocks, cliff edges, cracks, rock debris, water, or anything that could conduct a strike to you through the ground.

Here are the six most deadly common activities in lightning storms, in order: working or playing in open fields; boating, fishing, and swimming; working on heavy farm or road equipment; playing golf; talking on the telephone; and repairing or using electrical appliances.

## Poison Ivy & Poison Oak

Poison ivy grows on the East Coast, poison oak on the West. They are closely related, and the sap of both contains a highly allergenic substance that causes an itchy rash, or worse symptoms in sensitive people. Pictures of these nasty plants are found in chapters 6 and 17. It's best to avoid anything bearing a remote resemblance. I repeat the following chant to my children: "Stay on the trail."

If you think you have come into contact with either plant, wash the contact area with alcohol and soap strong enough to get off tree sap. The sap sticks to clothing and remains active for a long time, so wash anything that might have touched the plant. The rash takes 12 hours to 2 days to appear. Once it does, you have up to 2 weeks of misery ahead, longer if you scratch and it gets infected. Try hot baths and showers — as hot as you can stand — for up to 8 hours of relief from itching. Calamine lotion, aspirin, Aveeno oatmeal baths, and antihistamines such as Benadryl may help. Get medical treatment for extreme reactions.

## Seasickness & Motion Sickness

Being seasick or carsick is one of the worst feelings in the world. We've found children's chewable Dramamine to be effective. You have to take the pill an hour before you get on the boat or start the drive for it to be effective. It does make you sleepy — potentially a good thing for kids.

On a boat, take a child who feels seasick up on deck, where there's fresh air and you can see the horizon. Keeping your eyes on the horizon helps.

## Snake Bites

Usually, people are bothering a snake when they get bitten. Be careful turning over rocks, reaching into dark places, and gathering firewood. If you are bitten, symptoms quickly follow, starting with a funny taste in your mouth. You may want to bring a snake-bite kit, but in any event, get medical attention as soon as possible, keeping the bitten limb below the heart. Carry a person who has been bitten on the leg or foot.

## Sunburn

Most skin cancer in adults is caused by over-exposure to the sun decades before, as a child, whether tanning or burning. Severe sunburns can also ruin your trip. Wear sun hats with flaps or wide brims. Always apply sunblock with an SPF of at least 15, even on an overcast day. This is especially important at high elevations or on the water. An SPF higher than 15 doesn't offer much additional protection — just a few percentage points. Applying it heavily and often is much more important.

There's not much to do about a burn. Get out of the sun immediately. Aspirin, cool compresses, ointment, and cool baths with a half cup of baking soda added to the water are about all you can do for relief. Avoid lotions and creams, which can contain irritating alcohol or preservatives; oil-based ointments such as Vaseline are okay.

## Traffic

Your children are a lot more likely to be hit by a car than eaten by a bear on a national park trip. Many drivers are manning unfamiliar vehicles, such as rented RVs. Pedestrians have even been hit by big rear-view mirrors. Don't let your guard down in parking lots and on roadsides.

# The Eastern Seaboard

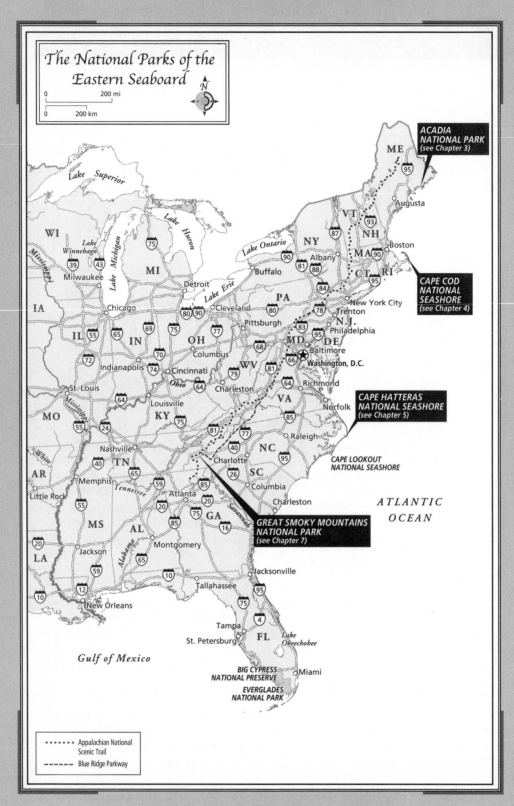

The National Parks of the
Eastern Seaboard

0 _____ 200 mi

0 _____ 200 km

N

ACADIA
NATIONAL PARK
(see Chapter 3)

CAPE COD
NATIONAL
SEASHORE
(see Chapter 4)

CAPE HATTERAS
NATIONAL SEASHORE
(see Chapter 5)

CAPE LOOKOUT
NATIONAL SEASHORE

GREAT SMOKY MOUNTAINS
NATIONAL PARK
(see Chapter 7)

BIG CYPRESS
NATIONAL PRESERVE

EVERGLADES
NATIONAL PARK

ATLANTIC
OCEAN

Gulf of Mexico

Lake Superior

Lake Huron

Lake Michigan

Lake Winnebago

Lake Ontario

Lake Erie

Mississippi

White

Mississippi

Ohio

Tennessee

Alabama

Savannah

Lake
Okeechobee

WI
MI
IA
IL
IN
OH
MO
KY
TN
AR
MS
AL
LA
GA
FL
ME
VT
NH
NY
MA
RI
CT
PA
N.J.
MD
DE
WV
VA
NC
SC

Milwaukee
Chicago
Detroit
Cleveland
Pittsburgh
Columbus
Indianapolis
Cincinnati
Charleston
Louisville
St. Louis
Nashville
Memphis
Little Rock
Atlanta
Montgomery
Jackson
New Orleans
Tallahassee
Tampa
St. Petersburg
Miami
Jacksonville
Columbia
Charleston
Charlotte
Raleigh
Norfolk
Richmond
Washington, D.C.
Baltimore
Philadelphia
Trenton
New York City
Boston
Albany
Buffalo
Augusta

39
43
75
80
90
69
65
55
72
70
74
64
24
55
40
65
59
20
75
85
16
65
59
10
12
10
75
95
4
81
77
26
40
95
85
64
79
81
66
95
83
78
84
88
90
81
87
93
95
90

● ● ● ● ● ● Appalachian National
Scenic Trail

─ ─ ─ ─ ─ Blue Ridge Parkway

34

# CHAPTER 2

# Moving Water, Moving Land

There are many ways to understand the power of the ocean. Feel a receding wave pull at your legs, taking the sand from beneath your feet. See a rocky shore shattered by the blunt smash of moving seawater. Think of all that has changed in the 400 years since European settlers first arrived on North America's eastern shore, and then notice how, even in the places where they landed, the ocean still rules, not people. Despite all the cities and roads we humans have built, we can't stop the ocean. The land we build on isn't permanent — it lasts only as long as the sea allows.

The national seashores and parks on the eastern seaboard teach all this and more. They're also among the best places anywhere for a young family to vacation. People from the region already know this, and for more than a century they have been going to the shore for the cool summer air, great swimming, boating, and other outdoor activities. In some places, that summertime tradition has brought a spreading mange of trashy tourist development. The boardwalks on parts of the New Jersey shore are an extreme example, but mini-golf courses, taffy shops, and arcades show up from Florida to Maine. Not so on shores protected as national parks and seashores. Here you find big, unspoiled areas and everything a family needs on vacation, a kid-friendly infrastructure of fun activities, casual restaurants and hotels, day camps, and well-thought-out nature programs.

Nowhere else in nature can children get in touch with the earth's wild side as easily as they can at the seashore. The gentle swell a toddler wades in one day can become a towering breaker that rearranges the landscape. The seashore is a unique, sharp boundary between completely different ecological systems and wildlife habitats. The sudden transition from land to water requires plants and animals to adapt in fascinating ways. The band between low and high tide is its own narrow world. Beginning naturalists who would never catch a good look at a bird or land mammal can find, pick up, and study sea animals that are twice as interesting. They can build sand castles and watch the tide come in and wash them away:

geology in action, identical to how it happens on the larger scale. To me, standing at the edge of the sea feels like standing at the top of a mountain — at the ultimate edge of my world, gazing into the bottomless expanse of another.

Unlike the big western parks, which draw visitors from everywhere, we found these parks mostly used by people from nearby states — we certainly didn't meet any fellow Alaskans. More families from other parts of the country should consider visiting, too. There's more for a family with young children to do here than almost anywhere. Besides nature and the outdoors, you can visit some of our nation's greatest historic and cultural sites.

## THE PARKS

**Acadia National Park** preserves a section of the rocky Maine shoreline, mostly on the east side of Mount Desert Island, a former resort for the very rich. Lovely, genteel carriage roads pass through the woods around the small, rounded granite mountains. Offshore, the park is a center for sailing, sea kayaking, and whale watching. There are lots of attractive campgrounds, both commercial and within the park, plenty of family-oriented motels and cottages, and several quaint towns.

**Cape Cod National Seashore** takes in the eastern beaches and sand dunes of Massachusetts's arm-shaped cape — the outer side from the elbow to the fist. The Pilgrims landed here, and the Cape is full of history; yet, the dunes and beaches remain wild and inspiring. There are museums, nature education facilities, and organizations offering summer day camps. The seashore has no campgrounds, but plenty of attractive campgrounds are nearby, as well as lots of good motels, cottages, and historic inns.

**Cape Hatteras National Seashore** protects 75 miles of the Outer Banks, a thin strand of sand islands draped around North Carolina's eastern coast 10 to 40 miles off the mainland. The ocean swimming and water sports are supreme, and miles of beach invite exploration and ecological interpretation. Nearby historic sites will fascinate most children and adults, including the Wright Brothers National Memorial and the site of England's first American settlement. The Park Service has several sandy seaside campgrounds, and there are plenty of hotel rooms and houses for rent.

# NATURAL HISTORY: THE CYCLES OF THE SEA

Waves never stop, even on the calmest day. Waves have steadily washed the earth since long before the birth of the first human being, or even of the first animal. They will not stop until the sun goes out. Like the tick of a clock, another wave always comes to shore, repeating the story of the last. Yet no two waves are identical, and from hour to hour the beat can change. Under a hot summer sun, waves might roll ashore in a slow, soothing rhythm. In a nighttime storm, they can roar urgently, crashing against the rocks or sand. But all waves are the same in having a low part followed by a high part and then another low part. That kind of repeating action is called a cycle. Waves are short cycles. The tides, the seasons, and other cycles in nature are much longer. Like waves, all these cycles change and cause change around them, but they always return, never stopping, always driven by the same forces. At the shore you can see the past and the future nearly to infinity by watching the cycles of the sea.

The swirling of ocean currents, the spinning of the earth, the fires of the sun, and the way our planet moves through space all tick the clock of cycles that affect each of us every day. Scientists have only begun to understand some of these cycles (and they don't agree on all of what I talk about here). Ocean currents

# THE EARTH'S CYCLES

| CYCLE EVENT | CYCLE TIME | CYCLE EVENT | CYCLE TIME |
| --- | --- | --- | --- |
| Ocean waves | 5–20 seconds | Sunspots | 11 years |
| Tides | 12 hours | Tide time and range | 18.6 years |
| Storms | 3–30 days | Sunspots | 22 years |
| Seasons | 1 year | Earth axis wobble | 21,000 years |
| Ocean eddies | 1 year plus | Earth tilt | 41,000 years |
| El Niño | 3–7 years | Earth orbit shape | 100,000 years |

can form eddies that last a year or more, and major changes in currents and weather come in cycles of more than 10 years. Changes in the currents change the temperature of ocean water and the weather over the land. The famous El Niño weather and current pattern comes each 3 to 7 years in the Pacific Ocean, changing the kinds and numbers of plants and animals that live there. The amount of energy that comes from the sun, feeding life on earth, changes with spots that show up on the sun's surface in cycles of 11 and 22 years. The tides change daily, but how much they change depends on the changing position of the moon, which goes through a cycle that lasts 18.6 years.

But these are tiny cycles, like ocean waves, compared to the earth's longer, larger cycles. The earth spins and circles the sun, wobbling and changing its path in cycles that affect the climate in big ways, as more or less sunshine reaches us. The most familiar wobble brings us winter and summer every year. But changes in the wobble also happen in cycles of 21,000 years. The tilt of the earth's spin changes in a 41,000-year cycle. And the earth's orbit around the sun changes shape according to a cycle of 100,000 years. These long cycles can each cause an Ice Age, bringing glaciers that grind down mountains, level plains, lower the oceans, cause animals to become extinct, and affect people in ways we can only imagine — since all of recorded

human history has happened since the last change of the shortest cycle.

## WAVES OF GLACIATION

Instead of saying "Ice Age," scientists use the words **glacial period,** because they understand that the coming of glacier ice to cover much of the planet is a regular cycle, not a one-time event. Our current 10,000-year period of relatively good weather is an **interglacial period.** Based on the movement of the earth in space, the shortest glacial cycle lasts 21,000 years, so we're about halfway to the next glacial period. When that period comes, colder temperatures and increased snow will bring glaciers back across North America. (For an explanation of how glaciers work, see "How Glaciers Work," in chapter 13, "The Nature of High Places.")

The granite mountains of Acadia National Park were once taller and connected to each other before Ice Age glaciers a mile thick piled up behind and plowed over them. Signs of this grinding collision show up all over the landscape. The bald granite mountaintops were cut from bedrock, which has not gathered enough soil since then to fully cover them with trees and plants. The mile-thick ice layer pushing across the rock also explains the mountains' rounded shape. On top of Cadillac Mountain, where you can drive or hike, you can see the scratch marks left on the rock by the glacier and a huge boulder brought from about 20 miles north and left here when the glacier melted, called a **glacial erratic.** Between the places with the hardest rock, the glacier carved out channels of softer rock where it could flow through more easily. These became the valleys that now hold Eagle Lake, Jordan Pond, Echo Lake, and Long Pond — notice on the Acadia map (see p. 60) how all of these point north and south, the direction the glacier flowed. The largest of the valleys that the glacier gouged became Somes Sound, the long, narrow bay that splits Mount Desert Island in half. It's the only true fjord, or glacier-carved bay, on the East Coast.

The rock that the glaciers ground off Mount Desert Island ended up far to the south, at the southern end of the glacier, in an area now known as the Georges Banks. The world's sea level was about 400 feet lower at that time because so much water was frozen in glacier ice. Today the Georges Banks are an underwater shoal and fishing grounds.

Cape Cod is another glacial moraine — a glacier's pile of leftovers. As glaciers plow through the landscape, they carry the sand and rock they pick up to the front edge of the glacier. The area of Cape Cod and the islands just to the south were the farthest south the glaciers came during the last glacial period. As these glaciers were drawing back and melting away, the area still stood well above sea level, so the sand and rock the glacier laid at its front edge piled up on the ground. When the water rose, much later, that pile became the southern Cape. The northern, forearm-shaped part of the Cape, where the national seashore is, grew from crushed rock left by rivers flowing from the glaciers (see the map on p. 85). That north-south section was the line between two adjoining glaciers that were both headed south. As the melt water ran out from the glaciers, it ran across this area, and the sand and mud it was carrying settled out on the ground. The sand and broken rock also buried huge pieces of glacier ice that remained frozen

after the rest of the glacier had melted away. When this buried ice melted, it left big holes called kettles. Some kettles filled with water, forming freshwater ponds like those at Nickerson State Park, or saltwater bays, such as Salt Pond at the national seashore visitor center in Eastham. Glacial erratics were left behind on the Cape, too — there's a huge one called Doane Rock a mile down Doane Road from the Salt Pond Visitor Center.

## THE TIDES

Invisible forces from outer space caused the glacial periods, and they control the daily cycle of life on the shore every day as the tide rises and falls. When the water is low, it leaves a mat of seaweed and weird undersea creatures slowly dying in the sun. Then the water slowly rises, saving the sea animals and filling the shoreline right up to where only land plants and animals still show. The tide rises and falls twice a day this way on the east and west coasts of America, affecting life from day to day and the shape the land takes over thousands of years.

The tides are caused by the gravity of the moon and sun pulling on the surface of the ocean. We're most familiar with gravity for the way it holds us down to the earth, but every physical thing in the universe pulls with gravity on every other. We notice the pull of earth's gravity most because, being so large and near to us, it pulls at us with a lot of force. We don't feel the gravity of the moon and sun because they are so far away. But because the oceans are very large and the water flows freely, even a tiny pull of gravity tends to pile up water in the spot nearest the thing that's pulling. As the moon passes over the ocean, that bulge of water follows along with it, growing a couple of feet high in the middle of the ocean. When the bulge of water reaches shore, however, it piles up much deeper against the barrier of land. The tide rises. (There are tides in all liquids on earth, even a glass of water, but they are much too small to notice.)

The earth spins once a day, so you would think the tide would be high once a day as the bulge of water moved around. But it's high twice a day. The reason is pretty surprising. The earth isn't standing still as the moon circles; the earth is also circling the moon. Imagine the earth and the moon as two balls on either end of a string. They're both spinning around the string, but from whichever ball you are standing on, it looks like the other one is circling around you. Now, if you really do swing balls (or one ball) around on a string, you will notice that the string pulls tight; as long as they spin, the ball or balls seem to try to get away from the center of the spinning. That's called centrifugal force. (You can feel it in your arms if you hold out two heavy objects and spin around.) With the earth and moon, gravity is the string holding the two together. Centrifugal force pulls in the opposite direction. On the side of the earth away from the moon, centrifugal force pushes up a bulge of water in the ocean, opposite to the bulge made by the force of gravity facing the moon. The two bulges, moving around the world as the day goes on, are the two high tides that rise each day.

At Acadia National Park, the difference between the high and low tides, or the tidal range, averages 12 feet. At Cape Cod National Seashore it's about 7 feet, and at Cape Hatteras it's only 2 feet or less. Some days the tide rises higher, and sometimes not so high. When you go to bed at night, you can predict whether the next day's tides will be big or small by looking at the moon. Big tides, called spring tides because the water springs up higher, happen when the moon is full or just a sliver (called a new moon). Little tides that don't come as high or fall as low are called neap tides. They come when the moon is half full.

To understand why this is so, you have to imagine the earth, sun, and moon in space. The sun pulls on the ocean the same as the moon does, but because the sun is so much farther away, its pull is a bit less than half as hard as the moon's. When the moon and sun both pull together, either because they are on the same side of the earth or because they are on opposite sides, their gravity and centrifugal force add together, and pull the water higher on those two sides. That's when we get spring tides. But when the moon is crossways to the sun compared to the earth, the two pull the water in different directions. With the two pulling against each other, not much water moves, so we get neap tides.

The moon gets its light from the sun. It looks so light on a dark night because it is a big rock in full sunlight while we are in darkness. If the moon is on the far side of the earth from the sun, you see one whole side of the moon lit up by the sun. The moon is full. If the moon is lined up toward the sun, you see only a sliver of the lighted part, called a new moon. Either way, the gravity of the moon and sun pull together to make spring tides. But if the moon is to the side of the earth, you can see about half of the lighted part, and then we get neap tides on earth.

The sun, moon, and earth also wobble and tip as they fly through space. Their paths in orbit, never a perfect circle, constantly change shape. All these motions alter the tides, too. By studying the motions, scientist found that the same pattern of tides repeats every 18.6 years. Using that knowledge, and measuring how high the tide comes at each point in the cycle in many different places, they have learned to predict how high the tide will be at any one time in any one place. The predictions are printed in tide books and even in the newspapers in coastal communities, where mariners and clam diggers need the information every day. (For more information or to get tide predictions, go on the Web to co-ops.nos.noaa.gov.)

## The Intertidal Zone

The strip of the shoreline between the high tide line and the low point, called the intertidal zone, is a window into another world.

Twice each day, this narrow section of the sea floor is uncovered for inspection. At Acadia National Park and on other rocky northern shores, shallow tide pools are little pieces of the ocean you can touch. There you'll find animals with no legs, eyes, or ears firmly rooted to the rocks, and tiny plants that swim freely through the water with microscopic arms. Barnacles, for example, look like plants, but they're really animals because they eat. Plants don't eat for the energy to live; they take energy from sunlight. (See "Read Aloud: Photosynthesis," in chapter 22, "Olympic National Park.") Barnacles (and people) get energy from eating plants or other animals, not directly from the sun.

Barnacles eat plankton, which consists of tiny plants, called phytoplankton, and tiny animals, called zooplankton. Phytoplankton are like plants on land because they turn sunlight, carbon dioxide, and minerals in the water into food and into oxygen which animals need to breathe. But phytoplankton are more important to life on earth than land plants. They make four-fifths of the world's oxygen. Near the coast, zooplankton are mostly baby animals, or larvae, of jellyfish, lobster, sea stars, crabs, snails, fish, or even barnacles. Like caterpillars that become butterflies, these animals begin life as living soup in the water before growing into something completely different. If you look at tide-pool water through a microscope, you can see the plankton paddling around.

Rocky tide pools also are good places for young scientists to grow and learn. Pick up a sea star and try to figure out how it eats (the answer is on p. 48). Put your finger in the mouth of a bright sea anemone and see what happens. This is a place full of new animals that can't get away from a child's inspection. They live only here, in the 10-foot gap between low and high tides. How have they adapted to survive the battering of heavy seas, winter ice, and hot, drying summer days? Places to go tide pooling include the rocky

shores at Acadia (see chapter 3, "Acadia National Park"), at Point Reyes National Seashore (see chapter 21, "Point Reyes National Seashore"), and at Olympic National Park (see chapter 22, "Olympic National Park").

The intertidal zones on sandy beaches such as those in Cape Cod and Cape Hatteras don't support as many animals you can look at during low tide as do rocky shores, because the sand on ocean beaches is always moving, leaving nothing for plants and animals to hold onto. But on the back side of Cape Cod, on Cape Cod Bay, and on the sound side of Cape Hatteras, where the water is calmer, low tide uncovers flats where you can see clams, snails, and crabs. Clams live under small holes in the mud; lines wandering across the sand may lead to periwinkles or moon snails. Hermit crabs are common on the mud flats at Cape Cod. Low tide also is a good time to find seashells on the ocean beaches, especially at the ends of Cape Hatteras National Seashore's barrier islands.

# THE WAVES
## Waves Are Energy

The shortest cycle on the seashore is the cycle of the waves, which come in every few seconds. Most waves are made by wind. How big they are depends on three things: how much open water they have to build up in, how strong the wind is, and how long the wind blows in the same direction. In a small body of water, or close to shore when the wind is blowing out from the land, the waves don't have enough space to grow large, even in strong winds. But crossing the ocean, a steady wind can push a wave for a great distance. Instead of going faster and faster, the wave takes in the energy of the pushing wind by growing larger.

Now, you might think that the wind pushing waves across the ocean would mean that all the water in the ocean would end up on one side, where the wind was blowing to. But waves on the ocean don't move water — just the energy, or pushing strength, of the wind. Watch a seagull floating on the waves: It goes up and down but doesn't move along with the waves.

A good way to understand how this works is to do an experiment: Have two people hold the ends of a rope with some slack in it, so that the rope hangs down a little, and then have one person slowly shake his or her end of the rope up and down. Waves will move along the rope, and the person on the other end will feel the shaking rope trying to move his or her own hand up and down, too. The rope is like the surface of the ocean. In both, waves store energy and move it from one place to another, but the material carrying the waves ends up where it started. The rope itself just moves up and down. Each individual drop of water in an ocean wave moves in a circle as a wave passes; together, the ocean's water sends the energy from the wind to the shore, where it is used up smashing water against the beach.

## Waves Shaping Rocky Shore

The wind across the Atlantic Ocean is strong enough to smash solid granite when it reaches the Maine coast, if you give it enough time. The Thunder Hole, along Acadia's Park Loop Road, is a place where you can see this happening. The waves have carved out a joint of weaker rock between harder granite to create a chasm where waves smash in with a boom. Even when the waves are not strong, they keep digging away at the hole by tossing boulders around. At low tide, you can sometimes see these rocks bouncing around in the waves in the Thunder Hole and slowly making it larger.

Waves do much more work during big storms. On the south side of Acadia's Baker Island, huge, round granite boulders are piled up on the bedrock in a chaotic mess, as if a giant child had scattered his toys here. Storm waves broke them off the rock just offshore and then tossed them around, battering the shore and breaking off still more boulders. All the bumping rounded the rocks off. At the Seawall area, at the southwest side of Mount Desert Island, similar granite rocks broke off in smaller rounded pieces and piled up in a wall-like storm berm, like a beach dune of stone. When the cities of the east coast were being built, workers gathered these stones to make into cobblestone streets.

## Surf on Sandy Shores

Waves shape sandy shores much faster. Sitting on the beach watching the rollers come in, you can see the Outer Banks or Cape Cod growing and shrinking, if you know what to look for. In deep water, as we saw above, a wave is just energy moving along the surface of the ocean, and the water moves only in circles. But on shallow coasts, the base of the wave rides up on the sea floor, and there isn't enough water to complete the circle carrying the wave's energy. The circle is forced to become an oval, and finally a line, as the energy of each wave throws water up onto the beach and it washes back again. The rising sea floor also slows the wave and forces it to change shape, growing steeper and narrower to carry the same energy in less water. The front of the wave slows first, as it enters the shallower water first, and that bends the wave forward, as if it were tripping on the beach. When the wave stacks up to a height that is one-seventh of its length, it can't stand any steeper and it falls, or breaks, crashing on the beach.

There are three kinds of breakers. Plunging breakers, the classic surfing wave, bend over and curl, making a tube of air before smashing straight down. Spilling breakers don't form the tube — the top of the wave just sloshes down the front. Collapsing breakers, made by small waves on steeper beaches, spurt out from the bottom of the wave and don't fall over at all. These are the hardest to see, but you sometimes can pick them out in the froth close to shore when two small waves meet and the water suddenly squirts up toward the beach.

## How Surf Moves Sand

When you stand in the surf, you can feel how plunging and spilling breakers suck sand away from the beach. As the wave approaches, the water around you pulls toward the ocean. Then the main part of the wave washes toward shore on top of you. And then the backwash pulls away from the shore again. Water always comes in on top and goes out underneath, so if you stayed on the bottom, you would only feel water going away from the beach. That means that plunging and spilling breakers, which come in rougher weather, especially in winter, pull sand off the beach and out into deeper water. But that sand doesn't disappear. It stays mixed up in the water only as long as it is being swirled by waves. A little offshore, where the water is deep enough that the waves don't touch the bottom, the sand settles on the sea floor. In time, a sandbar grows at that spot, building up until the water over it gets shallow, and waves start to break over the sandbar.

If the weather is still rough, the plunging and spilling breakers on the sandbar will pick up the sand and again move it farther out. But calmer weather may produce collapsing breakers. Collapsing breakers, which splurge out from their base when they break, create a current toward the shore on the bottom, pushing the sand back onto the beach. When they break on an offshore sandbar created by plunging or spilling breakers, they pick up the sand and slowly carry it back to where it came from. Sometimes you can see this movement in progress, when a sandbar sticks up close to shore at low tide.

## The Alongshore Current

Waves also make currents that run along the beach. Watch a wave that hits the beach at an angle. As the water flows back into the ocean, gravity pulls it straight down the beach, not back at the same angle that it came in. So the water in each angled wave ends up a little farther down the beach. That alongshore drift can move a lot of sand. In fact, it made the entire tip of Cape Cod, an area more than 6 miles long.

To understand how, remember that the high part of Cape Cod was left by glaciers in hills called moraines. As the last glacial period ended, the temperature began to rise, the ice began to melt, and sea level began to rise. That rise is still going on. Scientists studying fossils believe that the water rose about an inch every 10 years until 4,000 years ago, when it slowed down to about an inch every 80 years. The ocean got high enough to make Cape Cod a cape, rather than just a hill, 6,000 years ago, and that's when it started washing at the moraines left behind by the glaciers and flattening parts of them into beaches. The alongshore current moved the sand down the beach and left it at the end of the Cape, making the peninsula longer, one grain at a time. The picnic area at Pilgrim Heights, just north of North Truro, stands at the northern end of the glacial part of the Cape — looking north from this last bluff, the land is flat or rounded by sand dunes. The Province Lands, Provincetown, and Race Point are just sand that was put there by the alongshore currents.

## THE CAPES
## Narrowing Cape: Cape Cod

The sea cliffs along a 15-mile stretch of Cape Cod from Wellfleet to North Truro are still giving up sand. The 150-foot-high bluffs move back almost 4 feet a year, never to return. At this rate, the Cape has no more than a couple of thousand years left before it all washes away. At the historic site in Wellfleet where Guglielmo Marconi sent the first meaningful radio message across the Atlantic Ocean in 1903, you can stand on the bluff and imagine where his tower stood, at a spot that's now a couple hundred feet out to sea. In the opposite direction, you can see Cape Cod Bay, on the other side of the Cape. It's easy to imagine how this narrow strip of land could wash away.

But, as we learned earlier in this chapter, the sand doesn't disappear. It moves. Strong waves tend to hit the Cape straight on around Truro — on any particular day, they might come in on a different angle, but if you add all the waves together, they average out to coming straight in at this point. North of Truro, the waves angle toward the north, and the alongshore current moves sand to the tip of the Cape. As the current rounds Race Point into Cape Cod Bay, it carries sand around the corner, making the tip bigger and curlier. South of Truro, the waves angle toward the south, and the sand moves south, growing Nauset Beach and Monomoy Island.

These low beaches will probably last longer than the cliffs. Their sand washes away during rough winter weather, but comes back with the calm summer waves. Wind and storms build dunes at the back of the beach that protect plants behind them. The plants hold the sand in place. Over many years, grass, shrubs, and trees can grow on top, anchoring the sand and covering it with soil from fallen leaves for more plants to grow. Nauset Beach is a long barrier beach, protecting the shore and the bays behind it by absorbing the battering of the seas. It changes every year, but never disappears completely.

## Moving Cape: Cape Hatteras

Cape Hatteras, which is lower, narrower, and more vulnerable to the waves than Cape Cod, hasn't washed away with the rising sea level — it has moved closer to the mainland to make up for the rise. North of Cape Hatteras Lighthouse, the Outer Banks are moving toward the mainland at a rate of 5 feet a year. Geologists have measured the movement from old maps and aerial photographs and figured out how the sand is making the move from the outer side to the inner side. Currents carry sand around the islands, storms wash sand over the top, and wind blows it across. Unlike Cape Cod, which was made partly by glaciers, the Outer Banks are purely barrier islands, created and maintained only by the way the sea acts on moving sand. They have survived this way for thousands of years.

Scientists aren't sure exactly when or how the Outer Banks got started, or even why they stand so far into the ocean. Most of the world's barrier islands are close to the mainland, but the Outer Banks are 10 to 40 miles off the mainland, across a huge expanse of shallow, sandy water — Pamlico and Albemarle sounds. Driving along Bodie, Hatteras, and Ocracoke islands, it can be hard to imagine how such narrow, low strips of land could survive over time. But they have. Far to the west, on high ground on the mainland of North Carolina, geologists have found evidence of barrier islands that lay along this shore 85 million years ago, when the sea level was 300 feet higher than it is today. Interstate 95 roughly follows that old coast. Scientists have found the shapes of barrier islands underwater well out to sea too.

The Outer Banks we know today must have become islands sometime after the oceans started rising during the last Ice Age, probably when the rise in sea level slowed 4,000 years ago. Since then, they have changed shape, size, and place constantly, affected by each wave that hits the shore. And by changing, the islands have stayed alive.

## How a Salt Marsh Is Made

Salt marshes often form behind barrier islands and barrier beaches. At Cape Cod, it happens when the sand moving with the alongshore current reaches a bay and fills the opening with a sandbar. In time, the protected waters behind that barrier can fill with enough sand, mud, and rotted plant matter to form a salt marsh. At Cape Hatteras National Seashore, the whole place is a barrier island, and salt marsh runs pretty much the whole length of the sound side of the islands.

Salt marshes are like huge tide pools, filling and draining twice a day, but protected from waves by their sand barrier. The calm, slow-moving water makes a good home for grasses, insects, birds, small fish, snails, crabs, and other members of a unique system of plants and animals. Over many years, the living things die and sink in the water, building up its flat floor with rich muck that plants and worms love. As the bottom of the marsh slowly rises, it may become drier, or the rise may match the rise in the ocean level so that the marsh can thrive for a very long time.

## Inlets in Barrier Islands

Holes through barrier islands, where the ocean meets the sound, are called inlets.

Today there are five inlets along North Carolina's Outer Banks, but since Europeans first came to the islands more than 400 years ago, there have been as many as nine at one time, and a total of more than 24. They have opened and closed like elevator doors. A new inlet that opened during a hurricane in 1846 eventually killed off the town of Portsmouth, on an island southwest of Ocracoke Island. For its first 100 years, the townspeople made their living from the ships that came though Ocracoke Inlet, but when the hurricane opened the other inlet, the ships went that way instead. With no jobs unloading ships or storing cargo, the people of Portsmouth began to leave, and the town died entirely in 1971 when the last two residents left. Today, Portsmouth is a historic site, a ghost town you can visit at Cape Lookout National Seashore (see "Natural Places," in chapter 5, "Cape Hatteras National Seashore").

If you have ever built a dam of sand or dirt, you can imagine how an inlet could open so quickly. As long as no water at all flows over the dam, it can hold back all the water. But as soon as a trickle makes it over the top, the pressure of the water flowing behind it quickly washes out a channel that gets larger and larger until the dam washes away. The barrier island is like a dam holding back the tide. When the tide goes out, or ebbs, water has to flow from Pamlico Sound out to the ocean, and when it comes in, or floods, the flow goes the other way. When a few large storm waves break a small channel across the island, the rising and falling tides start flowing through the hole and quickly erode it into a path that's much larger and deeper.

Tidal currents can also fill inlets. The current runs fastest in the narrow inlet channel, carrying sand with the water. Past the inlet, when the current dies down in open water, the sand falls to the bottom and creates a delta, like the flat deltas at the mouths of rivers. Because of the alongshore current running on the ocean side of the Cape, the ebb tide delta stays fairly small — its sand is carried on down the beach. But the flood tide delta, inside the island, grows until it fills in the inlet with new land. It's another way the barrier island moves toward the mainland. In the case of an inlet on a salt marsh, the flow of sand slowly makes the marsh higher and drier.

Today, workers dredge the Hatteras and Oregon inlets to keep them open, digging with equipment on a floating barge. When a storm washes over the dunes, bulldozers sometimes push the sand back into place to prevent new inlets from cutting the islands in two. People don't like having their land wash away, and over the years they've tried many ways to stop the moving sand on the Outer Banks and Cape Cod. But their work has often made the problem worse. Engineers built breakwaters that stuck out from the beaches to catch the sand, and sea walls to stop the land from eroding more, but it was only the natural movement of the sand back and forth that had kept the land from disappearing in the first place. When walls stop the flow, they might temporarily protect a building, but they cause a problem somewhere else, where the sand normally would have gone. For these reasons, the national seashores no longer allow walls that try to stop the natural process of the sea.

## Plants & Wind Erosion

Wind causes the land to move, too. When gusts of wind hit the front of a dune, they pick up grains of sand and drop them on the downwind side. When the dune gets too steep on the downwind side, it avalanches, spreading out in that direction. If you look closely at the sand on a windy day, you can see how it moves, making tiny ridges the same way it makes large ones. In each season, the whole dune slowly moves in the direction of the most common wind. The sand of Parabolic Dunes, near Pilgrim Lake on Cape Cod, shows what happens when dunes are on the move: The blowing sand is filling the lake and sometimes covers Route 6. On the Outer Banks, migrating dunes — as dunes on the move are called — have covered up whole communities.

Plants can stop sand dunes. Nothing grows right on the beach, but several plants have adapted to grow on the dunes behind the beach, where they get washed by seawater only during the worst storms. On a low, sandy coast, there often are two or three lines of dunes that protect the shore from storm waves. American sea grass and sea oats start closest to the water, on the first two lines of dunes. Unlike most plants, which dry out and die when hit by salt spray from the ocean, sea grass and sea oats and a few other species adapted to survive the spray. These plants protect the dune by blocking the wind and by holding the sand together with their roots. More sensitive plants grow farther back, hiding behind the second or third dune or blocked from the spray by the sea grass. Thickets of bushes and small trees such as stunted eastern red cedar can grow where plants have fixed the dunes in place for a long time. The thick, tangled branches help these plants protect each other. Sometimes you can see how thickets grow taller farther from the top of the dune: The plants closest to the sea are partly killed back by the spray, but they shield the plants behind them, allowing the protected plants to grow a little taller. Farther back, underneath a thick roof of hardy trees, the ground is so well protected from the wind and spray that leaves can fall to the ground and rot without blowing away. The rotted leaves build up for thousands of years to make soil that traps fresh water and helps the trees grow.

When the Pilgrims first arrived in the New World, the Province Lands area was probably forest. Settlers cut trees on Cape Cod to farm the land and used the beach grass on Cape Cod and Cape Hatteras for grazing animals. Without being held in place by the trees and plants, the soil blew away and the sand started to move again. At the Province Lands, strong winter winds from the northeast pushed the dunes toward the southwest — toward Provincetown. By 1800, with the dune crests moving 90 feet closer to town each year, townspeople stopped grazing animals in the area and began replanting beach grass. Fifty years later, the dunes around the town stabilized. Other towns on Cape Cod and Cape Hatteras disappeared completely because of wind moving sand. The soil on Cape Cod blew away and the farmers had to become fishermen. Both capes were saved by local people and government agencies planting beach grass. That's why you should stay on trails when you walk through the dunes: Your footsteps could help the land blow away.

# THE LITTLE FIELD GUIDE

## MAMMALS & MARINE LIFE

In addition to the creatures here, you might also want to refer to some in other chapters: white-tailed deer, gray fox (p. 144), California mussel (p. 473), limpet, sea anemone, and sea urchin (p. 474).

Barnacle

## Barnacle

Barnacles live all over the world's shoreline wherever there's something solid to hold onto, and even on the bottom of ships. The northern rock barnacle shows up as far south as Delaware, and many other barnacles that look similar are found at Cape Hatteras too. On the West Coast, the acorn barnacle is common. When the tide is out, barnacles close the doors of their little white houses to avoid drying out. When moving water returns, they stick out a fanlike filter that catches plankton from the passing seawater. If you swish water past a closed barnacle with your finger, you often can see it open and wave its fan.

## Blue Crab

Found all along the East Coast, but most commonly from Cape Cod south, these tasty crabs grow up to 9 inches across. They live in calm, shallow estuaries where they can find dead animals to eat, but they also can swim fast enough to catch small fish and shrimp. You can catch a blue crab with a piece of smelly meat hung on a string, but look out for the scary claws, which can really hurt you when they pinch (see "Crabbing," in chapter 5).

Harbor Seal

## Harbor Seal

Harbor seals are among the most common seals. You can see them lazing on sandbars and rocks all along the East Coast as far south as South Carolina, and on the West Coast from southern California to arctic Alaska. Harbor seals grow 4 to 6 feet long, and their short-haired coats are gray or tan. Unlike sea lions, they have no visible ears. Seals are mammals, so they have to hold their breath when they swim underwater and come back to the surface for air. They eat fish.

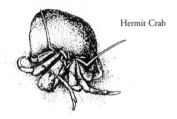
Hermit Crab

## Hermit Crab

The hermit crab is the most interesting common animal you'll see during tide-pool explorations on Maine's rocky shores; they can also be found on tidal flats at Cape Cod and Cape Hatteras and all along the West Coast. A dozen kinds of hermit crabs live in different habitats, but all are the same in that they don't have their own shells. They live in old snail shells they find empty. When a hermit crab gets too big for its home, it has to find a larger, unused shell somewhere in the intertidal zone. They're easy to catch for observation in a watery sand bucket before you let them go. The wonderfully illustrated book *Pagoo,* by Holling C. Holling (Houghton Mifflin), tells the story of a hermit crab and the whole tide-pool world; it's best for ages 8 and older.

Horseshoe Crab

## Horseshoe Crab

This weirdest of crabs is not really a crab, but an arachnid, like spiders and scorpions, which makes it seem even creepier. But horseshoe crabs are harmless, crawling along the sand to find food that they can grind up. They're the only animal I know that has four eyes on its back. Horseshoes often are called living dinosaurs because the fossil record shows that they look the same now as they did millions of years ago.

Humpback Whale

## Humpback Whale

More than 10,000 humpbacks migrate through the North Atlantic annually. Many pass by and feed off Cape Cod or off Acadia's Mount Desert Island, where shallow waters and upwelling currents bring food to the surface. Whales spend the winter mating and having babies in tropical waters but don't eat there. In the summer they come to northern waters, where there's more food, and bulk up with a year's worth of nourishment. The same pattern holds off the West Coast. Humpbacks grow to 56 feet in length and eat small fish. They appear on the surface in four postures: just cruising along and resting, when you can see the humped back arching slowly from the water; sounding, which is diving straight down into the water for several minutes, when you can see the huge tail sticking straight up into the air; lunge feeding, when they encircle a school of fish with a ring of bubbles and then surge up from beneath to gobble them up; and, if you're really lucky, breaching, when the whale leaps entirely clear of the water's surface.

## Northern Moon Snail

Found from Maine to North Carolina, this snail spends its time in intertidal sand flats digging for clams. When it finds one, it drills though the shell and sucks out the meat inside. (This may explain clam shells you find with holes in them.) The northern moon snail can grow to the size of a grapefruit, but more commonly the shell is around 2 inches. Smaller species of moon snails also show up at different places all along the East Coast; on the West Coast, the giant moon snail is much the same.

## Quahog (Hard Clam)

The gray shells that make good fences on the tops of sand castles often come from this tasty clam, which lives just below the surface of the sand in the intertidal zone or just offshore all along the East Coast. Clams reach to the surface of the sand with siphons — tubes they use to pull in and push out water and to catch particles of food and get oxygen. Quahogs grow up to 4 inches, but you usually find them smaller. People catch them from shore with rakes and shovels, and the whole thing is good to eat. Surf clams are similar but larger, more symmetrical, and yellowish white. Oysters are more oblong than quahogs, with wavy, bumpy shells. Scallops have shells that look like fans.

## Sand Fiddler Crab

Found at Cape Cod and Cape Hatteras, this is one of the amphibious crabs (meaning it lives in water and on land). It lives in a burrow in the beach sand, and at low tide it runs along the water to find little nuggets of food in the grains of sand where the foam licks the shore. Another is the ghost crab, which lives only south of Delaware and seems to appear at night from nowhere, like a ghost. You can have fun on the beach, watching the ghost crabs by the light of the moon or chasing them with a flashlight and putting them in a bucket (set them free when it is time to go). We did this one night on Ocracoke Island with a screaming mob of children; it was great fun. Both species are less than 2 inches in size.

Sea Star (Starfish)

## Sea Stars (Starfish)

There are many varieties of sea stars. The best place to find them is a rocky shore at low tide, but they show up on sand and mud too. All sea stars are predators. If you have an hour or two to watch, you can put one on a mussel or clam and watch how the sea star slowly grabs the outside of the shell with the suction cups on its arms (called rays), pulls the shell open, then inserts its stomach into the shell to digest its prey in place. Sea stars also have the amazing ability to grow back parts that are cut off. One that's cut apart can even grow into two or three sea stars.

## BIRDS

In addition to the birds here, you might also want to refer to the barred owl (p. 144), common loon (p. 475), golden eagle (p. 288), hairy woodpecker (p. 289), common loon, common murre, belted kingfisher, and great horned owl (p. 475).

Great Blue Heron

## Great Blue Heron

With their long legs and necks, these large birds like to stand on the edge of the marsh scanning for fish or frogs to eat. They spend the summer in the north and winter in the south. The heron looks similar to the egrets that you may see around Cape Hatteras, which also are impressive birds.

## Herring Gull

This is the classic seagull. It can be quite a pest: Never feed a seagull because you'll soon be surrounded by them, and they can be aggressive and pesky. Herring gulls are scavengers, and you can always find them at a garbage dump; but they also eat seashore animals. To open clams, they drop them from great heights on rocks and parking lots to smash the shell.

Osprey (Sea Hawk)

## Osprey (Sea Hawk)

Although it may look like a gull from a distance, up close you can see that the osprey is a member of the hawk family, with a sharp hooked beak for tearing apart prey. If you're lucky, especially at Acadia, you may see an osprey hunting. Using its sharp vision, it picks out fish in the water, then dives from the air down into the ocean and snatches fish in its sharp talons.

Sanderling

## Sanderling

These are little shorebirds that run in groups in front of incoming waves on sandy beaches, then run back toward the receding water to catch little shrimp and other food. They're small and have sticklike beaks and white bellies.

## Trees & Plants

In addition to the flora here, also refer to poison ivy (p. 146) and quaking aspen (p. 290).

### American Beach Grass

This common beach plant is an important defender of the front sand dunes close to a beach. It survives being buried in sand and washed by salt spray, and its roots can delve deep for water and help hold the dune together. American beach grass grows on Cape Cod and Cape Hatteras, and sea oats are even more common on Cape Hatteras. They have curlier leaves and fatter seeds.

### American Beech

Common at Acadia and found in a unique stand at Cape Cod's Province Lands, the beech grows all over the East Coast. Beechnuts feed squirrels and birds. The leaves are sharp-pointed ovals with edges like a saw. The leaf veins are all parallel. The bark is smooth.

### Eastern Red Cedar

This plant, also known as juniper, can grow as a seaside shrub, carved by the salt spray, or as a tall tree on Cape Cod and Cape Hatteras. The first Europeans to run across it were the colonists on Roanoke Island. Behind the dunes, it grows low in the sand, hiding from the full drying damage of the salt spray. Away from the shore, on Cape Cod, it grows tall on old farmland and has been harvested to make pencils and closet linings.

### Eastern White Pine

These tall, straight trees were used for the masts of great sailing ships in the days when ancient stands — all cut down since — had trunks 150 feet tall. The white pine is Maine's state tree and grows as far south as Georgia at higher elevations. The cones are narrow and up to 8 inches long. The needles come in bunches of five.

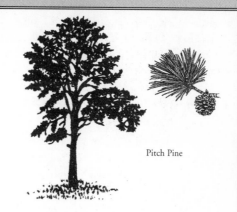

Pitch Pine

### Pitch Pine

These are the pine trees at Cape Cod. They grow in sandy and rocky soil and can survive salty spray. At Acadia, you find them on rocky ledges where there's not much soil. After fires, they can come back quickly with new sprouts. Although they can grow to be 50 feet tall, you'll usually see them scraggly and much smaller. Before people cut down most of the timber on Cape Cod, the area had a much greater variety of trees, but pitch pine took over land that had lost much of its soil. To tell kinds of pine apart, inspect the needles — yellowish pitch pine needles come three to a bunch, short and thick. Pitch pines don't grow at Cape Hatteras, where Loblolly pines are the common species. These are taller, straighter trees.

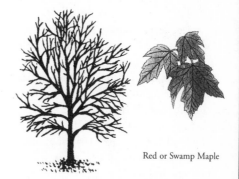

Red or Swamp Maple

### Red or Swamp Maple

The red maple grows from Maine to Florida, reaching 60 to 90 feet in height and 2½ feet in diameter. In the fall the leaves turn bright yellow, orange, and red, and at other times the tree has red flowers. It's found in Acadia, in wet areas on Cape Cod — where it has recolonized abandoned cranberry bogs — and occasionally even in marshes on the Outer Banks. Early settlers used the bark to make ink. The leaves look like the one on the Canadian flag.

# HISTORY & CULTURE: FIRST ENCOUNTERS

Imagine living on the edge of a sea no one you know of has ever crossed. No one knows what's on the other side. One day a ship arrives, larger and more technologically advanced than any your society has the ability to build. The people who get off look completely different from your people and carry tools you've never seen that can do things you never imagined possible. And they settle down to stay, forever, and to change your land in terrible and unexpected ways. It's hard to imagine how it would feel, so think of it this way: Tonight you see on the evening news that space aliens have arrived in a ship larger and more technologically advanced than anything humanity could build, carrying strange and powerful tools and weapons. They announce they'll settle down to live here and change the earth completely. And they don't really care if anyone already lives here. For the Native Americans in North America, the arrival of European colonists on the eastern seaboard 400 years ago must have felt much like the arrival of space aliens would to us today. The Native Americans' courage and initial hospitality is amazing, when you think about it that way.

What was it like for the first settlers? Their courage is amazing, too. For them, going to America must have been like going to another planet would be for us. They traveled in small wooden ships that often disappeared without a trace on long ocean voyages. If they ran into trouble or got sick, there was no one to help them, and if only a few people died on a trip, that was good luck because usually more died. Once they left port, there wasn't any way to communicate with family back home. And they were going to a place that no one knew anything about. They didn't even know what the coast looked like. As far as they knew, no one had ever been there — or at least no one who mattered, for as far as they were concerned, the Native Americans were hardly people at all. Out of this new, strange, and completely unknown land, they planned to make a home and a new country.

## ELIZABETH'S EXPLORERS

Sir Walter Raleigh sent the first English colonists to the New World to settle on Roanoke Island, just inside the Outer Banks. In 1584 he sent a pair of sailing ships to explore the area. Raleigh was a rich, popular friend of Queen Elizabeth I and Sir Francis Drake (learn more about Drake's adventures in chapter 21). At the time, Spain was the world's most powerful nation, thanks to Christopher Columbus's discovery of America in 1492. Spanish conquerors found fortunes in gold and silver in South and Central America, and each year sent treasure ships home. King Philip II of Spain used the treasure to hire soldiers and build ships. But Queen Elizabeth wanted a piece of America's wealth, too. Her way of spreading her empire was to have private investors like Raleigh do the work and pay her a tax for giving them permission to take the land in England's name. In July 1584, Raleigh's explorers arrived at an inlet in what is now Bodie Island (the inlet closed by 1657) and put up a post saying that the land now belonged to England.

The Croatoan Indians greeted the Englishmen with gifts and feasts. The English also offered gifts and traded copper objects, highly valued by the Croatoans, for furs. Captain Arthur Barlowe wrote: "We found the people most gentle, loving and faithful, void of all guile and treason, and such as lived after the manner of the Golden Age. The earth bringeth forth all things in abundance, as in the first Creation, without toil or labor." In fact, he was quite wrong: The Native Americans worked hard and traveled far to grow their crops, fish, and hunt for their food. And their tribes often fought over land and honor, warring with surprise attacks and ambushes, just like the Europeans.

The Native Americans' impression of the English was wrong, too. Some thought they were dead people who had returned to earth with supernatural powers — explaining their incredible wealth, ships, and guns. Wingina, chief of the Roanoke Indians, may have thought the English were possible allies to attack his enemies and make him more powerful. He even sent one of his people back to England with the explorers. A Croatoan named Manteo also went to England and learned to speak English. His mother was ruler of Croatoan Island, which now is part of Hatteras Island.

## THE ENGLISH OUTSTAY THEIR WELCOME

When you meet someone for the first time, on a short visit, it's easy to have fun and see only the good parts of your new friends and the place you've discovered. Raleigh's explorers came back to England describing a paradise in America. But when a visit lasts too long, both the host and the guest can get tired of each other and realize they don't like each other as much as they thought they did. This happened with a group of about 100 men Raleigh next sent to settle Roanoke Island, who planned to stay permanently.

At first, they were welcomed generously by Wingina and his people, who gave them a place to build a fort and planted a field of corn for them. John White and Thomas Harriot, a painter and a scientist, worked to learn the Natives' languages and ways, traveling from village to village to study the wildlife and geography of the area. The studies they produced were the best record ever made of Native American societies before contact with European ways.

But problems developed. The English governor, Colonel Ralph Lane, was a hotheaded military man. Instead of trying to build a colony that could support itself, he relied on Wingina to help catch fish and sell him corn. But the tribe members had to work hard to get by. In the summer and fall, they went to camps on the Outer Banks to fish and gather oysters, in the winter they hunted, and they grew corn most of the year. They didn't have enough to feed the English too.

After a year, the colonists were short of food; a ship they expected to bring supplies was late. The Roanoke Indians didn't want to trade their food for pretty but useless items the English offered because their own food supplies were running out. Wingina's people disappeared from their villages at times to avoid Lane, perhaps fearing that the English would attack and take the corn by force. The governor got suspicious. He heard rumors that Wingina was plotting with other tribes to attack the colony, and he decided to attack first, killing Wingina and his leading men in an ambush. Not long after, Sir Francis Drake arrived, planning to bring more colonists, but Lane grabbed the opportunity to leave for home with his entire group. When the expected supply ship arrived 2 weeks later, no one was around at Roanoke to supply. Eighteen men were left behind, but they were never heard from again. After the sneak attack by the Englishmen who had just left, it seems likely the Native Americans killed this next group.

## FAMILIES TO SETTLE AMERICA

Raleigh tried one more time in 1587 with a group of 120 colonists who could really build a community. Instead of the military men he had sent before, he sent families with children and with a variety of skills who could support themselves. John White, the painter who had developed friendships among the Native Americans, led the new colony, and he brought along his pregnant daughter and her husband. They set to work immediately building homes, farming, and fishing. Virginia Dare, White's granddaughter, was the first English child born in the New World.

Before the ships that had brought them left for England, the colony had serious problems. Lane's warlike way of dealing with the Native Americans had made enemies of most of the tribes, and fighting broke out as soon as the new colonists arrived. With the help of Manteo and the Croatoans, who were still friendly, White tried to set up peace talks, but the other tribes no longer trusted the English. The leaders of the colony got together and convinced White to go back to England on the ships that were still waiting in the harbor, to get more help. He didn't want to go, but he finally agreed.

White made it back to England and set up a convoy of ships to bring supplies back to the colony. But at the same time, Spain mounted an all-out attack to conquer England. The Spanish navy, called the Armada, was the largest ever built. The challenge to England was so great that all ships had to join the war, including the vessels intended to resupply the colony. White still tried to make it with two small vessels but was attacked on the way and had to give up. The English, led by Sir Francis Drake, beat the Armada in 1588. White worked desperately to get back to the colony but didn't have much help from Raleigh, who had gotten interested in another project in Ireland. In 1590, White finally got a ship to take him back to America. Even then, he went only as a passenger on a vessel whose real job was to attack Spanish ships and steal their cargo.

## THE LOST COLONY

Three years had passed when White arrived at Roanoke, and he found the colony deserted. The houses were gone, and a strong wooden fort had been built. On one of the logs, the word CROATOAN was carved. White took that as a sign that at least some of the colonists had gone to Croatoan Island, the home of the friendly tribe, and he intended to go there to find them. But he had more bad luck: The ship was out of fresh water and lost its anchor in a storm. The captain decided to sail south to the Caribbean for water and supplies. In the Caribbean, the ship got caught up in fighting the Spanish and never went back to the Outer Banks.

Over the following years, others tried to go back and find the colonists at Croatoan, but they didn't try very hard, and no one made it there for many years. In 1653, a visitor to Croatoan, which had become Hatteras Island, found Native Americans there who looked different from others — some had gray eyes — and who said they were partly descended from Englishmen. By then 66 years had passed since the colonists were left at Roanoke Island. Maybe some of them went to Croatoan to wait and, when no one ever came, they married Native Americans and lived out their lives as Croatoan Indians on the Outer Banks.

White believed that most of the colonists probably went north to the Chesapeake Bay to form a settlement there. When the Jamestown colony was formed on the James River in 1607, its leader, John Smith, tried to find the earlier colonists, hoping they would be able to help his struggling settlement. Powhatan, a fierce chief (his daughter, Pocahontas, twice saved Smith's life), told Smith that his warriors had killed off the Lost Colony. Some historians believe that the colony split up, with some people staying at Croatoan to wait for White, and others moving to the Chesapeake, where they joined with the Chesapeake tribe and were killed when Powhatan massacred the Chesapeakes. But no one really knows what happened. The best book on the Lost Colony is *Set Fair for Roanoke,* by David Beers Quinn (University of North Carolina Press). It's an academic text written on an adult level. Good material at a children's level is on the Web at www.nps.gov/fora.

When you visit, you can see where all this happened and two good museums about it, go on board an Elizabethan ship, and attend an evening performance about the story (see chapter 5). Besides wondering what happened to the Lost Colony, it's also worth wondering how things could have gone differently. What if the first colony — the one led by the soldier Lane — had tried to supply its own food and live peacefully with the Native Americans rather than dominate and take from them?

## THE GREAT EPIDEMICS

The Pilgrims were more cooperative with the Indians, but by the time they landed on Cape Cod, on November 9, 1620, some of the problems of working with the Native Americans had been cleared away for them. Most of them were dead, killed by diseases brought by newcomers from Europe. European explorers had been charting the coast for years. Different nations hoped to be the first to claim and hold the new land.

A French explorer, Samuel Champlain, sighted and named Mount Desert Island in 1604, met the local Native Americans at Otter Point, and mapped the area. The name, which means "island of barren mountains," was *l'Isle des Monts-déserts* in French. The French claimed much of what we now call New England as its new territory of "La Cadie," or Acadia. In 1613, France landed a party of Jesuit missionaries on Mount Desert, near the mouth of Somes Sound, but an English ship soon attacked and destroyed their mission. That left ownership of the island up in the air, and neither side did much with it for the next

150 years. The English did use Maine's waters for fishing each summer, returning home with their catch in the fall. And they kept exploring and meeting the Native Americans. Captain John Smith, from the Jamestown colony, traveled through New England making detailed maps for a new colony he hoped to start, and even tried to persuade the Pilgrims as an advisor.

Wherever the Europeans went, sickness and death soon came to the Native Americans. Epidemics of new diseases swept through their villages, sometimes killing every inhabitant. At Roanoke Island, the Native Americans thought the newcomers were killing them with invisible bullets that sickened them. We know today the true cause of the sickness: The Europeans were carrying diseases such as smallpox. Europeans had been living with the germs for thousands of years, and their bodies had the ability to fight off the illnesses. The Native Americans, on the other hand, had not been in contact with any of the European germs, and they died by the thousands when they picked them up from European sailors. (The same process continued across North America for the next 300 years. Alaska's tribes met with the terrible epidemics just 100 years ago.)

When the Pilgrims finally settled at Plymouth, they found good cornfields cleared and ready for their use. Three years earlier, the tribe that made the fields, the Patuxet, had been wiped out by sickness. The only survivor, Squanto, had traveled to London and learned to speak English. The Pilgrims believed God had killed the tribe so that they could take over the Indians' land, choosing the Pilgrims over the Patuxet because the Native Americans weren't Christians.

## THE PILGRIMS

The Pilgrims' religious faith made them decide to go to America and gave them the will to survive when others would have given up. They were Puritans, who believed that people's fates — whether they would go to heaven or hell — were decided before they were born. When they behaved well, this just proved that God had already chosen them to go to heaven.

These beliefs were different from the teachings of the Church of England, which was the official government church controlled by the king, James I. So the Pilgrims decided to leave the country. They went first to Holland, then decided to set up a new colony in America. They raised money for the trip by making a deal with some merchants in London to send back goods to sell. But, unlike the colonists sent by Raleigh, going to America wasn't a job for the Pilgrims, it was their own idea. Also, unlike Raleigh's first colony, many of the Pilgrims were families who planned to build homes where they could feed and defend themselves and wouldn't have to rely on others. Unfortunately, they knew almost nothing about how to do that in the place they were going. They were farmers, not fishermen, hunters, or soldiers. For the main crop they would rely on, corn, they didn't have seeds or knowledge of how to plant them.

The Pilgrims might not have survived without the help of the few Native Americans who had survived the epidemics, but their first meeting was not friendly. Cold winter weather had set in when their ship, the *Mayflower*, anchored in Provincetown harbor in 1620. The Pilgrims sent out groups to explore Cape Cod and decide if they should settle there. As far as they could see, it was a "hideous and desperate wilderness full of wild beasts and wild men," as one Pilgrim wrote. On the Cape, you can see several places they first found, such as the site at Pilgrim Heights, where the explorers found water. On the inside of the Cape, in Truro, they found a cache of the Native Americans' corn, which had probably been stored for seed for the next year's planting. It was just what the Pilgrims needed. After a long talk about whether it would be right to steal the corn, the Pilgrims decided to take it but to pay back the tribe it

belonged to if they happened to meet them. The place is still called Corn Hill. On their next exploring trip, they met a group of Nauset Indians, who attacked them with arrows. With a few shots from their muskets, the Pilgrims drove them off. The place in Eastham where that happened is called First Encounter Beach.

## NATIVE AMERICANS HELPING SETTLERS

The Pilgrims' first friendly meeting with the Native Americans happened after they decided to settle at Plymouth, across Cape Cod Bay. It could hardly have been more different from the landing of Raleigh's colonists 36 years earlier. A man named Samoset simply walked into the village and introduced himself in English. He had known English fishermen in Maine, he liked their food, and he was willing to tell the Pilgrims about the area and set up meetings with the head chief in the area, Massasoit. In the spring, when Massasoit came to visit with 60 warriors, each side was nervous and tried to impress the other with gifts and ceremonies. The Pilgrims introduced their governor with trumpets blowing and drums playing. But it was just show, for half of the 102 Pilgrims had died during the winter from disease.

The Native Americans showed the Pilgrims how to plant the cornfield left behind by the dead Patuxet tribe, placing seed and two or three fish in each hole. In the fall, the harvest was good, and the Pilgrims planned a feast, which they invited Massasoit's people to share. Ninety braves came for a party that lasted 3 days. The first Thanksgiving was like a huge, wild outdoor barbecue. The menu included roast goose, duck and venison, clams and other shellfish, eels, cornbread, vegetables such as leeks and watercress, and plums and dried berries for dessert. (They didn't have turkey or pumpkin pie.) They drank strong white and red wine made from wild grapes. The Native Americans and Pilgrims both contributed the food. It was a wonderful celebration and became a tradition the very next year.

The English colonists' relations with the Native Americans didn't stay so friendly after more Europeans moved to America and became more powerful. In the end, wars would be fought and the New England tribes all but eliminated. But for a while, at the beginning at least, the Pilgrims and the Native Americans who helped them showed that two could cooperate and live in peace.

# CHAPTER 3

# Acadia National Park

From on top of Acadia's Cadillac Mountain, you can see for miles along the Maine coast. The bumpy bedrock landscape, shaped like a lumpy bedspread over a restless sleeper, is filled in by the sea — a rounded green island pokes above the surface here and there like an elbow or a shoulder. You can gaze at it for hours, finding new details. This small national park has mountains and forests, ponds and marshes, rocky and sandy shores, marine and land animals. And people. By the time Acadia became a national park, the land and seashore already had been in use for centuries. On each island, behind every ridge, there are colonies of life.

Compared to other parks, Acadia gives us a different way to understand nature — with people as part of the picture. Most of the famous national parks out West set the land aside for us to visit and look at, preserved as much as possible to be as they were before settlers arrived. To feel a part of those places — and not just a viewer of a natural show — we have to leave our cars behind and hike away from other people into the wilderness. Acadia is different. People have been here long enough to have become threads in the fabric of the place. From the top of Cadillac Mountain the scene all fits together: the forests, the tiny islands, and the waterside villages with their boats passing back and forth.

Acadia doesn't have great wilderness areas and there is no backpacking, but its partly tame natural places are so inviting and easy to reach that the park may be the best of all for families. You don't need to be a sturdy hiker to get away from the car. Here a bike or a bike trailer towed behind a parent will carry you to quiet woodland ponds. Anyone who enjoys a boat ride or a shore ramble can have a close encounter with the natural world. You will find plenty to do at Acadia; after two visits, our family is well short of doing everything we want to there.

## BEST THINGS TO DO

- Bike the unpaved carriage roads that wind through the woods of Mount Desert Island, around placid ponds, and over arching bridges of cut stone.

- Canoe the lakes or learn to sea kayak in Frenchman Bay.
- Go sailing in lovely Great Harbor and Somes Sound.
- Explore rocky shores where the tide leaves behind pools of water full of strange little animals.

- Take a boat ride to see wildlife and a tiny, historic island.
- Climb granite Cadillac Mountain and buy a lemonade on top.

See "Activities" (p. 72).

# HISTORY: PUTTING A PARK TOGETHER

The map of Acadia National Park shows clumps of parkland patched across Mount Desert Island, with lots of holes in between. It looks that way, and the park feels so civilized, because of the island's unique history as a resort for fabulously wealthy families who lived a life of luxury here. Those visitors were even rich enough to buy a national park: Acadia was put together from gifts of land they bought and then donated to the government.

The rich members of high society first found out about Mount Desert Island in the 1840s and 1850s, when artists such as Thomas Cole returned to New York with paintings of glorious rustic scenes. Curious visitors began coming from the large cities of the East Coast, and big hotels were built to take care of them. Steam ships carried the tourists north in comfort. As time passed, wealthy summer visitors bought the land that made up the island's pretty views and began building houses like palaces, which they called "cottages." By 1880, the island was becoming the fashionable place to be for the richest of the rich, such as the Rockefellers, Morgans, Vanderbilts, Fords, and Carnegies. Their cottages had dozens of rooms — one had 80 rooms — and armies of servants tended to their whims. These people didn't come just for

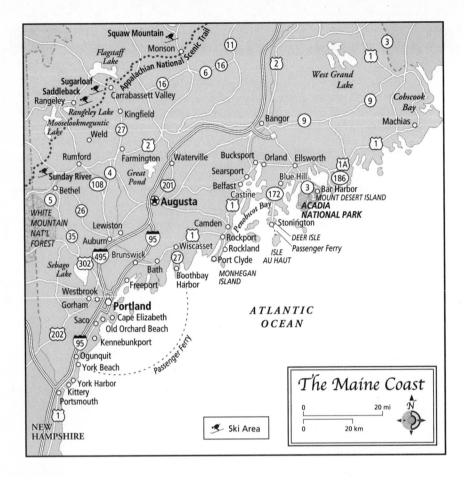

The Maine Coast

0 ——— 20 mi
0 ——— 20 km

N

Ski Area

nature walks. They were more interested in tennis, teas, golf, horse races, society balls, and private clubs.

In 1901, some of the island's major owners and summer people started thinking about protecting its natural beauty permanently. They feared that private owners might eventually cut down the trees for wood, spoiling the views. George Dorr, of Boston, became the project's main supporter. He dedicated much of his life to buying up Mount Desert Island and creating the park. He worked so hard on it that he didn't attend to his own textile business and lost the fortune he had inherited. A richer man, John D. Rockefeller, Jr., probably contributed the most money. His wealth came from his father, who had helped start the oil industry and was the world's richest man.

After coming to the island for the first time in 1900 and summering near Seal Harbor, Rockefeller began buying large areas of land, and eventually donated one-third of today's park area. (He also helped start Grand Teton and Great Smoky Mountains national parks, and others; see "History: Rockefeller to the Rescue!" in chapter 15, "Grand Teton National Park.")

Rockefeller built Acadia's carriage roads. Horseback riding and horse-drawn carriages were an important part of the royal lifestyle the wealthy summer people enjoyed. Even after cars became popular, they persuaded the Maine legislature to outlaw them on the island. The year-round residents didn't like that and finally won the right to drive in 1915. Rockefeller responded by building his own carriage roads where he could ride horseback without cars to bother him. These lovely forest ways, with granite walls and bridges, snake among the valleys, ponds, and hills. By agreement with Dorr, who ran the new national park which he had helped create, Rockefeller built carriage roads over the public lands too. He paid for the Park Loop Road and the road to the top of Cadillac Mountain, and helped design them. By the time he died in 1960, Rockefeller had built and maintained 57 miles of carriage roads with 16 beautiful granite bridges all over the eastern side of the island.

For Rockefeller, these special roads were a gift to the public, and building them was an interesting hobby. But many wealthy summer people opposed them because they didn't want to share the island with new visitors who weren't like them. As the years passed, the kind of people who came to the island did change. The outrageously rich lifestyle of Mount Desert's Golden Age ended during the Great Depression of the 1930s, with higher taxes on the rich, a worse economy, and new ways of looking at how people should relate to each other. The rich couldn't just do whatever they wanted anymore. A huge fire in 1947 wiped out many of the great houses and estates, so today you can't see how the island looked then. But the Rockefeller family stayed, and they still have their property near Seal Harbor, where their private carriage roads are open to walkers and horseback riders, but not bicyclists. The ordinary people that their very rich neighbors didn't want on the island *do* visit Acadia and enjoy the carriage roads by the millions.

# ORIENTATION

## THE ISLAND
Acadia National Park takes up much of Maine's **Mount Desert Island** (called MDI by locals), a little point to the east called the **Schoodic Peninsula,** and a smaller island to the west, **Isle au Haut.** Most of the park and the things to do are on MDI.

The largest town on the island is **Bar Harbor,** an attractive and historic seaside community that's been overrun by tourists. It's a center for activities, but too crowded and congested; we preferred the other, still-quiet towns and villages. Their names, in clockwise order around the island from Bar Harbor, are Seal Harbor, Northeast Harbor, Southwest Harbor (the largest after Bar Harbor), Bass Harbor, and Tremont. The villages of Northeast Harbor and Seal Harbor are in the town of Mt. Desert. The island is divided in half by Somes Sound, a lovely 7-mile-long fjord. The best of the park is on the eastern, Bar Harbor side, including the carriage roads, most of the publicly owned shoreline, the botanical gardens, and Cadillac Mountain.

Less of the western side belongs to the park, but there are many pretty and less-used spots, plus a swimming lake and some relatively unspoiled towns.

## THE ROADS
Unless you're in your boat, you'll approach Acadia along **Route 3.** The road leads from the town of Ellsworth (a good place to stop at a large grocery store) south through a ghetto of water parks and mini-golf courses, past the airport, and across the bridge to MDI. From the bridge, **Route 102** leads straight to the western part of the island and the town of Southwest Harbor; Route 3 leads 8 miles to the main visitor center at Hulls Cove (see "Visitor Centers," below), another 3 miles to Bar Harbor, and beyond that to the rest of the east side of the island. From the visitor center or Bar Harbor you can join the **Park Loop Road,** which circles many of the scenic points on the eastern shore of the island and passes through a fee station (the only time you're asked to pay the park fee).

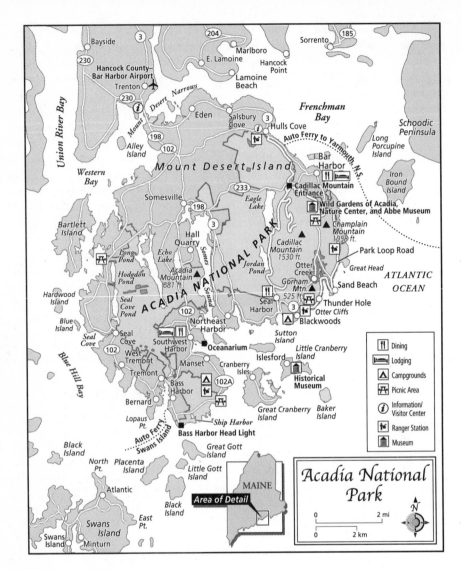

## MAKING THE ARRANGEMENTS

### WHEN TO GO

July and August are the most popular months to go to Acadia, during the summer break from school but after the worst of the bug season. Temperatures tend to be comfortable, with average highs in the mid-70s; days in the 90s are rare. Rain comes in the form of thunderstorms or longer episodes of drizzle, and you're likely to get wet at least once in any 3-day stay. The popular carriage roads and the

streets of Bar Harbor fill with people, hotels and excursions charge their highest rates, and traffic is at its worst during these months. If possible, avoid arriving on a weekend, especially the Independence Day and Labor Day weekends, which are the park's busiest times.

June is a calmer month, when many hotels advertise lower prices. June weather is slightly cooler than later in the summer, and mosquitoes and black flies are more plentiful. To

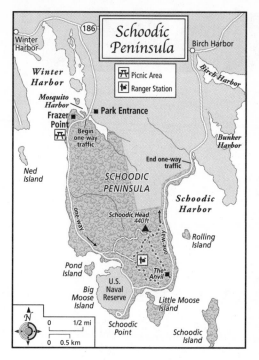

Schoodic Peninsula

⛵ Picnic Area
🏠 Ranger Station

■ Park Entrance

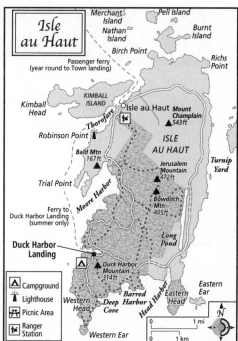

Isle au Haut

Passenger ferry
(year round to Town landing)

Ferry to
Duck Harbor Landing
(summer only)

**Duck Harbor
Landing**

🔺 Campground
⛯ Lighthouse
⛵ Picnic Area
🏠 Ranger Station

avoid crowds and pay even less, go in May and September, when average temperatures are 10 degrees cooler than in July and rates drop to bargain levels. Bugs are worse in May, less of a problem in September.

In winter, Bar Harbor shuts down and visitors are few. Snow is unpredictable. Spring break isn't a good option.

## How Much Time to Spend

It takes time to get to Acadia from most places — too long to justify less than 3 or 4 days. A week is best. There's plenty to do, and staying a week give you access to weekly rentals.

Don't underestimate the time it takes to get around Acadia. Although the distances on the island are small, the traffic is slow and the roads are winding. They were built for sightseeing, not for getting anywhere quickly. Plan your time carefully so that you spend the whole day in one general area and drive across the island only once a day.

## How Far to Plan Ahead

To get the dates and places you want, make hotel reservations for anywhere on the island by April for a July or August visit. June is easier to book. Cottages should be booked by early winter for the following summer. The **Blackwoods Campground** requires reservations in advance through the national system (see "National Park Campground Reservations," in chapter 1, "Planning Your Trip"). The **Seawall Campground** is first-come, first-served, but it's hard to get in during busy months. Several excellent private campgrounds mentioned below take reservations.

Commercial activities such as whale watching, carriage rides, and sea kayaking usually have openings on the same day, but call ahead to make sure. There are plenty of bikes to rent, but it's a good idea to reserve special equipment such as trailers or tandems a day in advance.

## WEATHER CHART: BAR HARBOR AVERAGES

|  | AVG. HIGH (°F) | AVG. LOW (°F) | PRECIP. (IN.) | OCEAN TEMP. (°F) |
|---|---|---|---|---|
| Dec.–Feb. | 34 | 17 | 19.7 | 39 |
| March | 41 | 25 | 4 | 38 |
| April | 53 | 34 | 4.2 | 43 |
| May | 64 | 43 | 3.8 | 50 |
| June | 72 | 51 | 3.2 | 55 |
| July | 78 | 57 | 3 | 59 |
| August | 76 | 56 | 2.7 | 62 |
| September | 68 | 50 | 4.3 | 58 |
| October | 58 | 41 | 4.6 | 54 |
| November | 47 | 32 | 5.9 | 52 |

## READING UP

Each of these books is available from Eastern National, listed at the beginning of the chapter, or at the Hulls Cove Visitor Center. The handy "Pocket Guide" series of little biking, hiking, and paddling books is published by Down East Books (www.downeastbooks.com). **Biking:** *Biking on Mount Desert Island,* by Audrey Minutolo, has maps and descriptions of carriage path tours rated by time, distance, and difficulty, and clear directions. **Hiking:** *Hiking on Mount Desert Island,* by Earl Brechlin, editor of the *Bar Harbor Times,* is a straightforward trail guide with the right amount of detail to get where you're going; buy a good map separately. **Paddling:** *Paddling the Waters of Mount Desert Island,* also by Brechlin, contains plenty of practical information and many nuggets of local knowledge; it is strongest on the freshwater areas. **Maps:** The best map of the whole island is published by National Geographic's Trails Illustrated (www.trailsillustrated.com); it has an amazing level of detail and is printed on plastic. **Nature for Kids:** *Discovering Acadia: A Guide for Young Naturalists,* by Margaret Scheid (Acadia Press), is an ingenious children's field guide and workbook. It is fun, challenging, and beautifully illustrated. **History:** *Mount Desert Island and Acadia National Park: An Informal History,* by Sargent F. Collier (Down East Press), is a light adult-level read with lots of historic pictures.

## GETTING THERE
### By Road

The fastest way to drive to Acadia is up Interstate 95 to Bangor, then southeast on Route 1A to Ellsworth and Route 3 into the park. This typically dull but speedy drive takes about 6 hours from Boston.

The other way to go is slow and potentially frustrating, but it's scenic and full of places to stop along the Maine coast. It turns the drive from Boston into a 1- or 2-day affair. Divert from I-95 at Brunswick (Exit 22) or later, and take mostly two-lane Route 1 through a series of cute, tourist-choked towns on the sea.

If you take an RV to Acadia, also take a car to get around in. RVs don't belong on these narrow, congested roads, and parking is difficult.

## By Air

The Hancock County Airport in Trenton, on Route 3 just off the island, is served from Boston by **Colgan Air** (☎ **800/272-5488** or 207/667-7171; www.colganair.com). A round-trip is around $200. **Hertz** (☎ **800/654-3131** or 207/667-5017; www.hertz.com) rents cars there.

If you want to save money and don't mind driving a bit farther, have your travel agent shop around for the best car-rental and ticket deals at different cities. Portland, a 3-hour drive away, and Bangor, a 1-hour drive away, receive the most flights in Maine; Portland has the most car-rental agencies. Or fly to Boston for the greatest number of choices — and possibly the greatest savings — and drive 6 hours.

## By Water

**The Cat,** a futuristic, high-speed car ferry, runs daily between Bar Harbor and Yarmouth, Nova Scotia, late May through late October. Traveling over the water at 55 mph, the 300-foot catamaran makes the trip in under 3 hours, saving a 630-mile drive. (Reserve at ☎ **888/249-7245** or 207/388-2295, or online at www.catferry.com.) One-way fares are $155 for large cars, $55 for adults, $25 for children, and free for those under 5. One-day excursion fares are the same as one-way passenger fares.

## WHAT TO PACK
## Clothing

You'll want to bring clothes for warm, cool, and rainy weather. You should do some boating while at Acadia; out on the water, you'll probably need sweaters and jackets, and even hats and gloves. Evenings on land can be cool, too, and rain and fog come often. Bring breathable rain gear so that you can get out in the woods during drizzle or light rain, and heavy, waterproof gear if you plan on serious boating. Bring a swimming suit for the lakes and pools. Good walking shoes will suffice for the island's well-tended trails. When you're exploring the tide pools and shoreline, tall rubber boots increase your freedom; you can get a pair for less than $20.

## Gear

Bring bug dope for flying insects and to keep off ticks that carry Lyme disease. Campers should bring good, waterproof gear, including a tarp or other roof for the picnic table. Summer nighttime lows are in the 40s and 50s.

If you're driving all the way from home, bring your bicycles and helmets. If you don't have a car bike rack, the cost of buying a good one is less than 2 days' bike-rental fees for a family of four. Fat-tired bikes are best for the unpaved carriage roads, but any touring bike will make it because the surface is smooth and packed.

# WHERE TO SPEND THE NIGHT

## CAMPING
## Park Service Campgrounds

The Park Service allows gathering of dead, downed wood for fires, but you won't find much; so pick up a couple of bundles at any of the roadside shops or at the grocery store.

**Blackwoods.** Rte. 3, Otter Creek (between Bar Harbor and Seal Harbor). May–Oct $18 per site; Nov and April $10; Dec–Mar free (bathrooms closed). 300 sites; tents or RVs. Campfire grates, cold-water bathrooms, dump station.

This huge campground at the southeast end of the island, near Seal Harbor, doesn't feel so big because the sites are thickly wooded — indeed, little direct sun makes it through the trees. You can walk to the steep, rocky shore of Otter Cove, on the Ocean Loop Drive, or join a long trail up Cadillac Mountain (see "Natural Places: Mount Desert Island," on p. 69), but although you're close to several of the park's other best spots, a lack of trails or sidewalks means that with kids you'll have to drive or take the shuttle. Blackwoods is the only reserved campground at Acadia, and sites go quickly (see "National Park Campground Reservations," in chapter 1, for details on the national reservation system).

**Seawall.** Rte. 102A, Manset (south of Southwest Harbor). Campground ☎ **207/244-3600.** $18 drive-in sites, $12 walk-in sites. 200 sites; tents or RVs. Campfire grates; cold-water bathrooms; dump station. Closed Oct to Memorial Day.

This well-wooded campground is on the southwest end of the island, far from the bustle of Bar Harbor and the carriage roads. Sites are well separated on mossy ground. It's near a cobbled beach and seaside nature trails, and a short drive from sailing at Southwest Harbor and swimming at Echo Lake. Half the sites are walk-in, requiring 100 feet or so of effort.

Reservations are not taken, so a line forms early in the morning for sites in July and August. As someone leaves, the first in line can take the site.

Just east of the campground, **Seawall Camping Supplies** (☎ **207/244-7006**) offers showers, laundry, food, supplies, canoes, lobster, and other country-store goods.

## Commercial Campgrounds

Mount Desert Island has some of the best private campgrounds anywhere.

**Bar Harbor Campground.** Rte. 3, Salisbury Cove (RFD 2, Box 1125), Bar Harbor, ME 04609. ☎ **207/ 288-5185.** www.barharborcamping.com. Tent sites $20, full hookups $27, tax included. No credit cards. No reservations. 300 sites. Hot showers; heated pool; play area; laundry; store; ATM.

Situated with other campgrounds in the touristy area on Route 3 as you approach Bar Harbor, this place is more of a resort than an ordinary campground. Besides the good-sized pool, facilities include basketball, an arcade, shuffleboard, and blueberry picking. Campers choose their own sites, either those in an open, grassy area with a great view across Frenchman Bay, or more secluded sites surrounded by trees. A grocery store, restaurants, and other tourist businesses are nearby.

**Mt. Desert Campground.** Rte. 198, Somesville, Mt. Desert, ME 04660. ☎ **207/244-3710.** $24–$32 per site, up to 2 adults and 2 children, additional adult $5, additional child $2. 150 sites; tents and RVs under 20 ft. only. Water and electricity at some sites; hot showers; ocean swimming and fishing; canoe rentals.

We've spent some of our happiest days at this family-operated campground, our favorite of the many we've visited all over the country. Sites lie among tall trees at the head of glittering Somes Sound, the long fjord that divides MDI, where the restricted tidal flow allows the water to warm to a temperature suitable for hearty swimmers (there's no lifeguard). At the dock, kids catch crabs with a piece of string, and rental canoes wait for exploration of the placid waters. The sites are larger than those at the Park Service campgrounds, and many have wooden platforms to help keep you dry. A real sense of community prevails among many campers who have been coming for years, blossoming in the evening at the Gathering Place, where you can buy an ice cream or a cup of coffee and visit. On the practical side, the bathrooms are clean and comfortable and water is always nearby. The campground is at the center of the island, 5 miles from Bar Harbor, Northwest Harbor, or Southwest Harbor, just west of the intersection of routes 198 and 233.

**Smuggler's Den Campground.** Rte. 102 (P.O. Box 787), Southwest Harbor, ME 04679. ☎ **207/ 244-3944.** Tent sites $23, full hookups $31 for 4 people; $6.50 per person additional person over age 6. 100 sites. Hot showers; heated pool; playground; laundry.

Attractive for RVers, but also great for tenters with kids who need room to run, this campground has lots of amenities, and it's within walking distance of the park's west-side hiking trails and the Echo Lake swimming beach. The campground is in a clearing in the woods just to the south on Route 102, with a huge mowed field for play. RVs camp out in the open, and tents hide back in the trees along the edge of the field. The swimming pool has a small slide and a shallow area for toddlers. A camp store sells the basics. Camp cabins rent for $475 a week in July and August.

## HOTELS

If you don't want to camp or spend a whole week in a cottage rental, you can visit Acadia by staying in a hotel in Bar Harbor or one of the other towns. Expect to pay $120 a night or more for your room in July and August. Rates may be lower in June and are much lower in May and September (I've listed only high-season rates). Most hotels are in and around Bar Harbor, where crowds and traffic take something away from a national park experience. I've also listed one in quiet Northeast Harbor.

**The Acadia Hotel.** 20 Mount Desert St., Bar Harbor, ME 04609. ☎ **207/288-5721.** www.acadiahotel.com. 10 units. High season $115–$135 double; low season $65–$85 double. $10 extra person (child or adult). MC, V.

This is a rare historic inn that accepts children. It has three rooms large enough to accommodate a family (lower rates apply for other rooms), and an apartment with cooking facilities. The classic New England house, with a wraparound porch, faces the town-square park in Bar Harbor. Inside, rooms have all been recently remodeled. A light, Victorian theme carries through the building, appropriate to its period. The proprietor, active in the community, is a great resource for guests. Rooms lack telephones but have TVs and air-conditioning.

**Bar Harbor Regency Holiday Inn SunSpree Resort.** 123 Eden St., Bar Harbor, ME 04609. ☎ **800/23-HOTEL** or 207/288-9723. Fax 207/288-3089. www.barharborholidayinn.com. 221 units. High season $155–$345; low season $95–$175. AE, DISC, MC, V. Closed Nov–Apr.

This luxurious resort of stone-faced buildings on the water near Bar Harbor will tempt you to stay on the well-tended grounds or in your large, quiet room rather than visit the park. The diversions include an attractive outdoor pool with a toddler pool and hot tub, tennis courts, a putting green, a sauna and fitness room, and several choices for dining. You can even get away from the children, signing them up for a day program of structured activities, including lunch and an evening movie (ages 4–11, $30 a day). Rooms, decorated in a colonial style, have high-end amenities, including refrigerators, big TVs, and fashionable bathrooms.

**The Golden Anchor.** 55 West St., Bar Harbor, ME 04609. ☎ **800/328-5033** or 207/288-5033. www.goldenanchorinn.com. 88 units. High season $110–$200 double; low season $45–$120 double. $10 each extra person 13 and over, $5 ages 5–11, free under 5. DISC, MC, V. Closed Nov–Apr.

This hotel feels like a seaside place, with a large swimming pool and hot tub right over the shoreline, but it's in the middle of Bar Harbor, on the main waterfront street where some of the whale-watching boats dock. A decent family restaurant is attached (see "Where to Eat," p. 78). The rooms have refrigerators and satellite TV. The decor is light, if somewhat dated, with wood-plank paneling. The more expensive ones have fine water views and balconies.

**Kimball Terrace Inn.** 10 Huntington Rd. (P.O. Box 1030), Northeast Harbor, ME 04662. ☎ **207/276-3383** or 800/454-6225 reservations only. Fax 207/276-4102. www.kimballterraceinn.com. 70 units. High season $130–$150 double; low season $66–$80. Additional person over age 5 $10, 5 and under free. AE, DISC, MC, V. Closed Nov–Mar.

Northeast Harbor retains a lot of the charm Bar Harbor has lost to crowds and traffic congestion, and this comfortable motel overlooking a lawn that slopes down to the harbor is an easy place to enjoy it. The rooms, in three levels with exterior entrances, are large and well kept, although not all have air-conditioners. Private balconies on the upper levels have a fine view, while the ground-floor patios open onto the lawn, with its good-sized pool and tennis courts. A lobby–sitting room is stocked with games, there is a quiet restaurant, and a short trail leads to Main Street.

**The Villager.** 207 Main St., Bar Harbor, ME 04609. ☎ **207/288-3211** or 207/288-3011. Fax 207/288-2270. www.acadia.net/villager. 63 units. High season $82–$118 double; low season $59–$89 double. $10 extra person, children under 5 free. AE, MC, V. Closed Nov to mid-May.

This is a friendly, basic motel with reasonable prices (for Bar Harbor) and ample parking right in town on a strip of good restaurants. The rooms, opening on the parking lot or an upstairs walkway, are utterly nondescript in a style you might call 1970s motel anonymous. Yet they're comfortable with two double beds and room for a crib, and there is a heated swimming pool on the parking lot.

## COTTAGES

If you're planning to stay for at least a week, renting a cottage makes more sense than staying in a hotel. Besides getting a place more like home, where you can relax and don't have to worry so much about making noise, you'll be able to cook for yourself, saving a lot on restaurant dining and avoiding the tension of eating every meal out.

Summer rentals go from Saturday to Saturday. Most of the attractive houses run $1,000 to $1,500 a week, but you can get into a two-bedroom house for as little as $650. Prices depend on size and location — rentals closer to the beach or in more fashionable neighborhoods cost more. Repeat visitors book a year ahead, and to have a full range of choices you should book by early winter for July and August. You will have to send a deposit — typically a third of the total rental — but agents here aren't as tough about requiring references as those at some other summer house areas. You will not be able to use a credit card for a house rental. Most houses provide linens and utensils, but check ahead for particulars on what to bring. Make sure to inventory any damage when you move in and when you leave to avoid unwarranted charges.

Below are a few of the agents on the island; you can contact others through the chambers of commerce (see "Acadia Address Book," on p. 57). The Internet helps find a cottage; you can browse by area and price, with pictures of each.

**Acadia Cottage Rentals Inc.** 77 Mt. Desert St. (P.O. Box 949), Bar Harbor, ME 04609. ☎ **207/288-3636.** Fax 207/288-5855. www.acadiarental.com.

These friendly folks have cottages all over the island and in towns along the coast.

**The Davis Agency.** 363 Main St. (P.O. Box 1038), Southwest Harbor, ME 04679. ☎ **207/244-3891.** Fax 207/244-9454. www.DaAgy.com.

This agency specializes in the Southwest Harbor area but has properties all over the region.

**Mt. Desert Properties.** P.O. Box 536, Bar Harbor, ME 04609. ☎ **207/288-4523.** www.barharborvacationhome.com.

This agency has properties all over the island, including some near each other for reunions or groups of families.

# WHEN YOU ARRIVE

## ENTRANCE FEES

Acadia charges entrance fees at a station on the **Park Loop Road,** half a mile from Sand Beach. Vehicles are $10 for 7 days. The Park Service intends the fee to apply to the whole park, but collecting it is impractical except on these few miles of scenic waterfront road. Essentially, it is an honor system. The fee supports park improvements.

## VISITOR CENTERS

Each of the visitor centers is seasonal. If you come in winter, stop at the park headquarters on Route 233 west of Bar Harbor.

**Hulls Cove Visitor Center.** Rte. 3 north of Bar Harbor. July–Aug daily 8am–6pm; mid-Apr to June and Sept–Oct daily 8am–4:30pm. Closed Nov to mid-Apr.

The main Park Service visitor center is atop a hill at Hulls Cove, off Route 3 north of Bar Harbor. It's a good idea to stop here when you arrive to pick up maps and sign up for ranger programs. Fifty-two granite steps lead up from the parking lot. The center itself is small and out-of-date, with a desk to ask rangers questions and sign up for programs, a small bookstore, a large relief map of the park, and an auditorium where a 15-minute film on the park shows every half hour.

**Thompson Island Visitors Center.** Rte. 3, on the bridge to Mount Desert Island. Open daily, hours vary. Closed mid-Oct to mid-May.

This small information center is run by the Park Service and the island's Chamber of Commerce. Located on Thompson Island as you cross the bridge from the mainland to MDI, the center offers information on lodging and activities, as well as the park.

**Acadia Information Center.** On the right side of Rte. 3 approaching the island. ☎ **800/358-8550** or 207/667-8550. www.acadiainfo.com. Daily 9am–6pm. Closed mid-Oct to mid-May.

This commercially operated center offers information on its many customers and maintains an updated lodging vacancy board and an extensive website.

## Town Visitor Centers

Each town has its own printed visitor guide, and three have walk-in centers where you can ask questions and get referrals.

Here are their visitor center locations:

**Bar Harbor:** Bar Harbor Chamber of Commerce, 93 Cottage St.

**Southwest Harbor:** Southwest Harbor/ Tremont Chamber of Commerce, 204 Main St., Southwest Harbor.

**Northeast Harbor:** Mt. Desert Chamber of Commerce, Sea Street at the marina, Northeast Harbor. Open seasonally.

## GETTING AROUND
## By Car

Although the distances aren't great, traffic is slow on these scenic, winding roads. Plan your days to spend as much time as you can in one area. Parking in Bar Harbor can be tough; try at Main and Park streets, near the big park. Trailhead parking is a problem, too; if you don't get there early, you might not be able to use the trail. RV sites with hookups are available at some commercial campgrounds, but if you bring an RV, plan to leave it in the campground and use a passenger car or the shuttle to get around, because the narrow, congested roads are not suitable for big vehicles.

## By Shuttle Bus

A free shuttle called the Island Explorer (☎ **207/288-4573,** summer only) runs seven routes all over the island and to the airport late June through Labor Day. By using it, you avoid parking problems in Bar Harbor and at trailheads. The shuttle also allows one-way hikes on some of the park's trails and has bike racks. Service covers all the park campgrounds

**Emergencies**   The island is in the process of installing a ☎ 911 system, which should be in place by the time you read this. In the meantime, you can call ☎ 911 in Bar Harbor. In Mt. Desert (Northeast Harbor or Seal Harbor), call the **Mt. Desert Police Department** ☎ 207/276-5111. In Southwest Harbor, call the **Southwest Harbor Police Department** ☎ 207/244-5552 (non-emergency 207/244-7911); Fire: ☎ 207/244-5233; Ambulance: ☎ 207/244-5030. Elsewhere on the island, call the **Hancock County Sheriffs Department,** ☎ 207/667-7575 (non-emergency 207/667-7577). For emergencies on the water, the **U.S. Coast Guard** unit at Southwest Harbor is at ☎ 207/244-5121. **Mount Desert Island Hospital** is at 10 Wayman Lane in Bar Harbor (☎ 207/ 288-5081; www.mdihospital.org). The **Community Health Center** in Southwest Harbor is at 9 Village Green Way (☎ **207-244-5630**).

**Stores**   A small grocery store is in each village around the island. **Don's Shop 'N Save** is on Cottage Street in Bar Harbor. Do major shopping as you arrive: **Shaw's** is at the corner of High and Foster streets in Ellsworth, on the right side of Route 3 on the way to Acadia. Walmart also is on Route 3 as you leave Ellsworth for the island.

**Banks**   Banks on Main Street in Bar Harbor have ATMs.

**Post Offices**   The main post office in Bar Harbor is on Cottage Street, across from the grocery store. Villages across the island also have post offices.

**Gear Rental**   Several bike and canoe rental and kayak agencies have shops in Bar Harbor, including **Acadia Bike and Canoe,** 48 Cottage St. (☎ **207/288-9605,** or 800/526-8615; www.acadia fun.com), and **Bar Harbor Bicycle Shop,** 141 Cottage St. (☎ **207/288-3886;** www.barharbor bike.com).

**Gear Sales**   An **L.L. Bean Factory Outlet** is at 150 High St. (Route 3) in Ellsworth (☎ **207/ 667-7753;** www.llbean.com). **Cadillac Mountain Sports,** 26 Cottage St., Bar Harbor, and 34 High St., Ellsworth (☎ **207/288-4532**), is a fancy, boutique-style sporting-goods store with high-quality gear for sale.

and attractions and most commercial camp-grounds, with all lines connecting at Bar Harbor's Village Green. Service is frequent near Bar Harbor, but becomes impractically far apart as you get farther afield. A shuttle schedule is published in the park newspaper.

## By Boat

Mail and tour boats take passengers to park sites in the Cranberry Islands. See "Boating" (p. 72) for details.

## KEEPING SAFE & HEALTHY

See "Dealing with Hazards," in chapter 1, for tips on poison ivy, sunburn, seasickness, and Lyme disease. Here are other things to watch out for at Acadia:

## Bike Safety

Keep to the carriage roads with children, carrying bikes from the rental agency to the trailhead on your car rather than riding through the streets (you can rent a rack). These busy roads aren't suitable for children.

## Falls

Tide pooling and exploring on the rocky shorelines can be dangerous because of the steep, slippery rocks. Sometimes you can't tell when a rock you're about to step on will be slimy with algae. Wear good shoes or boots and keep your children under good control; and don't venture into areas with drop-offs or moving waves.

# Enjoying the Park

## Natural Places: Mount Desert Island

### Cadillac Mountain

A bald granite peak on the east side of MDI, Cadillac Mountain, is the tallest mountain on the eastern shore of North and Central America. It's 1,530 feet tall, not much of a mountain compared to most places; but this old coast has been worn down by glaciers and weather for so long that Cadillac Mountain is the highest thing left, so from the top you can see a long way. It's said to be the first place the sun rises in the United States. The name came from a French aristocrat who tried to colonize the area in 1688 and later founded Detroit, and even later got a car named for him. See "Waves of Glaciation," in chapter 2, "Moving Water, Moving Land," to learn how Cadillac Mountain was made.

You can drive to the top of the mountain, where there's a small store, but consider hiking instead. The trails across the barren granite have great views and are fun places to hike as you pick your way from one rock cairn to the next and step over small ledges. These open areas are good for bird-watching too.

Trails climb the mountain from four directions. The **West Face Trail,** from Bubble Pond, is the shortest and steepest, at 1.4 miles (you can get to the trailhead on the loop road or the carriage roads). The easiest is the **North Ridge Trail,** paralleling the road 2.2 miles from just outside Bar Harbor. The **Cadillac South Ridge Trail** is one of Acadia's longer hikes, leading 4.2 miles from the Blackwoods Campground gradually up the mountain (you can cut 7/10 of a mile off by starting from Route 3).

### Along the Park Loop Road

The shoreline from Sand Beach around the southeast corner of the island to Seal Harbor is scenic and full of interesting places to stop. Traffic goes one-way, and you have to pay at the fee station. At Sand Beach you can join trails that climb half a mile up to rocky Great Head, or walk along the fairly level **Ocean Trail** that leads 1.8 miles to Otter Point, getting a closer look at the dramatic coast than is possible from the parallel road. **Thunder Hole,** where waves boom into a cave, is along the way, as are the impressive **Otter Cliffs. Otter Point,** at the end of the trail, offers great tide pooling at low tide (for more information, see "Activities," p. 72; the geology is explained in "Waves Shaping Rocky Shore," in chapter 2).

### The Ponds

Like the claws of a great animal scratching across Mt. Desert Island's granite back, ancient glaciers left deep north-south scratches in the stone. Filled with water, they are the park's intricate ponds and Somes Sound fjord (it's like the ponds, but open to the sea). Some of these ponds hide in the mountain clefts, discovered only by carriage roads or foot paths — Bubble Pond, Aunt Betty Pond, Witch Hole Pond. Gracious carriage roads encircle Eagle Lake and Jordan Pond, finding glittering views under a canopy of broad shade trees. At Jordan Pond's grassy southern lawn, the famous tea house serves popovers and visitors lazily examine a numbered nature trail (see "Where to Eat," p. 78). On the western side of the island, Long Pond branches in complexity, inviting exploration by canoe, and Echo Pond sounds with the voice swimmers (see "Activities," p. 72; see "Waves of Glaciation," in chapter 2, for how the ponds were created). These are places of childhood adventure and great places to be learned and appreciated.

## Frenchman Bay & Great Harbor

The water off Bar Harbor, with its many small islands, is Frenchman Bay, a rich ground for watching seals, osprey, and other wildlife. It is busy with sea-kayaking excursions, fishing, and wildlife-watching boat trips (see "Activities," p. 72). You can even walk to one of those alluring little islands. For 90 minutes on each side of low tide, the sandbar path to wooded Bar Island is exposed, starting at Bridge Street, off West Street.

Great Harbor, site of the Cranberry Isles, lies south and east of Mt. Desert Island, faced by Southwest Harbor and Northeast Harbor. It is a lovely area where small passenger ferries bound for the islands pass seals, birds, and quaint marine scenery (see "Boating," p. 72). These islands are inhabited — you can rent a cottage there for a week. There's a little park museum in the village of Islesford, on Little Cranberry Island, and a wonderful ranger program goes to the historic but now deserted Baker Island (see "Places for Learning," p. 72). The area is the essence of coastal Maine, bright and windy and full of life.

## Seawall Area

This is a peaceful area, off the park's beaten track, where you can get down to the wild seashore and see some classically picturesque Maine scenery. The seawall itself (near the picnic ground across from the campground) is a natural barrier of cobblestones built by the ocean, at one time removed from the beach to pave city streets in the northeastern United States. Just to the west, two flat paths lead over sandy ground about 1½ miles round-trip to a rocky shore, great for exploring and seeing birds; they're both fun, easy kid hikes. The **Wonderland Trail** ends at an exposed point with plenty of room to spread out; a little to the west, the **Ship Harbor Nature Trails** traces the edge of the tiny harbor in a loop, with interpretive signs on the way.

Less than a mile farther west, a lighthouse stands on Bass Harbor Head, with steps down the rocky point that allow you to get down in front and see the waves come in and to get a good picture of the light. It is a working Coast Guard station and is not open to tours, probably not worth a special trip.

## Natural Places: Isle au Haut

Much of the southern half of this island some 20 miles southwest of MDI is within the park, but few visitors make it here. Its relatively undeveloped lands are a different experience from the main part of the park; this is a place for solitude and contemplation in the woods and on the seashore, without cars or many tramping feet.

To get to Isle au Haut, take the passenger ferry from Stonington (Route 172 and Route 15 from Ellsworth). On the island you'll find a small village, a ranger station, and a campground with five lean-tos. A few trails follow the coast and cross the rounded, wooded hills in the center of the island.

Despite what some Park Service handouts say, you don't need a permit to visit the island unless you are bringing a large group. But you will need reservations for the campground, which are difficult to obtain. Reservation requests must be mailed to the park on April 1 with a $25 fee; from those postmarked on that day (but no earlier), the Park Service picks in order those who will get reservations during the whole summer. Call ☎ **207/288-3338** or write ahead for the reservation card and information on the system.

## Natural Places: Schoodic Peninsula

About 45 miles east of Bar Harbor by road, but less than 10 miles over the water, this part of the park takes in a rocky mainland point that you can see from Great Head or Otter Point on MDI. Most visitors just go for the 7-mile, one-way loop drive around the point. There are also a picnic area, a ranger station, and a few short trails to the 440-foot summit of Schoodic Head. To get here, take Route 1 east from Ellsworth, then go south on Route 186.

# Places for Learning

**Museum of Natural History, College of the Atlantic.** 105 Eden St. (just north of Bar Harbor on Rte. 3). ☎ **207/288-5395.** www.coa.edu/nhm/. Admission $3.50 adults, $1.50 teens, $1 children 3–12, free under 3. Summer daily 10am–5pm; winter Thurs–Fri and Sun 1–4pm, Sat 10am–4pm. Closed Thanksgiving to mid-Jan and middle 2 weeks of Mar.

Children will certainly enjoy an hour or two of a rainy day spent in this superb little museum on the grassy campus of the environmentally inclined college. Students have built wildlife dioramas that capture an entire story in the life of an animal: raccoons getting into garbage, voles emerging from a snowy burrow observed by a hungry hawk, a honey-raiding bear swarmed by bees. An excellent touch tank allows you to explore a living tide pool indoors, learning the creatures you can hunt for on the shore later. There are activities for children and adults, the museum offers interpretive programs, and a summer field study program leads children to the island's shores, forests, and ponds for ecological education.

**Mount Desert Oceanarium.** Rte. 3, Thomas Bay, Bar Harbor. ☎ **207/288-5005.** Also at 172 Clark Point Rd., Southwest Harbor. ☎ **207/244-7330.** Bar Harbor admission $10.95 adults, $7.95 children 4–12, free under 4; Southwest Harbor admission $6.95 adults, $4.95 children 4–12, free under 4. Discounts available to visit both sites. Mon–Sat 9am–5pm. Closed mid-Oct to mid-May.

These two privately owned facilities focus on teaching and entertaining children with facts and demonstrations about the Maine shore and its marine life. The Bar Harbor facility has a program about seals, a lobster hatchery and museum, and a marsh nature walk. The Southwest Harbor museum is in a well-worn waterfront building, with aquariums, huge lobsters, a boat kids can climb on, a tide-pool touch tank, and demonstrations. It's well done, with hands-on, personal attention; yet the prices are more than I could justify.

**Islesford Historical Museum.** Islesford, Little Cranberry Island. Free admission. Mon–Sat 10am–noon, 12:30–4:30pm; Sun opens 45 min. later.

Closed Oct to mid-May. See "Boating" (p. 72), for ferry information.

The neat thing about this little museum is that you take a 40-minute mail-boat ferry ride to get there. Islesford is a tiny island village with a restaurant and store and the museum, in an odd brick building. An island summer resident (who's buried out back) started the collection of ship models, dolls, nautical items, and antiques in 1927. Now it is run by the Park Service.

**The Abbe Museum.** 26 Mt. Desert St. and at Sieur de Monts Spring ☎ **207/288-3519.** www.abbemuseum.org. Bar Harbor: Admission $4.50 adults, $2 children 12 and under. July–Aug Wed–Sun 10am–9pm, Mon–Tues 10am–5pm; June and Sept daily 10am–5pm; Oct–May Thurs–Sun 10am–5pm. Sieur de Monts (see below for directions): Admission $2 adults, $1 children 12 and under. July–Aug daily 9am–5pm; spring and fall daily 10am–4pm; closed mid-Oct to mid-May.

The Bar Harbor location, planned to open after publication, expands the old museum in the park by eight times, providing more room to show a fine collection of baskets and other artifacts of Maine Indians, and to teach more about their life today. The small museum in the park will still operate seasonally. Its exhibits, while of interest to adults and teenagers, are unlikely to hold the attention of younger children for long.

# Sieur de Monts Spring Area

This area, the original core of the park, contains three places to learn about the island: a botanical garden, a nature center, and a branch of the Abbe Museum, a collection of Native American artifacts (covered above). Take Route 3 or the Park Loop Road about a mile south from Bar Harbor and follow the signs. Pick up the free guide booklet to follow the nature trail through the area.

We most enjoyed the **Wild Gardens of Acadia.** This small botanical garden was planted by volunteers to show Mount Desert Island's native plants in their natural habitats. A complex of gravel paths and a brook divide

12 habitat types where labels teach the names of plants and trees you encounter while biking or hiking. The children were delighted with the garden's map-reading, exploring, and imaginative opportunities.

The **Nature Center** is a room with animal and bird mounts and displays explaining natural processes and park management. It's a good place to get questions answered and to find out what the animals you may see look like up close. It is open July through August, daily 9am–5pm, sometimes shorter hours off-season; closed late September to mid-September.

## ACTIVITIES
### Biking

Acadia is the best national park for biking, and biking is one of the best ways for a family to get into the woods. All of the carriage roads are free of cars, giving kids wonderful new freedom. You gently swoop over mountains and past lakes; riding here is like a dream. (Learn more about the carriage roads under "History: Putting a Park Together," p. 57.) Most of the island's regular roads aren't safe for families to ride, but there are some spectacular exceptions, such as Sergent Drive, leading along the east side of Somes Sound north of Northeast Harbor, and, for more advanced riders, the Park Loop Road.

Some planning will improve your ride. We saw some out-of-shape riders who were suffering greatly on the carriage roads. All the trails are somewhat hilly — that makes them interesting — so sedentary people may have a hard time. The good guide book listed under "Reading Up" (p. 62) can help you choose a ride at your ability level, as can your rental agency. Even without the book, you will need a map. The Park Service and rental agencies hand out basic maps free, but because navigation is a big part of the fun for children, you may want to buy a better one with topographic lines (see "Reading Up").

Try not to start your ride in Bar Harbor. The ride through city streets is steep and scary with kids. Also, avoid the crowded Eagle Lake trailhead. I prefer to rent a bike rack for $5 (the park shuttles also have bike racks) and start out at Jordan Pond House, which is on the Park Loop Road, or at the Parkman Mountain Trailhead on Route 198 near Northeast Harbor, or at the Brown Mountain Gatehouse near Lower Haddock Pond. You will have these trails more to yourself, and they are among the park's most beautiful.

Don't let small children hold you back; they can ride a trailer or trailer bike (also called tag-a-longs). Trailer bikes attach to the back of an adult's bike to make it into a tandem that's sized just right for a kid. A brilliant invention, they bridge the gap when kids are too big for trailers but not ready to keep up with grown-ups on their own bikes — roughly ages 4 through 7. You feel like a real team riding together. Take it easy at first, however, because the parent often has to counterbalance a wobbly beginning rider. A trailer, carrying a baby or toddler, also can carry your picnic and jackets.

Bike-rental agencies are listed under "For Handy Reference" (p. 68). Adult bikes are around $18 a day, kids $10, with discounts for half-day, multiple-day, or weeklong rentals. Trailers and trailer bikes are around $10 a day; car racks, $5 a day. Bring your own bikes if possible; buying a good bike rack costs around $125, or less than 2 days of bike rental for our family.

### Boating

Besides the sailing, whale watching, canoeing, and sea kayaking opportunities covered below, the waters around Mt. Desert, with their wildlife and many islands, are a powerboat paradise. An afternoon boat ride can take you to a quaint island village or just to see the seals, osprey, and incomparable scenery.

The least-expensive choices are the passenger ferries and excursions that run from Northeast and Southwest harbors to the Cranberry Islands (see "Frenchman Bay and Great Harbor," p. 70), including Islesford

Historical Museum (see p. 71). A typical round-trip fare to Islesford or Great Cranberry Island is $10 or $12, with half off for children. **Beal and Bunker, Inc. (☎ 207/244-3575),** runs many times a day from the municipal pier in Northeast Harbor. **Cranberry Cove Boating Co. (☎ 207/244-5882** or 207/460-3977) goes from the upper town dock at Southwest Harbor. Others offer similar service, or rides to islands farther afield; check with the visitor center.

For slightly more money, you can take a guided tour, but if you don't have time for that or if you want to go from Bar Harbor, there are plenty of choices for prices ranging from $12 to $22 per adult or $7 to $15 for children. **Islesford Ferry Co. (☎ 207/276-3717),** the folks with the Baker Island boat, have other nature tours from Northeast Harbor, as does **Sea Princess Cruises (☎ 207/276-5352),** which offers a tour of almost 3 hours for only $15 for adults.

One of the most appealing boat tours from Bar Harbor is the Katherine, a 42-foot lobster boat, which hauls lobster pots on its 90-minute tours, bringing up sea cucumbers, hermit crabs, and starfish to examine, as well as lobster you can buy. It is operated by **Bar Harbor Whale Watch Company (☎) 207/288-2386;** www.whalesrus.com); they also offer a 2-hour Frenchman's Bay wildlife tour and the offshore whale-watch tours covered below.

Even better, rent your own boat. There's no sense of freedom greater than that when you're behind the wheel of a boat. **Harbor Boat Rentals,** 1 West St., next to the Town Pier in Bar Harbor (☎ **207/288-3757),** offers Boston Whaler and Mako powerboats for use in Frenchman Bay. (Sailboats are covered below.)

## Canoeing

Acadia is an excellent setting for beginning canoeists. The park's smooth, long ponds are safe, interesting places to paddle and learn the advantages of silent travel for watching birds and animals. The best way to go is probably to rent from **National Park Canoe Rental (☎ 907/244-5854;** www.acadia.net/canoe), which has an outlet at the north end of Long Pond, on Route 102 (Pretty Marsh Road) on the west side of the island (they also operate in Bar Harbor, **☎ 207-288-0007).** It's a big lake with a swimming float and lots of bays and channels to explore. You can also take your own canoe or one you rent in Bar Harbor with a car-top carrier to any of the other lakes (see "For Handy Reference," p. 68, for rental agencies). Echo Lake has the added advantage of the swimming beach, Jordan Pond has fish and gravel beaches for picnicking, and Somes Sound offers protected marine waters (easily accessible only if you stay at Mt. Desert Campground, p. 64). Launch spots are marked on the official park map. For a book with details on all the choices, see "Reading Up" (p. 62).

## Carriage & Horseback Riding

Younger children will enjoy carriage rides along the carriage roads that Rockefeller originally built for horses, not bikes. The carriages are carts with rows of seats, pulled by a team of two horses. Drivers offer a little commentary on the passing scenery, but mostly you just go for the ride. It's fun to watch the passing bicyclists below you, but perhaps not enough of a thrill for older children. **Wildwood Stables,** half a mile south of Jordan Pond House on the Park Loop Road, is the park concessionaire (☎ **207/276-3622;** www.acadia.net/wildwood/). One- and two-hour rides leave several times a day in the summer. An hour is plenty; that tour, which circles Day Mountain, costs $13.50 for ages 13 and up, $7 for ages 6 to 12, and $4 for ages 2 to 5. Two-hour tours go farther afield, allow better views, or stop for a snack at Jordan Pond House. Call ahead for times. You can make reservations with a credit card. Don't be late, and bring small bills to tip the driver. No horses are for rent in the park, but if you bring a horse you can stable it at Wildwood.

## Hiking

Acadia offers more good family day hikes in a smaller area than anywhere else I know. The park has more than 100 miles of trails, but few of them are more than a few miles long. Many cover wonderful terrain, passing through tall, quiet woods; rounding fresh, bright ponds; and mounting bare granite highlands. Old trails have granite steps or iron climbing rungs. I mentioned some easy and popular choices under "Natural Places," above, including the **Cadillac Mountain trails, Ocean Trail, Bar Island, Wonderland,** and **Ship Harbor.** But with such a wide choice, there's no reason to limit yourself to these. The Park Service gives away a list of trails rated by difficulty, which essentially means steepness. The book mentioned above under "Reading Up" provides much more information for planning a hike. Or, to take another approach, just get on a trail and start walking: There's a trailhead every time you turn around, and the distances are small.

## Sailing

You couldn't ask for prettier waters for a day sail than those of Great Harbor and Somes Sound, which is probably why Southwest Harbor's unique MDI Community Sailing Center exists (☎ 207/244-7905 or 207/244-3713). Members who demonstrate their sailing knowledge can use the center's fleet of sailboats all summer. A $300 family membership also includes a week of the Junior Sailing Program. Contact the center through Harbor House Community Center (p. 77). For just 1 day's sailing, **Mansell Boat Co.,** on Shore Road just south of Southwest Harbor (☎ 207/244-5625; www.mansellboatrentals.com), rents sailboats for $125 a day, and offers 3-hour lessons for $175. They rent powerboats too.

If you want to sail but don't want to handle your own boat, you can take one of several excursions aboard larger vessels that make short day trips from Mount Desert Island. **Downeast Windjammer Cruises** (☎ 207/288-4585; www.downeastwindjammer.com) operates a four-masted schooner, the Margaret Todd, on 90-minute to 2-hour Frenchman Bay cruises from the Bar Harbor Inn Pier (the ticket office is at 27 Maine St.). The trips cost $27.50 for adults and $17.50 for children under 12.

If you bring your own boat, Southwest Harbor has every service cruising sailors might need. The **Hinckley Company** (www.hinckleyyacht.com), builder of the classic yachts, is based here, on Shore Road. It charters sailboats as bare boats (☎ 800/492-7245 or 207/244-5008) or with crews (☎ 800/504-2305 or 207/244-0122). If you enjoy sailing, cruising the Maine coast on a comfortable yacht is sublime. Unfortunately, if you have to ask how much it costs, you probably can't afford it. Bare boats go for $2,250 to $5,500 a week; deposits and references on your sailing experience are required. Boats with crews start at $5,200 a week. In either case, reserve by March for summer.

## Sea Kayaking

Sea kayaking is a terrific family sport, a child in the front of a two-seat kayak while a parent sits in back. I first paddled with Robin when he was 7, but I have friends who have taken much younger children and even dogs. As long as you can trust your child (or animal) not to freak out, you should be fine. With a hull larger and flatter than a river kayak and a center of gravity lower than a canoe, a sea kayak is the most stable of the three. You skim silently along the surface of the sea, perhaps just inches off the shore. It's the closest thing to walking on water.

Beginners should go with a guide. **Coastal Kayaking Tours,** part of Acadia Bike and Canoe, 48 Cottage St. (☎ 800/526-8615 or 207/288-9605, www.acadiafun.com), offers several daily paddles, including a 4-hour outing for families with children as young as 8. The company has its act together; our guide was professional and friendly without being intrusive. Where you go depends on weather conditions. It's nice to go right in Frenchman Bay, but because fog or wind often make that too risky, you may have to ride a van to the northern side of the island. That's far from wilderness, but still a lot of fun. It costs $45 per person. Other trips range from 2½ hours to 3 days — trips that could include island camping or go from inn to inn. They also rent kayaks for $35 to $55 a day and offer instruction.

## Swimming

The ocean waters of Mount Desert Island are generally too cold for swimming, but there's a good beach where even young children can swim on **Echo Lake,** with changing rooms and a lifeguard. The beach is very gradual. Hiking trails to Beech Mountain and other peaks connect to the parking area, so some of you can have a more vigorous day while others swim, wade, and sun. Canoeing is permitted on the lake, too. To get there, turn right off Route 102 south toward Southwest Harbor.

## Tide Pooling

If you don't know how to go tide pooling, perhaps your children can teach you. It's all about climbing over wet rocks to find strange little animals; all you need is curiosity. You can bring an identification key and a magnifying glass if you want, but we've had more fun with a pail in which to temporarily imprison tiny fish and crabs. Do wear shoes with good traction and which you can get wet. And do choose a time when the tide is low and still has some time to go out; a table is published in the *Beaver Log,* the free park newspaper.

At Acadia, the difference between low and high tide is 12 feet: That's a lot of sea floor to explore. **Otter Point,** on the Park Loop Road, is one of the best spots, with a large parking lot and plenty of uneven rocky shore where tide pools can collect. Be careful of slips and falls — the rocks can be steep and slippery. Don't let squeamishness deter you — the creatures may be slimy, but there's nothing there to hurt you. Turn over rocks and brush aside seaweed to see what's underneath; but put everything and everyone back where you found them, and be careful not to trample living things. (See "Experiment: Tide Pool Plant or Animal?" on p. 76; "The Intertidal Zone," in chapter 2; and "Natural History: The Systems of Life," in chapter 20, "Ecology: Fitting It Together.")

The Park Service offers good ranger-led tide-pool excursions; check the schedule in the *Beaver Log.*

## Whale Watching

On an evening boat ride from Bar Harbor, we motored out of sight of land 30 miles into the Gulf of Maine and, as if by prior arrangement, met a pod of 20 or more humpback whales lunge feeding close on either side of the boat. When humpbacks feed, they spin a circular net of bubbles to contain schools of herring, then lunge upward through the school with open mouths to swallow the fish. Their upward momentum carries them explosively through the surface of the ocean, a startling and awesome sight. (For more on humpback whale behavior, see p. 47.)

Now the downside: Children 6 and younger may get bored, especially if the whales don't show up quickly. Indeed, these Gulf of Maine waters, because of their size, can be a hard place to find whales compared to predictable areas such as Cape Cod's Stellwagen Bank. This big open water also always has ocean swells, bringing on seasickness. Take Dramamine before setting out, and don't go if the weather is rough. Also, bundle up very warmly in sweaters, jackets, hats, and gloves.

**Bar Harbor Whale Watch Co. (☎ 800/ WHALES-4** or 207/288-2386; www.whales rus.com) offers 2½- to 3-hour whale-watching trips from 1 West St. in Bar Harbor with a high-speed catamaran. It costs $39 for adults; $25 for kids age 6 to 14; and $8 for kids 5 and under. They offer a 70% refund if you don't see any whales of any species. Reserve a day or two ahead if possible. Other tours by the same company add bird-watching for puffins or use

# EXPERIMENT: TIDE POOL PLANT OR ANIMAL?

One of the odd things about the life of tide pools is that it's not always easy to tell the plants from the animals. On land, you would assume you were looking at a plant if you came upon a living thing without eyes, ears, head, arms, legs, heart, or brain, and that is permanently rooted to one spot. Not so on the shore. None of the tide-pool life listed here has those things, but some of them are animals. Guess which is a plant and which is an animal. Then develop your own hypothesis (or idea) of what the real difference is between plants and animals. The answers are on p. 79, under "Tide Pool Answers." The page number by each name is where to find its picture.

**Barnacles** (p. 46): After a barnacle sticks to something hard — a rock, shell, or boat — it never moves again. Barnacles are shaped like tiny white smokestacks and they are as hard as bone on the outside. When they are under moving water, a door opens at the top and a tiny sweeper comes out to catch food drifting by. When the tide goes out and the barnacle is exposed to the air, the door closes to keep its inside moist. Plant or animal?

**Sea anemones** (p. 474): A bright flower with fleshy petals stands on a thick stalk on a rock, on a dock piling, or in the sand, a delicious sight to a small passing animal. But when anything touches the petals — such as a fish or your finger — they quickly close into a ball (they're not really petals at all). That's how the anemone catches its dinner. Plant or animal?

**Dinoflagellates:** If you put a drop of tide-pool water under a microscope, you likely will see lots of strangely shaped little things floating and swimming around. Dinoflagellates are probably among them. These little creatures, among the most common on earth, have two wiggly arms called flagella that push them through the water. They live by taking in energy from the sun and carbon dioxide and nutrients from the water around them. Plant or animal?

**Mussels:** The big mats of blue shells on the rocks are mussels, permanently tied to one spot by threads. One mussel by itself can easily tear off, but thousands of them together are safe; then, you can't even see the threads, just a solid area of hard blue shells. When the tide covers them, the shells open slightly and the mussels filter food from the water. Plant or animal?

(Answers are on p. 79.)

---

a different boat; their lobster fishing tour is described under "Boating." The whale season is mid-May to late August.

## PROGRAMS

Acadia National Park has some ranger-led programs that go beyond the lectures or short walks parks often offer. All are listed in the *Beaver Log* park newspaper. For some, you need to sign up in advance at the Hulls Cove Visitor Center, so be sure to pick up the *Beaver Log* and be ready to make some decisions when you go there (it is also on the park website, www.nps.gov/acad).

## Children's Programs

The park offers several programs a week aimed at children 5 to 12. The best may be the **Island's Edge** hike and tide-pool explore that Robin and I joined. Each child wore a magnifying glass around his or her neck to inspect the finds the ranger pointed out over 2 hours of walking, first in the forest and then on the shoreside rocks. The children's programs require advance sign-up at the Hulls Cove Visitor Center to prevent overcrowding.

The park's **Junior Ranger program** uses booklets that cost $1.50 at the Visitor Center, Sieur de Monts Spring Nature Center, or the campgrounds. Kids complete the worksheets and attend ranger programs to win a Junior Ranger pin, which you pick up at one of the visitor centers. The booklets, one for 7 and younger and one for 8 and older, are mostly rainy-day activities to do with a pencil. They will take time but won't be too hard for the intended ages with a little reading help. On the other hand, a much better book of this kind is listed under "Reading Up" (p. 62).

## Family & Adult Programs

Programs start as early as 7am, for a 3-hour bird-watching outing, or as late as 9:30pm, to watch the stars on Sand Beach. The best are the half-day, ranger-guided boat excursions for wildlife watching and visiting the little islands just south of Mount Desert. Robin still talks about the **Baker Island Cruise,** which took us to a small island with a lighthouse where a family subsisted 150 years ago — their story also is told in an engaging picture book, *Island Boy,* by Barbara Cooney (Puffin). You could almost see their children playing on the granite shores beside ours. We also saw seals and an osprey that day. Reserve directly with the **Islesford Ferry (☎ 907/276-3717).** The fare is $18 adults, $10 children 4 to 12, free under 4. The boat leaves from Northeast Harbor. Dress warmly. The ranger-led **Islesford Historical Cruise** visits quiet Little Cranberry Islands and the Islesford Historical Museum (see p. 71). It also requires boat reservations; see the *Beaver Log.* But many of the free adult programs don't require prior sign-up.

**Campfire programs** take place every night of the summer at Blackwoods and Seawall campgrounds. The topics, on natural history, conservation, culture, and even sing-alongs, are posted at the campground and printed in the *Beaver Log.* Anyone can come — you don't have to be camping. Times change during the year; check at the campground bulletin board.

## Summer Camps

Acadia is a place where, if you schedule a long enough vacation, parents and kids can split up for part of that time, each doing what they most enjoy.

**Camp Cadillac,** operated by the Mount Desert Island YMCA, 21 Park St. (P.O. Box 51), Bar Harbor, ME 04609 (☎ 207/ 288-3511; www.mdiymca.org), offers a tremendous array of nature, outdoors, learning, art, and sports activity camps for children ages 4 to 16. Besides using the 100-year-old Y's impressive facility in Bar Harbor, the camps roam over the national park and island, and some even go off the island for sea kayaking and the like. The day programs last from late June to late August and cost about $90 for a week of full days. Reserve well ahead.

**Harbor House Community Center,** P.O. Box 836, Southwest Harbor, ME 04662 (☎ 207/244-3713, www.mainetoday.koz. com/maine/harborhous), offers day camps for kids 2½ to 14. Groups up to age 9 go on field trips to museums and outdoor activities each day. Sailing camp, for ages 9 through 14, costs $110 a week. Camps run mid-June to mid-August, and you need to reserve by mid-May. They also operate the MDI Community Sailing Center (see p. 74).

## FUN OUTSIDE THE PARK

A section of lower-quality tourist development lies along Route 3 leading north and west

---

### PLACES FOR RELAXED PLAY & PICNICS

At times Acadia feels like a huge city park; it's not hard to find safe places to play or picnic. We made good use of the **Village Green** in Bar Harbor, at the corner of Main and Mount Desert streets, where there are a fountain, a gazebo, and a lawn to romp on. A much bigger park, with a fenced playground, is at Park and Main streets, near the YMCA. **Sand Beach** and **Echo Lake Beach** are also great spots to lie back and let the kids do whatever they want. **Seal Harbor** has a modest ocean beach and a village green.

from the Hulls Cove Visitor Center to Ellsworth, off the island. If you decide on an afternoon of empty-calorie fun, this is where you'll find mini-golf courses, water slides, and go-carts. Take a look on your drive to Acadia to decide what you want to do, then set aside time for the outing. It's 20 miles of slow driving from Bar Harbor to Ellsworth.

# WHERE TO EAT

## LOW-STRESS MEALS
There are no fast-food franchises on MDI, but you can get quick, familiar food in each town.

## Bar Harbor
A popular neighborhood pizza place, with the menu on the wall, is on Cottage Street, near the intersection with Main. **Epi's Pizza and Subs,** 8 Cottage St. (☎ **207/288-5853**), charges under $5 for a sub, around $10 for a large pizza. They're open daily in summer 10am to 9pm, winter Monday through Saturday 10am to 8pm, and they don't take credit cards.

The **Village Green** (☎ **207/288-9450**) is a casual restaurant and bakery with takeout, seating on the sidewalk, and a pleasingly worn indoor dining area with a high ceiling and a bar serving microbrews. They serve good, simple food which comes quickly; there's no children's menu for lunch, but there are plenty of inexpensive choices. Lunch is $6 to $8 and dinner entrees are around $13, with a kids' menu at $4.50. It is open daily 6:30am to 10pm, but closes at 2pm in mid-winter.

The **Pier,** at 55 West St. (☎ **207/ 288-2110**), is a dock restaurant associated with the Golden Anchor Hotel. The dining room is surrounded by big water views, but the decor and food suggest a typical family seafood restaurant, with a good children's menu and adult entrees around $12. It is a quick, handy spot for breakfast, with a buffet that costs $4 for kids, $8 adults. In summer it opens at 7:30am and stays open through dinner. Across the street, the **West Street Café** is another good choice, open for lunch and dinner.

## Northeast Harbor
The **Docksider Restaurant,** in a rough-hewn building on the way down to the harbor at 14 Sea St. (☎ **207/276-3965**), serves a broad and inexpensive choice of seafood, sandwiches, and deserts (PB&J $2, lobster crepes $16) in a small dining room hung with fishing nets, or outside, or for takeout. It's very casual; in fact, service was scattered. They serve lunch or dinner starting at 11am.

For pizza, try The **Colonel's Rest** (☎ **207/ 276-5147**), an airy deli and bakery with indoor or outdoor tables and takeout, down a walkway from Main Street. They're open daily in summer, 6am to 9pm.

## Southwest Harbor
**Beal's Lobster Pier** (☎ **207/244-3202**), on a dock at the end of Clark Point Road, is a classic Maine lobster pound, where your lobster, clams, and corn on the cob are served on wooden picnic tables. They're open 9am to 8pm daily in summer.

## BEST-BEHAVIOR MEALS
### In the Park
**Jordan Pond House.** On the Park Loop Rd. at Jordan Pond. ☎ **207/276-3316.** www.jordan pond.com. Lunch and dinner $9–$18. Kids' menu around $5. Summer daily 11:30am–9pm.

A meal here is a part of the Acadia experience. The historic 1870s restaurant, rebuilt as a huge brick-and-cedar structure after the original burned down in 1979, is a traditional stop on a park tour, and the experience remains pleasing and relaxingly genteel — after you get past the crowds. During the high season, make reservations for any meal or expect to wait up to an hour. Parking can also be a problem. You can dine in partly or fully enclosed dining rooms, or sit out on the lawn by the pond. The traditional afternoon tea (or another beverage) and popovers is $6.25 per person.

## Bar Harbor

**Mama DiMatteo's.** 34 Kennebec Place, Bar Harbor. ☎ **207/288-3666.** Dinner $9–$24. Children's menu $5. Summer 5–10pm; winter 5–9pm.

This is one of my favorite restaurants in the country, and it's a favorite of people in Bar Harbor too, where it is one of only a few popular enough to stay open year-round. First comes the attitude: They made our family feel like we'd arrived as honored guests at a celebration. The dining room is small and high-backed booths keep your kids from bothering anyone else. Then comes the food: a Tuscan grilled tuna that I just can't forget, and inspired, creative seafood and pasta dishes on an ever-changing menu. The children's selections are also very good.

**Poor Boy's Gourmet.** 300 Main St., Bar Harbor. ☎ **207/288-4148.** Dinner $10–$17. Children's menu $6. Nightly 4:30–10pm. Closed Nov–Apr.

Poor Boy's is just plain fun. Voices ring off the plank floors of the various rooms and porches of a big white frame house, the light and jollity spilling into Main Street. Servers pop in and out of doors, zooming around with big plates of pasta, or some of the 10 ways they make lobster, or one of the 14 nightly desserts,

baked in-house. We had Robin's birthday there (they brought him a free strawberry daiquiri), and soon the whole place seemed to be one big party, with the diners at the other tables in our room enthusiastically joining in. All that said, the food was good but not memorable, the service somewhat random.

**Rupunini.** 119 Main St., Bar Harbor. ☎ **207/288-2886.** Lunch $5–$7; dinner $7–$17.

Rupunini, a trendy bar and grill, allows parents to order from a long list of microbrews and a varied menu while their kids color, order from a good children's menu, and sit in indestructible outdoor iron furniture or well-contained inside booths. You don't have to worry about being too noisy in this pub atmosphere.

# CHAPTER 4

# Cape Cod National Seashore

Looking at our family pictures from Cape Cod, it's impossible to choose a single image that stands for our time there. We have camped there, we have stayed in hotels, and once we rented a couple of houses for 2 weeks and brought three branches of our family together. There's a hilarious shot of two fathers and a grandfather furiously digging sand for a sand castle while a 5-year-old watches calmly and doesn't get his hands dirty. Another shows the kids dressed up to go out for their grandparents' 40th anniversary dinner at a wonderful restaurant. There are a sailing excursion, a ferry trip off Provincetown, and kids in front of a weathered cottage. From one trip, we have a picture of our daughter, Julia, at 2, discovering ocean water for the first time, with limitless delight. From the next trip, the same wonderful moment, but this time with Julia's little brother, Joseph. And there were lots more we never photographed: the museums and old houses we saw, the nature trails. In my memory, I can see a line of puffy clouds, wildly colored by the setting sun, floating in a royal blue evening sky. Below, next to the rumbling surf, my wife, Barbara, and I walk on a deserted beach, alone for what seems like the first time in years.

Cape Cod is so famous, you might think you don't need to be introduced to it. You probably know what a weathered Cape Cod cottage looks like, and most people don't need instructions on how to enjoy the beach. But Cape Cod is a big, complicated place. It has long, lonesome places and traffic jams. You can go there to learn about an amazing variety of wildlife habitats, or to shop at an amazing variety of stores. On a busy Provincetown street, the Cape sometimes seems to be sinking under the crush of people, yet just across the highway lie miles of shifting sand dunes at the edge of the sea's pounding waves. There are 40 miles of beaches, some of them deserted all the time, patches of marsh and forest, privately managed nature preserves, a state park, and many other historic and interesting places. The famous side of Cape Cod is only the surface.

## Best Things to Do

- Go to the beach to swim, hike, fly a kite, build a sand castle, or just lie on warm sand.
- Canoe in Nauset Marsh or one of the other salt marshes full of birds and wildlife.
- Go sailing on the protected bays facing Cape Cod Bay.
- Take a nature walk in the coastal woods or bike one of the paved paths.
- Visit one of the kid-friendly nature or history museums.
- Take a whale-watching boat ride, or one of the other wildlife boat tours.
- Sign the kids up for a fun and educational day or residential camp while parents spend time alone together.

See "Activities" (p. 99).

## History: Finding the "Real" Cape Cod

More than most places, the idea of Cape Cod stands for a whole way of living, not just a spot on the map. For summer people, it is a way lived in slow days of sun amid the scent of salt water and pines, grains of sand always stuck to your feet, and the feeling that, even though it's an old place and you are a short-time visitor, you belong. Here, you can take the time to really see. See a bike leaning against a gray beach cottage in the sand. See the sun trickle through a roof of shade trees on a narrow colonial street. See a great blue heron balance on one foot in calm marsh water while the surf roars beyond a barrier beach. Protecting Cape Cod means more than keeping places from changing. It also means protecting the special way of living that produces these moments.

Of course, the Cape is different for everyone, and as time passes, it changes for each of us. The history of those changes created the place we enjoy today. Our easy summer days here would seem very strange to the hard-working farmers, boat builders, and whalers who built the towns where we play. Their Cape Cod is gone. As more and more people come to the Cape with their cars and new buildings, the Cape Cod I love is in danger of disappearing, too.

Every wildlife habitat has a carrying capacity — it can support just so many animals, and no more — and the version of Cape Cod I love may have reached its carrying capacity for people. Each summer, more visitors on shorter trips bring more traffic. Route 6 around Eastham turns into a slow-moving parade of cars. When it's sunny, everyone takes to the beach, where parking lots can fill and cars sometimes have to form lines to get in. On rainy days, the museums and other indoor activities get crowded. Reservations for summer houses fill while the snow is still falling the winter before. In the old, narrow streets of historic Provincetown, pedestrians gather so thickly that they spill from the sidewalks and take over the lanes, making a solid river of people from wall to wall.

The Cape the Pilgrims found was wild, barely populated by the survivors of bands of Native Americans who had been killed off by diseases brought by the first European explorers (see "The Great Epidemics," in chapter 2, "Moving Water, Moving Land"). Unlike the Cape today, which is mostly covered by short pitch pine and open, grassy dunes, the Pilgrims found old forests of towering oaks, maples, and cedars. After exploring, however, they decided that the sandy, windy land wouldn't be good for farming and went on to Plymouth, on the other side of Cape Cod Bay.

Later, colonists did settle the Cape, clearing forests for wood and land they could plant. They were the first to build the classic Cape Cod house, a simple, rectangular building, easy to expand and to heat with central

### PARK & NATURE INFORMATION

**Cape Cod National Seashore Headquarters.** 99 Marconi Site Rd., Wellfleet, MA 02667. ☎ **508/349-3785.** www.nps.gov/caco. Some of the best ranger-led activities require advance sign-up, so contact the park before your visit to make your reservation by credit card.

**Eastern National** (for books and maps). 470 Maryland Dr., Suite 2, Ft. Washington, PA 19428. ☎ **877/NAT-PARK.** Fax 215/591-0903. www.eparks.com.

**Nickerson State Park** (and Cape Cod Rail Trail). 3488 Main St. (Route 6A), Brewster, MA 02631-1521. ☎ **508/896-3491;** www.state.ma.us/dem/parks/nick.htm. Reservations ☎ **877-422-6762;** www.reserveamerica.com.

**Cape Cod Museum of Natural History.** Route 6A (P.O. Box 1710), Brewster, MA 02631. ☎ **508/896-3867.** www.ccmnh.org.

**Wellfleet Bay Wildlife Sanctuary; Massachusetts Audubon Society.** Off West Road (P.O. Box 236), South Wellfleet, MA 02663. ☎ **508/349-2615.** www.wellfleetbay.org.

### CHAMBERS OF COMMERCE

**Cape Cod Chamber of Commerce.** P.O. Box 790, Hyannis, MA 02601. ☎ **888/33-CAPECOD** or 508/362-3225. www.capecodchamber.org.

**Eastham Chamber of Commerce.** P.O. Box 1329, Eastham, MA 02642. ☎ **508/255-3444** or 508/240-7211. www.easthamchamber.com.

**Provincetown Chamber of Commerce.** 307 Commercial St. (P.O. Box 1017), Provincetown, MA 02657. ☎ **508/487-3424.** Fax 508/487-8966. www.ptownchamber.com. (Also see www.provincetown.com.)

**Wellfleet Chamber of Commerce.** P.O. Box 571, Wellfleet, MA 02667-0571. ☎ **508/349-2510.** www.wellfleetchamber.com.

---

fireplaces, and without a lot of expensive glass windows. It was covered on the outside with shingles of local cedar, and its steeply pitched roof shed snow. Farming lasted only a few generations, however, because without the trees and other natural plants, the sun dried up the soil and the wind blew it away. Farmers' sons turned to fishing, whaling, boat building, shipping, and salt-making — work that used the Cape's forests until they too were almost all gone.

Whalers made fortunes sailing from Wellfleet and Provincetown on voyages that lasted years and covered most of the world. They killed whales for oil to burn in lamps and for baleen, a material from the whales' mouths. Whales use baleen to filter food from water. People used it much as plastic is used today, for flexible items such as umbrella spokes and stiff parts in ladies' underwear. Cape Cod shipyards also built some of the world's fastest sailing ships, trading on routes up and down the East Coast, especially between Boston and New York.

Many sailors on those voyages died on the shore of Cape Cod — 3,000 shipwrecks have been recorded since the arrival of the *Mayflower,* which itself briefly got in trouble in those waters. The shifting sand that makes up the Cape's beaches extends far offshore

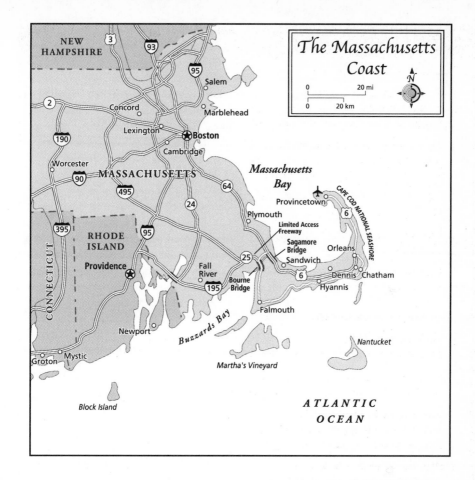

underwater, creating dangerous shoals. Sailing ships attempting to round the Cape were often caught in northeast winter winds that drove them toward the shore and upon the sandbars, where they got stuck and the surf bashed them to pieces. Some 3,000 ships sank here. Sailors froze or drowned trying to get to the beach. Many deaths were prevented by the Cape's lighthouses and by the U.S. Lifesaving Service. The brave surfmen of the service patrolled the beach, launching rowboats into the waves to save sailors. Or, if the surf were too high, the surfmen would fire a line to the ship with a Lyle gun and then pull victims ashore in an aerial contraption called a breeches buoy. The digging of the Cape Cod Canal in 1914 allowed ships to cut through rather than round the Cape and saved many more lives.

When Henry David Thoreau's book about the Cape was published in 1865 (after his death), it was still a lonely place. The tourism industry hadn't started yet; it was difficult to get around on the Cape, and most people didn't know what it was like out there. Thoreau explored all over the Cape, walking from Eastham to Provincetown and meeting the solitary scavengers, called wreckers, who collected driftwood and cargo that washed ashore from shipwrecks. He admired the simple towns and people and wrote philosophically of the wild, ancient sea. "The time must come when this coast will be a place of resort for those New Englanders who really wish to visit the seaside," he wrote.

That change began in 1873, when a railroad reached Provincetown, opening the Cape to visitors who could develop and enjoy it. Hunters and wealthy vacationers began to build large summer homes. Around 1900, Provincetown began to develop into an artists' colony, and dramatists, writers, and visual artists started coming to the Cape for the summer to create and share their work. The great playwright Eugene O'Neill joined the Provincetown Players in 1915 and saw his first Pulitzer Prize–winning play produced there. With the construction of highways, many more people came.

After World War I and even more after World War II, family car vacations took over Cape Cod. People who could afford only a week or two came to stay in simple vacation cottages. Today, the trend of more people on shorter visits continues. Instead of a week, more visitors come for long weekends. And instead of simple cottages of weathered boards, more people want standard hotel rooms, condo units, or houses with the same comforts they have at home. They want convenient shopping centers and modern things to do when they're not at the beach.

The Cape's communities have come to recognize that only so many people can fit on this hook of land before it will be spoiled for everyone. New zoning laws require larger pieces of land for building, so fewer houses can be built. But only wealthy people can afford houses built on large lots of such valuable land. As limits on development limit the supply of vacations and more people want to come, prices are rising. Some families have seen their favorite rental houses get too expensive and sadly moved on to other summer vacation spots. Cape Cod has long been a place where ordinary people can come from hot, dirty cities for family vacations in the outdoors. Will they still be able to afford to come?

We can't capture and preserve the perfect Cape Cod. It's hard even to say what the "real" Cape Cod looks like. Certainly, it doesn't look like a typical American strip mall or condo resort. On the other hand, Thoreau's Cape Cod was missing something, too. As beautiful and desolate as it must have been, there were no scenes of children splashing in the surf or paddling in canoes to learn about the salt marshes.

But even if we can't preserve Cape Cod, we can savor its natural smells and sights, have simple fun, and let tension drift away. Each family can help make Cape Cod the ideal place to visit. Plan enough time to really enjoy it, avoid unnecessary driving, and go to natural places rather than commercial centers. Don't add to all the crowds, traffic, and bustle. Our way of living here now could help set the future so that families can continue to summer the same way for a long time to come.

# ORIENTATION

## THE NATIONAL SEASHORE

The national seashore is 40 miles long, running from **Race Point,** at the northern tip of Cape Cod, to the thin barrier beaches of **Nauset Beach,** near the Cape's elbow. Our focus, however, is only on the Cape's forearm, the main part of the national seashore from Eastham north. On the park-managed ocean-facing beaches here you'll find fine, white sand; high bluffs and dunes; crashing waves; and relatively cold water for swimming. On the opposite, **Cape Cod Bay** side of the Cape, the water tends to be calmer and warmer, the sand coarser and muddier, and the beaches controlled by towns or private parties. In between, private and park land mix together around salt marshes, ponds, and forests.

## THE TOWNS

Towns mix smoothly into one another, but you need to know their names because that's how people give directions and define the part of the Cape they are talking about. We will

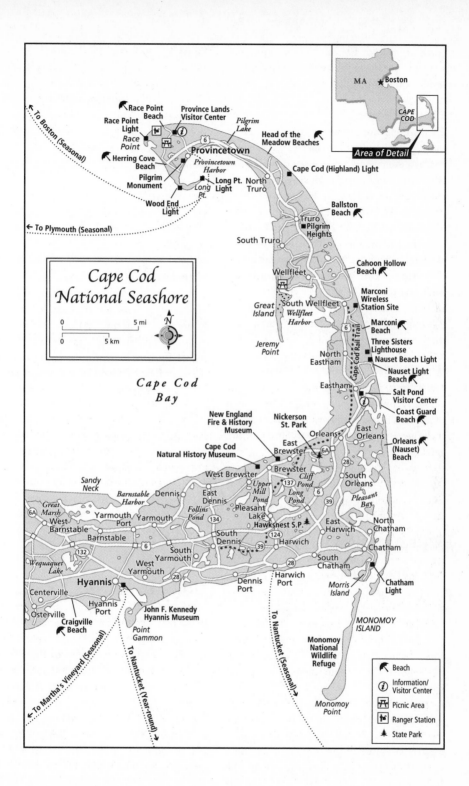

Cape Cod
National Seashore

0       5 mi
0       5 km

MA ★ Boston

CAPE COD

Area of Detail

To Boston (Seasonal)

Race Point Beach
Race Point Light
Race Point
Herring Cove Beach
Pilgrim Monument
Wood End Light

Province Lands Visitor Center
Pilgrim Lake

Provincetown
Provincetown Harbor
Long Pt. Light
Long Pt.
North Truro

Head of the Meadow Beaches

Cape Cod (Highland) Light

To Plymouth (Seasonal)

Ballston Beach

Truro
Pilgrim Heights

South Truro

Cahoon Hollow Beach

Wellfleet

Great Island
South Wellfleet
Wellfleet Harbor

Marconi Wireless Station Site

Marconi Beach
Three Sisters Lighthouse
Nauset Beach Light
Nauset Light Beach

Jeremy Point

North Eastham

Eastham

Salt Pond Visitor Center

Coast Guard Beach

Cape Cod Bay

New England Fire & History Museum

Nickerson St. Park

Orleans

East Orleans

Orleans (Nauset) Beach

Cape Cod Natural History Museum

East Brewster

West Brewster

Brewster
Cliff Pond
Upper Mill Pond
Long Pond

South Orleans

Sandy Neck

Barnstable Harbor
Dennis
East Dennis

Pleasant Lake

Pleasant Bay

Great Marsh

Yarmouth Port
Yarmouth
Follins Pond

Hawksnest S.P.

East Harwich

North Chatham

West Barnstable

Barnstable

South Dennis

Harwich

Chatham

Wequaquet Lake

South Yarmouth
West Yarmouth

South Chatham

Hyannis

Dennis Port
Harwich Port

Morris Island

Chatham Light

Centerville

Hyannis Port

John F. Kennedy Hyannis Museum

MONOMOY ISLAND

Osterville
Craigville Beach

Point Gammon

Monomoy National Wildlife Refuge

To Martha's Vineyard (Seasonal)

To Nantucket (Year-round)

To Nantucket (Seasonal)

Monomoy Point

Beach

Information/ Visitor Center

Picnic Area

Ranger Station

State Park

cover towns from Eastham north, with a few sites in Orleans and Brewster, towns on the inside of the Cape's elbow.

## Provincetown

This is the historic town of narrow streets at the tip of the Cape. It's clogged with people and best avoided on weekends and afternoons, when day-trippers from Boston add to the mob. Parking is terrible. Resign yourself to paying as much as $10 and pulling into a lot as you enter the town rather than getting stuck in traffic looking for a better spot. If you visit the Pilgrim Monument, however, it has ample free parking near downtown. Provincetown has many hotel rooms, museums, tour boats, and other activities, and is the only choice if you want to forgo a car during your stay, but I think the crowds spoil it.

## Truro

Quiet Truro is made up mostly of cottages along country roads with tree-branch canopies. There's hardly any town center, but there are lots of national seashore land and great beaches.

## Wellfleet

Grown-ups will enjoy a walk around the town. Its shops, art galleries, and narrow, tree-lined streets look like a movie set of a colonial New England town. It's the Cape's best mix of town and outdoors. Parking is a problem, so you may need to walk several blocks to the town center.

## Eastham

This diffuse town has several interesting historic sites and nature trails, plus the park visitor center.

## The Roads

Learning your way around is simple, but you'll need a good map for the details. Two-lane **Route 6** is the north-south spine of the area, running from the **traffic circle** at the south end of Eastham to Provincetown (where there is a short four-lane section). Because the Cape is narrow, everything is close to Route 6. At the traffic circle, 6 becomes a limited-access two-lane road leading off the Cape. Taking 6A from the traffic circle leads to Main Street in Brewster. Splitting from 6A onto Route 28 before Brewster puts you in Orleans.

# MAKING THE ARRANGEMENTS

## WHEN TO GO

Summer vacation is the busy season at Cape Cod, beginning solidly at Memorial Day and lasting through Labor Day. Crowds are somewhat smaller in June, when the water is cold for swimming. In May, rates are low and crowds few. If you're coming in the summer and plan to spend less than a week, avoiding weekends matters more than what month you come.

Rates go down before and after the summer season. September and early October are relatively quiet, and the weather is still okay. Many businesses shut down in the winter, especially on the Outer Cape where the

national seashore lies. A winter trip is romantic for couples, but not much fun for families.

## HOW MUCH TIME TO SPEND

From the Boston area, it may make sense to go to the national seashore for a weekend or even a day trip, but for anyone from farther afield, a week is the minimum. The best accommodations — houses, cottages, and some campgrounds — rent by the week, from Saturday to Saturday. Besides, Cape Cod isn't the kind of place where you can go and quickly hit the high points. There is a lot to see and do, and you should not do it quickly — relax and forget your cares for a while.

## How Far to Plan Ahead

Rental cottages and houses book up for summer in February. Many people go to the same place every summer, and they have certain properties sewed up years in advance. Try making your lodging reservations first, before you set your vacation dates — that way, you have a better shot at getting a good place. Hotels and motels don't fill up so soon. The best places fill for July and August 2 months ahead, but for midweek lodgings you often can find something without much lead time. If you need a car, reserve that well ahead, too, to avoid paying an outrageous rate.

## Reading Up

Eastern National (☎ 877/NAT-PARK; ebooks.com) operates the visitor-center bookstores and carries a modest selection of books online or by telephone order.

## Nature

*The Seaside Naturalist,* by Deborah A. Coulombe (Fireside Press), is clearly written and illustrated for children and adults.

## Getting There
### By Car

The route is simple, but read on for information that could save you hours of frustration.

From the south, split from Interstate 95 onto I-195 in Providence, then take Route 25 to Route 6. From the north, Route 3 takes you straight to Route 6. Head for the Sagamore Bridge over Cape Cod Canal and follow 6 the rest of the way to the national seashore (you can also take the Bourne Bridge, a little farther south, with slight added complication). The bridges are where tie-ups occur. Since weekly rentals on the Cape turn over on Saturdays, a large portion of the summer population tries to get across the bridges all at once. Backups can be 3 hours or more. The worst congestion occurs 2 to 8pm Friday and 8 to 11am Saturday. Avoid those hours. If you're not on a weekly rental, try not to arrive or leave on a weekend at all. Eastham is 5½ hours

from New York, 2 hours from Boston or Providence, assuming no traffic.

### By Plane

Commuter planes fly to the airports in Hyannis and Provincetown. Fly to Hyannis (also called Barnstable) airport from Boston, New York, or Providence. Carriers include **Cape Air** (☎ 800/352-0714 or 508/771-6944; www.flycapeair.com) and **US Airways Express** (☎ 800/428-4322; www.usairways.com). The fare from Boston is under $200 round-trip. Five car-rental agencies have desks at the airport, including **Budget** (☎ 800/527-0700 or 508/790-0163), **Thrifty** (☎ 800/367-2277 or 508/771-0450), and **National** (☎ 800/227-7368 or 508/771-4353). Only Cape Air flies to Provincetown's tiny airport. You can rent a car there from **Budget** (☎ 800/527-0700 or 508/487-4557).

### By Boat

Three passenger ferries operated by two companies connect Provincetown to Boston. We did this once, and it was fun. The boats make day trips from Boston, but we took it one-way on our way to Maine, missing the Cape traffic and seeing finback whales and dolphins on the way. In Boston we rented a car. Where the *Provincetown II* lands, Commonwealth Pier on Northern Avenue Seaport Boulevard, is a short cab ride from South Station, Amtrak's last stop in Boston. It's a large vessel, but also the oldest and slowest of the choices. It takes 3 hours each way; but the boat has lots of open space, and a children's entertainer was playing music and making balloon animals during our ride. The operator, **Bay State Cruise Company** (☎ 617/457-1428; www.baystatecruisecompany.com) also runs the Provincetown Express, which makes the run in 2 hours. **Boston Harbor Cruises** (☎ 877/733-9425 or 617/227-4321; www.bostonharborcruises.com) takes only 90 minutes to get across from Long Wharf on State Street in Boston aboard a 600-passenger, high-speed catamaran. Each

## WEATHER CHART: PROVINCETOWN

| | AVG. HIGH (°F) | AVG. LOW (°F) | PRECIP. (IN.) | OCEAN TEMP. (°F) |
|---|---|---|---|---|
| Dec.–Mar. | 42 | 28 | 3.8 | 37 |
| April | 53 | 37 | 3.6 | 46 |
| May | 64 | 46 | 3.3 | 55 |
| June | 73 | 56 | 3.1 | 55 |
| July | 79 | 62 | 2.4 | 71 |
| August | 78 | 61 | 3.4 | 72 |
| September | 71 | 55 | 3.5 | 67 |
| October | 62 | 46 | 3.7 | 59 |
| November | 52 | 38 | 4.5 | 50 |

*\* Water temperatures are for Woods Hole, Massachusetts*

boat has a snack bar. Fares on the slowest are $18 one way, $30 round-trip (free for infants, but otherwise children pay full fare); prices are higher for the faster service. Service on any of these boats is sparse or nonexistent in the off-season.

## WHAT TO PACK
### Clothing
The summer high is typically 10°F colder than on the mainland, averaging in the 70s. During the day, people wear shorts and T-shirts. In the evening, they dress a little better than at most beach places or national parks — perhaps a skirt or khaki trousers and a cotton sweater for going out to dinner at a nice restaurant. Hats and sunblock are necessities. Also bring raincoats for foggy days and occasional drenching rains.

### Gear
There are beach shops on Route 6, so you can pick up your beach umbrella and sand toys upon arrival. If you have a toddler, bring a backpack or jogger stroller so that you can go far enough down the beach to get away from the crowds. Bring your own bikes to save on renting. Conditions are mild for summer camping.

## WHERE TO SPEND THE NIGHT

### CAMPING
Cape Cod is great for camping. There are no campgrounds in the national seashore itself, but nearby are several superb commercial campgrounds and an extraordinary state park. In addition to the commercial campgrounds below, you can get a list of more campgrounds from the **Cape Cod Chamber of Commerce** (☎ 888/33-CAPECOD; www.capecodchamber.org), some of which are on their website.

As with everything at the Cape, campsites require reservations well in advance. Also, minimum stays often apply. Backcountry camping requires a high-clearance vehicle and a special permit; see "Off-Road Driving" (p. 103).

**Nickerson State Park.** 3488 Main St. (Rte. 6A), Brewster, MA 02631-1521. ☎ **508/896-3491;** www.state.ma.us/dem/parks/nick.htm. Reservations ☎ **877/422-6762;** www.reserve

america.com. $12 per site Massachusetts residents, $15 nonresidents. 418 sites; tents or RVs. Flush toilets, free hot showers, dump station (no hookups). Bathrooms closed Oct 15–Apr 15.

Nestled among towering white pine in seven groups, the sites here are thoughtfully arranged around the park's lovely kettle ponds so that it feels like wilderness. Few more appealing places to camp exist anywhere. There's more to do at this state park than at a lot of national parks: swimming and sailing in the ponds, long bicycle trails, and ranger programs and children's programs at the nature center (see "Natural Places," p. 96, and "Programs," p. 104).

Reservations for summer are essential, and are hard to get (mid-Oct to mid-Apr it's first-come, first served). Availability opens 6 months ahead, and you should book your dates as soon as they are available. Often scattered openings of a day or two remain after most of the time is booked, so still it's worth a try later. (For more on the reservation agency, see "Other Campground Reservations," in chapter 1, "Planning Your Trip.") Twenty percent of sites are held back for those who show up without reservations, but you have to wait for 3 to 5 days to get a site that way, first putting your name on a list and then coming back each morning at 10am to find out if your name is called.

**Atlantic Oaks Campground.** 3700 Rte. 6, R.R. 2, Eastham, MA 02642. ☎ **800/332-2267** or 508/255-1437. www.capecamping.com. Tent sites $30, full hookups $42 for 2; $7.50 each extra adult; $2 extra child 6–18; free for those 5 and under. 100 sites; tents or RVs. Hot showers, laundry, playground, evening movies. DISC, MC, V.

This well-wooded campground, with pull-through sites among shade trees, is intended for RVs. The price includes cable TV hookups. The location is half a mile from the Salt Pond Visitor Center and right on the rail trail. They require minimum stays on many weekends.

**Dunes' Edge Campground.** East side of Rte. 6 (P.O. Box 875), Provincetown, MA 02657. ☎ **508/487-9815.** www.dunes-edge.com. $28 per site for 2; $10 each extra adult; $3 each extra child; electric and water hookups $6 extra. 100 sites. Hot showers.

This is a simple, old-fashioned campground with large, well-screened sites similar to those at the better national park campgrounds. The hilly, overgrown dune terrain and thick oaks and pitch pine help. Race Point is a couple of miles away by bike, a reasonable ride for kids. Provincetown is just across the highway. The campground has a nice family feel and well-kept facilities, but no resort stuff — there's no playground other than the woods. Tenters will be happiest here, because only 15 sites accommodate trailers, there are no sewer hookups, and the 20-amp service won't support high-wattage gear. The office does not accept credit cards for reservations or payment.

**North of Highland Camping Area.** Head of Meadow Rd. (P.O. Box 297), North Truro, MA 02652. ☎ **508/487-1191.** capecodcamping.com. $20 for 2; $8 each extra adult; $2 each extra child. 237 sites. Hot showers; recreation building; laundry; store. No hookups, no trailers over 17 ft. DISC, MC, V.

Intended for tents, this campground sits on 60 sandy acres of twisted scrub pine surrounded on all sides by the national seashore. Head of the Meadow Beach is a short walk down a dirt road, and from there a secluded bike trail leads to Pilgrim Heights. The location is probably the most natural and isolated you'll find on the Cape, allowing you to forget about the car for a while. Everything seemed well maintained when I visited. During the peak season, weeklong minimum stays apply, with shorter minimums other times. Call well ahead to reserve.

## HOTELS

A startling number of places, including all but a few historic hotels and B&Bs, are off-limits to kids under age 12. Start looking for a room early, and be sure to ask about age limits right off. Prices are high for good rooms, generally over $100 a night. I've listed only high-season rates; after Labor Day and before mid-June, they drop 25%, and in winter are up to 40% lower. If you're staying a week, a cottage is a better bet for quality and price; however, cottages rent for a week at a time in the summer.

## Eastham

**Beach Plum Motor Lodge.** Rte. 6 (P.O. Box 282), Eastham, MA 02642. ☎ **508/255-7668.** 5 units. $63–$118 per unit. AE, MC, V. Closed Nov–Apr.

It's an old-fashioned place with small rooms, but this motel has something no other can claim: proprietor Gloria Moll, who loves her guests, especially children. She does it all, baking the breakfast, keeping up the blazing glory of the gardens, cleaning the rooms, and even sometimes producing cakes for kids who happen to be here on their birthdays. The rooms are cute and well maintained but have only showers, no tubs, and there's no room to spare. There are a small pool and room to play outside, where a rabbit roams, and the Salt Pond Visitor Center is nearby.

## Wellfleet

**The Even'tide.** 650 Rte. 6 (P.O. Box 41), South Wellfleet, MA 02663-0041. ☎ **508/349-3410.** www.eventidemotel.com. 31 rms, 8 cottages. $92–$155 double; $15 extra adult, $8 per extra child; cottages $595–$895 per week. AE, DC, DISC, MC, V. Closed Nov–Mar.

The family that built this Route 6 motel more than 30 years ago, and still runs it, knows how to make families comfortable. We felt the tension going out of our shoulders when we drove up. There are a play area in the courtyard and a huge, immaculate indoor swimming pool for rainy days. Rooms have refrigerators and coffee and other useful features for families, such as lots of counter space and practical floor coverings. Large family rooms are in their own building to reduce the chances you will disturb anyone. Although the motel fronts on the

highway, it backs on the national seashore, and Marconi Beach is three-quarters of a mile away on a forest trail. The rustic cottages are in the woods, by the Cape Cod Rail Trail. You must reserve many months ahead for the high season.

**Inn at Duck Creeke.** 70 Main St. (P.O. Box 364), Wellfleet, MA 02667. ☎ **508/349-9333.** www.capecod.net/duckinn. 27 units, 18 with bathroom. $70–$95 double; $15 extra person, $5 children under 5; $10 moving fee for cribs or cots. AE, MC, V. Closed Nov–Apr.

Standing a little out of the town center on a tidal creek, the inn's main white clapboard house was built around 1810 and has operated as an inn since the 1940s with the same furnishings, many of them antiques. Although creaky and rough in places, the inn has loads of period atmosphere, with plank floors, quilts, lace curtains, and charming, old-fashioned wallpaper, faded by the years. There are no TVs or telephones and air-conditioning is in the top floor only; these are far from standard accommodations and not a good choice if you want a modern hotel room. With the lawns, screened porch, sitting rooms, and shared bathrooms, I felt like my grandmother's house had been turned into an inn. Room rates include a light breakfast. The award-winning **Sweet Seasons Restaurant** is on the same grounds.

**Wellfleet Motel and Lodge.** Rte. 6 (P.O. Box 606), South Wellfleet, MA 02663. ☎ **800/852-2900** or 508/340-3535. Fax 508/349-1192. www.wellfleetmotel.com. 65 units $145–$155 double, $10 each additional person. AE, MC, V. Closed Dec 15–Mar 15.

Their motto is "squeaky clean," and, indeed, this roadside hotel has a pristine, almost antiseptic feel. Rooms come in two sets, the lodge and motel, in three buildings on large lawns screened from the highway by pines. The large rooms have a cool, solid feel. Although without character, there's nothing lacking that you would find in any mid-scale hotel chain. Indoor and outdoor pools are on-site.

**Emergencies**   Dial ☎ **911** for police, fire, or ambulance service. The **hospital** is in Hyannis at 27 Park St. (☎ **508/771-1800**). **Outer Cape Health Services,** a clinic with 24-hour on-call service as well as regular office hours, is at 49 Harry Kemp Way in Provincetown (☎ **508/ 487-9395**). The Wellfleet office, on Route 6 (☎ **508/349-3131**), is open daily year-round. The **Coast Guard's Provincetown Station** is at ☎ **508/487-0070.**

**Stores**   Each of the towns along the Outer Cape has a small country store where you can pick up milk or a few forgotten items. For a major shopping trip, there's a **Stop & Shop** in Orleans at the intersection of routes 6A and 28 just south of the Route 6 traffic circle. Provincetown has an A&P Superstore on Shank Painter Road and Route 6.

**Banks**   Various banks are represented in the area, with multiple ATMs in Provincetown, Wellfleet, Eastham, and Orleans, along Route 6, and on the town main streets.

**Post Offices**   Each town on the Cape has a post office. In Provincetown, it's at 211 Commercial St. (☎ **508/487-0163**).

**Gear Sales & Rental**   **Goose Hummock Shop,** on Route 6A in Orleans (☎ **508/255-2620;** www.moose.com), is a full-service sporting-goods store for outdoor equipment, and also rents canoes, kayaks, and fishing gear. Their website has loads of information on fishing and other activities. For bike rentals, see "Getting Around" (p. 93).

## North Truro & Provincetown

**Best Western Tides Beachfront.**   837 Commercial St. (P.O. Box 617), Provincetown, MA 02657. ☎ **800/528-1234** or 508/487-1045. Fax 508/487-3557. www.bestwestern.com. 64 units. $199–$209 double; $20 extra adult, free for kids. AE, CB, DC, DISC, MC, V. Closed Nov–Apr.

If what you want is a standard upscale American beachfront hotel, this is a good choice, with the well-kept but anonymous rooms you would expect. Just south of Provincetown, it faces Cape Cod Bay, with many rooms opening right onto patios and the white sand beach. There are a heated pool, a guest laundry, and a small restaurant for breakfast and lunch. Mention the kids when you make your reservation — families get ground-floor rooms only.

**Kalmar Village.**   Rte. 6A (P.O. Box 745), North Truro, MA 02652. ☎ **508/487-0585.** (Winter: 246 Newbury St., Boston, MA 02116; ☎ 617/ 247-0211.) kalmarvillage.com. 40 cottages, 15 efficiencies. Efficiencies $90–$145 double; $15–$17.50 extra child or adult; cribs free.

Cottages $1,085–$1,950 per week. DISC, MC, V. Closed Nov–Apr.

On the edge of Cape Cod Bay just south of Provincetown, Kalmar Village is a collection of trim, white cottages separated by green lawns, hedges, and roses. In the evening adults barbecue and socialize while their kids play on the broad private beach and splash in the outdoor pool. Motel rooms and efficiencies rent by the night, but the cottages are the thing. Airy and clean, with wood floors and glass doorknobs, they are cozy and self-contained and seem to have been beamed to the present from an ideal past. They have TVs, but no phones. Everything is provided, including clam rakes. For July and August, the weeklong cottage stays book up in February.

## COTTAGES & HOUSES

The traditional and still the best way to visit the Cape is to rent a place of your own for a week or two. You'll be able to settle in, play without bothering others, and cook relaxed family meals. You can rent a cottage in a compound, a house or cottage off by itself, or even a house where the resident family has gone on vacation. Two of the motels listed above also rent cottages.

The price range extends from rough little places that cost as much as a motel room to palaces renting for more in a week than most people make in a year. The least expensive one-bedroom cottages far from the water start around $700 a week, and you can get a three-bedroom house for $1,500 a week. But it's a renters market, and prices are rising as much as 10% a year. In the area we cover, prices are highest in Provincetown, lowest in Eastham, and about the same in Wellfleet and Truro (my favorite areas). A bigger factor in price is proximity to the beach or a cute colonial town center, which costs more.

Starting early — preferably by January — is critical. Not much is left by March. Develop an idea of what you want and how much you can pay; looking at houses on the Internet will help, but don't get attached to one house you see. You have to talk to an agent (such as the ones listed below) to find a place that fits your desires, dates, and budget. If you're flexible about where and when, you can get a better deal and better choice. Remember, there's nothing wrong with bare board walls and a bike ride to the beach — that, not a fancy condo, is the real Cape Cod. Staying 2 weeks also broadens your choices. Be sure to find out about the house's surroundings so that you don't end up on a busy street or otherwise undesirable spot.

Before you go, find out exactly what linens, appliances, kitchen items, telephone service, and other necessities are included. Plan all your meals in advance so that you can do one major shopping trip when you arrive. There are no large grocery stores between Orleans and Provincetown, and daily shopping wastes a lot of time in traffic. When you arrive, inventory any problems in writing, and do it again when you leave, to make sure you don't get hit for any unwarranted damages.

For cottages at motels, you can call directly and reserve with a credit card, but most rentals are handled by real-estate agents. They will request references, preferring a previous vacation rental. You'll likely have to pay a large deposit up front, or even the whole amount, by check, just to make a reservation.

Dozens of agents are listed on the website of the **Cape Cod & Islands Association of Realtors** (☎ **508/957-4300**; www.cciaor. com), with links to agencies' sites, some of which have pictures of houses. You can also find an agent through the chamber of commerce in the town you're interested in (see "Cape Cod Address Book," p. 82). Here are two of the larger agencies.

**Cape Cod Realty.** P.O. Box 719, Wellfleet, MA 02667. ☎ **508/349-2245** or 800/545-7670. www.capecodrealty.net.

This agency has many listings in Wellfleet, with a scattering in Truro and Eastham.

**Duarte/Downey Real Estate Agency.** 12 Truro Center Rd. (P.O. Box 2016), Truro, MA 02666. ☎ **508/349-7588**. www.ddre.com.

These knowledgeable folks represent as many as 300 homes, mostly in Truro but also spanning the area from Eastham to **Outer Cape Realty.** 5150 Rte. 6 (P.O. Box 1170), North Eastham, MA 01651. ☎ **508/225-0505.** www.outercape.com.

# WHEN YOU ARRIVE

## ENTRANCE & USE FEES

The national seashore charges fees in the summer to use the beaches it manages. Fees are $7 per day, or $20 for a season pass, for each vehicle. A person on foot or a bike pays $1. See "Beachgoing" (p. 99) for more details.

## REGULATIONS

Don't **climb** on the dunes and bluffs except on a marked path, because this speeds erosion. You need a permit from a visitor center (see below) for an open wood **fire.** Charcoal grills and camp stoves are okay in picnic areas and on ocean beaches. **Pets** must be kept on a short leash and are not allowed on bike or nature trails, on lifeguarded beaches, in shorebird nesting areas, or, from May 15 to October 15, in freshwater ponds.

## VISITOR CENTERS

**Salt Pond Visitor Center.** Rte. 6, Eastham, MA 02641. ☎ **508/255-3421.** Daily 9am–4:30pm, later in summer. Open year-round.

The center contains a fascinating little museum of Cape history and nature. Children can enjoy up to an hour with the displays on 19th-century Cape Cod life, plus lifesaving, whaling, and other nautical matters, presented with models and mock-ups to make the artifacts understandable. The center also has an information desk, a bookstore, an auditorium where a short orientation film is shown, and an amphitheater for evening ranger programs. Trails and canoeing starting here are covered below under "Nature Walks" (p. 102) and "Canoeing & Kayaking" (p. 101).

**Province Lands Visitor Center.** Race Point Rd., Provincetown, MA 02657. ☎ **508/487-1256.** Daily 9am–4:30pm, later in summer. Winter closures vary, usually around Thanksgiving to mid-Apr.

This hexagonal building has an upstairs viewing deck with vistas in all directions that take in the surrounding dunes, the sea, and Provincetown. Besides the information desk and a film, there are a few interesting displays, including placards telling how to recognize different kinds of ships, but its not worth a stop unless you have questions for the rangers.

**Provincetown Visitor Center.** MacMillan Wharf, 307 Commercial St. ☎ **508/487-3424.** June–Sept daily 9am–5pm; off-season shorter hours.

Run by the Provincetown Chamber of Commerce, the center helps find lodgings and serves as the ticket office for the ferry to Boston.

## GETTING AROUND
## By Car

Traffic is a big enough problem at Cape Cod to ruin days of your vacation if you're not careful. **Route 6** north of Orleans — the national seashore area — is the only way to get anywhere, and it's a two-lane country road with numerous intersections, traffic lights, and driveways. The section through Wellfleet and Eastham often turns into a long, slow line of cars. The solution is to reduce your trips. Plan to spend an entire day on visits to the opposite end of the area, such as going to Provincetown from Eastham or to Brewster from Truro, by putting together activities. Make a detailed menu plan before your trip so that you can do all your shopping at once when you arrive. There is no large grocery store between Orleans and Provincetown, so you don't want to be running to the store. If you plan to put your child in a day camp or spend a lot of time anywhere, get accommodations nearby. Use bikes for short hops.

## By Bike

The distances are too great and Route 6 is too dangerous to rely on bikes as your primary transportation, but you can bicycle for many of your shorter trips — to the beach, to a village center, or for outings along the **Cape Cod Rail Trail,** a bike path that follows the old railroad route for much of the length of the Cape. Several agencies in each town rent bikes, with good bikes available for $12 to $20 a day.

- **PROVINCETOWN: Ptown Bikes,** 42 Bradford St. (☎ **508/487-8735**); **Expedition Whydah Sea Lab,** 16 MacMillan Wharf (☎ **508/487-8899;** www.whydah.com).

- **WELLFLEET: Idle Times Bike Shop,** Route 6, Wellfleet (☎ 508/349-9161; www.idletimesbike.com).
- **EASTHAM: Idle Times Bike Rental,** 4550 Route 6, N. Eastham (☎ 508/255-8281; www.idletimesbike.com); **Little Capistrano's,** 341 Salt Pond Rd. (☎ 508/255-6515).

## Keeping Safe & Healthy

For health and safety tips on sun, seasickness, poison ivy, and Lyme disease, see "Dealing with Hazards," in chapter 1. Here are some other issues specific to Cape Cod.

## Drowning

Water on the oceanside beaches usually is too rough for children under age 8, and days come when swimming there is not safe even for older children and adults. The national seashore swimming beaches have lifeguards, but not some town beaches and/or any beach away from the parking lots. The water is usually calm on the Cape Cod Bay beaches, and little ones can wade far out on the gently sloping shore. Beach details are covered under "Beachgoing" (p. 99). Also see, "Practicalities: Swimming Safely in Surf," in chapter 5.

## Traffic

Cape Cod's lovely, narrow country roads leave little room for pedestrians and bicycles. In the towns, people often walk in the street. As a driver, take it easy. As a parent, hold hands with your children, and don't try to bike on Route 6 or other major roads.

# Enjoying the National Seashore

## Natural Places: Cape Cod National Seashore

### Province Lands

The tip of the Cape, set aside early on as a common area for the people of Plymouth Colony, is a broad lowland of sand dunes and a few woods, a kind of desert on the sea. It's a strange, unfamiliar place, where forests of weathered trees fight a slow-motion war with the dunes trying to smother them. The area is strung with bike and nature trails, and there are great ocean beaches for swimming or walking. See "Activities" (p. 99) for biking and beachgoing at the Province Lands.

Everything north of Pilgrim Heights, including Provincetown and all the Province Lands, is nothing more than a huge sandbar. For around 6,000 years, since the sea level rose high enough for waves to lick the Cape's bluffs, currents running north along the shore have washed sand from those higher shores and dropped it here. Early settlers stripped the area of a forest, and recovery has taken a long time. Photographs at the **Province Lands Visitor Center,** on Race Point Road

(see p. 93), show how the landscape has changed in a few generations.

A rare stand of beeches off Race Point Road near Route 6 is one of a few surviving patches of the kind of forest that covered much of the Cape when the Pilgrims arrived. In the long history of a piece of sandy ground, different kinds of plants follow each other as the capabilities of each match and change the soil (see "Plants & Wind Erosion," in chapter 2, and "Competition," in chapter 20, "Ecology: Fitting It Together"). The beech forest is the last step in this process of plant succession. The **Beech Forest Trail** winds for miles through this peaceful and shady environment, over steep dunes long ago locked down by roots and around a pair of ponds carpeted by lily pads. There are some steps, but it should be an easy walk for anyone over age 4.

An interesting building stands at the east end of the Race Point Beach parking lot, the 1898 **Old Harbor Lifesaving Station** (☎ 508/487-1256). A one-room display of lifesaving equipment is worth a look if you're at the beach anyway, but doesn't justify a special trip. Check with the visitor center or call the number above to find out about occasional demonstrations of the Lyle gun (see "History: Finding the 'Real' Cape Cod," p. 81, to learn about the lifesavers' work).

## Pilgrim Heights

This is an unusual place to see a sharp break between two kinds of land. The heights are the northern end of the Cape's glacial highlands (turn right from Route 6 as you head north from Truro); north of here the land has all been built by sand washing around in the ocean. It's also a historic spot, where the Pilgrims, on their scouting expeditions from Provincetown, first found water in the new world. A short **nature trail** leads to that spot. Another, the **Small's Swamp Trail,** crosses a swamp that was used for farming by Native Americans and by white farmers, with signs to explain the archaeological sites (pick up a trail guide brochure, too, at information centers or at the trailhead).

Looking over the bluff from the heights, you can see an area of salt meadow extending far to the sea, a field of dunes, covered with beach grass and decorated by oddly shaped little ponds. A picnic area, rest rooms, and an information kiosk are by the parking lot, and a **bike trail** leads to Head of the Meadow Beach.

## Outer Beaches

Walking along the Atlantic Ocean side of the Cape is like walking in a watercolor painting: a strip of beach, a strip of sea, a blue sky, and a bluff. The pale, sun-scented sand; the cool, pure ocean breeze; and the jagged, sparkling water rumbling lazily into froth. Everything is so bright, it all seems to vibrate.

These beaches are not only a place to lie in the sun and play in the surf, but also a unique and inspiring natural setting. The Cape's outer beaches make up a high-energy shoreline — that means they get hit by big ocean waves that have a lot of power behind them. The battering waves move the sand around and keep most plants or animals from being able to live here (see "Narrowing Cape: Cape Cod," in chapter 2).

Swimming on the outer beaches is for fit adults and big kids only. The beaches with bluffs extend from Wellfleet to North Truro. Low-profile beaches are at the Province Lands and from Eastham south. See "Beachgoing" (p. 99) for advice on where to go and what to do, as well as access issues.

## Bay Beaches

Although as close as a mile to the Atlantic-facing beaches, the shoreline along Cape Cod Bay feels completely different. The waves are smaller, the water is warmer, and the sand often is coarser, with more seaweed, clams, snails, and other creatures. This is a lower-energy beach. Waves don't have enough room on Cape Cod Bay to pick up much wind energy compared to waves on the wide Atlantic Ocean. Because the waves hit with less force, the sand moves around less, creating flatter beaches and allowing more plants and animals to survive. Most of the shore on this side is controlled by towns (see "Beachgoing," p. 99), except the wonderful area east of Wellfleet Harbor, site of the **Great Island Trail** (see "Nature Walks," p. 102).

## Salt Marsh

The salt marsh is a safe harbor for all kinds of life. Because it is completely protected from waves, it's the lowest-energy shoreline and produces the most plants, animals, and insects. (See "How a Salt Marsh Is Made," in chapter 2.) Water slowly flows in with the tide, bringing food and sediment to feed grasses, seaweed, crabs, clams, snails, fish, mice, voles, otters, and many varieties of birds, including herons and egrets. It can be a mysterious place, a maze of watery channels among the grasses where you feel as though you might find anything. The best way to explore the salt marshes is by canoe (see "Canoeing & Kayaking," p. 101), but you can get a sense for the areas and scope for birds on nature trails, among the

When the Pilgrims arrived, so many lobsters lived in the water off Cape Cod that in storms they washed up on the outer beach in long piles a foot and a half deep. For many years people thought they weren't good enough to eat, and lobster was buried as fertilizer and fed to servants and poor people. In the 1800s, more people started to eat lobster, and fishermen began catching them on purpose. As more people ate them, fewer were left in the sea. Today, lobsters are hard to find, and to get big ones lobstermen must go far offshore and put their traps (called lobster pots) in deep water. Lobster is among the most expensive types of seafood. All this goes to show that how much we value something often depends most on how hard it is to get.

Fish you buy in a restaurant or store usually has been caught by commercial fishermen who own big boats, nets, and other special gear. They make their money in a completely different way than people on land. On land, workers are paid by the hour. They sell their time and skills to the boss. Farmers plant crops on their land and sell their harvest to people who make it into food. All sell something they own. But fishermen don't own the fish until after they catch them. Fish are free to whoever gets them first. For a fisherman to make a living, he or she needs to catch as many fish as possible, as fast as possible, before anyone else gets them.

Today, valuable fish are gone from much of the water off the East Coast. In towns that once had a lot of fishermen, many have had to quit and sell their boats because they can't catch enough fish. One reason is overfishing. Fish need time to have offspring, making more fish. If you don't catch too many, those that are left keep growing and making more fish you can catch the next year so that you never run out. But if fishermen catch too many fish each year, there won't be enough left to have offspring, until almost all the fish are gone. Overfishing has happened many times and in many places through history. One example is whales. Some kinds of whales almost died out

best of which is the Nauset Marsh Trail (see "Nature Walks," p. 102).

## Lighthouses

Six lighthouses stand out on bluffs and sandy points from Chatham to Race Point. Starting in 1798, passengers on ships from Europe to America received their first sign that they had arrived at our continent in a flash of the **Highland Light** (also called Cape Cod Light) above the sea cliffs in Truro. The lights are generally not open for tours, but the **Highland House Museum** (☎ 508/ 487-3397; open daily 10am to 5pm in summer) stands near Highland Light on Light House Road, off South Highland Drive. **Chatham Light** dates to 1878; a light has stood on that point since 1808. **Nauset Light** is also relatively easy to get to, off Route 6, and may be open on summer Sunday evenings. **Race Point Light** is a good walk several miles west down Race Point Beach from the parking

lot, and **Wood End** and **Long Point lights** are on Long Point, an island in Provincetown Harbor that you can reach for $10 round-trip by an hourly pontoon boat from Macmillan Pier, operated by Flyer's Boat Rental (☎ 508/ 487-0898). The **Cape Cod Museum of Natural History** leads day and overnight trips to Monomoy Island and the light there, which it controls (see "Programs," p. 104).

## NATURAL PLACES
## Nickerson State Park

The park is a great place for camping, biking, hiking, lake swimming, and messing around in small boats, which are for rent by the hour. The 1,900-acre park itself surrounds a set of ponds created by big chunks of buried ice that were left behind when the glaciers melted. When these chunks melted, the ground caved in around them, forming kettle ponds. The area belonged to the wealthy Nickerson family until they donated it to Massachusetts

completely before the countries of the world agreed in the 1970s to stop hunting them. Even now, some kinds haven't started to come back because there aren't enough to have babies.

You might wonder, if everyone knows about overfishing, why don't they stop it? After all, it would be smarter in the long run to catch less fish each year if that meant you could keep fishing forever. But one fishing boat crew alone can't stop overfishing, because any fish left behind would just be caught by someone else. All the boats could get together and agree to catch fewer fish, but the next year more boats might start fishing and catch all the fish anyway.

Many people think the problem is that no one owns the ocean. If you owned all the fish, you wouldn't wipe them out with overfishing. In fact, you do partly own the ocean. All the water within 200 miles of our coasts and the fish swimming in it belong to all the people of the United States. The government decides how to use what we all own, and it has made laws in some places to try to stop overfishing. The laws seem to work best when they give the fish to the fishermen. In some places, the law says that certain people have permission to catch fish, and no one else. In other places, the law even gives a certain amount of fish to each boat. In those areas, the owner of the boat can sell the fish for someone else to catch. That saves the fish, but it also means the fish don't belong to all the people anymore. It makes fishermen like farmers, harvesting fish they own.

Sometimes when a thing belongs to everyone, it's the same as belonging to no one. Often, people don't take care of things they don't own and waste what they get free. Our national parks belong to everyone, and anyone can go there at any time. If too many people go at once, it spoils the park for everyone, much like too many boats catching all the fish. Do you think we can take care of the parks forever? How should we make sure we do?

in 1934. Civilian Conservation Corps workers during the Great Depression planted long rows of white pine, which have grown tall and grand. More recently, a small stretch of bay beach and salt marsh was added by the state. The park is in Brewster at 3488 Main St. (☎ 508/896-3491); take Route 6A west from Orleans. Also see "Biking" (p. 101) and "Camping" (p. 88).

## Wellfleet Bay Wildlife Sanctuary

The Massachusetts Audubon Society maintains 5 miles of trails that weave through a lovely 1,000-acre preserve of wetlands, woods, and meadows around the south end of Wellfleet Bay that began as a private bird research station in 1928. It's a great place for a family ramble. Learn about the plants and the birds while exploring paths well designed to unfold views and hidden places. Several trails get a close look at the salt marsh. Stop at the nature center to take a look at the aquarium and pick up a free map and, if available, a printed trail guide that explains what you see. The society also offers naturalist-guided walks, guided outings elsewhere on the Cape, and a summer day camp (see "Programs," p. 104). The sanctuary is off West Road in South Wellfleet (☎ 508/349-2615; www.wellfleet bay.org); there's a sign on Route 6. The trail fee is $3 adults, $2 children. In summer, the visitor center is open daily 8:30am to 5pm, the trails 8am to dusk all year. An exceptional campground is only for people who have been members of the society for a year or more.

## PLACES FOR LEARNING
## In Provincetown

**Provincetown Museum & Pilgrim Monument.** High Pole Hill Rd., Provincetown. ☎ **800/ 247-1620** or 508/487-1310. www.pilgrim-monument.org. Admission $5 adults, $3 children 4–12, free for children 3 and under. July–Aug daily 9am–7pm; Apr–June and Sept–Nov daily 9am–5pm.

The large, home-grown museum houses a lot of items that children will enjoy: a doll collection, a horse-drawn fire truck, and many models, including a large *Mayflower*, among other things. It's an old-fashioned place showing off the handiwork of local people representing their own history. You could spend a couple of hours looking at the exhibits while those who lose interest play outside on the broad lawn or climb the monument. It's a 252-foot tower of massive granite blocks, the tallest all-granite structure in the United States. It was completed in 1910, commemorating the Pilgrim's landfall at Provincetown on November 11, 1620. The tower can be seen from far out to sea and down the Cape, and the view from the top is amazing. The climb is not excessively scary, but the 116 stairs and 60 ramps should burn some excess energy; and it's fun to see the stones donated by different towns set in the walls of the stairwell. The museum has plenty of free parking, making it a good starting point for a visit to Provincetown. To avoid the pedestrian-dominated downtown streets, turn left from Route 6 onto Shankpainter Road, left again on Jerome Smith Road, right on Winslow Street, and left on High Pole Hill Road into the lot.

**Expedition Whydah Sea Lab and Learning Center.** 16 MacMillan Wharf, Provincetown. ☎ **508/487-8899.** www.whydah.com. Admission $5 adults, $3.50 children 6–12. High season daily 9am–7pm; low season daily 10am–5pm, except weekends only Nov 1–Jan 1; closed Jan–Mar.

This small commercial museum displays the discoveries of ongoing treasure hunts from two real pirate ships. The *Whydah* was driven onto the outer beach in a nor'easter storm in 1717 while returning from plundering the Caribbean. The survivors were hanged in Boston. The same expedition team recently uncovered the remains of Captain Kidd's flagship on an island off Madagascar. The museum is intriguing because it preserves the mystery of underwater archaeology instead of cleaning everything up. You can see lumps of material still waiting to be taken apart. The museum's office also sells tickets for the fast ferry to Boston and rents bikes and sea kayaks.

## In Eastham & Wellfleet

Paths at each of these two sites are covered under "Nature Walks" (p. 102).

**Marconi Station Site.** Marconi Site Rd., off Rte. 6, South Wellfleet (no phone).

From this high ocean bluff on January 18, 1903, Guglielmo Marconi started the era of instant radio communication with the first meaningful wireless message between America and Europe by Morse code. Most of the ruins either eroded into the sea or were dismantled after the station was shut down in 1917. Today there's an information kiosk, as well as incredible views over the bluff and clear across the Cape. A free guide brochure explains the site.

**Penniman House.** Fort Hill Rd., off Rte. 6 in Eastham south of the Salt Pond Visitor Center. No phone. Free admission. Mon–Fri 1–4pm; open summer only.

Captain Edward Penniman used whaling profits to build his fanciful yellow house with a cupola in 1868. The gate is a whale's jawbone. Penniman went to sea at age 11 and rose through the ranks to make his fortune. Inside the house you can see the interesting records of the voyages he took with his wife, each of which lasted years. The rooms are mostly bare, however, and will likely hold your interest for no more than 20 minutes.

## In Brewster

**Cape Cod Museum of Natural History.** Rte. 6A, Brewster. ☎ **508/896-3867.** www.ccmnh.org. Admission $5 adults, $2 children 5–12. High season daily 9:30am–5pm; low season Mon–Sat 9:30am–4:30pm, Sun 11am–4:30pm.

The museum has good exhibits, such as tanks of tide-pool animals and fish, mounted birds for identification, and simple, clear teaching tools on ecological concepts. But it's more of an educational center than a static museum. The enthusiastic staff and volunteers lead visitors outdoors to learn about the museum's extensive marsh and bay-front grounds, and beyond, on hiking, canoeing, and boating trips as far afield as the Monomoy Island National Wildlife Refuge. Many of the guided walks are free with the price of admission. (For more on the outings and children's day camps, see "Programs," p. 104.) Call or write ahead for the extensive calendar of shows, events, and trips. On rainy days, the museum organizes informal talks, microscope viewing, and the like.

**New England Fire and History Museum.** 1439 Main St. (Rte. 6A), Brewster. ☎ **508/896-5711.** Admission $4 adults, $2.50 children 5–12. Summer Mon–Fri 10am–4pm, Sat–Sun noon–4pm; closed Oct–May.

Children who want to be firefighters should visit and see many working fire engines, mostly antique horse-drawn models, and many fire-related artifacts presented by friendly volunteers. Those who don't share that fascination may not want to stay long enough to justify the trip and admission.

## ACTIVITIES
## Beachgoing

**ACCESS & FEES**   The beach itself is public everywhere on the Cape, but beach access is not. Beaches managed by the national seashore are open to all. Town beach access often is restricted to people living or renting a cottage or a motel room within town limits.

The Park Service charges $7 a day or $20 a season for a beach pass that's good for everyone in the car. If you walk or ride a bike, the fee is $1, but it doesn't always seem to be collected. National passes cover the fees (see "Passes & Fees," in chapter 1, for details).

Some town beaches are open for daily use for fees listed under "Town Beaches," below; others require a beach sticker on your car that only renters in the town can get. Renters buy the sticker for around $25 a week by showing a lease or a special form from a hotel at the town office. Get details from your host or landlord or the local chamber of commerce (see "Cape Cod Address Book," p. 82).

**CHOOSING A BEACH**   The beaches on the eastern, outer side of the Cape have fine sand for sand castles, limitless distances for beach walks, crashing waves to bodysurf in and to watch and listen to, relatively cold water, sea-polished shells, and some shorebirds. The beaches on the western, Cape Cod Bay side of the Cape are tamer and safer for young children to wade and swim in. The waves are smaller, the water is warmer and calmer, and the beaches are more gradual — waders don't have to worry about getting in too deep. At low tide, the beach widens and you can look for sea creatures and watch shorebirds feeding. The sand is coarser, and there's more seaweed and gunk.

**AVOIDING CROWDS**   The most crowded beaches are the national seashore beaches and the town beaches that are open to the public. Beaches in Provincetown and Orleans are usually more crowded than those in Truro and Wellfleet, with Eastham in between. Town beaches restricted to residents and renters in Truro and Wellfleet may be least crowded of all — a good reason to rent there and get access. These towns control many miles of pristine beach, usually without lifeguards, that are uncrowded even at the height of the season. Some of the parking lots fit only a couple dozen cars. The gatekeeper is a teenager in a lawn chair, or no one at all in the morning or evening, when you may be able to go without a permit. Also, no permit may be required in early June or in September.

When national seashore parking lots fill, cars form a line at the gate waiting for someone to leave. If the line is long, try another beach. But once you get in, you can be as solitary as you want by walking away from the access point. Most people either are lazy or like crowds, because they pack together tightly rather than take a short walk. If you have a good way to carry small children and you limit your beach baggage, you'll be able to go farther. Also, go to the beach in the morning, before the crowds arrive and while the sand isn't as hot as it is in mid-afternoon.

## National Seashore Beaches
The national seashore beaches, which generally are on the outer shore, have showers, bathrooms, and lifeguards, and, with a single exception, don't sell food or have any commercial services. You need to bring everything with you, including beverages.

- **Coast Guard Beach** is near the Salt Pond Visitor Center in Eastham. Most summer days you have to park a distance from the beach and take a free shuttle. The beach forms a thin barrier around Nauset Marsh.
- **Nauset Light Beach** is just a mile north from Coast Guard Beach on Ocean View Drive near the famous lighthouses. If you don't want to mess with the shuttle at Coast Guard, it's a good alternative.
- **Marconi Beach,** in south Wellfleet, is isolated at the end of a longish park road, with no other beach access over the towering cliffs for miles in either direction.
- **Head of the Meadow Beach** may be the least used of the national seashore beaches, down an unpaved road in North Truro. A

town beach is right next to it, and a park bike trail leads to the interesting Pilgrim Heights area (see p. 95).
- **Race Point** is a wide, north-facing, white-sand beach in the midst of the busy Province Lands area, and it has the historic Old Harbor Lifesaving Station (see p. 94). The beach is popular and many people bike there on the trails from Provincetown.
- **Herring Cove Beach,** near Provincetown at the southwest tip of the Province Lands, is the only national seashore beach facing west, toward Cape Cod Bay. It's halfway between a fine-grained, high-energy ocean beach and a calm, coarse, gradual bay beach. A food stand offers snacks. The parking lot often fills.
- **Remote Beaches,** tens of miles of them, are waiting, if you can get to them. One way is by off-road vehicle (see p. 103). Another is on a shuttle boat across Provincetown Harbor to Long Point (not part of the national seashore; see "Lighthouses," p. 96).

## Town Beaches
Below I've listed other town beaches open to everyone (not those that require a sticker), along with the daily nonresident fee at each beach:

- **Eastham** — Bay side: **Cooks Brook Beach** and **Sunken Meadow Beach,** off Massasoit Road; **First Encounter Beach,** off Samoset Road; and **Thumpertown Beach,** off Herring Brook Road. Daily fee $10.
- **Wellfleet** — Bay side: **Mayo Beach,** on Kendrick Avenue by the town pier. Free. Outer side: **White Crest Beach,** Ocean View Drive, and **Cahoon Hollow Beach,** Cahoon Hollow Road. Daily fee $10.
- **Truro** — Bay side: **Corn Hill Beach,** Corn Hill Road. Daily fee $5.

## Biking

The Cape has several recreational bike trails. The longest is the 24-mile **Cape Cod Rail Trail,** a state park path on the old rail line between Dennis and Wellfleet. The path is flat and has long straight sections through scrub pine, but it also passes by ponds, bay beaches, and Marconi Beach. It runs near the Salt Pond Visitor Center, where a 1.6-mile bike trail leads to Coast Guard Beach. At its midpoint, the rail trail crosses part of Nickerson State Park, where it meets an 8-mile bike trail that passes through the woods and past the campground and ponds. The park manages the rail trail (see "Nickerson State Park," under "Natural Places," p. 96), and a detailed trail guide and map is widely available.

An 8-mile bike trail, the **Province Lands Trail,** explores the strange area of dune and forest at the tip of the Cape (see "Province Lands," p. 94). The path starts at the visitor center or any of several other spots, and leads to Race Point Beach, the Beech Forest Trail, and Herring Cove Beach. This is a fun and interesting ride over steep, rippling hills and around sharp corners, but it's heavily used. The Park Service also maintains a less-used 2-mile trail that connects **Head of the Meadow Beach** to the **Pilgrim Heights picnic area** and High Head Road, a beautiful area (see "Pilgrim Heights," p. 95). The Park Service gives away a map of its three trails at the visitor centers, where you can also buy an inexpensive booklet, *The Cape Cod Bike Book,* which covers all the trails on the Cape and the connecting roads. Bike rental agencies are under "Getting Around" (p. 93).

## Canoeing & Kayaking

To quote Kenneth Grahame's *The Wind in the Willows,* "There is nothing — absolutely nothing — half so much worth doing as simply messing about in boats." The salt marshes and tidal estuaries of Cape Cod are the best sort of place for that. Paddling through the branching channels, you can easily imagine that you're discovering hidden places for the first time. This also is the best way to see a lot of birds, animals, and sea life, from snails and crabs to impressive great blue herons, egrets, and osprey. The marsh is biologically rich and the canoe is quiet. Canoeing here is easy over smooth, shallow water; but the currents can be strong and occasionally you run out of water and need to drag the canoe. Wear water shoes or rubber boots. (Read more in "How a Salt Marsh Is Made," in chapter 2.)

We had a great day, despite rain, exploring part of the huge **Nauset Marsh,** in Eastham. A launch spot and parking lot is near Salt Pond on Route 6, just before the turn for the Salt Pond Visitor Center. Paddling out a narrow channel puts you in the marsh, still more than a mile from the outer, barrier beach. Paddling into the channels from here, you are soon out on your own in a landscape of green grass and water, sand and mud,

## EXPERIMENT: SAND CASTLES VERSUS TIDES

Is the tide rising or falling? At the national seashore, high tide is 6 to 10 feet above low tide (see "The Tides," in chapter 2, to learn how tides work). Without checking a tide table, look for clues around you on the beach. Is the sand wet higher up the beach than the highest waves? Then maybe the tide is going out. Are the waves running into old footprints and getting close to people on beach towels? Then maybe the tide is coming in. Develop your hypothesis — your idea of which way the tide is going — and then come up with an experiment to test your hypothesis. My favorite way is to build a sand castle right down where the waves run out. A few waves always wash over my work, but if the tide is going out, that happens less and less often until the castle is high and dry. If the waves keep getting closer and start to wash my sand castle away, I know that the tide is coming in; I watch the water erode the castle away until the beach is flat again.

frequently encountering wildlife. The **Pamet River,** in Truro, also offers placid paddling and easy access.

Canoes and kayaks are for rent all over the Cape (see "For Handy Reference," p. 91), and several organizations offer **guided paddles** to learn about canoeing and nature. The Park Service offers trips almost every day in midsummer in Nauset Marsh from the visitor center, in Pleasant Bay in Orleans, or in ponds, for adults and children (age limits depend on the trip). For most of the paddles you need some idea how to paddle a canoe, but one is for beginners. A list of current offerings is printed in the park newspaper or on the website (www.nps.gov/caco). Tickets are $5 to $18 for paddles ranging up to 3 hours, and you need to reserve up to a week in advance. The best plan is to call the week before you go, because the trips fill fast. Reservations are taken in person at the Salt Pond Visitor Center starting at 9am 7 days prior to the trip, or starting at 9:30am by telephone (☎ **508/ 255-3421**). Pay when you register, by credit card only if by phone.

The **Cape Cod Museum of Natural History** offers guided nature paddles in the salt marshes and all over the Cape. The 4-hour trips run every day April through mid-September and take children as young as 7 with an adult. They cost $45 per boat and require no previous experience. Before June 1, reserve a day in advance; in summer, reserve 4 days in advance. The Audubon Society's **Wellfleet Bay Wildlife Sanctuary** also offers paddles for families with kids 12 and up. See "Cape Cod Address Book" (p. 82) for contact information for either organization.

## Nature Walks

The Cape's trails are short. Only the **Great Island Trail** (see below) extends more than a couple of miles. But several make good outings with children, showing off a varied environment. Among the best walks are the 5-mile network of trails at the **Wellfleet Bay Wildlife Sanctuary** (p. 97). The **Beech Forest Trail** is truly lovely (see "Province Lands," p. 94). The **Small's Swamp Trail** tours thick woods (see "Pilgrim Heights," p. 95). Here are some other choices:

- **Atlantic White Cedar Swamp Trail:** Starting from the parking lot for the Marconi Station Site (p. 98), at the end of Marconi Site Road in Wellfleet, the flat 1-mile trail crosses from the sandy shoreline habitat of scrub pines to a mossy, shady grove where, from a looping boardwalk, you can find frogs in swamp pools. Notice the different kinds of plants that grow near the sea and farther back in the swamp, and ask your kids why.

- **Buttonbush Trail:** Across the parking lot from the Salt Pond Visitor Center in Eastham (p. 93), the trail is designed to teach children what the outdoors are like to the blind. A grown-up can read the guide brochure while the kids close their eyes and feel their way along the guide rope. It's fun.

- **Fort Hill and Red Maple Swamp trails:** From the grounds of the Penniman House in Eastham (p. 98), the **Fort Hill Trail** circles 1½ miles through red cedar along Nauset Salt Marsh, to Skiff Hill, offering good views of the marsh and beaches and an old Indian sharpening stone. It's a great bird-watching trail. The trail joins the **Red Maple Swamp nature trail,** a short boardwalk loop where you can look for frogs, turtles, woodpeckers, and catbirds (a little gray bird that mews like a cat and may come out of hiding if it hears you mewing).

- **Great Island Trail:** The national seashore's only substantial hike is this glorious 4-mile (one-way) trail along the sandy strip of land that separates Wellfleet Harbor from Cape Cod Bay. The trailhead is near the end of Chequessett Neck Road, west of the Wellfleet town center. The woods and wild beaches feel like primeval Cape Cod, but in fact a village once stood here where people would beach whales to cook out their oil over wood fires. They cut all the trees to build the fires, and without trees erosion washed away the village. Archaeologists turned up ruins of a tavern in the forest that has recovered (there's nothing there to see), but the hike's main allure is its wildness. The final section is above water only at low tide.

- **Nauset Marsh Trail:** Starting from the Salt Pond Visitor Center (p. 93), the 1-mile loop trail rounds the shore of the pond and then overlooks the marsh from a bluff. With a scope or strong binoculars, it would be a good vantage for bird-watching. You also get to pass through thick shoreline vegetation of oak and eastern red cedar.

## Off-Road Driving

A section of the outer beach at the end of Cape Cod from Race Point Light to Head of Meadow Beach is open for over-sand driving during the summer and even beach camping in RVs with the right equipment. If you own a high-clearance four-wheel-drive vehicle and aren't afraid to put some accelerated wear and tear on it in the salty sand, this can be a fun way to get to fishing or remote beach walks. But call ahead or check the website (www.nps.gov/caco/activities/oversand/index.html) because you will need one of a limited number of $40 permits, and there are various regulations and an inspection to comply with (most vehicles lack the right tires, for example). The **Race Point Ranger Station** (☎ 508/487-2100) manages the system.

## Sailing

I doubt there are many places in the world like Provincetown's MacMillan Wharf, where you can shop for your choice of wooden schooners, as well as various other vessels, for day trips. The trips last a couple of hours and leave several times daily. Ticket booths and vessels are side by side on the dock, so you can choose the boat and the price you want. Fares range from $10 to $20 for adults, roughly half that for kids. If you want to plan ahead, call the schooner *Hindu* (☎ 508/487-0659) or

the schooner *Bay Lady II* (☎ 508/487-9308; www.sailcapecod.com).

You can have even more fun sailing your own boat for an afternoon. We had a wonderful time on a 19-foot boat in Wellfleet Harbor, a large, protected, but not-too-calm body of water. **Wellfleet Marine Corp.** (☎ 508/349-2233) offers boats from a booth at the town dock — prices range from $30 for the first hour to $115 a day — and has skiffs for fishing. In Provincetown Harbor, **Flyer's Boat Rental,** 131A Commercial St. (☎ 800/750-0898 or 508/487-0898, sailnortheast.com/flyers/), offers a wide range of sail- and powerboats, plus rowboats, kayaks, and fishing gear. Sailboats are $50 to $100 a day. Flyer's also offers sailing lessons by reservation.

## Whale Watching

Migrating humpback, finback, and right whales show up every day off Cape Cod, in **Stellwagen Bank National Marine Sanctuary** or **Cape Cod Bay Critical Habitat Area,** where the Pilgrims first saw whales and later colonists invented whaling. The whales stop here to feed on their way north for the summer, and the area has become a center of whale research and a popular place to see whales. All whale watching is from boats. It's hard to grasp how big these animals are until you're with them. Children are as impressed as adults, although young children may not have the patience to watch the whales for as long as grown-ups want to.

The **Center for Coastal Studies,** 59 Commercial St. (P.O. Box 1036), Provincetown, MA 02657 (☎ 508/487-3622; www.coastalstudies.org), works to study and protect the whales, especially the dwindling right whales, by untangling them from fishing nets and diverting ships that might hit them. The center has named more than 1,000 humpback whales and keeps track of their life stories — staffers can recognize individuals by the white markings on their tails that show when they sound. Contact the center if you want to learn more, or pick up a copy of the

*Whale Sighting Guide* chart sold by the Park Service, at the Center for Coastal Studies office, and elsewhere.

Several competing companies send boats from Provincetown's MacMillan Wharf several times a day to see the whales, competing fiercely on price and service on trips that last 3 to 4 hours. We went with **The Dolphin Fleet** (☎ 800/826-9300 or 508/349-1900; www.whalewatch.com). The boat was large and stable with ample deck room. More important, the guide was a naturalist from the Center for Coastal Studies who really knew his stuff and gave a fascinating commentary, including his firsthand stories of rescuing net-entrapped whales. The Dolphin Fleet has worked with the center for years, using these commercial whale-watching trips to count and identify the whales as part of its scientific work. On board you can consult a huge catalog containing the life story and ancestry of every whale you see. Of the many ocean tours we've taken from Alaska to Maine, this was the best guided. They run mid-April through late October, as often as nine times a day in midsummer. The peak season fare is $20 adults, $17 ages 7 to 12, free 6 and under; off-season is a dollar less. Reservations aren't needed. To avoid seasickness avoid going in rough weather; also see "Seasickness & Motion Sickness," in chapter 1.

## Programs

Four organizations promote naturalist offerings in the national seashore area, including the National Park Service, Nickerson State Park, Cape Cod Museum of Natural History, and the Audubon Society's Wellfleet Bay Wildlife Sanctuary. The last two of these also offer summer day camps for children. Each place is described earlier in this chapter, and contact information for all four is listed under "Cape Cod Address Book" (p. 82). I've also listed Cape Cod Sea Camps, which has day and residential camps. Many of the activities and all the camps require planning and advance reservations, so request details before your trip.

## Cape Cod National Seashore

The national seashore offers one of the most extensive schedules of ranger programs of any unit in the national park system. Choices are listed in the park newspaper and on the website (www.nps.gov/caco). They start from many sites. Campfires take place on the beaches after a walk away from the access point. Walks on the tidal flats and in the salt marshes teach about the plants and creatures there. Tours of historic houses, and musical and literary programs take place in various places. Some programs teach new skills and sports, including surf casting, canoeing, and shellfishing. Several programs are aimed specifically at families with children, and kids are welcome with their families on most. The best programs require reservations, and often carry a fee. I recommend mapping it all out before you come, planning your days to minimize driving and to make sure you get reservations for what you want to do.

The Park Service produces a good **Junior Ranger booklet** intended for children ages 8 to 12, which you can get for $2 at either visitor center. Younger children would enjoy some of the matching exercises and illustrated check-off lists of different kinds of Cape Cod architecture and animals, too, if not the writing activities. The booklet is designed to be used at home too, a recognition that you don't want to sit inside doing workbooks if the weather is good. To earn a Junior Ranger patch, children ages 8 to 12 complete six workbook activities, attend two ranger programs, and visit and write about park sites — not easy, but doable. Kids ages 5 to 7 do the same less the workbook activities to win a patch.

## Nickerson State Park

The state park's **Junior Ranger program** comes with an excellent 38-page book of outdoor activities aimed at school-age children who read well and have a good attention span. After completing 8 of the 12 activities and an evaluation form, kids get a patch and certificate from the Massachusetts Department of Environmental Management.

A kids' nature center near the park entrance has activities for children 6 to 14 just about every day of the summer. It's a casual, drop-off arrangement with a ranger who takes the children for a couple of hours for walks, games, and activities — they were making a pond when I visited. Parents can take off on their own. The park also has programs for families together, including guided nature walks, campfires, and the like.

## Cape Cod Museum of Natural History

The museum has day camps and programs for families. Contact them ahead for times and registration (see "Cape Cod Address Book," p. 82).

The price of admission alone gets you on some of the guided walks on the grounds, but the museum also offers some of the most famous and appealing outings on the Cape. Their boat trips to **Monomoy Island,** a sandy bar that extends south of the eastern edge of the Cape, are a chance to see birds and other wildlife and the truly remote national wildlife refuge there. The museum manages the Monomoy Point Lighthouse on South Monomoy Island, taking day-trippers for tours and offering overnights in the keeper's cottage. These are popular trips, with limits of 6 to 12 passengers per session, so you must reserve well ahead. Minimum ages are 7 for some trips, 12 for others, and prices range from $40 to $200. If you can't get on one of those trips, try a daily boat cruise through **Nauset Marsh** with a naturalist catching creatures to examine. There are guided hikes, stargazing outings, mudflat explorations, and more offerings (canoeing is covered under "Canoeing & Kayaking," p. 101). Get the catalog before you go.

Day camps for children as young as preschool and as old as 9th grade last through July and August. Many are just one or two sessions of a few hours, a chance for the family to split up and pursue individual interests without a huge investment of time. Sessions include nature encounters, artistic inspiration, and science skills — they might dig in the tidal mud or make casts of animal tracks. A typical session for kids 6 to 9 lasts 2½ hours and costs $30. The museum also offers a day camp of 5 full days for grades 1 to 6 and a field school for grades 7 to 9. Tuition is $175 to $250.

## Wellfleet Bay Wildlife Sanctuary

The Audubon Society offers programs at its sanctuary and afield focused on adults, families, and kids, and day camps for age 4 through 7th grade. Reservations are necessary for most programs, so contact them ahead for the catalog (see "Cape Cod Address Book," p. 82).

During the high season, many programs a day are in session, on many subjects other than birding. Children's programs cost as little as $5 or $6 — the cost of the aquarium tour, nighttime bug and critter prowl, or nature crafts, and many others. Family and adult programs include guided walks at the sanctuary for birding, shoreline study, and the like. Other appealing outings go afield, including the superb boat cruises: bird-watching through

---

### PLACES FOR RELAXED PLAY & PICNICS

You're never far from a picnic area in the national seashore. The **Pilgrim Heights** picnic area is mentioned on p. 95. A picnic grounds is located at **Doane Rock,** a boulder the size of a house left by a glacier near the Salt Pond Visitor Center. Others are at the starting points of the **Great Island Trail** in Wellfleet (p.102) and the **Beech Forest Trail** in the Province Lands area (p. 94). I've listed places that pack picnics under "Where to Eat" (p. 106). The towns generally have small public libraries and school playgrounds for downtime.

Nauset Marsh, pulling up sea creatures from under Wellfleet Bay, or watching gray seals off Chatham. There are several other choices, some aimed specifically at families. Fares are $35 or less.

The Audubon Society's July and August day camps are in five age groups, starting with 4-year-olds, who spend 5 fun mornings at the sanctuary learning about nature for a tuition of $140. The next two age groups have similar programs, while groups of grades 3 through 5 and grades 6 through 7 concentrate on a particular scientific topic all week, with outings on day cruises (and even overnight cruises). Tuition is up to $250.

## Cape Cod Sea Camps

This highly regarded camp with low staff-to-camper ratios is right on Cape Cod Bay. It has been in business since 1922. It offers all kinds of summer camp activities, but the specialty is sailing. Residential, day camp, or combination options are available for periods of as little as 5 days or up to 7 weeks, serving children ages 4 through 17. Prices start at $425 for a week of day camp. Most fill up by January 1, and you can register as early as October. Contact info: P.O. Box 1880, Brewster, MA 02631-0062 (☎ **508/896-3451** or 508/896-3626; fax 508/896-8272; www.capecodseacamps.com).

# WHERE TO EAT

## PICNICS & TAKEOUT

**Box Lunch,** with three locations in our area and more elsewhere, packs meals to go. The emphasis is on healthy ingredients and creative preparation. Most items are around $4; a kid's sandwich is $2, and the menu tops out at $10 for a lobster sandwich. The original location is in Wellfleet, just off the town center at 50 Briar Lane (☎ **508/349-2178;** www.boxlunch.com); also in Provincetown at 353 Commercial St. (☎ **508-487-6026**); and Eastham on Route 6 (☎ **508/255-0799**). All locations are open 7am to 7pm daily.

In Truro, a summer-only country store and deli called **Jams Gourmet Grocery** is at 14 Truro Center Rd., just off Route 6 (☎ **508/349-1616**). Although the prices will convince you not to do all your shopping there, the rotisserie chicken, gourmet pizzas, and baked goods make for an unforgettable picnic or great takeout for dinner.

## LOW-STRESS MEALS
### Eastham

The **Eastham Lobster Pool,** 4380 Route 6, North Eastham (☎ **508/255-9706,** takeout 255-3314; www.lobsterpool.com), perfects a

type: the rough-edged New England seafood joint. The floor is concrete and crab pots hang from an unfinished ceiling, but the fish is as good as you will find anywhere. For families, the side benefit is that it's hard to bother anyone. The service is fast and relaxed. The children's menu includes a half lobster for $8 and other items for $6 to $12. The grown-ups' menu changes every day according to fish availability and the chef's whim, but always includes the lobsters swimming around near the front of the place. Lunch prices range from $6 to $27, dinner $12 to $27. They don't take reservations, and it gets crowded; so dine early. They're open mid-April to mid-October 11:30am to 10pm daily in summer, closing at 9pm before Memorial Day and after Labor Day.

The **Red Barn Restaurant,** on Route 6 just north of the Salt Pond Visitor Center (☎ **508/255-4500**), is a pizzeria with a table or two inside and bench tables outside under a canopy. The pizza is good and they have an ice-cream window. Then, if the children deserve a treat, you can wander over to the mini-golf course and arcade.

## Wellfleet

The **Lighthouse,** 317 Main St. (☎ 508/ 349-3681), is a place for a traditional, filling meal, especially breakfast. Upstairs is a classic small-town diner, open daily 7am to 9pm, until 10pm in summer, with friendly, familiar service, a bulletin of local events, and enough noise to drown out the children. Lunch main courses are $4.50 to $8.50, dinner $8 to $17. Downstairs, there's pizza in the evening.

Out on Route 6, **Moby Dick's** (☎ 508/ 349-9795; www.mobydicksrestaurant.com) is a big family-run and family-oriented fish place with a long history, serving lobster, sandwiches, and fried fish. Lunch is $5 to $8, dinner $10 to $18. They're open 11:30am to 10pm in the summer, closing earlier in the spring and fall.

## Provincetown

**Clem & Ursie's Food Ghetto,** on Shank Painter Road near Route 6 (☎ 508/ 487-2333), is a masterpiece in chaos. Barbara found it a bit unnerving to walk into the noise, lines, and confusing arrangements of counters and fast-food–style tables, but the kids and I loved it when we got our bearings. And the food! Sophisticated seafood prepared in styles from all over the world for shockingly low prices, simple fresh fish, barbecue, home cooking, and even a $5 kids meal with a prize. Grab a table, then figure out the menu and order at the counter, where you pay and get a number. The food comes quickly. Entrees range from $4 to $21. They're open early April through mid-October, 10am to 10pm.

## BEST-BEHAVIOR MEALS

**Adrian's.** 535 Rte. 6, North Truro. ☎ 508/ 487-4360. www.adriansrestaurant.com. Dinner $10–$25, children's menu $5; breakfast $4–$8. Summer daily 8am–noon and 5:30–10pm.

Dining on the deck, you can watch a glorious sunset unfold far below on Cape Cod Bay while experiencing wonderful regional Italian cuisine. It includes a lot of seafood, but also Italian-style pizzas with ingenious combinations of ingredients. The service is quick and the atmosphere light and friendly. Children need to behave themselves, but the meal won't be tense.

**Aesop's Tables.** 316 Main St., Wellfleet. ☎ 508/ 349-6450. July–Aug Wed–Sun noon–3pm; daily 5:30–9:30pm; call for off-season hours. Closed mid-Oct–Apr.

This justly famous restaurant in a large, historic house serves creative cuisine made from food provided by Cape Cod's waters. We've had flawless dinners here, and a windy lunch on a flapping linen tablecloth under the tall shade trees above Main Street. The cuisine is creative and complicated, but always harmonious. The kids' menu, said to have been designed by local children, is cute, with names like "green worms in slime" for pasta with pesto, but far from a bargain in price. This is a place to choose for a special meal when you want to dress up and your older children will enjoy behaving correctly among the colonial furniture and relatively close quarters, while waiting the time required to serve fine food.

**The Lobster Pot.** 321 Commercial St., Provincetown. ☎ 508/487-0842. www.ptown lobsterpot.com. Entire menu served for lunch and dinner, $6–$24. Summer daily 11:30am–10:30pm, closing an hour earlier off-season.

This place is an institution, its narrow and lively dining rooms overlooking Macmillan Wharf humming like a town nerve center. Arrive early, because they don't take reservations, and children won't stand for the wait it requires to get a table. Other aspects do make sense for families, however, including the long and varied menu they serve all day, which allows one diner to have an inexpensive burger while another orders blackened tuna sashimi. It's a good choice for a special lobster dinner.

# CHAPTER 5

# Cape Hatteras National Seashore

Driving along Hatteras and Ocracoke islands on a narrow strip of sand with the ocean close on both sides, you may think that the Outer Banks seem like a geographic miracle. Why should this razor-thin rim of sand persist far out in the sea? How wild it seems, a land of windy beach with no end, always in motion, always vulnerable to the next, slightly larger wave. There's so much here to see and learn, and so much solitude to enjoy. You're like a passenger on an enormous ship, and unpredictable nature is the captain.

Oddly, many people don't see Cape Hatteras this way. When they think of the Outer Banks, they think of Nags Head or Kill Devil Hills, towns where tourist development has pushed right up to the edge of the sea and, in many places, gotten really ugly. Most visitors to the national seashore come only for the weekend, and just from the nearest states, to escape the damp heat of the Southern summer. On the Outer Banks, the wind almost always blows, so it feels cooler than inland. But people should come from all over the

United States because the parts of the Outer Banks protected by the national seashore and other nature preserves are wild and beautiful. Being here, it's easy to imagine what it was like when the first English colonists landed more than 400 years ago, or when the Wright Brothers flew the first airplane a century ago. Both events are well interpreted at their sites. Ecologically, the area is fascinating, too. Here, north and south meet, and the mix of ocean currents, climate, fresh and salt water, and geography create a fabulous diversity of bird and plant life at places like the Pea Island National Wildlife Refuge and Nags Head Woods Ecological Preserve (p. 128). (In this sense, the area is much like Point Reyes, its counterpart on the west coast, covered in chapter 21, "Point Reyes National Seashore.") And, for children, the national seashore is a huge sandbox. We saw more children having a great time here than anywhere else we went.

## BEST THINGS TO DO

- Pick a place to be alone on a hot, sunny beach, where you can find crabs and shells

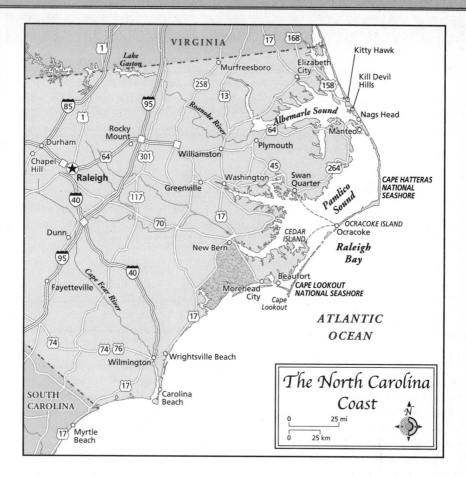

0        25 mi

0        25 km

and swim in surf that's so warm there's never a reason to get out.

- Visit Wright Brothers National Memorial, where the first flight occurred in 1903, and Fort Raleigh National Historic Site, where the first English colony in the New World was built and disappeared in the 1580s.
- Climb one of the nation's highest lighthouses, visit the aquarium, and climb

aboard a 16th-century ship replica.

- Hike a wetlands trail and look for interesting birds.
- Go fishing, sailing, or sea kayaking, or just wade into shallow sound waters to catch crabs.

See "Activities" (p. 131).

## HISTORY: ISLANDS IN TIME

As you drive south along the Outer Banks from Nags Head to Hatteras Village, then (after a ferry ride) to Ocracoke, you might feel as if you're driving backward in history toward a more isolated, more natural time. The drive starts where the seasonal shopping centers and rows of beachfront houses in the Nags Head area crowd the ocean. Farther south, the highway enters the national seashore, with its miles of wild, windy dunes and empty sand where

**Outer Banks National Park Service Group Headquarters** (for the national seashore and historic sites). 1401 National Park Dr., Manteo, NC 27954. ☎ **252/473-2111.** Cape Hatteras National Seashore, www.nps.gov/caha; Wright Brothers National Memorial, www.nps.gov/wrbr; Fort Raleigh National Historic site, www.nps.gov/fora.

**Eastern National** (for books and maps). 470 Maryland Dr., Suite 2, Ft. Washington, PA 19428. ☎ **877/NAT-PARK.** Fax 215/591-0903. www.eparks.com.

**Outer Banks Visitors Bureau.** 704 S. Hwy. 64/264, Manteo, NC 27954. ☎ **800/446-6262** or 252/473-2138. www.outerbanks.org.

**North Carolina Ferry System.** 113 Arendell St., Morehead City, NC 28557. ☎ **800-BY-FERRY** (eastern U.S. only) or 252/726-6446; Ocracoke ☎ 800/345-1665 or 252/928-3841; Hatteras ☎ 800/368-8949; Cedar Island ☎ 800/773-1094 or 252/225-3551. www.ncferry.org.

**Outer Banks Chamber of Commerce.** P.O. Box 1757, Kill Devil Hills, NC 27948. ☎ **252/441-8144.** www.outerbankschamber.com.

**Ocracoke Civic and Business Association.** P.O. Box 456, Ocracoke, NC 27960. ☎ **252/928-6711.** www.ocracokeisland.com.

---

breakers roll in day and night, unnoticed by anyone. On Ocracoke Island, the quiet town of Ocracoke sits among the trees in the wider part of the island, while the beachfront along the highway remains pretty much wild.

History set these patterns. Over hundreds of years, people decided which places to fill or leave open based on the jobs they had, the roads and bridges they built, and what they wanted to save for the future.

After Sir Walter Raleigh's Lost Colony disappeared in the 1580s (see chapter 2, "Moving Water, Moving Land"), several generations passed without Europeans on the Outer Banks. The islands were too remote and sandy for most people. Just getting there was difficult. On the stormy outer shore, surf constantly beat the beaches, making it a dangerous place to sail and an impossible place to land a ship. On the calm, sound-side shore, the water was too shallow for all but small boats, and only experienced sea pilots could find the way through channels that constantly shifted in the sand. These conditions were perfect, however, for one group of people: people who didn't want anyone to find them.

The Outer Banks became a hideout for pirates and other fugitives.

During wars, European rulers would allow private ship captains to attack any vessel from an enemy nation and keep whatever they could take. This was called privateering. When the War of the Spanish Succession ended in 1713, many of the privateers kept right on attacking and robbing other ships. With no war for an excuse, this was piracy — and if you got caught, the punishment was death. In 1718, in a battle near Ocracoke, the most notorious pirate, Blackbeard, was killed by the British navy, and the age of piracy ended (see "Read Aloud: Blackbeard's Ghost," p. 120). His treasure was never found.

The village of Ocracoke became a home for pilots who knew the shipping channels well enough to safely guide vessels through Ocracoke Inlet and across Pamlico Sound to larger towns on the North Carolina mainland. Just as pilots still do in many parts of the world, an Ocracoke pilot would take a small boat out to meet a ship, steer the ship through the channels, and then travel home again in the small boat. As the town was settled and

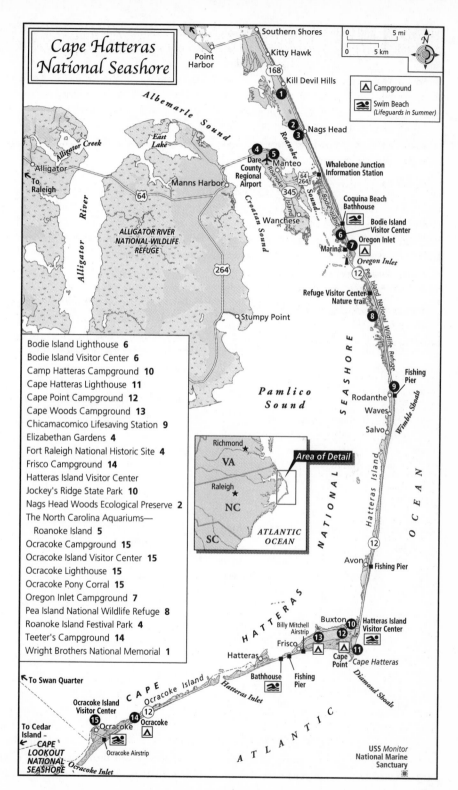

# Cape Hatteras National Seashore

Bodie Island Lighthouse **6**
Bodie Island Visitor Center **6**
Camp Hatteras Campground **10**
Cape Hatteras Lighthouse **11**
Cape Point Campground **12**
Cape Woods Campground **13**
Chicamacomico Lifesaving Station **9**
Elizabethan Gardens **4**
Fort Raleigh National Historic Site **4**
Frisco Campground **14**
Hatteras Island Visitor Center
Jockey's Ridge State Park **10**
Nags Head Woods Ecological Preserve **2**
The North Carolina Aquariums—
  Roanoke Island **5**
Ocracoke Campground **15**
Ocracoke Island Visitor Center **15**
Ocracoke Lighthouse **15**
Ocracoke Pony Corral **15**
Oregon Inlet Campground **7**
Pea Island National Wildlife Refuge **8**
Roanoke Island Festival Park **4**
Teeter's Campground **14**
Wright Brothers National Memorial **1**

built by pilots and their families, others settled there, too. People lived by piloting, fishing, carrying cargo in boats, grazing cattle and sheep on the beach grass, growing food in their gardens, and gathering valuables that washed up on the beach from shipwrecks.

Many ships sank on the Outer Banks and off Cape Hatteras. Sometimes ships wrecked trying to get through the dangerous inlets. Sometimes they wrecked just trying to get around the Cape. Look at a map: Cape Hatteras forms a turning point for ships going up and down the East Coast. If the wind were blowing the wrong way for a sailing ship to get around the corner, the captain would have to wait for the wind to change, sailing back and forth until it did. If he sailed too far out, he might get caught in a current that would carry his ship the wrong way. But a mistake in sailing around the shoals close to shore, or a storm that blew toward shore, could mean a ship would run into a shoal and get stuck. Once stuck in the surf, the ship would be smashed to pieces by the waves. This could happen miles offshore or right on the beach, and either way, the sailors would often drown in the breakers. Ocracokers and other Bankers (as year-round residents of the islands were called) would help those sailors lucky enough to wash up on the beach alive — but that didn't stop them from gathering the valuable cargo that also washed up, and using or selling it.

Shipwrecks, and avoiding them, brought jobs, too. The first Cape Hatteras Light was built in 1802. The lighthouse that stands in the village of Ocracoke today was finished in 1823; it's the oldest still standing in the area. Over the next 50 years, more great lighthouses were built on the Outer Banks. The current Cape Hatteras Light, the second, was finished in 1870, and is the tallest brick lighthouse in the United States, and probably the most famous. The Bodie Island Lighthouse was knocked down by Confederate soldiers during the Civil War — the Outer Banks were the site of furious sea battles — and was rebuilt after the war.

In the 1870s, the U.S. Life Saving Service built stations along the islands to rescue sailors and passengers in shipwrecks on the coast. When a wreck was spotted, horses would pull a boat down the beach, and if the waves weren't too rough, lifesavers would row to the grounded ship. Sometimes the lifesavers themselves drowned. When the waves were too big to even try rowing out, rescuers would fire a gun with a rope attached to the shell, fasten the line to the ship, and use it to bring in sailors one at a time. (See "Chicamacomico Lifesaving Station," p. 131.)

Even after steamships began to replace sailing ships, many people died on the Outer Banks when they made mistakes in navigation, lost engine power, or suffered storm damage to their vessels. In the world wars, the German navy took advantage of this "Torpedo Junction," the best spot on the East Coast to attack American shipping by submarine. In the first half of 1942, while the U.S. navy concentrated on fighting in the Pacific Ocean and left Cape Hatteras almost undefended, German U-boats sank some 80 ships within sight of the Outer Banks. Wreckage, oil, and bodies littered the beaches. The British sent ships to defend against the submarines, and on May 11, 1942, a British ship went down with all hands in a torpedo attack. Four British sailors washed up on Ocracoke and were buried by the islanders, who dedicated their little plot to England forever. You can see it on a walking tour of the village; it's a moving place.

The Outer Banks had a part in many wars. During the American Revolution, the Ocracoke pilots captured a British ship in their harbor. Vessels they guided through the inlet and sound helped supply General Washington at Valley Forge. When the first U.S. Census was taken in 1790, 25 families were listed on Ocracoke and Portsmouth islands. Among Ocracokers, the names are all still familiar, for the same families live there today. Over more than 200 years, they developed their own ways of doing things, and even their own accent and words that were spoken nowhere else. When babies were born, a local midwife attended, and when people died they were buried in family plots next to their homes. As you walk around the village, you can see the tiny cemeteries all around. In 1846, a hurricane opened Oregon and Hatteras inlets. Ships began to use them instead of Ocracoke Inlet, so the pilots weren't needed as much as they had been. But Ocracoke held on, despite its isolation, as if the people had become a permanent part of the land.

On the Outer Banks, where towns have come and gone and the population explodes every summer weekend, the permanent community of Ocracoke is rather special. Nags Head is more typical. There, summer visitors built the town, starting in the 1830s. The North Carolina mainland nearby is swampy, and at that time people believed that it gave off a poison gas called "miasma" in summer, causing malaria. The deadly fever killed many people, but it seemed that if they went to the Outer Banks, breathed the salty air, and spent a lot of time in the ocean, the miasma wouldn't make them sick. The truth was that malaria is caused by tiny parasites in blood carried from person to person by mosquitoes. Malaria wasn't a problem on the Outer Banks because mosquitoes can't fly in windy places. Miasma doesn't exist.

The Outer Banks began to wash away soon after the summer visitors arrived. Grazing animals ate and trampled beach grass that helps hold the sand in place. As the sand moved, it buried woods and flattened the barrier dunes that keep the waves back. By the 1930s, the wind had flattened the dunes so much that with each hurricane waves swept across large areas all along the Outer Banks. Some areas were just bare beach all the way across.

At the suggestion of a newspaper editorial, people started talking about a way to save the Banks from washing away. They proposed a park for the areas that hadn't yet been developed and a program to rebuild the dunes and to plant beach grass. The changes came fast. The Wright Brothers and Fort Raleigh sites were set aside, and in 1937 Congress authorized the creation of the national seashore by buying up land along the Outer Banks south of Nags Head, except places that were already towns. It was done, and the national seashore started, in 1952. Change stopped on most of the Outer Banks south of Nags Head. That's why we can drive back in time today, back to the village lanes of Ocracoke.

# ORIENTATION

## THE NATIONAL SEASHORE

Cape Hatteras National Seashore is 75 miles long and as narrow as a few hundred feet wide in some spots. It's made up of barrier islands off the coast of North Carolina. The protected seashore begins on the southern end of **Bodie Island** and includes most of **Hatteras** and **Ocracoke islands,** although small towns pop up along the way. Pea Island National Wildlife Refuge takes up the northern part of Hatteras Island. The water inside the barrier islands is wide, shallow **Pamlico Sound,** by Hatteras and Ocracoke islands, and freshwater **Arbemarle Sound** inside Bodie Island. The sound water is fairly calm, good for crabbing and for wading toddlers; the ocean side has great beaches and big surf. **Roanoke Island** lies between Arbemarle and Pamlico sounds, protected by Bodie Island on the ocean side; it's where the Lost Colony was, and where you'll find **Fort Raleigh National Historic Site. Wright Brothers National Memorial** is north of the national seashore, on Bodie Island. **Cape Lookout National Seashore** starts at the next island south of Ocracoke, protecting rugged barrier islands without visitor development.

## The Towns

**Kitty Hawk, Kill Devil Hills,** and **Nags Head** make up the generally unattractive tourist development that runs together along the road immediately north of the national seashore. There are some interesting places to visit in the area, however, plus large grocery stores and other services, and many motels and rental houses.

**Manteo** is a pleasant, year-round town on Roanoke Island with a variety of services, a nice redeveloped waterfront, major historic sites, and an aquarium.

Heading south through the national seashore, the towns get progressively more attractive as you go away from Nags Head. **Rodanthe, Waves,** and **Salvo,** a trio of tourist towns on the northern part of Hatteras Island, show the wear of years. **Avon** is a bit more upscale, but still mostly just a strip of beach houses. **Buxton,** at the corner where the island turns west, is a larger town on a wider piece of island, with houses back in the woods. **Hatteras,** at the south end of the island, has a harbor and some newer hotels.

The village of **Ocracoke,** on an island you can reach only by ferry, is the one town on the Outer Banks with real charm. Cut off from the rest of the world for hundreds of years out on this strip of sand, the people, called Ocracokers, developed their own island ways and unique form of English. The differences are fading with time, but Ocracoke still feels like an island.

## Roads & Ferries

It would be pretty tough to get lost here. Two-lane North Carolina **Highway 12** runs the length of the national seashore, meeting **U.S. 64** at an intersection known as **Whalebone Junction,** on Bodie Island at the north end of the national seashore. U.S. 64 connects the region to points west. Whalebone Junction is a major landmark, and mileage along the Cape is often counted from there. To the north, Highway 12 runs parallel with **U.S. 158,** which leaves the island above Kitty Hawk — that's the main way north.

To the south, Highway 12 leads to the **ferry** at the south end of Hatteras Island, where frequent free service runs to the north end of Ocracoke Island. Highway 12 then runs to Ocracoke village, on the south end of that island. Ferries also run from the village to the mainland. For more on the ferries, see p. 124.

# Making the Arrangements

## When to Go

The Cape Hatteras National Seashore and the nearby historic sites are busiest in July and August, followed by June. The temperatures are cooler than on the mainland, but still quite hot if you're not used to it, with highs averaging in the mid-80s and often going into the 90s. The trick is to stay in the wind, which is almost always blowing, and in the shade — even the hottest days don't feel that bad if you're under a beach umbrella and there's a strong sea breeze. Wind also helps with mosquitoes, which can be bad all summer, depending on the year. Weather is changeable during spring break, with highs in the 60s and 70s, but the water is too cold for swimming. The ocean water is warmest on Ocracoke. Swimming starts there around Memorial Day and on the east-facing islands in mid-June.

The best time to go — if you don't have to go during a school break — is October and early November, when the weather is cooler, birds and fish are plentiful, the bugs and crowds are gone, and the water is still fine. You'll also save on accommodations outside the peak summer months, but Park Service campgrounds are open only during the summer. Midwinter is stingingly cold on the Outer Banks; not much is open.

## WEATHER CHART: CAPE HATTERAS AVERAGES

|  | AVG. HIGH (°) | AVG. LOW (°F) | PRECIP. (IN) | WATER TEMP. (°F) |
|---|---|---|---|---|
| Dec.–Feb. | 54 | 39 | 14 | 49 |
| March | 60 | 44 | 4.3 | 52 |
| April | 67 | 51 | 3.5 | 59 |
| May | 74 | 59 | 4 | 68 |
| June | 80 | 67 | 4.1 | 74 |
| July | 85 | 72 | 5 | 77 |
| August | 85 | 72 | 6 | 80 |
| September | 81 | 68 | 5.3 | 76 |
| October | 72 | 59 | 5 | 70 |
| November | 65 | 49 | 5 | 58 |

*Cape Hatteras averages; precipitation is for the entire period covered*

Hurricane season runs June through November, with the most likely time for storms mid-August to the first week in October. If one comes, you may have to evacuate and forget about your whole trip. See p. 125 for important information about hurricanes.

## How Much Time to Spend

The Outer Banks draw millions of people from nearby states for weekends of beachgoing and fishing, but I'd recommend at least a week at the national seashore. You'll want plenty of time to enjoy the beach and other outdoor activities, a couple of days for the historic sites, and time to get down to Ocracoke Island to catch the slow rhythm of life there. Avoid arriving on weekends, especially for camping or sightseeing, because of the crowds. During the week, even in the high season, there aren't many people around.

## How Far to Plan Ahead

Summer weekends are busy, weekdays are not. For motels, 4 weeks should be enough lead time to reserve, and in the middle of the week there's a good chance of finding vacancies on the same day as the stay. For weekends, especially summer holidays, bookings may be needed months ahead. Weekly cottage rentals should be reserved in February or March for the summer. People who come back every year reserve a year ahead. Off-season, less lead time is needed for all accommodations.

For national seashore camping, only the Ocracoke Campground takes reservations, handled through the national system described in chapter 1, "Planning Your Trip."

## Reading Up

The National Park bookstores have good selections in history, nature, and the outdoors. You can order some of these by phone or online from Eastern National (☎ 877/NAT-PARK; www.epark.com).

## Nature

The best nature guide book I've found on this or any other area is *The Nature of the Outer Banks,* by Dirk Frankenberg (University of North Carolina Press). It explains seashore concepts in understandable terms using mile-by-mile commentary on what you see as examples. You can order directly from the publisher at ☎ 800/848-6224; uncpress.unc.edu.

## Fishing

The visitor centers sell an excellent 40-page booklet by Ken Taylor, *Fishing the Outer Banks,* for $3.95, a good purchase for any angler who doesn't know the area.

## GETTING THERE
### By Car

**From the north,** you leave I-64 or U.S. 13 in Norfolk. Two parallel routes from there are about equal, either Highway 168 or U.S. 17 and 158. Either way, you end up on U.S. 158 across Currituck Sound to Kitty Hawk, then south to Whalebone Junction and the start of the national seashore.

**From the west or south,** U.S. Highway 64 leads straight east from I-40 at Raleigh or from I-95 at Rocky Mount to Roanoke Island and Whalebone Junction. Or, if you are headed to Ocracoke, split from U.S. 64 to Highway 45 to the ferry at Swan Quarter.

**To Ocracoke,** you can drive through the national seashore on Highway 12 and then take the free ferry from Hatteras Village; or, if you are coming from the south or west, take the ferry across Pamlico Sound. You can stay in your car, parked on the deck, getting out to watch the water and scenery pass by from the rail; there's also a small indoor seating area. From the west, split from U.S. 64 onto Highway 45 to Swan Quarter. From the south, wend your way up the country roads to Cedar Island. The crossing from either point to Ocracoke is about 2½ hours, and the fare is $10 per car. Reserve in advance, because the ferries are small. Contact information is under "Outer Banks Address Book" (p. 110).

### By Air

You need a car to get around at Cape Hatteras. If you want to fly and rent one, the nearest major city airport is in Norfolk, Virginia, about 100 miles north. Major car-rental agencies are located there. To shop car-rental prices or airfares, Richmond, Virginia, and Raleigh, North Carolina, are each around 190 miles from the national seashore.

## WHAT TO PACK
### Clothing

During the summer season you'll spend most of your time in shorts, T-shirts, swimsuits, sandals or beach shoes, and sun hats. Also bring long pants and shirts for protection against insects, walking shoes for the historic sites and scratchy nature walks, and windbreakers or raincoats for summer thunderstorms. If you come in the off-season, bring more warm clothing. There aren't many places to wear formal clothing.

### Gear

Prepare for wind, sun, and bugs. Bring mosquito repellent and strong sunblock. You can buy a beach umbrella to get away from the sun, and sand toys for the kids, at surf shops all along the highway. If you have a toddler, bring a backpack or rent a sand cart to carry him or her over sand. You often have to hike over a dune to get to the water, and once there you may want to walk along the beach. A portable radio to keep track of the weather forecasts is a good idea, too.

If you're camping, bring lots of rope or cord. Camping on a windy sand dune requires you to tie out your tent to the picnic table, the bumper of the car, or anything else that won't move. Short, skinny tent stakes won't work; instead, you need the metal, blade-shaped stakes, and plenty of them (see chapter 1). Also, shade is rare at any of the campgrounds, so canopies and screen-house tents that can go over a picnic table are popular.

# WHERE TO SPEND THE NIGHT

## CAMPGROUNDS

We enjoyed camping at Cape Hatteras, surrounded by wind and sand and near enough the ocean to stroll from the tent to the water. But you do need shade and wind to escape the heat, and mosquitoes can be vicious when the wind is low or near the marshes. And life is gritty. Despite the cold showers, which are heaven on a hot day, you're always sandy.

## At the National Seashore

There are four Park Service campgrounds in the national seashore, all just behind the dunes on the ocean beach. The facilities generally are more modern and cleaner than those at most national parks. All the campgrounds have cold showers in booths — fine on a hot afternoon — and cold-water rest rooms with flush toilets. There are no hookups at any of the campgrounds; all but the Frisco Campground have dump stations.

Only Ocracoke takes reservations; the other three are first-come, first-served. On Sundays through Thursdays, that system works well, but on Friday and Saturday nights and holiday weekends, getting a site is difficult. The campgrounds often fill on Friday before noon; a waiting list is kept for Saturday in case someone leaves early. During the week, arrive before noon for your choice of prime sites, but even in late afternoon there's usually something left.

Campgrounds are listed here by their distance from Whalebone Junction, at the north end of the national seashore.

**Oregon Inlet.** On Hwy. 12, at the south end of Bodie Island. $17 per night. 120 sites. Closed Oct to mid-Apr.

Right across the highway from the marina and fishing center, where you can shop for food and fishing supplies, these grassy and sandy sites sit on the edge of and among the dunes. Many informal paths lead through a series of dunes to the broad beach, which is heavily traveled by off-road vehicles. It's an attractive campground, and a good place to stay if you want to be within the national seashore but still close to the historic sites. Lifeguarded Coquina Beach is several miles north.

**Cape Point.** At the Cape Point Beach access, near Cape Hatteras Lighthouse. $17 per night. 202 sites. Closed Sept to late May.

This campground occupies a big grassy lawn behind the dunes near the point where the Outer Banks make their sharp turn from north-south to east-west. The walk to the very end of the point is about 1½ miles each way. Of the four Park Service campgrounds, this one is the nearest to a lifeguarded beach. The Buxton Woods Nature Trail and the big lighthouse also are nearby, as is the town of Buxton, but the campground is at the end of a quiet road. It operates during a shorter season than the others.

**Frisco.** On Billy Mitchell Rd., off Hwy. 12, Frisco. $17 per night. 127 sites. Closed Oct to mid-Apr.

---

### PARK CAMPING BASICS: TOILETS, SHOWERS & LAUNDRY

The national seashore campgrounds and beach bathrooms lack hot water, but were quite clean when we visited. The visitor centers have hot water and soap. There are cold-water showers in booths at the campgrounds and out in the open at Coquina Beach and Sandy Bay Day Use Area, for both day-use visitors and overnighters. Do your wash at **Kill Devil Hills Amoco Launderette**, at milepost 6 on U.S. 158 (☎ 252/441-9520), or in Manteo at **Mr. Clean,** near the Post Office in the Chestley Mall (☎ 252/758-4928). A major inconvenience is that there are no public laundry facilities on Ocracoke. If you're renting a house, make sure it has laundry machines.

---

A few miles west of Cape Point, the Frisco Campground has a much more isolated, wilderness-like feel. Bushy dunes rise around the sites, many of which have good privacy (arrive early to get one of those and not some that are packed quite close together). From atop the dunes, there are sweeping views all the way to the lighthouse. The seaside is near, too. A mile away, on Highway 12, are the Frisco Market, Frisco Rod and Gun, a post office, and a Texaco that stocks everything a camper could need.

**Ocracoke.** On Hwy. 12, about 4 miles east of the village. $17 per night. 135 sites. Closed Oct to mid-Apr.

A grassy area stands behind a single dune, close to long, empty Ocracoke Beach. Don't set up camp on the other side of the campground near the road, where marshy, mosquito-ridden brush grows. To escape the bugs, you have to be in the wind. Reserve through the national system (see chapter 1), but because you choose your site on arrival, it pays to be early. Groceries are available in the village, but there are no laundry facilities on the island.

## Commercial Campgrounds

All rates listed here are for the high season; they drop off somewhat in the off-season.

**Camp Hatteras.** Hwy. 12 (P.O. Box 10), Waves, NC 27968. ☎ **252/987-2777.** www.camphatteras.com. Tent sites $30–$35, full hookups $48, up to 2 people; $4 per extra adult, $2 per extra child 6–17, free for children 5 and under. 400 sites. Indoor and outdoor pools, hot tubs, playground, clubhouse, tennis, sailing, minigolf, store, laundry.

I've never seen a place quite like this, although a similar KOA campground is right next door. Covering 50 acres all the way across the Cape, with long frontages on both shores, it has everything listed above and more — three stocked fishing ponds, for example. RVs couldn't do better for this kind of place, and tenters have a grassy area set aside for them on the sound, although it has only portable toilets.

The area is a bit tacky, with a lot of roadside tourist development, including amusement parks, mini-golf courses, and the like — a place for a fun kid trip, but not what you might think of as a national park trip.

**Cape Woods Campground.** Rte. 1232 (P.O. Box 757), Buxton, NC 27920. ☎ **252/995-5850.** Tent sites $23, full hookups $28, up to 2 adults and 2 children; $4 per extra adult, $2 per extra child 12 or under. 130 sites. Pool, playground, laundry.

In the woods next to a pond in Buxton, more than a mile from the ocean, this is a nicely landscaped, family-run campground. The sites are wooded and shady and have a natural feel.

**Frisco Woods Campground.** 53124 Hwy. 12 (P.O. Box 159), Frisco, NC 27936. ☎ **800/948-3942** or 252/995-5208. www.outer-banks.com/friscowoods. Tent sites $24–$29, full hookups $35–$40, up to 2 adults and 2 children, additional adult $6, additional child 16 and under $3. 163 sites. Pool, coin-op laundry, watersport rentals, playground.

This is an exceptional campground, combining a natural setting with enough activities to make you want to spend plenty of time. Set among trees and on lawns along with lots of frontage on Pamlico Sound, the family-run campground offers gear rental for playing on the water and even windsurfing lessons. There's a small beach. They also have cabins.

**Teeter's Campground.** On British Cemetery Rd., Ocracoke, NC 27960. ☎ **800/705-5341** or 252/928-3135. Tent sites $15, full hookups $20; $2 per extra person over age 6.

If you want to hook up your RV or camper in Ocracoke, or absolutely must have a hot shower, this campground under shade trees right in the village is the place to go.

## HOTELS

Motels are all along the islands in each town. They generally have pools — an advantage over most cottage arrangements — and some rent cottages too; read the section below if you are considering that option. Rates are highest in July and August, often declining in June and into the off-season. Many places have five or six levels of rates depending on the season. Here I've listed one or two nice places in each area, going from north to south, with peak weekday rates only. Higher rates may apply for weekends or holidays. All rooms have TVs, phones, and air-conditioning.

**Roanoke Island Inn.** 305 Fernando St., Manteo, NC 27954. ☎ **877/473-5511** or 252/473-5511. Fax 252/473-1019. www.roanokeislandinn.com. 8 rms, 1 bungalow. $148 double, $178 suite or bungalow, $30 each additional person, child or adult. AE, MC, V.

A huge but perfectly proportioned country house on elaborately landscaped grounds stands right on the waterfront in Manteo, with good restaurants within walking distance and bikes to head to the historic parks or aquarium. The house, still in the family that built its first section in 1860, was remodeled by its current architect owner. It feels just right. Guest rooms are comfortable and stylish, with wood floors, quilts, antique furniture, and reproductions. The parlor, site of the included continental breakfast and snacks, looks like a movie set, with a stunning ceiling mural painted by an artist from the Lost Colony show. Several rooms and the bungalow out back are big enough for families.

**First Colony Inn.** 6720 S. Virginia Dare Trail, Milepost 16, Nags Head, NC 27959. ☎ **800/368-9390** or 252/441-2343. Fax 252/441-9234. www.firstcolonyinn.com. 26 units. $170–$260 double; $35 per extra person, $15 child under 2. AE, DISC, MC, V.

The lovingly restored wooden building contains large rooms furnished in a colonial style with antiques, reproductions, and custom pieces. They have every amenity, from the usual ones such as VCRs and refrigerators to more exotic additions, including control heat and air and dedicated hot-water heaters. Children are welcome and well provided for, with an upstairs library stocked with games and an elegant, wooden-decked pool. You have to walk to the beach, across the road. The place doesn't quite fit the neighborhood, with the Dairy Queen and Blackbeard's Mini Golf

across the street, but the national seashore and Manteo are a short drive. Rates include a hot breakfast. Reserve well ahead, because some dates book up a year in advance.

**Hatteras Island Resort and Fishing Pier.** Hwy. 12 (P.O. Box 9), Rodanthe, NC 27968. ☎ **800/331-6541** reservations or 252/987-2345. www.hatterasislandresort.com. 32 rms, 35 cottages. $89–$109 double; $6 per extra person over age 8. Cottages $549–$949 per week. AE, DISC, MC, V.

I include this as a budget choice that has what families are looking for, despite being somewhat aged and worn. The important things are right: The pool is large, with a big kiddie pool, and clean, and there are a fishing pier and a game room on-site. The rooms, which have wood interiors, were clean on each of my visits, although the eight with cooking facilities had a food odor. They also have laundry facilities. There's no longer a need to ask for a room in the new building, because the old building washed away in Hurricane Dennis. The garish seaside amusements of the Rodanthe–Waves strip are nearby.

**Lighthouse View Motel-Cottages.** Hwy. 12 (P.O. Box 39), Buxton, NC 27920. ☎ **800/225-7651** or 252/995-5680. www.lighthouseview.com. 24 rms, 49 cottages. $118–$147 double; $5 each additional person; cottages $830–$2,400 weekly. AE, MC, V.

The large, modern, sun-drenched motel rooms feel like a beach house, with the sound and sight of surf ever present just beyond the dune. Standing on pilings, the weathered shingle buildings rise several stories around a sandy, grassy compound with an outdoor pool. Many rooms have decks, and there are many steps to climb. All I saw were well kept and smelled fresh, and some of the cottages are real showplaces: luxurious, current, and large. I counted five bathrooms in one. Check the complex rate card on the website; although not cheap, the rooms are a good value considering what you get. Off peak, some of the cottages rent by the night. If you can't get in here, right across the street is the Comfort **Inn Hatteras Island** (☎ **800/432-1441** or 252/995-6100), with very nice rooms for $129 double.

*Here's a scary story for the campfire. Beware — it has lots of blood and guts.*

Back before just about anyone lived on the Outer Banks, when there were no roads, towns, or bridges here, before our country even became the United States and was still part of England, pirates used the islands for their secret hideouts. The pirates had learned to fight in wars between the countries of Europe, when they had permission to attack ships that belonged to the other side and sell the valuables they took. That was called "privateering," and ship captains could get rich doing it. So when the war ended, some of them didn't want to stop. But without permission, they weren't privateers anymore — they were pirates.

A pirate ship had to be fast and carry a lot of sailors who were good fighters. The strongest and fiercest pirate was the captain, and he could rule his men only by fear and respect. When the pirates saw a ship on the horizon, they would chase it and fire cannons at it until they could come alongside and get on board. Ships carrying passengers and cargo didn't have enough sailors or weapons to defend themselves against the pirates, but navy ships did. If the pirates got caught by the navy, they would be hanged. So the pirates might kill everyone on board a ship they caught to keep anyone from telling what they had done.

One of the worst pirates was Blackbeard. His real name was Edward Teach. He grew up in England and went to sea as a privateer. After the war was over, he met a pirate named Captain Hornigold in the Bahamas, and Captain Hornigold put Blackbeard in command of his own ship. Blackbeard turned out to be a very scary pirate. He was a fierce fighter. Going into battle, he wore two gun belts across his chest and carried two pistols, and he made himself more frightening by braiding his hair and beard and tying slow-burning fuses in the braids. With the ship Hornigold gave him, Blackbeard soon captured a much larger ship of his own and loaded it with hundreds of pirates and 40 cannons. Within a couple of years, he had four ships and 400 pirates — his own little navy, able to beat anyone.

By that time, piracy had become such a serious problem in America that our king, George I (remember, this is before we were the U.S.A.) decided to offer the pirates a deal. He wouldn't punish them if they would agree to stop being pirates. Blackbeard decided to take the offer and settled down as a wealthy gentleman in Bath, North Carolina. He got rid of most of his ships and pirates; the worst of his pirates he marooned on an island. But pretty soon he went back to his old ways. Blackbeard set off on a voyage, saying he was going to trade cargo. When he came back he had a

**Holiday Inn Express Hatteras.** 58822 Hwy. 12, Hatteras Village, NC 27943. ☎ **800/361-1590** or 252/986-1110. Fax 252/986-1131. 40 rms, 32 suites. $130 double, $150 suite; $10 each additional adult, children under 18 free. AE, DC, DISC, MC, V.

Right by the ferry dock and marina at the south end of Hatteras Island, this fresh, modern hotel, shingled in yellow, has a pleasingly historic look to it. All rooms in the solid buildings are large and have microwaves and refrigerators and other extras, and they are crisply decorated with wallpaper and artwork. Those with views look out on the marsh. The pool is large, with a deck of brick. A coin-op laundry is on-site.

**Pony Island Motel.** Hwy. 12 (P.O. Box 309), Ocracoke, NC 27960. ☎ **252/928-4411.** Fax 252/928-2522. 50 units. $83–$147 double; $5 per extra adult, $2 per extra child under 12. DISC, MC, V.

There are other, more historic hotels on Ocracoke, but the newly remodeled rooms at this place on the edge of the village are just about perfect for families. In the new building, each of the large, airy rooms has a microwave, refrigerator, wet bar, and coffeemaker. The suites are like homes, and the

French ship, which he claimed he had just found floating in the ocean without anyone on board — as if anyone believed that! Then he shared the cargo with the governor and chief justice of North Carolina.

Soon Blackbeard went back to piracy, grabbing ships sailing up and down the coast, but the governor of North Carolina didn't do anything to stop him, maybe because he had gotten a share of the booty. People in North Carolina were angry and asked the governor of Virginia to help. In November 1718, that governor sent two British navy warships to stop Blackbeard, led by Lieutenant Robert Maynard.

Lt. Maynard found Blackbeard at his hideout in Teach's Hole, a small bay on Ocracoke Island, and attacked. Blackbeard was outnumbered and surprised. He fired his cannons at Maynard's ship and disabled it, but Maynard's sailors knocked out Blackbeard's rigging with their guns, and the pirate ship ran into a sandbar and got stuck. Maynard sent his men below decks to protect them from Blackbeard's guns while his ship drifted toward the pirates. When the the ships touched, the pirates jumped aboard, throwing bombs, and Maynard's men ran up on deck.

Blackbeard and Maynard met face-to-face and both fired pistols at the same time. Blackbeard was hit, but he drew his sword and fought on. Maynard's sword broke and Blackbeard lunged at him to finish him off, but just then one of the British sailors turned around and slashed Blackbeard's neck with a sword. Blood went everywhere, but Blackbeard and his men kept fighting. Blackbeard fought on even after he had been cut with swords five more times. Finally he fell to the deck. Seeing their leader fall, the other pirates jumped in the water and then gave up. Later, all but one were hanged.

Seventeen men died in the battle and 15 were injured. Maynard had Blackbeard's head cut off and hung from the bow of his boat as he sailed to Bath. Blackbeard's body was thrown into the ocean. His treasure was never found. He had never told anyone where it was hidden. Maybe you can find it on your visit to the Outer Banks. Local people hope to build a new "Graveyard of the Atlantic" museum that will include some of Blackbeard's stuff and other shipwreck items (it may open in 2002 or 2003).

Or maybe you'll see Blackbeard himself. People say his body was so strong that it swam around and around his ship after his head had been cut off, then sank to the bottom. And since then, late at night, his ghost has often been seen on the beaches of Ocracoke and along the rest of the Outer Banks. Blackbeard's body wanders on and on, looking for his head.

---

prices aren't out of line. Most of the older rooms have been remodeled and have wainscoting and similar details, but remain on the small side. A good-sized pool is in front by the highway. A popular restaurant is on-site, with some of the best breakfasts in town, and the hotel rents bikes for $2 an hour.

## COTTAGES

If you plan to stay a week or two, renting a summer house is the best way to enjoy the Outer Banks. You can relax and spread out, you don't have to worry about eating out with the kids, and you'll have a home base with a place to play and a sense of security. You'll have privacy from each other and from the rest of the world. The downside: You have to rent by the week, you usually won't have a pool, and prices can be high, especially if you want to be on the beach. You add the work of cooking, cleaning, shopping, and possibly bringing housewares and linens from home. During the season, rentals are for a full week, turning over on Saturday or Sunday. You may be able to negotiate shorter periods during the off-season, when a lot of places are empty.

Only families can rent some places, and the agent may ask for references. You, on the other hand, often must choose based on a photo and put up a lot of money before you even arrive. Ask plenty of questions, get a complete listing of what the rental comes with and what you need to bring, and make sure you understand the lease conditions. Most agencies sell insurance against unavoidable cancellations, which costs from 4% to 7.5% of the rental cost, depending on the agency and the time of year — hurricane season costs most. Your cash deposit often amounts to half of the rental cost and generally is not refundable if they can't rent it to someone else — even in case of hurricane — so the insurance seems like a good bet. When you arrive, inventory any damage so that you don't get stuck with a bill for it when you leave.

Rates are highest in July and early August, in some cases going down 10% to 20% in June and late August, and dropping as much as half in the spring and fall. Size, location, and view determine how much you pay, with beachfront properties commanding a high premium. Prices in the high season for beachfront houses range from around $1,200 a week for a two-bedroom house to more than $4,000 for a large place. On the sound side, prices are on the lower end of that range, sometimes as low as $800 for a place. Real-estate agents publish catalogs and websites of their summer rental listings, often with pictures of the houses, rates, and enough details to allow you to make a choice. Here are three

agencies; there are many others you can learn about from the chamber of commerce (see "Outer Banks Address Book, " p. 110).

**Hatteras Realty.** Hwy. 12 (P.O. Box 249), Avon, NC 27915. ☎ **800/428-8372** or 252/995-5466. www.hatterasrealty.com.

This agency lists dozens of houses from Avon to Hatteras Village in a highly detailed 200-page catalog. Renters get the major bonus of free use of Club Hatteras, a facility in Avon with a large pool, tennis courts, and a summer camp drop-off program for kids. Nonrenters can use the pool for $7 a day.

**Outer Beach Realty.** P.O. Box 280, Avon, NC 27915; local offices in Avon, Waves, and Hatteras. ☎ **800/627-3150** or 252/995-4477. Fax 800/627-3250 or 252/995-6137. www.outer beaches.com.

This agency has an extraordinary selection of more than 500 properties on Hatteras Island, all listed with interior and exterior photos in a 150-page catalog.

**Ocracoke Island Realty.** 1055 Irvin Garrish Hwy. (P.O. Box 238), Ocracoke, NC 27960. ☎ **252/ 928-6261** or 252/928-7411. www.ocracokeisland realty.com.

Martha Garrish offers 150 houses in Ocracoke with high-season prices ranging from $500 to $2,700 a week. Although the island has no beachfront housing, it does have some houses on the sound, a few with their own docks, and some where you can bring a pet.

# WHEN YOU ARRIVE

## ENTRANCE FEES
There are no entrance fees or beach fees at Cape Hatteras, but historic sites may charge fees (see "Places for Learning," p. 129).

## REGULATIONS
**Camping** is permitted only in formal campgrounds. **Fires** are allowed below the high-tide line, below the dunes. Put them out with water, not sand. **Fireworks** are not allowed

anywhere on the national seashore, including the beaches along the towns, because they cause too many fires. **Pets** have to be on a leash and aren't allowed at beaches with lifeguards.

## VISITOR CENTERS
**Wright Brothers National Memorial,** in Kill Devil Hills (p. 130), and **Fort Raleigh National Historic Site,** on Roanoke Island

**Emergencies**   Dial ☎ **911** in emergencies. To reach the Park Service or other emergency agencies from outside the area, call dispatch at ☎ **252/473-3444** north of Oregon Inlet, or ☎ **252/995-6111** south of the inlet. The **Regional Medical Center** (☎ **252/261-9000**; www.regionalmedicalcenter.com), at Milepost 1½ on Highway 158 in Kitty Hawk, has a wide range of services, open for urgent care 9am to 9pm. **Health East Outer Banks Medical Center** (☎ **252/441-7111**), 2808 S. Croatan Hwy., Nags Head, is open 24 hours a day. On Ocracoke, the **Ocracoke Health Center** (☎ **252/928-1511,** or 252/928-7425 after hours) is staffed by a physician's assistant and nurse practitioner; follow the sign off Highway 12 by the ferry terminal. It is on Back Road.

**Weather Forecast**   Call the **National Oceanic and Atmospheric Administration** (☎ **252/223-5757**). Links to various hurricane and other weather websites are on the Dare County site at www.co.dare.nc.us/LWeather.htm.

**Stores**   Each town along the Cape has a grocery store with most of what a summer visitor would need. There are large **Food Lion** stores on U.S. 158 in Nags Head and Kitty Hawk, and on Highway 12 in Avon, and a **Food-A-Rama** grocery in Manteo on U.S. 64. On Ocracoke, **The Community Store** on Silver Lake Road (☎ **252/928-3321**) is a classic country store and community center established in 1918.

**Banks**   ATMs are located in towns all up and down highways 12 and 158 and in Manteo and Ocracoke Village. **East Carolina Bank** has locations in Manteo (☎ **252/473-5821**), Avon (☎ **252/995-7900**), Hatteras (☎ **252/986-2131**), and Ocracoke (☎ **252-928-5231**).

**Post Offices**   Each town along the national seashore has a post office on Route 12, or Route 158 in Nags Head. In Manteo, the post office is at 212 B South U.S. 64/264.

**Gear Sales & Rental**   A very complete sportsman-oriented sporting-goods store, **Frisco Rod and Gun,** is on Route 12 in Frisco (☎ **252/995-5366**; www.friscorodgun.com). The website includes a message board full of fishing reports. Rental agencies for just about anything summer people might need are all along the Outer Banks. **Ocean Atlantic Rentals** (☎ **800/635-9559** for reservations; www.oceanatlanticrentals.com) rents all kinds of baby, beach, and household equipment, as well as bikes. It has offices at Mile 10, Beach Road, in Nags Head (☎ **252/441-7823**), and on Route 12 in Avon (☎ **252/995-5868**).

**Outdoors Activities   Kitty Hawk Kites** (☎ **877/FLY-THIS** or 252/441-4124; www.kitty hawk.com), with stores in Manteo, Avon, Hatteras, and Ocracoke, offers lessons, guided outings, rentals, or day camps for biking, hang gliding, kite surfing, parasailing, rock climbing, sailing, sea kayaking, and other sports; see "Activities" (p. 131).

near Manteo (p. 129), are good first stops for national seashore information. They are managed jointly by Park Service staff headquartered at the Fort Raleigh site. Both are open year-round. You can also ask questions at a seasonal information station at **Whalebone Junction,** at the north end of national seashore.

**Hatteras Island Visitor Center.** Near the Cape Hatteras Lighthouse, Buxton. ☎ **252/995-4474.** Year-round daily 9am–5pm; longer hours in summer.

The national seashore's main center occupies a small, historic building, moved along with the famous lighthouse it has so long accompanied. Displays cover the history of industry and war in the area with artifacts and written placards at an adult level. An information desk and a good little bookstore are downstairs. Many ranger programs start here; for details, see the park newspaper and "Programs" (p. 134).

**Bodie Island Visitor Center.** Near the Bodie Island Lighthouse west of Hwy. 12, 5 miles south of Whalebone Junction. ☎ **252/441-5711.** Summer daily 9am–6pm; off-season 9am–5pm.

This small center has an exhibit on lighthouses, but the light itself is not open for tours.

**Ocracoke Island Visitor Center.** Near the ferry dock in Ocracoke Village. ☎ **252/928-4531.** Summer daily 9am–6pm; off-season 9am–5pm.

The center mostly is a place to ask questions with a few exhibits.

## Town Visitor Centers

**The Outer Banks Visitors Bureau.** 704 S. Hwy. 64/264, Manteo. ☎ **800/446-6262** or 252/473-2138. Mon–Fri 8am–6pm, Sat–Sun noon–4pm.

This is a county information center covering commercial offerings for the whole region, including Ocracoke, which doesn't have its own center.

**Outer Banks Chamber of Commerce Visitor Center.** 101 Town Hall Dr., Kill Devil Hills. ☎ **252/441-8144.** Mon–Fri 8:30am–5:30pm.

If you're coming from the north, this may be the most convenient source of information on businesses.

## Getting Around
### By Car or RV

Driving is the only practical way around the national seashore. Traffic flows pretty well on Highway 12, but don't count on getting anywhere fast. Be careful stopping or trying to turn around on the highway; many vehicles get stuck on the sandy shoulders every day. For off-road driving see p. 133.

## By Ferry

To get to Ocracoke Island from the rest of the national seashore, you have to take the free state ferry from Hatteras Village, a fun ride that's part of what makes the place special. In the summer, the ferry runs from 5am to midnight, leaving on the hour and half hour during the day, on the hour in the early morning and evening. From November 1 to April 30, it runs on the hour only. If you time your arrival at the ramp perfectly to catch the boat, you may find that it's full and you have to wait for the next one. The ride takes 40 minutes. Contact information for the **North Carolina Ferry System** is under "Outer Banks Address Book" (p. 110).

## By Bike

Highway 12, the national seashore's main road, with its fast traffic and lack of shoulders, is not safe for children on bikes. If you're spending a week, you or the kids may enjoy taking a bike to the beach, or around the campground or cottage. Bikes can also come in handy in Manteo, where a paved bike trail leads from the village to the Fort Raleigh National Historic Site and elsewhere. In the village of Ocracoke, traffic is slow and there are quiet lanes safe for biking. Bike-rental agencies are listed under "For Handy Reference" (p. 123) and at the Pony Island Motel in Ocracoke (p. 120).

## Keeping Safe & Healthy

In addition to these tips, see the information on sunburn, dehydration, insects, poison ivy, and seasickness under "Dealing with Hazards," in chapter 1.

## Drowning

The fact is, a lot of people *do* drown every year in the surf of the national seashore, and that's why you see warnings posted every time you turn around. Some of the advice is easy, but also easy to forget: Don't swim in big surf, and don't let small children swim in little surf, which is proportionally much larger than they are. Have someone watching everyone in the water. Go to lifeguarded beaches. Red flags mean swimming is dangerous, so stay out of the water if you see one. In any weather, the gradual beaches and calm water on the sound side of the islands are better for little kids. For more tips, see "Practicalities: Swimming Safely in Surf," below.

## Foot Injuries

You can run into cacti, burrs, sharp shells, and hot sand unexpectedly, and they can cause great anguish and even injury. Tiny prickly-pear cacti grow all over Wright Brothers National Memorial, so heed the signs that tell you to stay on the path. Plants called sand spurs aren't dangerous, but they can hurt and upset kids. They're common in the seaside campgrounds; they stick to socks and soft shoes but don't seem to be as bothersome if they don't have fabric to cling to. Be cautious at the beach and at least carry shoes with you. The sand can burn, and sharp shells and washed-up debris can cut.

## Hurricanes

The storm surge, a bulge of water brought by the low pressure and wind of a hurricane, can submerge large parts of the Outer Banks. You really don't want to be here when it happens. Hurricane season is June through November, although hurricanes are most frequent mid-August through the first week of October. Keep tuned to a local station for forecasts. A **hurricane watch** means that hurricane conditions (winds over 74 mph) are expected within 36 hours; a **hurricane warning** means 24 hours. County officials give the word if it's time to go. Leave as soon as you can. Evacuation routes are published in the park newspaper and posted along the road, but they're pretty obvious, leading off the islands on routes 64 or 158. Ocracoke Islanders go north on the ferry to Hatteras, then north by road.

## PRACTICALITIES: SWIMMING SAFELY IN SURF

Only strong swimmers should swim in ocean surf, and that never includes younger children, whose size makes them vulnerable to even small waves. Even the strongest swimmers will be safer with some knowledge of how the waves work. (See "The Waves," in chapter 2, for more on wave mechanics.)

Ocean water is always moving, sometimes faster than you can swim. A rip current pulls directly away from the beach. It forms where water running back to the sea funnels through a channel in a sand bar. Rip currents are narrow and ease up as soon as the water gets deeper, so if you find yourself in one, don't swim against it. Instead, swim along the beach until you escape the flow of the rip current. Your biggest risk is fighting the flow and getting tired. Currents along the shore can move fast, too. To guard against them, always be aware of where you are, checking landmarks on the beach, and return to the beach before you're too far into waters you haven't observed carefully from shore. Never swim near piers or jetties, where the currents can be very strong. And don't swim near inlets, where the currents created by the tide rushing in and out of the sounds could sweep you away.

By paying attention to how the water moves you in the surf, you can learn how to take advantage of the waves. Developing that awareness also helps keep you from getting hit by a falling breaker, which can be scary and even dangerous. Dive into breaking waves. Go with the flow rather than fighting rushing water. For example, a backwash current, or undertow, is the water of receding waves pulling back into the surf. If you don't fight it, you're carried a short distance from the beach and then back toward shore with the next wave; if you swim against it, you can end up getting smashed down by the next breaking wave. When you do get tumbled in the froth of a breaking wave, try to relax and curl up rather than fighting it. The water will leave you on the beach or the undertow will carry you to calmer water, where you can surface.

Finally, remember that in case of trouble, you're on your own unless the beach has a lifeguard.

## NATURAL PLACES
## Outer Beaches

The entire length of the Outer Banks, 75 miles of it in the national seashore, is all brilliant sand and roaring waves. You really can be alone, getting over the dune from the highway at any of many deserted ramps and then walking until you drop in the sand. Even without swimming there's plenty to do and discover on the beach. (Beachgoing and off-road driving are covered below, under "Activities.") Collect seashells: The best places are at the end of the barrier islands, where the current wraps around. Hunt for sand crabs: This is great fun at night, with a flashlight and a sand bucket, but be sure to release all the crabs when you're done. See how close to the waves you can build a sand castle: What design holds up best against the waves? Walk back in the dunes, staying on trails so that you don't trample the beach grass, and see what kinds of birds and plants you can identify. Watch the water and see if you can find the three kinds of breakers discussed under "The Waves," in chapter 2.

---

### READ ALOUD: WHY THE STILTS?

Why do you think so many houses are built on stilts on the Outer Banks? Here's a clue: Early settlers built their houses far from the water, and they didn't need to put them up in the air. The answer is that in hurricanes and winter storms, waves can easily wash over the area where the beach houses are built. If the houses are up on legs, called pilings, the waves are less likely to do damage.

Now, why do you think people put those crisscrossed strips of wood between the pilings, called lattice? Today, it's done just for decoration, but when they first started building beach houses on pilings, these islands were used for raising cattle and sheep. The lattice kept the animals from going under the houses, which they always wanted to do to get out of the sun.

---

Cape Point, at the very tip of Cape Hatteras near the lighthouse, is a great place to do this. Think about how the waves are shaped by the sand and how they shape the sand.

## Sound Side

The inner coast of the national seashore, mainly facing the Sound, differs from the outer shore in many ways, most of which have to do with the energy of the waves that hit the coast. On this side, the waves don't have much distance to build, so they're smaller. Without being battered by large waves, the coast can develop into marshes full of delicate birds and animals.

Two kinds of marsh grow on the shore: freshwater marshes on Arbemarle Sound, to the north, and saltwater on Pamlico Sound, to the south. Many of the saltwater marshes also have freshwater parts nearer land, where rainwater trapped in the sand pushes out against the saltwater. You can see examples of both kinds, with excellent bird-watching, on the **Bodie Island Dike Nature Trail,** on the same road that leads to Bodie Island Lighthouse and Visitor Center. A guide brochure, available at the start of the trail or at the nearby visitor center, matches numbered posts. The trail loop is 6 miles long; don't overexert yourself on a hot day. This marsh and those just north on Highway 12 grew upon deltas of sand left behind by the flow of water through inlets to the ocean side. Four inlets existed at one time or another along here, including the one Sir Walter Raleigh's ships came through in 1585. Where the Cape is wider, it's often because a former inlet allowed the tide to move sand into the sound. Sand finally filled the inlet completely, connecting islands with the dry land we see today. Other great trails for marsh exploration are at Nags Head Woods Ecological Preserve (p. 128) and the Hammock Hills Nature Trail on Ocracoke Island (p. 133).

You also can explore the marshes and channels along the sound shore by exploring by sea kayak, rowboat, or other craft. Go crabbing along the way, about the most fun a kid can have. Since the water is so shallow, warm, and gentle, these waters are relatively forgiving, a good place to learn to sail or windsurf, kayak, or try other new water sports (see "Activities," p. 131).

Swimming is different on the sound side, too. The sand is coarser and the bottom is gradual — so gradual that an adult probably could walk miles out into the sound in places. Waves tend to be small. There are beaches, without lifeguards, at **Haulover,** just north of Buxton; **Sandy Bay,** between Frisco and Hatteras village; and **Jockey's Ridge State Park** (see p. 128).

## The Woods

You could easily visit the Outer Banks without ever noticing the woods, but two notable pockets of ancient forest survive amid the sand, making refuges of quiet and shade, marsh and ponds, and homes for wildlife. Nags Head Woods is described below, and Buxton Woods under "Nature Walks," p. 133; they're both well worth a visit. Before people caused increased erosion here by grazing sheep and cattle on the beach grass, woods covered much more of the barrier islands; without the beach grass, sand dunes buried some of the woods. The oak and pine of the woods grow where a large area is sheltered from salt spray by sand dunes and by plants that can handle salt. Over time, falling leaves and pine needles and dying plants build a layer of soil that can nourish generations of larger and more varied plant life. Finally, the woods grow thick and green, but you can still see the shapes of sand dunes underneath, sometimes holding ponds in between their ridges. Depending on how the islands move, these peaceful places, full of birds and animals, can last for thousands of years.

## The Lighthouses

The most impressive lighthouse you're ever likely to see is the great **Cape Hatteras Lighthouse** at Cape Point. At more than 200 feet tall, it's the tallest brick lighthouse in the United States; in clear weather, it's visible 20 miles out to sea. (To see how it looks right now, go to ww.nps.gov/caha/livecam.htm.) Visitors can climb 257 steps up an iron spiral staircase right to the circular balcony at the top for an amazing view, but it's a long, hot, and potentially scary climb. You'll want to pace yourself and hold your kid's hands (children 12 and under can go only with an adult). Children under 38 inches are not allowed, and I wouldn't recommend it for children under 5 or for anyone with a fear of heights. Carrying a child or any kind of backpack is rightfully prohibited. Admission is $3 adults, $1.50 kids under 12; national passes are not accepted. The light is open Memorial Day to Labor Day daily 10am to 6pm; it closes at 2pm in the spring and fall and closes entirely early October through mid-April.

The lighthouse was built well back from the beach in 1870, but erosion moved the shoreline closer, and by 1935 the Coast Guard gave it up for lost, with waves crashing at its foot. After 60 years of struggle to stop the erosion, the Park Service moved the light 2,900 feet in 1999, placing it back in the woods 1,600 feet from the beach. Today, the light looks like it has always been there, but you can see where the tracks lay that over the course of a summer very slowly inched the tower to its new home, without a crack, an amazing engineering achievement.

The **Bodie Island Lighthouse,** at the Bodie Island Visitor Center, and the **Ocracoke Lighthouse,** in Ocracoke Village, are picturesque historic buildings; but they lack the drama and scale of Hatteras, and you can't go inside.

## Ocracoke Pony Corral

In 1585, Sir Richard Grenville picked up some Spanish ponies in Haiti along with other supplies to help establish the colony at Roanoke Island; but on June 23 one of his ships, the *Tiger,* ran aground, and the ponies and other goods were put off. More than 400 years later, their descendants are still running around Ocracoke Island, today confined to a large fenced pasture off Highway 12 north of the village. At least, that's the most plausible explanation for how wild Spanish ponies got here. You can see them from a 600-foot boardwalk, and sometimes the rangers saddle them up and ride them on beach patrol. For more on the colony, see "History & Culture: First Encounters," in chapter 2.

## Parks & Preserves

**Pea Island National Wildlife Refuge.** Hwy. 12, north end of Hatteras Island. ☎ **252/473-1131;** visitor center 252/987-2394. alligatorriver.fws.gov/peaisland. Visitor center open summer daily 9am–5pm; winter hours vary.

This refuge at the north end of Pea Island, within the national seashore, protects an exceptional bird habitat, the best for bird-watching in the area. The cape's unique geography has contributed to an amazing 400 species identified. The refuge encompasses a sound-side marsh that contains both fresh and saltwater and freshwater ponds in the middle of the island. A few exhibits and bird mounts, and a spotting scope, are inside the visitor center. Outside, superb trails, with boardwalks, tour the wetlands and reach across a dike between the ponds with built-in spotting scopes. You can also see turtles.

**Nags Head Woods Ecological Preserve.** 701 W. Ocean Acres Dr. (see directions below), Kill Devil Hills, NC 27948. ☎ **252/441-2525.** Summer Mon–Sat 10am–3pm; off-season Mon–Fri 10am–3pm.

The Nature Conservancy protects and teaches about this uniquely diverse 1,400-acre forest, a shady mosaic of wetlands tucked between dunes that shield it from the salt spray on three sides. Five miles of nature trails with superb printed guides weave through the woods past ponds, sand dunes, orchids, herons, river otters, and ancient oaks, peaceful places a world away from the fast-food ghetto out on the highway. The conservancy offers marsh kayaking, bird-watching, and other programs from its small interpretive center, and superb weeklong nature day camps for many ages (there are few spaces, so reserve well ahead). The place is poorly marked. Southbound on U.S. 158 near milepost 9½, a small brown sign says NATURE CONSERVANCY, pointing down West Ocean Acres Drive toward the sound. Take it to the end.

**Jockey's Ridge State Park.** U.S. 158, Milepost 12, Nags Head. ☎ **252/441-7132.** www.jockeysridgestatepark.com. June–Aug daily 8am–9pm; Apr–May and Sept 8am–8pm; Mar and Oct 8am–7pm; Nov–Feb 8am–6pm. Visitor center closes a little earlier.

You can't miss the towering sand dune of this state park as you drive through Nags Head on Route 158, the tallest dune on the east coast. The wind blows northeast and southwest here, gathering up the sand and moving it back and forth across the crest, but not spreading it out much. The main attraction is a fun and bizarre walk and slide on the shifting and cascading sands. It's a place where you just can't help playing. The view at the top, about 100 feet up, is terrific. If you want to get serious, there is a route with numbered posts corresponding to a nature guide (not a trail, because it would soon disappear in the sand). On the sound shore of the park there is a calm swimming beach, a couple of feet deep on Roanoke Sound, and another nature trail; take Soundside Road, the first turn south of the main park entrance. The park offers kids' programs on various natural topics. Adults and kids can even learn to hang glide at a school at the park (see p. 133).

**Cape Lookout National Seashore.** 131 Charles St., Harkers Island, NC 28531. ☎ **252/728-2250.** www.nps.gov/calo.

The Outer Banks continue southwest of Ocracoke Island along 56 miles of truly wild, uninhabited barrier islands in Cape Lookout National Seashore. Visit to experience true wilderness and see a real ghost town. The town of Portsmouth, on the island nearest Ocracoke, lived from 1753 until the last two residents left in 1971, when it was abandoned to the wind. In Portsmouth, ships would stop and unload their cargo to be stored and loaded into smaller boats that could cross Pamlico Sound to the mainland. It was once was the largest and busiest town on the Outer Banks, with 500 people, a post office, a school, and a hospital. But on the night of September 7, 1846, a hurricane washed over a dune on Ocracoke Island, parting the sand to make a new inlet and washing away an old man's fig and peach orchard and potato patch. The new opening was Hatteras Inlet, now the northeast end of Ocracoke Island, and it allowed ships to sail right into Pamlico Sound. Portsmouth was no longer needed.

On a day trip, taking everything you need with you, especially mosquito repellent, you can explore though the town and go into a couple of buildings, now preserved as a historic site by the National Park Service. The islands themselves are mostly just low dunes and bare beaches extending for mile after mile. Day trips to Portsmouth from Ocracoke are offered by **Portsmouth Island Boat Tours** (☎ **252/928-4361**). The ride takes half an hour each way, and you stay on shore, self-guided, for 4 hours. It costs $20 for adults, $10 for children, free for 6 and under.

## Places for Learning
Roanoke Island has several exceptionally interesting sites to visit that will take at least 1 full day and can be reached by bicycle from Manteo, mostly on a separated trail. The Wright Brothers National Memorial, in Kitty Hawk, is a short drive from there. There are other museums on the Outer Banks, but they hardly bear mentioning compared to this complex of attractions.

**Fort Raleigh National Historic Site.** Off Rte. 64, 3 miles west of Manteo. ☎ **252/473-5772.** Free admission. Summer Sun–Fri 9am–8pm, Sat 9am–6pm; winter daily 9am–5pm.

This is where the Lost Colony likely stood, and the mounds of earth you can walk around may be the remains of a fort built by Colonel

## EXPERIMENT: SAND SLIDES

Make a hill of sand at Jockey's Ridge State Park or on the beach. The sand has to be dry and should be fine-grained. Add sand to the top of your pile until you set off avalanches that run down the sides. The question to answer with this experiment is, why does the sand avalanche down? Does it come down because the hill is too tall, or because it is too steep? How tall or steep can a sand pile be without starting an avalanche? Decide what you think (that's your hypothesis), then test your idea by building sand piles that are different sizes and shapes, big or small, steep or gradual, until you know if you were right.

**Here's the answer:** The size of the pile doesn't matter, but there is a limit to how steeply one kind of sand can be piled. Using careful observation, you can find the steepest angle possible for your sand, which is called the angle of repose. The size and shape of the individual grains of sand make the difference. Try it with different kinds of sand to see if the angle of repose changes. Also, pay attention when you walk on the side of the dune at Jockey's Ridge. Your footsteps make the sand avalanche down; it always keeps going until the sand on the slope organizes itself at the angle of repose.

Ralph Lane, the leader of the first group of English colonists who tried to settle America (see "History & Culture: First Encounters," in chapter 2). Or maybe not — archaeologists can't pin down exactly who built the fort, but it surely had something to do with Sir Walter Raleigh's project. With the mysteries surrounding the colonies, it makes sense that one of the weekly ranger programs is a hands-on lesson in archaeological digging (see "Programs," p. 134). The area was also a Civil War–era colony set up by the Union Army for escaped and former slaves. The Park Service is just starting to tell that story.

A good little museum in the visitor center concentrates on the Lost Colony, with artifacts, ship models, costumes, armor, and other interesting exhibits. Our son Robin was fascinated by a comparison of the food and technology of the Indians, colonists, and people today. The grounds have quiet, shady lawns, a picnic area, and several miles of walking and nature trails with exhibits that explain how people used the area's natural resources. This is a good place to rest and play during a break from a day of sightseeing. Most of it is navigable by strollers.

*The Lost Colony,* a summer performance that has played on the grounds of the historic site since 1937, tells the story of the colonists and Indians with music, dance, and re-creations of the events in a large outdoor amphitheater facing the water. It's a local institution, a required part of a trip to the Outer Banks, and popular with kids. The season runs from early June through August; performances are held at 8:30pm every night but Sunday. Tickets are $16 for adults, $8 for children 11 and under; reserve a week ahead if possible, and ask about nights with special ticket deals for children (☎ 800/488-5012 or 252/488-3414; www. thelostcolony.org).

Also at the historic site are the **Elizabethan Gardens** (☎ 252/473-3234), open daily from 9am to 5pm (to 8pm on nights when *The Lost Colony* is playing). This is a formal garden of the style planted at the estates of Sir Walter Raleigh's noble colleagues. The shady, symmetrical paths and fountains are charming and provide a window on the time. It's a good stop if you are visiting the historic site anyway; however, I wouldn't make a special trip. There's a good little gift shop of garden items. Picnicking is not allowed, and the paths are difficult for strollers. Admission to the garden is $3 for adults, free for children under 12.

**Roanoke Island Festival Park.** 1 Festival Park, Manteo. ☎ 252/475-1500. www.roanokeisland. com. Admission $8 adults, $5 children 6–18, free for children 5 and under. Summer daily 9am–7pm; off-season daily 10am–5pm.

This remarkable new state historic park, across a channel from the waterfront shops and restaurants in Manteo, is the Outer Banks' best cultural attraction, and should not be missed. It has several parts. A fanciful but

highly informative museum of the area's history will entrance children, who can learn to use an astrolabe, put on Elizabethan clothing, and listen to a mechanical pirate, among many other experiences. On the water, the *Elizabeth II* is docked, a superb replica of a 16th-century sailing ship, manned with sailors in period costume who stay in character; nearby, a small camp is similarly staffed, showing what the Lost Colony was like. An amphitheater stages performing-arts events all summer. Indoors, a 45-minute film, showing all day, tells the story of the Native Americans who lived here.

**The North Carolina Aquariums — Roanoke Island.** 374 Airport Rd., west of Manteo on Rte. 64. ☎ 252/473-3493. www.aquariums.state.nc. us. Admission $4 adults, $2 children 6–17, free for children under 6, $20 maximum per family. Summer daily 9am–7pm; off-season Mon–Sat 9am–5pm, Sun noon–5pm.

Reopened after a $16 million expansion in 2000, this aquarium on the edge of the sound brilliantly re-creates the local marine and aquatic environment in miniature. It's a place to learn about the habitat and animals you'll see on the Outer Banks and the sounds, why they live where they do, and how they live. Everything is in context. An atrium seems to put you right in the marsh with river otter, alligators, turtles, and other animals. Other displays are dramatic, too — divers sometimes swim in the shipwreck tank — but I was most impressed by how much I was learning. Children will love all of it, and the area especially for them is terrific, too. Programs included in the price of admission happen as often as five times a day in summer, for adults and children. The gift store is among the best in the area for natural history books and toys. The grassy grounds and waterfront area are suitable for a picnic.

**Wright Brothers National Memorial.** On Rte. 158, Kill Devil Hills. ☎ 252/441-7430. Admission $2 per person, or $4 per car. Summer daily 9am–6pm; winter daily 9am–5pm.

The Wright Brothers' story is truly inspiring: A pair of bicycle mechanics with no more than a high-school education studied and worked hard, and, by careful observation of nature, figured out how to fly. There was no luck involved. This is where they did it, in December 1903. A tall dune where the brothers tested a glider in the process of developing their successful plane has been stabilized with ground cover and topped with a huge marker. On the flat, a replica of their launch track and markers shows the takeoff and landing points for the four successful powered flights. The Wrights' bunkhouse and workshop also have been replicated. Keep to the paved paths that run throughout, staying away from sharp, hidden cacti.

Many activities are planned to mark the centennial of the first flight in 2003, including a reenactment put on by today's aeronautical experimenters. Check the memorial's website (www.nps.gov/wrbr) for a schedule (not set at this writing).

The memorial's fascinating visitor center, with its mock-up of the plane and museum on the Wrights' accomplishments, is closed at this writing due to structural problems, with no date set for reopening. Programs are operating from a temporary building. While this goes on, there is no entry fee at the memorial. Ranger talks continue frequently in the summer, and other flight-related programs take place at various times during the week. When we visited, they taught us to make kites from garbage bags, which flew well in the steady wind of Kill Devil Hills.

Inexpensive airplane rides are available at the memorial from **Kitty Hawk Aero Tours** (☎ 252/441-4460; www.kittyhawkaerotours. bizland.com). They are to the right of the circular drive by the monument. The 30-minute scheduled flights circle the Bodie Island Lighthouse, with the pilot pointing out spots of interest along the coast. Prices are $29 to $34 per person, depending on the size of your party, or $68 per person for a ride in an open-cockpit biplane.

**Chicamacomico Lifesaving Station.** Hwy. 12, Rodanthe (no phone). Free admission. Tues–Sat 11am–5pm. Closed Nov–Apr.

Local historical society volunteers are restoring this complex of buildings that date to 1874. Lifesavers once waited here for shipwrecks so that they could launch boats into the surf to save the victims. The museum contains their equipment and uniforms and objects from the wrecks. Each Thursday at 2pm in the summer, the volunteers bring out the beach cart with all the equipment necessary for a rescue and conduct a drill, complete with firing of the Lyle gun, which was used to shoot a rope to a grounded ship.

## ACTIVITIES
### Beachgoing
Surely this is how you'll spend most of your time at Cape Hatteras National Seashore. This 75-mile strip of sand is one of the best beaches anywhere, and the water is terrific for swimming. There are no fees for any of the beaches and none is really crowded. You can always be alone if you're prepared to walk a bit, or drive to a remote ramp. National Park Service lifeguard coverage changes each year depending on budgets, but generally lifeguards watch over **Coquina Beach,** near the north end of the seashore on Bodie Island; **Lighthouse Beach** in Buxton, near the big lighthouse; and **Ocracoke Beach,** just north of the village of Ocracoke. Coquina Beach has a bathhouse for changing, and cold, outdoor showers, as does the unguarded (as of this writing) **Sandy Beach Day Use Area,** on the sound side southwest of Frisco. Each of the campgrounds is within walking distance of the beach, too, with showers in stalls but no lifeguards. All along the seashore, ramps for off-road vehicles lead over the dunes, providing access to long areas of rarely visited beach. You can use these ramps to walk to the beach in remote areas, but be careful about parking because many people get stuck. North of the national seashore, town beaches have lifeguards in **Nags Head, Kill Devil Hills, Kitty Hawk,** and **Southern Shores.** I've described some other ocean and sound beaches, and some of the things to do here, under "Natural Places"

(p. 126), and safety information is under "Drowning" (p. 124) and "Practicalities: Swimming Safely in Surf" (p. 125).

## Bird-Watching

The Outer Banks' tremendous variety of bird sightings results from its location and variety of habitat types. The islands are on the eastern migratory flyway. They stick out into the Atlantic, making a resting place for exhausted birds that have accidentally wandered far from their normal homes. The habitat includes placid salt and fresh water of the sound and the marshes, rough ocean beaches and off-shore water, the Nags Head and Buxton woods, and the ponds at the Pea Island Refuge (see "Natural Places," p. 126). The refuge is bird-watcher's central, where you can meet other birders and get advice from rangers.

## Clamming

Clams live under the tidal flats of Pamlico Sound. With a rake, a bucket, and some local knowledge, you can harvest them to steam for dinner. No license is needed as long as you take fewer than 100. Pick up a copy of fishery regulations at a visitor center to get size limitations. **Hatteras Village Aqua Farm,** just north of Hatteras (☎ **252/986-2249**), offers the equipment, the knowledge, and a place for clamming daily from 10am to 5pm in the summer. It costs $5 for adults, $3 ages 6 to 11 (it's free for kids under 6), plus around 24¢ per clam, depending on the market. It's a good idea to call ahead for reservations. The farm sells seafood you don't have to catch, too.

## Crabbing

First you take chicken necks and leave them out in the sun until they get really stinky. Then you tie the bait to a string and dangle it in the water in a marsh where you think a blue crab might be sniffing around. When you see a crab, you hold the bait near it in a tempting way. When it grabs hold, you scream and wave your arms, then pull it in on the string, net it, and drop it in a bucket, trying not to

get pinched. Back home, steam or boil it and eat it.

For children, crabbing is a lot more fun than fishing, because you can see the crabs walking around in the shallow, marshy waters at the edge of Pamlico Sound from a rowboat or even on foot. You don't need a license, but get size and take regulations from a visitor center. The Park Service sometimes teaches this fine art in a ranger program that starts from the Bodie Island Visitor Center — check the park newspaper for details. Get the bucket and net at any sporting-goods store (see "For Handy Reference," p. 123), and buy chicken necks — or any other kind of meat — at a grocery store.

## Fishing

There are lots of ways to fish, places to go, and kinds of fish to catch at the national seashore, from common, pan-sized spot fish to the challenging 40-pound red drum. For children and beginners, the best choice may be one of the fishing piers along the outside beach. Anglers pay a fee, rent gear, and buy bait at the booth, where you can also get tips on how to fish. Fishing piers stick out all along the shore. Several are north of the national seashore and within its boundaries; piers are at **Rodanthe, Avon,** and **Frisco.**

For more accomplished fishermen, surf casting allows more of a solitary, natural experience. Pick anyplace you like along the islands away from swimmers; the best spots are in sloughs and holes, which smart fishermen scope out at low tide and come back to later. Fish on an incoming tide when wind and waves are light, casting just to the other side of the breaking waves. Tide tables run in the park newspaper. The Park Service sometimes offers a program teaching surf casting and provides everything but bait. Participants are chosen by lottery (see p. 135), so plan ahead. Places to buy and rent gear are listed under "For Handy Reference" (p. 123).

There are several places to charter a boat with a guide. The **Oregon Inlet Fishing**

**Center,** on Highway 12 on the north side of the bridge (P.O. Box 2089, Manteo, NC 27954; ☎ **800/272-5199** or 252/441-6301; www.oregon-inlet.com), has a huge fleet. Charter rates, which are controlled by the Park Service, range from under $300 for a half day on the sound in an open boat for four (a good choice with kids) to over $1,100 to go offshore all day for trophy fish. For peak weekends, you may have to book a year in advance. They also sell fishing gear, supplies, and deli sandwiches. **Hatteras Harbor Marina** (P.O. Box 537, Hatteras, NC 27943; ☎ **252/986-2166;** www.hatterasharbor.com) has trips at roughly similar prices and also rents inexpensive apartments by the night and has a deli. On Ocracoke, the **Anchorage Marina** (P.O. Box 880, Ocracoke Island, NC 27960; ☎ **252/ 928-6661;** www.theanchorageinn.com) has three large boats, and somewhat lower prices for Gulf Stream trips. From any of the operators, these full-day, offshore trips go 20 miles out to the Gulf Stream for tuna, dolphin, sailfish, marlin, and the like. For beginners and children, instead choose a short, easy trip on the sound. Independent charters also run out of Ocracoke.

## Hang Gliding

Jockey's Ridge State Park (p. 128) is the only place I've run across hang gliding as a family activity, but the school there run by Kitty Hawk Kites takes children regardless of age as long as they weigh at least 80 pounds, and also people with disabilities. They claim to be the world's largest hang-gliding school, in operation since 1974. Three-hour beginner classes take five flights from 5 to 15 feet high on the dune and cost $85.

## Horseback Riding

**Buxton Stables** (☎ **252/995-4659**) offers 1-hour rides in Buxton Woods for $30 and 3-hour beach rides for $65. Kids have to be at least 10, and in summer it's a good idea to reserve at least a week ahead.

## Nature Walks

The three-quarter–mile **Buxton Woods Nature Trail,** starting from the road to the swimming beach just south of the Cape Hatteras Light, is a very pleasant walk over wooded rises and past swamp ponds that formed on the sand dunes and dips that the woods now cover. Excellent interpretive signs explain the landscape. The **Hammock Hills Nature Trail,** on Ocracoke Island across the road from the campground, shows each of the typical ecological areas of the Outer Banks: forest, dunes, and salt marsh, with signs describing what lives there. Bring mosquito repellant. Other trails include the **Bodie Island Dike Trail** (p. 126), **Pea Island Trail** (p. 128), and **Nags Head Woods Ecological Preserve** (p. 128).

## Off-Road Driving

Large stretches of the national seashore on both sides are open to four-wheel-drive vehicles, if you follow rules designed to save the dunes, nesting birds, and sea turtles. Driving on the beach can be a lot of fun, and it's a practical way for families to get to beaches of their own. A map given away by the visitor centers tells you where you can drive, what the regulations are, and what equipment you'll need, and provides important tips on how not to get stuck — you can't really do without it. Find the same information at www.nps.gov/ caha/bdriv.htm. Ask about seasonal closures before you go.

More than 20 dune ramps allow vehicles access to the beach, from the Bodie Island area to the south tip of Ocracoke. They are marked by numbers that represent the mileage from Coquina Beach, with those farther south having higher numbers. On the sound side, drive only on designated jeep trails.

## Sailing/Boating

The sound side's calm, warm water and steady winds are just right for day sailing. **The Waterworks,** on the causeway between Roanoke Island and Whalebone Junction

(☎ 252/441-6822; www.obxwaterworks. com), and at other locations, has 15- and 18-foot sailboats for rent, as well as all kinds of motorboats, canoes, kayaks, and Windsurfers, and lots of guided tours and lessons. **Hatteras Watersports,** on the sound side in Salvo (☎ 252/987-2306), offers sailing equipment, parasailing, fishing, and kayaks at a big lawn, beach, and picnic area; kids were catching crabs when I visited. **Kitty Hawk Kites** (p. 123) also has sailboats and kayaks.

Sailboat rides on schooners are available, too. The 56-foot **Downeast Rover** (☎ 800/SAIL-OBX or 252/473-4866 or www.downe astrover.com) sails three times daily on 2-hour cruises from the Manteo waterfront. They cost $20 for adults, $12 for children 2 to 12, or $25 for adults or children on the evening trip. They're often full in summer, so reserve ahead.

## Sea Kayaking

The shallow coastal salt marshes on Pamlico Sound are prime sea kayaking areas, where the silent craft can sneak up on birds and animals. Unlike those in areas farther north, most rental agencies and guides on the Outer Banks seem to use open kayaks, which are like low canoes, not traditional closed-deck kayaks. You get wetter in this kind of craft, but with the water so warm, it probably doesn't matter.

Most agencies offer rentals, guided trips, and classes. **Kitty Hawk Kites** (see "For Handy Reference," p. 123) offers guided kayaking and rental, including a kayaking camp for kids 5 to 15. Many other operators compete, including those listed above under "Sailing/Boating." On Ocracoke, **Ocracoke Adventures/Wave Cave,** at the intersection of Highway 12 and Silver Lake Road (☎ 252/928-7873), offers kayaking and educational outings run by a former ranger and a real Ocracoker. They also teach surfing for adults or kids; you can leave your kids for lessons.

## PROGRAMS

The National Park Service offers programs at Cape Hatteras National Seashore, Wright

### PLACES FOR RELAXED PLAY & PICNICS

The beach is the best place for relaxed play, but if you want a change, you also could stretch out a blanket on the lawns of **Fort Raleigh,** around the **North Carolina Aquarium,** or at the **Roanoke Island Festival Park.** For active play, there's a great ship-theme playground on the Manteo waterfront, Kill Devil Hills has a **city park playground** at 1634 N. Croatan Hwy. (U.S. 158), and a school playground is at the north end of the town of Buxton. **Diamond Shoals Family Fun Park,** at milepost 9.75 U.S. 158, Kill Devil Hills (☎ 252/480-3553), has three water slides, paddleboats, a kiddy pool, 36 holes of minigolf, an arcade, a batting cage, and so on.

Brothers National Memorial, and Fort Raleigh National Historic Site. Other organizations have programs at Jockey's Ridge State Park, Nags Head Woods Ecological Preserve, Pea Island National Wildlife Refuge, and North Carolina Aquariums — Roanoke Island. All are covered under "Parks & Preserves" (see p. 128) and "Places for Learning" (see p. 129).

## Children's Programs

Each of the three National Park Service units gives a nice patch to kids who complete a list of tasks, but the instructional booklets they do to earn the patches emphasize rote learning — mostly just finding facts and filling them in on a single, two-sided piece of paper. Also, beware before you commit yourself to the project because getting the patch requires kids to attend as many as four ranger programs. While the ranger programs are certainly worth attending, you may not be planning so many trips back to the visitor centers.

The **Sand Castle Environmental Education Center** at Coquina Beach gives kids something meaningful to do while apart from their parents. The 30- to 60-minute activities have included shirt printing, low-tide beach walks, and studying seashells, and they take place frequently on summer days. Check the bulletin board at the beach or ask at a visitor center for details, because the program changes annually.

Nags Head Woods Ecological Preserve (p. 128) and Kitty Hawk Kites (see "For Handy Reference," p. 123) both offer day camps for kids, allowing parents to drop them off for half a day of environmental education at Nags Head Woods or outdoor activities in kayaks or sailboats at Kitty Hawk Kites.

## Family & Adult Programs

The schedule and a description of programs at up to six Park Service sites are included in the park newspaper. The national seashore offers lots of guided walks and lectures, which you can join by showing up at the appointed time and place. For hands-on sessions in surf casting, snorkeling on the sound, and net fishing in a salt marsh, there's a lottery for the limited number of slots. The lotteries are conducted at 4:30pm the day before the program at the visitor center that's running the program.

At the Wright Brothers National Memorial (☎ 252/441-7430), fun programs, like kite and paper airplane making, are scheduled at various times during the week. Fort Raleigh National Historic Site (☎ 252/473-5772) offers the usual lectures and children's stories, but also has free dramatic and musical performances on historic themes — most take place in the visitor-center auditorium — and other innovative programs.

# WHERE TO EAT

The strip of highway north of the national seashore, including Kitty Hawk, Kill Devil Hills, and Nags Head, has every fast-food joint you can think of, including, at one intersection near Milepost 9½, Pizza Hut, McDonald's, Wendy's, Burger King, and KFC. Below, I have included some of the better restaurants to the south, in the national seashore and Manteo.

## MANTEO & ENVIRONS

The redeveloped waterfront area of Manteo, facing the Roanoke Island Festival Park across a small bay, is a pleasant place to walk, window-shop, take boat tours, and eat. Besides Clara's, below, try The Full Moon Café (☎ 252/473-6666), which has a small dining room with a water view, serving tasty cuisine that combines southwestern and southeastern influences — a shrimp and crab enchilada, for example. (Lunch: $3–$15, dinner $3–$20, with a children's menu at $2–$4. Open daily in summer 11am–9pm, in winter Mon–Thurs 11:30am–3pm, Fri–Sat 11:30am–9pm.)

**Clara's Seafood Grill.** On the waterfront, Manteo. ☎ 252/473-1727. Dinner $9–$16; lunch $4–$17; kids' menu $3.25–$5.50. Summer 11:30am–9:30pm; winter hours vary; closed Jan–Feb. AE, DISC, MC, V.

This bright, noisy, fun place overlooks the harbor. The food is good, covering the local basics, but also stretching to a grilled portabella mushroom sandwich with a roasted garlic spread. The kids' menu includes a cheap hot dog and more ambitious fare at reasonable prices. Lunch lines can be daunting, so you may want to call ahead to find out how bad a wait you'll face. Reservations are not accepted.

**The Lone Cedar Café.** On the U.S. 64 causeway between Manteo and Nags Head. ☎ 919/441-5405. Lunch $7–$12, dinner $11–$22; children's menu $3–$5. Daily 11:30am–3pm and 4:30–10pm. DISC, MC, V. Closed Dec–Feb.

Known locally as Basnight's, for its State Senator owner, this is a good-time southern seafood place surrounded by Roanoke Sound. Friendly waitresses in shorts quickly bring big plates of fish, shrimp, and shellfish to tables with plastic tablecloths in a dining room rocking with noise and cheer. The preparation is generally simple, but the chef gets a chance to shine with a rich crab lump dip appetizer and the tasty crab cakes. Kids will enjoy it, too, except for the wait for a table at popular hours.

## HATTERAS ISLAND

There are casual eateries in each town along the island, places where families slip out of the beach house for a pizza when they don't feel like cooking. **Nino's Pizza** on Highway 12 in Avon (☎ **252/995-5358**) is one such place, and they also deliver. They're open summer Monday through Saturday 11am to 10pm, Sunday 4 to 10pm; winter closed Wednesdays and an hour earlier in the evening. They don't take credit cards. On Highway 12 in Buxton, Angelo's (☎ **252/995-6364**) serves pizza and delivers in the evening. Their hours are summer daily 11:30am to 2pm and 4:30 to 10pm; winter daily 4:30 to 9pm.

Also on Highway 12 in Buxton, near the turn for the lighthouse, the **Tides Restaurant** (☎ **252/995-5988**) is a casual, beach place decorated with local artists' work. The menu includes a lot of fried fish and regional ham and chicken, with entrees topping out at $15. For breakfast they have homemade biscuits and inexpensive omelets. They are open Easter to Thanksgiving 6am to 11am and 5:30 to 9pm.

**Fish House Restaurant.** On Hwy. 12 overlooking Buxton Harbor, Buxton. ☎ **252/995-5151.** Dinner $10–$18; lunch $3.25–$7. Summer daily 11am–2:30pm and 5–9:30pm; winter closes earlier. AE, DISC, MC, V. Closed Dec–Feb.

Among all the touristy stuff, here's an authentic-feeling old fish house turned long ago into a sound-side restaurant — the floor slopes because it once was used for draining water from fish boxes. The specialty is locally caught seafood, prepared simply, and it's done right and comes quickly. There's a decent kids'

menu and a beer and wine list. The plastic tableware adds to the funky Southern seaside feel and conserves water.

## OCRACOKE

The **Cat Ridge Deli** (☎ **252/928-DELI**) is in Albert Styron's Store, a well-preserved historic fixture on Lighthouse Road. It's a gourmet take-out place specializing in Thai cuisine and wraps, as well as more traditional deli fare. They're open summer 11am to 9pm, spring and fall 11am to 5pm; closed December to April.

**Captain Ben's Restaurant.** Hwy. 12, Ocracoke. ☎ **252/928-4741.** Dinner $11–$21; lunch $3.50–$16. Daily 11am–9pm. Closed Nov–Mar.

If you've spent much time in east coast seaside towns, this old-fashioned, nautical-themed place, 31 years in business, will be familiar as soon as you walk in. The service is fast and friendly, with a long menu that includes lots of seafood, prime rib, and something for everyone in the family. Our meals were good, plentiful, and straightforward.

**Howard's Pub and Raw Bar Restaurant.** Hwy. 12, Ocracoke. ☎ **252/928-4441.** Lunch and dinner $5–$17. Daily 11am–2am.

If you can get past the feeling that you're taking your children into a bar, this is a great place for families. You can eat away from the smoke on a screened porch or in a light, air-conditioned dining room with a wood floor that's been worn down by sandals and beach sand. Toys and games are stored on one side — as the proprietor said, it's the kind of place where the kids can get up and run around. The menu offers beef and seafood and items from an in-house smoker. The grilled tuna I ordered was done just right. There's a generous kids' menu. The beer list includes more than 200 brews, and they never close all year, even for hurricanes.

# The Great Smoky Mountains

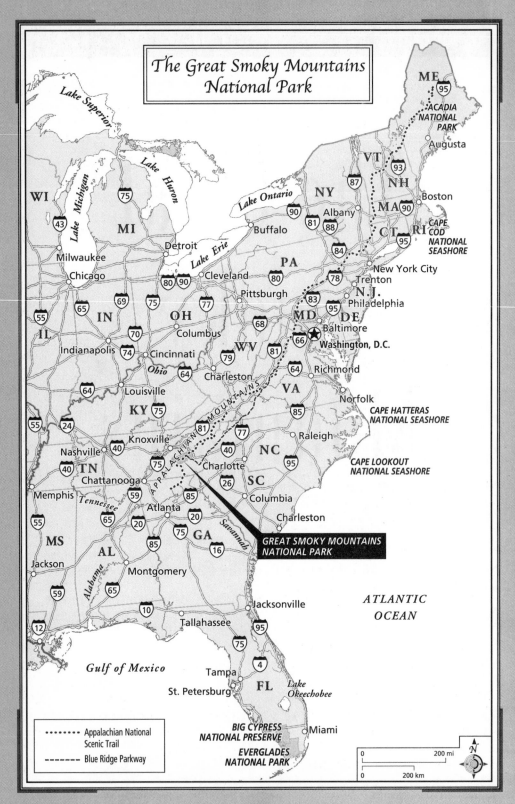

# The Great Smoky Mountains National Park

GREAT SMOKY MOUNTAINS NATIONAL PARK

........ Appalachian National Scenic Trail

– – – – Blue Ridge Parkway

# Bringing Back the Past

The Great Smoky Mountains poke up like an island amid the farms, cities, and freeways of the southeast United States. The mountains are indeed an island, in lots of different ways: The 6,000-foot peaks are among the highest in the eastern U.S. Atop them, cool weather supports islands of subalpine life normally found only much farther north. Lower, great forests of leafy trees shade a riot of amazingly diverse plant life—the most diverse of any American national park. In some areas, patches of especially magnificent trees grow. The Smokies are home to the largest areas of primeval forest (never cut by loggers) in the eastern U.S. They also serve as an island of survival for age-old wildlife, including black bears. Just outside the park's boundaries, unplanned commercial development has brought the ugliest of modern America right up to the shores of this island of nature, like a dirty froth in the surf. Inside, just a short distance off the park roads, real wilderness lives on, free of human development.

The Smokies are half in Tennessee and half in North Carolina, and almost entirely within Great Smoky Mountain National Park. They're part of the southern end of the Appalachian Mountains, a range that leads through the most populated part of the country all the way to Maine. Other areas of the Appalachians are protected, too, and the Appalachian Trail runs the length of the chain. But nowhere else along the range is such a large area preserved.

## NATURAL HISTORY: RESTORING NATURE

People have been in these mountains for at least 10,000 years—since the Ice Age. The Cherokee lived on the land, changed it, and used it. Two hundred years ago, white settlers changed it more, but mostly around the fringes. Then, in the past 100 years, industrial logging ripped across the mountains, and the national park turned them into a car-oriented recreational playground. We changed the mountains more in a few decades than the rest of nature had since the Ice Age.

Today, something completely different is happening. People are trying to erase most of the changes we made to the Great Smoky Mountains. The Park Service is trying to turn back the clock to the day before white settlers arrived, or, in some places, to the years when mountain farmers lived off the land without hurting it much. This work is called **restoration.** Like a carpenter who returns an old house to the way it looked when it was first built, the National Park Service since 1963 has tried to return nature in the parks to the way it was before we started changing it.

To restore a house, you might need to tear down a newly added porch or rip off perfectly good aluminum siding. To restore nature, you might have to kill plants and animals that didn't live there naturally, or you might intentionally burn trees that would have burned if people hadn't been around to put out the fires. Then you would try to put back what was missing. In the case of the house, you might look for the old furniture. In the Smokies, you would try to bring back the animals that had been killed off.

## THE PROBLEMS OF RESTORATION

Restoring nature isn't exactly like fixing up an old house. It's a lot harder. Unlike a house, nature never stands still, but changes constantly all by itself. Natural places might seem permanent and unchanging to us, but that's only because we're changing and moving so fast. You can spend a whole busy day without once noticing the slow changes in sunlight, but from morning to evening the sun crosses the entire sky. In a meadow, the same thing can happen over a human being's lifetime, as trees grow and throw new shadows, becoming forest home for different kinds of plants and animals. Nature makes huge changes to itself all the time, often in ways we don't understand and cannot predict. How do you restore that?

The Park Service's idea is to restore the nature of the Smokies to work the way it did so that the area can change the way it would have changed if people hadn't interfered. For example, in the southwestern part of the park, the forest of Table Mountain pine was being taken over by oak because the Park Service had put out fires there for the past 60 years. Pine seedlings grow best after a fire, because they need bare ground and heat opens the pinecones. The Park Service wants to restore the pine forest's way of regrowing itself—and keeping out the oak—by starting fires in the pines. In the future, fires that start naturally in the area won't be fought, as long as the fires don't threaten people, buildings, or special areas. That way, the natural process of change in the forest should return.

In a way, this kind of restoration is like fixing a machine. Once all the pieces are back in the right places, you shouldn't have to tinker with it all the time. For example, eastern white-tailed deer can become too many in the park, bringing starvation and disease on themselves. Once upon a time, wolves feeding on deer helped keep down their numbers, but people finished off the Smokies' red wolves by 1905. Hardly any red wolves are left in the world, but in 1991, the Park Service began putting a few wolves back in the park. They hoped the wolves would breed, form packs, and feed on the deer. But in this case, fixing nature wasn't much like fixing a car after all. Nature is unpredictable. The wolf pups died and the Park Service had to give up on the project.

Sometimes, we don't understand nature well enough to fix it like a machine. On the tops of some mountains in the Smokies, the first white explorers found lovely open meadows of grass and flowers, called **balds.** At the end of a hike through the forest, a bald opens up to the sky and the view around the mountain like the opening at the end of a tunnel. Settlers used the balds to graze sheep and cattle in the summer, but when the land became a national park, the settlers and their animals had to leave. Over the years since then, the balds have slowly filled in with bushes and trees, shutting off the fabulous views and threatening the wonderful and rare wildflowers.

The Park Service had a puzzle on its hands. The balds were open before the settlers arrived, but they didn't stay open unless the grass was being trimmed by the settlers' farm animals. So how did the balds stay open before the settlers? To this day, no one knows for sure. The Park Service believes in allowing nature to work without interference, the way it did before white settlers arrived, but it can't figure out how the balds worked—how they stayed bald. Instead of losing the balds and their rare plants completely, each summer biologists go to two of them that they are sure were open before white settlers arrived, Gregory Bald and Andrews Bald, and mow the small trees and bushes that threaten to fill them in. Is that restoration? Or is it just another way of altering nature to be more like we want it to be?

But the park is still working on fixing nature's machine. It's possible elk and bison helped keep the balds open, but elk died out all over the eastern half of the United States when logging and farming destroyed the forests, and none has been seen in this area in almost 200 years. Bison were killed off even earlier. Now more of the forests are back, more land is protected, and biologists think elk might survive at Great Smoky. In April 2001, they released 25 elk with radio tracking collars in the park's Cataloochie area to see how they will do. With success, biologists will release more elk each year. Someday, the elk may return to feeding in the balds and keeping them open.

Sometimes restoration works well. River otters were released again in the park, and now they live in many of the large streams where they did before. Peregrine falcons were killed off by a chemical called DDT, which was once used by farmers to kill insects. The last peregrine falcon to nest in the Smokies had been seen in 1947 in a crag on a cliff on Little Duck Hawk Ridge on the Alum Cave Trail. After many years of work to restore the birds to the park, rangers saw the first peregrine chick hatch in a nest in that same crack in 1997, exactly 50 years later.

## WHAT NEEDS TO BE RESTORED?

The Appalachians are old mountains that have been wearing down for a long time. They're older than the great ranges out West, and smaller because water and weather have worn at them so much longer. Their form today dates to the last ice age, or glacial period, when glaciers spread over most of North America. The ice didn't make it this far south, but the climate of the Smokies was cold enough to grow alpine tundra that you see today only in higher or more northern mountains—the green mat of low, heathery plants. When the ice melted and the weather warmed up, hardwood trees and rich plant life returned to the base of the mountains. At the highest points, the elevation kept the air cold enough for subalpine trees and plants normally found only much farther north. Those islands of plant life, so far from their kind, contain unique species that either didn't survive elsewhere or developed only here. One is the Fraser fir. Sadly, an insect accidentally introduced from Europe, the balsam woolly adelgid, has killed most of the park's Fraser firs. Now only short, Christmas tree–size firs remain, because the insects kill the trees as soon as they get old enough to have cones.

The Fraser fir is a good example of how changes brought by people can't always be changed back, and there were many artificial changes at Great Smoky. The mountains have been settled and changed by white people since before our nation gained independence. In the western United States, where white settlement came much later, creating national parks usually meant that the government just put aside its own land. Not much had to be restored, because not much had been changed. But by the time the idea of national parks developed, the Smokies already had been in use by private owners for more than 100 years. To put the mountains in a park, the government had to get the land by purchase or gift. Then the Park Service had to restore the workings of nature.

When President Franklin Roosevelt dedicated the park at Newfound Gap in 1940, the Park Service had a different idea of how to restore the park than it does now. Then, it thought of the park as being more for people than for animals. Rangers stocked the streams with rainbow trout so that fishermen could catch more and bigger fish than the local but unique brook trout. The rainbows made for better fishing, but they pushed the brook trout out of native streams. Today, one of the restoration projects aims to get the rainbows out of sections of stream where brook trout might be able to make a comeback. The Park Service also built a lot of roads in the park, and wanted to build more roads and campgrounds, which conservationists were able to stop. With the number of cars in the park today, it's frightening to think of the number there might have been if all the projects had gone ahead.

## FOREST RESTORATION

The damage done by the early Park Service was nothing compared to what came before. Around the beginning of the 20th century, logging companies bought up most of the Smokies to cut the trees for lumber and paper pulp. This remote area was the last in the eastern United States where old-growth forest still stood. **Old growth** (also called **virgin** or **primeval forest**) is forest that has never been cut. In the Smokies, it had been growing since the last glacial period, and many of the trees were huge. In a mature old-growth forest, trees die of old age and fall, rotting away to make soil for new trees. Those smaller trees slowly grow to replace the giants. A steady cycle of birth, death, and growth makes the forest seem to stand still in time in an unchanging balance. A walk in old-growth forest passes through shady areas with high ceilings of leaves, and areas with splashes of light where big trees have fallen and left a place for grass and new life. Great Smoky still has a few old-growth stands, such as Albright Grove on the Maddrone Bald Trail or along the Ramsay Cascade Trail, both in the northeast part of the park. Only 20% of the park was never cut, but it still contains the East's largest stands of old growth.

The logging destroyed more than trees. The loggers of the time didn't even try to protect the land. Their ways of getting huge logs out of the forest tore up the ground, caused erosion and severe fires, and ruined streams. Besides dragging out the logs or rolling them down hillsides, they built railroad lines all through the forests. Or they moved logs down the valleys by building **splash dams.** A creek would be gouged out, taking away rocks, snags, or bends (the turns and obstructions in the flow that make a stream a good place for fish), and then the logs that needed to be moved would be piled in the stream below a dam with a trap door. When the water was high enough, the trap door would be opened to send a flood smashing into the logs, whooshing them downstream.

Many loggers were careless about fire, leaving piles of **slash**—tree tops and branches— that could flare up with a spark from a passing coal-fired locomotive. Fire burned from cut lands through good timber. Where the hills were cut and scorched, soil washed away. Pines, which grow well in poorer soil and sprout after fires, took over land that had grown hardwoods for centuries.

The way to restore a forest is to do nothing. Loggers today replant the forests they cut, but the trees they put back are the fastest-growing kinds that can be cut again soon. That produces an unnatural forest without much variety of plants or animals. At Great Smoky, logging went on until the park was set aside. Logging companies resisted selling their land until they had cut all the good trees, and one of the largest companies would sell only with the agreement that it could go on cutting for 15 years. Much of the park had been cut by the time the Park Service took over. At that time, people thought the way to restore a forest was to bring in teams to plant valuable species like white pine in orderly rows. Fortunately, they didn't do that much here, but just let it grow. Sixty years later, many of the cut-over forests have grown trees as big as old growth. But it will take another 150 to 350 years for the forest to reach maturity, with an even mix of strong young trees, trees dying of old age, and sprouts growing from the rotted logs of giants.

## RESTORING HISTORY

People used to live in valleys all through this mountain country. When hiking a high valley that looks like wilderness, you might be walking on ground where generations of self-sufficient farmers grew crops, built homes, and lived and died. All trace is gone of about 1,200 farms that park founders bought to put Great Smoky Mountains National Park together. (More than 6,000 pieces of land were bought, but many were logging tracts or small lots with summer cabins.) Some of the farming families left willingly, some held out for the highest price they could get, and some refused to give up at all. The government finally forced everyone to sell whether they wanted to or not, but those who chose to live out their lives on their farms were allowed to stay until they died. Then their homes, like the others, were demolished and the fields left to grow back into forests.

In a few places, however, the park saved the best of the old buildings. By the 1940s, when the park was complete, the Park Service realized that the area's history was worth keeping. Today, we endlessly copy and repeat "country" style in everything from home decoration to popular music—but the imitations aren't anything like the real, hard lives of the those who really lived in these back woods. You can see what their lives were like at outdoor museums in the park, where their homes, farms, and mills were preserved (see "Places for Learning," in chapter 7, "Great Smoky Mountains National Park").

At Cades Cove, the park's most popular place to visit, and at the much quieter and more isolated Cataloochie area, roads and trails pass through pastures and woods where communities once stood. It's a little spooky. The houses, churches, and other buildings feel at times as if the people living there just left and that as a visitor you're intruding. Other houses stand empty and rattle in the wind like those in a ghost town. The 11-mile Cades Cove Loop becomes a big traffic jam, taking up to 3 hours to round on a summer afternoon. That's a frustrating pace, and it takes away from the experience of watching wildlife and the countryside go by. (You can avoid it by going to Cataloochie instead, covered in chapter 7.)

For the Park Service, the job of restoration has changed. The buildings and natural surroundings are in good shape. Now the park should work on ways to restore the experience of visiting Cades Cove by getting rid of the cars.

## FINDING A BALANCE

In the Smokies, we've chosen to restore some things but not others. By saving the best 75 pioneer buildings, the Park Service didn't choose to show history as it really was—to do that, it would have had to restore the poorest, worst-built houses too. Nor is it natural to have millions of cars touring the park on paved highways and a Motor Nature Trail, the great majority of visitors never getting far from their cars. Over the years some roads have been removed, and some unwise road projects have been stopped; but no one is talking about taking away the pavement to restore it to the way it was before the first settlers arrived.

Many other restoration projects will never be complete, no matter how hard the Park Service works. Wild European boars that escaped from a North Carolina game farm more than 80 years ago found their way into the Smokies and bred until more than 1,000 of them were here, tearing up the ground and eating food the native wildlife needs, and consuming lots of snails, crayfish, and salamanders. The Park Service hunts and traps the boars every year, cutting the number greatly, but they breed fast and are hard to find. They'll probably never be all gone, so the work can never stop.

It's hard to figure out what to restore and how to do it, and the work never ends. The Smokies will never be completely restored. If they were, we'd have no way of knowing it—after all, no one is left alive who remembers what the mountains looked like before the first white settlers arrived. But what has been done is amazing, and in many ways it's good enough. Park your car and hike a trail. Maybe the land you walk through was a logging slash, a farmer's garden, or even a road once upon a time. You'll likely never know, because it will feel just like wilderness.

## THE LITTLE FIELD GUIDE

### MAMMALS & MARINE LIFE
In addition to the creatures here, you might want to check out the black bear (p. 392).

Gray Fox

### Gray Fox/Red Fox
The gray fox's back is gray and the sides of its neck are red. The red fox is similar but larger and red on the back. The red fox is more common in the Smokies, but it's shy and likes to lurk in the underbrush. Be patient and make quiet squeaking sounds to help lure the curious animal out. Cades Cove or Cataloochie are good places to look.

### White-Tailed Deer
White-tailed deer are the common deer of the eastern United States, once rare from over-hunting and now so numerous that they're a nuisance in some places. To keep the population down, hunters outside the park are allowed to take great numbers. You're almost sure to see white-tailed deer in Cades Cove grazing on the grass in the fields, especially at dusk.

### Woodchuck (or Groundhog)
Woodchucks are about 2 feet tall when they stand and, especially when getting ready for winter, can be hilariously fat. They like open areas near roads or clearings. You can find them by locating the piles of dirt they leave near their burrows.

### BIRDS
Besides the birds listed here, you will see some described in other chapters, such as the raven (p. 54), the belted kingfisher and the great horned owl (p. 475).

### Barred Owl
If you hear an owl hooting while you're in your tent at night or while hiking during the day in the thick lowland forest, it's probably one of these big guys. One writer describes the cry as "who cooks for you, who cooks for you *all*." Barred owls are gray-brown with round heads and pronounced spectacles around the eyes. They come out at night, so to see one you have to explore the deep woods, following the hooting.

Ruffed Grouse

Flame Azalea

## Ruffed Grouse

This gray-brown bird, which looks something like a chicken, hides on the ground in underbrush, then bursts up into the air when people pass. That makes it a popular game bird. But the regrowth of big trees on logged land has made grouse more rare, because they like thick undergrowth and bushy clearings. The forests of big trees are the wild turkey's favorite habitat, so they are taking over where grouse lived.

Wild Turkey

## Wild Turkey

The male looks just like the cartoon turkey you see at Thanksgiving. The female lacks all the fancy feathers. Turkeys were hunted almost to extinction. Now, with protection and the return of their favorite habitat— mature forest without much undergrowth— they're becoming more common. You might run across them while you're hiking or at Cades Cove in the evening.

## TREES & PLANTS

In addition to the flora here, also refer to American beech, eastern red cedar, red or swamp maple, and eastern white pine (p. 49).

## Flame Azalea

This brightly blossoming shrub—in red, orange, and yellow—appears in its greatest profusion in early July on Gregory Bald and Andrews Bald. The spectacular show so impressed botanists and visitors that they helped persuade the nation to set aside the Smokies as a national park. Down below, flame azaleas bloom in June.

## Fraser Fir

This Christmas tree–shaped evergreen grows only here and on a few nearby mountaintops. These firs like high elevations, growing by themselves or mixed with red spruce a little lower. The mountaintops are islands of cool weather in the southern climate where these trees can survive. They should grow up to 30 feet, but an introduced insect, the balsam woolly adelgid, kills these trees as soon as they mature.

## Mountain Laurel

These pink and white flowers come out through May and June. The mountain laurel grows in cove hardwood forests and other areas with leafy trees.

Poison Ivy

## Poison Ivy

This bane of bare legs was discovered by Captain John Smith, leader of the Jamestown Colony. Its sap contains a substance called *urushiol,* which is so toxic that 500 people can get a rash from a drop the size of a salt grain. Poison ivy grows as a vine or as a plant on the ground with one or many stems. Avoid the three-leafed plant and any others that might be poison ivy at all costs. Wear long sleeves in the woods, and don't touch anything that might have touched poison ivy at any time in the past. Treatments are covered in "Dealing with Hazards," in chapter 1, "Planning Your Trip."

## Rhododendron

With their big leathery leaves, rhododendrons are easy to identify, and they grow all over Great Smoky. Catawba rhododendron grows only in the southern Appalachians on ridges and other high places, and has gorgeous purple flowers in late June. The more common rosebay rhododendrons have white flowers that bloom in June in the valleys and July on mountainsides.

Tulip Tree
(or Yellow Poplar)

## Tulip Tree (or Yellow Poplar)

This tall, straight tree has oddly shaped large leaves, each with four rounded points. It's a common tree of the low-level cove hardwood forest that's reclaiming old logged areas and farmland. A member of the magnolia family, this lovely tree has spring flowers shaped something like tulips. When white settlers arrived in North America, they found huge old-growth tulip trees. Some of the biggest left standing are in the park (see "The Cove Hardwoods," in chapter 7).

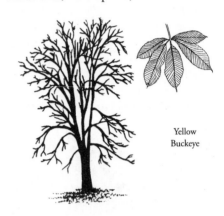
Yellow Buckeye

## Yellow Buckeye

Another tree of the cove hardwood forest, the yellow buckeye is common at Great Smoky and isn't found outside this region. The leaves are long and saw-toothed, lighter colored and hairy underneath, and appear in groups of five. The flowers are yellow. The seeds and shoots of this tree are poison, but Native Americans knew how to cook them to make them safe to eat.

# HISTORY & CULTURE: WHOSE LAND IS THIS?

Before Europeans arrived, Cherokee warriors controlled land across a great part of the Southeast that's now in eight states. The Smokies were a small part of that land. The Cherokee patrolled their borders and fought wars against other tribes to expand their territory. When whites from Europe started to arrive, the Cherokee fought some of them too.

## CHEROKEE WAYS

Cherokee customs were quite different from European ways. For example, in European culture, women were less important than men. They couldn't do much on their own, almost as if they belonged to their husbands or fathers. Among the Cherokee, women were equal to men in some ways, and even more important in others. Mothers owned the family home, and they could divorce and remarry. When Europeans first met the Cherokee, they were impressed by how civilized they seemed. By "civilized," the whites meant that the Cherokee's organized way of life reminded them of European society. The Cherokee were serious and dignified, they had age-old laws and met to discuss problems together, and everyone in their communities had a job. Looking back, they seem more civilized than the white traders, trappers, and settlers. Unlike the Cherokee, whites on the frontier often didn't respect any law and took whatever they could. The Cherokee even took baths a lot more often than the whites.

The British and French fought over the Appalachians in the 1750s in the French and Indian War. The Cherokee, like other tribes, got caught up in the war after being threatened by both sides. They fought on the British side against the French; but the Cherokee and British soldiers didn't get along, and soon they were fighting each other. Groups of Cherokee warriors massacred white settlers who were coming into their lands—they would swoop down and kill everyone. Like violent people in many societies, some Cherokee just liked killing, and they tortured and killed any vulnerable white they saw.

The British also did hideous things. When a group of 25 or 30 chiefs came for a peace conference, a British commander tricked them and took them prisoner. The Cherokee played the same trick back, and the British then killed all the chiefs. Soon, both sides were killing anyone they could find. When the war with the French was over, the British came into Cherokee country with a large army and destroyed all their villages, all their crops, and everything they had, and left them to starve in the cold.

## BECOMING ASSIMILATED

Over the years of war, some Cherokee leaders came to believe that the only way they could survive was to get some of the special powers the whites had. They needed more than guns—they also needed tools and knowledge. Most important, they needed to know how to read and write and use the white laws. Our first president, George Washington, met with Cherokee leaders and agreed that they should be protected from the whites. He promised to give them what they needed to fit in as part of the new United States of America. He sent plows, seed, and men to teach the Cherokee how to farm the land, and spinning wheels and looms so that they could make cloth of the cotton they grew. The Cherokee invited Christian missionaries into their land to build churches and schools where the children could learn to read and write. The most forward-looking even sent their children away to school. John Ridge, the son of one of the most important chiefs, became a lawyer and married a woman from Connecticut who came back to live in the Cherokee Nation.

The Cherokee believed that if they became as "civilized" as the white Americans, they might be left alone and allowed to keep the land that hadn't already been taken from them. John Ridge helped create a government for the Cherokee that was like the U.S. system—it had a constitution, two elected bodies like the two houses of Congress, a head chief who was like the president, and a supreme court. Sequoyah, an uneducated Cherokee man, created a language with 86 letters so that the Cherokee language could be written and read as well as spoken. (Sequoia trees in California, the world's largest, were named for him.)

The Cherokee Nation built a capital city, New Echota, with a newspaper published in English and Cherokee. When the whites had trouble with other eastern tribes, the Creek and Seminole, at different times, the Cherokee volunteered to fight on the side of the government. General Andrew Jackson led armies of white and Cherokee soldiers into battle. The Cherokee were among his best troops and officers. Over the years, Cherokee chiefs met with U.S. presidents many times, and they signed treaties that said the Cherokee could keep their land forever.

## PRESSURE TO LEAVE

As time passed, more and more white settlers came to Georgia, North Carolina, and Tennessee, surrounding the Cherokee. The Cherokee had worked hard and succeeded in the white ways. They owned mills, schools, miles of roads, tens of thousands of livestock, houses, ferries, sawmills, cotton-weaving machines, and even slaves. But there were a lot more whites in Georgia than Cherokee, and many of the whites were poorer. They wanted the Cherokee's land, no matter what the law said and no matter how well the Cherokee had taken on white ways. In 1828, the Georgia legislature passed a law saying that all the Cherokee land within the state belonged to the state.

Also in 1828, the Cherokee's old war comrade, Andrew Jackson, was elected president. They turned to him for help and protection from the whites in Georgia. But Jackson declared that all Indians should be taken from land east of the Mississippi River and moved out West. He told the Cherokee to go and offered them land in Arkansas and money if they would agree to leave. Georgia and the other states surrounding the Cherokee did more to force them out. The states changed their laws so that they would not protect the Cherokee, and they threw Christian missionaries and teachers in jail if they helped protect the Cherokee. Without the law to stop them, whites began stealing from the Cherokee, attacking them, and taking their land. The Cherokee, having accepted white ways, tried to fight back using the whites' rules. They took Georgia to court. In 1832, the U.S. Supreme Court, the highest law in the land, ruled that the Cherokee were in the right and that Georgia had no right to take their land. But President Jackson, whose job it was under the U.S. Constitution to enforce the court's order, simply ignored it and told the Cherokee they had to leave anyway.

## TRAIL OF TEARS

Most Cherokee refused to go, so Jackson sent the U.S. Army to force them out. Soldiers would show up at a house and tell the family to grab what they could carry—they had to leave immediately. Whites were waiting to steal everything that was left behind the moment a Cherokee family was gone. Georgia raffled off the land and houses to whites, including the big plantations of the richest Cherokee. About 12,000 Cherokee were forced to walk to Arkansas, more than 1,000 miles away, and hundreds died on the way. The route was called the **Trail of Tears.** Later, when the whites in Arkansas decided that they wanted that land too, the Cherokee were sent to Oklahoma.

A small number of Cherokee managed to stay behind in North Carolina because of a difference in the laws relating to their land. Their reservation remains just south of Great

Smoky Mountain National Park. In the town of Cherokee, you can see their museum, tour a re-created village, and take in an outdoor performance on their history (see chapter 7).

There was never an excuse for white settlers taking Native American land, as they did all over, but the unfairness of it was never more clear and outrageous than in the case of the Cherokee. The laws and customs the whites held up to demonstrate their superiority didn't matter as soon as they wanted what the Cherokee had. The Cherokee turned out to be more civilized even than the President of the United States, Andrew Jackson, who betrayed his old war comrades, broke the promises made by his country, and ignored his duty under the Constitution to enforce the law.

## BUYING THE PARK

People started talking about a national park in the Smokies in the 1880s, and city folk and state legislatures quickly supported it. More people joined in support of the park after 1900, when logging companies began their destructive tree cutting in the mountains (see "Forest Restoration," p. 142). The lumbermen were rich and influential, however, and they persuaded Congress not to pass any laws creating the park for many years. Only in 1925 did Congress approve the park, but it set aside no money to buy the land. That would have to come from private sources and the neighboring states.

The children of Knoxville, Tennessee, collected their change to help the park. They gave a total of $1,391.72. Unfortunately, $12 million was needed. The biggest chunk of it, $5 million, came from John D. Rockefeller, Jr., the heir to one of the largest fortunes in the world. He also was the biggest contributor to Acadia and Grand Teton national parks, and he helped set aside 21 other parks and natural places around the country. After much of the money was raised, the U.S. government gave some, too.

A government commission (a committee) was in charge of spending the money. Buying the Smokies wasn't easy. The commission spent years fighting in court with lumber companies that didn't want to sell. The lumbermen kept cutting as long as they could, even agreeing in one case to sell only if they could cut trees for another 15 years. Most of the park's trees were cut before the land sales were completed.

## THE PARK TAKES OVER

The small landowners—the descendants of those who moved into Cherokee land—were treated better than the Native Americans had been. Only one-sixth of the park was owned by people other than big logging companies, but that one-sixth represented 6,200 little pieces of land. About 1,200 were farms. Many of the farmers were happy to sell their land for the good prices the government commission offered. The Great Depression was going on, and the farmers could move on and find better land with the money. But about a third didn't want to sell, and the government used its power of **eminent domain** against them—a law that allows the government to buy anyone's land if it has a good reason, whether or not the owner wants to sell it. Instead of making the owners leave, however, the National Park Service allowed those who wanted to stay to continue to use their homes until they died.

About 60 years passed from the time the park was thought of until it was dedicated in 1940. By that time, the mountain people's way of life had become a museum piece. Their homes remain in Cades Cove, Cataloochee, and a few other places in the park that you can tour.

# Great Smoky Mountains National Park

The deep woods of the Smokies are closer to my idea of the paradise of Eden than anywhere else I've ever been. The place I'm thinking of has tall, graceful trees, a nearly solid roof of green, brightly flowering rhododendron, and a babbling stream of clear, clean water on a leafy bed of black rock. My senses are filled: the sound of the birds and water; the scent of green, growing things; the sensation of warm, moist air; and then the delicious chill of a mountain stream as I plunge into one of its glassy pools, feeling totally alone in a fairy-tale wilderness.

It's a feeling you might not expect in the busiest of all the national parks, which you share with about 10 million other visitors a year. But it's a big park, and fewer than a third of the visitors ever get away from their cars. One out of six never even turns off the engine, touring only places like Cades Cove and the Roaring Fork Motor Nature Trail with many other cars, looking at the old buildings, fall foliage, and animals like visitors at a museum or game park. The park protects big, unique natural places within a half day of most of the population of the eastern U.S. The Park Service used to accommodate all the visitors by emphasizing car-based touring and believed that the best way to protect the park from people was to keep them in their cars. Only the resistance of local conservationists stopped even more roads from being built.

Fortunately, the park isn't completely crisscrossed with pavement, and you don't have to experience it only from behind a windshield. You use the senses of touch, smell, and hearing, as well as sight, and feel the rewarding weariness in your legs that comes at the end of a good hike. Moreover, you can have the trail mostly to yourself, because many people who do get out of the car hike only the five most popular trails. Those trails become crowded masses of people, but other trails remain rarely used and can even be overgrown. I backpacked 25 miles in early September and saw only one other person. That's when I found Eden.

## BEST THINGS TO DO

- Hike a trail in the deep woods to a waterfall, old-growth forest grove, or mountaintop.
- Play in a creek on a hot day or tubing downstream just outside the park.
- Put on a pack to camp out a few miles into the backcountry, or use a long-haul trail for an expedition as long as you like.
- Ride horseback through the forest or mountain-bike on many miles of unpaved road.
- Visit the historic abandoned communities of Cades Cove and Cataloochie and other sites showing backwoods life.
- Take in the museum and other Cherokee Indian attractions in their reservation just south of the park.

See "Activities" (p. 170).

## ORIENTATION

### THE PARK

Great Smoky Mountains National Park is a rectangle roughly 60 miles by 20 miles, running east and west and taking in the Great Smoky Mountains in the southern Appalachian Mountains. The high ridge line running the length of the park divides Tennessee and North Carolina. The tops of the mountains are more open than the thick forests below, but because the Smokies' tallest 6,000-foot peaks are still below tree line, big views open only at special places. Valleys in the lowlands on the north and south sides of the mountains are called **coves;** this is where the largest and most diverse forest grows.

### THE ROADS

Roads surround and thread through the park to allow access to many less-used points on every side, including Cosby, Big Creek, Cataloochee, paths near Fontana, and Abrams Creek, in addition to the four gateway towns mentioned below. Many of these country ways are slow and winding, including the madly

---

## GREAT SMOKY ADDRESS BOOK

**Great Smoky Mountains National Park.** 107 Park Headquarters Rd., Gatlinburg, TN 37738. ☎ 865/436-1200. www.nps.gov/grsm.

**Great Smoky Mountains Natural History Association** (for books and maps). 115 Park Headquarters Rd., Gatlinburg, TN 37738. ☎ 865/436-0120. www.smokiesstore.org.

**National Forests in North Carolina** (Nantahala and Pisgah national forests). 160A Zillicoa St., Asheville, NC 28801. ☎ 828/257-4200. www.cs.unca.edu/nfsnc.

**Cherokee National Forest.** P.O. Box 2010, Cleveland, TN 37320. ☎ 865/339-9700. www.r8web.com/cherokee.

**Cherokee Tribal Travel and Promotion.** P.O. Box 460, Cherokee, NC 28719. ☎ 800/438-1601 or 828/497-9195. www.cherokee-nc.com.

**Gatlinburg Chamber of Commerce.** 466 Brookside Village Way, Suite 8 (P.O. Box 527), Gatlinburg, TN 37738. ☎ 800/900-4148. www.gatlinburg.com.

**Swain County Chamber of Commerce.** P.O. Box 509, Bryson City, NC 28713. ☎ 800/867-9246 or 828/488-3681. www.greatsmokies.com.

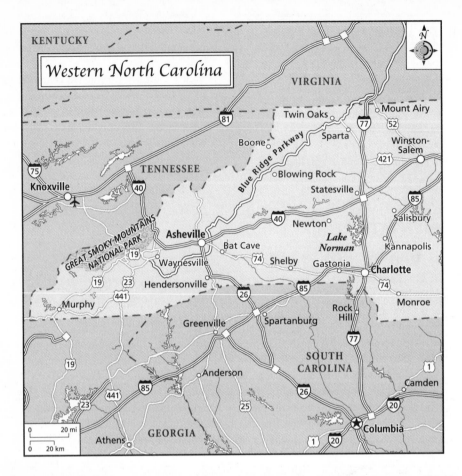

Western North Carolina

twisting U.S. 129 west of the park, which motorcyclists come from all over the world to try out. None of them is a speedy way to get around, and it's wise to plan on averaging no more than 45 mph. The major exceptions are **Interstate 40,** which passes by the east side of the park, and the isolated sections of the **Foothills Parkway,** a round-the-park route begun in 1951 but stalled since 1986 by environmental concerns. Most useful of its three fragments is the spur from U.S. 441 that allows you to bypass Gatlinburg from Pigeon Forge to the Sugarlands Visitor Center, saving much time in traffic. The parkway portion on the western side of the park is spectacular. (The Blue Ridge Parkway is covered under "Getting There," p. 156.)

Unpaved roads also penetrate the park at several points, often following the narrow roadbeds of abandoned logging railroads. These mostly seasonal, often one-lane routes have many narrow, wooden bridges, and even ford streams; while generally passable by passenger cars, they are really more suitable for mountain bikes (see p. 172). You can get an inexpensive map and guide called *Auto Touring* at visitor centers.

The following two roads are the park's major travel routes. Even they were built for slow traffic, and sightseeing brings them to a crawl. Although speed limits are faster, count on making no more than 25 mph.

## Newfound Gap Road

This 32-mile drive is the park's centerpiece, crossing the back of the mountains, more than 5,000 feet high, and allowing you to see how the elevation changes the plants and trees on the way. The road itself is interesting, too, as it snakes and even crosses itself with a bridge on the way up the mountain. Despite the slow traffic, this road is also the quickest way across the park. It runs from Gatlinburg to Cherokee.

## Sugarlands to Cades Cove

A winding route leads from the Sugarlands Visitor Center, near Gatlinburg, to Cades Cove, where a loop circles the valley and its historic buildings. From the visitor center, the scenic drive to Cades Cove on Little River and Laurel Creek roads totals 25 miles. The Cades Code Loop itself is only 11 miles (see p. 167), but congestion can make the tour very slow.

## THE TOWNS
### North Side
#### GATLINBURG

This is the park's main northern gateway, near the headquarters at the Sugarlands Visitor Center. It's easy to see how Gatlinburg, laid out on winding streets in a narrow valley, was once an attractive community. Tourist development has spoiled it entirely, turning the streets into carnival midways of wax museums, gift shops, indoor minigolf, and anything else you can imagine. The largest choice of hotels and restaurants is here.

What they couldn't fit in Gatlinburg, tourism boomers built along a four-lane strip a few miles north, erasing the villages of **Pigeon Forge** and **Sevierville** with a solid strip of schlock that goes on for miles. You can find anything you want here but beauty or serenity.

East of Gatlinburg on U.S. 321, cabins and other businesses typical of a rural highway extend to the east side of the park.

#### TOWNSEND

On my last visit, it looked like this quiet, sparsely developed highway town near Cades Cove had caught the same disease as Pigeon Forge, with franchise businesses busily digging up the pastures for new stores. Still, there is a beautiful commercial campground and a quiet, attractive motel (see p. 160 and 162).

### South Side
#### CHEROKEE

The highways around the town center of the Cherokee reservation at the park's main southern entrance are fronted with old-fashioned roadside motels and Indian curio shops, new chain motels, and a huge video gaming casino. But there are some cultural attractions of significant interest, and outside town Big Cove Road has a collection of good commercial campgrounds.

#### BRYSON CITY

Although it lacks a direct connection to the main park roads (you have to drive 10 miles east to reach Newfound Gap Road in Cherokee), Bryson City does have a fine back door on the park. It's a charming, old-fashioned Southern town, with plenty to do. There are waterfall trails, a park campground, and inner-tubing.

#### MAGGIE VALLEY

Along U.S. 19 near the southeast end of the park, the Blue Ridge Parkway, and the Cataloochee area, this is a small, relatively quiet highway town.

# MAKING THE ARRANGEMENTS

## WHEN TO GO

The visitor season at Great Smoky is long, starting with spring break and running through October, when the leaves turn brilliant colors. Summer and the foliage season are the busiest times, with weekends heavier than weekdays, and often commanding a premium hotel rate. The Smokies are rainy all year, with precipitation just shy of rain-forest proportions: 87 inches a year at Clingmans Dome. The midsummer months and early spring are wettest.

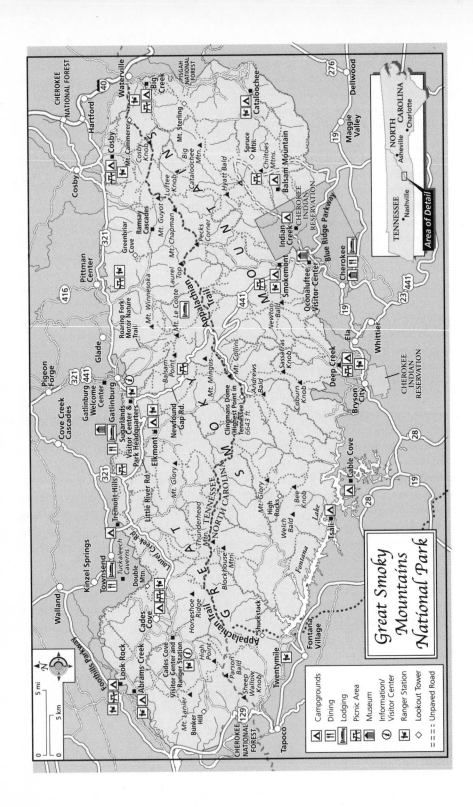

Great Smoky Mountains National Park

The park is an excellent choice for spring break. Roads and other facilities start to open in the second half of March. The weather can still be changeable, with occasional snowstorms at the top of the mountains. Farther down, you'll need sweaters in the evenings. Snow is gone from trails in April and May, when wildflowers arrive with the warming temperatures. Hotel rates don't rise until June at many places. These are the quietest of the good weather months.

Locals prize their cool summer weather, but that's mainly in comparison to the unbearable temperatures at lower elevations in the region. At Gatlinburg, around 1,500 feet, summer highs average in the upper 80s, with high humidity. Up in the mountains, highs in the mid-60s make for a delicious break and perfect hiking weather. July is the park's most crowded month, and its rainiest, with an average of 13 rainy days. June is less busy. For inner-tubing, spring through early summer is best, because water levels can dwindle from July on.

A drier, crisper fall weather pattern sets in starting sometime in September. Leaves change in early October in the mountains, late October down below. People out to see the bright foliage clog park roads, and hotel rates shoot up to their annual peak. Reservations are hard to get. Snow hits the highlands in November and is heavy through the winter; little snow falls in the valleys. Hotels are empty and inexpensive during the winter season.

## How Much Time to Spend

The many folds and surprises of the Smoky Mountains make a large area seem even larger. Few people can hope for a comprehensive visit. A week would be adequate to explore a couple of parts of the park and see the main highlights. A 3-day visit would allow you a couple of hikes or activities in one area and some sightseeing. Anything less than 3 days will be mostly a drive-through.

## How Far to Plan Ahead

The reservation campgrounds often fill up from Memorial Day into the fall. Call as soon as you can after the system opens for your dates (the national reservation system is covered in chapter 1, "Planning Your Trip"). Out-of-the-way campgrounds more often have sites unclaimed except on summer holiday weekends.

You'll never see more motel rooms in a concentrated area. A week ahead is often enough to reserve motel rooms during the week, but weekends book up earlier, especially in the busy fall foliage season. Cabins and rooms in country inns need more planning.

## Reading Up

The Great Smoky Mountains Natural History Association (GSMNHA) operates the visitor center bookstores and sells online and by phone (☎ 865/436-0120; www.smokiesstore. org). The material they publish on the park is exceptionally good, including a collection of inexpensive map-guides on topics such as wildflowers, day hikes, and waterfalls.

### Hiking

*Hiking Trails of the Great Smokies,* edited by Don DaFoe, Beth Giddens, and Steve Kemp (GSMNHA), is a truly extraordinary trail guide, covering every hike in exquisite detail, that comes with a map.

### Maps

The maps sold by the park for $1 or included with the book above are adequate, but a finer-scale map with topographic lines makes it easier to really figure out where you are. The plastic Trails Illustrated edition is up to date and loaded with information.

### Nature

Rose Houk's *A Natural History Guide: Great Smoky Mountain National Park* (Houghton Mifflin), is a good introduction to the park's natural systems.

| | AVG. HIGH (°F) | AVG. LOW (°F) | PRECIP. (IN.) GATLINBURG | PRECIP. (IN.) CLINGMANS DOME |
|---|---|---|---|---|
| Dec.–Feb. | 51 | 28 | 4.4 | 8.6 |
| March | 61 | 34 | 5.5 | 8.8 |
| April | 71 | 41 | 4.5 | 6.5 |
| May | 78 | 49 | 4.9 | 5.4 |
| June | 84 | 71 | 5.4 | 7.8 |
| July | 86 | 74 | 6.2 | 8.4 |
| August | 85 | 60 | 5.1 | 6.3 |
| September | 80 | 54 | 3.7 | 5.1 |
| October | 71 | 42 | 3 | 5.5 |
| November | 60 | 33 | 4.2 | 7.8 |

*Temperatures are about 20°F cooler at Clingmans Dome than in Gatlinburg.*

## GETTING THERE
### By Car

Interstates run close to the park from every direction, with **I-40** touching the park's east side. Navigation is simple, but if you want to make time, stay off the country roads until you are as near your destination as possible.

The **Blue Ridge Parkway** is the ultimate scenic route. The two-lane road follows the top of the Blue Ridge Mountains 469 miles from Shenandoah National Park, in Virginia, to the south entrance of Great Smoky. There's lots to see and do on the way. Contact the Blue Ridge Parkway at 199 Hemphill Knob Rd., Asheville, NC 28801 (☎ **828/298-0398;** www.nps.gov/blri). Get business information from the **Blue Ridge Parkway Association,** P.O. Box 2136, Asheville, NC 28802 (www. blueridgeparkway.org), which has a comprehensive website. The road is closed in the winter.

### By Plane

Knoxville's **McGhee Tyson Airport,** south of the city and 48 miles northwest of Gatlinburg, is the easiest place to fly in and rent a car. It's served by five major airlines, including **Delta** (☎ **800/221-1212**), **United** (☎ **800/241-6522**), and **Northwest** (☎ **800/225-2525**). Most of the national car-rental agencies operate there. If you want to shop ticket and car prices, Charlotte and Atlanta are each around 4 hours from Cherokee.

## WHAT TO PACK
### Clothing

The Smokies are famous for rain, so you should come well prepared at any time of year. The dampness comes in the form of mists and haze, steady showers, and ferocious thunderstorms. Up in the mountains, it can be chilly in the spring and fall, and blizzards come in mid-winter. Down in the valleys, Northerners will find the weather mild on all but cold winter days, and sometimes warm and muggy in summer. Bring a variety of clothing, from short sleeves for down below to sweaters and raincoats for up in the mountains. You won't need anything heavier unless you spend the night in the mountains off-season. There are some nice restaurants in Gatlinburg, but dress generally is casual. Bring good hiking shoes or boots because the trails are often rough.

## Gear

Make sure your camping gear can handle rain. Bring a couple of extra plastic tarps if you have room. A screen tent for the picnic table will make eating and sitting more comfortable with rain or summer bugs. Bring floating toys for the creeks.

# WHERE TO SPEND THE NIGHT

## CAMPING

The campgrounds listed below are open year-round unless otherwise noted.

## Park Service Campgrounds

The 10 campgrounds within the park fall into two categories.

Three large campgrounds—Cades Cove, Elkmont, and Smokemont—lie on the main spine of paved roads. They are booked through the national reservation system (see chapter 1) and are often full during the season. Campers using these campgrounds tend to be visitors from outside the area. Sites are not reserved November through May 15, and rates are $3 lower during that period.

The other seven campgrounds, on the fringes of the park and often reached by unpaved roads, don't take reservations. They are seldom all full (Cosby rarely fills) and are used more by locals coming up for a weekend. Some of these campgrounds are idyllic, out-of-the-way discoveries with the feel of back-country camping.

All campgrounds in the park have flush toilets. Campfire programs are held, in season, at Cades Cove, Smokemont, Elkmont, Cosby, Deep Creek, and Balsam Mountain.

### CAMPGROUNDS ACCEPTING RESERVATIONS

The reservation system is covered in chapter 1.

**Cades Cove.** At the western end of Laurel Creek Rd. on Cades Cove. Mid-May to Oct $17 per site; Nov to mid-May $14. 159 sites; RVs and tents. Dump station; store and bike rental.

This large, flat campground among widely spaced shade trees is a center of activity at this end of the park. It has a store (open in the summer only), ranger station, and stable. If you spend a couple of nights here, you can cover the Cades Cove Loop on rented bikes or by car just after dawn or at dusk, when there's little traffic and wildlife is most active. The area also makes a good base for hiking. The sites lack much screening from each other but have gravel tent pads. And the campfire amphitheater is covered—a good idea.

**Elkmont.** 1½ miles up spur from Little River Rd., about 4 miles west of Sugarlands Visitor Center. Mid-May to Oct $17; Nov and Apr to mid-May $14. 220 sites; RVs and tents. Dump station. Closed Dec–Mar.

These grassy sites lie along the Little River under shade trees, without much separating them. River valley walls enclose the area. A nature trail leaves from the campground, as does the **Little River Trail**. It leads 5.1 miles up the valley, connecting with four other trails on the way, and passes some good swimming holes on the Little River. The first is about one-third of a mile beyond the gate.

**Smokemont.** Newfound Gap Rd. (Hwy. 441), near the south entrance of the park. Mid-May to Oct $17 per site; Nov to mid-May $14. 142 sites; tents and RVs up to 27 ft. Dump station.

Along a rocky, rushing stream (the Bradley Fork of the Oconaluftee River), campsites sit in a narrow valley beneath tall trees. It's a perfect setting. A stable for trail rides is nearby, as are several excellent trails. One is the 5.7-mile

**Smokemont Loop,** which comes right back to the campground. It passes by a pioneer cemetery one-third mile back into the woods from the Bradley Fork trailhead end. No other trace remains of the town that once stood where the campground is now.

## FIRST-COME, FIRST-SERVED
## CAMPGROUNDS
**Abrams Creek.** Off Hwy. 72/129, west side of the park. $12 per site. 16 sites; tents or RVs up to 16 ft. Closed Nov to mid-Mar.

Not many find their way down the 7 miles of country roads from the extreme west end of the park to this very lovely spot under the trees. About half of the sites are right on clear Abrams Creek, a very welcoming spot for a dip. The campground also makes a promising spot to start a family backpacking trip, because several loops are possible from two different trailheads with campsites closely spaced. Abrams Falls is about 5 miles and Cades Cove 7.5.

**Balsam Mountain.** About 7 miles up Heintooga Ridge Rd. from Blue Ridge Pkwy., north of Hwy. 19. $14 per site. 46 sites; tents or RVs. Closed Oct to mid-May.

This is the park's only mountaintop campground, at 5,310 feet. It's an old campground (the bathrooms are built of stone), and the sites, while grassy, are unscreened. The trees are small and bushy. Firewood is for sale on the honor system. The beautiful **Flat Creek Trail** follows the ridge and creek south, reaching two-tiered Flat Creek Falls after 1½ miles. The Heinooga Road to the campground from the parkway is paved, but from here onward one-way Balsam Mountain Road is a one-lane adventure, weaving through the woods to meet remote trailheads at the start of some backpacking loops. I thought the road looked like a better mountain-biking route than drive. Open only in summer, the road ends at Big Cove Road, behind Cherokee.

**Big Creek.** Off Rte. 32, near I-40 Exit 451. $12 per site. 12 sites; tents only. Closed Nov to mid-Mar.

This is a remote-feeling backwoods campground that's quite accessible, just off the interstate. All sites are walk-in, but unlike walk-in sites at most campgrounds are close together. Many front on the creek, which has a good swimming spot, and all have gravel tent pads. An unpaved road runs through the mountains south to Cataloochie, a promising mountain-bike ride or slow drive.

**Cataloochee.** 11 miles up Cove Creek Rd. from the intersection of U.S. 276 and I-40. $12 per site. 27 sites; tents or RVs. Closed Nov to mid-Mar.

The winding, partly unpaved, sometimes muddy road and remote location protect this idyllic internal valley from too many visitors; it's my favorite place at Great Smoky. (Signs are inadequate: Where U.S. 276 exits I-40, turn northwest on Cove Creek Road, then keep the faith until eventually you reach the park.) I've covered the historic buildings, hiking, and mountain biking on p. 170 and 172. The campground itself is flat and shaded, with large sites, about half of which are on a creek. Be sure to stock up, because it's a long drive to a store.

**Cosby.** Off Rte. 32 in the NE corner of the park. $14 per site. 175 sites; tents and RVs up to 25 ft. Dump station. Closed Nov to mid-Mar.

This is a quiet, less-visited area of the park, more than 15 miles east of Gatlinburg, and consequently you can almost always find a site at this large campground on a hillside. There's good ground cover, and the large, well-designed sites are shielded from each other by brush, while shade trees shelter all. Most sites have gravel tent pads. A 1-mile nature trail with a guide brochure is at the campground, and many longer trails radiate from here, with loops suitable for family backpacking. The **Gabes Mountain Trail** starts at the campground and passes Hen Wallow Falls after 2.2 miles. The tiny Park Entrance Grocery is a couple of miles away, but generally the area is quite rural.

**Deep Creek.** West Deep Creek Rd., 2½ miles north of Bryson City. $14 per site. 108 sites; tents and RVs up to 26 ft. Dump station. Closed Nov to early Apr.

The sites in this pleasant campground are on tiers above the creek, like seats in a theater. There are big trees, along with little ones that provide a sense of privacy to some sites. Gravel pads help keep your tent dry. The creek is one of the area's best for inner-tubing, and a superb network of trails, relatively little used, leads from the campground to waterfalls a short distance away and connects to longer backpacking trails. Riding stables and inner-tube rental outlets are nearby, as is a little country store.

**Look Rock.** On Foothills Pkwy. 18 miles from Townsend. $14 per site. 92 sites; tents or RVs. Closed Nov to mid-May.

This exceptional campground is along the scenic ridgetop parkway west of the park. Sites gain total privacy by their distance from the road or a step down in elevation, a clever design that makes use of the ridge location. The sunset views from the tower, a half-mile walk away, or from some of the parkway pull-outs, are unforgettably grand and graceful.

## Forest Service Campgrounds

The Nantahala National Forest's **Cheoah Ranger District** (☎ 828/479-6431) has two campgrounds on the south side of Fontana Lake, west of Bryson City; take Route 19 to Route 28. Sites are first-come, first-served, for tents or RVs.

**Cable Cove.** Forest Rd. 520, 1.4 miles off Rte. 28. $8 per site. 26 sites. Flush toilets; boat ramp.

This grassy campground is quiet and lightly used, with huge sites, many set far back, that are supplied with tent pads.

**Tsali.** Forest Rd. 521, 1½ miles off Rte. 28. $15 per site. 42 sites. Flush toilets, showers; boat ramp.

Fifteen miles west of Bryson City, this very attractive, grassy campground is set among rhododendrons, maples, and other broadly separated trees. Sites are far apart and have

tent pads. Showers are included in the price. Four highly rated single-track mountain-biking trails nearby network 40 miles through the woods; their use carries a $2 fee. The lake is popular for fishing and boating.

## Backcountry Camping Permits

To camp along the trail on a backpacking or horseback-riding trip, you need a free backcountry permit. It couldn't be much easier to get. The first step is to get the Park Service's *Great Smoky Mountains Trail Map,* which costs $1 and includes trail mileage, permit rules, and campsite locations. Before you go, the backcountry office (☎ 865/436-1297) will send you a copy of the trail map free, which you pay for on the honor system. (Trail guides and better maps are listed under "Reading Up," p. 155.) There are about 100 backcountry sites and 16 three-sided shelters in the park. The shelters, along the Appalachian Trail, are in high demand. You can reserve shelters and some campsites—those shown on the map in red—by calling the **backcountry office** (☎ 865/436-1231) up to a month in advance. If you just want information but aren't ready to reserve, call ☎ 865/436-1297. It's open daily from 8am to 6pm.

The great majority of campsites, shown in green on the map, are open without

---

### PARK CAMPING BASICS: TOILETS, SHOWERS & LAUNDRY

All the campgrounds have flush toilets, even the small ones, but only the **Tsali Campground** in Nantahala National Forest has showers. On the north side of the park, you can take a shower and wash your clothes at **Compton's Laundry,** 1231 East Pkwy., Gatlinburg (☎ 865/436-2103). On the south side, you'll find laundry machines at the **Washpot** (☎ 828/497-4932) in the Frontier Shopping Center in Cherokee.

reservations. There's enough room at each campsite for several parties, and no need for rationing. If you plan to use only those sites, you can self-register at any ranger station or visitor center when you arrive. Be sure to read up on the regulations on avoiding bears, storing food, and other issues on the back of the Park Service map. Also see "Backpacking" (p. 170).

## Commercial Campgrounds

### CHEROKEE

Big Cove Road, which leaves Cherokee to the northeast, has a series of campgrounds in a wooded river valley. You can drive along the road and take your choice. The two I've listed are at opposite ends of the road, and opposite ends of the range between natural and developed camping.

**Cherokee KOA Kampground.** Big Cove Rd. (S.R. Box 39), Cherokee, NC 28719. ☎ 800/825-8352 or 828/497-9711. Fax 828/497-6776. www.cherokeekoa.com. Full hookups $37–$42 for 2, tent sites $30–$35; $5 per extra adult, children under 17 free. Lower rates off-season. 420 sites. Showers, store, pool, hot tub, playground, tennis, volleyball, basketball, activity center, game room, trout fishing ponds.

This is a true camping resort with enough activities to keep you entertained for a good part of your vacation. They've got everything found at the fanciest resort campgrounds, plus some I haven't seen elsewhere, such as an adults-only center with a big-screen TV and dataports. The campground is in a nice spot, too, on a river where the family can go inner-tubing. It even serves meals, has a tour desk, and has a bus to town. Don't look here for a natural camping experience, however, because it feels more like a camping city. For not much more than the cost of a campsite, 106 camping cabins are for rent.

**Indian Creek Campground.** Bunches Creek Rd., off Big Cove Rd. (S.R. Box 75A), Cherokee, NC 28719. ☎ 828/497-4361. indiancreek campground.com. Tent sites $20, full hookups $22 for 2 people; $4 per extra adult, $1 children 4–18.

70 sites. Showers, laundry, store, playground. Closed Dec–Feb.

At the confluence of two creeks below steep mountains, with trout fishing right from a few secluded sites, this thickly wooded campground is more like what you usually find inside a park than a commercial operation. Ask for the kind of site you want, because they range in quality. It's run by a family and has a relaxed country feel. It's also more than 8 miles from town. Trailers and cabins are for rent, too.

### GATLINBURG

**Twin Creek RV Resort.** U.S. 321, 2 miles east of Galinburg (P.O. Box 1395), Galinburg, TN 37738. ☎ 800/252-8077 or 865/436-7081. www. twincreekrvresort.com. $35 full hookup site for 2, $4 each additional person over age 3. RVs only. Pool, whirlpool, playground.

The campground is near enough to Gatlinburg to be on the trolley route, but the peaceful streamside grounds are a world away from the tourist bustle there. The grounds are lovingly landscaped, more like a pleasure garden than a campground, and each paved site has its own seating deck. Hookups include cable TV. The pool and children's pool are both large. They don't accept tenters.

### TOWNSEND

**Tremont Hills Campground and Log Cabins.** Hwy. 73 at the park entrance (P.O. Box 5), Townsend, TN 37882. ☎ 800/448-6373 or 865/448-6363. www.tremontcamp.com. Full hookups $28–$32, tent sites $16–$19 for 2 people; $2 per extra person, children under 5 free. 150 sites. Showers, laundry, pool, children's pool, store, playground, game room, basketball.

This beautifully maintained grassy campground overlooks the Little River right at the park entrance, only 7 miles from Cades Cove. It's an unspoiled area, but close to other businesses. You can go fishing and inner-tubing nearby. The pleasant cabins are reasonably priced, with full kitchens and fireplaces.

# HOTELS & CABINS

I've listed only summer rates below; off-season rates drop in a somewhat unpredictable pattern. Some places have just two seasonal rate schedules; others have complicated schemes with rates that rise and fall as occupancy changes by the week. Generally, lows are two-thirds to one-half of summer rates. October rates might be $10 higher than summer rates. Weekends often carry a premium, too.

## In the Park

**LeConte Lodge.** On top of Mt. LeConte, 5 miles up the Alum Cave Trail (and other trails). ☎ **865/429-5704.** 15 cabins and rms. $78.50 per adult, $63.50 children ages 4–10, free 3 and under. Price includes all meals. No credit cards. Closed mid-Nov to mid-Mar.

There's no more beautiful or authentic lodging than these log cabins looking out from the top of the park's third-highest peak, but to get here you have to climb the mountain. The spectacular 5-mile hike up the **Alum Cave Trail** is crowded at first, then thins out over the 2,500-foot climb. Trails radiate from the lodge. When I visited, they were getting ready for the season, lowering cases of Chardonnay from a helicopter; it's $7 for a bottomless glass. (Llamas also bring in goods.)

The cabins are rugged but perfect, with wooden bedsteads and kerosene lanterns that the pioneers would recognize. Flush toilets are in a central building, but there are no showers. Meals are family-style Southern cooking—chipped beef and gravy, cornbread, grits, and so on. Reservations open for the following year October 1 and are full within a few weeks.

## Gatlinburg

This gateway town has 6,500 motel rooms, with some chains represented several times. More are nearby. Except for holiday weekends, you should have no trouble finding a budget room. Cabins are for rent in the area, too, so you can get out of the bustle of town.

**Whitlock's Mountain Rentals,** P.O. Box 1565, Gatlinburg, TN 37738 (☎ **800/972-2246**), has cabins east of town with many amenities renting for $125 a night in summer.

**Best Western Twin Islands Motel.** 539 Pkwy., Gatlinburg, TN 37738. ☎ **800/223-9299** or 865/436-5121. Fax 865/436-6208. www.ogles properties.com. 113 units. $100–$130 for up to 4 people. AE, CB, DC, DISC, MC, V.

The hotel occupies an island on Little Pigeon River, which surrounds the motel, but stands right in the center of town, saving guests all the parking and traffic hassles. In the middle of the island, the motel's landscaped courtyard has a protected feeling, with a pool, a playground, covered picnic tables, and barbecue grills. Around the edge, kids can play in the water and anglers can catch the regularly stocked trout. Rooms were comfortable, attractively decorated, and quite clean on my visit. All have refrigerators and coffeemakers and other such amenities, and the better rooms are quite posh. There are a restaurant and a coin-op laundry on-site, and more restaurants are a block away. The same people rent the **Laurel Estate** log cabins 4 miles out of town.

**Gatlinburg Holiday Inn SunSpree Resort.** 520 Historic Nature Trail, Gatlinburg, TN 37738. ☎ **800/435-9201** or 865/436-9201. www. 4lodging.com. 400 units. High season, $99 double; children 12 and under stay free. AE, CB, DC, DISC, JCB, MC, V.

These are good, standard American hotel rooms, decorated with attractive fabrics and wallpaper borders, with good-sized bathrooms, and extras such as small refrigerators, coffeemakers, and hair dryers. The newer rooms are larger and lighter. The common areas and the program for families are exceptional. The hotel has three pools (two indoors) and a 1-foot toddler pool, an arcade, table tennis, barbecue grills, and picnic tables. A park is nearby, and the Little Caesar's pizzeria on-site delivers to the rooms. When you stay on the grounds during the summer, the staff will take the children off your hands for games, arts and crafts, nature hikes, pajama parties, and all sorts of summer-camp fun. There's a sit-down restaurant too.

**Mountain Loft Resort.** 110 Mountainloft Dr., Gatlinburg, TN 37738. ☎ **800-456-0009** or 865/436-4367. www.mountainloft.com. 266 units. $109–$249 per unit. AE, DISC, MC, V.

On a hill just east of Gatlinburg, the resort consists of a wooded condo development in freestanding chalets and apartment-like units in larger buildings. It's all new and lavishly furnished and decorated, with every amenity of a quality home, including laundry machines, full kitchens, VCRs, stereos, whirlpools, and so on. The least expensive units are the equivalent of a luxurious hotel suite and sleep 4, renting for $109 a night; the largest sleep 10. A clubhouse has indoor and outdoor pools.

## Townsend

**Talley Ho Inn.** 8314 State Hwy. 73, Townsend, TN 37882. ☎ **800/448-2465** or 865/448-2465. www.talleyhoinn.com. 46 rms, 1 cottage. $49–$72 double; $5 per extra person, children 12 and under free. AE, DC, DISC, MC, V. Closed Dec–Feb.

In a quiet town on expansive grounds just outside the park, a family has kept this group of motel buildings well-maintained and landscaped for more than 40 years. Rooms include basic motel rooms, cozy ones with big brick fireplaces, others with terraces, plus a four-bedroom cottage. There are an outdoor pool, tennis courts, and a family restaurant, open in the summer only.

## Cherokee

Near the park entrance on U.S. 441, the **Best Western Great Smokies Inn** (☎ **828/497-2020;** www.bestwesterncherokee.com) has a nicely landscaped courtyard with a pool and children's pool and large room for $90 double in the high season. Some of the best rooms in Cherokee are at a group of chain hotels on Highway 19 west of town. The **Comfort Inn** (☎ **800/228-5150** or 828/497-2411; www. comfortinn.com) has rooms overlooking the Oconaluftee River for $85–$95 in the high

season. The **Holiday Inn of Cherokee** (☎ **800/HOLIDAY** or 828/497-9181; www. hicherokee.com), across the road, has large indoor and outdoor pools, a laundry, and newly remodeled rooms with lots of extras. They go for $89 on summer weekdays, $10 more on weekends.

## Bryson City

This town has a lot of authentic Southern character and plenty to do nearby. The kids will have to behave if you stay at one of these historic inns, but unlike most of what you find around the park, it won't be a plastic experience.

**Folkstone Inn.** 101 Folkstone Rd., Bryson City, NC 28713. ☎ **888/812-3385** or 828/488-2730. Fax 828/488-0722. www.folkstoneinn.com. 10 rooms. $82–$108 double; $10 per extra adult or child. Rates include breakfast and afternoon wine and cheese. DISC, MC, V.

This welcoming old farmhouse full of antiques could make your trip. It stands in a peaceful country setting one-fourth of a mile from the little-used waterfall trails and inner-tubing at the Deep Creek entrance to the park, 2 miles north of Bryson City. The eager-to-please Snodgrass family serves a two-course breakfast and afternoon wine and cheese, included in the price of charming rooms with quilts, wood floors, and claw-foot tubs. They take only children over 5, and kids need to behave in this genteel setting.

**Fryemont Inn.** Fryemont Rd., off Veterans Blvd. (P.O. Box 459), Bryson City, NC 28713. ☎ **800/845-4879** or 828/488-2159. 32 rms, 1 cabin. $135 double; extra adult $35, extra child 2–10 $18. Rates include breakfast and dinner. DISC, MC, V. Main lodge closed Thanksgiving–Easter.

On a hill above Bryson City, thickly shrouded in eastern hemlock, the bark-covered exterior immediately takes you back to 1923, when the inn started operation. Inside, an authentic nostalgic sense hangs over the wood floors and walls; I couldn't get over the beloved scent of my grandmother's house, and women who looked a lot like her were taking tea in the parlor. Each room is different, with furniture that ranges from antique to just plain old. Most are quite old, especially a four-bed suite. They lack air-conditioning or television. There's an outdoor pool among the trees. Best of all, sophisticated and traditional southern meals from an extensive menu come with the room; there's a good kids' menu too. You save a lot by staying here. Nonguests are also welcome for dinner.

## Maggie Valley

**Jonathan Creek Inn.** 4324 Soco Rd. (P.O. Box 66), Maggie Valley, NC 28751. ☎ **800/ 577-7812** reservations or 828/926-1232. Fax 828/ 926-9751. www.jonathancreekinn.com. 43 rms, 4 villas. $70 double; $5 per extra adult, kids stay free. AE, MC, V.

Sixteen miles east of Cherokee, near Cataloochee or I-40 on Highway 19, an industrious couple has transformed this roadside motel into a delightful country inn. The rockers, wreaths, decorative borders, quilts, and other warm touches give it a cozy feeling, and the large rooms are a real bargain. Refrigerators, microwaves, coffeemakers, big TVs, and other amenities are standard, and some have fireplaces and Jacuzzis. Kids can play in a playground or the trout-stocked creek that flows out back by the hot tub, or swim in the glass-enclosed pool by the parking lot. For a longer stay, they have four luxurious houses on the other side of the creek, renting by the week for around $1,000.

# WHEN YOU ARRIVE

## ENTRANCE FEES

The Park Service charges no fees to enter the park.

## VISITOR CENTERS

**Sugarlands Visitor Center.** Newfound Gap Rd., 2 miles from Gatlinburg. Summer daily 8am–6pm; winter 8am–4:30pm.

The park's main visitor center has a natural history museum where you can learn about the different life zones and plant communities, with specimens, animal mounts, and written explanations. It can be quite crowded. A film in the brand-new, high-tech theater covers the park's highlights and scenery. It shows on the hour and at 20 and 40 minutes past; admission is 50¢. A well-stocked bookstore and the main backcountry office are here, too.

**Oconaluftee Visitor Center.** Newfound Gap Rd., 1½ miles from the south entrance. Daily 8:30am–4:30pm, varying longer hours in summer.

The visitor center has a small exhibit space and a bookstore. A backcountry office is in an adjoining building, and the Mountain Farm Museum is nearby (p. 168).

## Commercial Visitor Centers

**Gatlinburg Welcome Center.** Hwy. 441 between Pigeon Forge and Gatlinburg. ☎ **865/ 436-0519.** Sun–Thurs 8am–6pm, Fri–Sat 8am–8pm.

Before you plunge into Gatlinburg, you can stop here to pick up information about the park and accommodations in town. A board lists available rooms. There's also a 15-minute orientation film and a bookstore. A trolley runs into Gatlinburg in the summer.

**Cherokee Visitor Center.** Main St. (Hwy. 19), Cherokee. ☎ **800/438-1601** or 828/497-9195. Summer daily 8am–8pm; fall daily 8am–6pm; winter and spring daily 8am–4:30pm.

Pick up brochures and information about attractions and rooms in Cherokee and the rest of the reservation here.

## GETTING AROUND
## By Car

A private car is the only practical way around most of the park for families. The most important thing is to be patient and allow plenty of time, because driving is very slow. Plan your visit carefully to group your activities. If you

**Emergencies**   Call ☎ **911** in emergencies within or outside the park. To reach park dispatch, call ☎ **865/436-1294**; for **Gatlinburg Police**, call ☎ **865/463-5181**, and for **Cherokee Police**, ☎ **828/497-7405**. **Fort Sanders Seier Medical Center** (☎ **865/453-7111**) is in Sevierville on Middle Creek Road, 15 miles north of Gatlinburg; **Swain County Hospital** (☎ **828/488-2155**) is in Bryson City.

**Stores**   **Mountain Market** is on U.S. 441 in Gatlinburg as it enters the park. Huge stores are on the strip in Pigeon Forge, just north of Gatlinburg. In Cherokee, an **IGA** grocery store is near the casino on Highway 19.

**Banks**   ATMs are plentiful in stores in the gateway towns. **Tennessee State Bank** is at Highway 321 East in Gatlinburg. In Cherokee, **First Citizens Bank** is on Highway 441 North.

**Post Offices**   In Gatlinburg, the post office is on Highway 321 near Newman Road. In Cherokee, it's on 441 North (which becomes Newfound Gap Road). The Bryson City post office is on Flote Street.

**Gear Sales & Rental**   In Gatlinburg, the **Happy Hiker** (☎ **865/436-6000**), behind the Burning Bush restaurant, just outside the park entrance on U.S. 441, sells camping gear and rents backpacks. The **Smoky Mountain Angler**, 376 E. Pkwy. (☎ **865/436-8746**), carries fishing gear and offers guided trips. In Pigeon Forge, the **Trailhead**, 912 Wears Valley Rd. (☎ **865/429-1973**), sells and rents bikes and runs tours. On the south side of the park, the **Nantahala Outdoor Center**, 13077 Hwy. 19 W., west of Bryson City (☎ **800/232-7238** rafting, ☎ **888/662-1662** biking; www.noc.com), offers guided river floats and mountain-bikes rides, rents gear for both, and has a full-service bike shop, among other offerings (see "Rafting, " p. 172).

want to see two different areas, plan a longer trip and stay in two different places. Roads and shortcuts are covered on p. 172.

## By Trolley

Various trolleys run routes in Gatlinburg and Pigeon Forge, with fares less than $1.25 per trip. You can pick up route maps at the welcome center. Gatlinburg driving is congested and parking can be difficult.

## By Bike

There are quite a few appealing mountain-biking routes in and near the park (although not on park trails), and on Saturday and Wednesday mornings you can bike Cades Cove without cars; but traffic congestion on the park's main roads limits the utility of bikes for transportation. See "Mountain Biking" (p. 172) for recreational biking.

## KEEPING SAFE & HEALTHY

In addition to the particulars below, see "Dealing with Hazards," in chapter 1, for information on giardia, hypothermia, lightning, Lyme disease, and poison ivy. A black bear killed a hiker at Great Smoky in 2000, the first such death ever in a national park, so it's time to take bear avoidance seriously here.

## Carsickness

If you are susceptible, you're likely to get carsick on twisting, tree-shaded roads such as Little River Road to Cades Cove (avoid some of it by going through Townsend) and many of the country roads. U.S. 129, at the west end of the park, is understandably world famous for its crazy curves. Newfound Gap Road has a few wiggles, too. Other than avoiding these segments, which is only partly possible, prepare kids by administering children's chewable Dramamine an hour before setting out (see "Seasickness & Motion Sickness," in chapter 1).

## Yellow Jacket Stings

These wasps live in the ground, and stepping on a nest can mean a lot of painful stings from a swarm. Stings can cause horrible swelling and, if you get enough of them, illness. Benadryl and other antihistamines help with the swelling. Extreme symptoms mean that you need to see a doctor immediately, because allergic sting reactions can quickly be fatal. (See "Sting Allergies," in chapter 1.)

# ENJOYING THE PARK

## NATURAL PLACES
### The Cove Hardwoods

The coves, or valleys, at the foot of the Smokies feed their forests with the perfect mixture of dampness, warmth, and soil to grow trees and plants fast and fancy. The trees are tall, roofing over the land with a high green canopy, and come in an amazing variety. If you're not from around here, hiking through these woods is full of surprises and wonder. You'll see brand-new trees and plants, or kinds that you have seen before only in botanical gardens, not wild woodlands. In the spring, everything seems to flower. Near openings and streams, the brush is thicker than in the full shadow of the trees, with huge rhododendrons, twining wild grapes, and other jungle-like growth. The forest can feel truly enchanted.

A handy and inexpensive map-guide published by the Great Smoky Mountains Natural History Association (see "Great Smoky Address Book," p. 151) shows where old-growth and selectively cut forests survive in the park, and which trails lead through them to the different forest types. There are lots of ways into the rich cove hardwoods. Five miles up Newfound Gap from the north end, the **Cove Hardwood Nature Trail** is a loop less than 1 mile long.

A 4-mile trail rises 2,000 feet through some huge old-growth tulip trees and other cove hardwoods to Ramsay Cascades, the park's highest waterfall. The **Ramsay Cascade Trail** also leads past swimming holes on the Little Pigeon River. The trailhead is on Greenbrier Road, off Highway 321, 6 miles east of Gatlinburg. Like other waterfall trails, it is among the park's busiest. One less-used trail leads to an old-growth forest of enormous cove hardwoods, including a tulip tree 25 feet around: the **Albright Grove Loop.** The loop starts about 3 miles up the Maddron Bald Trail, 15.4 miles east of Gatlinburg on Highway 321 (turn on Laurel Springs Road). After hiking along an old farm road and past a farm cabin and overgrown fields, you reach the ancient primeval forest of huge mossy trees, a natural spiritual refuge.

You needn't stick to these trails to see cove hardwoods, however; indeed, they cover much of the park, and many trails pass through them for great distances.

### The Pine-Oak Forest

Higher in the hills above the cove hardwoods, where the weather is a bit colder and the soil drier on the western and southern slopes, a forest of oaks and pines grows. Pines are the first to grow on land disturbed by fire. Trees like the Table Mountain pine open their cones in the heat of fire and need soil cleared by flames to get started. After 50 or 60 years, if not renewed by fire, these trees grow old and oaks begin to fill in where they decline.

Trails in the southwestern part of the park, where the land is the driest, pass through more of this kind of forest, but you might encounter it in patches on many trails. The **Abrams Falls Trail,** starting on the west end of Cades Cove and going 2½ miles one way along Abrams Creek to the falls, rises and falls gently from pine-oak ridges to thick hemlock and rhododendron by the creek. It ends at the wide, roaring falls. The trail can be crowded.

## The Mountaintops & Balds

High in the Smokies you can look down on ridges that tangle like tree roots, spreading out into the dim distance. Clouds wash against the green mountainsides like a rising flood, white mist seeping into the valleys between the ridges. At the top, the air is crisp and smells fresh—your head clears from the scent of sleepy rot you smelled among the big trees down below—and the sky opens among rocks and small spruce and fir trees. At the grassy, brushy mountain balds, big views open in all directions, and in season, flowers shout out to the sky.

The easiest way to the mountaintops is **Newfound Gap Road.** The **Appalachian Trail** meets the road at the ridge of the Smokies. Drive west to Clingmans Dome on a 7-mile spur road (closed in winter) to see sweeping mountain views from a tower that stands at the highest point in the Smokies, 6,642 feet high. The paved, half-mile walk from the parking lot is steep, but the view is well worth it. Some excellent trails lead from the Clingmans Dome and Newfound Gap roads. **The Alum Cave Trail,** on Newfound Gap Road, is gorgeous, but often quite crowded until the steepness weeds out the weaker hikers. For an easy, uncrowded walk, try one of the paths along the road marked Quiet Walkway. These are former road segments. The *Newfound Gap Road Guide* booklet, available at the visitor centers, describes each.

Reaching the summit of a mountain can be a letdown at Great Smoky when you find that the summit is a thick forest with no view, but the balds are great mountain destinations with fine views. For reasons unknown, these areas stayed grassy and open amid the trees (see "The Problems of Restoration," in chapter 6, "Bringing Back the Past"). You can see a long way, feel a cool breeze, and enjoy the sun. The flowers can be extraordinary, especially the flame azaleas blooming in June and July. And,

since it takes some work to get there (you can't drive), these areas are not crowded with cars or people.

**Andrews Bald** is a reasonable family hike, 1.8 miles down a steep and rocky trail from Clingmans Dome Road. The views are sublime and the bald is large and easy to lose yourself in; it's a perfect picnic destination. **Gregory Bald,** above Cades Cove, is an all-day hike or an easy overnight. Two backcountry campsites are nearby. The trail rises 2,500 feet over 4½ miles from Parson Branch Road on the south side of Cades Cove.

## Waterfalls & Streams

Clouds from the Gulf of Mexico float over the south, full of water, then bump up against the Smokies and mist, drip, or slosh down upon its mountainsides. The streams from that water have worn these mountains down from towering peaks to the branched ridges and valleys they are today. On a hot summer day, the streams can be wonderful places to play. Rarely do you find a hole deep or wide enough to swim more than a few strokes, but there are plenty of places to feel the thrill of cold water all over your hot body, splash around, and experience a unique joy. Streams are everywhere; sometimes it's a battle to keep hiking when swimming (see "Inner-Tubing & Swimming," p. 171, for safety and other tips).

Waterfalls happen when a streambed runs from a harder rock to a softer rock. The water wears away the softer rock faster, leaving a drop-off at the place where the harder rock ends. Because of the old and complicated geology of the Smokies, different kinds of rock meet in many places. And so there are many waterfalls. They make good destinations for hikes, and the visitor centers sell an inexpensive map-guide with descriptions of each fall. The popularity of waterfall hikes also means that these are the most crowded trails in the park. The Ramsay Cascade and Abrams Falls trails are described above in this section. Some easy and less-traveled waterfall hikes start in the peaceful Deep Creek area, near Bryson

City, including **Indian Creek Fall, Juney Whank Falls,** and **Toms Branch Falls. Mingo Falls,** on the Cherokee Reservation, is the highest in the area, with a 120-foot drop; to get there, take the first left on Big Cove Road to Mingo Falls Campground, which is less than a quarter mile from the falls. **Hen Wallow Falls** is about 2 miles through old-growth trees from the Cosby Campground, at the east end of the park.

## PLACES FOR LEARNING

**Cades Cove.** West end of Laurel Creek Rd. Visitor center. No phone. Spring–fall daily 9am–6pm; winter daily 9am–4:30pm.

Settlers began clearing trees and building farms in this lovely mountain valley in 1819, when the state of Tennessee got the land from the Cherokee in a treaty. As many as 700 people lived here, and some of their churches and hand-hewn log houses have been saved in an **open-air museum,** arranged around the edge of the fields in the center of the cove. Walking through these buildings and cemeteries is fascinating and ghostly. You can almost hear the ordinary people who lived here. The Park Service leases the pastures for grazing cattle to keep them from going back to the forest. The open vistas and grass make this among the park's best places to see wildlife. Animals are most often seen at morning and dusk.

An **11-mile scenic loop** road circles the cove, passing by buildings and trailheads on the way. A $1 auto tour booklet, available at visitor centers or the start of the loop, explains the sites by number; you need it to understand the tour. At the back of the loop, the **Cades Cove Visitor Center** is a place to ask questions about the cove's history and buy a book. But ask general questions at the ranger station at the Cades Cove Campground rather than taking the slow drive to the visitor center.

The problem with Cades Cove is crowding. The road is one lane, and people tend to stop traffic while they watch deer or look at a cabin. At peak times the loop takes up to 3 hours, without stops—an unbearably slow

pace. The solution is to go early or late in the day, and if the pace is just too slow, take one of the shortcut roads across the pastures. Or rent a bike at the Cades Cove campground. On Saturday and Wednesday before 10am, only bikes are allowed in the Cove. Even at other times, you can have more fun and move faster by going around the cars. Buggy rides or hayrides go through the cove every day, some with rangers along to give commentary (see "Horseback Riding & Hayrides," p. 171). The other alternative, and my preference, is to skip Cades Cove entirely and spend the time instead at Cataloochee, which I cover next.

**Cataloochee.** Cove Creek Rd., off Hwy. 276 (complete directions under the "Cataloochee" campground listing, p. 158).

Up in the mountains at the end of a rough, twisting gravel road, this ghost village is like a version of Cades Cove without crowds. There are pastures great for wildlife viewing and spooky old buildings you can walk through, including cabins, farmhouses, a barn, a church, and a school. One house holds an interesting little museum. Even better, several hiking trails lead into dark hardwood forest past more buildings, including the extraordinary church at Little Cataloochee, several miles beyond where car-bound tourists can see. The narrow, unpaved roads limit driving, but seemed to me like they'd be good mountain-biking routes, especially the road from Big Cataloochee to the Little Cataloochee trailhead, which continues north to Big Creek, on the northeast corner of the park; on maps, it is marked as "Old NC 284."

**Mingus Mill.** Newfound Gap Rd., across from Oconaluftee Visitor Center. Daily 9am–5pm. Closed Nov–Apr.

This working mill grinds corn under a stone powered by creek water passing through a cast-iron turbine propeller that dates to 1886. When I visited, a couple of old guys in overalls were running the machinery and passing the time, much as workers might have 100 years ago. Depending on the volunteers' time,

It's fun to identify trees. Even little kids can learn the difference between a pine, an oak, and a hemlock. As you get better at noticing differences, you can recognize beeches, birches, maples, and magnolias. If you put a little more effort into it, with a good field guide you can puzzle out what kind of pine you are looking at. There are more than 100 types of trees in the Smokies. Eventually, you're bound to ask why there are so many.

Look at the trees and think about what makes them different. Soon you'll notice there are two main groups: trees that drop their leaves in the fall and have flowers in the spring, and trees that stay green all year and have cones. Oak, birch, beech, poplar, magnolia, and maple all drop their leaves and make their seeds with flowers. They are called **deciduous trees. Evergreen trees** look the same all winter and drop their leaves, which we usually call **needles,** only a few at a time, so you don't notice they're gone. Most evergreens are **conifers**—trees that grow their seeds in cones instead of flowers. Pine, spruce, fir, and hemlock are conifers.

By studying fossils of plants, scientists have figured out which kinds came first, and how they developed into the forests we see today. (See "Reading Rock Layers," in chapter 8, "Layers upon Layers," and the sections that follow it, to learn about how they came up with a timeline of life on earth.) **Ferns** came first, around 400 million years ago, and were the main kind of plant on earth for more than 100 million years. Ferns don't have seeds—they grow **spores** that fall off and make another tiny plant. When the new plant gets soaked with water, it develops eggs for a new fern. Around 360 million years ago, some ferns developed with seeds instead of spores. The first conifers showed up about 290 million years ago.

A seed has all the makings of a new plant inside, including the food to get it started. But to make a seed, a plant egg needs to be combined with pollen, or **fertilized.** On conifers, the seed grows in one cone and the pollen in another, smaller cone. The wind blows the pollen to the egg and a seed forms in the cone; then, the cone falls to the ground and sometimes grows into a new tree. Plants and trees that make their seeds with flowers first grew roughly 100 million years ago. Instead of relying on luck for the wind to carry pollen for fertilization from one cone to another, they grow flowers that attract bees and other insects, which carry the pollen from flower to flower. Because the seeds don't need to catch pollen in the wind, the plant can protect them within an ovary so that they won't be eaten by insects.

The development of one kind of plant or animal into a new, more successful kind is called **evolution.** It works this way: Sometimes, by accident, a plant grows with a slight difference from the parent plant—a new fern has seeds instead of spores, for example. The new fern plants its seeds and reproduces, growing more ferns with seeds. If, in a particular place, having seeds helps the new kind of fern reproduce more copies of itself than it could with spores (if seeds work better than

---

the hours and season of operation may be less or more than noted above.

**Mountain Farm Museum.** Newfound Gap Rd., behind the Oconaluftee Visitor Center, at the park's south entrance.

Buildings saved from around the Smokies have been set up in a pasture to show what a pioneer farm might have looked like. When the government bought the land for the park, there were about 1,200 mountain farms in the Smokies. Each was mostly self-sufficient, with family members working together to raise and store grains, vegetables, fruit, and meat. Today, when we rely so much on others to survive, it's interesting to see how you might be able to do it alone. Get the inexpensive guide booklet at the visitor center before starting.

## Cherokee Sites

The Cherokee have created an oasis of meaning in the midst of the exploitative roadside tourist businesses outside the park. These

spores), then over time there will be more and more ferns with seeds. The old, less successful ferns with spores slowly will give up land to the new kind, becoming extinct or surviving only in special places where they still do better than the new kind. Ferns evolved into seed plants, and seed plants into flowering plants, because the new ways worked better.

Today, most of the plants on earth are the kind that came last—the kind that makes seeds with flowers. They produce most of the food we eat and cover most of the land. Ferns and conifers remain mostly in places where they still have an advantage: dark, moist places for most ferns; and high, cold, dark, or dry places for most conifers.

How a plant makes more of itself, or reproduces, is not the only thing that can help it win land from other plants. Anything that allows it to grow stronger or live longer helps it reproduce more. Some scientists think flowering plants took over most of the world because their flowers allowed them to evolve faster and to change and fit their surroundings. That process is called **specialization.** The amazing variety of flowering plants and trees in the coves and low mountainsides of the Smokies—the best growing lands—seems to say that's right. Each plant has evolved to take advantage of its place within a small area thanks to pollination by insects, which take the right kind of pollen to the right kind of flower. These plants might not have been able to specialize as well if they had had to count on the wind to move the pollen.

Leafy, deciduous trees evolved a trick that works well in places with big differences in the weather between winter and summer. In the summer, when there is plenty of sun and warmth to help them grow, they open big, flat leaves that catch a lot of energy and turn it into food. When cold weather comes, with less light and with snow and ice that could break branches, they lose their leaves and become dormant. That ability gave them a big advantage over the conifers, and they took over the best growing areas.

Conifers evolved to make the most of the areas that are left over, including most of the western United States. Many grow in a Christmas tree shape that helps them hold a lot of snow without breaking so that they can survive high in the mountains. Some do well in areas where forest fires often burn, although deciduous trees might take over if the fires are continually extinguished. On mountaintops and places where the wind blows all the time, conifers have advantages over most deciduous trees, because their needles don't blow off. In places where conditions allow them to grow very tall, as hemlocks do in protected rain forests in the Pacific Northwest or stream valleys in the Smokies, conifers shade the ground, so deciduous trees cannot grow.

When you identify a tree, also try to figure out what makes it special so that it can grow in the particular place where you found it.

three sites are on the reservation just outside the south park entrance.

**Museum of the Cherokee Indian.** 589 Tsali Blvd. (Hwy. 441 and Drama Rd.), Cherokee. ☎ **828/497-3481.** June–Aug Mon–Sat 9am–8pm, Sun 9am–5pm; Sept–May daily 9am–5pm. $8 adults, $5 children 6–12.

The museum uses technology and artifacts to effectively put you in a place and time, following the Cherokee story from the deep past and through the Trail of Tears. I'd be surprised if

the experience of the exhibit doesn't inspire tears in many visitors. It starts with a 5-minute film on the creation myth in a mock campfire circle, so you may have to wait a few minutes.

**Oconaluftee Indian Village.** Off U.S. 441 North, Cherokee. ☎ **828/497-2315,** or 828/497-2111 off-season. www.oconalufteevillage.com. $12 adults, $5 children 6–13. Daily 9am–5:30pm. Closed late Oct to late May.

Cherokee guides lead visitors on a 1-hour tour through a shady re-creation of a 1750s village, stopping to look in the buildings and see demonstrations of traditional crafts and life-ways; the kids on our tour were fascinated by the blow gun. It's nicely done and well worth the hour, although the expense of the admission price may exclude those without a particular interest in the Cherokee.

**Unto These Hills.** Off U.S. 441 North, Cherokee. ☎ 866/554-4557 or 828/497-2111. www.oconalufteevillage.com. $16 reserved seating, all ages; $14 adults, $6 ages 6–13 general admission. Performances mid-June to late August 8:30pm.

This is a huge summer outdoor drama telling the story of the Cherokee from the arrival of De Soto in 1540 to the Trail of Tears. (see "History & Culture: Whose Land Is This?" in chapter 6). The drama has run since 1950.

## ACTIVITIES
## Backpacking

Great Smoky is a good place for beginning or advanced backpackers. Beginners can plan short days, because there are plenty of campsites, many of them close together. Backcountry permits are easy to get without advance reservations (see p. 159). Cold weather is rare in summer and fall, and although climbing a mountain with a backpack on a hot summer day is sweaty work, you can usually stop and dunk yourself in a creek to cool off. Spring-break temperatures are perfect for backpacking, although it's often muddy at the top. In any season, count on rain and mist, and be prepared to hike through it. The park's trails include many loops, so you can plan a trip that returns to your car without covering the same trail twice. Volunteer rangers in the backcountry office are helpful in choosing a route, but I recommend preparing before you leave home with the superb trail guide mentioned under "Reading Up" (p. 155). Opportunities for guided backpacking in groups with naturalists and outdoors experts are described under "Programs" (p. 173). However you go, read up on how to avoid black bears, which are common in the Smokies and can be dangerous. The park uses food-hanging cables at the backcountry campsites, so you will need a bag to put your food in and a way to attach it to the hook. Keep everything with any odor hanging on the cable. See "Dangerous Wildlife," in chapter 1, for more on bear safety.

## Fishing

Anglers go for rainbow, brown, and rare Southern brook trout in Smoky's streams. Keeping brook trout is not allowed. The truth is, the fishery isn't very productive. Experienced locals might do well, but tourists spend a lot of time flogging the water. That's okay if you enjoy standing for hours on the edge of a sparkling mountain stream under huge, waving trees, but children might lose patience. A fishing license from either Tennessee or North Carolina is good anywhere in the park; you also need a special permit for the Cherokee reservations or the town of Gatlinburg. Get a list of regulations at a visitor center. Licenses are widely available. See "For Handy Reference" (p. 164) for information on gear.

For easy kids' fishing, **Cooper Creek Trout Farm** (☎ 828/488-6836) gives you the gear, cleans the fish, and charges $3 a pound for what you catch. Take Cooper Creek Road off Highway 19 between Cherokee and Bryson City; it's open March to October 10am to 6pm, November 10am to 5pm; closed December to February.

## Hiking

Smoky is one of the great hiker's parks, with many hundreds of miles of trails through fairy-tale forests with few other people in evidence. Despite the great numbers of visitors, only 30% ever leave their cars, and only 5% of that number go beyond certain popular trails that total about 20 miles—famous routes and short paths to waterfalls. Starting out on a hike early one morning, I had the Alum Cave Trail to myself, returning around midday to the trailhead surrounded by dozens of people struggling upward in the hot sun in an almost solid line. After the delicate scent of spring flowers and mountain air up the trail, I thought I would choke on the thick odor of after-shave and perfume. On another trip, I chose a more obscure trail and never encountered another hiker; indeed, at points the trail was overgrown. Yet the hike was beautiful. I came to a gorgeous waterfall, an abandoned rail trestle, and many more swimming holes than I could use. The lesson: Hike early on popular trails or choose less-known routes. Choosing an uncrowded trail is made much easier by a book called *Hiking Trails of the Great Smokies* (see "Reading Up," p. 155), which indexes hikes by popularity as well as other ways. In fact, it's the best trail guide I've ever come across. Each trail description is a thoughtful essay on its area's nature and history, as well as a lode of practical advice. You'll also need a map, also covered under "Reading Up."

I've described several trails elsewhere in this chapter: the Little River Trail at Elkmont Campground (p. 157), the Smokemont Loop Trail at the Smokemont Campground (p. 157), the Flat Creek Trail at Balsam Mountain Campground (p. 158), the Gabes Mountain Trail at Cosby Campground (p. 158), the Alum Cave Trail under LeConte Lodge (p. 161), the Ramsay Cascade Trail and Albright Grove Loop under "The Cove Hardwoods" (p. 165), Abrams Falls Trail under "The Pine-Oak Forest" (p. 165), Andrews Bald and Gregory Bald trails under "The Mountaintops & Balds" (p. 166), and Cataloochee trails (p. 167).

## Horseback Riding & Hayrides

About half of the trails at Smoky are open to horses, and five stables offer scheduled day trips in the park for families with children ages 5 and up. Charges are around $15 for a 1-hour ride, $28 to $35 for 2 hours, $50 to $65 for 4 hours, $100 for all day. At **Cades Cove,** ½-hour horse-drawn buggy rides and 2-hour tractor-drawn hayrides let you see, with younger children or nonriders, some of the

area as the settlers did. Some hayrides have rangers along to give commentary. Hayrides are $6, buggies $8 per person. The cove's trails are flat, so the stable allows children under 5 to ride horseback in front of their parents, as long as their combined weight is less than 250 pounds. Call the **Cades Cove Stables,** at the General Store at Cades Cove (☎ 865/ 448-6286), for reservations.

The friendly folks at **McCarter Stables,** near the Sugarlands Visitor Center (☎ 865/ 436-5354), have been operating in the same family since 1931. Their steep trails require riders to be 200 pounds or less, and they don't take reservations. The **Smokemont Stables** are near the campground of the same name on the North Carolina side (☎ 828/497-2373). **Smoky Mountain Riding** (☎ 865/436- 5634) is a few miles east of Gatlinburg on Highway 321; their weight limit is 225. **Deep Creek Riding Stables** (☎ 828/488-8504) is at the Deep Creek Campground, near Bryson City, where you can ride to the waterfalls. All close for the winter months.

## Inner-Tubing & Swimming

Few ways of spending a hot summer afternoon could be more fun than floating down a creek on an inner tube—or "tubing," as they call it around here. There are no rules about where you can swim or tube in the park, but use your common sense. For tubing, it's wisest to go where you see others; even at popular spots you can get banged up, so going where you aren't sure of the conditions is foolhardy. Many businesses and campgrounds outside the park rent or sell tubes on streams where you can jump right in. You'll need a swimsuit, lifejackets for kids, and shoes you can get wet. Perhaps the best spot for really wild tubing is at **Deep Creek,** near Bryson City. The lower portion near the campground is reasonable, but if you want real white water, losing your tube and getting bumped around, you can hike a mile higher. The **Deep Creek Tube Center** (☎ 828/488-6055; www.kiz.com/ deepcreek) is one of the operators there, with tubes and changing rooms, charging $3 to $5 a day. As the summer wears on and water levels subside, tubing becomes more difficult; at Deep Creek, good tubing lasts from April through June and possibly July.

For swimming, almost any inviting pool or hole in a slow-moving river will do. I've mentioned swimming holes all through the chapter, especially with the campgrounds, but it's really unnecessary to plan around a particular spot. Few spots are big enough to really swim, but many creeks have holes as big and deep as a large hot tub, enough to cool down and splash around. The season does make a difference, however, so it's a good idea to stop at a visitor center and ask about water conditions. Never swim in the seemingly appealing pools under waterfalls, because they often have strong currents that can pull you into danger. Of course, there are no lifeguards.

## Mountain Biking

Bicycles are not permitted on trails, but the park is rich in one-lane dirt roads through the mountains where you can ride as sunlight flashes through the leaves of overhanging trees. I've mentioned Balsam Mountain Road with the Balsam Mountain Campground (p. 158) and the route in the east of the park known as Old NC 284 in Cataloochee (p. 167). A route over Forge Creek and Parson Branch roads leads from the south side of the Cades Cove Loop, in the west end of the park, over Hannah Mountain to twisty U.S. 129. On any of these rides, you will need to either backtrack or have someone pick you up on the other end, because families shouldn't ride in the traffic of the paved roads. The most unusual of the park's bike routes is the scenic **Lake View Drive,** better known as "the road to nowhere." It leads from Bryson City partway around the north side of Fontana Lake and through a 1,100-foot-long tunnel before ending at the point construction had reached when environmental concerns halted the project in the 1960s. I've covered biking in Cades Cove itself on p. 157. Outside the park, the national forests have famous single-track trails where bikes are allowed. The **Nantahala National Forest** near Bryson City offers many choices, including the 40-mile trail network near the Tsali Campground (p. 159). Shops offering bike rental and guided outings are listed under "For Handy Reference" (p. 164), of which Nantahala Outdoor Center is the best established and nearest to these trails.

## Rafting

There's no rafting within the park, but you'll find good rides outside its boundaries. The **Nantahala Outdoor Center** (see "For Handy Reference," p. 164) is the region's best-established service and something of an institution in the Bryson City area. It offers trips on five different rivers every day during the season. Relatively easy floats on the Nantahala River are for beginners, but still have class III rapids; children must weigh at least 60 pounds. You can rent a raft and gear for the run for around $20. The guided 3-hour trips cost around $30. You can ride one way on the Smoky Mountain Railroad and raft back for $69 adults, $54 ages 12 and under. At the other end of the spectrum, ferocious water and overnights on the Chattooga River are for fit adults and teenagers only and cost considerably more. The center also offers canoe and kayak instruction and mountain-bike rentals and trips; rents cabins; and has showers, laundry, and three restaurants on-site.

## Wildlife Watching

The best places to see wildlife are in open areas where you have a wide field of vision and where there's grass and undergrowth for animals to eat: **Cades Cove, Cataloochee,** and **the balds.** You're most likely to see deer, woodchucks, other small mammals, and wild turkeys. More than 1,000 black bears live in the park, more than the natural habitat can easily support. Visitors see the bears mostly in the spring when they're looking for food after hibernating. In June, they head into the hills and woods. In October, more sightings occur

The woods and stream banks are places to play together. If you're looking for play facilities, there's a **city park** in Gatlinburg on the hill above Historic Nature Trail; take that road uphill, turn right on Cherokee Orchard, and then turn right again on Asbury Way. In Bryson City, the **Swain County Recreation Park** is a family facility on the way to the park's Deep Creek Campground with a pool, playgrounds, tennis, and basketball. The pool fee is under $2. For information, call the county parks department at ☎ **828/488-6159.** There are many picnic grounds in the park, marked on the official park map. Some of them, on the main roads, are huge areas with dozens of tables and bathrooms with flush toilets.

again as the bears fatten up for hibernation. Be careful to avoid attracting bears with food odors. Prepare for bear encounters by reading "Dangerous Wildlife," in chapter 1.

# PROGRAMS
## Children's Programs

The park has a **Junior Ranger** program for kids ages 5 to 12, although those on the younger end of the range will need help reading and completing some of the activities. Buy the $1 workbook at a visitor center. Children complete the pages (some teach natural history, some don't), pick up trash, and attend a ranger-led program; they then present the work at any visitor center to receive a Junior Ranger badge.

## Family & Adult Programs
### PARK SERVICE

During the summer and fall, rangers lead an excellent program of hikes; talks on flowers, forests, birding, and other natural history topics; history walks and talks; films; and so on. Children can go along, if you think they'll be

interested in the topic. Many programs start from the Sugarlands Visitor Center, with something always about to start in season. Others start at trailheads or other areas around the park. The schedule is published in the *Smokies Guide* park newspaper, available for 25¢ at the visitor centers. The programs are free, and there's no need to sign up in advance.

Rangers also offer evening **campfire programs** at Elkmont, Cades Cove, Smokemont, Cosby, Deep Creek, and Balsam Mountain campgrounds. Check the park newspaper for times.

**Smoky Mountain Field School.** The University of Tennessee Professional and Personal Development, 600 Henley St., Suite 105, Knoxville, TN 37996-4110. ☎ **865/974-0150.** www.outreach.utk.edu/smoky.

The University of Tennessee and the Park Service offer a full catalog of 1-day classes and multiple-day outdoor learning expeditions March through November. Most are open only to adults, but on many summer weekends, there are programs especially for families. Sessions might cover subjects like mountain life and song or reptiles and amphibians. They cost around $22 for adults, $14 for children 6 to 12. Check the catalog online to find out what's on when you'll be visiting.

## Summer Camps
**Great Smoky Mountains Institute at Tremont.** 9275 Tremont Rd., Townsend, TN 37882. ☎ **865/448-6709.** www.nps.gov/grsm/tremont.htm.

The institute, with dormitories and classrooms in a mountain valley in the northwest part of the park, offers intensive sessions for adults all year, and summer camps for ages 9 to 17 during the summer. Campers backpack in the park, do fun activities, and learn from naturalists. The National Wildlife Federation offers some sessions. Some 5-day camps, for ages 9 to 12 or 13 to 17, are less than $300. Reserve well ahead.

# Fun Outside the Park

## Gatlinburg

The Gatlinburg area is a prime habitat for water parks, country music theaters, freak museums, go-cart tracks (outdoor and indoor), bumper boats, bungee jumping, an aerial tram, and the most amazing variety of mini-golf courses I've ever seen. The attractions are unlimited, and I don't doubt many are fun; but they're just a distraction from the park, and I found it a relief to escape the carnival atmosphere. Get information at the welcome center or the Gatlinburg Chamber of Commerce (see "Great Smoky Address Book," p. 151).

## Cherokee

The museums and performance operated by the Cherokee are covered on p. 168.

## Bryson City/Dillsboro

The **Great Smoky Mountains Railroad** (☎ **800/872-4681** or 828/586-8811) operates excursion trips around the mountainous countryside every day of the season. Many are pulled by a steam engine. Special trains include dinner trains and a river-rafting train that goes to the Nantahala Outdoor Center (see "Rafting," p. 172). Fares start at $28 for a 3½-hour ride, half price for children 3 to 12. Request a timetable in advance (☎ **800/872-4681,** ext. R; www.gsmr.com).

# Where to Eat

## North Side of the Park
### Low-Stress Meals

In Gatlinburg and Pigeon Forge, you can get any kind of franchised fast food you might want. On U.S. 441 as it enters Gatlinburg, you'll find **Pizza Hut, McDonald's,** and **Applebee's,** a chain pub restaurant that also treats children well. Across the street from Applebee's, **Atrium Pancakes** (☎ **907/430-3584**) is a good version of a very common type around here, the friendly, bustling breakfast place. The name owes to the two glass-sided dining rooms. Breakfast is $4.25 to $7.50, lunch $2.75 to $6.75. They're open 7am to 3pm.

### Best-Behavior Meals

**Burning Bush Restaurant.** 1151 Parkway, just before the park entrance in Gatlinburg. ☎ **865/436-4669.** Breakfast $8–$12, lunch $6.50–$9, dinner $14–$23, children's menu $4. Summer daily 8am–9pm; winter 8am–8pm.

Finches flittering about in glass cases perfectly accent the stylish dinning rooms, each for a different mood, arranged throughout this large restaurant. It's an oasis in Gatlinburg, especially the atrium that looks out into a woodland scene in the park, which starts here. The menu varies in price and style, with dinners of trout, beef, ham, various kinds of poultry, and seafood prepared as Southern or ethnic cuisine. My meals have been excellent and service has been both warm and perfect.

## South Side of the Park
### Cherokee

Cherokee has plenty of places to get fast food, including **Dairy Queen, McDonald's,** and **Big Boy** restaurants just outside the park, and there are many casual coffee shops; but I never found a place that got me excited. **Myrtle's Table,** in the Best Western Great Smokies Inn (☎ **828/497-2020**), is a comfortable place, decorated with squared log walls. **Pizza Inn** (☎ **828/497-9143**), near the visitor center, is a typical family pizzeria, and has a lunch buffet. The **Holiday Inn,** on Route 19 heading west (☎ **828/497-9181**), has a pleasant restaurant, the Chestnut Tree, with good grown-up and children's menus, including pizza. It's also lighter than most of the restaurants in town.

## Bryson City

The restaurant at the **Fryemont Inn** (☎ 828/488-2159) is one of the best restaurants in town (p. 162). There are lots of choices for fast or casual food, too, including **McDonald's, Hardee's,** and **Pizza Hut.** But my favorite was a place on the east side of town, at 1245 Main St., called **Na-Bers Drive-In** (☎ 828/488-2877). This is a real, unreconstructed, old-fashioned drive-in, where cars pull into stalls and the driver orders through an intercom for someone to carry the food out. There's also a small dining room decorated with 1970s country music album covers (Glenn Campbell, for example). A burger is $1.65, but I decided to splurge with the barbecue pork sandwich with coleslaw on top, in the North Carolina style, with fries and a soda. Everything was great, and it set me back $3.76, including tax.

## Maggie Valley

**Joey's Pancake House** (☎ 828/926-0212), at 4309 Soco Rd. (U.S. 19), is the best of its kind I've ever dined at. The pancakes are fluffy and delicious (the mix is fantastic, too, and needs only water); the dining room is light, clean, and comfortable with many booths; and the service is quick, friendly, and old-fashioned. People come from afar for breakfast here. They're open only for breakfast, 7am to noon except Thursday, and closed in March.

# The Southwest

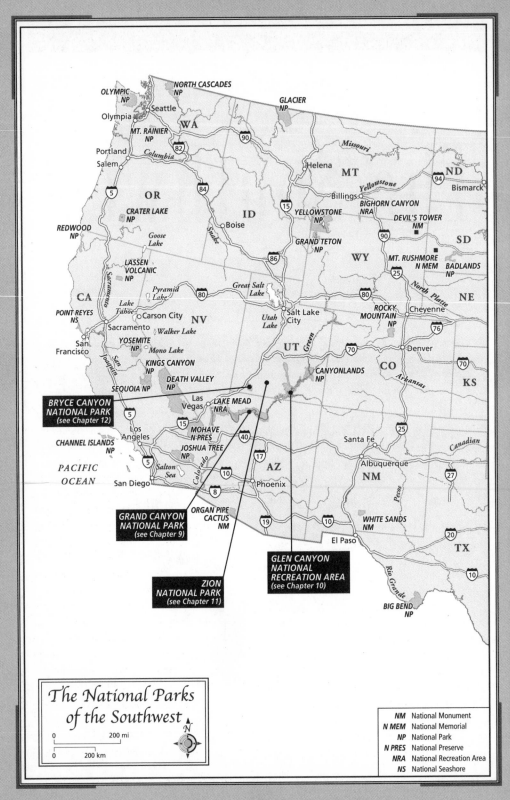

The National Parks of the Southwest

| | |
|---|---|
| 0 | 200 mi |
| 0 | 200 km |

| | |
|---|---|
| NM | National Monument |
| N MEM | National Memorial |
| NP | National Park |
| N PRES | National Preserve |
| NRA | National Recreation Area |
| NS | National Seashore |

BRYCE CANYON NATIONAL PARK (see Chapter 12)

GRAND CANYON NATIONAL PARK (see Chapter 9)

ZION NATIONAL PARK (see Chapter 11)

GLEN CANYON NATIONAL RECREATION AREA (see Chapter 10)

# Layers upon Layers

Driving north of the Grand Canyon along U.S. 89A, on a section of straight desert highway across a flat, featureless floor of land, a wall towers to the north. The map says it's called Vermilion Cliff. It's obviously big, but there's no telling how big because the empty landscape holds nothing to compare it to — no trees, no buildings, certainly no people. It must be big, because as you drive, nothing seems to change. The lines on the road flicker by, but the flat land and the wall are so large that the speed of the car doesn't seem to make any difference. They always look the same.

Then the road quickly rises away from the cliff into a forest of thick, green pines and cool, fragrant air. Another layer, and another world. Vermilion Cliff is only one step on the Grand Staircase, a series of huge cliffs that rise like stairs. They run more than a day's drive northward through northern Arizona and southern Utah, from desert floor to snowy alpine slopes of heather. A national monument also uses the name Grand Staircase, but the staircase steps start near the Grand Canyon; and each plateau is notched by Glen,

Zion, or Bryce canyons, all national parks or recreation areas. Each step on the staircase holds a different layer of life as the rising elevation brings cooler temperatures and more moisture. At each step a sharp line divides different kinds of living things. There are layers within the steps, too. Rock laid down over the past two billion years — half of the earth's history — was cleanly sliced by weather into cliffs and canyons. As the steps rise, the layers of rock they expose also grow younger, step-by-step. Together, they form a nearly continuous record from the bottom of the Grand Canyon, laid down when life was dawning on earth, to the relatively recent red rocks at Bryce.

Seeing far into the distance over desert ground that's mostly bare, the earth's inner workings seem to stand out clearly. It's as if a hand too large for us to see set up a magnificent natural-history exhibit to teach about the sheer size, age, and strength of the earth. Take in the lesson by climbing around the rocks and looking at the plants and animals that have learned to live among them. Feel the hot, dry sun. Climb a trail up the sandstone cliffs of

Zion Canyon, higher than the tallest skyscraper, and look down on the backs of soaring birds. See the mile-high walls of the Grand Canyon from below as well as above. Walk among the bright red, bizarrely shaped towers of rock in Bryce Canyon. Dive into the clear, cool water that fills Glen Canyon and climb out on a bulge of sandstone bedrock, as round and warm as a giant's shoulder. Strange as this landscape seems, few places are better for a family to spend 2 weeks playing and learning.

## THE PARKS

Under "Exploring the Region" (starting on p. 195), I've included information on how to link the parks on a single vacation tour of 1 to 3 weeks. Included are descriptions of some of the national monuments and other stunning natural sites where you may want to stop along the way. Here are quick sketches of each park to help orient you.

**Grand Canyon National Park** protects one of the world's most famous and admired natural wonders, the incredible canyon through northern Arizona made by the Colorado River. Most visitors to the park come to the edge and look in, arriving by car at the visitor village on the South Rim, or the higher and less visited North Rim. Hikers can get down into the canyon and see much more; how far you can go depends on your group's physical abilities.

**Glen Canyon National Recreation Area,** up the Colorado River east of the Grand Canyon, is a version of the same thing, filled most of the way with water. The Glen Canyon Dam holds back Lake Powell, an unnatural but beautiful body of water that provides families with much better access to the backcountry than they have at the Grand Canyon or the other canyon parks. Houseboats, speedboats, and tour boats fan out from marinas along more than 1,000 miles of shoreline into a strange, mazelike landscape along the border between Arizona and Utah.

**Zion National Park** contrasts the rugged immensity of the Grand Canyon, to the southeast, with smooth, soaring shapes. Ancient sand dunes formed into the park's gracefully waving Navajo sandstone. Among the billowing rocks, the river, trees, and plants add to the serenity. Strong hikers also can follow paths up canyon walls that stand 2,000 feet high.

**Bryce Canyon National Park** surrounds some of the oddest and most strangely beautiful land forms at any of the parks. North of Zion in Utah, high in the pines at the top of the Grand Staircase, erosion has carved soft, red rock into amazing towers and channels you can walk among. The park offers a more intimate experience than the vast cliffs and canyons. Most hikes are easy, and there are other activities for families at the park and just outside.

## NATURAL HISTORY: LAYERS OF ROCK, LAYERS OF LIFE

How can we know what happened before the first person was born? Or, before the first dinosaur cracked its way out of an egg? Or, before anything lived on earth bigger than a speck of dust? Geologists have theorized from the rocks of the Grand Staircase.

How do they do it? Scientists start from the tiniest grains that make up a rock. Then they look around and try to see how nature works today that could make a rock like that. And when they figure that out, they have the first small clue about what happened so long ago, when that rock was young.

## CLUES TO THE PAST

This is one of the best places on earth to look into the past. It's a dry region where most of the ground isn't covered by trees and plants. The rocks are right out there to see. And most of the rocks lie in flat layers. They were made by loose stuff, like soil, sand, or mud, slowly buried and crushed together into rock. The stuff that was buried is called **sediment,** and the rock it made is called **sedimentary rock.** When geologists study sedimentary rock, they figure out what kind of sediment made it, and that tells a lot about what was going on back then. For example, if a rock was made from ocean mud, it must have been underwater. Sedimentary rock often has fossils in it, too. If geologists find fish and seaweed fossils in the rock, they can start to imagine what kind of sea covered the area when the layer of rock was put down.

Our biggest help in seeing into the past is that here, like nowhere else, water running through canyons and over cliffs has cut away the edges of sedimentary rock like a knife through a layer cake. When you see the layers in the sides of the Grand Canyon, you're looking at a step-by-step record of the earth's history going back about halfway to the original formation of the planet. Nowhere else on earth can you see such a thing. The bottom layers were laid down first, the next-highest layer next, and the top layer last. At the base of Zion Canyon, the bottom layer is the same kind of rock as the top layer at the Grand Canyon, so the story continues up through the top of Zion. At Bryce Canyon, Zion's top layer of rock shows up at the bottom; Bryce's layers finish the story.

## READING ROCK LAYERS

Geologists use the layers to figure out the order in which things happened — what the area was like first, next, and so on. For example, looking into the Grand Canyon, you can see a steep red wall called the Redwall Limestone, which makes one of the most noticeable stripes along the canyon wall (actually, the red is a stain from the rocks directly above). Limestone is made of calcium and carbon, or calcium carbonate, the same stuff bones and shells are made of, and this Redwall Limestone layer has many fossils of coral and other sea animals with shells. When this layer was being made, the area must have been underwater. The calcium carbonate must have fallen to the bottom of the ocean from seashells, dead animals, and other sea sediment. Judging from what we know about the oceans today and what kinds of fossils are in the rocks, it must have been a warm, shallow sea, like the ones in the tropics today.

The next layer higher on the canyon, which looks like a flatter ledge of red rocks, is completely different. It is sandstone and **siltstone** — rock made of sand and silt or clay that was pressed together and heated inside the earth. The fossils here are of moss, ferns, and the footprints of **amphibians** — animals like frogs, toads, and salamanders that live on land and in the water. This area must have been swampy and damp, but not underwater. With these clues, a story starts to develop: The area was under the ocean, then it rose enough so that it became land, but it still was low, warm and moist.

## DATES FOR THE LAYERS

Each layer covers a different part of the story. Studying rocks from different places, geologists can even figure out what was going on long ago over big parts of the country. But that doesn't tell how long ago any of these things happened, just the order in which they happened — what was first, second, and so on. Scientists use **radiometric dating** to find out exactly when the rocks formed. Here's how it works.

Almost everything is made of **atoms,** which are so small no microscope using light could ever see one all by itself. Atoms are made mostly of protons and neutrons, which are even tinier. Different elements, such as iron or sodium (salt), have different numbers of protons in their atoms. Iron has 26 protons and sodium has 11, for example. That's what makes them what they are. In some elements, having a certain number of protons and neutrons works very well, and they stick together so that they almost never come apart. Those are stable elements. But some elements, like uranium, which has 92 protons and 146 neutrons, are unstable, and their atoms tend to fall apart. The protons and neutrons break off into smaller groups that make atoms of different elements. These unstable elements are called **radioactive elements.** When they break up, it's called **radioactive decay.**

A tiny number of radioactive atoms are in almost everything around us, including the rocks. One of the handy things about them is that how long they take to fall apart, or decay, is always the same. That amount of time is called the **half-life.** For example, the half-life of uranium is 4.49 billion years — that's how long it takes half the atoms in a piece of uranium, with 92 protons and 146 neutrons, to decay into lead, with only 82 protons and 124 neutrons. If you want to know the age of a rock, you find out exactly how much of those two elements are in it, then compare them. If it's exactly half and half, you know that the rock is 4.49 billion years old. (There aren't any rocks that old on earth, but you get the idea.) Other radioactive elements have different half-lives and can be used for dating rocks in different situations.

Once you know the age of the rocks in a particular layer, it's a safe guess that other rocks in the same layer are around the same age. Scientists match up the radiometric dates with the story they pieced together from the fossils and sediment in the rocks. That's how they can tell what was going on in the area of the Grand Staircase from 2 billion years ago until the present, except for a few gaps when, for whatever reason, no rock layers were left behind. The earth is about 4½ billion years old, and the oldest rocks ever found anywhere are about 3.8 billion years old. That means the rocks from the bottom of the Grand Canyon to the top of Bryce Canyon cover about half the history of earth and most of the time anything has been alive on our planet.

## THE STORY IN THE LAYERS

You can follow the story the geologists figured out when you look out across the Grand Canyon. Climbing down at least partway to the river, you can see up close the layers of rock laid down over the history of the earth. The end of that story, at the top of the canyon, picks up at the bottom of Zion Canyon. When it ends at the top of Zion, it starts again at the bottom of Bryce Canyon. Glen Canyon's rock layers mostly cover the same times. With this guide, you can figure out the age and history of the rocks you see as you look into the canyons or hike their sides. The order I've used, from older to younger, goes upward on canyon walls; if you're going down, reverse the order. (See "Read Aloud: Evolution & Trees," in chapter 7, "Great Smoky Mountains National Park," to learn some of the biology of the process.)

**2 billion years ago:** Sand, mud, and ash from volcanic eruptions settle in a shallow sea and slowly form sedimentary rock. No fossils from this period have been found; the only things living on earth were bacteria and other things the size of germs.

**1.7 billion years ago:** The sedimentary rock is buried deep in the earth, where heat and pressure soften and fold it. It becomes a new kind of rock, which finally hardens into the Vishnu Schist now found at the bottom of the Grand Canyon. Later, molten rock pushes up from below into cracks in the schist, leaving veins of Zoroaster Granite. A mountain range forms and erodes away to nothing.

**1.2 billion to 800 million years ago:** The ocean repeatedly floods the land, leaving behind layers of sediment, and then runs back out again. Harder rock forms islands where softer rock eroded. Finally, the whole thing is broken and tipped by movement of the earth's crust, leaving the rock in blocks sitting at an

## Bryce Canyon And Cedar Breaks Area

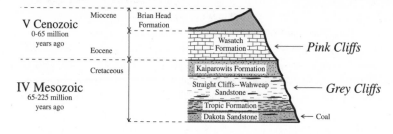

| | | |
|---|---|---|
| **V Cenozoic** 0-65 million years ago | Miocene | Brian Head Formation |
| | Eocene | Wasatch Formation — *Pink Cliffs* |
| **IV Mesozoic** 65-225 million years ago | Cretaceous | Kaiparowits Formation |
| | | Straight Cliffs--Wahweap Sandstone — *Grey Cliffs* |
| | | Tropic Formation |
| | | Dakota Sandstone ← Coal |

## Zion Canyon Area

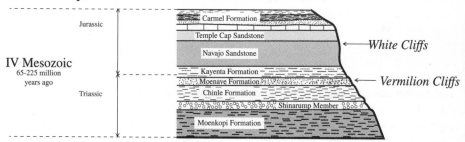

| | | |
|---|---|---|
| **IV Mesozoic** 65-225 million years ago | Jurassic | Carmel Formation |
| | | Temple Cap Sandstone |
| | | Navajo Sandstone — *White Cliffs* |
| | Triassic | Kayenta Formation |
| | | Moenave Formation — *Vermilion Cliffs* |
| | | Chinle Formation |
| | | Shinarump Member |
| | | Moenkopi Formation |

## Grand Canyon

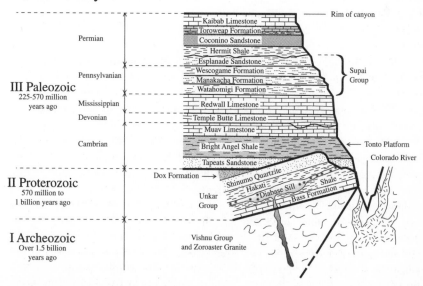

| | | |
|---|---|---|
| | | Kaibab Limestone ── Rim of canyon |
| **III Paleozoic** 225-570 million years ago | Permian | Toroweap Formation |
| | | Coconino Sandstone |
| | | Hermit Shale |
| | | Esplanade Sandstone |
| | Pennsylvanian | Wescogame Formation } Supai Group |
| | | Manakacha Formation |
| | | Watahomigi Formation |
| | Mississippian | Redwall Limestone |
| | Devonian | Temple Butte Limestone |
| | | Muav Limestone |
| | Cambrian | Bright Angel Shale ← Tonto Platform |
| | | Tapeats Sandstone ── Colorado River |
| **II Proterozoic** 570 million to 1 billion years ago | | Dox Formation → Shinumo Quartzite, Hakati, Diabase Sill, Shale, Bass Formation Unkar Group |
| **I Archeozoic** Over 1.5 billion years ago | | Vishnu Group and Zoroaster Granite |

angle. The angled lines of the layers show up in the Inner Gorge. These rocks have fossils of algae, which are like tiny plants that float around in water.

**550 million years ago:** An ocean rises from the west, slowly pushing a beach back across the region over the course of 30 million years. Beach sand that becomes the Tapeats Sandstone forms the lowest of the steep cliffs in the canyon, just above the Inner Gorge. Next, as the water gets deeper, underwater mud mixed with sea worms and other primitive sea animals collects on top of the sand. Under pressure, the mud becomes the Bright Angel Shale, which makes a ledge above the cliff called the Tonto Platform. Finally, as the water gets even deeper, calcium carbonate from seashells and seawater settles on top of the mud to leave ooze that turns into Muav Limestone, which is also part of the platform.

**400 million years ago:** Another layer of limestone fills in channels that formed in the lower rocks. Around this time, the first fish develop.

**330 million years ago:** The Redwall Limestone forms a vertical cliff about 500 feet high all around the canyon. The calcium and carbon that make up the rock come from a shallow tropical sea, and lots of seashell fossils are in the rock. (The red color comes from a stain that later drips down from the rock above.)

**300 million years ago:** Now the sea is gone and silt and sand are being left behind, along with moss, ferns, snails, and some plants from dry land. They form sandstone called the Supai Group. This soft rock makes for a less steep part of the canyon, called the Esplanade, the first fairly flat part below the rim. Some of it is red because of rusty iron in the rocks.

**275 million years ago:** The environment is still much the same — swampy. The swamp mud forms the red Hermit Shale instead of sandstone below, and shale holds together better, making the steeper cliffs above the Esplanade.

**265 million years ago:** Sand dunes blow across the swampy land, burying it 400 feet deep. Scorpions and early reptiles live here. Their tracks have been found in the white Coconino Sandstone that forms cliffs near the top of the Grand Canyon.

**255 million years ago:** The ocean returns, leaving behind more limestone that forms steep cliffs, the Toroweap Formation. Clams and other ocean fossils that look more like what we see today show up in these rocks.

**245 million years ago:** The ocean is still here, creating another thick layer, the Kaibab Limestone, that forms the steep rim of the Grand Canyon. Fossils of sharks' teeth have been found in this layer. The first dinosaurs will appear soon. There are higher layers of rock upstream on the Colorado River, but they are soft and probably eroded away at the Grand Canyon. The Kaibab Limestone also shows up on a cliff at the bottom of Zion Canyon.

**235 to 200 million years ago:** The story continues at Zion, although it can't be seen as clearly as in the striped layers of the Grand Canyon. The sea that made the Kaibab Limestone draws back, and now the region becomes a low, flat plain that's sometimes underwater and sometimes dry. Then it turns into a low, wet, tropical area with lakes, streams, and swamps. The fossils of freshwater animals, fish, and finally dinosaur footprints remain in the mud and sand that turn into rock.

**200 to 150 million years ago:** A huge desert of windblown sand dunes spreads over much of the region, burying Zion more than 2,000 feet deep. This sand becomes the Navajo Sandstone, the most noticeable feature of the park, making the towering cliffs of Zion Canyon and the solid rock dune shapes along the Zion–Mt. Carmel Highway. Navajo Sandstone also gives Glen Canyon National Recreation Area some of its most beautiful areas, including the Rainbow Bridge.

**150 to 60 million years ago:** The sea returns, leaving limestone with fossils of shallow-water creatures in Zion park's mountains. A thin layer of sand from the beach makes a sandstone called the Dakota Formation, the last rock at Zion and the first at the bottom of Bryce Canyon. The age of dinosaurs ends.

**60 to 30 million years ago:** A great uplift of land pushes up the Colorado Plateau and the Grand Staircase, bringing the rock layers far above the sea. (More about this lifting is in the next section, "Raising the Grand Staircase.") A ring of mountains makes an area where streams bring water to huge lakes. The lakes get bigger and smaller as time passes, and each time they leave behind different layers of sediment: muddy, sandy, gravelly, and calcium carbonate, with some fossils of turtles, snails, and reptiles. All this makes the Claron Formation (also called the Pink Cliffs), which later erodes into the strange and brightly colored shapes of Bryce Canyon.

**2.5 million years ago:** Humans appear on earth, but not in North America until about 15,000 years ago.

# RAISING THE GRAND STAIRCASE

For most of earth's history, the land we call the American West was low and swampy, or even underwater. But it wasn't the American West back then. When the rocks at the bottom of the Grand Canyon were formed, this land was in the southern part of the world, and it was connected with a continent that was shaped nothing like North America. Even the oceans were different. Over time, this great continent moved to where it is today, and its western part lifted up, miles high. The evidence that this happened is in the rocks. We know from the fossils and kinds of rock layers, now high in the mountains, that they once were deep in tropical seas. So how did they get here?

All land and all of the sea floor on earth is made of solid plates of rock that float around on the hot, squishy inner layer of the planet. Western North America's plate moved northeast and spun around a bit to get where it is

now. As it moved, it slowly passed through different climates. That's why animals that live in tropical waters and warm, wet places show up in rock layers. Starting about 65 million years ago, the North American Plate, going west, ran into the Pacific Ocean Plate, going east, and the Pacific Plate slid underneath. As it pushed under the land, the land got higher. To the east, the Rocky Mountains grew as the land crumpled. Here on the Colorado Plateau, on the other hand, the rocks didn't break so much, pushing up more like an elevator. (A deeper explanation of this is under "Mountain Building," in chapter 13, "The Nature of High Places.")

# CUTTING THE STAIRS & CANYONS

The steep canyons and sharp cliffs that slice across flat layers of rock in these deserts were cut with liquid water. As strange as it might seem, a dry climate makes that happen faster than a wet one. Not many plants grow here, so there's not much soft topsoil to soak up any rain that does fall. When a thundercloud bursts, water rushes madly across the desert and through the canyons, carrying away rocks and logs in flash floods that smash and wear down the rock along the way. Even more water comes from the Rocky Mountains, to the east. They're so tall they catch clouds that pass right over the rest of the West (see "Natural History: Making Great Mountains & Weather," in chapter 13, "The Nature of High Places"). Deep snow that falls in Rocky Mountain National Park melts in the spring to start the Colorado River flowing. More snowmelt washing down creeks, streams, and rivers joins the Colorado from all over the Rockies. By the time it gets to the desert plateau, the Colorado has a lot of power, and its water cuts like a knife. Since not much rain falls on the desert, the river's canyon walls aren't worn down. The cliffs stay as steep as the river made them.

Water also took away rock layers to create the steps of the Grand Staircase, which rise up to the north with a combined gain in height greater even than the Grand Canyon. Where water ran over layers of soft rock, it cut down steeply, making cliffs. Where water met hard layers of rock, it ran on top until it reached a cliff, making plateaus. The cliffs and plateaus make the steps of the staircase. The Vermilion Cliffs, north of the Grand Canyon, are the first obvious step, carved from rocks around 200 million years old. The White Cliffs, made mostly of Navajo Sandstone, are the next up; Zion Canyon is a notch in that step. The Gray Cliffs were cut from sandstone around 70 million years old. Bryce Canyon is a notch in the Pink Cliffs, the top step. All this is too large to see at once, but from Rainbow Point, 9,000 feet up in Bryce Canyon National Park, you can see a lot of it. A vivid graphic at the Bryce Canyon Visitor Center shows how it fits together.

We really don't know how the Grand Canyon came to be exactly where it is, but the puzzle is interesting to think about. Scientists used to believe they knew, and anyone who tells you so has probably read one of those older books. When you are figuring out something that happened long ago, it's always possible you are wrong, and new evidence has persuaded most scientists to drop the old explanation of the canyon. The problem is this: The Grand Canyon cuts right through a high place, a bulge of land with lower ground on each side. Why would a river do that? Why wouldn't it just flow around? And here's another mystery: The canyon is much younger on its downstream end than it is upstream. How could that happen? There are several clever theories (or ideas) that try to explain how these facts fit together, but each theory has reasons why some people don't believe it, and no one has found evidence yet that convinces most scientists to accept one and drop the others. No doubt a new explanation will eventually win out, but in the meantime all the confusion is a good reminder of how little we really know. We think we can read the story of the earth from ancient rocks, but really we're only making educated guesses at the meaning of what we see.

## CLIFF EROSION & HOODOOS

Flowing rivers explain the deep canyons — the Grand Canyon, Glen Canyon, and Zion Canyon — but not Bryce Canyon, which is really just a notch in the Pink Cliffs. The Bryce Amphitheater, the park's main attraction, is a rounded gap in the cliffs 12 miles wide and 800 feet deep. When you walk down into it, you can see there's no river there, and no way a river could have made the delicate red shapes. They reminded me of fringes of lace hanging straight up into the sky.

Here's how geologists believe Bryce came to be and is still being carved. Snow that falls above the cliffs in the winter melts on warm spring mornings into water that trickles down through cracks in the rocks. As the weather changes, cooling at sunset or during a cold snap, water that seeped into the cracks freezes. Frozen water takes up more space than liquid water, so the ice pushes the sides of the cracks apart, making them larger. When the morning sun again thaws the ice in a crack, a big hunk of rock might fall off a cliff. Water trickling through the rocks can make them weaker in warm weather, too. Some kinds of rock slowly dissolve in water, as salt does. Other rocks might slowly come apart when the water seeping down brings acids from rotting plants or other chemicals from the air. Finally, melt water and runoff from thunderstorms wash away the broken rocks and gravel.

Water and ice could have made a straight cliff at Bryce, but instead it wore down in strange and amazing shapes because of the way different kinds of rocks are mixed up here. These pink and red rocks started out as sediment that fell to the bottom of lakes. The lakes came and went over time, getting deeper and shallower and sometimes drying up completely. The water in the lakes came from rivers that started in many different places and brought sediment from many different kinds of rock. So the red Bryce rocks are a mixture of minerals. Some dissolve easily in water and some block water so that it can't flow through. Some come apart when they're touched by acids and some are hard and break down only very slowly.

The hoodoos are an easy example to understand. **Hoodoos** are the skinny towers of red rock along the edge of the Bryce Amphitheater. On the trails near Sunset and Sunrise points, you can walk among the hoodoos, feeling as though you're walking in a forest of stones. Each hoodoo started with layers of softer rock under a layer of harder rock. Water and ice carved down through cracks in the harder rock until it reached the softer rock, then started carving much faster. Pieces of the hard rock above stayed solid, like a hat protecting the soft rock underneath it from water. Those protected rocks stayed tall, forming fins or sharp ridges. Then cracks in the sides of the ridges eroded the same way, cutting them off from the cliff. But where a piece of hard rock stayed on top, the soft rock under the hat still stood tall, like a column. You can still see the hat on some of the hoodoos. The mixture of different kinds of rocks of different hardness works in other ways all over the park to make odd shapes.

## LAYERS OF LIFE ZONES

I'll never forget climbing the West Rim Trail in Zion Canyon in March. Down below, the morning sun was T-shirt warm. The canyon around the Virgin River was a green oasis, but the desert was near at hand. The path, climbing through switchbacks and steep ledges chipped from the sandstone, rose 1,500 feet upward. I stayed warm enough with a hard climb, but I could feel the air cooling around me. In a narrow side canyon, pine trees appeared in the shade of the rocks — I hadn't seen any of those down below. On top, the crisp freshness of the air, the light, and the views from 1,000-foot cliffs made me feel like an eagle. But I started to get a little chilly. As I hiked on into the mountains, the pines and rock outcroppings reminded me of the high

country at Yosemite. And then, turning into a shaded valley, I ran into deep snow. In a couple of hours, I had hiked from spring back into winter.

This experience happens frequently all over these parks. At the Grand Canyon, we camped amid snow, mud, and pinyon pine. A short hike over the rim, and we were in hot, arid desert, craving water. As you drive certain highways, your speed brings the change of plants and air even more suddenly, seasons changing as if at a flip of a switch. One of the best examples is Route 89A, over the Kaibab Plateau near the Grand Canyon's North Rim. It climbs from desert below 5,000 feet to over 8,000 feet in less than 20 minutes. From a flat and seemingly barren table of Sonoran Desert, you enter a lush forest of ponderosa pine, blue spruce, fir, and aspen — a so-called Canadian life zone.

Across the Grand Canyon, less than 10 miles away but 2,000 feet lower on the South Rim, the environment is different yet again. Pale, rocky ground without much covering it grows thin pinyon and juniper trees, the kind that border the Sonoran Desert. These different forests, and the barrier of the canyon between them, make two different kinds of homes for animals, too. On the North Rim, the Kaibab squirrel is black with a white tail, fitting in with the dark forest. It's found nowhere else. On the south side, the Abert's squirrel has a gray body that matches its rocky home. Scientists believe that the two squirrel varieties were one before the canyon divided their world in half. Each has since adapted to its own surroundings. (Pictures are on p. 190.)

## A HABITAT IS A HOME

People are the only animals who can put on an overcoat or a sun hat, build a house with a furnace or an air-conditioner, turn on a water tap, or shop in a supermarket. That makes us the only animals who can live almost anywhere we choose. Other animals can live only where the environment provides food, water, and shelter in the way their bodies need: the right kind of food, enough water, and weather that's not too hot or cold. For each animal, the place where it fits in is its **habitat.** The same is true of plants. Some need a lot of moisture, soil, and shade; some like dry ground and hot sun.

In this part of the world, elevation is the most important difference between habitat areas. Higher land is cooler, which means there's more rain and snowfall, and water takes longer to dry. (See "Elevation & Air Pressure," in chapter 13, "The Nature of High Places," to find out why higher elevations are cooler and moister.) These elevation differences cause changes in habitat like the changes you see going from the southern to the northern part of North America. In the south, in Mexico or southern Arizona, hot deserts grow varieties of cactus and other plants like the creosote bush that can survive heat. In the north, in interior Alaska or Canada, the weather might be just as dry, but plants grow such as heather and blueberry, and trees such as fir and spruce, which survive in cold weather. Around these parks, going up 1,000 feet in elevation brings a change in plant and animal habitat the same as going north 400 miles. The North Rim of the Grand Canyon is more than 6,000 feet above the Colorado River at the canyon's floor. You can do the math yourself, but here's a clue: The plants at the bottom are like what you'd find in Mexico's Sonoran Desert, and the forest on the top is like Canada.

## ELEVATIONS OF LIFE ZONES

One of my favorite things about traveling in this part of the country is seeing how the habitat changes with elevation. While driving a highway, you can sometimes guess how high you are by what you see growing. More often there are no exact lines between the life zones, and plants from two zones frequently mix. (See "The Little Field Guide" that follows, for pictures or descriptions of some of the plants and animals.)

**Below 4,500 feet:** You're in the desert. In the Painted Desert, east of the Grand Canyon on the drive to Glen Canyon along Route 89,

broad landscapes with almost no plants pass by your window. In other desert places, you might see plants such as prickly pear and cholla cacti, and creosote bush. These plants have roots that can gather what little water is available in the ground and store it in their stalks through long droughts. Near year-round rivers at the bottom of Zion Canyon and similar places, Fremont cottonwoods and other lush plants grow.

**4,500 feet to 6,500 feet:** You're in a zone called the Upper Sonoran zone, or the pinyon-juniper belt. A lot of these parks and the surrounding land are at this level. The ground is rocky and dry, and rain and snow bring only about 10 inches of water a year. It's hot in the summer, but not as hot as the desert. This is a halfway stage between desert below and forest above, and it's half of each. The pinyon — a small, twisted pine tree — and the Utah juniper grow with plenty of space between. Yuccas and other desert plants, like sagebrush and the twiggy ephedra, commonly grow at this level, too.

**6,500 to 8,000 feet:** You're in the pine-oak belt, or the transition zone. The ground is sandy but gets more moisture — 20 to 25 inches of water a year in rain and snow. This is truly a forest, with a variety of leafy plants and trees. The main tree is the ponderosa pine — the great, straight, tall pine that towers over much of the West. The big trees often stand far apart, allowing light to reach the forest floor, where bushes can grow.

**8,000 feet or more:** At these high elevations, sometimes called the Canadian life zone, the forests become thick with fir, aspen, and, above 9,500 feet, spruce. The rain and snow amount to three times or more than falls in the pinyon-juniper belt, helping lots of bushes, plants, and trees grow in the topsoil that is created when they drop their leaves. Snow, wind, and cold challenge even the hardy trees, and above about 11,000 feet, trees can't grow at all. This is the alpine zone, with low tundra plants similar to those found in the arctic.

# THE LITTLE FIELD GUIDE

## MAMMALS & OTHER DESERT CRITTERS

Besides the plants and animals pictured here, you might also see elk, mountain lion (p. 288), and bobcat (p. 392).

Coyote

and about 2 feet tall. Jack rabbits are active at night, and you often see them in your headlights when driving. If you're camping, keep an eye out for their eyes reflecting the light of your fire or lantern from the woods.

Mule Deer

## Coyote

These wild dogs are midway in size between wolves and foxes. Their natural habitat is in the deserts and grasslands of the West, but when bounty hunting killed all the wolves in the lower 48 states, coyotes spread out over most of the country and changed their behavior. They now act more like wolves, hunting in packs and going for bigger game, like deer. In the Southwest they're more solitary, eating reptiles, rodents, insects, and fruit.

## Mule Deer

You might see elk, which are larger, but mule deer are much more common in this region. They are 4 to 6 feet long, have big ears like a mule, and have brown coats in the summer. Generally, mule deer in groups are females with offspring, while bucks travel alone.

Rattlesnake

Jack Rabbit

## Rattlesnake

Watch out for these guys, and if you find one, just back off. Most people who get bitten step on one accidentally or are messing with the snake; it attacks an animal as large as a person only in self-defense. (See "Dealing with Hazards," in chapter 1, "Planning Your Trip," for what to do if someone gets bitten.) Rattlesnakes are dormant in the winter and come out only at night in the hot summer months. There are many kinds, including one that lives only in the Grand Canyon, but I

## Jack Rabbit

You can tell a jack rabbit by its long ears and strong back legs. This rabbit is tan and white

wouldn't recommend getting close enough to check which one you're seeing.

## Side-Blotched Lizard

There are 3,000 kinds of lizards in the world, many of which look alike, and you often don't see them for long — be happy just to say it was a lizard. This one is 4 to 6 inches long and is brown with spots. Like snakes and other reptiles, lizards are cold-blooded. They use the environment around them to set their body temperature, hiding in the shade or basking on warm rocks to get it right. (We're called warm-blooded animals because our bodies burn fuel to stay the same temperature.)

Abert's Squirrel

Kaibab Squirrel

## Squirrels

You might see many kinds of squirrels, but the relatively rare **Abert's squirrel** is noticeable because it has tall tufts of hair that stick up behind its ears. The back is gray, with white running on the underside from the belly to the tip of the tail. It's found only in pine and juniper forests, especially on the South Rim of the Grand Canyon.

The rare **Kaibab squirrel,** on the North Rim, evolved separately after the canyon formed and has an all-black body and a white tail.

## BIRDS

In addition to the birds below, you might also spot a golden eagle (p. 288) or a hairy wood-pecker (p. 289).

Raven

## Raven

You can see the raven, a black bird like a larger version of a crow, and hear its throaty caw all over the West into Alaska. The raven is common in the stories of many Native American cultures as a wily trickster and pow-erful creator. Ravens *are* extremely intelligent birds, able to solve problems. They eat many kinds of food, but a favorite seems to be garbage.

## Western Bluebird

This is a striking bird, with a bright blue back and a red breast. Males compete for nest holes, using a red breast like the robin's to show other males that they're willing to fight for their place. Look for them in open areas where there are trees for nesting.

## Trees & Plants
## Cholla

Chollas are cacti that look like trees, with branches that reach out, often from a central trunk. They live in the desert. Like other plants, cacti need to absorb carbon dioxide from the air through tiny holes called **pores** and combine it with sunshine to make food. But unlike other plants which do that during the day, chollas, prickly pears (see below), and other cacti know how to open their pores at night to take in carbon dioxide, store it, and then put it together with sunshine the next day. That way they can keep their pores closed under the hot sun so that they don't waste water. ("Read Aloud: Photosynthesis," in chapter 22, "Olympic National Park," explains how plants make food of sunlight.)

## Creosote Bush

The dark green bushes that dot deserts all over the Southwest are often this tough shrub. Resin coats the leaves to save water, and when the weather gets very dry, the bush drops the leaves altogether. When rain comes, it quickly adds new leaves and branches. A bush can live for more than 100 years by adding rings of branches when old ones die. The creosote bush is a source of many natural medicines for Native Americans.

## Ephedra

The ephedra is a strange-looking plant that can show up at elevations of 2,000 to 7,500 feet. It has no leaves, only light-green twiggy branches, and cones instead of fruit. Also known as Mormon tea and used to make tea by the Navajo, ephedra shows up in remedies at health-food stores. Hunt for it on hikes — it's not as common as some of the other plants here.

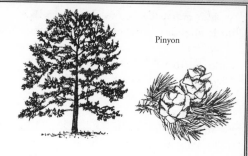

Pinyon

## Pinyon

These small pines grow in lower, rockier places than the big ponderosa. The pinyon has adapted to its environment by growing slowly, and a tree with a trunk 6 inches thick could be more than 100 years old. The needles are short for a pine and grow in tufty groups, attaching in bundles of two. Under their scales, the smallish pinecones contain tasty nuts that are harvested and sold.

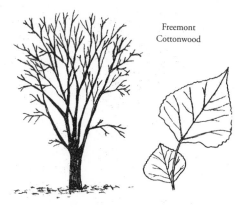

Freemont
Cottonwood

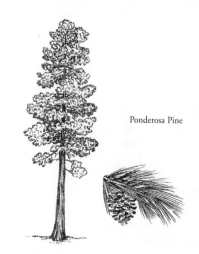

Ponderosa Pine

## Fremont Cottonwood

The long, high branches of this tree shade the campgrounds at Zion National Park, along the Virgin River, and show up in other wet places in the pinyon-juniper belt. It's a tall and graceful tree, with rough gray bark and roughly triangular leaves with saw-tooth edges.

## Ponderosa Pine

For most kids, learning to recognize any pine will do. Telling two dozen varieties apart is a fun but tricky puzzle that requires a good field guide. The ponderosa and pinyon (above) are a relatively easy starting point. The ponderosa, which grows up to 150 feet tall and 4 feet thick, is an impressive tree that provides as much lumber as any other in America.

Varieties of ponderosa grow all over the West; the kind in this area has long needles in bundles of three.

Utah Juniper

Prickly Pear

## Prickly Pear

This is a cactusy-looking cactus, and you'll most likely find it in low, desert places, such as around Glen Canyon. There are various kinds, but they all have flat pads that work as leaves, branches, and places to store water and grow spring flowers. Watch out for the sharp thorns. Prickly pears turn their pads toward the sun.

## Utah Juniper

Found commonly in the same habitat as the pinyon, especially on the South Rim of the Grand Canyon, the Utah juniper has green branches like a cedar tree. Some people call it a cedar — that's how Cedar Breaks National Monument got its name. It grows only about 15 feet tall. The trunk has shredded bark, and the branches start close to the ground. The Hopi use juniper for medicine and make beads of the berries.

Sagebrush

Banana Yucca

## Sagebrush

A common plant on dry, rocky places over 4,500 feet, sagebrush has hairy, silvery leaves. They look a little like the herb sage but are nothing like that member of the mint family. At times, sagebrush takes over an area and nothing else can grow.

## Yucca

There are many kinds of yucca, each with pointy leaves growing from the center in a shape like a sunburst. Various tribes used the banana yucca, which is among the most common plants growing in dry places above 4,500 feet, as one of their main foods. They ate its fruit fresh or roasted, or ground it up, dried it, and made it into cakes.

# HISTORY & CULTURE: HOW DO PEOPLE LIVE HERE?

Today we have cities in the desert, like Phoenix and Las Vegas, with green lawns and cool restaurants that serve food from far away — you can have lobster, fresh from a saltwater tank, whenever you like. But how many people could live here, and how well could they live, if we didn't have the freeways, trucks, airplanes, electrical and water systems, and all the fuel to make everything work? The stuff that keeps these cities alive comes from somewhere else, mostly beyond the desert. For the millions of people here, life itself depends on keeping the machines running. Without machines, these places would be pale, thirsty deserts where most of us wouldn't know how to survive for a week.

But people did live here before the first Europeans arrived in 1539. The Native Americans of the Southwest not only survived, they built villages of stone with sports arenas and temples, systems to bring water to their fields, and roads. They traded with other cultures, created works of art, and practiced complicated religious rituals. They formed communities organized so that each person had a job that contributed to the group's survival and success. They built projects that took generations to finish. You can see big ruins they left behind at the national monuments and parks all over the region, several of which I've described below. These are places where a civilization came together and fell apart before Christopher Columbus ever crossed the ocean.

There's a lot to think about when you visit stone ruins of buildings like the ones at Wupatki (pronounced wuh-*pot*-key) National Monument. It's fun to imagine the men and women, boys and girls who lived in those small rooms so long ago. It's interesting to try to understand what the rooms were for and to wonder what games people played in the ball court. But take it one step further, if you can.

The people who lived here, and in many other villages, called **pueblos,** left because they had used up the environment that supported them. They had to move to new places and leave behind the many things they had built. Could that ever happen to our civilization? How do you think it would happen? Where would we go if it did?

## RISE OF A GREAT CULTURE

The earliest natives in the Southwest arrived during the Ice Age, more than 10,000 years ago. Cool weather and moisture made the region a grassy hunting ground for bison and other animals that are now extinct, such as the mammoth, a woolly elephant. When the weather changed, making the area desert, and the animals left or became extinct, these **Paleo Indians** followed with their spears and temporary camps, looking for greener areas. Then, around 7,000 years ago, new people came into the area and learned how to survive in the desert. These **archaic** people hunted, but they also gathered food and made clothing from plants, moving to the best areas as the seasons changed. They did well enough that their descendants spread all over the Southwest, but not well enough to leave much behind for us to find except tools and other simple items.

Farming was the big discovery that made people rich enough to erect beautiful buildings. The people of the Southwest learned from people in Mexico to plant seeds and tend their crops. About 2,500 years ago, farming started to take over the region, and groups of families began settling down in permanent houses near their fields of corn, beans, and squash. Archaeologists (scientists who study the remains of past cultures) have found leavings from several groups of people. The people who lived in the area we're covering were the **Ancestral Puebloans** (also called Anasazi) and the **Hakataya.** The Ancestral Puebloans built the biggest and most complex villages — preserved at places like Chaco Culture National Historical Park in New Mexico — but the groups also mixed. At what's now Wupatki National Monument, Hakataya groups such as the Sinagua and Coconino lived near the Ancestral Puebloans, and they learned each other's ways.

## WUPATKI & A PEOPLE'S DECLINE

Wupatki became a cultural center after the Sunset Volcano erupted in 1064 (it's in another interesting national monument just to the south). Volcanic ash spread over the area. The volcano drove away a few families who had scratched out a life in the desert, but they soon returned when they discovered that the ash improved farming. It held water in the ground instead of allowing it to run off or evaporate. Soon, many more people moved into the area, built impressive buildings, had babies, and filled several towns with people. Archaeologists believe that 2,200 people were living here 100 years after the eruption. They have found thousands of sites where things were left behind. Three of the best are the Sinagua's Wupatki and the Ancestral Puebloan's Wukaki and Lomaki ruins.

The people who lived here had to know how to manage planting and water to support a large population in this dry, hot place. But it didn't last. Within 200 years of the eruptions, everyone left. No one knows for sure where they went or why, but they probably left because the land couldn't support them anymore. Farmland needs to rest. It is ruined if farmers use it too hard or the topsoil washes away. This farmland had grown well only because of the precious layer of ash. If that layer was damaged, the villages wouldn't have enough food for everyone. Maybe too many people moved into the area and had too many babies and the land was used up when farmers tried to provide for them all.

All over this region, people left their villages starting around this time and for the next couple of hundred years. The greatest accomplishments of the Southwest natives became ruins as the Ancestral Puebloans and other groups moved out. Hotter weather that made farming harder was one reason, but too many people trying to live on this difficult land might be a more basic explanation. Archaeologists believe that in some places, too many trees were cut down to build the great pueblos and to provide firewood. The lack of trees allowed the soil to wash away, and that ruined the farms. Archaeologists also believe that social structures — the way people work together — might have fallen apart with too many people to feed. People might have begun to fight for what they needed. When people can't work in cooperation, they can't get as much done, and even less food is grown. You might hear tales about the mysterious "disappearance" of the Anasazi, whom we now call the Ancestral Puebloans. The truth is simpler and more important to know: They didn't disappear, they developed their villages beyond the capability of their environment to support them, and they had to leave.

## THE HOPI & US

Today's **Hopi** people, Pueblo Indians, are descendants of the Ancestral Puebloans; they have asked people to use the name Ancestral Puebloans instead of Anasazi because of their relation to those ancient people. Through their culture, and that of other tribes of the pueblo people, the traditions of the ancient civilization live on. After the arrival of conquerors from Spain more than 400 years ago, much of the culture and history of the area was destroyed. Many native people died of new European diseases, in war, and under slavery. A rebellion in 1680 drove the Spanish out, and although they returned in 1692, the Hopi of Arizona were never again conquered. They knocked down Spanish churches built to force a new religion on them and tried to keep their old ways. Today, at Hopi pueblos on their reservation in Arizona, people still understand an ancient and complicated religion that measures and helps cause the changing seasons — knowledge that must have helped the Ancestral Puebloans be such good farmers.

Archaeologists have tried to figure out the story of the Ancestral Puebloan's fall by listening to Hopi legends (I've retold one in "Read Aloud: A Hopi Story," in chapter 9, "Grand Canyon National Park"), but they never got clear answers about what happened other than what we can learn from the ruins. You can draw your own conclusions from those ruins, too. Many cultures have become great and died out in the world's history. Usually they fell because of their own problems, not because of what someone else did to them. Our civilization is strong today, but in the future we might have to work to avoid what happened to the Ancestral Puebloans. The questions they should have asked apply to us as well. Are we using our land and water wisely so that it will last forever?

## EXPLORING THE REGION

The Southwest has many wonderful national parks, recreation areas, and monuments fairly close together. Most people visit more than one. I have covered four main parks in the following chapters, and nearby state parks and national monuments below in this chapter, but there are other parks a bit farther away that I haven't included, such as Capitol Reef, Canyonlands, and Arches. It's possible to visit them all in one trip, and many people do, driving through quickly for the star attractions. We believe in more meaningful visits to fewer parks. On that slower kind of tour, you could cover the areas we describe in 2 weeks. Take more time if you want to really relax and dig in at a park. The chapters also stand alone for a visit to a single park.

### GETTING THERE

Small cities are near most of the parks in the section, so you can fly almost all the way. Towns and airports are described in the individual chapters. But consider using Phoenix, Las Vegas, or Salt Lake City as a gateway. By going to one of these larger hubs, you will likely save money on plane tickets and car rentals. A travel agent should be willing to shop rates for each city, or you can do it on the Web. If you plan to rent an RV (a great way to go in this region), you should certainly start out at one of these hubs. (For RV rental, see "Practicalities: The RV Advantage," p. 198.)

### LINKING THE PARKS

Bryce Canyon National Park is the farthest north, on scenic Route 12, along the path east to Capitol Reef, Canyonlands, and Arches national parks. (For details on these three parks, which are not covered in this book, see *Frommer's Utah*.) Zion, Glen Canyon, and the North Rim of the Grand Canyon roughly form a triangle. The South Rim is off to the south and west. The highways connecting these parks are two-lane roads. They're straight and you can make good time, but expect no services along the way.

### U.S. 89

Route 89 is the main highway linking these parks. Interstates 17 and 40 meet U.S. 89 in **Flagstaff,** which is a hub for the Grand Canyon. Route 180 is the most direct route from there to the South Rim. U.S. 89 is the main road north, passing Wupatki and Sunset Crater national monuments, then crossing the Painted Desert to the town of **Page** at Glen Canyon National Recreation Area.

From Page, 89 turns west to the funny little tourist town of **Kanab,** then north to access routes to Zion and Bryce Canyon national parks (from the Route 89 side, the entrance to Zion involves a low-clearance tunnel on the Zion–Mt. Carmel Highway; see "Getting There," in chapter 11, "Zion National Park"). U.S. 89 finally meets I-70, near I-15 on the way to Salt Lake City. Other than the Painted Desert portion, the scenery along 89 isn't memorable.

## Route 89A

This older, alternate route branches off from Route 89 south of Page and goes west, past Lees Ferry and the Vermilion Cliffs. It climbs to the **North Rim** of the Grand Canyon, at over 8,000 feet, then descends to Kanab and rejoins 89. **Lees Ferry** and the standing rocks are worth a visit (see p. 198), and the forests of the North Rim are special and not as mobbed as the South Rim. If you're going both ways, take the spectacular drive on 89A at least one way.

## MAKING TRAVEL PLANS

More than most areas, the extremes of the Southwest demand you plan how you will travel.

## Camping

Tent camping in this dry country has a special attraction. At night the air is cool enough for sleeping even in the heat of the summer, and the desert air smells good in the morning. The drawbacks are the extreme daytime heat in the summer at low elevations and the unpredictable spring weather at higher altitudes. Since you'll be at many elevation levels during your trip, it can be hard to prepare. One solution is to camp where you expect the right climate and to stay in hotels at the other places. That also gives you a chance to clean up and sleep on sheets every so often. This is the least expensive way to visit the region, with park campgrounds charging around $15 a night.

## Hotels

There are good hotels at or near each park. They get you out of the heat and cold, but you have to eat your meals out. Generally, the choice of restaurants at these parks isn't that exciting. Also, you need to reserve far ahead to get rooms within the parks. Expect to pay $100 a night for a room and $75 a day for food.

## Renting an RV

This is a good compromise for families: You have a kitchen and beds, you aren't tied to hotels, and the kids can play in the campgrounds. It's not a way to save money, however, because RV rentals and related costs amount to as much as a hotel room, rental car, and restaurant meals combined. An intermediate-size unit for 10 days costs about $1,600 in the high season, 20% less in the low season, including spring break. Also budget $400 for gas on a 10-day trip and $22 a night for campgrounds (an average of park and full hookup places). See "Practicalities: The RV Advantage" (p.198) for more specific advice.

## STOPS ALONG THE WAY
## Towns

### FLAGSTAFF

This attractive college and skiing town also serves as a hub for the Grand Canyon, the nearby national monuments, and northern Arizona. It's at the junction of I-17, I-40, and U.S. 89, about 2 hours north of Phoenix. The drive to the Grand Canyon, about 77 miles away, takes a bit over an hour.

You could spend a couple of days here, or more if you want to ski. Among the attractions are the **Arboretum at Flagstaff,** 4001 S. Woody Mountain Rd. (☎ **928/774-1442;** www.thearb.org); the **Museum of Northern Arizona,** along Route 180 on the way to the Grand Canyon (☎ **928/774-5211;** www.musnaz.org); the **Lowell Observatory,** 1400 W. Mars Hill Rd. (☎ **928/774-2096;** www.lowell.edu); and, 35 miles east on I-40, the **Meteor Crater,** a private attraction with a museum and theater around a well-preserved impact site called by Scientific American the world's best for visiting (☎ **800/289-5898** or 928/289-2362; www.meteorcrater.com). The **Flagstaff Convention and Visitors Bureau** (☎ **800/217-2367** or 928/779-7611; www.flagstaffarizona.org) has an information center at 323 W. Aspen St., just off Route 66, or you can write ahead to 211 W. Aspen, Flagstaff, AZ 86001.

The local airport (☎ **928/556-1234**) is served by **America West Airlines** (☎ **800/235-9292** or 928/774-0404). Cars are available from **Budget** (☎ **800/527-0700** or 928/779-5235) and **Avis** (☎ **800/331-1212** or 928/774-8421), among others.

### KANAB

On the way to Zion or Bryce Canyon National Park, just north of the Arizona border on U.S. 89, this funny little cattle and tourist town has a few Western-style attractions of interest to younger children. It's a good stop for groceries or fast food. If you need a place to stay, a nice **Holiday Inn Express** is on the east side of town at 815 E. Rte. 89, Kanab, UT 84741 (☎ **800/574-4061** or 435/644-8888). A **visitor center** offering information on the region is at 78 E. 100 South, Kanab, UT 84741 (☎ **800/733-5263** or 435/644-5033; www.kaneutah.com).

## Parks & Monuments

All these sites are along the routes between the parks. Also see Kodachrome Basin State Park and Cedar Breaks National Monument, both near Bryce Canyon National Park. (See "Natural Places Just Outside the National Park" in chapter 12, "Bryce Canyon National Park.")

### NEAR FLAGSTAFF

**Wupatki and Sunset Crater Volcano national monuments.** On Rte. 89, 12 miles north of Flagstaff. ☎ **928/679-2365** (www.nps.gov/wupa) for Wupatki, ☎ **928/526-0502**

(www.nps.gov/sucr) for Sunset Crater. Admission to both $3 per person, free for children 16 and under. Visitor centers, daily 8am–6pm in summer, shorter hours the rest of the year.

These two monuments lie on a 36-mile road that loops from Route 89 through Coconino National Forest and next to the Navajo Indian Reservation. **Sunset Crater Volcano National Monument** is to the south, closer to Flagstaff. A 1-mile nature trail crosses a lava flow from the volcano that blew in 1064; another ascends a cinder cone. Interesting exhibits at the visitor center explain the site. Depending on your interest, you could spend 30 minutes to 2 hours here.

We found the **Wupatki National Monument** extremely interesting. The main ruins of a Sinagua pueblo are behind a first-rate visitor center, about 20 miles north of Sunset Crater. You really can imagine what it was like to live here 800 years ago when you walk among the rooms and ball court. A natural rock formation called the **blowhole** — which appears simply as a hole in the ground — sucks or blows air harder than a vacuum cleaner into and out of hidden caves in the underlying Kaibab Limestone. The air flow is caused by the air pressure in the cave trying to equalize with changing barometric pressure outside. Thousands of minor ruins have been found within the boundaries of the monument. Don't miss Wukaki, a lonely castle of red rock built by the Ancestral Puebloans. The monument has a **Junior Ranger program** with a good workbook, if you want to spend the time. There are pleasant picnic grounds at Doney Mountain, northwest of the visitor center, where a trail leads to a high overlook for views of the area and the Painted Desert.

**Bonito Campground,** in the national forest across the road from the Sunset Crater Visitor Center, has 44 sites for $12 a night, picnic tables, bathrooms, and running water. It's open from May through mid-October; call the **Forest Service** at ☎ **928/526-0866.**

# PRACTICALITIES: THE RV ADVANTAGE

As a tent camper, I've at times been puzzled and annoyed by big motor homes. Bringing along a home on wheels, with air-conditioning, beds, a kitchen, and other comforts, seemed to defeat the purpose of camping, which is to experience the outdoors. But in the Southwest, much more than in other parts of the U.S., RVs are everywhere, and after trying it for a couple of weeks, I understand why. RV camping in this part of the country is fun and makes a lot of practical sense.

If an RV insulates you from the outdoors somewhat, that's often a good thing in this land of extremes. In many ways, spring break is the best time to visit the Southwest — that's when we went for our research trip, and we found no crowds and comfortable daytime temperatures. But higher elevations were too cold for tent camping at that time of year. Most people visit in the summer, when the weather is too hot during the day. Because of the way climate varies with elevation, you run into both extremes on a single trip. Our coldest night was in the 20s and our hottest day nearly 100°F. We were glad to have air-conditioning and a heater. We spent as much time outside as we liked, but we didn't have to worry about the elements because home was always close by. We also got used to having a sink to do the dishes in and a bathroom on board.

An RV has major advantages over staying in hotels, too. You have your own cooking facilities and dining table, so you don't have to spend time and money eating stressful meals with kids in forgettable restaurants. If you want to eat out, you still have the opportunity. You also have greater flexibility and don't have to worry so much about reservations. During busy seasons, park accommodations in the region are booked up many months in advance; your itinerary has to be locked in long before you know how you'll feel about different areas. Campgrounds often require reservations, too, but not as far ahead; and if you change your mind you're out a lot less money than if you cancel a guaranteed hotel reservation. Finally, camping gives kids more freedom to be themselves than a hotel room can. Your campsite is a built-in playground.

Of course, there are disadvantages too. One is cost. Renting an RV is expensive and can cost as much as or more than staying in a hotel, renting a car, and eating out for all your meals. (A comparison is on p. 196 under "Making Travel Plans.") RVs also use prodigious amounts of gasoline, with a gallon typically taking you less than 10 miles. Another disadvantage is reduced mobility. Ungainly RVs are justifiably outlawed from many crowded park areas. In some parks, RV rental drivers and the accidents they cause have become notorious (I don't know how many times I've heard stories of people bashed in the head by passing RV side mirrors). It's often best to set up camp and then find some other way to get around — on a park shuttle or bicycles, for example.

Also, someone has to drive the thing and drain the sewage tanks. Even smaller RVs take a lot of concentration and awareness to drive, because the vehicle fills the lane, you don't have much power, and you have huge blind spots. Now that I've driven one, I steer well clear of them on the highway. And draining the tanks can be revolting. We made it a rule to use campground toilets

**Walnut Canyon National Monument.** 7 miles east of Flagstaff on I-40; take Exit 204 and drive 3 miles south to Walnut Canyon Rd., Exit 3. ☎ 928/526-3367. www.nps.gov/waca. Admission $3 per person, free for children 16 and under. Summer daily 8am–6pm; spring and fall daily 8am–5pm; winter daily 9am–5pm.

You can explore Sinagua cliff dwellings built in cave ledges in lovely Walnut Canyon just east of Flagstaff. Pace yourself, because the air is thin, and coming back out of the canyon requires climbing more than 200 steps. The visitor center includes a museum and ranger talks. Guided hikes to off-trail cliff dwellings and other sites usually off-limits are offered from June through August.

## ON U.S. 89A

**Lees Ferry.** Rte. 89A, 14 miles west of the Bitter Springs junction with U.S. 89 in Arizona, 37 miles

whenever possible, but just dishwashing water forces you to drain the tanks every few days. There's a lot of gadgetry to learn, too. Go slowly through your rental briefing and take notes. Finally, kids who get carsick might easily find that the configuration of seats and windows in an RV sets them off.

On balance, we found that the advantages outweigh the annoyances. If you decide to do it, here are some tips we learned:

- **Shop on the phone by gateway city as well as agency.** Prices may vary widely in the region's major cities — Las Vegas, Salt Lake City, and Phoenix. Often you'll pay a mileage charge if you go over a certain limit (1,000 miles a week, for example), so you should plan your departure point with that in mind. You'll probably have to research this by calling around yourself, because travel agents don't have a simple way of comparison shopping.
- **Off-season rentals are a great bargain.** In the slower seasons, you can shop and even dicker for a deal. In the early spring, the agencies have RVs sitting idle. If you're daring, you can show up without a reservation and shop around town for a really low price.
- **Rent the smallest vehicle you can be comfortable in.** A bigger RV will cost more, use more gas, and make it more difficult for you to navigate and fit into campsites.
- **Reserve early for the high season, and get all the details before you commit.** What is provided and what do you need to bring? What are the security deposit arrangements? Are there any restrictions on where you can go? How old is the vehicle? What will the agency do if the vehicle breaks down? What are the insurance conditions and deductibles? Are there any extra costs for full coverage? What tax rate will you pay? Will the agency pick you up at the airport? How far is it from the rental office to a grocery store and an attractive campground?
- **Reserve popular campgrounds well ahead.** You can always change your plans.
- **Do as much grocery shopping at one time as possible.** You'll want to avoid taking the RV on unnecessary shopping trips. Plan meals and make a shopping list before you leave home.
- **Ask the rental agency for boards to put under the wheels in campsites.** Most RVs have propane refrigerators that work best when the vehicle is level.

Below are some of the major agencies in the Southwest. We had a good experience with Cruise America, the national leader in these rentals. You can also get information from the **Recreation Vehicle Rental Association** (☎ **703/591-7130**; www.rvra.org).

- **Cruise America.** Las Vegas, Salt Lake City, Phoenix, Albuquerque, other locations nationally. ☎ **800/327-7799**; www.cruiseamerica.com.
- **Bates Motorhome Rental Network.** ☎ **800/732-2283** in Las Vegas, ☎ **800/435-4678** in Phoenix, and ☎ **800/461-0456** in Salt Lake City; or check the website www.batesintl.com.
- **Access RV Rental Group.** Salt Lake City. ☎ **800/327-6910**; www.accessrvrental.com.

from Page. ☎ **928/608-6404.** www.nps.gov/glca. Admission $10. Navajo Bridge Interpretive Center: mid-Apr to Oct daily 9am–5pm; early Apr and Nov Sat–Sun 10am–4pm; closed Dec–Mar.

The area where the Paria River and the Colorado River meet is part of Glen Canyon National Recreation Area. Even if you plan to skip Lake Powell, you might want to stop here to get close to the river and see this section of unflooded canyon.

Start at the **Navajo Bridge Interpretive Center,** on Route 89A, where you can learn from the exhibits and cross a pedestrian walkway over the old Navajo Bridge across the Colorado River. Before the bridge, a ferry on the river was the main way for early Mormon settlers to cross. Drive down to Lees Ferry to see the ranch built by the ferry's Mormon pioneers, and other historic buildings. A worthwhile $1 booklet leads you through.

Lees Ferry is also your only chance in many miles to get close to the Colorado River by car and get a sense of its power to carve canyons. Fishermen and rafters use the Park Service dock and facilities here for trips on the Colorado. They float down from Glen Canyon and from here down through the Grand Canyon (covered in the park chapters that follow). Several hiking trails of varying levels of difficulty traverse the surrounding canyon floor and walls, and a challenging 34-mile backpacking trip down the Paria ends here. To plan that hike, get information from the public land agencies in the area (see "Backpacking," in chapter 10, "Glen Canyon National Recreation Area"). For day hikes in the area, drop in at the ranger station for guidance.

We enjoyed **camping** at Lees Ferry during spring break. The campground stands on a hill overlooking the river, surrounded by the canyon walls. This low ground is desert-like and warm, and each site has a sun shade. The first-come, first-served campground, open year-round, is $12 a night and has cold-water bathrooms. There's a dump station down at the dock.

Back up on Route 89A, there are a couple of businesses and the bizarre **standing rocks.** The huge red boulders stand atop thin pillars of softer rock that has eroded under them. Pull off and take some pictures.

## NEAR KANAB

**Pipe Spring National Monument.** 14 miles west of Fredonia on Rte. 389, Fredonia, Arizona; 21 miles from Kanab, Utah. ☎ **928/643-7105.** www.nps.gov/pisp. Admission $3 per person over age 17. June–Sept daily 7:30am–5:30pm (guided tours 8am–4:30pm); Oct–May 8am–5pm (guided tours 9am–3:30pm).

This monument represents cowboy and Mormon history. A ranch of red sandstone was built here as a fort to defend against Navajo raiders and to raise cattle. Park Service guides lead tours of the ranch house every half hour, or you can use a self-guided map to tour the grounds. There are often living history demonstrations, such as pioneer cooking and blacksmithing, during the summer.

**Coral Pink Sand Dunes State Park.** Off Rte. 89 north of Kanab, Utah. ☎ **435/648-2800,** 800/322-3770 for camping reservations. $4 day-use fee; $13 camping fee; $6.25 reservation fee. 22 camping sites; tents or RVs. Flush toilets, showers, dump station.

These sand dunes are popular among off-road vehicle enthusiasts, but there are also hiking trails, and kids will enjoy playing in the sand. Stop for a picnic on the way, or stay in a well-developed campground. You can reserve camping sites 3 to 120 days in advance.

## A SIDE TRIP TO DINOSAUR NATIONAL MONUMENT

**Dinosaur National Monument** is in northeast Utah and northwest Colorado. It isn't near the parks covered in this chapter, but it might be in your path if you're coming from that direction or visiting the Rockies (see part V, "The Rockies"). I include it mostly because it's among our favorite places in the national park system and a paradise for kids interested in dinosaurs.

The main attraction is the **dinosaur quarry,** where an ancient river full of dead dinosaurs fossilized into a cliffside tangle of thousands of bones of 10 different species. They've been uncovered and left undisturbed. The quarry is in a building where you can stand on a balcony over the bones and use a $1 guide map booklet to figure out which of your favorite dinosaurs you're seeing. There are also some bones you can touch. Rangers give frequent talks and answer questions. Scientists last excavated in 1991, but they continue to work in a lab at the site; and you can watch them through a large window if they happen to be working during your visit. The site is 150 million years old. No place or exhibit I've seen does a better job of conveying both the science and the wonder of paleontology.

The monument is at the edge of the Great Basin Desert, where the Green River cuts through rocky cliffs. The land is full of weird and varied rock formations. It's a grandly beautiful place on a manageable scale. Dinosaur is a popular spot for hiking and rafting on the Green River. The 1½-mile Desert Voices nature trail is at Split Mountain, where the Green carves through a high mound of rock. It's ingeniously aimed at adults and kids, with kids' signs made by kids. The monument's interpretive materials are exceptionally good and will guide you to the petroglyphs, hiking trails, and other activities.

The **Green River Campground** has 88 sites on the river under spreading shade trees. There are flush toilets, and the campground is generally open from April through September. Camping costs $12. Other, less developed campgrounds are available, too.

The monument lies on U.S. 40 just east of Vernal, Utah, partly in Colorado and just south of the Wyoming border. The **Park Headquarters** (☎ **970/374-3000;** www.nps. gov/dino) is on the Colorado side and open during the week. There you can ask questions and get into the backcountry and to a scenic drive through the Colorado section of the monument without paying the entrance fee. The **Quarry Visitor Center** (☎ **435/789-2115**), at the west end of the park, is the only place in the monument to see dinosaur bones. It's open daily from 8am to 7pm in the summer, and from 8am to 4:30pm in the winter. To get to it and several other popular areas in the Utah section of the monument, you must pay $10 per vehicle at a fee booth on the road (passes apply). In the summer, the small parking lot at the quarry is often full, and free shuttle buses run from a lot with a covered waiting area below. For more information, write to **Dinosaur National Monument, 4545 E. Hwy. 40, Dinosaur, CO 81610-9724.**

# CHAPTER 9

# Grand Canyon National Park

Nothing prepares you for it. The first sight of the Grand Canyon is a shock, no matter how many pictures you've seen. Coming from the south, you've been driving through pines and desert, with your eyes focused at the usual distance on the world around you. Then, all of a sudden, the earth in front of you disappears. There's nothing but air for 1 mile down and 10 miles across. I found my mind slipping its gears, not quite able to take in all I was seeing at once. I couldn't grasp all the layers of rock, carved into so many shapes, shadow and searing brightness, tiny and massive rocks fitting together. We all reacted the same way, silent and with wide eyes. Julia, only 2 at the time, wanted to be held high to gaze in the canyon for a long time. She broke the silence with a hushed comment: "Lots and lots of castles!" That's how I've thought of the Grand Canyon ever since.

Over the following days, however, we learned of the drawbacks of visiting the Grand Canyon with young children. There's not much for them to do other than just look at the canyon. The hiking trails are either flat, paved paths along the rim or brutally steep descents into the furnace of the canyon, too tough for young kids. The famous mules serve fewer than 100 visitors a day — 1 in 1,000 visitors gets to go. The famous trails are terribly crowded. Most people make short visits to the park, just driving in, taking a look, and passing on. The average stay is 4 hours. In the summer, visitors clog the South Rim area with cars. With the parking at the overlooks full, people park along the roads and walk through the woods to the canyon rim. It's dangerous, leaves ugly lines of cars all along the road, and destroys the plants and trees that are trampled. But what else can people do?

You need to plan carefully to avoid these pitfalls. Plan far in advance to obtain backcountry permits so that you can get away from the throngs. Visit the quieter North Rim. Get up before dawn to beat the heat and the crowds on canyon trails, catching the spectacular morning vistas.

## BEST THINGS TO DO

- See the canyon at dawn or sunset, when the angle of the sun picks out the folds in the rock.
- Rise before dawn to hike down into the canyon, seeing how its extraordinary walls look from close up.
- Get a backcountry camping permit so that you can hike farther, away from the crowds.

See "Activities" (p. 218).

# HISTORY: THE STRUGGLE FOR PRESERVATION

The human history of the Grand Canyon mostly has to do with how people tried to get across it or down it. The canyon is so long, so deep, and so steep that it divides the Southwest. It has blocked animals and plants as well as people. Living things that cannot survive in the heat at the bottom of the canyon could never cross. For people, the canyon was hard to cross because of the steepness of the sides. Even today, with bridges and dams that help us go around the canyon and over the Colorado River, the area to the north is remote and not many people live there. Those who live on the strip of Arizona that lies north of the canyon connect more with southern Utah than with the rest of their own state.

Native Americans who lived here didn't have written language, so scientists try to figure out their history from the things they left behind: ruins of houses, tools, baskets, and so on. Explorers of hard-to-reach caves have found models of animals made of willow and cottonwood twigs that were split, bent, and tied together. These were about 4,000 years old, from before the time when southwestern Natives learned about farming or settled down in villages. Scientists think that hunters might have used the animal shapes to magically help their hunt.

Later, after they learned to farm, Native Americans lived in the canyon and on the rim in small villages, but the Grand Canyon area

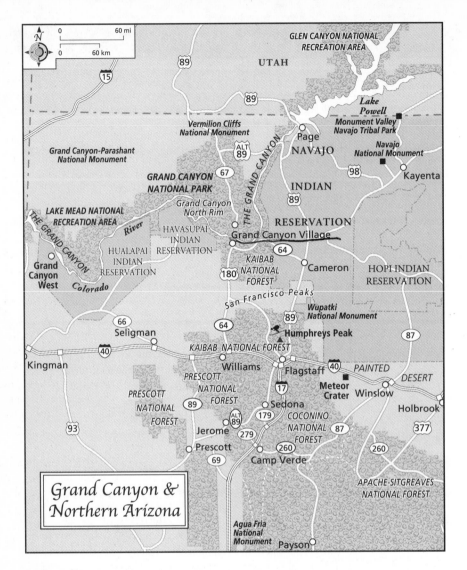

Grand Canyon &
Northern Arizona

never was a center of large, complicated villages like the great stone pueblos farther south and east. This area was the edge of the Ancestral Puebloan (also called Anasazi) territory, where they mixed with other, simpler cultures. You can see one of their villages at the Tusayan Museum and ruin (see p. 217). The last natives who lived in the Grand Canyon Village area left some 600 years ago, but the Havasupai still live along Havasupai Creek, to the west.

Explorers from Spain first saw the Grand Canyon in 1540, but they couldn't find a way

down. No one figured out how to get across until 1776, when a group led by a pair of Spanish missionaries set out to find a route from Santa Fe, New Mexico, to Monterey, California. They crossed the Colorado River in Glen Canyon and also discovered, but did not use, the crossing at Lees Ferry. Later travelers used those routes, but the Grand Canyon still wasn't explored even after Mexico gained independence from Spain. In 1846, the United States attacked Mexico and in 2 years of the Mexican War won most of the American West south of Oregon and west of

Santa Fe. The U.S. government sent explorers to map the area, looking for routes for railroad lines. In 1857, one of the military groups found the Grand Canyon and decided it was impossible to survey. The party reported back that it was beautiful but useless, and said there was no reason for anyone else to go back.

A member of that group convinced the Grand Canyon's most famous explorer, John Wesley Powell, to float down the Colorado in 1869 with a party of 10. Powell took wooden boats all the way from the Green River in Wyoming to towns below the Grand Canyon. Think about his courage: No one knew whether the trip was possible. There might be huge waterfalls. If he ran into trouble with the boats, there might be no way out, up the canyon walls and across the desert. When one of his boats crashed in the rapids, three of his group said they'd had enough and tried to hike out, and when they reached the canyon rim they were killed, probably by Indians. But Powell made it, then did it again 2 years later. He was a geologist, and he carefully wrote down his exciting discoveries, which are still studied. He never expected any waterfalls. Looking at how dirty the river was, he knew it must be eroding the rock quickly and would have eroded any rock shelves that would make a waterfall.

Prospectors explored the canyon and found valuable metals in the 1870s and 1880s, but they didn't make much money mining because it was too expensive and difficult to get the ore they found from inside the canyon to where people could use it. In the 1890s, the miners started to realize that they could make money showing the canyon off to tourists, and they began building hotels and trails. In 1901, a railroad punched through, and President Theodore Roosevelt came in 1903 (see "Read Aloud: Teddy Roosevelt Toughens Up," in chapter 14, "Yellowstone National Park"). In 1908 he made the canyon a national monument, protecting it for visitors to enjoy.

Since then, the history of the park has been about protecting it from human needs. The people of the Southwest need the water in the Colorado River, so dams catch it in a series of lakes. The Glen Canyon Dam, holding back Lake Powell above the Grand Canyon, controls the wild flow of the river. That changed the nature of the canyon in ways scientists still study. Environmentalists defeated a plan to build a dam that would have backed up water in the Grand Canyon itself (see "Read Aloud: Should Glen Canyon Dam Be Unbuilt?" in chapter 10, "Glen Canyon National Recreation Area").

Perhaps most difficult of all, the canyon suffers from too much love. About five million tourists come each year, crowding beautiful places and bringing their garbage and other waste. On a summer day, 6,500 cars may try to fit into the 2,000 parking spaces. Down in the canyon, the dry weather preserves anything that's left behind — early films show rotting trees still in the same places after 100 years. Garbage lasts just as long, so the Park Service works hard to keep any from being left. For example, backpackers are encouraged to carry out their bowel movements in plastic bags, and rangers haul the contents of some backcountry toilets up to the rim on mules. Crowds overwhelm the South Rim in the summer.

The Park Service has decided to limit the number of cars in the park and expects someday to have to limit the number of people. The Park Service aims to keep the Grand Canyon as close as possible to the way it was when Powell first floated down the Colorado, no matter how many people visit. History will tell whether that's possible.

# ORIENTATION

The Grand Canyon has three main areas for visitors: the South Rim's **Grand Canyon Village,** the **Desert View area** on the eastern end of the South Rim, and the **North Rim.**

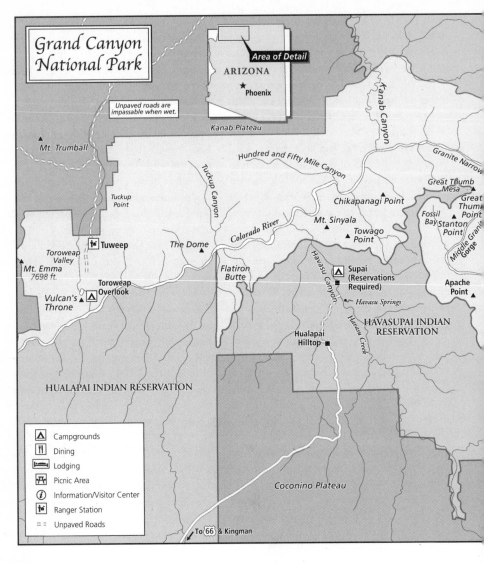

Tusayan is the touristy highway town just outside the entrance near Grand Canyon Village.

## THE PARK
## The South Rim:
## Grand Canyon Village

The Grand Canyon Village area is the traditional center of visits, with the main entrance at the tourist town of Tusayan. In the village area are historic hotels, the area's largest campground, several trailheads that lead to the canyon, and the Park Service headquarters. Long-term plans call for removing most cars from this overcrowded area.

## Desert View

This area is 25 miles east of Grand Canyon Village on a highway that runs along the rim. It has the Route 64 entrance, a campground, a store, and a few miles to the west the Tusayan Ruin and Museum. It is a quieter place to camp than the village, but you spend more time driving to the trailheads.

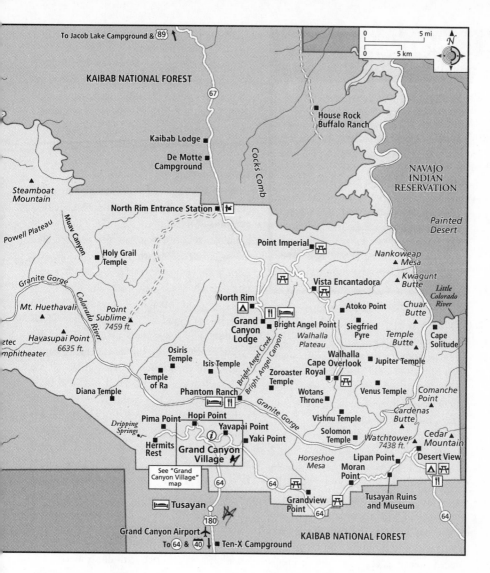

## The North Rim

The North Rim of the canyon is open only from mid-May to mid-October, depending on weather. It's a more rustic area, with a lodge, store, visitor center, and campground. The North Rim is a 5-hour drive from the South Rim. Glen Canyon National Recreation Area and Zion National Park both are closer to the North Rim by road than the Grand Canyon's own South Rim.

# MAKING THE ARRANGEMENTS

## WHEN TO GO

For families with school obligations, only a winter holiday break offers much chance of avoiding the crowds. It can be a delightful time to visit the South Rim, but snow and ice can make hiking tricky. Spring break (mid-Mar to Apr) is a bit less busy than mid-summer, but still crowded. You might get snowed

## A NOTE ON THE NEW TRANSPORTATION PLAN

The National Park Service has been unable to implement its grand plan to get rid of most of the cars in the village area. The changes were supposed to be finished by 2001, but the cars keep coming. The latest delay was a decision in December 2000 by the U.S. Congress to order more study. Now the Park Service hopes for a mass transit system to be in place by 2005, with day visitors parking outside the park entrance and only campers and hotel guests driving in. The Park Service publishes updates on the plans, which you can get by calling ☎ **800/638-7888**, or from the website (www.nps.gov/grca).

on even through May on the South Rim, and the North Rim is closed until mid-May. Spring-break high temperatures in the canyon are often in the 70s, the best hiking weather. An added bonus of off-season visits: more sleep, because you don't have to get up as early to see the sunrise in the canyon.

Summer down in the canyon is very hot, with temperatures frequently topping 100°F, with high temperatures along the rim usually in the 80s. Those conditions aren't suitable for hiking the steep canyon trails, and backpacking is miserable. Of the summer months, June is best and July hottest. The Park Service asks hikers to avoid midday hiking in the summer because so many people get into trouble. Because the rim is typically 15°F to 20°F cooler than the inner gorge, summer can be pleasant at the top, but the crowds are extreme.

## How Much Time to Spend

On a 1-day visit to the park, you can enjoy the spectacular views and take a walk. In view of the distance you have to drive, you'll want to spend a night somewhere relatively near, such as Flagstaff, 77 miles to the south; Williams, 56 miles to the south; or just outside the park's south entrance in Tusayan.

For a family that isn't up to strenuous hiking, 2 or 3 nights should be enough time for a complete visit to the South or North Rim, including seeing the canyon at different times of the day, which is important. More time could be boring for the kids. If you're up to a backpacking trip, a few days of rugged day hiking, or a rafting trip, you'll need more time.

## Reading Up

Park bookstores at the visitor centers are operated by the Grand Canyon Association (☎ **800/858-2808** or 928/638-2481; www. grandcanyon.org); you can also order online or by phone. **Maps:** The $6 inexpensive *Earthwalk Press Hiking Map Guide* offers adequate detail; the plastic Trails Illustrated map ($10) is more durable. The association also sells $3 map guides to each park trail. **Trail Guides:** The association carries *Hiking the Grand Canyon,* by John Annerino (Sierra Club), which includes a map and has all the park trails recently updated. I used and liked Scott S. Warren's *100 Classic Hikes in Arizona* (The Mountaineers), which gives details on hikes and backpacking trips in the canyon, and many other alternative hikes beyond the park that are easier and less crowded. It is not listed on the association's website. **Archeology:** *Southwestern Archeology in the National Park System,* by Robert H. and Florence C. Lister (Southwest Parks and Monuments Association), is clearly written at an adult level and rich with illustrations.

## How Far to Plan Ahead

If you can plan your trip to the Grand Canyon a year or two ahead, you have a better chance at some of the special activities, like taking a mule ride or staying at Phantom Ranch, in the bottom of the canyon. River-rafting outings also book a year or more ahead (see "Rafting," p. 220). For hotel rooms, you need 6 months for a decent selection in the summer, less for the off-season. Reservations for blocks of rooms may be canceled close to the date, so

## WEATHER CHART: CANYON TEMPERATURES & DAYLIGHT

| | SOUTH RIM ELEV. 7,000 AVG. HIGH/LOW (°F) | NORTH RIM ELEV. 8,400 AVG. HIGH/LOW (°F) | CANYON FLOOR ELEV. 2,600 AVG. HIGH/LOW (°F) | SUNRISE/SUNSET TIME (1ST DAY OF PERIOD) |
|---|---|---|---|---|
| Dec.–Jan. | 43/19 | 39/18 | 56/37 | 7:21/5:14 |
| February | 46/22 | 40/18 | 64/42 | 7:29/5:26 |
| March | 50/24 | 44/22 | 72/48 | 6:58/6:24 |
| April | 59/29 | 52/28 | 82/55 | 6:14/6:51 |
| May | 70/37 | 62/33 | 92/63 | 5:36/7:16 |
| June | 80/46 | 73/40 | 103/73 | 5:13/7:40 |
| July | 85/53 | 77/47 | 106/77 | 5:15/7:49 |
| August | 82/52 | 74/46 | 103/75 | 5:36/7:33 |
| September | 75/45 | 69/39 | 96/69 | 6:00/6:56 |
| October | 64/36 | 58/31 | 83/58 | 6:24/6:12 |
| November | 51/27 | 46/25 | 68/46 | 6:51/5:32 |

keep calling. Campgrounds book up for the high season soon after they become available on the national reservation system (see "National Park Campground Reservations," in chapter 1, "Planning Your Trip"). Off-season, you might find mud or snow, but you'll also have more choices.

## GETTING THERE

See "Exploring the Region," in chapter 8, "Layers upon Layers," for advice on traveling to and around this part of the Southwest and linking a Grand Canyon visit with a trip to another park.

## By Car

If you're coming **from the north** by way of the other parks in this section, see the descriptions of U.S. 89 and 89A in chapter 8.

From the east or west, Interstate 40 runs through northern Arizona. **From the east,** turn north from Flagstaff on Route 180. **From the west,** turn at Williams on Route 64.

**From the south,** I-17 leads 140 miles from Phoenix to Flagstaff; stop off at Montezuma's

Castle National Monument or camp in Oak Creek Canyon and see Sedona.

## By Air

The closest major airports are in Phoenix and Las Vegas. The Grand Canyon Airport in Tusayan has commuter flights from Las Vegas on **Scenic Air** (☎ **800/634-6801;** www.scenic.com). **Budget** rents cars at the airport (☎ **800/527-0700**).

## By Train

A good alternative to driving to the South Rim is to park in Williams, on I-40, and take the train. The run isn't scenic, but the staff works hard to make it entertaining for families, using historic equipment. During the summer, the machinery includes a steam engine to pull the train. If all you want to do is look at the canyon for a few hours and leave, you can ride the train both ways in 1 day and skip the hassle of finding accommodations or parking. The train leaves Williams at 10am for a 2¼-hour ride; you should check in earlier. It spends 3¼ hours at the canyon and gets back to Williams at 5:45pm. Round-trip coach class tickets are $54.50 for adults, $24.95 for kids 2 to 16 (babies under 2 sit on their parents' laps free); higher classes are $20 to $85 more, plus the park entrance fee and sales tax. The **Grand Canyon Railroad depot** is on Grand Canyon Boulevard in Williams (take Exit 163 from I-40); call ☎ **800/843-8724** or 928/773-1976, or check www.thetrain.com for more information.

## WHAT TO PACK
### Clothing

Pack for two climates, the desert of the lowlands and the cooler high country. You'll need light-colored, lightweight, breathable clothing and sun hats for hiking trips into the canyon or in the desert outside the park. In the spring and fall, you'll also need sweaters and jackets for cool nights on the rim. Bring clothes you can layer to adjust to changes in elevation and temperature. In the summer, the canyon is too hot for much hiking, and while nighttime lows on the rims are in the 40s and 50s, you'll mostly need hot-weather clothes.

A shirt with a collar and long pants will do nicely at all the park restaurants. For hiking in the canyon, you need sturdy footwear, such as hiking boots or shoes, not sneakers. In the winter and spring you'll likely encounter snow and mud at the rim and ice on the high parts of the trails. Crampons, which are ice-walking spikes that attach to your shoes, are for rent at the store in the South Rim Market Plaza. They're a necessity on the canyon trails in case of ice.

### Gear

Tent camping on the rim during spring break is iffy. It could be comfortable, or you might be buried in snow. Weather changes are quick and extreme. The temperatures are good for tenting in the canyon in the spring, but that's only for backpackers. The unpredictable conditions make RVs an especially attractive choice for this region; see "Practicalities: The RV Advantage," in chapter 8, for tips on renting one. In the summer, tent camping at the rim is great, but it's very hot down below. Bring gear to stay warm down to freezing on spring nights, and light gear for summer.

For day hiking, bring hats, water bottles, a small backpack, and the footgear described above. Strollers can manage most walks at the rim, but a baby backpack will give you more options.

## WHERE TO SPEND THE NIGHT

### CAMPING
#### Park Service Campgrounds

Besides the car camping campgrounds listed here, campgrounds and campsites for backpackers are below the rim, including the Bright Angel Campground, allocated through the backcountry permit system (see p. 212).

#### CAMPGROUNDS ACCEPTING
#### RESERVATIONS

Permits for **Mather** and **North Rim** campgrounds should be reserved when sites become available on the national reservation system covered under "National Park Campground Reservations," in chapter 1.

**Mather.** Grand Canyon Village, behind the commercial area. $10–$15 per site. 320 sites; RVs or tents. Flush toilets, laundry, and showers nearby. Open year-round; reservations accepted Mar–Nov.

This large, partly shaded campground sits among the pinyons back from the rim and commercial area in Grand Canyon Village. You can walk to the store, showers, visitor center, and rim, but you'll need to use the shuttle or a bike to get to trailheads and restaurants. There's little ground cover, so sites don't have much privacy.

**North Rim.** Bright Angel Point, Rte. 67 at North Rim. $15–$20 per site. 82 sites; tents or RVs. Showers and laundry nearby. Closed mid-Oct to mid-May. Reservations available.

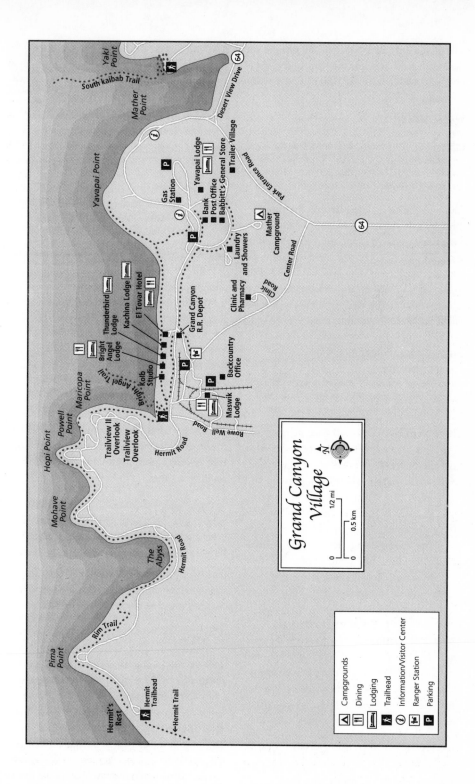

## Grand Canyon Village

Yaki Point

South Kaibab Trail

Mather Point

Yavapai Point

Desert View Drive

64

Park Entrance Road

P

Yavapai Lodge

Gas Station

Bank

Post Office

Babbitt's General Store

Trailer Village

64

Mather Campground

Center Road

Laundry and Showers

P

Clinic Road

Clinic and Pharmacy

Thunderbird Lodge

Kachina Lodge

El Tovar Hotel

Grand Canyon R.R. Depot

Bright Angel Lodge

Maricopa Point

Bright Angel Trail

Kolb Studio

P

Backcountry Office

P

Maswik Lodge

Powell Point

Hopi Point

Maricopa Point

Trailview II Overlook

Trailview Overlook

Hermit Road

Rowe Well Road

Mohave Point

The Abyss

Hermit Road

Rim Trail

Pima Point

Hermit's Rest

Hermit Trailhead

← Hermit Trail

1/2 mi

0.5 km

0

0

N

### Legend

- ◭ Campgrounds
- 🍴 Dining
- 🏠 Lodging
- 🚶 Trailhead
- ℹ Information/Visitor Center
- 👤 Ranger Station
- P Parking

This is the only Park Service campground on the North Rim. It's near the store and gas station, and within walking distance of most of the trails.

**Trailer Village.** East of Yavapai Lodge at Grand Canyon Village. $20 for 2, $1.75 per extra person. DISC, MC, V. 84 sites; RVs only. Full hookups, showers and laundry nearby. Open year-round; reserve through Amfac, the park concessionaire (☎ 303/29-PARKS; www.amfac.com).

Although the long-range plan calls for improvement, this was just a line of bare parking spaces with a few scattered shade trees when I saw it. It's conveniently in the park, with hookups for your rig. You'll need to use bikes or the shuttle to get to restaurants and trailheads. Amfac takes reservations up to 23 months in advance; call as far ahead as possible.

### FIRST-COME, FIRST-SERVED CAMPGROUNDS

**Desert View.** Rte. 64 at east entrance to the park. $12 per site. 50 sites; RVs or tents. Flush toilets. Closed mid-Oct to mid-May. No reservations.

This eastern end of the park is more open and desert-like than the village, quieter and farther from the center of things. But the major trailheads at the village are 25 miles away, and other than the Watchtower and Tusayan Museum, which take less than half a day, there's not much to do in the Desert View area. The campground doesn't take reservations, but at busy times you need to get there well before noon for a chance at a site; as people leave, those in line take their sites.

## Forest Service Campgrounds

The Kaibab National Forest has several campgrounds near the park. Each can accommodate tents or RVs. The Forest Service campgrounds don't take reservations. At busy times, you need to get there early for a chance at a site; as people leave, newcomers take their sites. For more information, contact the Kaibab National Forest (www.fs.fed.us/r3/kai) on the North Rim at the **North Kaibab Ranger District** (☎ 928/643-7395), which

operates a visitor center at Jacob Lake daily from mid-May to mid-October; for the South Rim, contact **Tusayan Ranger District** (☎ 928/638-2443).

### SOUTH RIM

**Ten X Campground.** Just south of Tusayan on Rte. 64/180. $10 per vehicle per site. 70 sites. Pit toilets. Closed Oct–Apr.

This is the Forest Service campground nearest to the park's main, south entrance. In the summer it offers campfires, and sites shaded by ponderosa pines.

### NORTH RIM

**Jacob Lake.** Rte. 89A and Rte. 67, about 30 miles from the North Rim. $15 per site. 54 sites. Flush toilets. Closed mid-Oct to mid-May.

This campground is near the Forest Service visitor center at the turn to the North Rim high on the pine-covered Kaibab Plateau.

**Demotte.** Rte. 67, 5 miles outside the park boundary. $15 per site. 23 sites. Closed Nov–June.

This is the closest campground outside the north side of the park, with a woodsy setting at an 8,760-foot elevation.

## Backcountry Permits

To camp in the canyon you need a backcountry permit. The only other way to sleep in the canyon is to spend the night at Phantom Ranch (p. 214). You don't need a permit to day hike, but the bottom of the canyon is too far for a family to do a round-trip in a day.

Planning ahead and knowing the system is important at the Grand Canyon because so many people are chasing so few permits (typically, one permit for every four applications). Begin planning in the fall for a spring-break hike. First, figure out where you want to go. See "Backpacking" (p. 218). Get a trail guide, a topographic map, and the Park Service publication *Backcountry Trip Planner.* It's a newsprint guide with good advice, a map of the permit areas, and a form to request a backcountry permit. Order the planner from the park (see "Grand Canyon Address Book," p. 203), or download the information and permit form from www.nps.gov/grca/grandcanyon/trip_planner/backcountry/. Backcountry rangers answer questions by phone Monday through Friday from 1 to 5pm at ☎ **928/638-7875.**

Permits cost $10 plus $5 per person, per night; you can pay by check, Visa, or MasterCard. The permits are issued starting the first day of the month 4 months before the trip, so permits for all of March start to disappear on November 1 of the preceding year. Applications are taken by mail (use the main park address), by fax (**928/638-2125**), and in person at the **Backcountry Office,** at the Maswik Transportation Center across the railroad tracks from Maswik Lodge. Applications postmarked before the first of the month are discarded. Overnight deliveries are accepted, but faxes with a credit-card number make the most sense — you can get ahead of the day's mail by faxing first thing in the morning or right after midnight. In-person applicants are taken as they come in, giving them priority, but that isn't practical for most people.

If you arrive without a permit, show up at the backcountry office in Grand Canyon Village before 8am; that's when permits that aren't picked up are given away to people on a standby list. You can usually get a permit through a cancellation within 2 or 3 days, but you have to be at the office at 8am each morning or your name is dropped from the list.

## HOTELS

Besides the hotels within the park, a strip of motels lies along the road just outside the entrance in Tusayan. Offerings include a **Holiday Inn Express** (☎ **888/473-2269** or 928/638-3000), a **Quality Inn** (☎ **800/228-5151** or 928/638-2673), a **Best Western** (☎ **800/622-6966** or 928/638-2681), a **Rodeway Inn** (☎ **800/228-2000** or 928/638-2414), and **Moqui Lodge** (☎ **928/638-2424**), which is owned by the park concessionaire, Amfac, and is open April through October only.

The hotels described below are in the park, operated by Amfac (see "Grand Canyon Address Book," p. 203). By staying near the rim, you can be gazing into the canyon just after sunrise and just before sunset, when it is at its most scenic. The most desirable rooms, such as the rim cabins at Bright Angel, go a year in advance. Some dates in the high season book up 6 months ahead all over the park. If you're flexible with dates and choices or travel in the fall or winter, you can find rooms 1 or 2 months in advance. Because Amfac allows cancellations without penalty up to 48 hours in advance, you can sometimes grab a room at the last minute, even at the busiest times, by directly calling the Grand Canyon Lodges switchboard (☎ **928/638-2631**). This is also the number to call to contact lodging guests. Only El Tovar has air-conditioning. Children under 16 stay free with their parents, and Amfac takes all major credit cards.

**Bright Angel Lodge.** 89 rms and cabins. $63–$121 double, $7 per extra adult.

This is one of my favorite national park hotels, not because of the luxury or style, but for the incomparable location on the canyon rim and the quirky and unmistakable character of the buildings and rooms. The hotel is of stone and logs, strange angles and disconnected lines, Spartan backpacker rooms and charming little cabins with views that would make a vacation by themselves. A pleasant social flow passes through as tourists saunter past the patios of rim cabins and wait in front of the lobby's huge stone fireplace to see if they can join a mule ride. The accommodations range from crude to delightful; some have no amenities at all, while others have telephones and refrigerators.

**El Tovar.** 78 units. $116–$174 double, $199–$284 suite; $11 per extra adult. TV TEL.

This big log structure on the rim dates from before the canyon was set aside as a park. Although not likely to be confused with a luxury hotel or resort elsewhere, there's a rustic elegance fitting to the park, and the location along the canyon rim couldn't be better. The suites are spacious, although the rooms can be small for families, and you may worry about making too much noise.

**Kachina and Thunderbird Lodges.** 104 units. $114–$124 double, $9 per extra adult. TV TEL.

These ugly concrete buildings look and feel like something from a 1970s community college campus yet occupy some of the world's best real estate, on the canyon rim. The park's long-range plan calls for them to be demolished, but in the meantime, they offer good standard rooms; those with a canyon view cost $10 more.

**Maswik Lodge.** 278 rms and cabins. Rms $73–$118 double, $9 per extra adult. Cabins $63 double, $7 per extra adult. TV TEL.

These two-story wooden buildings are set back from the rim in the village area but are still convenient to most of what you'll want to see. The rooms in the newer and more attractive northern section are large, with high ceilings, tables, and two queen-size beds. They cost $40 more than the south rooms, which are comfortable but unmemorable. The cabins are rustic.

**Yavapai Lodge.** 358 units. $88–$102 double, $9 per extra adult. TV TEL. Closed Nov–Mar.

Near the business area, away from the historic part of the village, these buildings offer basic motel rooms a step below the best at Maswik, but still quite serviceable. Yavapai East is at the higher end of the range and has standard rooms in two-story wooden buildings. Yavapai West, in one-story brick buildings where you can drive right up to your door, has rooms that cost $15 less. They're out-of-date, and certainly unattractive from the outside, but inside they're more than adequate and might be just the kind of low-key place you want.

## North Rim

**Grand Canyon Lodge.** 201 rms and cabins. $85–$110 double, $10 per extra adult. TV TEL. Closed mid-Oct to mid-May.

The only hotel on the North Rim stands out on a point above the canyon, with basic motel units and cabins that range from rustic to almost luxurious. The only accommodation for this area of the park, it's a center of activity, with a gift shop, bookstore, restaurant, and snack bar. The attractive stone building is in the rustic national park style.

## In the Canyon

**Phantom Ranch** is a famous and beautiful lodge at the bottom of the canyon. The only ways to get there are on foot, by mule, or on a raft. If you manage to book an overnight mule ride (see p. 219), a night in a cabin is included in the reservation and price. Hikers sleep in single-sex dorms and can reserve meals in the dining hall, but those slots book a year in advance through **Amfac Parks and Resorts** (see "Grand Canyon Address Book," p. 203). A dorm bed is $23.37 (including tax) per person per night.

# WHEN YOU ARRIVE

## ENTRANCE FEES

The fee to enter Grand Canyon National Park is $20 per vehicle, or $10 per individual arriving by train from Williams. If you're visiting several parks in the region, a $50 National Parks Pass makes sense; it's good for all parks and monuments operated by the National Park Service for a year (see p. 18).

# VISITOR CENTERS
## South Rim

**Canyon View Information Plaza.** Near Mather Point. Buildings open daily during daylight hours; outside displays available 24 hours.

This new visitor center was built as the initial stop-off for the new mass transit system, which now is delayed at least until 2005. At this writing, there was short-term parking within walking distance at Mather Point, or you can get there on the shuttle bus. Rangers and outdoor displays explain what to do in the park. Nearby are a large bookstore and a paved path leading to the Rim Trail.

**Desert View Information Center.** Near the east entrance, at the Watchtower. Daily 9am–5pm.

A small, one-room station with a ranger to answer questions and a few books for sale serves as the visitor center at the east entrance.

## North Rim

**Kaibab Plateau Visitor Center.** U.S. 89A and Rte. 67, Jacob Lake. ☎ **928/643-7298.** Daily 8am–5pm. Closed Mid-Oct to mid-May.

The exhibits and ranger programs at this U.S. Forest Service facility about 44 miles north of the North Rim are the most extensive you'll find in the area.

**North Rim Visitor Center.** Just north of Grand Canyon Lodge. ☎ **928/638-7864.** Daily 8am–6pm. Closed mid-Oct to mid-May.

This small visitor center, with restrooms in back of the building, has a few exhibits, but primarily just offers a place to ask questions.

# GETTING AROUND
## By Car

The current driving and parking arrangements in Grand Canyon Village are horrible in the summer and difficult at other times; park your car and leave it. You can get around by shuttle. West of the village, to Hermits Rest, you have to take the shuttle in the sum-

mer. Only a car can get you to the North Rim. It's a 5-hour drive from the village: east to Desert View on Route 64, then north on U.S. 89 to 89A, then west to Jacob Lake, and south to the rim on Route 67. The park's most spectacular drive for private cars is on the South Rim from the village east along Route 64, to Desert View and out of the park. (The planned new mass transit system is described on p. 208.)

## By Shuttle

Once you get the hang of it, the current shuttle system makes getting around the park fairly easy, but it's a good idea to carry the map of shuttle-bus routes, widely available at the park. Having the map also will put you up-to-date on changes in the system, which are likely. At this writing, shuttles were running on three loops: The Village Route, which circles the developed village area; the Kaibab Trail Route, which makes a circuit from Canyon View Information Plaza to Yaki Point and back; and the Hermits Rest Route, which runs from the west end of the village area to Hermits Rest and back. The Village and Kaibab Trail routes operate year-round. The Hermits Rest Route is currently operated from March to November only, but park officials hope for funding to run it year-round. The Village and Hermits Rest shuttles run every 10 to 15 minutes (with less frequent runs early and late in the day), while the Kaibab Trail route shuttle runs every 30 minutes. Use of the shuttles is free and unlimited, and no tickets are needed.

## By Bicycle or on Foot

Given the traffic crunch and the plans to solve it, it's a wonder the park hasn't developed bikes as an option by now, but it hasn't, and biking generally isn't safe for families on these clogged roads. In the village, if you stay at Maswik Lodge or one of the hotels right on the rim, you can walk most places, but it's too far to walk from Yavapai Lodge or the campgrounds.

**Emergencies**    Dial ☎ **911** in emergencies. Dial an additional 9 first from a hotel room within the park. **Grand Canyon Clinic** (☎ **928/638-2551**) is in Grand Canyon Village; it's open Monday through Friday 8am to 8pm, Saturday 9am to 1pm, with shorter hours in winter.

**Stores    Canyon Village Marketplace** (☎ **928/638-2262**) in Grand Canyon Village, at Market Plaza, is a full grocery store and has camping equipment rentals and some sporting goods too. Prices are a bit high, so it makes sense to stock up in Flagstaff, Williams, or whatever town you're coming from. Smaller branches are at Desert View and at the North Rim near the campground.

**Banks    Bank One** is in Market Plaza in Grand Canyon Village and has an ATM. There's another ATM in Tusayan at the IMAX theater.

**Post Offices**    On the South Rim, Market Plaza has a post office. On the North Rim, there's a window in the lodge.

**Gear Sales & Rental    Canyon Village Marketplace** (☎ **928/638-2262**), in Grand Canyon Village, and a small store near the **North Rim campground** are the main places to get gear in the park. They rent crampons for winter hikes and cross-country skis. At this writing, bikes were not for rent at the canyon.

## KEEPING SAFE & HEALTHY

In addition to the tips here, see "Dealing with Hazards" (chapter 1), for information on dehydration, elevation, hypothermia, sunburn, and snake and insect bites.

## Falling

People are killed every year falling into the Grand Canyon, sometimes for very stupid reasons (suicide is the most frequent cause). Visitors have fallen in while sitting on a railing, getting dizzy on a precipice, or backing up to have their picture taken. There are no guard rails along much of the Rim Trail, so one wild move could be the last. No child has ever died from a fall, which tells you about the intelligence of some adults. We made sure to hold hands whenever we were near the edge with our kids, and we got no arguments from them.

## Heat Exhaustion

Most people who die or have to be rescued at the Grand Canyon overestimate their ability to climb out. Walking down into the canyon is easy and alluring; going back takes twice as long and many times as much energy. For a strenuous 3-hour hike, you have to turn around after an hour. In the summer, rangers see dozens of people a day, usually casual day hikers, who need treatment or rescue because they went too far down and didn't bring enough water or food. Some die every year. Preparation and knowing your limits are key. Always take and drink plenty of water. Eat, too, because you also need electrolytes, and the water can leach nutrients from your system, causing a dangerous condition. Know the symptoms of and treatment for heat exhaustion and heat stroke (see chapter 1).

## Knee Problems

A friend who backpacked into the canyon found the steep descent the hardest part because walking downhill all day is so hard on knees and hips. Know your limits if you have joint problems.

# Enjoying the Park

## Natural Places
## The South Rim

The South Rim of the Grand Canyon is a great spot to see a vast and amazing natural place, but the rim itself is crowded and developed. You can find overlooks and pathways without many people, but they are the exception. That doesn't mean you can't have fun; you just have to ignore or enjoy the other people and plan ways to avoid the thickest crowds. Use the less-known trails, such as the Hermit Trail (p. 219), and get out at sunrise, one of the prettiest and least crowded times of day. Sunset is also very pretty, but the overlooks are most crowded. Other fun things to do: Take picnics to different places along the rim, and walk the Rim Trail at different times to see how the sun changes the canyon as the day passes; enjoy meeting other families at the campground or hotel; try to figure out the many foreign languages being spoken.

## Below the Rim

Everyone who visits the Grand Canyon should go at least a little way over the edge. The cliffs look completely different from down there, because you're walking across them on the trails. You get a better perspective when you see the individual rocks and folds of the canyon, and a better grasp of its sheer size. Also, as soon as you're on the exposed rock of the canyon side, you can feel the climate change. The air gets warmer, and yuccas and twigs of desert plants start to disappear until you're in a sterile landscape of broken, sun-heated rocks. It's hard to believe how quickly the change happens. See "Hiking" (p. 218) for ideas on where to go.

## The North Rim

One-tenth as many visitors go to the North Rim as the South. The area is quieter and more relaxed, and facilities intentionally have been kept rustic. Getting there takes time, so people who just want to drive through stay away. Only one trail from the developed area descends into the canyon, but more explore the pine woods at the rim. That allows families who can't tackle a steep canyon trek to have a good hike — something that's lacking on the South Rim. If you want to get away from the crowds, **Cape Royal Road** and **Point Imperial Road** connect with various overlooks and trails with fantastic views.

The North Rim is usually open only from mid-May to mid-October for overnight visitors. People can keep coming in just for the day until the snow flies, as late as December, but you have to be ready to leave quickly in case of a storm. The higher elevation — over 8,000 feet — makes the air thinner and cooler at the North Rim, and the forest of ponderosa pine is thicker and has more shade and more wildlife.

## Places for Learning

**Kolb Studio.** Grand Canyon Village at the Bright Angel Trailhead. Daily 8am–7pm, shorter hours off-season. Free admission.

The Kolb Brothers were early photographers of the canyon, and this house over the Bright Angel Trail was their studio and shop. There's a good bookstore on the upper level and there are frequent art exhibits down below.

**Tusayan Museum.** Rte. 64, 3 miles west of Desert View. Daily 9am–5pm. Free admission.

The small museum and nearby Ancestral Puebloan (Anasazi) ruin make up the park's best cultural display. The museum occupies a single room in a small stone building, with artifacts from the site displayed to show how the native people of the region lived and used their environment. The ruin amounts to low lines of stones where a pueblo stood for about 30 years 800 years ago. Signs do a good job of helping you imagine what it was like. The bathrooms are limited to portable toilets, but Desert View has full facilities. There are regular ranger-led tours of the ruin.

**Watchtower.** Hwy. 64, at Desert View. Daily 8am–5:30pm. 25¢ adults, ages 7 and under free.

The Santa Fe Railroad commissioned revered park architect Mary Jane Colter to build this odd structure, intended to replicate an Ancestral Puebloan (Anasazi) watchtower. The views from the top room, with telescopes, are great, and the big front patio is a good place for pictures. The ground floor is a big gift store.

**Yavapai Observation Station.** Yavapai Point, just east of the commercial center. Daily 8am–7pm, shorter hours off-season.

The station is a place to look out on the canyon and compare its layers to a geological cross section, and to see a few other exhibits. There's a small bookstore.

## ACTIVITIES
## Backpacking

To get into the canyon overnight and really see it, you'll probably need to hike in carrying your gear. For first-timers, it's a good idea to stick to the corridor of the Bright Angel and South Kaibab trails, which have campgrounds and water and can be connected into a 2- or 3-night loop. (Trails are described below, under "Hiking.") For example, hike down the South Kaibab, camp at the Bright Angel Campground at the bottom of the canyon, then take the Bright Angel Trail to Indian Garden Campground, halfway up, and then complete the final leg back to the top. It's a good spring-break trip for a family with elementary school–age children. See "Backcountry Permits" (p. 212) about reserving your trip and getting necessary advice.

Wherever you choose to go, remember that this steep desert hiking is different from what you might be used to. Especially in the summer, plan short days you can cover in the early morning and evening to avoid the midday heat. You also can lighten your load by having a **pack train** haul some of your stuff back up the canyon. The service costs $48.50 one-way for every 30 pounds; contact **Amfac** (see

"Grand Canyon Address Book," p. 203). Information about getting a bed at **Phantom Ranch,** at the bottom of the canyon, is on p. 214.

## Flightseeing

Helicopters and small planes from the Grand Canyon Airport in Tusayan swoop across the canyon many times a day. Seeing the canyon from the air gives you a better sense of its size and allows you to take in more angles and areas that you wouldn't see otherwise. But the experience is expensive for families and far from indispensable — it's just a fun add-on. Among companies offering flights are **Papillon Grand Canyon Helicopters** (☎ **928/628-2419** or 800/528-2418; www.papillon.com), which runs flights all day. A 30-minute tour is $99 for adults, $80 for children 2 to 11. Fixed-wing flights are offered by **Grand Canyon Airlines** (☎ **800/528-2413** or 928/638-2407; www.grandcanyonairlines.com), with a 50-minute tour for $75, $45 for kids 2 to 12.

## Hiking

The best way to see the Grand Canyon is to walk in and around it. Unfortunately, the main trails are strenuous and extremely crowded. The Park Service understandably tries to scare off unprepared hikers with its extreme warnings. I saw some of the idiots they have to deal with, including a woman on the South Kaibab Trail walking along a precipice in high heels and a tight skirt with a video camera in front of her face. But if you're cautious and follow some simple advice, there's no need to let the warnings stop you from enjoying the park.

During the hot months, hikers get into trouble with heat and exhaustion in the middle of the day. Experienced desert hikers stay put during the hot hours. If you start down at 6am and hike 90 minutes into the canyon, you can be back by 10:30am (remember, you have to allow twice as long to come up as to go down). Hikers going any distance over the rim should bring along ½ to 1 gallon of water per person per day, salty snacks, a sun hat, and sunblock. If you want a long hike, especially on a less-used trail, buy a topographic trail map and trail guide (see "Reading Up," p. 208). Bring a flashlight, a mirror for signaling, a jacket, and a first-aid kit.

Here are some of the main park trails:

**THE RIM TRAIL**  In the Grand Canyon Village area, the trail along the top of the canyon is paved and suitable for strollers. To the west of the village, it's rougher but still basically level, extending all the way to Hermits Rest, 8 miles away. There, or at points along the way, you can catch a shuttle back.

**THE BRIGHT ANGEL TRAIL**  This is the main foot highway into the canyon from the heart of the south rim's Grand Canyon Village. It's an incredible trail, with switchbacks and holes blasted in the rocks, but also incredibly crowded and slippery with manure from the mule trains that use it. There are good places 1.5, 3, 4.6, and 6.1 miles down to get water (during the warm months) and turn around. **Bright Angel Campground,** across the Colorado, is 9.5 miles and more than 5,000 vertical feet down, too far for a round-trip day hike.

**THE SOUTH & NORTH KAIBAB TRAILS**  These trails link the two sides of the canyon. The **South Kaibab Trail** descends from Yaki Point, a few miles east of the village. The trail itself is beautiful, an engineering masterpiece blasted out of the rock. A good goal for day hikers is Cedar Ridge, 1½ miles and less than 1,000 feet down; it's enough to give you a sense of the canyon but makes a manageable day for younger or less-fit hikers. The next major stop is Bright Angel Campground, at the bottom, 6.4 miles away — again, the round-trip is too much for a day hike. No water is available on the trail.

The **North Kaibab Trail** links up there after running 14 miles from the North Rim. If

you're at the North Rim, you'll want to hike at least part of the way down. Roaring Springs is 4.7 miles and 3,400 vertical feet down from the rim, a tough but rewarding day hike.

**THE HERMIT TRAIL**  For a hike that's not too tough, but still gets you below the rim to great views, this is the route to choose. The trail leads into the canyon from Hermits Rest, at the west end of Hermit Road. Board the shuttle from the village before dawn to be at the trailhead at sunrise. Because it is out of the way, the trail is less crowded than the others; it's also not as steep in the early going, although it is rugged, and unmaintained. You descend through a basin. The views are good, but not the sweeping vistas of the Bright Angel and South Kaibab trails. Santa Maria and Dripping Springs are possible goals, 2½ and 3 miles down; bring your own water or treat what you find.

**OTHER TRAILS**  There are eight other trails in the North Rim area, which are listed in the park newspaper that covers that part of the park. Several, such as the **Ken Patrick Trail** and **Widforss Trail,** offer good, long day hikes in the woods and canyon rim without huge elevation changes.

## Mountain Biking

Biking isn't allowed on the hiking trails. Dirt roads in the North Rim area and adjacent Kaibab National Forest offer some long rides with lots of solitude and the advantage of high altitude, which means cooler temperatures. A strenuous 42-mile round-trip ride with sweeping canyon views leads from Highway 67 near the park's north boundary, ending at Sublime Point. At this writing, there was no bike shop or rental agency near the park, so you must bring your own bike.

## Mule & Horseback Riding
### SOUTH RIM

Only about 60 people a day get to ride a mule from the South Rim into the canyon; many more than that would like to, because it's the only way down other than your own two feet. Reserve with Amfac, the concessionaire (see "Grand Canyon Address Book," p. 203). Tickets book up on the first day of the month 23 months before the ride; they're all booked before the end of the day except for rides in midwinter. You could get lucky, because there are cancellations. Put your name on the waiting list at the transportation desk in the Bright Angel Lodge. The outings are sold as day trips or 1- to 2-night stays at Phantom Ranch, the dormitory at the bottom of the canyon. Day trips are $111.25, overnights $314.25 for one person, $563.50 for two, plus $259.75 for each additional person, all-inclusive.

Riding the mules is hard on your behind and not for people afraid of heights — you're just along for the ride while the mule picks his way down the trail over steep drop-offs. Children under 4 feet 7 inches, pregnant women, and people over 200 pounds are not permitted.

**Apache Stables,** based at Moqui Lodge in Tusayan (☎ **928/638-2891;** www.apache stables.com), just outside the park, offers **horseback and wagon rides** in the Kaibab National Forest. Half-day rides include a canyon view. Prices for horseback rides range from $30.50 to $95.50 and wagon rides cost $12.50; call for details.

### NORTH RIM

Grand Canyon Trail Rides (☎ **435/679-8665;** www.onpages.com/canyonrides) offers mule trips into the canyon from the North Rim and along the rim. Hour-long rides along the rim for adults and kids as young as 7 are only $20, and half-day rides along the rim or into the canyon for those 8 years old and up are $45. They're easier to book than the South Rim trips. The longest, full-day rides go as far as Roaring Springs on the North Kaibab Trail for $95 per person. Riders on that must be at least 12 years old and less than 200 pounds.

## Rafting

If what you have in mind is a family day trip on smooth water, the Grand Canyon is out — instead consider a float on the Colorado starting at Glen Canyon Dam (see "Activities," in chapter 10). If, on the other hand, your children are 12 or older and you want a long white-water expedition with extraordinary scenery, the Grand Canyon may be a good choice. But you must be patient. River-rafting trips with commercial operators book a year or more in advance, and going on your own is impractical, even for experts, because the waiting period for self-guided river-trip permits is 10 years. (People die waiting, but to get one of those cancellations, you must still be on the list. About 700 people apply annually for 270 permits. Filing an application costs $100 and launching is $100 per person.)

Commercially guided trips last from 3 to 19 days. Sixteen companies have permits to offer the trips; the park can give you a list (see "Grand Canyon Address Book," p. 203). Some go by motorized raft, which speeds up the time between rapids, others on quieter oared or paddled rafts, dories, or kayaks. Generally, the company provides everything. Most floats begin at Lees Ferry. One major operator with a choice of trips is **Wilderness River Adventures,** run by ARAMARK, a park concession company in several large national parks (☎ **800/992-8022** or 928/645-3296; www.riveradventures.com). A weeklong float costs about $2,000 per person.

## PROGRAMS
## Children's Programs

The Park Service has a series of ranger programs aimed at children. One offering is a children's fossil walk. Pick up a schedule at the visitor center.

The **Junior Ranger program** is aimed at kids ages 4 through 14, with an activity booklet divided into three age levels. The younger kids will find it most interesting; older children are asked to do crossword puzzles and the like, which don't have much to do with nature.

All ages have to attend one ranger program or walk and collect a bag of trash and recycling goods. Get the booklet at a visitor center and go back when it's done for a Junior Ranger certificate and a badge. An embroidered patch is also available for a fee.

## Family & Adult Programs

Rangers offer walks and talks every day at the North Rim, Grand Canyon Village, and Desert View/Tusayan Museum. Schedules are published in the park newspapers. Some walks range as far afield as Cedar Ridge on the South Kaibab Trail — a good day hike. No walks are aimed specifically at children, but programs on fossil finding, archaeology, and geology will interest older kids.

**Evening programs** take place in the North Rim Campground and Lodge. On the South Rim, evening programs are in the Shrine of the Ages Auditorium in the colder months, and in the Mather Amphitheater after it gets warmer in May.

**Grand Canyon Field Institute.** P.O. Box 399, Grand Canyon, AZ 86023. ☎ **928/638-2485.** www.grandcanyon.org/fieldinstitute.

This nonprofit organization, affiliated with the Park Service, offers a catalog of multiple-day workshops, backpacking, and float trips, all with educational themes about the canyon or learning backcountry skills. Difficulty ranges from stationary workshops to trekking beyond the trails for more than a week. Most classes are for adults only, but the institute recently began a series of family classes, for adults and children 8 and older, including short day hikes along the rim, multiday camping and river trips, and photography workshops. Rates for the family classes range from $85 to $165 per person. Reserve well ahead.

# FUN OUTSIDE THE PARK

Other than the tourist strip of Tusayan and other rather desolate highway-side attractions, there's not much near the Grand Canyon. Here's the one major temptation:

**Grand Canyon IMAX Theater.** In Tusayan. ☎ **928/638-2203.** www.grandcanyonimaxtheater.com. Daily Mar–Oct 8:30am–8:30pm; Nov–Feb 10:30am–6:30pm. $9.50 adults, $6.50 children 3–11, including tax.

The super-big-screen theater shows a historical film about the Grand Canyon, starting on the half hour all day. There's a food court that includes a Pizza Hut and Taco Bell in the building, too. The movie tells the story of the Powell expedition and has lots of spectacular aerial photography of the canyon. Children 8 or older should enjoy it. On the other hand, why not skip it and go see the real thing a few miles down the road?

# WHERE TO EAT

You don't go to the Grand Canyon for food, but you will find a couple of good fine dining rooms, plus good family restaurants and relaxed cafeterias where you can eat inexpensively. The restaurants inside the park are all managed by the concessionaire, Amfac. Outside the park in Tusayan, you can find familiar fast food such as Wendy's, McDonald's, and, at the IMAX Theater, small versions of Taco Bell and Pizza Hut.

The Hopi people say that the Grand Canyon, which they call Öngtupqa, is where people first came to live on the earth. People came out of the underworld there, at a place called Sipaapuni. As they came out, they met a great being who already lived on the earth and was its ruler. He gave careful instructions about where the people should go and how they should behave. But among all the races of people, only the Hopi did as they were told.

The Hopi traveled on a great journey to find a place where the great being sent them, called Tuuwanasavi, or Earth Center. Along the way, they left ruins of the buildings they lived in, which you can see in national monuments near the Grand Canyon and across the Southwest. Today, archaeologists who study these ruins believe they were built by the Ancestral Puebloans (also called Anasazi) and other native people who, over many generations, left the ruins behind and became Hopi and other Pueblo peoples. So, on that point, the Hopi legend and the scientists seem to agree. In the end, the Hopi say, they found Tuuwanasavi, and that's where they still live today, on mesas in northern Arizona on the Hopi Reservation. The Hopi believe that people don't own the earth — we are only visitors here. And when a Hopi person dies, he or she is said to return home to Öngtupqa.

Here is a traditional Hopi story that might have been told to children long ago. It's adapted (with permission) from *Hopi Coyote Tales: ISTUTUWUTSI,* by Ekkehart Malotki and Michael Lomatuway'ma (University of Nebraska Press). In this book, the authors collected and translated stories told by Hopi elders.

Coyote lived by hunting. One day when he got hungry, he set out to find something to eat. But poor Coyote wasn't a very good hunter, and he searched for a long time without finding anything. Finally he decided to go to a place he knew where a village sat on a table-shaped hill called a mesa. The people who lived there threw away their garbage over the edge. Coyote thought, "Maybe I can find an old shoe to eat."

As he was searching through the garbage, Coyote heard a voice speaking to him. It was Wren, sitting up on top of a hill enjoying the sunshine. (A wren is a bird with a long, thin beak shaped like a knitting needle.) Wren asked Coyote what he was doing, they talked awhile, and pretty soon they made friends.

## LOW-STRESS MEALS

Large cafeterias at **Maswik** and **Yavapai lodges** serve thousands of meals a day in the quick, low-key style that families often want. Maswik is in the village, back from the rim; Yavapai is just east of Market Plaza. Both dining rooms are light and airy. The food is perfectly adequate, with burgers, pizza, and other familiar foods, plus healthier fare. Yavapai is especially popular among park employees for its definitely un–heart-healthy fried chicken. Both cafeterias are open daily from 6am to 10pm.

Located on the canyon rim at Bright Angel Lodge, the **Bright Angel Fountain** sells hot dogs, prepackaged sandwiches, soft drinks, ice cream, and the like, for takeout only. Hours vary with the season and payment must be in cash.

## DELI & PICNIC SUPPLIES

The deli in **Canyon Village Marketplace,** a concessionaire-operated grocery store near the south entrance in the village, makes sandwiches for picnics. A **snack bar** with a very limited menu operates from a window at Hermits Rest at the end of Hermit Drive.

## BEST-BEHAVIOR MEALS

**Arizona Room.** Facing the rim at the Bright Angel Lodge, Grand Canyon Village. ☎ **928/638-2631.** No reservations. Dinner $12–$25. Daily 4:30–10pm. Closed Jan–Feb.

This beef place, which also offers several chicken and seafood dishes, is aimed at adults,

Wren said, "What do you want to do?"

And Coyote said back, "I don't know. What do you want to do?"

"Let's play hide and seek," Wren suggested.

Coyote thought that would be fun, and said he would hide first, but Wren said that since the game was his idea, he should get to hide first. So Coyote closed his eyes while Wren went to hide. Wren found a great hiding place: He flew to one of the garbage piles, dug a hole, and buried himself in the garbage, with just his beak sticking out. Then he called out to Coyote: "Ready!"

Coyote searched for Wren for a long time and couldn't find him. He even looked in cracks and underneath rocks — places Wren couldn't possibly be hiding. Finally, he said, "Okay, I give up, you can come out now!" But nothing happened. Wren didn't come out. So Coyote searched a little longer, and then gave up and went back to looking through the garbage for food. While looking, he found a needle sticking up out of the pile. "What a find!" he said. "It's a needle I can take home to my grandmother to sew my shirts with." He grabbed the needle and gave it a strong pull.

The needle cried out, "Ouch, ouch, stop — that's my beak." It was Wren. Coyote had won the game.

Then it was Coyote's turn to hide while Wren closed his eyes. Now, Coyote isn't very original: He always does what he sees others do. So he, too, dug a hole in the garbage, and buried himself with just his nose sticking out for air, and said, "Ready!"

Wren looked for Coyote for a long time and couldn't find him. He decided Coyote must have run home. Wren thought, "Coyote is foolish and silly and he probably forgot all about the game." So he stopped searching and started picking through the garbage for a snack instead. And in the middle of the pile, he saw a little, shiny black bowl. "What luck!" Wren said, "I'll take this bowl home to my grandmother to cook our dinner in." And he grabbed the bowl with his beak and pulled it as hard as he could.

"Ouch, ouch, ouch — that's my nose," Coyote yelled.

Each had won the game, and they'd had a lot of fun. As they parted, Coyote and Wren promised to get together and play again another day.

but older children who can behave themselves might enjoy it for the view. It's right on the South Rim, where you can watch the sunset and the people passing by. Arrive early for a window seat.

**Bright Angel Restaurant.** At the Bright Angel Lodge, Grand Canyon Village. No reservations. Breakfast and lunch $4–$12, dinner $8–$20. Daily 6:30am–10pm.

This bright, bustling family restaurant with a Southwest theme knows how to treat kids, giving parents a chance to have real food brought by a real waiter without having to worry about the children getting bored or not being able to eat what they want. The food is predictable.

**El Tovar Dining Room.** In the El Tovar hotel, Grand Canyon Village. ☎ **928/638-2631.** Reservations necessary for dinner, not accepted for breakfast and lunch. Breakfast $7.50–$12, lunch $8–$18, dinner $15–$50. Daily 6:30–11am, 11:30am–2pm, and 5–10pm.

This restaurant in the historic El Tovar hotel tries for formality to match the setting. The service is accommodating; but a meal with kids takes a long time, and they're not prepared for young children. We held a grown-up's birthday there, and the kids did well — but I wouldn't choose it for a family dinner for anything less than a special occasion. It's worth arriving early for a window seat for lunch, with views of the passing crowds and the canyon.

Where to Eat  **223**

# CHAPTER 10

# Glen Canyon National Recreation Area

Lake Powell looks like a mirage the first time you see it. The water looks like part of the sky has fallen and been caught raggedly among desert cliffs of white sandstone. It shimmers like a mirage, and the edges have the same unlikely borders as a mirage — without plants or normal shoreline shapes. The water simply starts where the desert stops. Sand dunes that formed into white Navajo Sandstone millions of years ago still have their undulating shapes. Sticking out of the water, they look like the shoulders, knees, and hips of naked giants. Lake Powell often seems no more real than a daydream.

The lake started as a daydream, or at least as an idea. The Glen Canyon Dam stopped the free flow of the Colorado River here in 1963. It took 17 years for the river to flood a vast network of canyons on a scale with the Grand Canyon, which is just downstream. Since 1980, Lake Powell's smooth, shining water has extended 186 miles from the dam through countless side canyons and among towering rock mountains. All the twists and turns make the shoreline almost 2,000 miles long. The lake is unnatural, but it offers families a wilderness opportunity unequaled in the region. Here's a chance for anyone, no matter how young or unfit, to experience extended trips into an amazing, roadless wonderland of rock. No backpacks or wild raft rides are required, and an escape from the heat is a dive away.

An hour out of Wahweap Marine, we were exploring a deserted beach and mounds of rounded rock in a side canyon. Barbara and I were traveling with her 60-something mother, as well as Robin and Julia, 5 and 2 at the time. It was the first time we'd taken a toddler to such a remote place, and it changed my whole outlook on what we could accomplish with little kids. And I made another discovery: Little kids are much better at enjoying empty, beautiful places than the athletic adult hikers who can usually go there. It was one of the best days we had ever spent at a national park, and we've since become avid boaters, taking babies and toddlers to ever wilder places.

**Glen Canyon National Recreation Area.** P.O. Box 1507, Page, AZ 86040. ☎ **928/608-6404.** www.nps.gov/glca.

**Glen Canyon Natural History Association** (for books and maps). P.O. Box 581, Page, AZ 86040. ☎ **877/453-6296** or 928/645-3532. Fax 928/645-5409. www.pagelakepowell.com.

**ARAMARK** (doing business as Lake Powell Resorts and Marinas), park concessionaire. Main reservations: P.O. Box 56909, Phoenix, AZ 85079. ☎ **800/528-6154.** www.visitlakepowell.com.

- **Wahweap Lodge and Marina.** P.O. Box 1597, Page, AZ 86040. ☎ **928/645-2433,** or 928/645-1111 for boat rentals.
- **Bullfrog Resort and Marina.** P.O. Box 4055, Lake Powell, UT 84533. ☎ **435/684-3000.**
- **Hall's Crossing Marina.** P.O. Box 5101, Lake Powell, UT 84533. ☎ **435/684-7000.**
- **Hite Marina.** P.O. Box 501, Lake Powell, UT 84533. ☎ **435/684-2278.**

**Page/Lake Powell Chamber of Commerce.** P.O. Box 727, Page, AZ 86040. ☎ **888/261-7243** or 928/645-2741. www.pagelakepowellchamber.org.

**Escalante Interagency Visitor Information Center.** P.O. Box 246, Escalante, UT 84726. ☎ **435/826-5499.**

**Bureau of Land Management,** Kanab Resource Area. 318 N. 100 East, Kanab, UT 84741. ☎ **435/644-2672.** www.ut.blm.gov.

Everything at Glen Canyon National Recreation Area is related to outdoor activities, and a good visit takes time, money, and some effort. The popular activity at Lake Powell is renting a slow pontoon vessel, which is like an RV of the sea. Some are simple floating campers, while others are big, ostentatious affairs with dishwashers, air-conditioners, and slides into the water. All can take you up the lake to a spot of your choosing, where you can run up on a beach and spend a few days to a couple of weeks exploring, swimming, and being away from the rest of the world.

## BEST THINGS TO DO

- Taking a houseboat or speedboat into the desert for sightseeing, hiking, swimming, fishing, and isolation.
- Taking on a tough backcountry hike in the desert.
- Taking a day-trip tour boat to the amazing Rainbow Bridge National Monument.
- Joining a smooth-water float downriver to Lees Ferry.
- Touring Glen Canyon Dam.

See "Activities" (p. 236).

## HISTORY UNDER WATER

People lived in Glen Canyon at least 8,000 years ago. The first were the archaic people — Native Americans who hunted big game animals, always migrating across the land after their prey. Later came farming people who settled down and built villages and food-storage granaries that scientists study thousands of years later. Communities of Ancestral Puebloan people (also called Anasazi) lived here and then disappeared. (See "History & Culture: How Do People Live Here?" in chapter 8, "Layers upon Layers.")

The Spanish had no use for the area and marked it on their maps as *terra incognita*, or "unknown land." They first found a way across the canyon in 1776, when a party of

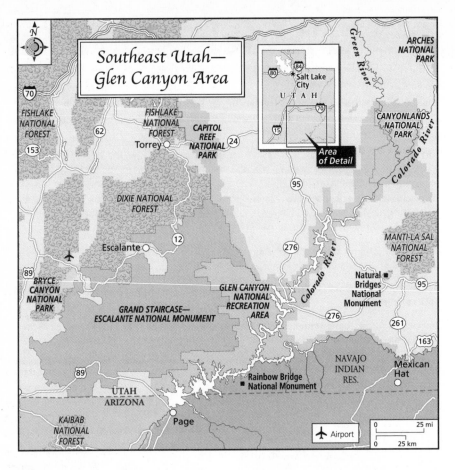

Southeast Utah—
Glen Canyon Area

explorers led by a pair of missionaries found a passage on the Colorado, later called "Crossing of the Fathers." It became an important route for wilderness travelers, but still Europeans didn't make much use of the rugged landscape. John Wesley Powell was the first to describe the area on his heroic river voyages of 1869 and 1871. The lake is named for him.

On his float trips along the Colorado River through Glen Canyon, Powell reported various archaeological discoveries, including ruins of stone villages left by the Ancestral Puebloans. Within 20 years, explorers were looting these places, taking away anything they found to sell or put in museums all over the world. The San Juan Canyon, now partly flooded in Glen Canyon National Recreation Area, was one of the first places in the Southwest where archaeologists began looking for the old villages. They found tons of ancient artifacts they could take back or sell. It was here that archaeologists first discovered the early Ancestral Puebloans.

Today when archaeologists find these kinds of treasures, they try to keep them near where they came from. They use the artifacts to help figure out what the people who lived there were like. They try to respect the cultures they're studying, letting Native people decide how the remains of their ancestors should be treated rather than just digging them up and taking them away. But in the 1880s, when archaeologists started finding the Ancestral Puebloan villages, they weren't so careful. The good ones took pots and human bones to museums; the bad ones sold them for as much as they could get.

In 1956, Congress voted to build Glen Canyon Dam and fill the canyons with water, and the National Park Service began a rush to study the ruins before they were flooded. Archaeologists explored a canyon area almost 200 miles long as fast as they could. They found more than 2,000 historic sites and dozens of ruins of communities and other buildings left by people long ago. They saved as much information about these places as they could; but the work was rushed, and ways we have today of finding out when things were made hadn't been invented yet. Work stopped in 1963, when Lake Powell began to fill behind the finished dam. In 1980, the lake finally was full, and most of the discoveries were under deep water. In 1971, the Park Service took over the management of recreation on the lake and the protection of the natural and historic treasures. Since then, researchers have found hundreds of historic sites above the waterline. Visitors can reach some by boat (see "Natural Places," p. 235). We can only imagine how much more lies beneath the waves.

# ORIENTATION

## LAKE POWELL

The lake is the overwhelming feature of the national recreation area. You can get onto the lake from the four marinas described below, where the concessionaire rents houseboats and motorboats; some also have tour-boat trips. A fifth marina, **Dangling Rope Marina,** about 40 miles from the dam and accessible only from the water, has a ranger station, store, and gas dock. In addition, there is a boat ramp at **Antelope Point,** a day-use area northeast of Page, and plans call for the development of a marina there sometime in the future.

## Wahweap Marina

The main marina and hotel are at Wahweap, near the town of Page and the dam. If you're also visiting the Grand Canyon, Zion, or Bryce Canyon, or coming from Phoenix or Las Vegas, this is the most convenient way onto the lake. It's also the most heavily used end of the lake; to avoid summer crowds, use one of the marinas mentioned below. There are restaurants, campgrounds, a sporting-goods store, and other facilities at the marina area. This small corner of the lake is the only part of the recreation area in Arizona; the balance is in Utah. Arizona does not use daylight saving time and Utah does, so in the summer

the time is an hour later north along the lake than at Wahweap.

## Bullfrog Basin & Hall's Crossing Marinas

At mid-lake, about 95 miles above the dam, a car ferry connects these two marinas on opposite sides of the canyon. The 3-mile ride cuts 150 miles of driving along Route 276, which connects both marinas to Route 95, a north-south highway that rounds the east end of Lake Powell near Hite. This is a more remote, less-developed option than Wahweap. Bullfrog has a hotel, restaurant, and visitor center. Hall's Crossing has only a few mobile homes for nightly rentals and no restaurant. Both have campgrounds with showers and laundry facilities. Use these marinas or Hite, below, if you're coming from Capitol Reef, Canyonlands, or Arches national parks, or other points to the north and east.

## Hite Marina

This marina at the head of the lake, 139 miles above the dam, has the fewest services and the smallest selection of boats. It offers access to a remote, scenic area that's on the lake and just upriver, where the Colorado passes through Narrow Canyon. Route 95 runs north and south nearby.

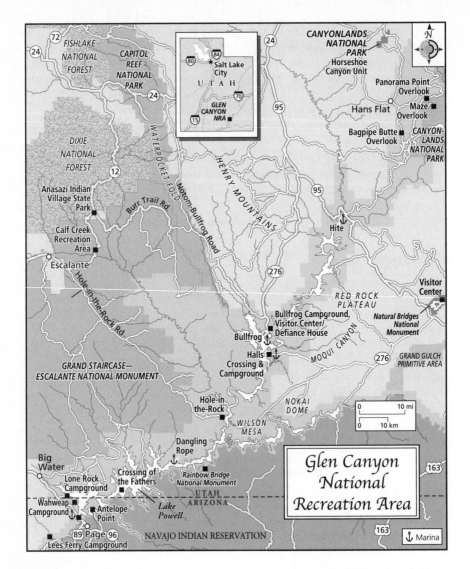

Glen Canyon National Recreation Area

## PAGE

Page (pop. about 8,000) is the only significant town near the lake. It was built to house construction workers for the Glen Canyon Dam and is now a regional center, with large stores and chain hotels arranged on broad, straight streets. Wahweap Marina is 15 miles away.

## OFF THE LAKE

Only 13% of Glen Canyon Recreation Area is underwater. The **Lees Ferry** area, described under "Exploring the Region," in chapter 8, is downriver from the dam. It's a place for camping, hiking, and fishing. There are hikes near Wahweap and Bullfrog marinas, and you can reach many more from the water, where the opportunity for casual exploring is unique. (See "Natural Places," p. 235.)

The Escalante River area, which links with Grand Staircase–Escalante National Monument, is a deep wilderness. You reach its many backpacking routes by dirt roads from Escalante, a town east of Bryce Canyon National Park and more than 180 miles from Wahweap by paved roads.

# Making the Arrangements

## When to Go

Summer is hot at this elevation, around 3,600 feet, with average highs in the 90s and lows in the 60s. It's also the season of daily afternoon thunderstorms that whip up winds, forcing boaters to seek sheltered water and bringing flash floods down narrow canyons. Backpacking is not advisable in the summer. Summer is also a time of warm swimming water — 79°F in August. Sleep under the stars on the top deck of your houseboat and dive into the water whenever you feel hot. The lake is full of boats, with some coves looking like cities, and the waves created by boat wakes make the channels choppy (to get away from people, use one of the marinas up the lake rather than Wahweap). Reservations for houseboats have to be made a year ahead.

Rates drop 25% from the beginning of April to mid-May and in October. High rates last longer at Wahweap than at the other marinas. High temperatures are in the 70s and lows in the 40s at this time of year. The fall might be best, with warm swimming water and reasonable daytime temperatures. The water is chilly during spring break, but you have the lake largely to yourself. Spring is the best time for hiking.

From November to March, the recreation area mostly shuts down. You can have the lake completely to yourself, but the weather is unpredictable, fine or cold and stormy. The water is too cold. Rates drop by 40% from the summer.

## How Much Time to Spend

There's not much point in going to the recreation area for less than a full day. If you have only a few days, you can take a boat tour and perhaps a day trip on a rented powerboat or a hike. The best visits are longer. Houseboats rent for a minimum of 3 days, but for all the effort of setting up housekeeping afloat and motoring out into the lake, you'll want to spend at least 5 days to a couple of weeks. An in-between option is to rent a speedboat and go tent camping in the backcountry. You don't need a backcountry permit and speedboats go four or five times faster than houseboats; so you can get to remote areas more quickly.

## How Far to Plan Ahead

The Park Service limits the number of rental boats on the lake, so during the most popular summer months, houseboats are booked a year in advance. In the off-season, you often can walk in and get one, but reserve as far ahead as possible to make sure. Reserve speedboats at the same time you book a houseboat. If you want a speedboat but not a houseboat, call as soon as you can; if you strike out, there's a good chance you can get one when you arrive by calling the marina.

## Reading Up

The recreation area's bookstores are operated by **Glen Canyon Natural History Association** (☎ 877/453-6296; www.pagelakepowell. com). At this writing they were planning an online catalog.

## Maps

Everyone uses the *Stan Jones' Boating and Exploring Map,* widely sold in the area for about $4 on paper and $10 laminated. Besides navigational information, it is loaded with information about the lake, including fishing advice. **Boating Guide:** Michael R. Kelsey's self-published *Boater's Guide to Lake Powell* is exhaustively detailed, concentrating on hikes accessed by boat, but difficult to use and apparently unedited. However, I could find no better. Buy it anywhere in the area or online from www.amazon.com.

## Getting There
### By Car

Glen Canyon makes a good stop on the way from the Grand Canyon to Zion or Bryce Canyon National Park. Wahweap Marina and

## WEATHER CHART: AVERAGE HIGHS & LOWS

|  | AVG. HIGH (°F) | AVG. LOW (°F) | WATER TEMP. (°F) |
|---|---|---|---|
| December–February | 42–51 | 24–30 | 46–51 |
| March–May | 58–80 | 36–53 | 54–64 |
| June–August | 91–97 | 62–69 | 71–79 |
| September–November | 55–85 | 35–58 | 61–74 |

Page are 117 miles from Zion, 130 miles from the North Rim of the Grand Canyon, and 141 miles from the South Rim, all on good two-lane roads. U.S. 89 runs northwest to Zion and south into Arizona, and U.S. 89A runs west to Lees Ferry and the North Rim. Flagstaff is 221 miles away, Phoenix and Las Vegas around 275. The marinas in the northeastern part of Lake Powell are closer to Arches, Canyonlands, and Capitol Reef national parks. For more on the highways, see "Linking the Parks," in chapter 8.

## By Air

The airport at Page, about 6 miles from Wahweap Marina, is served from Phoenix by **Great Lakes Airlines** (☎ **800/554-5111;** www.greatlakesav.com). **Avis** (☎ **800/331-1212** or 928/645-2024) rents cars at the airport. If you don't want to rent a car, a free ARAMARK shuttle will take you to Wahweap Lodge and Marina.

**Sunrise Airlines** (877/978-6747; www.sunriseair.net) offers charter service to Bullfrog, Hall's Crossing, and Hite marinas. ARAMARK's shuttle (free 8am–5pm; a fee at other times) takes you from the airstrip to Hall's Crossing Marina; call ahead (☎ **435/684-7000**).

## WHAT TO PACK
### Clothing

In the summer, prepare for highs often in the 100s. Besides swimsuits and summer clothes, you'll need sun hats, light long-sleeved shirts, and long pants. Rain other than thunderstorms is rare; about 6 inches fall all year. For spring break, bring shorts and T-shirts for the sunny days, but also sweaters and jackets and clothing you can layer for the cold evenings and sometimes-cool days. Most spring swimming will be in pools. Either time of year, bring boat shoes — canvas tennis shoes will do — that can get wet, are cool, and have good traction. Also pack sturdy hiking shoes or cross-trainers for canyon hiking and shore explorations. You'll find little use for anything but casual clothing.

## Gear

If you reserve a houseboat, the agency sends you a list of the items it provides and other things you might need, such as bedding. Agencies provide most kitchen needs. Of course, you're responsible for your food, and you should pack everything you might need for the whole trip. Plan all your menus, snacks, and drinks carefully; be realistic, because running out of something could really mess up your trip. Shop from a well-thought-out list when you arrive. Keep perishable items to a minimum.

If you're camping from a speedboat, you'll need backcountry camping gear, including a camp stove, a first-aid kit, and emergency supplies. Lists are included in chapter 1, "Planning Your Trip," but edit downward from that; reducing the bulk of your gear is important on a small boat, which you can easily overload with your family and stuff. The

Park Service protects the water by requiring everyone to use chemical toilets for overnight trips. Check on requirements when you reserve the speedboat. You might have to stop at Wal-Mart in Page and buy a toilet for around $30. For more on the speedboat-camping option, see "Boating" (p. 237).

# WHERE TO SPEND THE NIGHT

## HOUSEBOATS

Information on houseboating is included all over this chapter (especially see "Keeping Safe & Healthy," p. 234). Here I review the accommodations on board the different kinds of vessels, and the rates. Spring and fall rates are 25% less than those quoted below, and winter rates are 40% off. Various packages are available at different seasons from **ARAMARK;** you can also see pictures and floor plans of the boats on their website (see "Glen Canyon Address Book," p. 225). Minimum rentals in the summer are 3 days, off-season 2 days, but that much time hardly justifies all the trouble. You turn in the boat at 2pm on the last day, so a "2-day" rental is for only 1 night.

For more on how to boat on Lake Powell, see "Boating" (p. 237).

**Standard/Commander Class.** 36–50 ft. long. Sleeps 6–12. High season $1,765–$2,640 per week.

These relatively stripped-down boats make up the majority of the fleet, and only this class is available at Hite. It's perfectly comfortable, on a par with a large RV. It has a propane refrigerator and stove, linoleum on the floor, a shower and tub, and bunks with limited privacy; but no marine radio, air-conditioning, TV, stereo, slide, or other extras found on the more luxurious versions. Bring a cell phone for emergencies.

**Deluxe and Luxury/Captain and Admiral Class.** 54–59 ft. long. Sleeps 10. High season $3,475–$5,885 per week.

There are various versions with different amenities, ranging up to the Admiral, which has necessities such as big TVs and VCRs, full kitchens with dishwashers, and an extra bathroom. The rooms are carpeted and wood paneled, and bedrooms are divided so that couples can have privacy. It's basically a condo afloat. Nice, if you have the money to spend, but a level of luxury that's not really necessary to enjoy the natural setting.

## LAKESIDE CAMPING

One option is to explore the lake by speedboat and camp onshore each night. You will save a lot of money and have far more mobility than with a slow, gas-guzzling houseboat, able to go farther to more remote spots. Besides, a houseboat's TV and VCR only distract from the stars and the desert. Camping is allowed without a permit almost anywhere you choose. You will need a portable toilet and other backcountry camping equipment (see "Gear," p. 230). Details on the boats are under "Boating" (p. 237). It is legal to collect firewood below the high-water line and to build fires on much (but not all) of the lakeshore, but it's better to bring your wood along and burn on a metal platform or frying pan. Wood is hard to come by in popular camping areas, and fires leave a scar.

## Park Service Campgrounds

The Park Service's **Lees Ferry Campground** is covered under "Exploring the Region," in chapter 8. The only other Park Service campground in the recreation area is the primitive **Lone Rock Campground,** on the lakeshore off U.S. 89 north of Wahweap Marina. The fee is $6 a night to camp in an area with pit toilets and without designated sites. Reservations are not needed, and there should always be plenty of space.

## Concessionaire Campgrounds

ARAMARK operates campgrounds at each of the marinas except Hite, which has only primitive tent camping. Dangling Rope Marina is just a supply dock. RV sites at the other three marinas have full hookups for $28 in summer, $18 in winter, for two adults, plus $3 for each extra person over age 6. Tent sites are $15 per night and cannot be reserved in advance. Reserve RV sites (AE, DISC, MC, V) throughout the recreation area at ARAMARK's main number unless you're within a week of your stay, in which case you should call the marina directly (see "Glen Canyon Address Book," p. 225, for phone numbers).

At **Wahweap,** a large RV park with 123 sites with full hookups sits on a hill above the lake. Rigs park in rows under mature shade trees. There are a convenience store, a laundry, and bathrooms with two sets of showers — one without timers for RV park guests, and one operated with quarters for everyone else. An attractive tent campground with flush toilets faces the water down the hill from the RV park. A nice spot, but the desert vegetation doesn't offer much privacy.

**Hall's Crossing** has a small RV park with 17 spaces and a 50-site tent campground. Tenters can use free cold showers, or pay $2 for hot showers that are open to the public at the supply store. A coin-op laundry is available.

**Bullfrog** has 24 RV spaces and close to 100 tent sites, with free hot showers for campers and showers costing $2 for others.

## HOTELS

There are several chain hotels in Page, 15 miles from Wahweap Marina. They include a **Courtyard by Marriott** over the town golf course (☎ 800/851-3855 or 928/645-5000), **Best Western at Lake Powell** (☎ 888-794-2888 or 928/645-5988), and **Super 8** (☎ 928/645-2858).

The places described below are operated by **ARAMARK,** the recreation area's concessionaire (see "Glen Canyon Address Book," p. 225). Rates listed here are for the spring, summer, and fall seasons; November through March rates are about 30% to 35% lower. Children under 18 stay free with their parents.

Ask about packages when you reserve, because you may be able to save on tour-boat rides.

ARAMARK also rents housekeeping or family units at the three marinas up the lake from Wahweap. The **three-bedroom mobile homes** have full kitchens with utensils, TVs, two bathrooms, picnic tables and barbecue grills, and swamp coolers, but no phones. At Hall's Crossing, 20 are available; at Bullfrog, 8; and at Hite, 5. They rent for $185 a night for up to six guests in the high season, $10 for each additional adult up to eight.

**Defiance House.** Bullfrog Marina. 50 units. TV TEL. $110–$120 double, $10 per extra adult.

This hotel up the lake has rooms with private balconies where you can stay before or after a boat trip.

**Lake Powell Motel.** Hwy. 89, 2½ miles from Wahweap Marina. 24 units. AC TV TEL. $94 double, $6 per extra adult. Closed Nov–Mar.

This simple, one-story motel offers decent budget rooms nearer the marina than Page is, but without much around it.

**Wahweap Lodge.** At Wahweap Marina, 6 miles north of Page. 350 units. AC TV TEL. $159–$169 double, $12 per extra adult.

This beautifully landscaped compound of eight stucco buildings above the lake contains immaculate, attractively decorated rooms. The lovely pool looks out on the lake. The hotel serves as a frenetic activity center, with a desk that sells tour-boat tickets and a dock where tours depart. In the summer buffets are served for all three meals. The restaurant is open, in summer, from 6am to 2pm and 5 to 10pm.

# WHEN YOU ARRIVE

## RESERVATIONS & FEES
The Park Service charges $10 per vehicle. It's free to visit the dam, but you'll have to pay to reach any of the marinas or Lees Ferry. The fee is good for up to 7 days. National passes apply (see "Passes & Fees," in chapter 1).

## WATER-QUALITY REGULATIONS
It's important to keep sewage out of the lake. Everyone is required to carry out their waste and dump it at stations at the marinas and at floating restroom/pump-out facilities at various locations on the lake. Houseboats are equipped with toilets and holding tanks. Tent campers using speedboats must take and use portable toilets. Using a hole on the shore isn't okay, because the lake's water level can change more than 60 feet over the season, and human waste ends up in the water. Pets are permitted on the lake, but you must gather all waste and dispose of it in a marina dump station.

## VISITOR CENTERS
**Carl Hayden Visitor Center.** At the Glen Canyon Dam near Page. Summer daily 7am–7pm; off-season daily 8am–5pm.

Named for a late U.S. senator, this is the main information center for the recreation area. Plan your stop with an hour to spare before closing time for the dam tour, mentioned on p. 236. The visitor center has a big topographic model of the lake and displays about the dam and natural history.

**Bullfrog Visitor Center.** At Bullfrog Marina. Mid-Mar to Oct daily 8am–5pm; closed Nov to early Mar.

The center up the lake has exhibits and a ranger to answer questions; it also sells books and maps.

## Outside the Recreation Area
Stop for town information at the **Page–Lake Powell Chamber of Commerce** at 644 N.

Navajo Dr., Suite B. The office is open in summer daily from 9am to 6pm, and in winter Monday through Friday from 9am to 5pm. You can also get local information at the **John Wesley Powell Memorial Museum,** at the corner of North Lake Powell Boulevard and North Navajo (☎ 928/645-9496; www. powellmuseum.org), which documents Powell's expedition with photographs, etchings, and artifacts.

For backcountry trips north of the recreation area, contact the **Escalante Interagency Visitor Information Center** (☎ 435/826-5499), 755 W. Main St., Escalante. The town is more than a 3-hour drive from Wahweap between Bryce Canyon and Capitol Reef national parks on Route 12. A **contact station** on U.S. 89, 44 miles east of Kanab, offers information for trips down the Paria River Canyon.

## GETTING AROUND
For information on getting around the recreation area by boat, see "Boating" (p. 237).

### By Car
Connecting the different marinas over land is a major expedition that serves little purpose. If you spend most of your time boating, especially on an extended trip, you don't need a car — get everything you need at the marina or have it delivered (see "For Handy Reference," p. 234) and use the shuttle from the airport (See "Getting There," p. 229).

### By Ferry
The 154-foot **John Atlantic Burr ferry** (☎ 435/684-7000; www.canyon-country. com/lakepowell/ferry.htm) connects Bullfrog and Hall's Crossing marinas. The 3-mile run takes 25 minutes and saves several hours of driving. It runs six times a day each way in the

**Emergencies** The ☎ **911** emergency number doesn't work everywhere in the area, and in some remote areas it might not get you the best response. Instead, call the **Park Service emergency line** at ☎ **800/582-4351** or 928/608-6300. The Park Service also monitors Marine Band Channel 16 for emergencies. If you won't have a Marine Band radio, bring a cellular phone. They work over much, but not all, of the lake. **Page Hospital (☎ 928/645-2424)** is at North Navajo and Vista Avenue in Page.

**Stores** Each of the four marinas up the lake has a store for necessities, but you wouldn't want to do all your shopping there; instead, go to Page. **Bashas' Supermarket** is in the Gateway Shopping Center at 687 S. Lake Powell Blvd. in Page (☎ **928/645-3291**; www.bashas.com), where you'll also find a Wal-Mart. Basha's will deliver a phone or online order to your houseboat at Wahweap, but it would be cheaper to rent a car and drive: They charge 10% plus a $65 delivery fee.

**Banks** There are ATMs at the Bullfrog Marina and at Gateway Shopping Center, mentioned above. **Community First National Bank** is at 480 N. Navajo Dr. in Page (☎ **928/645-3223**).

**Post Offices** In Page it's at 44 Sixth St. On the lake, all four marinas have postal services and mail delivery for boaters; have the mail sent to the marina addresses listed under "Glen Canyon Address Book" (p. 225).

**Gear Sales & Rental** A sporting-goods store, open in season only, is near the boat ramp next to the Wahweap Lodge. It rents fishing gear, and stores at the other marinas sell fishing supplies. You can rent all kinds of motorized boating equipment plus kayaks and water toys from **ARA-MARK,** the park concessionaire at the marinas. The dive shop **Twin Finn**, 811 Vista Ave., in Page (☎ **928/645-3114**; www.twinfinn.com), offers lessons and organized dives. It also rents sit-on-top and sea-touring kayaks for $35 to $50 a day (4 days pays for a week). Straps and padding to carry a kayak on your vehicle are included free.

summer, four times a day in the winter. The fare is $2 for adults, $1 for children ages 5 to 11, $9 for vehicles under 20 feet.

## KEEPING SAFE & HEALTHY

All the warnings about desert hiking go for this very hot area. See "Dealing with Hazards," in chapter 1, for information on dehydration, hypothermia, sunburn, and snake and insect bites. Here are some items specific to Glen Canyon.

## Boating Accidents & Drowning

For the number of visitors, Glen Canyon is the second riskiest of the national parks (after Lake Mead National Recreation Area). Surely that's because of all the boating. Boating safety depends on good judgment, caution, and preparation. Pick up the Park Service's safety rules. Children must wear life jackets. Don't dive into water until you've checked it for rocks and depth. Don't swim alone. Don't drink and drive a boat. Slow down near shore or rocks; the water level changes greatly, so you can't always be sure of the depth. When you rent the vessel, ask enough questions to make sure you really understand everything. The instructions can be hard to remember, so take notes. If bad weather comes up while you're on the water, find a sheltered cove where you can wait it out; it rarely lasts long. See "For Handy Reference," above, for emergency communication information.

## Carbon Monoxide

Investigators established in 2000 that carbon monoxide from houseboat generators is a major danger on Lake Powell, killing 9 people and injuring more than 100 over the previous decade (the cause of those incidents had gone undetected). Exhaust poisons can gather around swimmers, quickly overcoming them. It doesn't take much to kill. Lake Powell rental houseboats have carbon monoxide detectors and exhaust vents away from the swim decks, but it's still important not to swim while engines or generators are running or until the area has been well aired afterward. Ask about this issue when you rent. If you are using a private boat, which may have an exhaust vent under the rear swim deck, use extreme caution.

## Flash Floods

The narrow canyons of the region — silent, shaded slots of rock hundreds of feet deep and only a few feet wide — are spectacular places to walk. Flash floods from thunderstorms carved them, and when the water comes down, it can strip away everything in its path. It did just that in 1997, when 11 hikers died in a flash flood in the narrow slot of Antelope Canyon, on Navajo land just outside Page. A thunderstorm 50 miles away caused the flood. People still hike down Antelope Canyon. There's no totally safe way to predict flash floods. In any event, certainly don't set out when there are thunderstorms in the area. Call the **Park Service** at ☎ **928/608-6301** to check the weather before you set out. Canyon hikes are safer in the spring, when thunderstorms aren't so common.

# ENJOYING THE RECREATION AREA

## NATURAL PLACES
## The Lake & Canyons

You can make your own discoveries in the 96 canyons that join Lake Powell on its nearly 2,000 miles of coastline. Because the canyon walls are so steep, boats can often go places little wider than they are. One of the weird and fascinating things about this odd place is that a shore that looks simple and straight from a distance changes when you approach it in a boat, opening onto hidden bays and beaches and narrow channels through rock. When you land, there's even more to find — caves and ruins, hidden places where grown-ups can doze in the sun while kids' imaginations feed on the adventure.

To choose where you will explore, get the map or boater's guide book mentioned under "Reading Up." But, although a good map is an essential safety tool, don't overlook the opportunity for spontaneity the lake offers. A boat can give a family an expansive new sense of freedom. Suddenly you have the ability to go anywhere. The youngest member of your crew can point to a shore upon which to land, and who knows what you will find there?

If you'd rather not set out on your own, consider taking a **boat tour.** The Rainbow Bridge tour described below is the best choice, but ARAMARK also offers shorter, less expensive boat rides from Wahweap Marina and one tour from Bullfrog. These give you a brief taste of boating on Lake Powell, but not the opportunity to get off and enjoy the shore. A 1-hour ride on a paddle wheeler is $13 for adults, $10 for kids 11 and under. A sunset dinner cruise is $44.50 each for adults and children. There are other tours of different lengths, too; get details from **ARAMARK** (see "Glen Canyon Address Book," p. 225).

## Rainbow Bridge National Monument

The bridge is truly an amazing sight. Shaped just like a rainbow, Rainbow Bridge stands 290 feet tall and 275 feet long; it's the largest natural bridge in the world. (A natural bridge is formed by water; other forces make natural arches.) This place is sacred to various Native American peoples, and it's easy to see why. Before the creation of Lake Powell, getting to the monument was difficult. There are no roads there, which adds to the grandeur.

Instead, you take a boat up the narrow waters of a twisting, flooded canyon, 50 miles from Wahweap, Bullfrog, or Hall's Crossing marinas. Floating signs show you the way through the mazelike corridors. At the end, a dock (with a toilet) connects to a quarter-mile paved trail that leads to the bridge. Try to keep that sense of quiet awe, and stay on the path — remember, this is a holy place to many people, and you are a visitor.

Bridge Creek eroded the bridge after the great uplift of this entire region 65 million years ago (see "Raising the Grand Staircase," in chapter 8). The creek meandered back and forth, cutting a canyon with big loops around narrow walls. Floods, washing down with more force, broke through one of these loops in a more direct path, starting an opening that slowly wore away, forming the Rainbow Bridge. The rock of the upper bridge is white Navajo Sandstone, the common, soft rock of the area. It formed from sand dunes that were pressed together. All over the lake you can see dune shapes in this rock layer from more than 150 million years ago.

**Tour boats** visit Rainbow Bridge from Wahweap and Bullfrog marinas. They leave most frequently — up to seven times a day — from Wahweap. If you don't care to operate your own boat, this is a good way to get out on the water, and it makes an excellent introduction to the lake even if you do plan to rent a vessel of your own. Rides of different lengths involve more or less commentary or stops on the way. A 5-hour trip from Wahweap stops at the Dangling Rope Marina and spends about half an hour at the monument. The fare is $75 for adults, $55 for children 3 to 11, free for children under 3. Full-day trips are $100 for adults, $70 for children. Book with **ARAMARK** (see "Glen Canyon Address Book," p. 225).

## PLACES FOR LEARNING

In addition to the places below, see "Exploring the Region," in chapter 8, for details on **Lees Ferry,** down the Colorado River from the dam.

**Glen Canyon Dam.** U.S. 89, just north of Page. ☎ **928/645-3532.** Daily 8am–5pm, 7am–7pm in the summer. Last tour starts 1 hr. before close.

Guided tours go over and inside the 700-foot-tall dam that holds back Lake Powell. It's fun to walk high on the dam and then ride the elevator far down to the base, where you can watch the generators spinning.

## Ruins & Archaeological Sites

Ancestral Puebloan (Anasazi) and Fremont people left stone dwellings, granaries, and rock art all along the canyons. Several of these sites are open for exploration, and you can visit but not enter others. Pick up directions and explanatory handouts from the visitor center, and use a good map like the one mentioned above under "Reading Up" (p. 229). **Defiance House,** a small Ancestral Puebloan pueblo found in the middle fork of Forgotten Canyon in 1959, is one of the open sites, with several well-preserved rooms and pictographs. The canyon is up the lake from Bullfrog Marina, 106 miles from the dam. **Hole-in-the-Rock** is the site of a trail built by early Mormon settlers seeking to colonize the area. It's 66 miles up from the dam, with displays that attest to their hardships.

## ACTIVITIES
## Backpacking

The area north of Glen Canyon is an unspoiled land of deserts and canyons that's among the most remote in the lower 48 states. A famous 35-mile trek runs down the **Paria River** in a narrow red canyon, starting from a Bureau of Land Management ranger station on U.S. 89, north of Glen Canyon Dam, and running to Lees Ferry. It's a challenging route where you walk in a riverbed for 4 to 6 days. You'll need local knowledge and a permit for overnights on the Paria or in other BLM areas north of Glen Canyon. Contact the **Bureau of Land Management,** Kanab Resource Area, 318 N. 100 East, Kanab, UT 84741 (☎ **435/644-2672**). Various routes branch from dirt roads along the Escalante River drainage, and you can reach some routes in the area from the lake. Experienced desert backpackers don't go in the summer, when heat and thunderstorms add danger and discomfort.

## Boating

The lake allows families to visit the desert by water for hiking, swimming, fishing, and enjoying the sun. That's what most of this chapter is about. Guided boating tours are covered under "Natural Places" (p. 235). Here are some of the basics on renting houseboats and motorboats you drive yourself.

**HOUSEBOATS** Whether you go with a basic houseboat or a luxury model, the vessel floats on pontoons filled with a living structure and big outdoor decks where you can sun and play, generally with ladders leading to a top deck (the choices and rates are under "Where to Spend the Night," p. 231). The decks have railings, but if you are bringing a toddler you may need to install netting between the rails and to block access to the ladder. Large outboard motors drive the boats through the water at around 10 mph, using 14 to 24 gallons of gas an hour. In a week's trip, it doesn't make sense to go more than 40 or 50 miles from the marina. Since the boats are so slow and unmaneuverable, most people find a good place to beach it and stay there for a while, exploring and swimming from that base. The water is generally too deep to anchor. Be careful not to get stuck on the beach: The lake can drop 3 inches in a day. For more mobility or for water-skiing, you can rent a motorboat you pull along behind. Reserve at the same time you reserve the houseboat. A sea kayak, available from ARA-MARK or in Page, is a quieter and less-expensive alternative (covered under "For Handy Reference," p. 234).

**SPEEDBOATS** Another option, if you don't have the time or money for a full-blown houseboating expedition, is to rent a powerboat for

## IMPORTANT TIPS ON RENTING A BOAT

Reserve well ahead, of course. When you do, ask for details on insurance, credit cards, and what identification you'll need. If you don't have to buy the rental agency's insurance, you'll save $10 to $25 a day.

The lines at the rental office are long in the morning, which wastes a lot of time, so think about picking up the night before, or be there when the office opens. Hours at the Wahweap Marina rental office are daily from 7am to 8pm in the summer, 8am to 5pm in the winter (remember, Arizona is always on standard time). The rental agent will ask where you're going; get a map or guidebook (see "Reading Up," p. 229) and have some ideas ahead of time.

Try to be well organized and have your gear packed so that it won't take too long to get on board. You'll receive a briefing on the vessel when you board. Bring a pad to write notes that will help you remember key points, have more than one person listen to the briefing, and ask questions about anything you don't understand.

a day trip or a few nights of lakeshore camping (see p. 231). ARAMARK rents 14-, 18-, and 19-foot boats. The 14-footers have small 25hp engines and not much room on board — they're fine for fishing or towing behind a houseboat, but not for seeing the lake. The larger boats have large outboards and zoom along at more than 45 mph, giving you a lot of freedom. The larger engines burn around 14 gallons of gas an hour. The boats are easy and fun to drive. Even if you have only a day, pack a picnic and take a speedboat out. You can rent a boat by the hour, but take one for a full day to have a full outing. High-season daily rates are $130 for a 14-footer, $255 for an 18-footer, and $305 for a 19-footer; off-season rates are up to 40% less. The weekly rate roughly equals five times the daily rate.

## Fishing

Lake Powell yields largemouth, smallmouth, and striped bass; sunfish; crappies; walleyes; and catfish. The lake is full of huge carp too. You can buy fishing licenses at the marinas. Pick up a copy of the regulations at the same time. Decide where you will fish before buying the license — or you might need to buy two, because the lake is in two states. Seven-day nonresident licenses are $21 in Utah and 5-day nonresident licenses cost $26 in Arizona. One-day licenses are $8 in Utah and $12.50 in Arizona. Children under 14 don't need a license in either state. For instructions on where and how to fish, get the map mentioned under "Reading Up" (p. 229). Downriver from the Glen Canyon Dam, you can fish for trout in the Colorado River, launching from Lees Ferry (see "Exploring the Region," in chapter 8).

## Hiking

If you're out boating on the lake, you'll find places to hike up the side canyons without trails.

Near Page and Wahweap Marina, there are a couple of day hikes. The **Horseshoe Bend View** is less than a half mile to a good view of the canyon below the dam. Drive about 5 miles south from the visitor center on U.S. 89 to a dirt road to the west near highway marker 545.

The **Wiregrass Canyon** leads about 3 miles from a trailhead to Lake Powell past a pair of natural bridges and some balanced rocks, as well as side canyons you can climb. Drive north on U.S. 89 to Big Water, Utah, turning right between mileposts 7 and 8 at the sign that says BIG WATER CITY. Follow signs for Glen Canyon National Recreation Area — State Highway 12 and Wiregrass Canyon Back Country Use Area about 5 miles from Route 89.

## Rafting

Below the dam, Glen Canyon is smooth water for 15 miles to Lees Ferry. **Wilderness River Adventures,** managed by ARAMARK (see "Glen Canyon Address Book," p. 225), offers motorized floats for families even with young children. The half- and full-day trips include commentary and a chance to get off and look at Ancestral Puebloan petroglyphs. It's the one chance in the area for most people to get on the Colorado below towering canyon cliffs. The fare for the half-day trip is $55 for adults, $47 for children; and the full-day trip, including lunch, costs $77 for adults and $69 for children.

## Swimming & Water-Skiing

During the summer and fall, when the water is warm enough, swimming in Lake Powell is one of the main attractions of boating here. The concessionaire rents water-skis and other toys to tow behind a boat. Know the safety rules first, of course. A sandy swimming beach, without a lifeguard, is just north of the Wahweap Marina.

## Programs

A **Junior Ranger** booklet produced by the Park Service and given away at the visitor centers will keep kids occupied for quite a while with activities that teach about the area. It

---

### PLACES FOR RELAXED PLAY & PICNICS

The atmosphere at the marinas is pretty relaxed, and there's lots of open space. Out on the lake, almost everything around you is a place for relaxed play. The Park Service has picnic areas at Wahweap and Bullfrog marinas. At Wahweap, a sandy swimming beach is just north of the boat-rental operation. There are grassy areas near the lodge and a minimal playground at the RV park up on the hill.

Playgrounds in Page, open to visitors when school is not in session, are at **Desert View Elementary School,** 462 S. Lake Powell Blvd., and **Lake View Elementary School,** 1801 N. Navajo Dr.

---

contains some good read-aloud material on the canyon's history. Kids who pick up at least 10 pieces of litter and complete as much of the booklet as they can get a free Junior Ranger badge at the Carl Hayden or Bullfrog Visitor Center. They can also send the booklet to the Glen Canyon National Recreation Area (see "Glen Canyon Address Book," p. 225).

# WHERE TO EAT

You'll probably stock your houseboat or speedboat with groceries rather than rely on restaurants. For local supermarkets, see "For Handy Reference" (p. 234).

## WAHWEAP MARINA & PAGE
In addition to the restaurant at Wahweap Lodge (p. 232) and the dinner cruise (see "The Lake & Canyons," p. 235), the concessionaire operates a pizza place above the boat ramp near Wahweap Lodge in the summer. The lodge also packs box lunches.

In Page, you'll find every fast-food franchise on the downtown strip. **Denny's, open around the clock,** is just west of town, near U.S. 89, at 169 Scenic View Dr. (☎ 928/ 645-3999). We found one memorable local place, **Strombolli's,** 711 N. Navajo (☎ 928/ 645-2605), open daily from noon to 9 or 10pm in summer, with shorter hours the rest of the year. It's a terrific little Italian family restaurant with good service and solid, well-prepared food. You can eat out front on a covered porch. It also offers takeout and free delivery.

## BULLFROG MARINA
**Anasazi Restaurant,** in the Defiance House hotel, is the only restaurant on the lake outside of Wahweap. In the summer, it's open 6am to 2pm and 5 to 9pm. There's a breakfast buffet on summer weekends. Menu prices range from $9 to $16 for dinner.

# CHAPTER 11

# Zion National Park

Zion Canyon simply amazed me the first time I saw it, and not only because of the height of the sheer sandstone cliffs. After all, the Grand Canyon, which we had just left, is much larger. Zion just felt so intentional, as if it had been made specifically to say something spiritual. In fact, the Virgin River made the canyon by cutting down through layers of rock for millions of years — there's no reason to believe that God had more of a hand here than anywhere else. But that's not how it feels when you stand in the quiet evening shadows under the ash and cottonwoods and see, through their broadly spreading branches, the corners of white cliffs catching the setting sun far up in a deep blue sky. At those moments, this valley floor is like a garden in a great cathedral. It's a peaceful and gentle place, a place of respite after the severe and pitiless desert.

In the summer, it's also a place of crowds. Like other parks with a single star attraction, Zion attracts many visitors who just want to stop by, look around, and move on. The average visit is about 2 hours. Over the years, those day-trippers have clogged the two-lane roads into Zion Canyon with cars. Thankfully, the Park Service has recently gotten most cars out of the canyon itself, using shuttle buses to get people in, saving it from feeling like a huge parking lot. You also can escape the crowds by hiking, sightseeing early or late, and visiting less-known park areas.

## Best Things to Do

- Hiking Zion is its only exceptional activity. Zion is for hikers. Spend a few days climbing the trails and testing your limits. Steep, challenging routes lead to cooler mountain air, a change to a different plant and animal community, and incredible views.
- Mountain biking along some good routes in the lands outside the park.
- Taking a horseback ride along the Virgin River in the canyon.
- Floating on an inner tube in Springdale, just outside the park.

See "Activities" (p. 252).

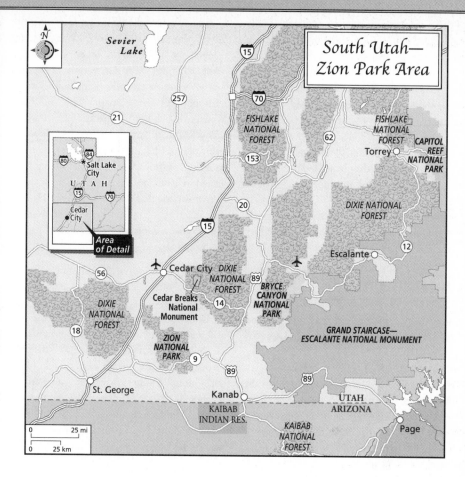

# A SPIRITUAL HISTORY

Zion Canyon made people think of God from the start. The first white explorer who came to the area, a Mormon missionary named Nephi Johnson, and a later visitor, Methodist minister Frederick Vining Fisher, both gave the place spiritual names such as West Temple, Pulpit, Angels Landing, and Great White Throne. The name of the canyon came from a Mormon settler who is said to have called the mountains temples as good for worship as the temples of Zion, the Promised Land in the Old Testament.

But we don't know what the first people here thought of the place. The earliest remains that archaeologists have found were left by Ancestral Puebloan (also called Anasazi) people who farmed the riverside bottomlands and hunted in the forests of the highlands. Sites of houses, granaries, and rock art are scattered around the park (but very few are open to the public). From the evidence, archaeologists believe that only a small community lived here, and those who did were on the fringe of their people's region and a little behind the times. About 700 years ago, when the Ancestral Puebloans left their pueblos elsewhere in the Southwest, they abandoned Zion too. Southern Paiute used the canyon now and then for the next 600 years, until they were pushed out by the Mormons.

The Mormons were members of the Church of Jesus Christ of Latter-day Saints, a religious group that started on the East Coast but was forced to leave by people who didn't like their beliefs. They came to Utah in 1847 when the area hadn't been explored and was still part of Mexico — the U.S. won it from Mexico in a war that ended in 1848. Mormons settled along the Virgin River from the beginning, and the church's great leader, Brigham Young, sent Nephi Johnson upriver to explore the Zion Canyon area in 1858. Other settlers followed, founding the town of Springdale and building farms in the canyon, including in the flat area around the Zion Lodge.

John Wesley Powell, the explorer who first floated the Grand Canyon, came to Zion Canyon in 1872. With other scientists he made maps and wrote descriptions of the area. Their reports drew others, including artists who painted the canyon. The St. Louis World's Fair of 1904 — dedicated to showing many wonders from the West — displayed paintings of the canyon that people simply could not believe. A government survey party visited in 1908, and its report on the area was so enthusiastic that President William Howard Taft made the canyon a national monument the next year. Zion became a national park in 1919.

# ORIENTATION

Zion has two main parts: the Zion Canyon area and Kolob Canyons & the High Country.

## THE ZION CANYON AREA

Zion Canyon and the approaches to it, on the south side of the park, draw most of the people. Unlike the arrangement at some other canyon parks, visitors enter at the bottom of the canyon, not the top. A dead-end road, **Zion Canyon Scenic Drive,** leads to the lodge, pullouts, and trailheads on the canyon floor. Most hikes and activities start there. From early April through late October, only shuttle buses and bicycles are allowed on this road.

### ZION ADDRESS BOOK

**Zion National Park.** Springdale, UT 84767-1099. ☎ 435/772-3256. www.nps.gov/zion.

**Zion Natural History Association** (for maps and books). Zion National Park, Springdale, UT 84767. ☎ **800/635-3959.** www.zionpark.org.

**Zion Canyon Chamber of Commerce.** P.O. Box 331, Springdale, UT 84767. ☎ **888/518-7070** or 435/772-3757. www.zionpark.com.

**Route 9** leads across the south of the park and meets the scenic drive. Campgrounds, the visitor center, the main entrance, and the town of **Springdale** are on the western side of the park along Route 9. Farther westward, it reaches Interstate 15 near the city of St. George. To the east, Route 9 becomes the amazing **Zion–Mt. Carmel Highway** on the way to the tiny town of Mt. Carmel and U.S. 89. See "Getting There" (p. 244) for restrictions on RVs on this road.

## KOLOB CANYONS & THE HIGH COUNTRY

The northern area of the park is in the high country, where summers are cooler, spring is snowy, and the trees are pinyon, juniper, and ponderosa pine. There are no commercial services. A pair of scenic drives leads among the steep-walled, red rock Kolob Canyons. To drive to this area of the park, take I-15 north from St. George. To hike there from the Zion Canyon area is a significant backpacking trip.

In the center of the park, the **Kolob Terrace Road** is a way into the backcountry. The long, partly paved route branches north from Route 9 west of Springdale. It cuts across

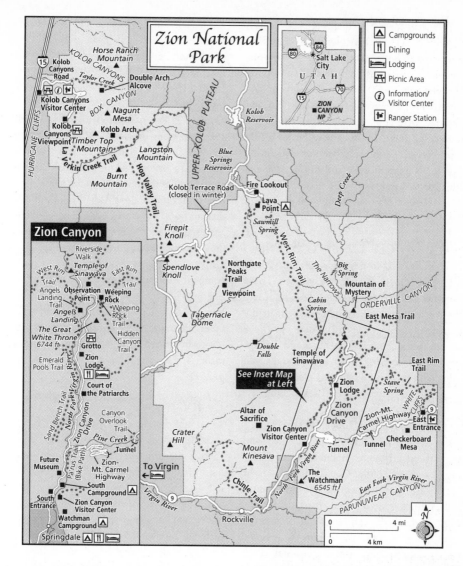

*Zion National Park*

the middle of the park's high country and meets several remote trails, leading ultimately to dirt roads north of the park and the primitive campground at Lava Point. The road is closed in the winter.

# MAKING THE ARRANGEMENTS

## WHEN TO GO

Summer is busy and hot at Zion. Thunderstorms are frequent in July and August, with daytime highs in the canyon almost always in the 90s and often over 100. The rim is 10°F to 15°F cooler. A ranger I met swore the park is overcrowded from May to October, but the 3 summer months are heaviest. The fall is perfect, with bright yellow leaves on the cottonwoods (foliage in the canyon peaks in late Oct), reasonable temperatures, and fewer crowds. Heavy snow is unlikely before November.

We went for a March spring break, and it was glorious. There were plenty of people, but it was easy to find a parking space or campsite, and the easier trails were busy but not too crowded to be fun. Down in the canyon, day-time temperatures were in the low 70s and evenings were cool. But up above, snow still buried the trails, limiting how far we could hike. For that reason, and because early spring weather is unpredictable and can be severe, a later spring break would be better. The final disappearance of snow is different each year, but all trails should be clear by early May.

## How Much Time to Spend

Zion lends itself to day trips, and that's how most people see it. In that case, you won't have time for any but the easiest hikes and a trip down the scenic road — not enough, in my opinion. If you can spend 3 days, you'll be able to take a couple of day hikes and perhaps enjoy some bicycling, inner-tubing, and a trail ride. With even more time and plenty of planning, Zion is spectacular for backpacking.

## How Far to Plan Ahead

Zion is crowded during the summer, and reservations for rooms should be made 3 to 6 months ahead at the Zion Lodge. The best Springdale rooms book up 2 or 3 months early, but less-special places are available later. Most of the park's campsites can be reserved from spring to early fall through the national reservation system (see "National Park Campground Reservations," in chapter 1, "Planning Your Trip").

## Reading Up

**Zion Natural History Association** (☎ 800/635-3959; www.zionpark.org) operates the park bookstores. Its wares are listed at the website.

**Maps:** A topographic trail map printed on paper by the natural history association covers the park in good detail and costs $4. **Hiking:**

The association also publishes *Zion: The Trails,* compiled by Bob Lineback, a pocket-sized, spiral-bound guide of 39 pages.

## Getting There
### By Car

Zion is just east of Interstate 15. Las Vegas is 158 miles away on fast roads. Zion is also on the way from the Grand Canyon and Glen Canyon to Bryce Canyon National Park and other parks and attractions to the north. Bryce is 86 miles north along U.S. 89, or a bit farther up I-15 by way of Cedar Breaks National Monument (see "Natural Places Just Outside the National Park," in chapter 12, "Bryce Canyon National Park"). Glen Canyon National Recreation Area is 114 miles southeast on U.S. 89, the Grand Canyon's North Rim is 120 miles, and the South Rim is 250 miles. Taking U.S. 89 means first driving the not-to-be-missed Zion–Mt. Carmel Highway through the east entrance of the park (see p. 251).

### By RV

To come from the other parks to the east via U.S. 89, you'll need to take Route 9, the Zion–Mt. Carmel Highway, through a long, narrow tunnel. Vehicles over 11 feet, 4 inches tall — almost any RV or bus — have to drive down the middle of the tunnel to fit through the arched ceiling. If yours is over 13 feet, 1 inch tall or over 40 feet long, you can't go through at all. To allow RVs to drive down the middle of the road, rangers have to radio ahead and stop oncoming traffic from the other end. To do this, you pay a $10 fee when you enter the park. Save the receipt, which is good for the return trip in the same vehicle up to 7 days later. The tunnel is staffed only from 8am to 8pm daily, March through October; if you're late, you're stuck. In the winter, RV drivers must call ahead (☎ 435/772-3256) to arrange for passage through the tunnel.

## WEATHER CHART: AVERAGE HIGHS & LOWS

|  | AVG. HIGH (°F) | AVG. LOW (°F) | DAYS/MONTH OVER 90°F |
|---|---|---|---|
| Dec.–Feb. | 52–57 | 29–31 | 0 |
| March | 63 | 36 | 0 |
| April | 73 | 43 | 1 |
| May | 83 | 52 | 8 |
| June | 93 | 60 | 21 |
| July | 100 | 68 | 30 |
| August | 97 | 66 | 28 |
| September | 91 | 60 | 18 |
| October | 78 | 49 | 3 |
| November | 63 | 37 | 0 |

## By Air

The nearest major airport is in Las Vegas, within a few hours' drive. You can rent a car or RV there (see chapter 8, "Layers upon Layers," for tips on RV rentals). St. George, Utah, less than an hour to the west, has a small airport. **Delta/Skywest** (☎ **800/453-9417;** www. skywest.com) flies between Salt Lake City and St. George), and **United Express/Skywest** (☎ **800/241-6522;** www.skywest.com) flies between Los Angeles and St. George. Car rentals at the airport are available from **Avis** (☎ **800/331-1212** or 435/634-3940; www. avis.com) and **Hertz** (☎ **800/654-3131** or 435/652-9941; www.hertz.com).

## WHAT TO PACK
### Clothing

The main thing is to bring good hiking shoes or boots. Up-and-down hiking can really chew up your feet in sneakers. (That goes for kids too.)

In the summer, pack for hot days in the canyon, with hats and light, reflective clothing. The evenings are pleasant. Up on top, you can wear light clothing in the summer, but you might need a sweater in the evening. Thunderstorms come often in the summer, so you might want jackets or ponchos, especially if you plan longer hikes.

For spring and fall visits, bring light clothing, but also layers of sweaters and jackets to make the transition from hot days in the canyon to cold evenings, especially higher up. You won't need clothing more formal than a clean pair of long pants and a shirt with a collar.

## Gear

In the summer, light camping gear will do. In the spring and fall, be prepared for chilly nights with heavier sleeping bags or a layered arrangement. If it's convenient, bring your bikes to use on Zion Canyon Scenic Drive and the one paved path here open to bikes; otherwise, you can easily rent. Hiking in the high country in early spring or winter might require snowshoes, which you will have to bring from home.

# WHERE TO SPEND THE NIGHT

## CAMPING
### Park Service Campgrounds

Reservations are accepted spring through early fall for Watchman Campground's 231 sites, but never for the 126 sites at South Campground or the 6 sites at Lava Point Campground. (See "Camping & Hotel Reservations," in chapter 1.) In the busy season, getting a first-come, first-served site can be difficult. Many people camp at a commercial campground outside, then show up at the park campgrounds early in the morning in hopes of getting a site when someone leaves.

**Watchman and South Campgrounds.** Rte. 9 near the Springdale entrance. $14 per site; $16 per site with electric hookups. 357 sites; RVs or tents. Flush toilets, dump station.

These lovely campgrounds next to each other along the Virgin River are shaded by Fremont cottonwoods and other shade trees, but there's not much to shield some sites from each other. The most coveted sites are along the water, but the whole place has a special feel, under the chiseled stone peaks on either side of the valley. The slightly smaller South Campground closes in the winter; Watchman is open all year, takes reservations in season, and might have slightly larger sites. In addition, Watchman has two loops with electric hookups. It's an easy walk or bike ride on the paved trail to town, where you can buy firewood from a stand just outside the park or at a handy grocery store. The **Watchman Trail** leaves from the service road near the Watchman Campground registration station, climbing a few hundred feet over 1 mile to a viewpoint of the valley. The **Zion Nature Center,** which has a Junior Ranger program (see "Programs," p. 254), is at the entrance of South Campground.

**Lava Point Campground.** At the end of Kolob Terrace Rd., 40 miles from the Zion Canyon Visitor Center. No fee. 6 sites. Vault toilets, no water. Closed mid-Oct to May.

This remote campground at the end of a dirt road is near high-country backpacking trails. The campground is on a plateau point at about a 7,900-foot elevation. Vehicles over 19 feet are not recommended, and any creekwater you find should be treated before drinking.

## Backcountry Camping

Backpackers camping anywhere outside a campground need a backcountry permit that costs $5 from either visitor center. You can't reserve ahead; permits are given out only in person, starting 3 days before the hike. Once out, you can camp in designated sites in the West Rim, and in the East Rim areas anywhere that's out of sight and sound of a trail and at least a quarter mile from a spring. In the Kolob Canyons area, you have to use designated sites. Contact the Park Service to get the *Backcountry Planner,* with all the regulations, a map of sites and camping areas, and essential advice (see "Zion Address Book," p. 242).

## Commercial Campgrounds

Besides the two RV-oriented campgrounds listed here, tent campers should read about **Zion Ponderosa Ranch Resort** (p. 248).

**Zion Canyon Campground.** 479 Zion Park Blvd. (P.O. Box 99), Springdale, UT 84767. ☎ 435/ 772-3237. www.zioncanyoncampground.com. Tent sites $16, full hookups $20 for 2; extra person ages 5–15 $2, extra person 16 and older $3.50. DISC, MC, V. 200 sites; all sizes of RVs. Hot showers, laundry, playground, game room, river swimming, store, restaurant.

This grassy campground with shade trees and a duck pond is far more pleasant than many arid, parking-lot–style RV parks that dot the region. Sites with picnic tables descend from the main street in Springdale to the edge of the Virgin River, where kids can splash around with inner tubes. The same couple has run the campground for close to 30 years. It's a popular place, and reservations are important for the busy season. Try to make them a month in advance. Inexpensive cabins are for rent, too.

**Mukuntuweep RV Park and Campground.** East of the park on Rte. 9 (P.O. Box 193), Orderville, UT 84758. ☎ **435/648-2154.** www. expressweb.com/zionpark. $15 tent sites, $19 full hookups for 2; $3 per extra person, kids under 12 $1.50. AE, DISC, MC, V. 150 sites; tents and all sizes of RVs. Hot showers, laundry, recreation hall, store, restaurant.

Along the sparsely developed highway east of the park toward U.S. 89, this campground is on a large plot of mostly open ground. Its best feature is its proximity to the park entrance. There are also six basic but comfortable log cabins, a hogan, and a teepee that share the campground's bathhouse ($25).

## HOTELS

Only **Zion Lodge,** described below, is within the park, but Springdale has delightful hotels and is so close you might as well be in the park. With a population of about 300, Springdale is developing fast, with new hotels and tourist businesses, but thoughtful community planning has helped it retain the atmosphere of a charming mountain resort community. Try to reserve a couple of months ahead for the busy season. In addition to the choices listed below, **Driftwood Lodge** (☎ **888/801-8811** or 435/772-3262) is nice, and **Best Western Zion Park Inn** (☎ **800/ 934-7275** or 435/772-3200) has lots of good standard accommodations. High-season rates run from March to October, with low-season rates about 25% less.

**Canyon Ranch Motel.** 688 Zion Park Blvd. (P.O. Box 175), Springdale, UT 84767. ☎ **435/ 772-3357.** Fax 435/772-3057. www.canyonranch motel.com. 21 units. High season $58–$88 per room (2–5 people). AE, DISC, MC, V.

This is an excellent budget choice. Although the stucco duplex and four-plex cottages look a bit old-fashioned, inside they're well kept. They sit on a grassy compound with a pool and swings. Kitchenettes are available, pets are permitted with a fee, and you can drive right to your door.

**Cliffrose Lodge and Gardens.** 281 Zion Park Blvd., Springdale, UT 84767. ☎ **800/243-UTAH** or 435/772-3234. Fax 435/772-3900. www. cliffroselodge.com. 36 units. High season $119– $145 double; $10 each additional adult, children under 18 stay free with parents. AE, DISC, MC, V.

On 5 beautifully landscaped acres along the Virgin River, this lodge has good standard hotel rooms with balconies and large bathrooms. The buildings have long, pitched roofs and warm wood siding above stone foundations. There are flower gardens, a playground, a sandbox, and a swimming pool.

**Flanigan's Inn.** 428 Zion Park Blvd. (P.O. Box 100), Springdale, UT 84767. ☎ **800/765-RSVP** or 435/772-3244. Fax 435/772-3396. www. flanigans.com. 33 units. $79–$99 double, $149– $169 suites; $10 per extra person over age 12. AE, DISC, MC, V.

Flanigan's combines a rare set of qualities. The stylish, handcrafted small hotel feels like a resort and is more than friendly to families — in fact, it positively courts them. The grounds are a small paradise of stone walls and hedges, with a swimming pool on a terrace, an ornamental pond, a children's play area with a tree house, and a nature trail that snakes off into the desert. The rooms are large and have features such as vaulted ceilings and original art. All have coffeemakers and some have kitchenettes; some of the nicely appointed "suites"

---

### PARK CAMPING BASICS: TOILETS, SHOWERS & LAUNDRY

**The nicest public restrooms are in the visitor centers and at Zion Lodge.** There are also toilets in Zion Canyon at the Temple of Sinawava, Weeping Rock, and Grotto Picnic Area. The campground bathrooms have cold water and no soap, and Lava Point Campground has no water at all. There's a coin-operated laundry in Springdale at the Zion Canyon Campground, listed below. It also offers hot showers to the public for $3.

are actually separate houses. See p. 255 for details on the restaurant, The Spotted Dog Café.

**Zion Lodge.** Zion Canyon Scenic Dr., inside Zion National Park. ☎ **435/772-3213.** Fax 435/772-2001. www.zionlodge.com. (Reservations ℅ Amfac Parks and Resorts, 14001 E. Iliff Ave., Suite 600, Aurora, CO 80014. ☎ **303/297-2757.** www.amfac.com.) 121 units. $95–$105 double, $105–$110 cabin; $5 per extra person over age 16. AE, DISC, MC, V.

The park lodge, a collection of buildings with massive stone foundations, spreads out over a large campus under shade trees in the middle of Zion Canyon. The lobby, restaurant, and auditorium building is a center of activities where you can reserve horseback rides, eat at the snack bar, and play on the big lawn. The modern motel rooms are in a pair of brown wood-framed buildings; each has a balcony and two beds. The rooms lack TVs but have air-conditioning, telephones, and tubs with showers. The cabins, in duplex and four-plex buildings, have a national park atmosphere, with vaulted ceilings, light wood moldings, and gas-burning stone fireplaces.

**Zion Ponderosa Ranch Resort.** East of Zion National Park (2 miles east of the park entrance, then 5 miles north on North Fork Rd). P.O. Box 5547, Mt. Carmel, UT 84755. ☎ **800/293-5444** or 435/648-2700. www.zionponderosa.com. 28 cabins. $65–$239 per person, all-inclusive lodging packages. $65 per person, all-inclusive camping packages. DISC, MC, V.

This lodge is in a remote area just outside the park, only a couple of miles from Zion Canyon on the East Rim Trail. Among the many services is a hiking shuttle to pick you up at the other end. There are trail rides, mountain biking, horseback riding, skeet and trap shooting, fishing, rappelling, climbing, and numerous other activities. In the summer a day camp takes care of the kids for up to 7 hours while adults tackle more ambitious activities. There are a pool and hot tub, tennis courts, and other sports equipment. Rates are complicated and include all activities and meals; there are discounts for children. In the off-season, you can just rent the lodgings or camp without buying a complete package. Large cabins have TVs, smaller cabins do not. There are no telephones except in the largest unit, and there's no air-conditioning.

# WHEN YOU ARRIVE

## ENTRANCE FEES

The entry fee is $20 per vehicle, $5 for individuals on their own. National park passes are accepted and a good buy if you will visit other parks in the region. RVs pay an added $10 fee for traveling through the tunnel on the Zion–Mt. Carmel Highway; see an important note on that under "Getting There" (p. 244).

## VISITOR CENTERS

The **Zion Nature Center** is listed below, under "Children's Programs" (p. 254). In addition, plans are underway for a new Human History Museum, scheduled to open in summer 2002 in the park's former visitor center, just outside Zion canyon.

**Zion Canyon Visitor Center.** On Rte. 9, just inside the south entrance station along the road to Watchman Campground. ☎ **435/772-3256.** Daily 8am–7pm in summer, 8am–5pm in winter.

The large new visitor center contains a ranger desk, a large bookstore, a few natural history exhibits, and many outside displays. It's a good first stop but by no means indispensable.

**Kolob Canyon Visitor Center.** At the northern park entrance, Exit 40 off I-15. ☎ **435/586-9548.** Daily 8am–7pm.

This center answers questions and offers orientation about the park's high country.

**Emergencies**   Dial ☎ **911,** or call ☎ **435/772-3322** to reach the Park Service in emergencies. There's a **medical clinic** at 120 Lion Blvd. in Springdale (☎ **435/772-3226**), open daily May through October and 1 day a week the rest of the year. The nearest hospital is **Dixie Regional Medical Center,** 544 S. 400 East, St. George (☎ **435/634-4011**).

**Stores**   The park's commercial services are mostly in Springdale. **Canyon Super Market** (☎ **435/772-3402**) is just outside the park entrance, at 65 Zion Park Blvd. It sells groceries, limited camping supplies, and firewood. It's open daily 8am to 10pm in the summer, 9am to 6pm in the winter.

**Banks**   **Zions Bank** is at 921 Zion Park Blvd. in Springdale, and has an ATM (☎ **435/772-3274;** www.zionsbank.com).

**Post Office**   Inside Zion Lodge and on Route 9 in Springdale.

**Gear Sales & Rental**   At least two bike-rental shops operate on the main drag in Springdale. Both rent bikes and carts, have inner tubes and a shuttle service for floating the Virgin River, and are happy to give advice on mountain-biking destinations. **Bike Zion,** 1458 Zion Park Blvd. (☎ **800/475-4576** or 435/772-3929; www.bikezion.com), also offers guided tours. **Scenic Cycles,** 202 Zion Park Blvd. (☎ **435/772-BIKE**), has electric and tandem bikes, and kid-size tandem attachments for the back of a grown-up's bike. For other outdoor gear (for sale or rental), advice, and "engaging in the human experience," visit **Zion Adventure Company,** 36 Lion Blvd., Springdale (☎ **435/772-1001;** www.zionadventures.com). These friendly young guys make a specialty of outfitting, guiding, and teaching skills in the park and the surrounding outdoors. Stop in and talk with them, especially if you plan a canyon trek. They also rent dry suits for walking in the water of the Narrows.

## GETTING AROUND
### By Car or RV

You'll need a car to get to Zion, to see the Zion–Mt. Carmel Highway, and to get to the Kolob Canyons area of the park, 45 miles from the Zion Canyon Visitor Center by way of Route 9 and I-15. In the off-season, the Zion Canyon Scenic Drive is open to vehicles, but if you're driving an RV you'll find it difficult because of the narrow roadway and limited parking. RVs also have special restrictions on the Zion–Mt. Carmel Highway, the eastern portion of Route 9 (see "Getting There," p. 244).

### By Shuttle

A new shuttle-bus system in the main part of the park reduces traffic congestion, pollution, and noise. The system has two loops: one in the town of Springdale and the other along Zion Canyon Scenic Drive, with the loops connecting at the new transit/visitor center just inside the south park entrance. From early April to October, you can travel the Zion Canyon Scenic Drive (off Route 9) only on shuttle buses, on foot, or by bike, except that overnight guests at Zion Lodge can drive as far as the lodge. Shuttles run roughly every 6 minutes at peak times from 5:30am to 11pm daily, and have room for packs, coolers, and strollers, plus two bicycles. Off-season, you can drive the full length of Zion Canyon Scenic Drive in your own vehicle.

### By Bike

During high season, when the Zion Canyon Scenic Road is closed to private vehicles, bikes are the most enjoyable way to explore the park. A paved bike trail, the **Pa'rus Trail,** leads through the woods along the Virgin River from the campgrounds and main entrance near Springdale roughly 2 miles to the intersection of Route 9 and the Scenic Drive. From there, bike into the canyon trailheads and viewpoints. During the off-season, however, when the road is open to private vehicles, biking is appropriate only for older and more experienced cyclists.

Bike rentals are available from the agencies listed under "For Handy Reference" (p. 249).

## KEEPING SAFE & HEALTHY

The blazing summer heat in the canyon and chilly spring and fall weather on the rim demand caution. Please read the sections on dehydration and hypothermia in "Dealing with Hazards," in chapter 1. Also review the notes on lightning and snake and insect bites. Here are a couple of specific things to be aware of at Zion.

### Falls

Many trails run along precipices, some of them with sheer drop-offs of more than 1,000 feet. Carelessness could be fatal. Also, knocking rocks off these high places endangers people below. Even if your route is safe, be aware of the fears of other members of your party. Have them turn back before they freeze in a frightening spot.

### Drowning

The swift-flowing river helps give the park its wonderful sense of life, and kids will enjoy playing near it. But be careful, especially in the spring, because they easily can fall in and be swept away. Don't let kids near water without supervision.

# ENJOYING THE PARK

## NATURAL PLACES
## Temple of Sinawava & the Narrows

This is the heart of the park, at the end of the Zion Canyon Scenic Drive. Here Zion Canyon becomes too narrow for the scenic road on the floor of the canyon to continue north. It ends in a magical space, nearly encircled by vertical cliff walls 1,600 feet high.

How did it get this way? The Virgin River made it. At this point, the river jogged, making a bow that remained as its bed eroded and left a towering cliff that reaches around and blocks the view down toward the mouth of the canyon. The Virgin River starts high on the Markagunt Plateau, at 9,000 feet. It ends 200 miles south and 8,000 feet lower in Lake Mead, a part of the Colorado River held back by Hoover Dam. Water flows fast over its steep course, especially in spring floods that come as snow melts in the high country and after summer thunderstorms. When that happens, water roars down the canyons and chips away at the soft rock with harder rock it picks

up along the way. Currently, water is wearing away about a foot of canyon every 1,000 years.

North from the parking lot, a flat, paved trail, **Riverside Walk,** runs along the Virgin River between the narrowing walls of the canyon. This corridor through rock shrinks and twists until it feels as though you're walking down a secret passage into the heart of the earth. Wildflowers grow from cracks in the walls where water seeps out. Signs along the way explain what you're seeing.

After 1 mile, the canyon runs out of room for a trail. This is the start of the **Narrows,** a 16-mile-long route, much of which is a slot canyon that's as little as 30 feet wide and 2,000 feet deep. Why is Zion Canyon so narrow here and wider back toward its mouth? The steep cliffs are mostly Navajo Sandstone, a grainy rock of light tan to red that wears away easily a grain at a time but stays in one piece as it is being carved up. Just below the layer of sandstone lies shale from the Kayenta Formation, which breaks into bigger pieces than the sandstone and doesn't hold together as well in cliffs. In the Narrows, where the canyon is only as wide as a large hallway, the river is still wearing through the sandstone and hasn't reached to the shale, so it only carves a thin, deep crack. Where the canyon gets wider, the river has reached the layer of shale. There the river washes shale away from underneath the sandstone, which then falls down, making the canyon much wider but still just as tall.

There's no trail through the Narrows, because water covers the canyon floor, but people do hike it by wading in the river. Because it's so difficult to hike against the current, most go downstream to traverse the whole thing, which requires a permit. Starting from the bottom, you can explore upriver without a permit, being careful not to overextend yourself and checking the weather for flash-flood warnings first. The river bottom is slippery, and a walking stick is a good idea. Just start wading. The scene is amazing right from the start. About 2 miles upstream, you come to the meeting of the Orderville Canyon, probably the most beautiful spot on the hike and a good turnaround destination. Of course, wading against a stream is only for strong hikers.

Going downstream the whole 16 miles is a unique and exceptionally challenging hike. Apply for a $5-per-person permit at the Zion Canyon Visitor Center 24 hours before the hike. Permits are available only if rangers deem the weather forecast and water levels suitable. Everyone in the party must be at least 12 years old and 56 inches tall. You can get directions to the trailhead, which is outside the park, from the Park Service when you get your permit or from the map listed under "Reading Up" (p. 244). Special dry suits for hiking in the river are for rent (see "For Handy Reference," p. 249).

The water level and temperature in the river determine the difficulty of the hike and what equipment you'll need. The water usually drops to a reasonable level in mid-June. In late July through early September,

thunderstorms create too much risk of deadly flash floods. From late September until winter, you can do the hike, but you might need 2 days because there's less daylight. If you're thinking about this interesting challenge, stop by the visitor center for advice a couple of days beforehand so that you can prepare.

## Weeping Rock

The most common rock formations at Zion are from the 2,000-foot-thick layer of Navajo Sandstone and the Kayenta Formation of shale that lies right under it. The sandstone was made from huge dunes that were pressed and heated into rock about 1 mile under the earth. The Kayenta rocks started out as mud and silt in a swampy environment, forming shale and siltstone when they became rock. An important difference between the two kinds of rock is that water seeps through the sand grains of the sandstone but can't get through the finer grain of the shale. Where the layers meet, water from the sandstone flows on top of the shale until it finds a way out. That's what happens at Weeping Rock. A spring coming out of the rock feeds hanging gardens of wildflowers (in season) that seem to grow from the cliff. It's only a quarter mile from a parking lot on the scenic drive. More ambitious trails climb the canyon from the parking lot here, too.

## The Zion–Mt. Carmel Highway

The red asphalt highway that enters the east side of the park is a wonder because of the strange and beautiful land it passes through, and because of the amazing effort it took to build the road. Plan to use this road on your way into or out of the park, allowing plenty of time to enjoy the scenery and take a walk. If you need to use the western entrance to come and go, take a half-day excursion to the Zion–Mt. Carmel Highway. (Practical information about the highway, also known as Route 9, is covered under "Getting There," p. 244.)

Starting from the east, on the way into the park, you go through a mountain valley of ponderosa pines and rounded sandstone outcroppings of white, tan, orange, and red, known as **slickrock country.** These rocks were sand dunes in a vast desert more than 150 million years ago, during the Jurassic Period or the age of dinosaurs. Many of the shapes look like sand dunes or huge waves of blowing fabric. Even more interesting, many of the mounds of rock have patterns of lines. These lines show the way the sand was arranged by the wind during the Jurassic Period.

How exactly did this happen? When wind blows over sand dunes, it picks up grains of sand from one side and moves them across the top to the other side. When the sand piles up more steeply than the "angle of repose" (34 degrees in this case), it avalanches down the side of the dune. (For more on this idea, see "Experiment: Sand Slides," in chapter 5, "Cape Hatteras National Seashore.") As sand is buried deep, it starts to stick together, and the patterns of lines left by the little avalanches are preserved. When the wind changes, the pattern changes, leaving a different set of lines. You can still see those lines clearly, crisscrossing on **Checkerboard Mesa** and many other places along the road.

This bedrock is inviting for walking, but be careful, because it's easy to slide off the steep slopes. A single trail branches off the road between its two tunnels. The half-mile **Canyon Overlook Trail** leads to an impressive view of Zion and Pine Creek canyons. Get a guide booklet at the trailhead or visitor center.

The second tunnel along the highway is more than a mile long; on the other side you pop out in completely new terrain, perched high on the side of a deep canyon. The road was built in 1930, and it's fun to imagine how they managed it. On the way down, you'll want to stop and take in the view a few times — you certainly don't want the driver taking his or her eyes off the road.

## The Canyon Rim

Zion Canyon is a notch in the White Cliffs, a step in the Grand Staircase that leads up a series of plateaus from Northern Arizona to Bryce Canyon National Park and Cedar Breaks National Monument, north of Zion in Utah. Few other places allow you to see so clearly how elevation affects the habitat for plants and animals. As you go higher, the weather gets cooler and damper, just as it does when you go north. By one estimate, 1,000 feet up equals 400 miles north in this area of the country. In a day hike at Zion, you can climb 800 miles north, from the desert Southwest on the canyon floor to pine forests more like those in Idaho. It's fun and easy to identify a few plants at the bottom, to note when they disappear on the way up, and to note the appearance of new plants as you rise. For an idea of what to look for in each elevation zone, see "Elevations of Life Zones," in chapter 8.

## Kolob Canyons Area

The northern area of the park, an hour's drive from Zion Canyon on Route 9 and I-15, includes canyons at the edge of the high Kolob Terrace. The red rock cuts steeply along narrow canyons, with many odd and interesting formations. A 5-mile scenic drive leads from the visitor center in front of the cliffs and up to a high overlook. Pick up a copy of the road guide at the visitor center (see p. 248). Two trails lead into the area; both are described below under "Hiking."

## ACTIVITIES
## Backpacking

Zion's trails link to create a network from one end of the park to the other. By carrying your gear and camping in the backcountry, you can take advantage of the trails and really get away from people. Below, under "Hiking," I've described some of the main trails. Before your trip, get a topographic map (see "Reading Up," p. 244) and a backcountry permit from the Park Service (see p. 246).

# Hiking

Setting out on Zion's trails is the best way to see the park. Unlike the Grand Canyon, with its risk of getting exhausted and stuck at the bottom, Zion hikes mostly start out going steeply uphill and if you tire you just walk back down again. Be sure to take good shoes or boots, and in hot weather take sun-protective clothing and plenty of water. A handy list of trails — with mileage, elevation gain, and the Park Service's conservative estimates of time and difficulty level — is included in the park map and newspaper you get when you arrive. Here are some of your choices, listed by area in order of difficulty. In addition, the **Riverside Walk** and hiking through **the Narrows** are covered under "Temple of Sinawava & the Narrows," p. 250; **Weeping Rock** is on p. 251; and the **Canyon Overlook Trail** is under "The Zion–Mt. Carmel Highway," p. 251.

## ZION CANYON

**THE EMERALD POOL TRAILS** The lower pool trail is a 1.2-mile paved loop; the upper pool trail adds another .8 mile that's a bit rougher. A stroller is possible but not easy on the lower trail, and impossible on the upper trail, but this is a great hike for young children. It leads to interesting places, they can manage the whole thing, and it isn't just another flat nature trail — there's some challenge to it. The trail crosses the Virgin River on a footbridge and then climbs a short way up the east side of the canyon to a series of pools, a lovely stream, and a pair of glorious waterfalls — part of the trail passes behind one of these. Go early to avoid crowds and the heat. Swimming in the pools is not allowed.

**THE SAND BENCH** It's possible to hike much of the length of Zion Canyon on the west side of the river, away from the road, without much elevation gain. This 3.6-mile loop trail is the south end of that network. It gradually gains about 500 feet. It's used by the horseback-riding concessionaire for trail rides in summer (see "Horseback Riding," p. 254), making it a bit less attractive to hikers.

**EAST RIM, INCLUDING HIDDEN CANYON** Starting from the Weeping Rock parking lot in the canyon, the **East Rim Trail** is one of two that climb to the canyon rim (the other is West Rim, below) up a spectacular and challenging series of switchbacks. It joins a network of high-country trails and ultimately leads to the east entrance station on the Zion–Mt. Carmel Highway, 11.6 miles away. Short of that goal, the **Hidden Canyon Trail** branches off partway up to explore a side canyon, making a 2-mile round-trip. At the top, you can strive for incredible lookouts on Observation Point or Cable Mountain. The trail has many scary points, with long drop-offs, and it's steep and hard work; but the rewards are great. Fit, energetic grade-school children should be able to make it.

**WEST RIM, ANGELS LANDING** The incredible **West Rim Trail** has even more elevation gain than East Rim, climbing steeply over 3,500 feet. Join it from the footbridge across the river at the Grotto picnic area on the scenic drive. The trail is a wonder, especially the flurry of switchbacks near the top built out of cut stone. They're called **Walter's Wiggles** after the park superintendent who built them. The awesome views start at the beginning, so this is a good trail to try even if you're not sure you'll make it to the top. Most of the way up, after 2 miles, the path branches to **Angels Landing,** a scramble out to a knife-edged ridge with vertical drops of more than 1,000 feet on each side. There's a chain to cling to, but I wouldn't take children or anyone who isn't completely fearless.

You can keep going up the West Rim to the high country of ponderosa pine and exposed sandstone. Ultimately, the trail leads 14 miles to Lava Point, at the end of Kolob Terrace Road. From there it joins other trails that cross all the way to the Kolob Canyons entrance, a backpacking trip of several days.

## KOLOB CANYONS AREA

**THE TAYLOR CREEK TRAIL**  The trail follows the middle fork of the creek into one of the canyons, a round-trip of 5.4 miles, with less than a 500-foot elevation gain. It offers a chance to see the steep-walled structures up close. The trailhead is a few miles beyond the visitor center on Kolob Canyons Road.

**THE LAVERKIN CREEK TRAIL**  The trail leads to 310-foot Kolob Arch — the largest natural arch in the world — after a one-way walk of 7 miles. It's an ambitious hike, descending into hot canyon bottoms, and the start of several multiple-day backpacking trips that go all the way back to Zion Canyon.

## Horseback Riding

**Canyon Trail Rides** (☎ 435/679-8665; www.onpages.com/canyonrides) offers two rides a day, starting at the corral across the road in front of Zion Lodge. The reservation desk is in the lodge. The guides offer commentary on plants and the history of landmarks on the way. Children as young as 7 can join the 1-hour ride along the Virgin River, which costs $20 per person. It starts by fording the river and goes as far as the Court of the Patriarchs. Children who are at least 8 years old are welcome on the half-day trip, which uses the Sand Bench Trail and costs $45 per person. Riders must be no heavier than 220 pounds. Book ahead in the busy season; you can reserve up to a year ahead, but a few days is probably enough.

## Inner-Tubing

When the Virgin River slows down and the weather heats up, families play in the water, especially where it passes through Springdale. The two bike shops mentioned under "For Handy Reference" (p. 249) rent tubes and shuttle floaters between the start and end points, both of which are outside the park. You'll need a bathing suit and shoes that can get wet.

---

### PLACES FOR RELAXED PLAY & PICNICS

The grassy lawns under shade trees near **Zion Lodge** reminded me of a campus. You can spread out, throw a ball, and walk over to the snack bar when you get hungry. Just up the canyon is the well-shaded **Grotto picnic area,** with plenty of running-around room and raised grills. In Springdale, there's a **city park** with a playground, tennis courts, and volleyball, on Lion Boulevard, behind Flanigan's Inn.

---

## Mountain Biking

See "By Bike" (p. 249) for details on road biking in the park. Bikes aren't allowed off pavement within the park, but the nearby Bureau of Land Management territory has many exceptional and undiscovered mountain-biking routes, some good for kids and some very challenging. The bike shops mentioned under "For Handy Reference" (p. 249) can help you find these places. One of them, **Bike Zion,** has a lot of pictures of the slick rock biking routes on its website (www.bikezion.com).

## PROGRAMS
## Children's Programs

**Zion Nature Center** (☎ 435/772-0169), at South Campground, is a miniature natural history museum for kids and their families. It's open only in the summer. The **Junior Ranger program,** a half-day ranger-led educational session that lets children earn a patch, takes place here. It runs from 9 to 11:30am or from 1:30 to 4pm daily in the summer.

## Family & Adult Programs

Ranger-led programs in various areas of interest are available all summer. You can find out when and where only by checking the bulletin boards at the campgrounds and the visitor center.

# FUN OUTSIDE THE PARK

The **Tanner Summer Series** presents performing arts in the 2,000-seat outdoor **O. C. Tanner Amphitheater,** on Lion Boulevard just off Zion Park Boulevard in Springdale. Concerts range from symphonies to cowboy poetry, beginning at 8pm every Saturday from Memorial Day through Labor Day. Tickets are $8 per person. Call ☎ 435/652-7994 to find out what's on.

The **Zion Canyon Cinemax Theatre,** 145 Zion Park Blvd. (☎ 435/772-2400; www. zioncanyontheatre.com), shows films on a massive screen in a complex that also has a deli, shops, a photo processor, and an ATM. The regular offering, *Zion Canyon — Treasure of the Gods,* presents the cliffs, rushing water, and spectacle of the place, plus a little pop history, in 37 minutes. Shows start on the hour all day. From March to October, the theater is open from 9am to 9pm; November through February, hours are 11am to 7pm. Admission is $7.50, $5.50 for seniors, $4.50 for children ages 3 to 11, and free for babies under 3.

# WHERE TO EAT

## LOW-STRESS MEALS

There are no fast-food franchises at Zion Park or Springdale, but you'll find plenty of places to get sandwiches and takeout. In the park, the snack bar at **Zion Lodge** serves full meals. You can sit down inside or take your food out to the lawn.

In Springdale, you can get good homemade pizza to eat in or take out at Zion Pizza & Noodle, located in a former church with a turquoise steeple at 868 Zion Park Blvd. (☎ 435/772-3815). It's open daily from 4pm with reduced hours in winter and closed January and February. Deli sandwiches, fresh-baked muffins and cinnamon rolls, gourmet coffee, and the like are for sale at **Zion Park Gift & Deli,** 866 Zion Park Blvd. (☎ 435/ 772-3843), open Monday through Saturday 8am to 9pm in summer, with shorter hours in winter. There's a deli at the **Zion Canyon Cinemax Theatre** complex, 145 Zion Park Blvd. (☎ 435/772-2400); see above for hours.

## BEST-BEHAVIOR MEALS

None of these places is really formal, but because you do sit down and get waited on, some patience is required.

**Bit and Spur Restaurant & Saloon.** 1212 Zion Park Blvd. ☎ 435/772-3498. Reservations recommended. Dinner $7–$16.50. Daily 5–10pm; closed Tues–Wed Dec–Jan.

Despite the Western saloon ambiance, the sophisticated Mexican and Southwestern cuisine here is popular with families. They sit in their own dining room or on the patio.

**Spotted Dog Cafe.** At Flanigan's Inn. 428 Zion Park Blvd. ☎ 435/772-3244. Reservations recommended. Dinner $9–$18. Daily 7–11:30am, 5–10pm; reduced hours in winter.

The creative cuisine here uses fresh local ingredients, including vegetables from the inn's garden. The food is served on a sidewalk patio or in a light, tiled dining room with high ceilings and original art. The menu includes many vegetarian selections, and prices are reasonable. The children's menu is comprehensive and inexpensive. Microbrews are on tap.

**Zion Lodge.** Zion Canyon Scenic Dr. ☎ 435/ 772-3213. Breakfast $5–$10; lunch $4.75–$13; dinner $9–$20.25. Daily 6:30–10am, 11:30am–3pm, and 5:30–9pm. Dinner reservations required in summer.

The lodge's huge main dining room, upstairs in the main building, is decorated with historic photographs and has an unforgettable view of the canyon walls. The room and service are formal, but the customers aren't. The standard American fare is good, if unmemorable.

Where to Eat  **255**

# Bryce Canyon National Park

Each of the parks in the Grand Staircase part of the Southwest has its own character, and Bryce is the friendliest. The other, bigger canyons impress you with their hugeness, which turns a single person into only a speck. Bryce, on the other hand, is a land of details. It invites you in. At the Bryce Amphitheater, natural red rock statues sit up like spectators in a great half-bowl, watching the sky's eternal show of drifting clouds. Paths draw you down into tiny canyons like aisles in a theater full of stone giants. With each step, the scene changes. Each tower has a different weird shape, each narrow alley twists to show a newly framed view of an unearthly landscape. A pair of fir trees reaches from the bottom of a canyon called Wall Street, just wide enough for their trunks and the pathway. A red rock balances high on a tall, skinny stone needle that looks as if a strong wind would topple it. The place is huge, but it wasn't the size that amazed me — it was the feeling that no matter how carefully I explored, no matter how closely I looked, there always would be something smaller and finer to discover.

The statue-like pillars of stone are called **hoodoos.** They and the other strange shapes at Bryce were created and are still being carved by water as it works on ground where hard and soft rocks are mixed together. How it all works is explained under "Cliff Erosion & Hoodoos," in chapter 8, "Layers upon Layers."

The park and other nearby public lands — **Dixie National Forest, Kodachrome Basin State Park,** and **Cedar Breaks National Monument** — include habitat that ranges from the hot, dry desert to the alpine zone, above 10,000 feet (see "Elevations of Life Zones," in chapter 8). In a little time in the car, or a bit more on foot, you can go from winter to spring to summer. On the plateau at Bryce, you stand at 8,000 feet amid tall ponderosa pine and look out on land where not much grows and snow can stick well into spring. If it's cold at Bryce, you can go down to Kodachrome Basin at 5,800 feet and warm up. If it's hot, head up over 10,000 feet to Cedar Breaks.

## BEST THINGS TO DO

- Hiking among the bewitching hoodoos are well within the reach of school-age children (and strong preschoolers).
- Riding horseback through the rock formations and on the desert plateau outside the park.

- Winter is long at this elevation and excellent cross-country ski trails span much of the rim area.
- The thin, clear air can make for visibility of more than 100 miles and superb stargazing.

See "Activities" (p. 268).

## HISTORY AT THE EDGE OF CIVILIZATION

Bryce Canyon was never used much by people before it became a park. Like other high-elevation parks in the West, the cold, snowy land was harder to live on than nearby lower areas that were warmer and free of snow during more of the year. The Ancestral Puebloans (also called Anasazi) and Fremont people visited only for summer hunting or gathering, and didn't build much for anyone to find later. After they were gone, the Southern Paiute came to the area on occasion. Their legends said that the hoodoos were ancient people who were turned to stone by the powerful Coyote, an animal spirit from early times.

In the 1870s, government explorers, including the famous John Wesley Powell, found the canyon, named the parts of the area with Paiute words, and reported their discoveries to the world. At around that time, Mormons settlers forced out the Southern Paiute and tried to settle near Bryce, but they couldn't hold on with the hard weather and poor land. Among them, Ebenezer and Mary Bryce arrived around 1875. Besides his name, which stuck to the canyon when he built a

logging road, Ebenezer also left behind a famous comment that helps you imagine how hard it must have been to ranch here; he said it was "a hell of a place to lose a cow." Later settlers were able to make it by building a 10-mile ditch to bring water over the plateau. As you drive east from the park, you can see the dry little towns they built. The biggest, grandest, and most lasting buildings remain the churches of the (Mormon) Church of Jesus Christ of Latter-day Saints.

Bryce Canyon itself became a place to live and work only when people started coming to see it. A road was built in 1915, and in 1919, Ruby and Minnie Syrett built a tourist rest lodge near the rim. The Union Pacific Railroad developed tourism, building the beautiful lodge that stands today near the rim of the Bryce Canyon Amphitheater. In 1923, Bryce became a national monument. The Syrett family still owns Ruby's Inn, a huge hotel, campground, and activity complex just outside the park entrance. But the plateau remains mostly empty land, a place where human history hasn't really happened yet.

## ORIENTATION

### THE PARK

Bryce Canyon National Park is a long, narrow strip of land. It takes in the cliffs and bluffs of the eastern edge of the Paunsaugunt Plateau, with a rim at around 8,000 feet elevation. These Pink Cliffs are the highest step on the Grand Staircase that descends to the south. There's no canyon, really — just this edge and

the places where erosion has dug notches. The biggest notch is the 5-mile-wide, 3-mile-long, 800-foot-deep **Bryce Amphitheater.**

An 18-mile dead-end road, the extension of **Route 63** that branches south from Route 12, runs most of the length of the park. It goes from the visitor center near the only entrance, at the north end, to Rainbow and Yovimpa

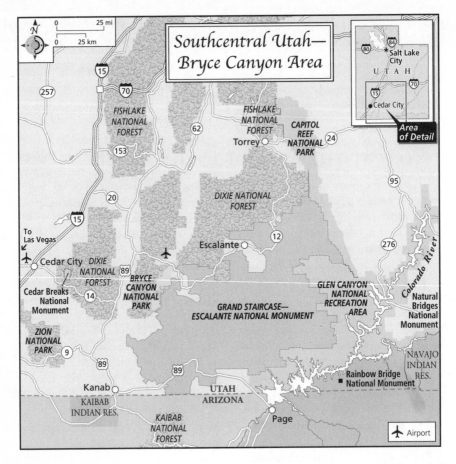

points, 9,100-foot overlooks at the south end of the park. From there you can see all the way to the Grand Canyon's Kaibab Plateau and Navaho Mountain, south of Glen Canyon. Overlooks and trailheads are all along the way. The lodge, campgrounds, and Bryce Amphitheater are all within a few miles of the visitor center. **Ruby's Inn**, the area's commercial center, is just outside the park on Route 63.

## BEYOND THE PARK

**Dixie National Forest** surrounds the park and takes in the land to Cedar Breaks National Monument to the west and Capitol Reef National Park to the east. **Route 12** descends the plateau from Bryce to a turnoff for Kodachrome Basin State Park, then continues toward Escalante and Capitol Reef. To the west, the highway passes through the national forest's Red Canyon area to north-south **U.S. 89.** Most of these areas are covered below under "Natural Places Just Outside the National Park" (p. 268). The nearest substantial town is **Panguitch,** Utah (pop. 1,500), about 24 miles from the park entrance, west on Route 12 and north on 89.

# MAKING THE ARRANGEMENTS

## WHEN TO GO

Summer is glorious — not too hot for hiking at this high elevation — but crowds fill the trails and hotels. Fall is less crowded, and the weather stays reasonable into October, although September snowstorms are not unheard of.

**Bryce Canyon National Park.** P.O. Box 170001, Bryce Canyon, UT 84717. ☎ **435/834-5322.** www.nps.gov/brca.

**Bryce Canyon Natural History Association** (for maps and books). P.O. Box 170002, Bryce Canyon, UT 84717. ☎ **888/362-2642** or **435/834-4600.** www.nps.gov/brca/nhamain.htm.

**Best Western Ruby's Inn** (commercial and activity center outside park entrance). P.O. Box 1, Bryce, UT 84764. ☎ **800/468-8660** or 435/834-5341. Fax 435/834-5265. www.rubysinn.com.

**Cedar Breaks National Monument.** 2390 W. Hwy. 56, #11, Cedar City, UT 84720. ☎ **435/586-9451.** www.nps.gov/cebr.

**Dixie National Forest.** 82 N. 100 East, Cedar City, UT 84720. ☎ **435/865-3700.** www.fs.fed.us/dxnf.

**Kodachrome Basin State Park.** P.O. Box 238, Cannonville, UT 84718. ☎ **800/322-3770** (campground reservations) or 435/679-8562. parks.state.ut.us/parks/www1/koda.htm.

**Garfield County Travel Council.** 55 S. Main (P.O. Box 200), Panguitch, UT 84759. ☎ **800/444-6689** or 435/676-8826. www.brycecanyoncountry.com.

Bryce is open all winter, but at this elevation it's quite snowy, and the lodge is closed. The clear, clean air allows exceptional star viewing and expansive vistas. The views of the red rock formations, highlighted by snow, make the season spectacular, but most of the hiking trails become impassable. Cross-country ski trails cover much of the plateau portion of the park, and Ruby's Inn, open year-round, offers winter activities and events.

Spring break is marginal but feasible. Snow and very cold nights last through March. The lodge opens around April 1. Snow and ice sometimes don't leave the trails completely until mid-May, but they can be passable much earlier. Spring offers cool days and a lack of crowds.

## How Much Time to Spend

Most visitors just drive through the park, which is possible to do in a few hours if you don't care about seeing it in-depth. But I recommend spending a minimum of 2 full days and 3 nights, and I would enjoy staying 5 days. For a 2-day stay, you could spend a day getting oriented and driving the park road and a day hiking or horseback riding. With more

time, you could take more and longer hikes or go backpacking, and add visits to nearby Kodachrome Basin, Red Canyon, and Cedar Breaks National Monument.

## How Far to Plan Ahead

For a midsummer visit, people who want to stay in rooms at the lodge or Ruby's Inn start reserving more than a year ahead. Make plans 6 months in advance to ensure a good selection. But don't give up. Large tour groups routinely cancel at Ruby's 1 month ahead. On the day of a visit, you may also snag a last-minute cancellation by calling around checkout time. It's far easier to find rooms at other motels, less attractive and farther from the park. The Park Service doesn't take camping reservations at Bryce, but campsites are almost always available at Ruby's Inn if you can't find one in the park.

## Reading Up

**Bryce Canyon Natural History Association** (☎ **888/362-2642** or **435/834-4600;** www. nps.gov/brca/nhamain.htm) operates the visitor center bookstore and lists its catalog online.

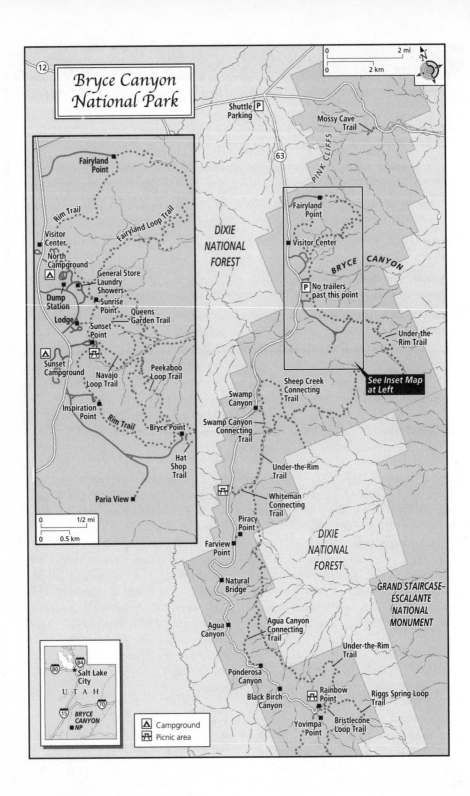

Bryce Canyon
National Park

12

Shuttle Parking
P

63

PINK CLIFFS

Mossy Cave Trail

DIXIE
NATIONAL
FOREST

Fairyland Point

Visitor Center

BRYCE CANYON

P No trailers past this point

Under-the-Rim Trail

See Inset Map at Left

**Inset Map (left):**

Fairyland Point

Rim Trail

Fairyland Loop Trail

Visitor Center

North Campground

General Store
Laundry
Showers

Dump Station

Sunrise Point

Queens Garden Trail

Lodge

Sunset Point

Sunset Campground

Navajo Loop Trail

Peekaboo Loop Trail

Inspiration Point

Rim Trail

Bryce Point

Hat Shop Trail

Paria View

0          1/2 mi
0     0.5 km

**Main map (continued):**

Sheep Creek Connecting Trail

Swamp Canyon

Swamp Canyon Connecting Trail

Under-the-Rim Trail

Whiteman Connecting Trail

Piracy Point

Farview Point

DIXIE
NATIONAL
FOREST

GRAND STAIRCASE-
ESCALANTE
NATIONAL
MONUMENT

Natural Bridge

Agua Canyon

Agua Canyon Connecting Trail

Under-the-Rim Trail

Ponderosa Canyon

Black Birch Canyon

Rainbow Point

Riggs Spring Loop Trail

Yovimpa Point

Bristlecone Loop Trail

0          2 mi
0     2 km

N

80  84
★ Salt Lake City
U T A H
15   70
BRYCE CANYON NP

△ Campground
⊼ Picnic area

| | AVG. HIGH (°F) | AVG. LOW (°F) | AVG. SNOW DEPTH |
|---|---|---|---|
| January | 36 | 9 | 11 |
| February | 39 | 12 | 15 |
| March | 46 | 17 | 11 |
| April | 56 | 25 | 3 |
| May | 66 | 31 | 0 |
| June | 76 | 31 | 0 |
| July–August | 80–83 | 45–47 | 0 |
| September | 74 | 37 | 0 |
| October | 63 | 29 | 0 |
| November | 51 | 19 | 2 |
| December | 37 | 10 | 6 |

**Auto and Trail Guide:** The association's $4 *Bryce Canyon Auto and Hiking Guide,* by Tully Stroud, hits all the high points, but, with its lavish illustration, it is pitched as more of a souvenir book than a practical hiking guide. It lacks useful maps. **Trail Guides:** The association offers hiking guides for day hikes or backpacking for less than $2. **Maps:** The plastic Trails Illustrated topographic hiking map of the park contains adequate detail to plan day hikes or a backpacking trip without any other resource. It costs $10.

## GETTING THERE
### By Car

The park road intersects with scenic **Route 12,** which meets **U.S. 89,** running north-south just west of the park. **Interstate 15** is about 40 miles farther west. If you're coming from Zion National Park, 80 miles away, or the other parks in this section, U.S. 89 is the backbone you will follow (see "Exploring the Region," in chapter 8). Glen Canyon's Wahweap Marina is 150 miles away, the Grand Canyon's North Rim is 160 miles, and the South Rim is 300 miles.

If you're coming from the southwest, or you want to pass through Cedar Breaks National Monument (56 miles away) or the Kolob Canyons area of Zion, take I-15, then cut to the east on **Route 14.**

To the east of the park, Route 12 is a beautiful drive through sections of Grand Staircase–Escalante National Monument to Capitol Reef National Park, and it connects with other state highways to some of the region's other parks. Visitors often link them with the others in this section in a Grand Circle route. Unless you have a long vacation, however, going to so many parks over so many miles will mean a lot of driving broken by short, superficial visits to the parks.

### By Air

Bryce is about 240 miles from Salt Lake City and 250 miles from Las Vegas. If you want to fly close, Cedar City airport is 87 miles from the park, served by **Delta/Skywest** (☎ 800/221-1212 or 435/586-3033; www.skywest.com). Rental cars are available there from **Avis** (☎ 800/331-1212 or 435/586-3033; www.avis.com) and **National** (☎ 800/227-73368 or 435/586-7059; www.nationalcar.com).

## WHAT TO PACK
### Clothing

Be ready for a great range of temperatures. Evenings are cool all year. Even in midsummer, the temperature could drop to freezing at night at Bryce while, just a few miles away, off the plateau, the next afternoon could be over 100°F. Typical summer days are in the 70s and 80s. The best way to deal with this variability is with layered clothing. You'll want cool clothing for hot weather, plus long sleeves, pants, sweaters, and jackets you can add. Thunderstorms are frequent in July and August. The sun is powerful at high elevations at any time of year, so bring sun hats and sunscreen. Good walking shoes or boots will help you enjoy the steep trails. There's never a need for formal clothing.

In winter, spring, and fall, Bryce is often cold and snowy. It's a beautiful time, with good cross-country skiing and snowshoeing, but cold for camping or inactive time outdoors. Warm winter clothing may be necessary October through April.

### Gear

For summer tent camping, prepare for chilly nights. Most of your camping at other parks in the region will be at lower, warmer elevations, so you may want to prepare with layers, which could include sleeping-bag liners, summer bags, thermal long underwear, and a single heavy bag to use as a comforter over you all. Tent camping before May or after October is only for the hardy because the nights are frigid. If you come in the winter, you can bring cross-country skis or rent them at Ruby's Inn. Bring your own snowshoes if you want to go over the edge, because the Park Service lends them only for use on the plateau. See "Cold Weather Preparations," in chapter 1, "Planning Your Trip."

# WHERE TO SPEND THE NIGHT

## CAMPING
### Park Service Campgrounds

Two campgrounds within the park offer sites only on a first-come, first-served basis. If you're not at the campgrounds by 1pm during the high season, your chances of getting a site are slim; the earlier you arrive before that, the better your chances. The two campgrounds have a total of 216 sites.

**North.** Entrance across from the visitor center and near Sunrise Point. $10 per site. Tents or RVs. Flush toilets, dump station ($2 self-service fee).

The campground is extremely convenient, within walking distance of the visitor center and the canyon rim, yet the design makes it feel remote and woodsy. Sites are well separated among ponderosa pines, and some have little terraces built up with stone blocks. **Loop A,** nearest the visitor center, is open all winter, for those few who care to camp in the snow.

**Sunset.** Across main park road from turnoff to Sunset Point. $10 per night. Tents or RVs. Flush toilets. Closed Oct–Apr.

This campground has sites separated by ponderosas and shrubs. It's back from the rim across the main park road, making it a little quieter than North.

### Backcountry Camping Permits

To camp in the backcountry, along the **Under-The-Rim Trail** or **Riggs Spring Loop,** you need a permit that costs $5 at the visitor center. These permits cannot be reserved; they are available only on the day of the hike or the day before, from 8am until 2 hours before the visitor center closes. The number of permits issued is limited, but park officials say they seldom run out.

### Outside the National Park

Besides these campgrounds, **Cedar Breaks National Monument** (see "Natural Places Just

Outside the National Park," p. 268) has a 30-site campground that does not take reservations. Open only in the summer, the campground has flush toilets and evening ranger programs.

**Ruby's Inn RV Park and Campground.** On Rte. 63 just outside the park entrance (P.O. Box 22), Bryce, UT 84764. ☎ **435/834-5302** summer, 800/468-8660 or 435/834-5341 winter. Fax 435/834-5481. www.rubsysinn.com. Tents $15.50 for 2, full hookups $25; $1.50 per extra person over age 5. AE, DC, DISC, MC, V. More than 200 sites; tents and all sizes of RVs. Swimming pools, activities, game room, showers, laundry, dump station. Closed Nov–Mar.

This is an exceptional commercial campground, on the edge of a pond among small pine trees. It's next to the activity center of Ruby's Inn, where you can use the indoor pools, laundry, and other facilities, or watch the rodeo, and the campground also has its own outdoor pool. RVers who need hookups should reserve ahead, but I've been told that there's almost always room for more self-contained campers, in tents or vehicles. In the winter, RVs can plug in behind the hotel, where the employees live.

**Kodachrome Basin State Park.** South of Cannonville, east of Bryce Canyon National Park on Rte. 12 (P.O. Box 238), Cannonville, UT 84718.

---

## PARK CAMPING BASICS: TOILETS, SHOWERS & LAUNDRY

The Park Service provides flush toilets in the campgrounds, at the visitor center, and at Sunrise, Sunset, and Rainbow points. There's even a vault toilet below the rim, on the Peekaboo Loop horse trail. From mid-April to mid-October, coin-operated showers and laundry machines are available at the **Camper Store**, near Sunrise Point. Public showers that are open the same months are at **Ruby's Inn** and cost $2.50. Ruby's also maintains a large year-round coin-op laundry.

---

☎ **800/322-3770** (campground reservations) or 435/679-8562. parks.state.ut.us/parks/www1/koda.htm. $13 per site. 27 sites. Tents or RVs. Ranger station and store, activities, flush toilets, free hot showers.

The sites here are separated and screened, well maintained and grassy, with concrete pads. When we visited, the bathrooms were remarkably clean and had showers without the usual coin-fed meters. In the spring, when it's too cold to camp at Bryce Canyon National Park, this lower, desert area is warmer and free of snow. I've described this wonderful little park more on p. 257. From Bryce, drive about 14 miles east to Cannonville, then turn south, following the signs 7 miles to the park.

## Dixie National Forest
See "Bryce Address Book" (p. 259) to contact the national forest.

**Red Canyon.** Rte. 12, west of Bryce. $9 per site. 37 sites. Tents or RVs. Flush toilets, showers. Reservations available with additional fee (use the system described under "Other Campground Reservations," in chapter 1). Closed Sept–May.

This is a well-developed campground near the canyon of red rocks and the visitor center on Route 12. This is a good mountain-biking area. The campground often stays open after Labor Day, depending on the weather.

**Kings Creek Campground.** Rte. 087 south from Rte. 12, east of Bryce. $8 per site. 34 sites. Tents or RVs. Flush and pit toilets. No reservations. Closed Sept–May.

The campground is at the end of a 7-mile gravel access road, on the Tropic Reservoir, a popular fishing hole along the Sevier River.

## HOTELS
**Bryce Canyon Lodge.** 1 Bryce Canyon Lodge, Bryce Canyon, UT 84717. ☎ **435/834-5361.** Fax 435/834-5464. www.brycecanyonlodge.com. (Reservations c/o Amfac Parks and Resorts, 14001 E. Iliff Ave., Suite 600, Aurora, CO 80014. ☎ **303/297-2757.** www.amfac.com.) 70 rms, 40 cabins, 3 suites. Rooms $93–$99 double, cabins $103–$108 double; $5 per extra person over age 16. AE, DISC, MC, V. Closed Nov–Mar.

The lodge and cabins built by the Union Pacific Railroad in 1924 are among the most beautiful examples of the national-park style. The huge pine logs and long, cedar-shingled roofs give an eternal feeling to the perfectly proportioned lodge building, which sits among towering ponderosa pines. The location is perfect, too, right in the center of things, just back from the Bryce Canyon rim.

Cabins come in two types, which go for the same rate. Those built of huge cut stones and logs with their bark still intact are works of art. Their high ceilings, stone fireplaces, and interiors tastefully balance comfort and the rustic park tradition. Other, less grand cabins are still comfortable. The motel rooms are standard. Rooms all have phones, but no TVs. Reserve 6 to 8 months ahead for the high season, or call or stop in to try for a cancellation.

The **restaurant** has the best food in the area, with a menu that includes vegetarian choices, and surprisingly reasonable prices. It's open from 6:30am to 4:30pm and 5:30 to 9:30pm, and makes box lunches.

**Best Western Ruby's Inn.** P.O. Box 1, Bryce, UT 84764. ☎ **800/468-8660** or 435/834-5341. Fax 435/834-5265. www.rubysinn.com. 368 units. High season $95–$110 double; low season $46–$63 double; $5 per extra person over age 12. AE, DC, DISC, MC, V.

The visitor complex built by the park's pioneering Syrett family dominates the landscape just outside Bryce's gates. It has huge motel buildings, a prominent Texaco gas station, the pond where the family homes are located, the spread-out campground, another gas station (Chevron), and a row of false-front businesses across the road. Inside are two pools, a grocery and gift store, an art gallery, and a sort of mall for tours and activities. It's a remarkably well-run place. The rooms lack much character but are loaded with amenities — some have VCRs, modem ports, and Jacuzzis, for example. People start to reserve more than a year in advance, but because many tour groups cancel 1 month ahead, you often can get rooms then. Rates vary many times through the year; I've listed only the highs and lows above.

**Bryce View Lodge.** Utah 63 across from Best Western Ruby's Inn (P.O. Box 64002), Bryce, UT 84764. ☎ **888/279-2304** or 435/834-5180. Fax 435/834-5181. www.bryceviewlodge.com. 160 units. $44–$60 double; $2–$3 per extra person over age 12. AE, DC, DISC, MC, V.

This basic motel consists of four two-story modular buildings, set back from the road and grouped around a large parking lot and attractively landscaped area. Rooms are simple but comfortable, recently refurbished, and are quite quiet. Owned by the same company that operates the Best Western Ruby's Inn, guests here have access to the swimming pools and other amenities across the street at Ruby's.

**World Host Bryce Valley Inn.** 199 N. Main St., Tropic, UT 84776. ☎ **800/442-1890** or 435/679-8811. Fax 435/679-8846. www.brycevalleyinn.com. 65 units. Apr–Oct $55–$65; Nov–Mar $35–$45; rates are for up to 4 people. AE, MC, V.

In the tiny town of Tropic, 10 miles east of the park on Route 12, this motel is a group of large wooden buildings with good, standard rooms, each with two queen-size beds. A 24-hour laundry facility is on-site, as is the Hungry Coyote Restaurant & Saloon, a pleasant but typical Western roadside cafe.

# WHEN YOU ARRIVE

## ENTRANCE FEES

Park admission is $20 per vehicle, or $15 total for the occupants of a vehicle left outside the park who use the free park shuttle (see p. 265). National park passes apply (see p. 18 for details).

## VISITOR CENTERS

**Bryce Canyon Visitor Center.** Near the entrance station. ☎ **435/834-5322.** Summer daily 8am–8pm; fall daily 8am–6pm; winter daily 8am–4:30pm.

This is the park's only visitor center. Besides the usual bookstore and desk where you can ask questions, the center also has an exceptional little museum about the history and nature of the area. A topographical model and graphic display explain the Grand Staircase, and an orientation slide show plays in an auditorium every half hour.

**Red Canyon Visitor Center, Dixie National Forest.** Rte. 12 between U.S. 89 and Bryce Canyon. ☎ **435/676-2676.** Daily 8am–6pm. Closed Sept–May.

The center has rangers to tell you about activities in the Red Canyon area and other national forest lands along Route 12. There are some interpretive exhibits, and books and maps are for sale. Outside is a short nature trail.

**Cedar Breaks National Monument Visitor Center.** Rte. 148, south entrance of monument. ☎ **435/586-9451.** Closed mid-Oct to May.

The center has a bookstore, rangers to answer questions, and exhibits on the geology, history, and biology of the monument.

## GETTING AROUND
The park's one 18-mile road carries visitors to more than 15 scenic overlooks.

## By Shuttle Bus
A voluntary, free **shuttle service** carries visitors on the park's only road to reduce increasing congestion. It operates mid-May through September from 7am to dark. Park at the staging area at the intersection of the entrance road and Highway 12, 3 miles from the park boundary, to ride the shuttle into the park and save $5 on entrance fees. You can use the shuttle if you drive in, too.

The system has three lines. The **Blue Line** travels between the staging area and the visitor center about every 15 minutes with stops at Ruby's Inn and Fairyland Point. The **Red Line** traverses the developed core of the park,

making eight stops on roughly a 15-minute interval. The **Green Line** departs the visitor center at 9am and 2pm daily for a 2½-hour drive to Rainbow Point in the southern part of the park, stopping at viewpoints on the return trip. Backcountry hikers can ride the Green Line to trailheads, but should inform the driver if they will not be returning to the bus. Seating on the Green Line is limited and should be reserved at the visitor center up to a day ahead.

## By Car or RV
The park road overlooks all face east, so it makes sense to drive from the north entrance all the way to the south end and then make your stops on the way out so that you make only right turns. Parking and traffic are a problem at the overlooks during the middle of the day from May to September, especially for RVs, which cannot use spaces marked for buses. Vehicles over 25 feet are not allowed at the Paria Overlook. If you're pulling a trailer, you have to leave it in your campsite or parked at a designated trailer turnaround area while you tour the park.

## By Bike
There are no bike trails in the park and mountain bikes aren't allowed on hiking trails. If you're bringing bikes anyway, you'll find them useful in the campgrounds and around the lodge. In the past, mountain bikes have been for rent at **Ruby's Inn,** just outside the park, but check on current availability. There's great mountain biking in the region (see p. 270).

## KEEPING SAFE & HEALTHY
The main risks at Bryce are from weather and falls. To protect against falls you need good shoes, common sense, and control of your children. For tips on dehydration, hypothermia, and lightning, see "Dealing with Hazards," in chapter 1.

# Enjoying the Park & Environs

## Natural Places in the Park
### Bryce Amphitheater

The park is a strip of land along cliffs that form the eastern edge of the Paunsaugunt Plateau, which itself is a portion of the Pink Cliffs, the top step in the Grand Staircase. Bryce Amphitheater is a dent in the cliff, the largest natural amphitheater among many along the park road. No river made this canyon. As you walk down through passages among the many fins of rock, you'll see that a river couldn't have done it because a river would have made one deep channel instead of many. Instead, the water from melting snow and thunderstorms parted the rock as it trickled down from the plateau. Soft layers wore away fast and made slots between hard layers. (The process is explained more in chapter 8, under "Cliff Erosion & Hoodoos.")

Lots of other trails wander through the hoodoos, allowing hikers to match a route to their energy level and time. You will need a map of some kind, because it's easy to get mixed up. The trails start from three of the four overlooks on the amphitheater's rim (the exception is Inspiration Point). A fairly flat, 11-mile **Rim Trail** connects the overlooks and Fairyland Point to the north.

Sunset and Sunrise points lie in the park's front parlor, between the amphitheater and the lodge, campgrounds, and services. The half-mile section of the rim trail between these points is paved and okay for strollers, but to go much beyond the crowds here you'll need a way to carry toddlers. Both points have picnic areas, and Sunset Point has bathrooms. Climb down at least the **Queen's Garden Trail** or **Navaho Loop Trail**, both less than 2 miles in length and descending 300 to 500 feet from Sunrise and Sunset points, respectively. A superb 2.8-mile hike links the two trails and takes you through some of the park's best highlights; it's manageable by any fit school-age child.

Bryce Point is farthest south in the amphitheater. The **Peekaboo Loop Trail** connects it to Sunset or Sunrise points, extending the Navaho Loop or Queen's Garden trails and allowing access to some more amazing terrain (add 3.5 miles to the connecting trail to get the total distance). You have to share the way with horses on this trail (see "Horseback Riding," p. 270, about riding). There is a vault toilet. Also from Bryce Point, the 4-mile round-trip **Hat Shop Trail** is a relatively challenging path that's less crowded than most of the park's hikes, and leads to some balanced rocks. That route continues as the backcountry's **Under-the-Rim Trail** south into a portion of the park with less fanciful topography.

## The Park Road

The road south through the park and the overlooks off the plateau to the east are a main feature of the park. Beyond Bryce Point, however, erosion has worked down through the red Claron Formation that makes the strange shapes in the Bryce Amphitheater. Cliffs south of there tend to be steeper and not as fancy because the layer below the Claron Formation is softer and washes away more easily. That undercuts the Claron rock and breaks it off before it has a chance to erode into long rows of hoodoos.

Here are some highlights from north to south, the way the road goes. If traffic is bad, you may want to take the overlooks from south to north so that you make only right turns, or take the shuttle. Stop at the visitor center for a map and possibly the guide book mentioned under "Reading Up" (p. 259).

## Farview Point

The road rises from the park entrance at about 7,800 feet, where ponderosa pines in the transition life zone take over from the treeless high desert. Here, at 8,800 feet, the transition zone gives way to the higher, moister Canadian life zone, with spruce and fir trees. That zone extends up to 9,115 feet at Rainbow Point, the beginning of the alpine zone (see "Elevations of Life Zones," in chapter 8).

## Natural Bridge

This 85-foot-long, 125-foot-high arch was formed by water expanding inside an eroded fin of rock and splitting away the opening below a harder layer above. Later, running water made it deeper.

## Ponderosa Canyon

Here you can see how elevation makes different kinds of habitats. Where you stand is a forest of spruce and fir of the Canadian life zone, and over the rim of the canyon you can see warmer, lower ground that supports ponderosa pine of the transition or pine-oak zone. The 1.6-mile **Agua Canyon Connecting Trail** leads down to the Under-the-Rim Trail.

## Rainbow Point, Yovimpa Point

From the park's high point, over 9,100 feet, you can see all the way back down the Grand Staircase. The view stretches over 100 miles to the south, to the high Kaibab Plateau, site of the North Rim of the Grand Canyon, and Navaho Mountain, on the south shores of Lake Powell. The jagged pink cliffs here are the top step. Look for high-elevation alpine plants and trees, including short, twisted bristlecone pine trees up to 1,800 years old. The 9-mile **Riggs Spring Loop Trail** is a popular backpacking route with several backcountry campsites, but strong hikers can do it as a day hike. It leaves from Yovimpa Point and descends gradually some 1,600 feet through forest with views of the pink cliffs. The **Under-the-Rim Trail,** which runs 23 miles to Bryce Point, ends at Rainbow Point.

## Fairyland Canyon

This relatively small canyon at the northern end of the park is full of strange rock shapes. It's less visited because the spur road to the overlook is a mile long and splits off from the main road north of the visitor center. The area along the rim here is a central part of the cross-country skiing loops because it connects the Ruby's Inn trails with the park trails. The

**Fairy Land Loop Trail,** usable only in the warm months, descends 900 vertical feet into the canyon, climbs back up to Sunrise Point, and then returns along the rim trail, a total distance of 8 miles. You will see fewer people than on the easiest trails right in the Bryce Amphitheater and will pass through lots of interesting rock shapes and a forest of pinyon and juniper.

## NATURAL PLACES JUST OUTSIDE THE NATIONAL PARK

### Kodachrome Basin State Park

East of the national park, Route 12 descends steeply from the plateau into hot semidesert, past arid ranches and tiny towns, 14 miles to Cannonville. There a 7-mile spur road leads south to this wonderful little state park. In the spring, when it's chilly in the national park, the weather is warm here, at 5,800 feet elevation, in the Upper Sonoran life zone of pinyon and juniper. Spring highs average in the 70s, summer in the 80s and low 90s. The whole park is on a comfortably small scale, perfect for families. The day-use fee is $4 per vehicle. The campground is covered on p. 263. Park contact information is under "Bryce Address Book" (p. 259).

The basin was named by the National Geographic Society in 1949. It sits in a desert-like landscape below pastel-colored sandstone cliffs. The rocks have many odd shapes (although nothing to compete with those at Bryce Canyon). The narrow columns of rock are called chimneys because they stand as straight and round as a chimney. (Before *National Geographic* came along, the area was called Chimney Rocks.) The chimneys were probably formed by sediment that filled hot water vents like the geysers of Yellowstone National Park. When the softer surrounding rock eroded away, the shape molded by the vent remained.

Six **nature trails** ranging from one-quarter mile to 3 miles meet the paved and dirt park roads. South and east of the park, dirt roads for mountain bikes and four-wheel-drive vehicles

continue 10 miles to the 99-foot Grosvenor Arch, in Grand Staircase–Escalante National Monument. From there, they run down the Cottonwood Canyon and Paria River all the way to Glen Canyon National Recreation Area. Get advice from the state-park ranger station before attempting that trip.

Also in the park, **Trailhead Station** (☎ **435/679-8536** or 435/679-8787) operates a small store with camping supplies, food items, and the like, and also offers horseback and stagecoach rides. Trailhead Station operates April through October; store hours are daily from 9am to 5pm, later in midseason. You can join horseback rides there ($15 for 1 hr., $45 for 3 hr.; minimum age 5), and 1-hour stagecoach rides that cost $12 for any age, except free for those 2 and younger. The company also rents six cabins with full bathrooms and refrigerators for $65 per night for up to four people. (MasterCard and Visa are accepted.)

### Cedar Breaks National Monument

The monument rises to over 10,000 feet west of Bryce Canyon and north of Zion National Park. A spectacular 2,500-foot-deep amphitheater of multicolored limestone falls from the edge of the plateau. At this elevation, there's alpine life that you might recognize from the Rockies: Englemann spruce, subalpine fir, quaking aspen, and meadows of wildflowers. There are a couple of hiking trails, a visitor center (p. 265), and a campground (p. 262). The entrance fee is $3 per person 17 and older, free for children. To reach the monument, take Route 14 east from I-15 or west from U.S. 89, then Route 148 over the scenic 5-mile drive through the monument. Monument contact information is under "Bryce Address Book" (p. 259).

## ACTIVITIES

### Backpacking

Carrying your gear into the backcountry for 1 to 3 nights is the best way to get off by yourself

For a person with curiosity about nature, the bright red rocks of Red Canyon almost seem to tap you on the shoulder and ask: Why are some rocks red? For that matter, why are the rocks at Bryce pinkish red, yellow, purplish, and white? To answer this question, you need the sciences of geology, chemistry, and physics. You may not have known what a complex question you were asking!

The answer from geology is that the red and pink rocks contain hematite, which is mostly iron. Pure hematite is an ore that is mined for the iron we use in cast-iron skillets and steel beams. Iron rusts, and when it does it turns red. Often it takes only a small amount of iron to turn a rock red. In these sedimentary rocks — rocks made of sand, mud, bones, and other stuff called sediment — the red color often comes from just a tiny amount of a mineral that holds together the grains. It works the same for other colors. Something like rust produces yellow rocks, such as limonite, and purplish manganese oxide. Copper turns green (like the Statue of Liberty) and green rocks you see in the desert probably have some copper in them.

So what causes this rust? To answer that, you have to get into chemistry. Rust is a common word for **oxidation.** In the case of these rocks, it happens when iron or manganese combines with oxygen. The oxygen comes from the air around us or from water, both of which have a lot of oxygen in them. That's why an iron tool rusts in the rain. Oxidation turns copper green and affects other elements.

Material oxidizes when the atoms it is made of trade parts called electrons. Almost everything around us is made of atoms. Each atom has a hard center called a nucleus that's made of protons and neutrons, and a less solid outer part made of tiny electrons that spin around the center like planets around the sun. The number of protons in the center decides what kind of atom it is — oxygen, iron, copper, and so on. The number of electrons likes to match the number of protons. But the outside electrons spinning around an atom aren't stuck on as tightly as the others. Sometimes when they get near another atom, the outermost electron can slip off and start spinning around the other atom instead. Oxygen takes an electron from iron very easily. That's oxidation, or rust.

So why does that make the iron turn red? Electrons and the way they orbit the nucleus decide how an atom reflects light. When iron rusts and loses an electron, the light that bounces off the remaining electrons comes off red.

---

in the park. Campsites are scattered along the trails under the rim south of Bryce Point. You'll need a $5 Backcountry Camping Permit from the visitor center (see p. 262). Backcountry camping isn't allowed in Bryce Amphitheater, but you could hike through on your first or last day. The park is small, and the longest trail, the **Under-the-Rim Trail** that leads north from Rainbow Point to Bryce Point (the more downhill direction), is only 23 miles. Take the shuttle to Rainbow Point and hike back (see "By Shuttle Bus," p. 265). You can shorten the route with any of various spur trails that reach up to the park road along the way. The trail has a lot of ups and downs, and because the thin air slows you down, it's easy to overestimate how much ground you can cover.

The other route is the **Riggs Spring Loop Trail,** mentioned in "Rainbow Point, Yovimpa Point" (p. 267). Without hiking an entire trail, a family can get out under the stars to a not-too-remote backcountry campsite and spend a couple of nights of solitude there, making day hikes and playing during the day. In any event, you'll need a good topographic map (see "Reading Up," p. 259).

## Flightseeing

You can buy tickets for flights over the park in helicopters or a fixed-wing plane in the lobby of **Ruby's Inn.** Various tour operators also have desks there. **Bryce Canyon Scenic Flights** (call ☎ 800/468-8660 or 435/834-5341 and ask for the flight desk) charges $55 to $250 for narrated flights lasting 15 to 70 minutes, with discounts for families and groups.

## Hiking

If you don't hike at Bryce, you're missing a lot. Choose a hike at the Bryce Amphitheater to see the park's most famous and impressive rock formations, trails which also get the heaviest use. They include the Rim Trail, Queen's Garden Trail, Navaho Loop Trail, Peekaboo Loop Trail, and Hat Shop Trail, all covered under "Bryce Amphitheater" (p. 266). From north of the amphitheater, the Fairy Land Loop Trail is a longer path with fewer people (see p. 268). By going south of the amphitheater, you hike away from the most interesting rock formations, but also away from most of the people. The trails here tend to be longer and more rugged. The Riggs Spring Trail is under "Rainbow Point, Yovimpa Point" (p. 267). The Under-The-Rim Trail is under "Backpacking," above. Maps and guides are covered under "Reading Up" (p. 259).

## Horseback Riding

Rides are available from a park concessionaire down into the Bryce Amphitheater and from another operator outside the park. The inside-the-park rides feature descents among the weird shapes of the canyon. The outside-the-park outfit offers longer rides.

**Canyon Trail Rides** (☎ 435/679-8665; www.onpages.com/canyonrides) offers rides that start from the corral near Sunrise Point and descend a horse trail north of the point into the canyon. A 2-hour ride, open to children as young as 7, goes down the trail to the canyon floor twice a day. It's $30 per person. A half-day ride follows the Peekaboo Trail, which crosses most of the Bryce Amphitheater. It costs $45 and is okay for children 8 and over. A 220-pound weight limit applies to both rides. Reserve by phone or at the lodge.

Rides offered by **Ruby's Red Canyon Horseback Rides** (☎ 800/468-8660 or 435/834-5341) all leave from Ruby's Inn, where the company has a desk, and go into

nearby Red Canyon. Kids must be 8 or older and riders under 220 pounds; half-day rides cost $40 and full-day rides, which include a box lunch, cost $75.

## Mountain Biking

The trails within the park are off-limits to bikes, but the vast public lands nearby offer great mountain-biking routes. Red Canyon, in Dixie National Forest (see "Bryce Address Book," p. 259), may be the best. You may need to bring your own bikes, because the bike-rental situation at the park is in flux (see "For Handy Reference," p. 267).

## Skiing & Snowshoeing

The high elevation usually makes for a good snowpack from December to February (it's wise to call about snow conditions before going). The colored rocks are even more beautiful against white snow. There are two connecting sets of trails. Ruby's Inn grooms more than 30 kilometers of track for both classical and skate skiers. They connect with the Park Service trails, which are set with tracks for diagonal stride skiing but are not regularly groomed. The park's easy trails run to Fairyland Point, then hug the rim from near the inn south to Inspiration Point, and then follow a forested 5.6-kilometer loop near Paria View. Snow machines are allowed on some of the Ruby's Inn trails but can't come into the park. (You have to bring your own snow machine; none are for rent here.) The set trails go over generally gentle terrain. The Park Service warns against trying to ski down into the canyon because of the danger, but skiing is permitted everywhere in the park if you want to break trail. **Ruby's Inn** rents skis, offers inexpensive lodging packages, and stages a 3-day winter festival with races, clinics, children's events, and entertainment each February.

The Park Service lends snowshoes free at the visitor center. Snowshoeing is fun and much easier to learn than skiing — it just takes a little coordination and energy. The Park Service won't let you take its snowshoes down into the canyon, though, and asks that snowshoers not disturb cross-country ski tracks.

## PROGRAMS
### Children's Programs

The park puts out an inexpensive *Kids Guide to Bryce Canyon,* aimed at children ages 5 to 10.

A **Junior Ranger program,** mostly based on worksheet activities such as a crossword puzzle and a word hunt, is available free from the visitor center. Kids who do the activities, attend ranger programs, and collect a bag of trash or recycle goods, get a badge and certificate. Ranger programs for children are sometimes offered in the summer; check at the visitor center for sign-up procedures and age limits.

### Family & Adult Programs

During the busy summer season, five or six ranger programs run every day. In addition to guided hikes, rangers lead evening sky viewing, which is exceptionally good thanks to the clean air, elevation, and lack of pollution. Evening talks are presented at Bryce Canyon Lodge, and campfire programs take place nightly at both campgrounds. The schedule of programs is posted at the visitor center.

## FUN OUTSIDE THE PARK

Ruby's Inn offers kids' amusements from a strip of false-front businesses just outside the park. There are a free trick horse show twice a day during the summer, gold panning ($4 pan rental), and an exhibition rodeo at 7pm daily in the summer. It costs $7 for adults, $4 for children under 12.

## WHERE TO EAT

One drawback of a long stay at Bryce is the lack of restaurants. Those you will find emphasize beef and cowboys, not fine cuisine. The best restaurant is at the Bryce Canyon Lodge (p. 263). World Host Bryce Valley Inn (p. 264) also serves food.

At Ruby's Inn, the large **Cowboy's Buffet and Steak Room** is a comfortable family restaurant with a heavy Western theme and plentiful, reasonably priced meals. Dinners are $5.50 to $20. The service was good, but the food was more institutional than subtle. It's a good place for a grown-up, sit-down meal where you don't have to worry about the kids. It serves three meals a day all year. Hours are 6:30am to 10pm in summer, 6:30am to 9pm in winter.

In the summer, Ruby's offers fast food at the **Canyon Diner,** with burgers, sandwiches, pizza, chicken, and so on. Dinner is $3 to $8.50.

From June to September, Ruby's offers a **chuck wagon dinner** at a covered wagon camp featuring a Dutch oven dinner, country music show, and hoedown in a meadow. It starts at 6:30pm every evening except Sunday. The 2½-hour program starts and ends with a covered wagon ride, and kids are sure to enjoy it. Barbecued chicken is the main course. Tickets are $30 for adults, $26 for kids 9 to 15, $18 for those 4 to 8, and free for children under 4. Tickets are available at Ruby's Inn.

# The Rockies

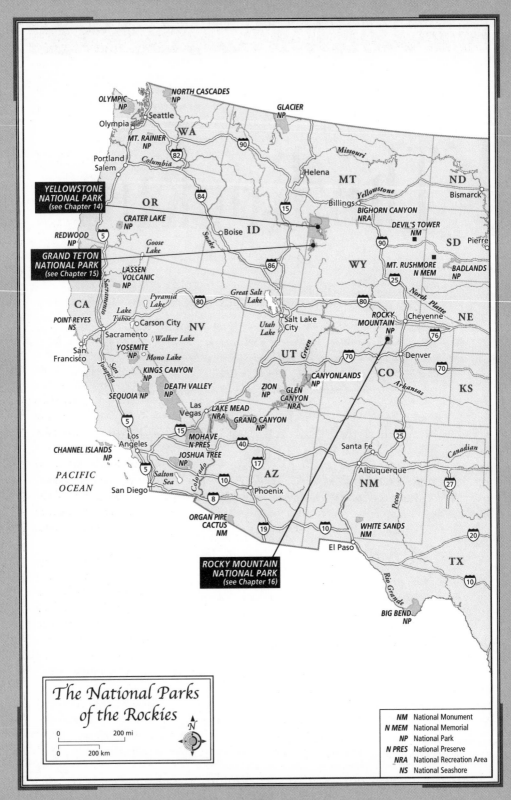

OLYMPIC
NP

NORTH CASCADES
NP

GLACIER
NP

Olympia

Seattle

WA

MT. RAINIER
NP

Portland
Salem

Columbia

82

Helena

Missouri

MT

ND

Bismarck

Billings

Yellowstone

YELLOWSTONE
NATIONAL PARK
(see Chapter 14)

OR

84

BIGHORN CANYON
NRA

CRATER LAKE
NP

DEVIL'S TOWER
NM

15

Boise

ID

90

SD

Pierre

REDWOOD
NP

5

Goose
Lake

Snake

86

WY

MT. RUSHMORE
N MEM

BADLANDS
NP

GRAND TETON
NATIONAL PARK
(see Chapter 15)

LASSEN
VOLCANIC
NP

25

North Platte

CA

Pyramid
Lake

Great Salt
Lake

80

POINT REYES
NS

Lake
Tahoe

Carson City

NV

Salt Lake
City

Utah
Lake

ROCKY
MOUNTAIN
NP

Cheyenne

NE

Sacramento

Walker Lake

80

76

San
Francisco

YOSEMITE
NP

Mono Lake

UT

Green

70

Denver

70

KINGS CANYON
NP

CO

San
Joaquin

DEATH VALLEY
NP

ZION
NP

CANYONLANDS
NP

Arkansas

KS

SEQUOIA NP

GLEN
CANYON
NRA

5

Las
Vegas

LAKE MEAD
NRA

GRAND CANYON
NP

Santa Fe

25

Los
Angeles

15

MOHAVE
N-PRES

40

CHANNEL ISLANDS
NP

JOSHUA TREE
NP

17

AZ

Albuquerque

Canadian

27

PACIFIC
OCEAN

5

Salton
Sea

Colorado

10

Phoenix

NM

Pecos

San Diego

8

ORGAN PIPE
CACTUS
NM

19

10

WHITE SANDS
NM

20

El Paso

TX

ROCKY MOUNTAIN
NATIONAL PARK
(see Chapter 16)

Rio Grande

10

BIG BEND
NP

## The National Parks
of the Rockies

0          200 mi

0      200 km

N

| | |
|---|---|
| NM | National Monument |
| N MEM | National Memorial |
| NP | National Park |
| N PRES | National Preserve |
| NRA | National Recreation Area |
| NS | National Seashore |

# CHAPTER 13

# The Nature of High Places

My fingers and then my arms began to tingle, and when I touched the rocks they hurt the way your arms and legs hurt when they "fall asleep" from being in a funny position too long. I watched the mountaintop scene as if all this were happening to someone else, someone I didn't care that much about. My legs kept climbing. My eyes could see the rocky summit, just ahead, so bright and sharp in the strong, clear light that it seemed more real than regular things. On top, I sat down on a rock — just another rest stop, really — and tried to take in the endless view. My mind, as fuzzy as it was, thought, "So this is how the thin air feels above 13,000 feet. No wonder not many plants and animals live here." I caught as much as I could in my memory, then got up and began the walk back down to the everyday world.

Going down again is the safe thing to do when you feel the physical effects of high altitude. Different people feel it at different levels. My wife, Barbara, felt ill at near 12,000 feet, at the visitor center on Trail Ridge Road through Rocky Mountain National Park. For me, it was a bit higher, on a hike. Everyone has an upper limit, where the air becomes too thin for the body to work right until it has had a few days to get used to the elevation. As you descend from the heights back to safe, thick air, it makes you think about how narrow a place we live in. Almost all people, plants, and animals live in a layer of air only 2 miles thick. That's one reason the high places of the Rockies feel so special. Up here, with the clear light and pure air, you're in a higher world, apart from ordinary life below.

The parks of the Rockies all have this magnificent sense of elevation. They're also among the nation's largest parks outside Alaska and among the best for finding your way into the wilderness. There are few distractions from glorious hiking, canoeing, skiing, and camping. Few places offer as good an opportunity to see wildlife. People haven't managed to spoil even the fringes of the parks. Each park has its star attractions — the shocking geysers of Yellowstone, the awesome peaks of Grand Teton, and the broad alpine vistas of Rocky Mountain — but in this wonderful region, even more than others, to go for a drive-through vacation would be a crime. This is a place to come for a couple of weeks, when you're ready to abandon yourself to your family and the outdoors.

## THE PARKS
### Yellowstone National Park
The first national park and the largest outside of Alaska, Yellowstone is packed full of amazing sights. It has geysers, the Grand Canyon of the Yellowstone River, bison and elk that walk close to roads, glorious alpine meadows, and Yellowstone Lake. You can drive through in a few days, ogling these places, but then you'd miss an incredible network of trails and campgrounds. Yellowstone lies in the northwest corner of Wyoming and on a strip of Montana and Idaho. You reach it by road from four directions, but there's not a large town in any.

### Grand Teton National Park
Nearly touching Yellowstone on the south side, Grand Teton has a single great show rather than many sideshows, but it's an unforgettable one. The ferocious daggers of the Teton Range rise straight up from the flat stage of a valley and lake. The overwhelming view meets you almost everywhere, but the best of the park for families is down below, on lakes and hiking trails rich in wildlife. Just south of the park, the fun town of Jackson, Wyoming, offers downhill skiing and a pleasant dose of civilization.

### Rocky Mountain National Park
Just north of Denver, Rocky takes in one of the highest parts of the nation's greatest

## A NOTE ON PLACE NAMES

In the old-time West, mountain men called valleys **holes.** Jackson Hole is the big valley that faces the Teton Mountains and makes up much of Grand Teton National Park. The town south of the park is often called Jackson Hole too, but many locals just call it Jackson. To keep them straight, I'm calling the town Jackson and the valley Jackson Hole.

mountain range. It's unique in permitting easy access to broad areas of alpine terrain, much of it over 10,000 feet in elevation. The camping and hiking are supreme and include opportunities for walking without trails on the tundra above tree line. Small towns on either side of the park offer cute and friendly places to stay, eat, and shop.

### Dinosaur National Monument
In northeast Utah, the monument is a stop not to miss on the way to any of these parks from Salt Lake City. The dinosaur quarry is likely to be the highlight of your trip, and the campground and hiking trails justify a stay of a couple of days. For details on making this side trip, see "Exploring the Region," in chapter 8, "Layers upon Layers."

In the area around Rocky Mountain National Park, we have the same problem. Open, grassy valleys are called **parks.** Estes Park is a town, but it's also a valley. I've tried to keep clear which I'm talking about in the text, but you may run into the word used either way when you visit.

## NATURAL HISTORY: MAKING GREAT MOUNTAINS & WEATHER

A great wall of mountains thousands of miles long curves through Alaska, Canada, the Western United States, and Mexico like a backbone. This ridge is called the North American Cordillera, and the Rocky Mountains are a link in its great chain. Rivers flow from here, down the western slopes toward the Pacific Ocean, and down the eastern slopes to the Atlantic. The exact line where the water splits into the two journeys runs along the peaks, called the Continental Divide. The Rockies influence the weather, too. The mountains are so high they create thunderstorms, calm down other storms headed east across the continent, and grab the moisture out of the sky, collecting it as snow. When the snow melts in the spring, it feeds the nation's great rivers, the Colorado and Columbia to the west and the Missouri to the east. Look at a map of North America to trace these rivers to the ocean and see all the places they go. They provide water for people and farms, habitats for fish, and navigation for ships over most of the United States. The mountains where they start simply are the biggest things in North America, and among the most important.

The high elevations also make a special realm for plants and animals. At the top, it's like the arctic. The mountainsides wear low green tundra for the few months without snow. The ground underneath never thaws. Lower down, trees grow; but the winters are harsh and snowy and the country is not much taken over by people, even outside the parks. Wildlife still wanders free, within certain limits, and the chance to see large mammals behaving naturally is better than at any other area in the United States outside Alaska. The elevation, which makes the world so cold and life so hard, has kept humankind away — people like to live where it's warmer and easier to grow crops. You might say the Rockies are at the edge of our natural habitat.

## ELEVATION & AIR PRESSURE

At high elevations the air tends to be colder, and more rain and snow falls. Lower down, it's usually warmer and drier. Why? Because we're at the bottom of a deep ocean of air called the **atmosphere.**

Our atmosphere is a layer of air about 180 miles thick. Gravity holds it to our planet. Air is made of **molecules** of oxygen and nitrogen, tiny pieces of the stuff we breathe. Where the atmosphere meets outer space, there aren't many air molecules, and there's lots of room between them. But gravity does pull them down toward the Earth, so they do have weight. That weight presses down on the molecules of air below. Adding the weight of those molecules, the air even lower down is even heavier and presses down even harder on the air below it. At sea level, the entire atmosphere is pressing down and squeezing the air together so that it's nice and thick, the way we're used to it.

Air presses on us with a force as hard as 15 pounds per square inch. The reason we don't feel it is that it pushes from all sides at once. When you swim underwater, you don't feel its weight either, but think how much the water above you would weigh if you tried to pick it up in a container. You normally don't feel changes in air pressure either, but your body won't work as well if you go to a higher elevation. Rising 10,000 feet reduces the air pressure — the amount of air in the same amount of space — by about one-third. Your lungs stay the same size, so at that elevation they pull in one-third less air with each breath. You'll notice that you get tired more easily and you may feel light-headed. As you get higher, you may feel other symptoms of altitude, like tingling fingers and disorientation. Your body and brain aren't getting enough oxygen. It can be dangerous, and the safe thing to do is get down to below 8,000 feet. As you go down, you may feel your ears pop. That means the tubes inside your head are filling with higher pressure air from outside. (See "Dealing with Hazards," in chapter 1, "Planning Your Trip," for more on altitude sickness.)

## MEASURING AIR PRESSURE

Since we don't feel air pressure, it can be hard to believe that an ocean of air is pushing down on us. If we were fish under the sea, we might have the same trouble believing water weighed anything. Here's a simple experiment that allows you to weigh air pressure (and also gives you an excuse for using bad manners in a restaurant). Fill a straw with water, or any other liquid, and block the upper end with your finger. Lifting the straw out of the liquid, you'll notice that the water doesn't come out. Release your finger, and it flows out normally. Why?

The reason the liquid stays in the straw is that the weight of the air pressure pushing into the open end is greater than the weight of the water pushing out. Imagine a balance scale with 180 miles of air on one side and a few inches of water on the other. The air is heavier. When you open the top end of the straw, the air pressure on each end is the same, so the liquid slips out.

With a longer straw, you could add more water until it weighed as much as the air, just as if you were adding more weight to one side of the balance scale. When the water and the air weighed the same amount, more water wouldn't stay in the straw. But to do that experiment, you would need a three-story-tall straw. Anything shorter, and the water wouldn't weigh enough to balance the weight of the air. When I was in college, my physics professor built such a thing, using heavy tubing that went all the way up the stairwell of the physics lab, more than 36 feet high.

It's easier to weigh the air if you use a heavier liquid, because then you don't need as much of the liquid to balance the air's weight. **Mercury,** a shiny liquid metal, weighs 13 times as much as water. With mercury, you don't need a 36-foot tube. Just 32 inches of mercury weighs as much as our 180-mile-high atmosphere. A tube of mercury like that is called a **barometer.** We use barometers every day to measure small changes in air pressure that cause changes in the weather. When air pressure is high, the mercury in the barometer goes up, and you can usually expect good weather. (But that's another story.)

Air pressure can tell you how high you are, too. As you go higher, less air is above you, so the air around you is lighter, or under less pressure. By measuring that change in pressure, you can tell your elevation. A device that takes such a measurement is called an **altimeter.** A mercury barometer could do the job, too. Every 1,000 feet higher equals about 1 inch of mercury in the barometer. If the barometer reads 30 inches at sea level, then at 10,000 feet the mercury will read 10 inches lower, or 20 inches. But carrying around a 32-inch glass tube of mercury is pretty inconvenient, so altimeters, and most barometers, use a different method of measuring air pressure. Instead of weighing the air with liquid, they measure changes in the size of a sealed drum of air. As the air pressure outside the drum gets lower, the air molecules inside the drum have to spread out to match that lower pressure, forcing the drum to get bigger. A gauge moves with the size of the drum, pointing to a dial marked with lines showing altitude or inches of mercury.

To learn how to build your own altimeter out of a party balloon and baby bottle, see "Experiment: Making an Altimeter," in chapter 16, "Rocky Mountain National Park."

## PRESSURE & TEMPERATURE

Thinner air is colder. That's obvious when you drive up into the mountains. On top of the Rockies the air is deliciously cool even on the hottest days in the plains. The tundra plants here are the same kinds you would find in cold, northern places like the arctic of northern Canada or Alaska (see "Layers of Life Zones," in chapter 8).

In dry, still conditions, air gets cooler by 5.4°F for each 1,000 feet higher you go. Of course, the air usually isn't perfectly dry or still, so it's commonly closer to 3.5°F cooler for each 1,000 feet. Go up 10,000 feet into the Rockies, and you can expect the temperature to go down 10 times 3.5°F, or 35°F. So if it's 100°F at sea level, at 10,000 feet it will be 100 minus 35, or 65°F.

To understand why, you have to understand what heat really is. Heat is the movement of the tiny molecules that make up almost everything around us. The faster the molecules move around, or vibrate, the hotter they are. Just hitting something can make it hotter by making the molecules inside wiggle more. Scientists also have been able to slow molecules down until they almost stop, and that's as cold as anything can ever be.

You can speed up molecules by pressing them together. The energy of your pressing goes into their movement, and as they fit into the more crowded space they bump into each other more. More movement means more heat. This doesn't work only for air. The sun and other stars burn because the force of gravity on their huge size presses them together so hard. The core of the sun, where the pressure is greatest, is 27 million degrees. The surface, where there isn't as much pressure, is 11,000 degrees. As you go higher on the Earth and the air gets thinner, the same thing happens — less air pressure, less energy making molecules move, less heat.

## MAKING CLOUDS & RAIN

That explains why high places are cool, but not why so much water falls on the western slope of the Rockies. It's the cold that draws the water out of the air. Water has three forms: solid, when it is ice; liquid, when you can drink it or swim in it; and gas or **vapor,** when it floats around invisible with the other kinds of molecules in the air. If you've ever seen a car window or bathroom mirror steam up, you've seen water turning from vapor to liquid. Invisible vapor forms into tiny droplets of liquid on the glass. If the glass is very cold, the water becomes ice, in the form of frost.

Sometimes when you breathe out on a cold day, a little cloud of steam comes from your mouth. Air can only hold so much water vapor without having it turn into liquid water,

and warm air can hold more vapor than cold air. The air in your breath is warm and it holds a lot of invisible water vapor. The cold air outside your body can't hold nearly as much. When you breathe out, and your breath cools, some of the vapor has to turn into liquid water. The steam cloud is made of many tiny droplets of liquid water that form when the vapor becomes liquid. The steamy car window and the bathroom mirror work the same way: Wet air hits a cold surface, and the water turns from vapor to liquid.

The word for water vapor turning into liquid water is **condensation.** As it gets colder still, the liquid water turns into solid water, or ice, which is called freezing. Going the other way, from colder to warmer, ice turning into liquid is thawing, and liquid water turning into vapor is **evaporation.**

All these changes happen for the same reason, because of the changing speed of the water molecules. When we heat liquid water, its molecules move faster, some fast enough to fly right through the surface of the water into the air. Once a molecule of water is floating around in the air, it is water vapor, not liquid. That's evaporation. When we cool vapor, the molecules in the air slow down, some slow enough that when they run into each other they stick together. When enough molecules of water vapor glob together they get big enough to be visible droplets of liquid water. That's condensation. When you breathe out on a cold day, what you really see is invisible water molecules from your hot breath slowing down in the cold air such that they stick together and make a little cloud of water droplets. Freezing and thawing work basically the same way (see "Read Aloud: Why Both Snow & Granite Sparkle," in chapter 16).

In case you haven't guessed by now, clouds up in the sky are made by condensation, too. The sun warms air near the ground or the ocean, and water evaporates. Air weighs less when it warms because the faster-moving molecules take up more space, so it pushes upward to a thinner level of the atmosphere. As it rises, air pressure lessens, the air cools, and the water vapor inside turns into tiny water droplets. The water droplets are so small that they float on the rising air in big groups that look like fluffy white blobs, otherwise known as clouds. When the droplets of water get large enough — usually after they freeze onto a tiny piece of dust — they get too heavy to float and start to fall. In warm weather, they melt on the way down and turn into raindrops. In the winter, they stay frozen and land on the ground as snow.

That's how it usually happens, but mountains as big as the Rockies change the way things work. Here, the air moving east across North America bumps into the mountains and slides up them like a ramp. As it rises, it cools and forms clouds, and they drop snow and rain on the western side of the mountains. That's why those places are damp enough to fill our great rivers and why, at the lower elevations, they grow great forests. As the air passes over to the east side of the mountains, the opposite happens. Much of the water has already fallen as snow or rain on the western side. Then, as the air is forced downward on the ramp of the eastern mountainside, it grows warmer and can hold more water vapor. Clouds disappear and evaporation begins again. That's why eastern valleys and the Great Plains are so dry and grow plants that don't need much water. (To see just how big the difference is, see the weather chart showing the snowfall in Grand Lake and Estes Park, towns on opposite sides of Rocky Mountain National Park, in chapter 16.)

## How Thunderstorms Work

One evening at the geyser basin in Yellowstone, where Old Faithful shoots off every 90 minutes or so, I watched a series of ferocious thunderstorms rampage across the sky. I'd been drenched several times already that week while hiking. I had run around in the dark in my underwear trying to find ways to keep puddles out of my tent as rain roared down so hard it shook the tent frame. So I wasn't thrilled to see another thunderstorm coming. But this thunderstorm was one of the most dramatic natural events I had ever seen.

The sky blackened until the valley was shut off, waiting in dusk to see what would happen next. The storm was coming. People ran for cover. The rain hit. Bolts of lightning struck with the punch of quick thunder, lighting the geysers and steam vents, which still spewed hot water onto a desolate plain. The rain grew into a waterfall, gushing onto the ground and over the buildings, then switched to hail. White hailstones the size of marbles bounced noisily off cars, like a shower of gravel, and covered the grass a couple inches thick. Clouds of steam from the geyser basin floated through the scene.

Appreciate the beauty of thunderstorms because you'll see them often in the summer in the Rockies. These are among the most powerful events we ever get to see. A single thunderstorm can release more energy than a large power plant produces in a month. Learn to plan around them — hike in the morning and leave vulnerable ridges and mountaintops before the afternoon storms hit. And visit the Moraine Park Museum at Rocky Mountain National Park during the rain to find out what makes thunderstorms work.

In summer, the sun cooks basins and mountains all over the West. The hot air rises. On days without thunderstorms, the rising air cools as it goes up and stops rising. But when thunderstorms are coming, the upper air is colder than usual, so the rising air cannot cool fast enough. It stays warmer than the air around it and keeps shooting upward. Air near the ground rushes in to take its place. In the summer, that new air often comes from warm ocean waters south of Los Angeles or on the Gulf of Mexico. The ocean air is moist, ready to condense into big clouds. When it gets to the hot land, it rises, too, and draws in even more wet air from the ocean. This system is called the **monsoonal flow,** and in the Rockies it usually lasts June through September.

The ramp of the mountains, pushing air upward, gives storms a boost. The dampness in the air helps even more. When water condenses from vapor to liquid, it warms slightly. As the vapor in the rising air condenses into clouds, it warms the air even more, and that added heat makes the air rise even faster. As this strong draft of air shoots upward, it makes a huge, tall cloud called a **thunderhead.** A thunderhead is the easiest kind of cloud to recognize. It is flat on the bottom and fluffy and wide on top, and it stands higher than any other cloud, towering as high as 8 miles up.

Lightning happens because of the electric charge that builds up in thunderheads. This is electricity like you get from a wall outlet, but much stronger and made in a different way. In fact, scientists don't really know how it is made — they have different theories and are doing experiments to figure out which theory is right.

What we *do* know is that the bottom of a thunderhead builds up a lot of the tiny particles that carry a negative electric charge, called electrons. The ground has the opposite electric charge, so a lot of electricity could flow between the cloud and the ground if a wire were running between them. But air doesn't normally carry electricity because its molecules have balanced positive and negative electric charges. Until the electric charge in the cloud gets very large, nothing happens.

When the cloud's charge is large enough, a thin strand of electricity flashes down toward the earth in a series of short, jagged legs. At the same time, a strand rises up from the highest point on the ground. These strands of electricity split the molecules in the air, making them electrically charged particles called **ions.** A path of ions is good at carrying electricity, like a wire. When the two strands meet, that wire of ions suddenly connects the cloud to the ground, and a huge amount of electricity flows through all at once. That's when you see the flash and hear the boom of thunder. Thunder is the sound of the lightning instantly heating the air it passes through to about 18,000°F, so that the air explodes.

The amount of power in a lightning strike is really amazing. Its electrical current can reach 10,000 times the current from an outlet in your home. Lightning kills about a hundred people a year in the United States. See "Dealing with Hazards," chapter 1, for tips on avoiding lightning.

## MOUNTAIN BUILDING

The unique way the Rockies affect the weather and water across our continent shows how special they are. Most of the world is flat, so big mountains like these really stand out. To see what I mean, look at a globe or map of the world that shows elevation and ocean depth. You will see that most of the Earth's surface is at two levels: land that is near sea level, and sea floor about 2 miles deep. There are high mountains on land and deep trenches in the oceans, but they're unusual, like the Rockies.

One of the first people to wonder why the world looks that way was a scientist and arctic explorer named Alfred Wegener. He noticed that the way the continents sit up above the deep sea looks similar to the way sheets of ice float on arctic seas, breaking apart and bumping into each other. When big ice sheets hit each other, they can crack into ridges like little mountains, but mostly, they're flat with sharp edges, like the continents. Wegener supposed that the continents might be floating around on the Earth the way the ice was floating on the sea. If he was right, it would explain why fossils of tropical creatures ended up in the arctic, and why the shape of South America looks like a puzzle piece that should fit together with Africa. But not many people believed Wegener. His idea was too new, and he couldn't explain what force could be moving whole continents around. He died on an

## EXPERIMENT: HOW FAR AWAY IS LIGHTNING?

Many times, lying in a tent at night, I've watched the flash of lightning, heard the roar of thunder, and tried to judge how far away the thunderstorm was. I've figured if the storm was getting nearer or going away, and estimated how long before I would get wet. Not that knowing helps in any way, but it's more fun than just waiting.

The longer the time between a flash of lightning and a thunderclap, the farther away is the lightning. If the light and noise are getting farther apart with each lightning strike, the storm is moving away. If they're getting closer together, it's coming toward you. If both come at the same time, the lightning is quite near. You can even figure out roughly how fast the storm is moving.

The reason this works is that light travels very fast and sound travels much slower. Light is made of photons, the fastest things in the universe, with a speed of about 186,000 miles per second. Light from a lightning bolt gets to you practically instantly. Sound, on the other hand, is like a wave on the ocean. The thunderclap moves the air and the air moves your ear and you hear. (That's why you can feel the deep rumble of thunder and other loud noises, and it's also why there is no sound in outer space, where there is no air.) The speed of sound depends on the temperature and moisture of the air. For a round number, call it one-fifth (or 0.2) of a mile per second (720 miles per hour).

Let's say you see a flash of lightning and hear the thunder 5 seconds later. You know the light got to you instantly and the sound took 5 seconds to come from the same spot. So if you figure out how far sound can travel in 5 seconds, you will know how far away the lightning struck. The figuring is pretty simple: Sound travels one-fifth of a mile per second, so in 5 seconds it travels 1 mile ($\frac{1}{5} \times 5 = 1$). The lightning must be 1 mile away. In 10 seconds, sound will travel twice as far, or 2 miles. The simple rule to remember is 5 seconds per mile. Start counting when you see the lightning, stop when you hear the thunder, and divide by 5. If you get up to 50, stop counting. You're unlikely to hear thunder more than 10 miles away.

You can even figure how fast a storm is approaching or moving away (although you can only get its actual speed if it is on a line over your location). Just compare the distances you get with your counting. If the first strike is 2 miles away, and 5 minutes later a strike is 1 mile away, then it has come closer by 1 mile in 5 minutes, and you probably have 5 minutes or less before you get wet.

---

expedition in Greenland in 1930. About 30 years later, other scientists started to realize he was right.

It turns out the surface of our planet is a solid layer of rock only 10 to 100 miles thick. Down below, for the other 8,000 miles to the other side of the Earth, some of the planet is gooey rock, some liquid rock, some solid, and all very hot. The stiff upper layers slowly float around on top of the hot, squishy rock below in pieces called tectonic plates. Along the middle of the oceans, hot new rock comes out of the Earth, adding to the ocean floor. As the ocean plate grows larger, a few inches a year, it carries islands and other land along like boxes on a conveyor belt.

New ocean floor is being made all the time, but the planet isn't getting any bigger to hold it all, so something has to give. In the Atlantic Ocean, one big continent split apart and made two — those puzzle pieces of South America and Africa that Wegener noticed. About 70 million years ago, a collision between the Pacific Plate and North America started building the Rockies. Continental plates generally are lighter than ocean plates, so the continental plate tended to ride up on top of the ocean plate. At places, the continental plate buckled and folded from the pressure of the collision, the way the sheet metal of a car bends into ridges when it hits something. That's what the Rockies and the rest of the North American

Cordillera are — a very big smashed fender. That big event helped raise the Colorado Plateau and all of the west.

That's the general idea, anyway; the details aren't so simple. The mountains weren't built all at once, and it took erosion by water and ice to carve them into the mountains we know. And, at Yellowstone, volcanoes built mountains and blew them up. That point in North America's plate is passing over a hot spot within the Earth. Even today the hot spot is raising the park on a cushion of molten rock and hot water. The hot spot could cause the area to explode again within the next half-million years.

## MAKING THE TETONS

There was a mystery about the Tetons' birth. Here are some of the clues. On the east side, the mountains rise out of the flat valley of Jackson Hole as steep as a knife blade, but on the west side, away from the park, they are far less impressive, rising slowly in a ramp of rounded hills. Their age is odd, too. The Tetons are only 7 million years old, quite young as mountains go, but they are made of some of the oldest rock in North America, gneiss that was laid down about 2½ billion years ago, when life on Earth wasn't much more advanced than single cells.

It took some clever scientific detective work to figure out how the Tetons got here. Geologists looked at the shape of the mountains and tried to imagine what could have made such a sharp break from a flat valley to a nearly straight wall of rock, while the other side of the same mountains looked like a ramp. It made sense if there was a fault at the base of the mountains. A **fault** is a place where the crust of the Earth is cracked. During earthquakes, one side of the crack would rise while the other side would fall, creating a steep cliff. That would explain why there were no foothills on one side of the mountains and there were on the other. Imagine the fault as a partly opened trap door in a floor. The open

edge of the door is a steep break, but the edge with the hinge is like a ramp.

To test this theory, geologists drilled down into Jackson Hole, looking for the same kinds of rock they had found up in the mountains. If they could find the same layers of ancient gneiss, they would know where the mountains came from. It worked. Far below the valley, the drills hit layers of rock that fit the layers of rock up in the mountains the way two pieces of a broken teacup fit together. But to put the pieces together, the valley would have to be higher, or the mountains lower, by 30,000 feet.

The layers must have been one flat piece before the fault started moving 7 million years ago. A block rose along one side of the fault while the block on the other side sank lower. Rivers and ice wore down the higher rocks and carried broken rock and sand down into the valley, filling it in as it dipped down so that the valley floor came out flat, as it is today. The fault stopped moving, but the mountains, made of hard, old gneiss, resisted wearing away and became sharp and pointed.

## HOW GLACIERS WORK

Glaciers once covered most of North America. They shaped the Rocky Mountains, the Sierra Nevada, the Olympic Mountains of Washington State, and Mount Desert Island in Maine, and they left behind Cape Cod, which is mostly a pile of leftover glacial rocks and dirt. The Ice Age began about 2½ million years ago, and since then ice has covered a large part of the world and melted back again almost 50 times. Scientists call these 50 cycles of freeze-and-melt **glacial** and **interglacial periods.** About 10,000 years ago, an interglacial period started that we're living in now. The Earth's climate warmed up and the great ice sheets melted, leaving planed-off prairies, U-shaped valleys, rounded mountains, and huge boulders standing mysteriously out in the middle of fields as evidence that glaciers had been there. (See "Experiment: Finding

Glacier Tracks," in chapter 18, "Yosemite National Park," for an explanation.)

Glaciers start when more snow falls in the winter than melts in the summer. Old snow packs down deeper and harder until it turns into hard, heavy ice. It takes about 100 feet of snow to pack down into glacier ice 1 foot thick. When the ice gets about 100 feet thick, the pressure at the bottom is strong enough that the ice starts to flow slowly downhill without melting. The ice slides until it reaches a lower level on the mountain, where the air is warm enough to melt the ice at the bottom as fast as it is added up above. Now it is a glacier — a slow, solid ice river, keeping the same shape while moving new ice down the mountain.

Glaciers' movement is too slow to see, but when scientists set up movie cameras and take one picture of a glacier each day for months, then run the pictures quickly through a movie projector, the glacier looks just like a weird, jerky river. Then you can see the cracks on the back of the glacier open and close as the ice flows over bumps and into dips. Today, the weather is too warm in most of the United States for glaciers, although they are common in Alaska. In the Lower 48, strong hikers can get to glaciers at Olympic and Rocky Mountain national parks and in the Sierra Nevada.

Many parks have places where glaciers changed the landscape. Imagine the force of ice hundreds of feet thick grinding over anything in its path. Glaciers can pulverize solid rock, demolishing mountains and gouging out valleys. Besides rubbing with their immense weight, glaciers also crack rock with water. The underside of a glacier is cold, but it also is under so much pressure that liquid water won't freeze even well below the normal 32°F freezing point. Very cold water stays liquid under a glacier until it can seep down into tiny cracks in rock underneath to a place where it can freeze. When water freezes, it gets slightly bigger, as you've noticed if you have ever put a sealed can of liquid, such as a soda, in the freezer. When water fills a small crack inside a rock and then freezes, it pushes the sides of the crack apart to make room for itself. Water is strong enough to break huge pieces of bedrock. When it does, the glacier removes the pieces. During the last Ice Age, when the ice buried North American mountains thousands of feet deep, great valleys were dug everywhere.

All the rock that a glacier takes from the mountains has to go somewhere. That's the other part of how glaciers change the landscape: They make hills and flatlands from broken pieces of mountains. The mountain rocks come down in boulders, cobbles, pebbles, and dust called rock flour or silt. Under the glacier, rivers carry some of the smaller stuff down and spread it out in front of the glacier. Huge gravel riverbeds, sometimes miles wide, form in front of a glacier with narrow braids of channels where an undersized river switches back and forth, spreading out glacial silt and pebbles. Eventually — in thousands of years — grass and bushes grow on the higher gravel bars between the channels, slowly spreading and turning the flat table of sand and gravel into a meadow or forest.

Glaciers also move their refuse of broken rock down from the mountains in the flowing ice. Rocks are carried along inside and under the glacier, or they could fall on top from valley walls the glacier cuts into. Dirty glaciers can even grow trees on their backs, but the trees don't have time to become a forest, because the glacier keeps moving like a conveyor belt, slowly carrying everything to its face and edges, where the ice melts and leaves everything in a pile. Over time, the rocks pile up at the glacier edges into hills and ridges called **moraines,** which, as I mentioned earlier, is how Cape Cod came to be (see "Waves of Glaciation," in chapter 2, "Moving Water, Moving Land").

## GLACIERS SHAPED THE ROCKIES

Glaciers helped shape the landscape of the Rockies, and small bits of glacier still sit in bowls atop some of the highest mountains. During the last Ice Age, which ended around 11,000 years ago, glacier ice probably filled the valleys thousands of feet deep, allowing only the pointed mountaintops to stick up. All that ice slowly slid downhill, pulled along by gravity, and ground the rocks away into valleys and rounded mountains. Only up above, where the peaks stuck out of the ice, did sharp shapes survive.

Shapes made by glaciers are easy to pick out on a mountainside. The valleys tend to be rounded, as if carved out by a big scoop. Valleys made by rivers look more like something cut by a thin knife. When glaciers slide over a high place, they leave it rounded. But a peak that looks jagged and cracked probably was shaped by freezing and thawing water. (See "Experiment: Finding Glacier Tracks," in chapter 18, for more on what to look for.)

Glacial moraines are quite noticeable at Grand Teton National Park, where they sit on the table-flat Jackson Hole (*hole* is a local word meaning valley). Trees grow on them, even though they can't grow on the plain, because the moraine's finer soil holds more water. Moraines dam the south shore of Jackson Lake and hold in three sides of Jenny Lake. At Rocky Mountain National Park, Moraine Campground is named for one of these features.

## HOW GEYSERS WORK

Echinus Geyser starts as a round pool of water, bubbling slightly and spilling over its rim at the Norris Geyser Basin. It's not Yellowstone's biggest geyser, nor is it similar to many other geysers — each has its own character. But every hour or so you can sit right next to Echinus and watch the pool splashing and spilling more and more, then suddenly bursting and being hurled high into the air by the swimming-pool-full. This isn't a narrow squirt of water, as I had imagined from seeing pictures of geysers. Thousands of gallons of boiling water shoot up in big, rumbling sploshes. It's really weird. And the weirdest thing, to me, is the way geysers do nothing for a long time — an hour to tens of years — and then suddenly erupt in wild towers of water. You would think that if they had hot water to get out, they would do it all the time instead of waiting to explode! It took scientists a long time to figure out how they work.

The power behind all the steam and hot water at Yellowstone comes from melted rocks below the surface. Most of the park is a huge, sleeping volcano that erupted as recently as 70,000 years ago and that blew up the entire area 600,000 years ago. The cap of solid rock plugging the volcano is 2 to 5 miles thick, compared to rock roughly 60 miles in most places. The volcano's heat comes from a hot spot deeper within the planet. As I explained above, under "Mountain Building" (p. 281), North America is floating on the hot, gooey interior of the Earth. Yellowstone is floating southwest at about an inch a year over its hot spot. There are other hot spots in the world — one created the Hawaiian Islands; another, Iceland — but except for Yellowstone, they're almost all under the ocean or near the coast. At Yellowstone, a hot spot right in the middle of the continent shapes the land. Much of the park is rising a couple of inches a year as the sleeping volcano bulges with molten rock and hot water. Someday, that stuff may come out on the surface again in another volcanic eruption.

The boiling water spewed by Yellowstone's steam vents, bubbling mud pots, and hot springs starts on the surface as rain and snow. Water trickles down through cracks to the hot rocks, heats up, and boils back to the surface. The geysers are a bit more complicated. Their water comes from the same source, rain and snow, but it has a harder time getting back to the surface because of the shape of narrow cracks it must flow through. Only certain kinds of rocks and minerals can create those special cracks. Yellowstone has the water, the heat, and the right kind of rocks, and that's why most of the world's geysers are here.

The special ingredient for geyser plumbing is a mineral called **silica.** Granite contains a lot of silica, and there is a lot of granite under Yellowstone. When granite melts and flows out on the surface as lava, it forms a rock called **rhyolite,** which is common at Yellowstone thanks to the volcanoes. (See "Read Aloud: Why Both Snow & Granite Sparkle," in chapter 16, to learn how granite, rhyolite, and obsidian are related.) Rhyolite is important because its silica dissolves in hot water. The water that seeps down from the surface heats up and dissolves the silica and paints it to the sides of underground cracks, like glaze on a clay pot. That glaze makes the cracks narrow and watertight, as they must be for geysers. You can see hardened silica, called sinter, when you watch geysers: The cone on top of many is made of sinter.

A geyser has a narrow, watertight crack leading to the surface but more space for water down below, like a wine bottle with a narrow neck. When water seeps into the larger spaces below the neck, the hot rocks there heat it up. Nearer the surface, however, the rock at the neck of the bottle isn't as hot. Water there stays cooler, sitting like a cork holding down the hot water underneath. Normally, when water reaches a certain heat it boils and turns into steam, which takes far more space than the water alone. But with the cork on the bottle of the geyser, that can't happen, so the water down below keeps getting hotter without boiling — as hot as 400°F, twice the normal boiling point at the surface.

With greater heat, pressure in the geyser water builds. On the surface, you can see evidence of that pressure. When a geyser is getting ready to go off, water starts to spill from the pool on top. The cork of cooler water is being pushed upward and overflowing. Finally, enough of the cork of cooler water spills that it can no longer prevent the superhot water below from flashing into steam. Steam and water shoot upward toward the lower pressure at the surface.

The most famous of the geysers, Old Faithful, has a crack only 4 inches wide, 22 feet before the surface. Every time it erupts, Old Faithful shoots out 3,700 to 8,400 gallons of boiling water through that narrow crack at speeds faster than the speed of sound. It lasts a few minutes. Then, with the underground cracks empty and the pressure released, water flows back in and starts heating again for the next eruption, in about 70 minutes.

# THE LITTLE FIELD GUIDE

## MAMMALS
In addition to the creatures here, you might also want to check out the white-tailed deer (p. 144), mule deer and rattlesnake (p. 189) and the black bear and bobcat (p. 392).

## Bighorn Sheep
The strong bodies and huge curling horns of bighorns are unmistakable. In the fall the males fight for the right to mate by bashing their horns together. You can hear it a mile away. At Rocky Mountain, you can often see

Bighorn Sheep

bighorn in the late spring and early summer on Highway 34 at Sheep Lakes in Horseshoe Park, where they come to eat minerals they don't get enough of in their winter diet. They come to the area so predictably that the Park Service posts crossing guards on the highway. Later in the year, you can see them in alpine areas, sometimes along Trail Ridge Road or on the Crater Trail.

Bison (or Buffalo)

## Bison (or Buffalo)

When whites first came to the West, 60 million buffalo roamed in huge herds across the plains. By 1890, excessive hunting had left fewer than 1,000 alive. Now there are more than 200,000 in North America, mostly on farms. The wild herds at Yellowstone and Grand Teton national parks are rare, and number a few thousand animals. Bison eat grass, often near roads where you can see them. In Yellowstone, the Hayden Valley and Lamar Valley are good spots to see them; in Grand Teton, look in the Antelope Flat area and along the Snake River. Amazingly, we saw people walking right up to bison. These animals are the size of a small truck and can run fast. People get hurt every year. For more on bison, see "History & Culture: Managing Nature" (p. 291).

Grizzly Bear

## Grizzly Bear

Grizzly bears once lived in much of the United States, but they need large areas of undisturbed land; and now some biologists fear they don't have enough room left even in their last Lower 48 habitat, in the northern Rockies. Only about 400 live in Yellowstone. About 30,000 live in Alaska. The best way to tell a grizzly from the smaller and more common black bear is by the hump on the grizzly's back and the black bear's straighter face profile. A grizzly's brown or blond color isn't a good guide, because blacks can be brown and grizzlies can be black. Grizzlies mostly eat roots, berries, and the like, but they are predators. Adult males weigh more than 500 pounds in this area. (For bear safety tips, see "Dealing with Hazards," in chapter 1.)

Moose

## Moose

Moose are the largest member of the deer family, with large males growing to 1,600 pounds. They like brushy areas, willows, and swamps or shallow ponds, where they stand deep in the water and eat weeds from the bottom. They're excellent swimmers. Look for moose along the Snake River and near Jackson Lake Lodge at Grand Teton, and in the Kawuneechee Valley at Rocky Mountain. Only the males have antlers.

Mountain Lion

Pika

## Mountain Lion

Your chances of seeing a mountain lion are slim because they're rare and appear only when they want to — and if a mountain lion wants you to see it, then you could be in danger. They are big cats and feed on large mammals like deer. Attacks on humans are rare but have happened, and are another good reason to keep your children near when you are hiking, especially in brush.

## Pika

The pika is a cute little animal that lives in rocky areas high in the mountains. Pikas grow to 8 inches and are related to rabbits but don't have long ears. Their coat blends in with the rocks, so look around carefully to see them. There is a good children's picture book called *A Pika's Tail*, by Sally Plumb (Grand Teton Natural History Association).

## BIRDS

Besides the birds listed here, you may see some that are described in other chapters, such as the raven and western bluebird (p. 190), Steller's jay (p. 393), and the pelican (p. 476)

North American Elk
(or Wapiti)

Golden Eagle

## North American Elk (or Wapiti)

These large, noble-looking deer show up all over the Rockies, spending the summer in alpine meadows and moving down for the winter. They show up at many places in all three parks; at Yellowstone you commonly see them along the road. In the winter, elk are fed at a refuge between Grand Teton National Park and the town of Jackson. Only the males have antlers.

## Golden Eagle

The majestic golden eagle has a wingspan of over 6 feet; it glides in the air before swooping down and grabbing a rabbit or other rodent in its ferocious talons. This eagle is all brown, with a lighter brown neck.

## Hairy Woodpecker

The hairy woodpecker is the size of a robin, with black and white feathers; the male has a red spot on his head. It lives in deciduous forests (where trees have leaves). Male woodpeckers have long, hard beaks that they hammer against tree trunks to make holes. Females have shorter beaks that are better for prying. Together, they dig insects out of the wood.

Mountain Chickadee

## Mountain Chickadee

This little bird looks a lot like the common black-capped chickadee but has an extra white stripe on its head and gray sides. It is easy to find high in the mountains, hunting insects and flitting around the alpine forests.

Trumpeter Swan

## Trumpeter Swan

These huge, graceful white swans are among the largest birds in North America. They are easy to find on the lakes of Yellowstone and Grand Teton national parks, but are found nowhere else except Canada and Alaska. They nearly disappeared, but conservation brought them back. *The Trumpet of the Swan,* by E.B. White (HarperCollins), is a funny and beautifully written novel to read aloud. It tells the story of Louis the swan, who has no voice and so learns to play the trumpet.

## TREES & PLANTS

In addition to the flora here, also refer to the ponderosa pine (p. 191), sagebrush (p. 192), columbine (p. 393), and poison oak (p. 394).

Subalpine Fir
(or Rocky Mountain Fir)

## Subalpine Fir (or Rocky Mountain Fir)

This dark green evergreen tree with thick needles is among the last to give up growing near the tree line on the mountains. As you go up, it gets smaller until it is a shrub, providing forage for many animals. Lower down, it can be 100 feet tall, shaped like a narrow cone. The branches hang near the ground and sometimes take root when snow holds them down. These trees grow in thick, shady forests with Engelmann spruce, a tree used for piano sounding boards and other musical instruments.

Indian Paintbrush

Lupine

## Indian Paintbrush

Various kinds of Indian paintbrush show up all over the West. They're pretty to look at and easy to identify. Bright, pointy flowers that look like artists' paint brushes top tall stalks. The giant red paintbrush commonly grows in clumps in mountain meadows and clearings. Orange-flowered desert paintbrush likes dry, sagebrush areas.

## Lupine

Lupines have hairy, star-shaped leaves and juicy stalks with vertical rows of flowers. The most common varieties are blue and violet. In the Rockies, they grow in open meadow or stream bank areas. They bloom most of the summer, and in the fall the flowers are replaced with fuzzy seed pods like peas. Peas and lupines are related. Cows that eat lupine can give poison milk.

Lodgepole Pine

Quaking Aspen

## Lodgepole Pine

The lodgepole got its name because it was useful for building lodges, teepees, and litters. The trees are as straight as telephone poles with branches well above the ground. Needles are longish, in bunches of two. The Rocky Mountain lodgepole pine has adapted to forest fires. Some of the cones open in the heat of a fire, so lodgepoles are the first tree to come back, with large, open forests. They cover 40% of Yellowstone. At a pull-out south of Bridge Bay along Yellowstone Lake, a sign points out a sharp line between a lodgepole pine forest and a forest of subalpine fir and Engelmann spruce. A fire must have come just to this point long ago.

## Quaking Aspen

In the mountains just below the spruce-fir forest, aspens grow quickly after forest fires, then die out as the conifers (trees with cones) take over. In the Rockies they spread by sending out new trees from their roots; when many trees cover a whole hillside, they may really be one plant, sometimes called the largest single living things on earth. In the moister northeastern United States, aspen spread with seeds. The roundish leaves are shiny on one side and dull on the other, and beautiful when they shake in the breeze.

# History & Culture: Managing Nature

The first explorers to visit Yellowstone could hardly believe their eyes, and when they got home and told of the geysers and steam vents, they were called liars. A government expedition went to the area in 1871, and the researchers' photographs and paintings proved the stories. The next spring, Congress passed and President Grant signed a law making Yellowstone the first national park in the United States or the world (see "Park History: A Good Idea," in chapter 14, "Yellowstone National Park"). You might think that would be the end of the story and that Yellowstone lived happily ever after. The problem is, we're still trying to figure out exactly what a national park is.

The park President Grant created was a place where hunting continued and thousands of elk and bison were killed. People in nearby towns used the land for their own purposes. In 1886 the U.S. Army built a fort at Mammoth Hot Springs — today the brown stone buildings are the park headquarters — and outlawed hunting, logging, and damaging the geysers. But the government still wanted to get rid of wolves and paid a bounty all over the United States for each one killed. Many of the people who wanted to protect the wild animals in the park felt that way only because they thought it would mean there would be more animals for hunting outside the park.

## What's Nature For?

When Yellowstone became a park, most people believed — as many people believe today — that God created the land and all the animals for human beings to use and take care of. That doesn't mean these places and animals should be wasted. They believe the land should be protected and managed to keep giving people what we need forever. If predators like wolves kill good and useful animals like elk, these people might say, then nature could be improved by getting rid of the wolves. If

forest fires destroy beautiful and valuable trees, then people have an obligation to fight the fires so that the wood and vistas can be saved. They would say the purpose of national parks is to promote tourism and recreation, and when we need roads and hotels so that visitors can enjoy the parks more, those things should be built. People who see things this way believe that the natural world should be managed the way a wise and careful farmer manages his land. Most of the land in the world today is managed by people following this philosophy.

Another group of people sees nature as something that's good all by itself, even if it doesn't help people. This view began to develop around the time Congress set Yellowstone aside, but didn't become popular until the 1960s. These people don't think we can make nature any better, and when we try, we tend to change things in damaging ways we don't even understand. One example is killing off the wolves. After they were gone, around 70 years ago, the numbers of elk went up, and park rangers started killing elk to keep them from eating everything in sight. These people think forest fires should burn to keep the forest young, with food for many different kinds of animals. In their minds, parks are not for people, they're for nature. If people fit into the picture, that's fine, but people shouldn't damage natural places to make it easier for tourists to see them. It took millions of years for the wildlife, landscapes, and natural systems of the Rockies to develop. Human beings, who have been here such a short time, have no right to try to destroy something so beautiful and irreplaceable.

The disagreement between these two points of view has been a main issue in the history and politics of the American West for the past 100 years. Westerners seem to argue about how to use land, water, and wildlife every time someone wants to build a road, dig a mine, or protect a park. Because the largest single natural area in the main part of the United States is in and around Yellowstone and Grand Teton national parks, this is where the hottest disagreements rage. (For more on how ideas about nature have changed, see "History & Culture: Changing Values," in chapter 17, "Rock, Life & Change.")

## NATURE THAT'S NATURAL

When the U.S. Congress created the National Park Service in 1916, the parks were meant to serve people, not nature. The parks' basic purpose, written in law, was to allow people to enjoy them in a way that would protect them "for the enjoyment of future generations." The reason to preserve nature in the parks was so that we could keep enjoying nature forever, not for nature itself.

The first park managers were conservationists compared to most other people at the time, but they still thought of the parks much as we do city parks, as places that could serve people better if they were not as wild. They thought they could make the parks better by getting rid of the "bad" animals. That's an idea that makes sense only from a human point of view — nature doesn't choose good and bad animals, only strong and successful ones. "Good" animals included trout, which rangers stocked in lakes and rivers to improve the fishing for visitors — even though the new species often drove out native fish. Horace Albright, an early park leader who helped found Grand Teton National Park (see "History: Rockefeller to the Rescue," in chapter 15, "Grand Teton National Park"), said good animals were "animals desirable for public observation and enjoyment," and bad ones were "enemies of those species."

The main enemies were **predators,** or animals that eat other animals. The Park Service and other government agencies killed them, including cougar, wolf, coyote, lynx, bobcat, fox, badger, mink, weasel, fisher, otter, and marten. At one time, they even destroyed eggs of the rare America white pelican, which feeds on trout, so that there would be fewer pelicans and more fish for Yellowstone visitors to catch. The pelicans survived; but wolves were gone from Yellowstone by the 1940s, and few survived anywhere in the Lower 48 states, although plenty remain in Canada and Alaska. And the rangers' plan worked. Without predators, the "good" species increased in numbers, so much so that the park service soon was killing or moving elk to reduce their numbers on Yellowstone's Northern Range.

But national park philosophy slowly changed through the years, led by scientists who learned about amazing park ecosystems that cannot really be improved upon. In an **ecosystem,** plants, animals, the land, and weather all relate to each other to gather energy and create life (see "Natural History: The Systems of Life," in chapter 20, "Ecology: Fitting It Together"). If one kind of animal eats away a certain kind of plant, another plant might grow more that benefits another animal. Different kinds of plants and animals might cover different areas, but overlap at certain times or places and feed on each other there. At Yellowstone, many kinds of wildlife migrate to the areas of hot springs and geysers in the winter because of the warmth and melted snow, then spread out across different areas in the summer. Fires help animals that eat young plant growth and hurt animals that need tree cover. We don't completely understand how these systems work, much less how to make them better. When rangers removed a part of an ecosystem, they didn't improve it, they simply changed it in big, unexpected ways, like taking a random piece out of a working machine. In the 1960s, the Park Service began managing the parks to interfere with nature as little as possible. And they began trying to put back together the pieces they had broken.

In 1995 and 1996, rangers released 31 gray wolves from Canada in Yellowstone. The wolves did well. They fed on the elk and moose, had lots of pups, and spread out across part of the area where wolves had been removed long before. After 5 years, there were 115 wolves in 11 packs. The moose had forgotten they were supposed to be afraid of wolves, so for a few years the wolves had an easy time in their hunting, but then the moose relearned their fear and returned to their natural, cautious behavior. The wolves mostly ate elk, taking 9 to 14 each month of the winter from the herd of up to 20,000 elk in Yellowstone's Northern Range.

Unfortunately, the wolves also killed more than 120 sheep, 25 cattle, and a few dogs, horses, and other animals outside the park in the first 5 years after their return. Wolves ignore park boundaries. They see domestic animals as an easy meal. Knowing this, ranchers had helped kill off the wolves in the first place, and they didn't want them back. Here was a clear example of a disagreement between those who thought nature should serve people and those who thought it was worth protecting just for itself. A conservation group called Defenders of Wildlife offered a compromise. They paid ranchers for animals killed by wolves. The bill for the first 5 years was about $50,000. People still come first: Nature is something we have to pay for.

In the early years, the parks also tried to improve wildlife viewing by controlling animals' movements. At Yellowstone they kept bison in pens for many years, and, until 1942, rangers fed bears from platforms so that visitors could watch. Grizzlies continued to eat at open garbage dumps at the park until 1970, with tourists parked nearby taking pictures. Bears got so used to taking their food from people that they would often climb up on cars, looking for a handout. Bears that get used to people are dangerous, and at Yellowstone they hurt about 45 park visitors every year. Traffic on park roads often tied up around begging bears.

The situation was far from natural, or even safe. Besides, you can see what a bear looks like at any zoo or game park (such as the good one in West Yellowstone, in chapter 14). Only in the wilderness can you see how a bear behaves when it is free. The garbage dumps were shut down, and the Park Service did a good job of cutting off the bears' human food by installing bear-proof garbage cans and teaching people not to let the bears get at their groceries. Without the extra food, fewer bears survived and the remaining bears went back to living away from people. Today, you usually see grizzlies only in the backcountry, and then rarely. On average, only a single visitor out of three million who go to Yellowstone each year is hurt by a bear. (Tips on bear safety are under "Dealing with Hazards," in chapter 1; also see "Read Aloud: How to Save a Bear," in chapter 18.)

But some bear experts think the park made the wrong decision. When the dumps closed, so many grizzlies died that they were at risk of disappearing completely. As few as 200 may have survived in the park at one time. Today, there are around 350 to 400 grizzlies in the park, only about one every 10 miles if they were evenly spread out.

## NATURAL REGULATION

If we could go back to the time before white settlers first arrived at Yellowstone, managing the park would be easy. Elk and bison would range freely, their herds kept from growing too large by wolves, bear, and mountain lion. Lightning would set off small forest fires that would burn old trees and underbrush, making room for aspens and willows that moose and elk like to eat and opening the cones of the lodgepole pine, which lets go of its seeds in the heat of a fire. Eagles, osprey, and pelicans would swoop down to feed on plentiful cutthroat trout; there would be no fish species that don't belong here eating the natural species. Park rangers wouldn't have to restore bear or wolves. Since life first appeared on earth, nature has taken care of itself, finding its own balance of plants, plant eaters, and predators. Without the changes people have made, that balance could go on as before; maybe it can even with the changes.

Letting nature find its own balance is called **natural regulation.** After so many years of trying to adjust the mix of animals in the park, the Park Service decided in 1968 to follow the rule of natural regulation at Yellowstone. The idea seems simple. It fits in nicely with the idea that the nature at the park has its own value and was not made to entertain people. But even after more than 30 years, there are strong disagreements about natural regulation and whether it can work.

Under natural regulation, the Park Service stopped killing or relocating elk. They thought natural elk deaths and the birth of fewer fawns could do the job of keeping too many elk from filling the park. But the elk kept breeding and their herds kept getting larger. Some people said the aspen and willow trees elk feed on were disappearing and grasses were being eaten down to the ground, causing soil to wash away and less grass to grow. They suggested it was too late for natural regulation. Maybe human beings had already changed the natural balance too much by killing wolves and mountain lions — which used to keep the numbers of elk down — and now the only solution was for us to do the job of thinning the herd. According to this view, people can't step out of the picture, because nature needs us.

The Park Service launched a major scientific research project — its largest ever — to find out if too many elk really were hurting the environment. The answers weren't simple and there is still much to learn, but the main answer park managers got from the study was that they were right. Natural regulation worked, but to keep at it, people needed to adjust how they looked at the environment. The elk did crop the grass low, and that looked bad to visitors from cities who were used to green lawns and to ranchers who would not allow their cattle to eat so much on their own land. But the scientists found that, however it might look, the elk weren't damaging the land — in fact, more plant life grew as a result. The elk herd might get too large in some years, but then a hard winter would come and kill off as many as a fourth of the animals.

But that doesn't mean natural regulation will work. People and our way of looking at the park are a part of the ecosystem now, and we may demand that it look the way we like (see "History & Culture: Human Ecology," in chapter 20). In 1988, natural regulation meant that a fire burned across a third of Yellowstone. The Park Service believes the great fire was a natural event that comes every century to renew the forest, but many people were upset that lovely green forests turned into fields of standing gray deadwood, which remain more than a decade later. The fire was too big to stop anyway, but afterward, people started questioning if natural regulation really was what they wanted.

In the winter of 1996–97, the idea of natural regulation ran into another problem. Bison began wandering out of Yellowstone. The herd had grown, and when a hard winter came, the animals went looking for food, ignoring the park boundary. Outside the park, natural regulation isn't the law. There, land is used to grow cattle, and cattle ranchers feared that their animals could catch a disease called brucellosis from the bison. Although the disease does not threaten humans, if cattle in Montana caught it, the ranchers would have to destroy their herds to keep it from spreading. Montana state officials couldn't allow that, so they shot the bison that left the park that winter — almost 1,100 of a herd of about 3,500 bison. Since then, the Park Service has set up a plan to chase, or haze, bison back into the park. If they won't go back, they are held in pens and checked for brucellosis; those that carry the disease are killed and the rest are let go.

The edge of the park is like the border between two worlds, with park rangers acting as border guards and customs agents for bison that cross the line. Outside the line, the world is run for people; inside, nature still rules.

## THE GREATER YELLOWSTONE ECOSYSTEM

The line around Yellowstone National Park doesn't make much sense for bison or other animals. Congress drew the line before anyone thought about ecosystems. Grand Teton, Rocky Mountain, and many other parks have the same problem. They don't include the whole area needed by their wildlife. Yellowstone and Grand Teton together include about 2.5 million acres of land, but the Greater Yellowstone Ecosystem is 18 million acres, including parts of seven national parks, three national wildlife refuges, and lots of state and private land. The related animals and plants in that region naturally depend on each other, and some of them, like grizzly bear and elk, travel over huge areas.

Seven herds of elk live in Yellowstone National Park, but only one herd spends both winter and summer there. When the snow comes to the Rockies, elk go down to valleys on the east side of the mountains, where not much snow falls and it is easier to move around and find food (see "Making Clouds & Rain," p. 279, for an explanation). Some elk migrate into the park on the Northern Range, while others descend from mountains at the center of Yellowstone and Grand Teton to lowlands where more people live.

Before settlers came to the valley of Jackson Hole, it was like a corridor for many of Yellowstone's elk to migrate in winter down from the mountains to the lowlands. But about 100 years ago, people started building the town of Jackson across the southern end of the valley. Their roads and buildings closed off the elk's route like a door at the end of the corridor. Elk that couldn't get to their winter feeding starved in great numbers at the north end of town. People hated to see that happen, so they began feeding the elk to get them through the winter. You still can see the herd of elk there in winter, feeding on bales of hay in the National Elk Refuge on the southern edge of Grand Teton National Park. It is a patch on a broken ecosystem, and it's not a perfect solution. With humans providing food, the elk's natural wintertime die-off doesn't happen, so the herd in Yellowstone in the summer is larger than it would be under natural regulation.

Human property lines often are straight and ignore the shape of the land. We don't have to worry about ecosystem areas because we can change the environment to meet our needs. If the weather is too cold, for example, you don't have to migrate, you can just turn up the heat in your house. Wildlife can't do that. They have to find a place that suits their needs, with the right temperature, food, water, and shelter. Such a place is called an animal's **habitat.**

Grizzly bears at Yellowstone eat elk calves, plants, rodents, dead animals, cutthroat trout, and berries. They like cool weather and a den in which to hibernate in the winter. Life here isn't easy for bears — there are fewer berries and fish than in places like the coast of Alaska, where the same species grows much larger and in greater numbers. A single male grizzly in the Great Yellowstone Ecosystem ranges over half a million to 1.3 million acres of ground to find what it needs to live (females use up to 350,000 acres). More than one bear can overlap in that area, but only so far: This habitat grows enough food for just one bear every 5 miles (if they were evenly spread out).

## HOW MUCH HABITAT?

Grizzlies used to live all over North America; but hunters got rid of them and they're not coming back. People use their habitat now. We've built cities, farms, and subdivisions on top of it. Each time a new house is built, there is less room left in our country for animals.

We have set aside the national parks as areas for wildlife habitat, but they are small islands in the large human habitat that covers most of the land. Some scientists think those islands of wildlife habitat are too small for grizzly bears to survive far into the future in the Lower 48 without being fed by people. The Greater Yellowstone Ecosystem is their last good hope.

Wildlife habitat is expensive. Some of the best habitat is also good for feeding livestock. Farmers or ranchers own that land, or the government owns it and lets them use it to help produce food. Everyone who eats needs America's farms and ranches, so we all have a stake in these decisions. Instead of wildlife habitat, parks tend to focus on scenery, which animals don't care much about. It has always been easier to make parks of rugged mountain areas, beautiful country that people don't want to use anyway. Unfortunately, not many animals want to live in the mountains in the winter, either.

Everyone agreed that the rocky Teton Mountains themselves should be set aside as Grand Teton National Park, but when conservationists started talking about adding the flat, grassy land of Jackson Hole to the park, they had a fight on their hands. Ranchers were using the land to raise livestock and to run dude ranches for visitors. They thought the

- **Crazy Games:** You start with a normal card game or word game, like the one above. When his or her turn comes around, each person gets to make up a new rule, which everyone then has to follow. The point is to make the game silly and complicated — for example, that every third person has to sing his or her part.
- **License Plate Collecting:** This game is hard to resist at the big western parks, where you can get almost all the state license plates very quickly. To make it challenging, also look for the Canadian provinces and the different plate designs from each state. Keep your list on a piece of paper. Sightings of rare plates are good conversation starters with other families, since everyone does it.
- **Postcard Collection:** Make a journal of your trip by buying postcards everywhere you go (even gas stations) for your child to put in a cheap photo album or otherwise make into a book. He or she can write on the back of the postcards, or draw pictures, and put them in the album. Rearranging, editing, and showing off the book will use up a lot of time. And when you get home, it's a good souvenir.
- **Joint Storytelling or Drawing:** In the verbal version, each person adds a sentence to a story in turn, which usually gets silly fast. In the visual version, kids take turns adding to a picture — preferably one of actions or mishaps, like a Richard Scarry illustration.
- **Interpreting the Landscape:** Talk about how the land you are driving through might have come to look the way it does. Why are the hills or fields shaped as they are? Why do certain plants grow there? What do the people do to make a living, and how has that affected the way things look? What might it have looked like before people arrived?
- **Scavenger Hunt:** A grown-up calls for an item — a boat trailer, a sign with a certain word, a truck carrying food — and the kids holler out and get a reward when they see it. Try a couple of things at once.
- **Exercise Breaks:** Stop for a spontaneous break for foot races, a game of tag, or just romping around.
- **Real Conversation:** The time in the car is a perfect opportunity to find out more about your kids. The best way to keep a conversation going is to ask questions. Make a game of it by taking turns asking each other questions.

needs of people were more important than the needs of wild animals. The park was finished only when a very rich man, John D. Rockefeller, Jr., secretly bought the ranch land and donated it to the government (see "History: Rockefeller to the Rescue!" in chapter 15). Most of the wildlife habitat in Grand Teton National Park is on the added land in Jackson Hole, not in the original mountain area of the park.

Rocky Mountain National Park is like Grand Teton would have been without the lower land that Rockefeller helped save. Rocky's protected wildlife habitat is much too small and changed by human settlement to work the way it used to. Elk leave the park in the winter for valleys in the mountain's eastern rain shadow, where they often wander in the streets of Estes Park. Before the Estes Park valley became a ranch and then a town, wolves, grizzly bear, and other predators would kill the elk, keeping the herd from growing too large. But people killed off the predators and the remaining habitat is too small for them to come back. Now, to reduce the herd, hunters kill elk when they migrate out of the park.

People sometimes can help wildlife survive in small pieces of remaining habitat. In the spring and early summer, bighorn sheep at Rocky Mountain visit Horseshoe Park, where they can find certain minerals they need. The bighorn's winter diet doesn't give it everything it needs for good health, but by licking or eating the ground at Horseshoe Park, the sheep add what their usual food lacks. To get there, however, they have to cross Highway 34. Bighorn are skittish around people and they were afraid to cross the highway until Park Service posted rangers as crossing guards to help them get over. With that help, the sheep have spent more time eating the minerals and their health has improved. It's a good solution, but a better one would be not to have the highway there at all. But no one is talking about doing that: Even in the parks, human needs often come first.

## THE WHOLE ECOSYSTEM

The people who believe most strongly in wilderness dream of protecting more complete ecosystems. They want to put together larger safe areas for wildlife where the animals can live in natural combinations as they did before white settlers came. When forest fires break out, they'll burn, clearing away the old trees and brush and opening pinecones. Wolves, grizzly bears, and mountain lions will roam freely, feeding on the elk and keeping them in balance with the plant life they need. Human land uses will be kept away.

But we'll still need meat from cattle, wool from sheep, grain to make bread, roads to travel on, and forests to grow trees for wood and paper. People will still control the earth. Today, we use 3% of the United States for national parks; 4% for cities, towns, and roads; and more than 40% for raising food. Every day when we decide what to eat, what to wear, and how to live, we also decide how much more of the earth we need to use, how much we can save, and how much we can give back to the wilderness.

# CHAPTER 14

# Yellowstone National Park

My cousin Carl, his wife, Teresa, and daughter, Carla, each had a goal at Yellowstone. Carl wanted to see geothermal features. Theresa wanted to see waterfalls. Carla wanted to see big animals. They entered the park at West Yellowstone, headed toward Norris, and within the first hour saw boiling water shooting out of the ground, water roaring over Gibbon Falls, and elk wandering near the road. Who knew it would be so easy? The same thing happened when we first arrived. I stopped to look into a pasture where elk wandered among plumes of steam rising from the ground. I thought I had stumbled on the kind of scene photographers wait years for, and it was hard to get back into the car and go on. Ten minutes later, there was the same sort of vista again. My wife, Barbara, hoped earnestly to see elk and bison; by the time we left, she was cursing elk and bison for all the traffic jams they were causing.

With so much to see right by the road, driving can get addictive. But, as with other addictions, there is a price to pay. In this case, the price is traffic and crowding. The trick *at Yellowstone is to say "enough," break from the car after seeing some highlights, and go deeper into the country. Fewer than 1% of Yellowstone visitors ever get more than one-quarter mile from the road, so it takes little effort to leave people behind. We thought we'd go crazy in the Canyon area one day: too many people, too hectic. Then we set out on the Clear Lake/Ribbon Lake Trail, and found ourselves walking over grassy, flower-specked hills, a herd of bison in the distance, and finding a fascinating white waste of an acidic thermal area. And no other people.

This is the center of the country's largest area of preserved lands outside Alaska. Going there and staying in a car the whole time makes as much sense as going to an art museum and refusing to take off your sunglasses.

## BEST THINGS TO DO

- Take a look at the geyser basins in the Old Faithful or Norris Geyser Basin areas and climb over the weird shapes of Mammoth Hot Springs.

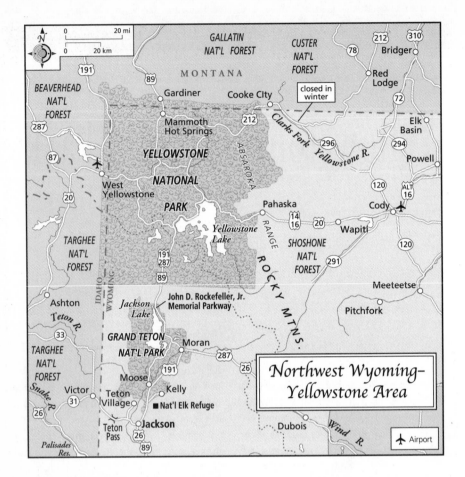

Map labels:

0 20 mi
0 20 km

GALLATIN NAT'L FOREST
CUSTER NAT'L FOREST
212  310  Bridger
78
Red Lodge
72
MONTANA
191
89
BEAVERHEAD NAT'L FOREST
Gardiner  Cooke City
closed in winter
287
Mammoth Hot Springs
212
Elk Basin
87
YELLOWSTONE
296
294
Powell
20
West Yellowstone
NATIONAL
120
ALT 16
PARK
Pahaska
Cody
ABSAROKA RANGE
14 16  20  Wapiti
TARGHEE NAT'L FOREST
Yellowstone Lake
191 287
SHOSHONE NAT'L FOREST
291
120
89
Meeteetse
IDAHO WYOMING
Ashton
Jackson Lake
John D. Rockefeller, Jr. Memorial Parkway
ROCKY MTNS.
Pitchfork
Teton R.
33
GRAND TETON NAT'L PARK
Moran
287
26
TARGHEE NAT'L FOREST
Moose
191
Snake R.
Victor  Teton Village
31
Kelly
Nat'l Elk Refuge
26
Teton Pass
Jackson
26
Dubois
Wind R.
89
Palisades Res.

Northwest Wyoming–
Yellowstone Area

✈ Airport

- See huge herds of bison and elk wandering through the meadows of the Hayden Valley or Northern Range.
- Take a day hike or an overnight on one of America's best networks of trails.
- Ride horseback on Yellowstone's spectacular Northern Range.

- Come in winter to see the countryside under deep snow by snow coach or on cross-country skis.

See "Activities" (p. 325).

# Park History: A Good Idea

The story of Yellowstone National Park is simple, and it's one that helped to change the world. This is the first national park not only in the United States, but anywhere on earth. Yellowstone started the idea of national parks, and with it the idea that some natural places should be preserved as God created them.

Just 125 years later, it seems strange that people didn't always value wilderness as we do today. But when Yellowstone was set aside as a national park, much more of the natural world was left unchanged. Explorers were still discovering parts of the planet. To most people, the world seemed limitless. Wild land and

**Yellowstone National Park.** P.O. Box 168, Yellowstone National Park, WY 82190-0168. ☎ **307/ 344-7381.** TDD 307/344-2386. www.nps.gov/yell.

**Yellowstone National Park Lodges,** operated by AmFac Parks and Resorts, park concessionaire. P.O. Box 165, Yellowstone National Park, WY 82190-0165. ☎ **307/344-7311.** TDD 307/ 344-5395. www.travelyellowstone.com.

**The Yellowstone Association** (for books, maps, programs, and the Yellowstone Institute). P.O. Box 117, Yellowstone National Park, WY 82190. ☎ **307/344-2293.** Fax 307/344-2486. Retail sales or course catalogs ☎ 877/967-0900 or 406/848-2450; Institute 307/344-2294. www. YellowstoneAssociation.org.

**Gallatin National Forest.** Federal Building (P.O. Box 130), Bozeman, MT 58771. ☎ **406/ 587-6701.** www.fs.fed.us/r1/gallatin.

**Shoshone National Forest.** 808 Meadow Lane, Cody, WY 82414. ☎ **307/527-6241.** www. fs.fed.us/r2/shoshone.

**Cooke City Chamber of Commerce.** P.O. Box 1071, Cooke City, MT 59020. ☎ **406/838-2495** or 406/838-2272.

**Gardiner Chamber of Commerce.** P.O. Box 81, Gardiner, MT 59030. ☎ **406/848-7971.** Fax 406/848-2446. www.gardinerchamber.com.

**West Yellowstone Chamber of Commerce.** P.O. Box 458, West Yellowstone, MT 59758. ☎ **406/646-7701.** www.westyellowstonechamber.com.

**The Total Yellowstone Page.** www.Yellowstone-Natl-Park.com.

---

animals didn't have the same value they do for us today, partly because there was so much. That feeling probably had something to do with Yellowstone becoming a park, too. Why not set aside this one special place, when there was so much of the West left to settle? Later, creating the smaller Grand Teton National Park, just to the south, was much harder because people wanted the land for other uses.

Native Americans used Yellowstone mostly in the summer. As in other high Rocky Mountain country, they came to hunt when the snow melted, then returned to warmer lowlands when winter arrived. The Crow, Shoshone, Blackfoot, Arapahoe, Flathead, and Nez Perce were all using the area that's now the park when white men arrived. The area has many archaeological sites of primitive Native American camps, some in areas around

geysers — disproving stories that the Indians were afraid of them.

A Shoshone band called the Sheepeaters, who lived by hunting mountain sheep, probably used hot water from the geyser basins to straighten the sheep's curled horn for excellent bows. Other ancient tribes, not identified for certain, mined Obsidian Cliff, in the northwest area of the park on the road between Mammoth Hot Springs and Norris Geyser Basin. (Don't break the law and help destroy the park by taking obsidian, or any other rocks. You can buy obsidian from outside parks in rock shops.) Obsidian is a glassy rock made by thick lava that comes to the surface and cools very quickly. (See "Read Aloud: Why Both Snow & Granite Sparkle," in chapter 16, "Rocky Mountain National Park," for an explanation of how it forms.) Although it's

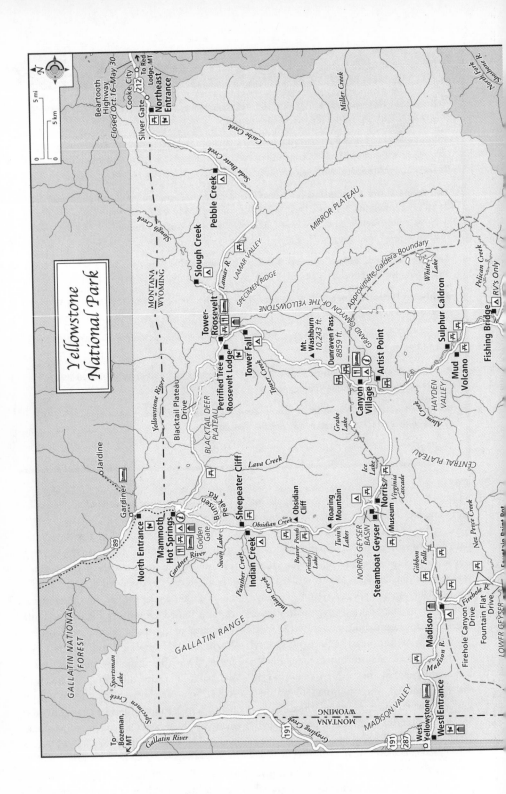

Yellowstone National Park

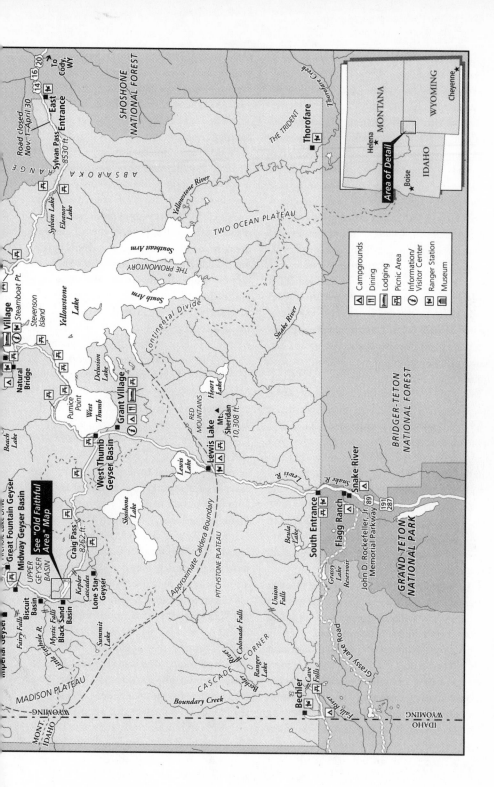

usually black, obsidian is natural glass, and it breaks in sharp flakes. If you don't have metal, flakes of obsidian make the best possible points for spears and arrows. Native Americans traded rocks from Obsidian Cliff with other tribes who could give them valuable items from other parts of North America. By studying the exact mixture of elements in Yellowstone obsidian, scientists have proved that ancient points found far away came from here. They've found this obsidian in archaeological sites in Ohio, Washington, North Dakota, Colorado, Manitoba, Alberta, Saskatchewan, and other, closer places.

Yellowstone's history of white settlement is unique: No sooner was it officially discovered than it became a park. "Discovered" is a funny word, because what it means always depends on your point of view. Native Americans discovered Yellowstone at least 10,000 years ago. John Colter, a member of the Lewis and Clark expedition, first passed through while hunting for furs in 1807. Fur trappers wandered through the area for decades after Colter. But part of discovery means reporting what you find back to people who don't know about it, and having them believe you. People probably made fun of Colter for his descriptions of the place, which they must have thought had to be lies. Most of the settlers didn't know how to read and write, and even if they had, it's doubtful leaders back East would have paid attention.

Gold prospectors began to come through in the 1860s and came across the geysers and hot springs that the trappers and Colter had found before them. That inspired a group from Helena, Montana, to explore the area in 1869. Their report of the canyons and geysers was rejected by East Coast publications as not believable, but it interested Henry Washburn, the official surveyor for the Montana Territory. (A surveyor is a person who measures and maps land.) He visited the next year. Members of his group returned to the East and lectured about what they had seen. Dr. Ferdinand Hayden, director of the U.S.

Geological and Geographical Survey, heard one of the lectures in Washington, D.C. His job was to draw the map of America. The next year, 1871, he went out West and "discovered" Yellowstone, bringing back photographs and paintings to prove it.

When you're expecting to see a geyser, it's amazing enough. Imagine how you would feel if you were hiking across the country and saw one shoot off in front of you, completely unexpectedly! Geysers show up in only a few places in the world, most of them here, and discovering them was big news. People starting thinking right away about how to make money from them. Soon after Hayden returned from his trip, the Northern Pacific Railroad joined him in pushing to have the thermal area protected as a park. The railroad wanted to carry tourists to the area on its trains. The law setting aside the park passed quickly, and President Grant signed it on March 1, 1872.

Yellowstone was not the first land in the United States to be preserved. Earlier, Congress gave California the Yosemite Valley and some areas of big sequoia trees, with the agreement that the land would not be used except as a state park. California later gave the land back to be a national park (see "History: Fight for the Valley," in chapter 18, "Yosemite National Park"). But Yellowstone was the world's first national park, and here people have fought hardest over the years about what a national park should be.

When Yellowstone became a park, land in the West was pretty much open for people to use as they liked, taking whatever valuable minerals or trees they might find. In the East, most land belonged to someone, and lines on a map showed who owned what. In the West, land was free for the taking. Poor people from the East could move here and get land of their own without much money. They would find a place they liked, mark the boundaries, and file papers at a government office. If they built a farm or ranch and lived on the land for a few years — called "proving their claim" — they normally received permanent ownership of the homestead. The first to arrive homesteaded the best land, closest to a railroad line or in valleys good for farming. The next families might go a bit farther out. Much of the private land in the West was settled this way, one homestead at a time.

At first, creating the national park just meant no one could homestead at Yellowstone. That was easy enough to agree on, because no one wanted to homestead there anyway. The area was too rugged and too far from towns to be worth much. After Yellowstone became a park, people still treated it as open land. They killed animals by the thousands for fur and took away whatever they wanted, breaking pieces off geysers and even plugging them up with coins and garbage. In 1886, the U.S. Army took over control of the park with the mission of protecting it. The army stopped the hunting and patrolled the backcountry to keep out poachers, people who kill wildlife when hunting is not allowed. Strange as it seems to us today, the soldiers thought of wolves, cougars, and coyotes as poachers, too, and killed them to keep them from killing other animals. People soon learned that the "good" animals in the park couldn't be protected without also protecting some of their habitat outside the park's boundaries. Forest land was then set aside around Yellowstone in

1891, stopping homesteading and uncontrolled hunting there too. President Theodore Roosevelt made these areas into the first national forests in 1905.

Eventually, all of the West was divided up into either private land or government land, each area with a certain purpose. The private land came in homesteads, railroad lands, and other government gifts. The government lands were national parks, national forests, national wildlife refuges, and land controlled by the Bureau of Land Management, called the BLM. Each kind of government land is managed by a different agency with a different purpose. Most of the land, including the national forests and BLM lands, are managed for multiple use. That means they aren't just for recreation and wildlife habitat, but also for logging, mining, and livestock range.

The great political debates in the West today are about how each of these lands should be used — if they can be used up, if they should be used in a sustainable way that can go on forever, or if they should be preserved and set aside like the national parks. Lands that are preserved for nature and wildlife are a small part of what's left from the old West. Yellowstone National Park, the first of these lands, is still the largest in the lower 48 states.

# ORIENTATION

## THE PARK

Yellowstone is a square roughly 60 miles on a side lying across the Continental Divide. It's mostly in northwest Wyoming, with a strip of Idaho on the west and Montana on the north. Much of the park is a mountain plateau 7,000 to 8,000 feet high, with mountains over 10,000 feet ringing it. The park's **Northern Range** is a lower, grassy valley, with grandly rolling terrain. Geysers and other thermal features show up all over the park, but the most

impressive are on the **western side** of the park, at Old Faithful, in the southwest quadrant, Norris Geyser Basin, near the midpoint, and Mammoth Hot Springs, in the northwest corner. On the **eastern side** of the park, the water of the Yellowstone River has created the most notable attractions. It flows north from the huge Yellowstone Lake, in the southeast part of the park, and through the impressive Grand Canyon of the Yellowstone and Tower Fall in the northeast part.

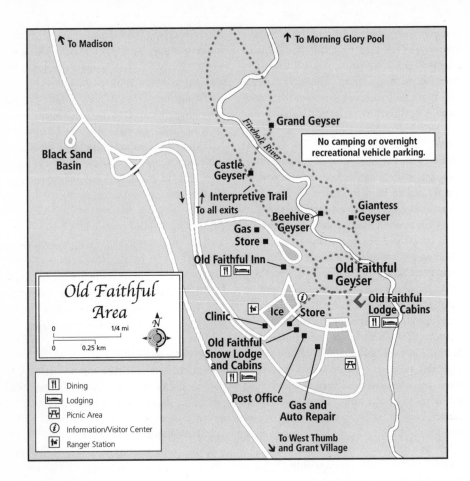

**Old Faithful Area**

To Madison

To Morning Glory Pool

Grand Geyser

No camping or overnight recreational vehicle parking.

Black Sand Basin

Castle Geyser

Interpretive Trail
To all exits

Giantess Geyser

Beehive Geyser

Gas Store

Old Faithful Inn

Old Faithful Geyser

Clinic

Ice Store

Old Faithful Lodge Cabins

Old Faithful Snow Lodge and Cabins

Post Office

Gas and Auto Repair

To West Thumb and Grant Village

*Firehole River*

0        1/4 mi
0    0.25 km
N

Dining
Lodging
Picnic Area
Information/Visitor Center
Ranger Station

# THE ROADS

The road system at Yellowstone has two connected loops, like an "8," with five tails leading to entrances in five directions (described below). Most visitors tour around these loops, park at the overlooks, and stop to watch geysers and take nature walks along the way. At a fast, superficial pace, each road loop takes a day of touring. Even driving across the park without stopping takes half a day because the roads wind and the traffic is frequently backed up by people looking at wildlife or scenery. My advice is to spend a week on one side of the park and get out of the car. The open route in the winter is the link through the Northern Range from the north entrance, at Mammoth Hot Springs, to the northeast entrance, near

Cooke City, Montana. Other roads close in November and reopen in April or May, depending on snow conditions.

# VISITOR AREAS

Choose one or two of the series of developed areas in the park for your base. Six areas have lodgings and visitor centers, and several others have campgrounds, museums, or other attractions. Details are in the appropriate sections below; here I've summarized each in an overview, moving clockwise from the north.

## Mammoth Hot Springs

At the north entrance, near the town of Gardiner, Montana, this historic area includes the park headquarters, two restaurants, a post office, historic lodgings, a store, a gas station, a clinic, a campground, and the most extensive visitor center and commercial services. Nature walks circle the bizarre, terraced hot springs. The terrain is relatively low, warm, and open.

## Tower–Roosevelt

This quieter, less developed area in the northeast part of the park has a ranger station and rough lodgings in cabins at Roosevelt Lodge. It's a center for horseback riding in the open, grassy land of the Northern Range. There are a restaurant, store, and gas station. Tower Fall and the campground are a few miles south of Roosevelt Lodge.

## Canyon Village

Near the falls on the Grand Canyon of the Yellowstone, the village is crowded with more than 500 cabins, a hotel, a huge campground, a general store, three restaurants and a cafeteria, a gas station, a post office, public showers and laundry, and a visitor center. It lies at the eastern connecting point of the upper and lower loop roads.

## Fishing Bridge, Lake Village & Bridge Bay

These three areas, within a few miles of each other on the northern shore of Yellowstone Lake, have lots of lodging and camping choices, from fine historic lodgings to falling-down cabins. There are restaurants, stores, a post office, and a gas station. The marina and a large campground are at Bridge Bay and an RV park is at Fishing Bridge.

## Grant Village

On Yellowstone Lake along the route to the south entrance, the charmless village has three restaurants, a hotel, a large campground, stores, public showers and laundry, a post office, a gas station, and a visitor center. The lakeside West Thumb geyser basin is just to the north.

## Old Faithful

The famous geyser is surrounded by a semicircle of hotels (including the park's best and worst), a visitor center, stores, restaurants, a post office, a gas station, and a clinic. Lots of other geysers are nearby on nature walks. This is the only major developed area without a campground, but there's one to the north at Madison. The stretch of road in between is the park's richest in geysers and other thermal features.

## Norris

There are two museums and a great campground near the spectacular Norris Geyser Basin but no lodgings or other commercial services. This is the connecting point of the two road loops on the west side, opposite the other intersection at Canyon Village, 12 miles east.

## GATEWAY TOWNS

Details on the towns appear below in the appropriate sections. Here's an overview.

## West Yellowstone

This Montana boomtown at the park's west entrance is the most developed and touristy of Yellowstone's gateways, with large chain hotels, a museum, a theater, and a small zoo. The town is high and snowy. There's an airport that's open in the summer.

## Gardiner

Near the north entrance and Mammoth Hot Springs, Gardiner, Montana, is a tourist-oriented town with lots of motels, but it still has some real Western character. Come here for rafting trips on the Yellowstone River, outside the park. The low elevation helps keep deep snow away.

## Cooke City

Cooke City, Montana, is a small town in a beautiful setting, with basic motel rooms. It stands outside the northeast entrance.

# MAKING THE ARRANGEMENTS

## WHEN TO GO

The park's main visitor season is July and August. At this elevation, the weather is seldom too hot. Brief afternoon thunderstorms are common.

Until mid-June, trails remain snowy or muddy at the 7,000-foot elevation of most of the park, and some facilities don't open. Campgrounds open between mid-May and mid-June, except for Mammoth, which is open all year. Yellowstone Lake ice generally clears in May, but sometimes doesn't go out until early June.

Spring-break visits aren't practical, with the park still largely snow-bound and few facilities open. Campgrounds start closing in early September. In September and October, crowds are gone and hotel rates drop steeply, but lodgings start closing in stages in early September. The air gets frosty at night in October, with few campgrounds left open. Roads close with the November snows. The Mammoth Hot Springs Hotel and Old Faithful Snow Lodge are open for the winter and summer seasons, but not in late fall and early spring.

The park is beautiful in snow, and wildlife congregates at the geothermal hot spots. At this writing, however, the most popular activity, snowmobiling, is being phased out, with the last, limited rides planned in the winter of 2002–03 (See "Note: No More Snowmachines," p. 329.) Visitors will still be able to get around in buslike snow coaches and recreate by cross-country skiing. The winter visitor season lasts from late December to the 2nd week in March. For tips on planning a winter vacation, see "Winter Sports & Sightseeing" (p. 329).

## HOW MUCH TIME TO SPEND

Just driving around the park and seeing the highlights takes 3 days, and for a good visit you need at least 5 days and preferably more time for hiking, boating, riding, and other activities away from the road. With 2 weeks, you could try various activities in more than one area of the park, or add a side trip to Grand Teton National Park (see chapter 15, "Grand Teton National Park").

## HOW FAR TO PLAN AHEAD

Yellowstone gets more than 3 million visitors each year, and virtually all spend the night. Hotels and five campgrounds in the park take reservations up to a year ahead, through the park concessionaire, Yellowstone National Park Lodges (contact information is under "Yellowstone Address Book," p. 301). You can get a campsite 6 months ahead of a summer date, but choices start to fill up after that. Seven campgrounds managed by the Park Service give sites away on a first-come, first-served basis; but they can be difficult to get and you shouldn't count on them. Backcountry sites are easier to get, but top choices are awarded in a lottery on April 1 for the whole year. If you need lodgings, you should have your rooms booked 4 to 6 months in advance. Reserve a table in the better hotel dining rooms at the same time, because they, too, book months ahead (you can always cancel). Hotels outside the park have openings later, but because anything near Yellowstone fills up in the summer, last-minute planning isn't a good option. The concessionaire enforces a 2-day cancellation policy in the summer, 14 days in the winter; you may find a room by checking when those deadlines hit, or by grabbing a room the morning of a stay if a guest doesn't stay over.

## READING UP

These items are for sale at visitor centers or by mail order or online from **The Yellowstone Association** (☎ **877/967-0090;** www.yellowstoneassociation.org). You will also find a deep mine of travel and scholarly information on the park's website, at www.nps.gov/yell.

## WEATHER CHART: OLD FAITHFUL AVERAGES

|  | AVG. HIGH (°F) | AVG. LOW (°F) | SNOWFALL (TOTAL IN.) |
|---|---|---|---|
| Dec.–Feb. | 27–33 | -2–1 | 119 |
| March | 40 | 9 | 33 |
| April | 47 | 18 | 21 |
| May | 56 | 27 | 9 |
| June | 65 | 34 | 2 |
| July–August | 73 | 36–39 | 0 |
| September | 64 | 28 | 2 |
| October | 51 | 20 | 7 |
| November | 35 | 7 | 34 |

*The elevation of Old Faithful is approximately 7,200 feet.*

**Hiking:** *Yellowstone Trails,* by Mark Marschall (The Yellowstone Association), is full of useful details and is organized to help find a hike at your ability level and near where you are. **Maps:** The park is too big to fit on one useful trail map, but American Adventure Association publishes two adequate paper maps each covering half, for $4. Much better maps, in a quartet to cover the park, are published on plastic by Trails Illustrated, for $8 each, and show the locations and numbers of all the backcountry campsites and trailheads compatible with the park's backcountry permit process. **Geology:** *Windows into the Earth,* By Robert B. Smith and Lee J. Siegel (Oxford University Press), is a stunningly illustrated and clearly written explanation of the geological processes of Yellowstone and Grand Teton national parks. **Ouch:** *Death in Yellowstone,* By Lee Whittlesey (Roberts Rinehart), chronicles more than 300 deaths at the park, including every one that wasn't caused by a vehicle. The morbid fascination doesn't last through all 300, but you will likely end up more cautious.

## GETTING THERE
### By Car

Yellowstone isn't near any large cities. Salt Lake City is a 350-mile drive, Denver 600, and Seattle 800. The closest interstate east-west highway is **I-90,** and the nearest north-south route is **I-15.** Two-lane U.S. highways enter the park at five places on routes that are fairly easy to follow on any highway map.

### By Air

There are several towns where you can fly in and rent a car linking to hubs in Denver, Salt Lake City, or Seattle. Air fares seem to differ greatly for each portal, depending on where you are coming from. If that's not a factor, you can plan around the driving distance to the point at which you plan to enter the park.

If you're staying at Mammoth Hot Springs, you can fly into **Bozeman,** Montana, 79 miles away. Bozeman is served by **Delta (☎ 800/ 221-1212;** www.delta.com), **Northwest (☎ 800/225-2525;** www.nwa.com), and other carriers. You can rent cars there from **Budget (☎ 800/527-0700** or 406/586-2575; www.budget.com) or **Practical Car Rental (☎ 406/586-8373).**

If you're staying in Grant Village, Jackson is 55 miles from the south entrance, covered under "Getting There," in chapter 15 (you can rent an RV there, too).

Cody, Wyoming, is 53 miles from the east entrance. Cody is served by **United Express**

(☎ 800/241-6522; www.ual.com) and **Skywest** (☎ 800/453-9417 or 307/ 587-9740; www.skywest.com). Car rentals are available from **Hertz** (☎ 800/654-3131 or 307/587-2914; www.hertz.com) or **Budget** (☎ 800/527-0700 or 307/587-6066; www. budget.com).

West Yellowstone, Montana, is at the west entrance. It's served only during the summer by **Skywest** (☎ 800/453-9417 or 406/ 646-7351), with car rentals available from **Budget** (☎ 800/527-0700 or 406/646-7882; budget.com) and **Big Sky Car Rentals** (☎ 406/646-9564).

If you don't mind driving a little farther, have your travel agent shop for ticket and car rates at Idaho Falls and Billings. Major carriers and car-rental agencies serve both.

## What to Pack
### Clothing

Summer weather may call for short or long pants and shirts, sweaters, or jackets, depending on the day and elevation. Summer highs are in the 70s, but afternoon thunderstorms are common. Summer lows are typically in the 40s, and get lower as you go higher. Everyone will do a lot of walking, even if you don't go on hikes, just to see the geysers and hot springs, so bring good shoes. Two fine restaurants demand better than outdoor clothing, so if you plan to eat there, bring nice casual clothes.

In the winter, West Yellowstone is often the coldest spot in the United States outside Alaska. Temperatures below zero Fahrenheit are no surprise. For outdoor sports such as cross-country skiing, bring layers of synthetic long underwear, fleece pants and tops, and wind clothes. For more sedentary sightseeing, add heavy winter clothing, including parkas and well-insulated winter boots.

### Gear

As at all hiking-oriented parks, a good baby backpack makes your group more mobile. A stroller is usable on most nature trails around the geysers and other famous sites. Quality summer-weight camping gear is okay for Yellowstone from June to early September with an extra layer for especially cold nights (long synthetic underwear or a heavy bag to cover all of you). Your tent should be ready for brief, heavy rain. It gets quite chilly in the fall, when you'll need winter-weight gear.

# Where to Spend the Night

## Camping
### Park Service Campgrounds

There are 12 campgrounds in the park, with varying facilities. An RV park and the four largest, most developed campgrounds are operated by the concessionaire, Yellowstone National Park Lodges, and they do a better job than the park service of making the grounds comfortable and welcoming. You can reserve up to a year ahead, and should call at least 6 months ahead for the high season (see "Yellowstone Address Book," p. 301). The other seven campgrounds, generally quieter, more isolated choices with larger sites, are run by the Park Service and don't take reservations.

During July and August, people often show up at these campgrounds early in the morning to grab a site from someone leaving. The last sites usually go at the 10am checkout time. It's not a good idea to count on one of these sites with no fall-back option, especially on a travel day. (These patterns change, however; in 2000, sites went vacant many nights.) At six of the more developed campgrounds, RV generators are allowed (noted in the listings below). They can run only from 8am to 8pm, but that can be enough to drive you crazy if you're tenting next door. Fishing Bridge RV Park is the only campground with hookups; generators there can run from 7am to 10pm.

## Campgrounds Accepting Reservations

These campgrounds, managed by Yellowstone National Park Lodges, resemble Park Service campgrounds in most ways but have more generous features, including soap in the bathrooms and vending machines for ice, newspapers, and soft drinks. All have flush toilets and dump stations, and all allow tents and RVs and generator use.

**Bridge Bay.** At Yellowstone Lake, near the marina. $15 per site. 430 sites. Closed mid-Sept to mid-May.

This huge campground has an attractive half and an area to avoid. The good sites have pine trees and sit on a higher bench overlooking Yellowstone Lake across a grassy meadow, including loops E through J (F is best). The other area, with loops A through D, is a large, flat field, completely without screening; full of tents and RVs, it looks like an updated Civil War encampment. You can ask for a certain site when you reserve, but it is not guaranteed; so arrive early if you can. The campground is near the marina and across the road from Yellowstone Lake, making it a good choice for anglers.

**Canyon.** In Canyon Village. $15 per site. 272 sites. Showers, laundry. Closed Sept–May.

This thickly wooded campground sits on a hillside above the hotel, visitor center, and other services; at 8,000 feet, it's the highest campground in the park and closes early in September. If you want to be near showers, restaurants, and a full general store, it's a good choice. Mountain trails and the Grand Canyon of Yellowstone are nearby.

**Fishing Bridge RV Park.** North end of Yellowstone Lake. $28 per site, full hookups, 4 people; $3 per extra adult. 344 sites; hard-sided RVs only. Showers, laundry. Closed Oct to mid-May.

This RV park is green and pleasant, but the sites are small and closely spaced, with room for little more than your rig and a lawn chair, and they lack tables or fire pits. The lake is across the highway. The visitor center and other facilities are a little way down the road.

**Grant Village.** At Yellowstone Lake, on the way to the south entrance. $15 per site. 425 sites. Showers, laundry. Closed Oct to mid-June.

The campground goes on and on along the shore of the lake. Although closely spaced, the sites are mostly wooded, and some have good lake views. Restaurants, the visitor center, and other comforts are nearby. The location makes some sense if you plan to spend time at Old Faithful, which has no campground (Madison Campground makes even more sense), but Grant isn't close to most of the park's most interesting areas.

**Madison.** Near the west entrance. $5 per site. 280 sites. Closed Nov–Apr.

The campground is in a pleasant spot among small pines on the banks of joining rivers. It's the closest campground to Old Faithful and a good base to explore the geyser basins, but it doesn't have a park village nearby to add crowds and activity. Sites, however, are small and not well screened. The lower elevation means a longer season and warmer air, and the park's best river swimming is from the banks at the campground and nearby on the Firehole River, water that is warmed by the earth (see "Swimming," p. 328).

## First-Come, First-Served Campgrounds

These campgrounds, managed by the Park Service, are more primitive than those above, which the concessionaire runs. RVs or tents are allowed at all, but most do not allow generators, a plus for tenters. Be at the gates early to get a site.

**Indian Creek.** South of Mammoth Hot Springs. $10 per site. 75 sites. Vault toilets; no generator use. Closed mid-Sept to May.

The campground is quiet, well off the park road, and the nearby creek is good for fishing or swimming. The area burned, and young pines now screen the many well-separated grassy sites, although some are built too closely together. The vault toilets weren't in great shape when we visited.

**Lewis Lake.** Near the south entrance. $10 per site. 85 sites. Vault toilets, no generator use. Closed Nov to mid-June.

Most campsites here sit far apart, in thick forest on the edge of a placid mountain lake, although not near much else. The lovely lakeside sites are walk-in only. A boat launch and dock make a portal to the backcountry, if you bring along a boat, canoe, or kayak.

**Mammoth.** North end of the park, at Mammoth Hot Springs. $12 per site. 85 sites. Flush toilets, dump station; generators okay. Open all year.

The campground occupies a bend in the highway that leads down to the north entrance and Gardiner. It's on an exposed hillside below the developed area, where the hotel, visitor center, and many services are located. Owing to the low elevation, it can be warm in summer and stays open in winter. Sites are well separated among grass, sagebrush, cottonwood, aspen, and juniper trees. It's a pretty spot, if a bit noisy because of the road.

**Norris.** Near Norris Geyser Basin, west side of the park. $12 per site. 116 sites. Flush toilets; generator use permitted. Closed Oct to mid-May.

Norris is one of my favorite Yellowstone campgrounds. Sites are large, arrayed on a grassy hillside among large pine trees. A creek and the ranger museum are at the bottom of the hill. Ice and firewood are for sale, but there's no busy park village area nearby. The location makes a convenient base, near the Norris Geyser Basin 12 miles from the Canyon area, 21 miles south of Mammoth, and 30 miles north of Old Faithful, and near several trailheads.

**Pebble Creek.** Near the northeast entrance. $10 per site. 32 sites. Vault toilets; no generator use. Closed Oct–May.

This is another quiet, out-of-the-way campground, down a gravel spur from the park road.

**Slough Creek.** East of the Tower-Roosevelt area. $10 per site. 29 sites. Pit toilets; no generator use. Closed Nov–May.

This isolated campground is tucked away in a river valley several miles up a gravel road from the highway.

**Tower Fall.** Across from the falls parking lot. $10 per site. 32 sites. Vault toilets; no generator use. Closed mid-Sept to mid-May.

The campground is on a steep hillside well above the road in a dramatic area on the edge of the mountains overlooking the Northern Range.

# Backcountry Permits

The best campsites in Yellowstone are away from the roads, reached by hiking trails or, on the lakes, by boat. The 300 backcountry sites have no facilities, just a place to hang your food away from the bears. You must be self-sufficient, but if you're up for it, it's simply magical to be off in your own beautiful place without other people. Backcountry sites are in less demand than hotel rooms or developed campground sites, and you can almost always get one somewhere, without a reservation, 48 hours in advance. But if you have a special area in mind, submit a reservation application in advance.

You'll need permit application forms and a copy of the *Backcountry Trip Planner*, a newspaper full of information and a map showing site locations. To order them, write to the Park Service at the address listed under "Yellowstone Address Book" (p. 301), call the main backcountry office at ☎ **307/344-2160** or 307/344-2163, or download them from www.nps.gov/yell/publications/pdfs/backcountry/index.htm (the files are quite large). You'll also need detailed topographic maps and a trail guidebook (see "Reading Up," p. 308).

Submit your advance reservations by mail or in person along with a $20 reservation fee. The fee is good for your whole trip, but you must pay again each time you start at a trailhead. Checks, traveler's checks, or money orders are accepted. Have your application in by April 1 to be entered in an initial random drawing for sites with more than one application. After that date, sites are assigned as requests come in. The Park Service will send you a confirmation, which you must turn in at a backcountry desk by 10am on the day of the trip to get your permit.

Forty percent of sites are held back for walk-ins, with no reservation fee, starting at opening time 2 days before your trip. Check at any of the 12 backcountry desks at visitor centers and ranger stations all over the park. You can go to any of the desks, which are linked by computer, but you may get better information from rangers closer to where you intend to go. Rangers will help you figure out where to go and what's available, and you'll be required to watch a safety film that's mostly about avoiding bears.

## Forest Service Campgrounds

Yellowstone National Park is surrounded by national forests that take in millions of acres of land. There's a lot of wilderness to explore, and the campgrounds also take park overflow. They're relatively primitive, with pit toilets and few services, but they're often in wonderful places, with fishing, boating, and hiking opportunities right at your site.

All the campgrounds I've listed are in **Gallatin National Forest** and **Shoshone National Forest,** with main contact information under "Yellowstone Address Book" (p. 301). Gallatin also has ranger district offices in West Yellowstone (☎ 406/646-7369) and Gardiner (☎ 406/848-7375), and a desk at the West Yellowstone visitor center. I've included campgrounds within 10 to 15 miles of the entrances, listed by the park entrance that is closest. Many other Forest Service campgrounds are farther afield. Reservations are taken only where noted; use the National Forest Service reservation system explained in chapter 1, "Planning Your Trip."

## NORTHEAST ENTRANCE

Soda Butte, Colter, and Chief Joseph campgrounds are in Gallatin National Forest, and Fox Creek and Crazy Creek campgrounds are in Shoshone National Forest. More campgrounds are along Highway 212 farther away.

**Chief Joseph.** Hwy. 212, 7 miles east of entrance. $8 per site. 6 sites; tents or RVs. Vault toilets; drinking water. Closed Sept–June.

**Colter.** Hwy. 212, 5½ miles east of entrance. $8 per site. 23 sites; tents or RVs. Vault toilets; drinking water; on a mountaintop with great views. Closed Sept to mid-July.

**Crazy Creek.** Hwy. 212, roughly 15 miles east of entrance. $9 per site. 19 sites; tents or RVs. Vault toilets; drinking water. Closed Nov–May.

**Fox Creek.** Hwy. 212, roughly 10 miles east of entrance. $9 per site. 27 sites; tents or RVs. Vault toilets; drinking water. Fishing stream nearby. Closed Oct–May.

**Soda Butte.** On Soda Butte Creek, Hwy. 212, 5½ miles east of entrance. $8 per night. 21 sites; tents or RVs. Vault toilet; drinking water. Closed Sept–June.

## NORTH ENTRANCE

**Eagle Creek.** From Gardiner, take dirt Jardine Rd. 2.2 miles. $6 per sites. 12 sites; no parking aprons; tents or RVs. Vault toilet; no fresh water. Open all year.

This campground in Gallatin National Forest has corrals if you bring your horse.

## WEST ENTRANCE

These three campgrounds are in Gallatin National Forest, near West Yellowstone. Stop at the visitor center there for information on other campgrounds a little farther afield.

**Baker's Hole.** Hwy. 191, 3 miles from park entrance. $12 per site. 72 sites; RVs only. Vault toilets; drinking water. Fishing in the Madison River. Closed Sept–May.

Toilet arrangements at each campground are listed with each. The Canyon and Grant Village campgrounds and Fishing Bridge RV Park have public showers and coin-op laundries, and Lake Lodge also has a laundry. In West Yellowstone, **Canyon Street Laundry**, 312 Canyon St. (☎ **406/646-9733**), has coin-op machines and showers open 7am to 11pm. In Gardiner, there's a public coin-operated laundry at the **Yellowstone Village Inn** on Route 89 (1102 Scott St.; ☎ **406/848-7417**).

**Lonesomehurst.** On Hegben Lake, 11 miles from park entrance. From West Yellowstone, go 6.5 miles west on Rte. 20 to sign, then 3½ miles to campground. $12 per site. Reservations accepted with additional fee. 26 sites; tents or RVs. Vault toilets; drinking water. Lakeside, with boating and swimming. Closed Sept–May.

**Rainbow Point.** On Hegben Lake, 11 miles from park entrance. From West Yellowstone, take Rte. 191/287 north 4.6 miles and follow signs. $12 per site. Reservations accepted. 85 sites; RVs only. Vault toilets; drinking water. Boating, fishing, and swimming on the lake. Closed Sept–May.

### EAST ENTRANCE

These two recently improved campgrounds are on U.S. 14/20 in Shoshone National Forest, Wapiti Ranger District (☎ **307/527-6921**). Grizzly bears are common; observe the food storage rules. Several more campgrounds are scattered along the highway east to Cody.

**Eagle Creek.** 8 miles east of entrance. $9 per site. 20 sites; hard-sided RVs only. Vault toilets; drinking water. Fishing in the North Fork of the Shoshone River. Closed mid-Sept to May.

**Three Mile.** 4 miles east of park entrance. $9 per site. 33 sites; RVs only. Vault toilets; drinking water. Closed mid-Sept to May.

## Commercial Campgrounds

**Rocky Mountain Campground.** 14 Jardine Rd., Gardiner, MT 59030. ☎ **406/848-7251.** $26 full hookups, $15 tent sites, for 2 people; $2 per extra person. 100 sites. Showers, laundry, store, playground, game room.

Atop a hill with great views near the lower-elevation north entrance to the park, this family-run park makes sense for RVers who want full hookups, but the tent sites are too exposed for my taste. The Yellowstone River Trail starts here.

**Yellowstone Grizzly RV Park.** 210 S. Electric St., West Yellowstone, MT 59758. ☎ **406/646-4466.** www.grizzlyrv.com. $38 full hookups, $25 tent sites. 158 sites. Showers, laundry, store, game room, small children's playground.

The open, grassy park is right on the edge of the town and a few blocks from the west entrance to the park. It's a trim, modern place, a good choice for RVers looking for full services.

## HOTELS
## Within the Park

The accommodations within the park are operated by **Yellowstone National Park Lodges** (see "Yellowstone Address Book," p. 301). They include some superb rooms in new and historic buildings, but also a great many units that embarrass the site managers who put guests in them. Some cabins, in fact, were in such deplorable condition on my last visit that, back home, they would not be considered fit for habitation. The reasons for this state of affairs are complex, having to do with the nature of the contract between the concessionaire and the Park Service, and will not be resolved for several years (although I've seen improvement since the first edition of this book). When I talked to the head of concessions at the Park Service headquarters in Washington, I found she didn't appreciate just how bad some of these places had gotten. A room doesn't have to be fancy, and I enjoy crude wilderness cabins; but peeling paint, worn-out floor and wall coverings, holes in walls, and advanced rot are unacceptable.

In any event, I've inspected all the accommodations to steer you toward good rooms. The hotel rooms tend to be far better than the cabins. Some of the cheapest cabins are nice, with bare boards and wood stoves, because they don't try to be anything but old-fashioned frontier shelter (these are often called Rough Rider class). The worst are the mid-range cabins that are trying to be like motel rooms, but have deteriorated into slums (some of these are Pioneer, Economy, or Budget class). Even many of the top "Western" class cabins are drab and out-of-date, while some are charming. The basic problem with almost all is that they were built 50 to 80 years ago with no thought of having them used this long.

Unless I've noted otherwise, rooms and cabins have private bathrooms but no telephones, TVs, or air-conditioning. It's critical to reserve as early as possible. Dinner at some of the hotel dining rooms should be reserved when you reserve your room, months ahead (see "Where to Eat," p. 330). Yellowstone National Park Lodges accepts American Express, Diner's Club, Discover, Japan Credit Bank, MasterCard, and Visa. Rates are for two people in the room; extra adults are $10 each, kids 11 and under free. You can check availability and reserve online at www.travelyellowstone.com.

**Canyon Lodge and Cabins.** Canyon Village. 79 rms, 540 cabins. $121 double room; $42–$111 cabin. Closed Sept–May.

A new hotel lodge in the classic park style includes some really special rooms, with phones and other modern facilities, and exceptional attention to detail. Those buildings stay open until mid-September. Most people end up in the 540 cabins, however, and they are nothing to write home about. The best, Western class, was clean, with newish carpet, drapes, bedspreads, and tub enclosures on my last visit, but that couldn't erase the 1950s ranch-style tract house design, with small bathrooms, cheap paneling on the walls, and acoustic tile ceilings. The lower-priced, Pioneer unit I saw was drab and depressing, with stained carpet, a decrepit shower stall, peeling paint inside and out, and disintegrating linoleum.

**Grant Village.** Near Yellowstone Lake on the way to the south entrance. 300 units. $89–$101 double. Closed Oct–May.

Six two-story gabled buildings, built in the 1980s with plywood siding, face the lake in tiers. The standard motel rooms are clean and modern and have telephones, but they lack character and, on my inspection, were ready for new carpet. Noise carries through the lightweight construction, so you will have to keep the kids quiet.

**Lake Lodge Cabins.** Near the Lake Yellowstone Hotel. 186 cabins. $50–$111. Closed mid-Sept to mid-June.

The 1920s log-and-stone lodge building, full of cane-backed chairs for sitting in front of the fire, belies the cabins out back. The Western-class units I saw were no more than acceptable. Quite out-of-date, they had worn carpet and peeling brown exterior paint. A tiny, low-ceiling, plank-walled Pioneer-class cabin looked like a piece from a museum on the dust bowl (some date even earlier), with a door that latched like a gate or garden shed and a hot water heater out in the room. However, it was clean and, for $50 a night, a dry place to sleep.

**Lake Yellowstone Hotel and Cabins.** Yellowstone Lake. 194 rms, 102 cabins. $100–$150 double; $392 suite; $83 cabin. Closed mid-Oct to mid-May.

This yellow 1891 hotel has been carefully restored to 1920s style. The common rooms and lodgings in the main building are as stylish and posh as they were during its golden age, a real experience that adds to your trip. These rooms go for $150 and up, and they have telephones. Rooms in an annex are $50 less; they are basic and lack phones. The Frontier-class cabins out back are barely acceptable; the bathrooms were renovated, but the rooms themselves are drab and worn out, with the yellow exterior paint peeling off.

**Mammoth Hot Springs Hotel and Cabins.** Near the north entrance. 97 rms, 116 cabins. $89 double with bathroom, $63 double without bathroom; $261 suite; $52–$84 cabin. Open Oct to mid-Dec and Mar–Apr.

The Mammoth is an impressive 1930s hotel, with a well-preserved exterior and common areas. The rooms, while not the restored showplaces of the Lake Hotel, are still pleasingly old-fashioned and comfortable. Some bathrooms have shower stalls, some old-fashioned tubs without showers, and some rooms use large shared bathrooms. The rooms have phones. The cabins are better kept than in most of the park while preserving a fun 1930s style. They're set around a grassy compound with picnic tables, and some have hot tubs. The hotel is a base for cross-country skiing, ice-skating, and other winter sports.

**Old Faithful Inn.** 327 units. $91–$149 double with bathroom, $68 without bathroom; $251–$334 suite. Closed mid-Oct to mid-May.

You'll never see a more amazing hotel lobby than the one at this historic landmark. It's made of logs and more than 70 feet tall, like a trapper's cabin mated to a Gothic cathedral. It sounds preposterous, but somehow it feels grand and cozy at the same time. In the evening it comes to life on various levels, including kids' programs on the huge balcony. Architect Robert Reamer also designed the lovely Fishing Bridge Visitor Center and other wood-and-stone buildings in the park, helping establish the rustic national park style. The 1904 inn contains an extremely wide range of rooms down long, confusing corridors. The premium rooms, in a 1920s wing, are luxurious and thoughtfully renewed for their period (they have phones). The "Old House," on the other hand, has the fairly crude, shared-bathroom original rooms with log walls and other untouched details. The smallish mid-range rooms are comfortable but unmemorable. Many rooms have views of the geysers.

**Old Faithful Lodge Cabins.** 97 cabins. $42–$65. Closed mid-Sept to mid-May.

The lodge building is an impressive example of the rustic park style and a good place to get an ice cream or meal while waiting for Old Faithful to go off. The cabins, once the park's worst, are in the process of improvement, with many of the grimmest gone. A remodeled Frontier-class unit was very clean, with white walls and new carpet and plumbing, although the bathroom remained tiny. The Pioneer and Budget cabins, however, were still drab and unappealing.

**Old Faithful Snow Lodge.** 100 rms, 24 cabins. $131 double. Closed mid-Oct to mid-Dec and mid-Mar to April.

This award-winning new lodge contains the park's best standard rooms. They've re-created the solid, rustic, communal feeling of the park's best classic architecture in rooms and common areas with sumptuous, current comforts and details, including handcrafted furniture and design touches. All rooms have two double beds and telephones. The cabins are more recent in construction than others in the park, too.

**Roosevelt Lodge Cabins.** In the northeast section of the park. 82 cabins. $84 with bathroom; $46 without bathroom. Closed Sept–May.

Built in 1919 to resemble a dude ranch, the place has returned to standards that really do resemble a good wilderness lodge. Remodeled Frontier cabins are cute, with white walls and wainscoting, while those that haven't had the treatment remain worn and dreary. My choice, however, would be the shared-bathroom Rough Rider units, real old west cabins with plank floors and rag rugs, heated by cast-iron wood stoves. (The bathhouse was remodeled, too.) The central lodge is a fine old building of logs and stone. The area is beautiful, great for horseback riding.

## Outside the Park

A normal motel room rents for about $90 a night in the summer and winter, much less in spring and fall. I've listed only summer peak rates. Unless otherwise noted, all have TVs, telephones, and air-conditioning.

## WEST YELLOWSTONE

The tourist town of West Yellowstone has the most motels, including national chains. Contact the chamber of commerce at www. westyellowstonechamber.com/accomoda.htm (see "Yellowstone Address Book," p. 301).

**Three Bear Lodge.** 217 Yellowstone Ave. (P.O. Box 1590), West Yellowstone, MT 59758. ☎ **800/646-7353** or 406/646-7353. three-bear-lodge. com. 75 units. $70–$80 double, $5 per extra person. DISC, MC, V.

This is a good, reasonably priced family motel, with an outdoor pool. The rooms are large enough for families, with two queen-size beds, and they offer a selection of two-room family suites for $115 or less. All were nicely kept up when I visited. They have a little movie theater and a western-style family restaurant on-site.

**Holiday Inn SunSpree Resort West Yellowstone Conference Hotel.** 315 Yellowstone Ave. (P.O. Box 470), West Yellowstone, MT 59758. ☎ **800/646-7365** or 406/646-7365. Fax 406/646-4433. www.yellowstone-conf-hotel.com. 123 units. $129–$139 double, $8 per extra adult, free for ages 18 and under. AE, DC, DISC, MC, V.

This place strives to be the best in town, with an attractive indoor pool and an activities director at a desk in the lobby to arrange park and fishing outings. They also rent bikes and operate their own snow coach. The guest rooms are large and immaculate, with sofas, microwaves, coffeemakers, and other extras. Family suites with a king- and two queen-sized beds in two rooms, two TVs, and even two bathrooms, in some, rent for $199. The hotel offers a free children's program that takes them off your hands for an hour or two of arts and crafts or popcorn and a movie. The railroad-theme decor includes an impressive 1903 VIP railroad car that has been restored, brought indoors, and made into a museum. The hotel's Oregon Short Line Restaurant

serves steak, elk, buffalo, salmon, and other entrees for $14 to $25.

## GARDINER

**Absaroka Lodge.** Rte. 89 at Yellowstone River bridge (P.O. Box 10), Gardiner, MT 59030. ☎ **800/755-7414** or 406/848-7414. www.yellow stonemotel.com. 41 rms, 3 cabins. $90 double, $5 per extra person, children 12 and under free. AE, CB, DC, DISC, MC, V.

This friendly, family-run hotel occupying a striking building is perched above the Yellowstone River right in town, each room with a balcony over the water. The rooms are light and airy, although unadorned by art or decoration. For $10 more, you can get a kitchen suite with a dining table.

**Yellowstone Village Inn.** 1102 Scott St. (P.O. Box 297), Gardiner, MT 59030. ☎ **800/228-8158** or 406/848-7417. Fax 406/848-7418. www. yellowstoneinn.com. 40 rms, 3 condos. $79 double, $6 per extra person, children 12 and under free. $135–$155 condos. AE, DISC, MC, V.

This is a good, family-oriented motel, with a good-sized indoor pool, a grassy play area, and a basketball court in the large parking lot. The country sportsman decor carries from the lobby into the good standard rooms and the large condos. All of it is quite clean and up-to-date. They offer a free continental breakfast, and a coin-op laundry is on-site.

## SOUTH ENTRANCE

**Flagg Ranch Resort.** John D. Rockefeller, Jr., Pkwy. (Rte. 89/191/287), between Yellowstone and Grand Teton national parks (P.O. Box 187), Moran, WY 83013. ☎ **800/443-2311** or 307/543-2861. Fax 307/543-2356. www.flaggranch.com. 92 cabins. Summer $135 double; winter $110 double; children 17 and under stay free in parents' cabin. Campground: $35 full hookups, $20 tent sites. AE, DISC, MC, V. 20 sites. Open year-round.

The log resort lodge and four-plex cabins sit among small pines between the two parks, offering modern, year-round accommodations, but lacking proximity to any of the main attractions or trails. They offer their own guided outings or rentals for fishing, riding, rafting, or cross-country skiing and have a daily snow coach to Old Faithful. A laundry, store, and restaurant are on-site. The camp-ground, with free showers, is best for RVs but does have tent spaces.

# WHEN YOU ARRIVE

## ENTRANCE FEES
The park admission fee is $20 per vehicle, and it's good for 1 week at Yellowstone and Grand Teton national parks.

## VISITOR CENTERS
## Park Service
Each of these centers has a bookstore, a desk where you can ask questions, and, except as noted, offices for backcountry permits. Ranger stations, where questions are answered and permits issued, are at many other sites around the park. Check the free park map, website, or *Yellowstone Today* park newspaper for locations.

**Albright Visitor Center.** Mammoth Hot Springs. ☎ 307/344-2263. Summer daily 8am–7pm; winter daily 9am–5pm. Open year-round.

Housed in a stone building in historic Fort Yellowstone, this large center contains a rich two-story museum. Highlights include the art and photographs that first revealed Yellowstone to the world and led to the park's creation, and vivid animal dioramas. It's worth up to an hour of your day, despite being dark and lacking adequate signs. A film on park history shows all day.

**Canyon Village Visitor Center.** ☎ 307/242-2550. Summer daily 8am–7pm; fall daily 9am–5pm. Closed Oct to mid-May.

The center has a fascinating little museum on buffalo, with large dioramas, videos, and other presentations that children will find interesting.

**Fishing Bridge Visitor Center.** North side of Yellowstone Lake. ☎ 307/242-2450. Summer daily 8am–7pm; fall daily 9am–5pm. Closed Oct to mid-May.

The two-room museum on the natural history of Yellowstone Lake and its animals isn't that exciting, but the stone-and-timber building is a wonderful architectural piece. The lakeside site is a nice place to play. Go to the ranger stations at the Lake and Bridge Bay areas for backcountry permits.

**Grant Village Visitor Center.** On Yellowstone Lake at the southern end of the lower loop. ☎ 307/242-2650. Summer daily 8am–7pm; fall daily 9am–6pm. Closed Oct to mid-May.

The center contains an exhibit on the great fire of 1988 and the natural history of forest fires in general, an explanation of the big areas of standing deadwood you have passed on the road. Most of it is well oriented to children. There's a slide show on the same theme.

**Old Faithful Visitor Center.** ☎ 307/545-2750. Summer 9am–7pm; fall and winter 9am–5pm. Closed Nov to mid-Dec and mid-Mar to mid-Apr.

The estimated times of upcoming geyser eruptions are posted on the wall of this utilitarian center, and you can see a seismograph, a film on the park, and the plans for a needed replacement center. For backcountry permits, go to the combination ranger station and clinic across the west parking lot.

## COMMERCIAL CENTERS
Contact information is under "Yellowstone Address Book" (p. 301).

**West Yellowstone Chamber of Commerce Visitor Center.** Corner of Yellowstone and Canyon sts., West Yellowstone. ☎ 406/646-7701. Summer daily 8am–8pm; winter Mon–Fri 8am–5pm. Open year-round.

The center has desks staffed by the local chamber of commerce, the National Park Service,

**Emergencies**  ☎ **911** works all over the park. Clinics are located at Mammoth Hot Springs (☎ **307/344-7965**), Old Faithful (☎ **307/545-7325**), and Lake Village (☎ **307/242-7241**). The clinic at Mammoth is open year-round, the others only during the visitor season. There's also a year-round **clinic** at 236 Yellowstone Ave., West Yellowstone (☎ **406/646-7668**).

**Stores**  **Hamilton Stores Inc.** (☎ **406/646-7325**; www.hamiltonstores.com) operates general stores, which sell groceries, gifts, and sporting goods, at Mammoth Hot Springs, Fishing Bridge, Lake Village, Canyon Village, and Grant Village. Smaller convenience stores are at Old Faithful, Tower Fall, Bridge Bay Marina, and Roosevelt Lodge. Each of the three towns around the park has grocery stores.

**Banks**  There are ATMs at stores and hotels all over the park. **First Security Bank** of West Yellowstone is at 23 Dunraven St. (☎ **406/646-7646**).

**Post Offices**  Stations are at Mammoth Hot Springs year-round, and seasonally at Old Faithful, Canyon Village, Grant Village, and Lake Village.

**Gear Sales & Rental**  The **Hamilton Stores** (☎ **406/646-7325**; www.hamiltonstores.com), with locations listed above, have limited sporting goods. You can also get gear and clothing in West Yellowstone. Boats and canoes are for rent at **Bridge Bay Marina**; see "Boating" (p. 326). For winter gear rental, see "Winter Sports & Sightseeing" (p. 329).

and the U.S. Forest Service. There's room to rest and look at information from many businesses and agencies.

**Gardiner Chamber of Commerce.** 222 Park St., Gardiner. ☎ **406/848-7971.** Summer Mon–Fri 9am–5pm, Sat–Sun hours vary; winter Tues–Thurs 9am–4pm.

Stop here for information about businesses outside the north entrance or to use the public computer.

**Cooke City Chamber of Commerce.** Hwy. 212, Cooke City. ☎ **406/838-2495** or 406/838-2272. Daily 10am–5pm. Closed mid-Oct to mid-May.

The center outside the park's northeast entrance has an information desk and brochures.

## GETTING AROUND By Car or RV

Driving is the only practical way for a family to get around the park. People do tour by bicycle; but the distances are great and I wouldn't recommend taking children on these narrow, heavily trafficked roads except before they open to vehicles in May (see "Biking & Mountain Biking," p. 326). Even in a car, the park is large, and to cover it efficiently takes planning. You can't get anywhere fast and it's pointless and frustrating to try. Minimize driving by breaking your trip into two or three different areas, exploring each from a home base within a limited radius before moving on to a new home base in another area. Better yet, relax and spend your whole trip in one part of the park. The fact is, after you've seen one geyser basin, you don't need to visit them all.

## KEEPING SAFE & HEALTHY

In addition to the special tips here, see "Dealing with Hazards," in chapter 1, for information on bears, hypothermia, and lightning.

## Bison

Signs are posted everywhere, and still people walk up to bison to take their pictures. These animals are the size of pickup trucks, have sharp horns, and can get mad unexpectedly. They run 30 m.p.h., faster than the fastest sprinter. Use your common sense, and stay safely back.

## Burns

Visitors have been scalded to death in the hot springs. The danger isn't just falling into a pool of boiling water, but also slipping into hot mud that looks like solid ground.

Prevention is simple: Stay on the trail when you are near thermal features, and keep good control of your children.

## Swimming

The swimming is great at Yellowstone (p. 328), but not in hot springs or water running entirely from hot springs, where the water can carry nasty bugs, including potentially fatal amoebic meningitis. The lakes are too cold for swimming.

# Enjoying the Park

## Natural Places

I've described the places in clockwise order, starting at the north entrance.

## Mammoth Hot Springs

Where the springs come to the surface, the flowing water has built high mounds of weirdly contoured rock called travertine. The rock continues to grow, sometimes 2 feet a year, engulfing trees and boardwalks. Scallop-edged pools of pastel stone steam and trickle like fountains in a pleasure garden, but the patterns are so complex and diverse that only nature's randomness could be so creative. Elk often come here to bask in the warmth from the earth. A **boardwalk nature trail** circles the lower area of the springs, and a traffic-clogged one-lane loop road goes through the less-active upper area. Strollers can roll on many of the boardwalks, but some amazing areas require a stiff stair climb. An excellent map and guide to the site is on sale for 25¢ at the visitor center; however, the most active and interesting areas change constantly, so you need to explore on your own.

The water for the springs falls as rain and snow, probably coming down 21 miles south near the Norris Geyser Basin. The earth heats it and mixes it with carbon dioxide, making carbonic acid. Then the acidic water flows to Mammoth through an underground crack called a fault. The underground limestone at Mammoth, outside Yellowstone's volcanic rim, started out as seashells and other muck on the bottom of an ancient ocean. Limestone dissolves in carbonic acid. When the acidic water from Norris gets to Mammoth, the acid dissolves the limestone and carries it to the surface. When the carbon dioxide gets to the surface, it floats off into the air, leaving the limestone behind. The limestone sticks back together and forms the travertine rocks you see at the hot springs.

Bacteria growing in the springs give the rocks their colors. Different water temperatures grow bacteria of different colors, and it's possible to find out how hot a pool is by what color it is. See if you can figure out which colors grow in the hottest and coolest pools, then check your answer in the guide map.

## The Northern Range

The broad mountain pastures along the northern leg of the park loop are an important wildlife habitat and a good place to find animals in the winter, when the lower elevation harbors thousands of elk and bison. Hiking and horseback riding in this area are glorious because of the open sky and wonderful views, but it can be warm in the summer. Paths lead from several points along the highway between Cooke City and Mammoth across the valleys and into the canyon of the Yellowstone River, routes suitable for a day hike or overnight. Horseback riding starts from the stable at Roosevelt Lodge. See "Hiking" (p. 327) and "Horseback Riding" (p. 328).

## Tower Fall

A short paved walk leads to an overlook, then a steep half-mile trail gets you to a much better view at the base of the falls. Unfortunately, it's often crowded. The waterfall is a creek spilling over into the canyon of the Yellowstone River. A spur leads farther down to the Yellowstone, a good place for supervised riverside play. The road south from this area to Canyon Village passes through the park's grandest mountain terrain and leads to trailheads for the popular hike up **Mt. Washburn,** 3 miles one way from Crittenden Road or Dunraven Pass. The alpine trail, leading over 10,243 feet, offers views over much of Yellowstone and a good chance to see bighorn sheep.

## Grand Canyon of the Yellowstone

The Yellowstone River has cut up to 1,200 feet deep through yellow rock and mud to create the canyon, which is still deepening. Besides being huge, it is fascinating to look at because the view changes so much from different places. Each point has a different scene of chaotic shapes of colored, broken rock, gushing water from two huge waterfalls, and trees that grow in seemingly impossible places. The paths and overlooks join the road a mile from Canyon Village, at the eastern midpoint of the loop roads. Many overlooks are crowded near the road, and the less-crowded canyon top trails can be scary for parents. Our strategy was to go take a quick look with everyone else, then head out on an uncrowded trail from the Wapiti Trailhead, just south of the canyon, to Clear Lake, a strange body of water fed by hot springs. The terrain there is beautiful rolling meadows. The 25¢ Canyon map and guide explains the natural history of the canyon and shows all the trails; get one at the visitor center.

The canyon's yellow rock is rhyolite which formed from lava flows. The geologic story of the canyon hasn't been clearly figured out, but we know that various lava flows poured out over thousands of years after the big eruption 600,000 years ago. The volcano also caused the earth to bulge, causing giant cracks that water could widen much later into the canyon. There was once a geyser basin here, too. The hot water helped weaken the rhyolite rock so water could cut easily. You still can see steam plumes in the canyon in places and around Clear Lake. At the end of the last Ice Age, about 10,000 years ago, a series of ice dams probably formed at the edge of Yellowstone Lake. When the dams would break, flash floods would wash down this way, quickly carving the canyon. Today's waterfalls mark spots where a flow of harder rhyolite forms a shelf over a softer flow. The softer rock wore away faster, leaving a steep drop. The rock is yellow because it contains iron that is oxidizing, or rusting, in the air.

## Hayden Valley & Mud Volcano

On the drive south from the Canyon area to Yellowstone Lake, the Hayden Valley is a spectacular mountain meadow along the Yellowstone River. This is one of the park's best areas to see groups of buffalo and elk from the road, or to hike off the road for more wildlife viewing (trails here can be tricky because the bison knock down the markers). To the south, **Mud Volcano** and **Sulphur Caldron** belch nastiness for the nose, eye, and ear right by a parking lot, definitely worth a quick stop, even if they are less impressive than the park's other thermal features (get the 25¢ guide at a visitor center). A ⅔-mile nature trail loop brings you to other such weirdness on a smaller scale.

## Yellowstone Lake & West Thumb

The lake is unique for its size, 20 by 14 miles, and its elevation, 7,733 feet, but if you could see underneath, you would be much more impressed. Exploration by a robot submarine in 1999 found craters up to half a mile across, spires of rock more than 110 feet tall, and canyons, including the lake's deepest spot, up to 390 feet deep. It's a wild volcanic scene down there. The lake bed itself is lifting up, tilting more toward the south. On the north, the lake bed is becoming exposed, and on the south, water has flooded former forest. At one time, the lake probably drained that way, flowing down the Snake River and eventually to the Pacific Ocean instead of going down the Yellowstone River and winding up in the Atlantic. Maybe it will switch again some day.

The best place to get an idea of what violence is happening under the water is at the **West Thumb Geyser Basin,** north of Grant Village. West Thumb is a large bay formed by a volcanic explosion 150,000 years ago. On a map, it looks a little bit like a thumb. At the geyser basin, a **nature trail** follows mostly flat boardwalks around deep, hot pools that seem to flow with rich, pure colors. The springs and vents are right on the lakeshore, often mingling the hot and cold water. Get the 25¢ trail guide and map. A small information station has a bookstore and a ranger to answer questions.

The hot water coming up underneath helps Yellowstone Lake sustain more life than would normally be found at this high, cold elevation by speeding the growth of algae and bacteria. Insects and other small creatures eat that growth, and they become food in turn for larger creatures, such as trout. The native cutthroat trout in turn get eaten by eagles, white pelicans, bears, and many other animals. Recently, however, lake trout somehow were introduced to the lake, and they threaten to wipe out the cutthroat if they aren't stopped. Rangers have been netting lake trout, and they encourage anglers to take as many as they can. You'll need to learn to identify the fish accurately, because any lake trout you catch must be kept and shown to a ranger intact (then you can eat it), but all native fish must be released

to swim again. (Always check on current regulations before you fish). Anglers can rent boats or engage guides at Bridge Bay marina (see "Fishing," p. 327).

Without fishing, you can get out on the lake in a rented canoe, or get a lift to one of the backcountry campsites on the lakeshore from the concessionaire at Bridge Bay (see "Boating," p. 326). They also offer narrated 1-hour **boat tours,** leaving from the marina all day in the summer. Fares are $8.75 for adults, $4.75 for children 2 to 11. The tour we took was expertly done, but, as much as I love boats, there just wasn't enough to see to make it worthwhile. In fact, I think the lake area as a whole has less to offer than the north or west parts of the park.

To the south, forested **Lewis Lake** is on the road to the park entrance. It has a campground and provides access for canoeists and kayakers to take an appealing backcountry trip to **Shoshone Lake,** which is untouched by roads and has a significant geyser basin on its southwest shore.

## Old Faithful & Nearby Geyser Basins

Walkways, hotels, restaurants, stores, and parking lots circle halfway around Old Faithful. If it ever stops shooting off hot water, the area will look awfully funny because everything focuses on that one spot. The time between eruptions has lengthened because of earthquakes, but so far, the geyser is still going strong. It erupts roughly every hour and a half and shoots up to 180 feet high, as it has at least since it was first described in 1870. The visitor center posts the predicted time of the next eruption for Old Faithful and some other geysers in the area; getting that information and the 25¢ guide maps of this and the nearby geyser areas when you arrive will greatly improve your tour. The guide maps also list the usual intervals between eruptions for various geysers. The best of the buildings around the geyser, especially the **Old Faithful Inn,** also are worth a stop (check out the hotel's lobby). These were the first experiments with designing buildings to fit a national park.

Many other geysers in the area benefit from more natural settings. One-fifth of the world's geysers — 140 of them — are within a mile of Old Faithful. You can tour them on a network of trails several miles long that starts from Old Faithful and on the road to the north. Steam and water shoot up from sterile plains of white mud and rock. It always turns my imagination to other worlds. This white material is sinter, or geyserite. Silica in the rocks below dissolves in the geysers' water, then solidifies on the surface into this white or gray rock. The ground all around you hisses and groans unexpectedly. Shoots of steam bloom, and strange mineral smells rise up.

There are more geysers and hot pools in the park than will interest most people, but you can spend a fascinating full day just walking around these basins. Some paths are open to bicycles too. A drive circles through the Firehole Lake area, with geysers and huge ponds of hot water. Don't worry too much about choosing where to go. The best geyser is one that's going off at the moment, and, with a few exceptions, that's unpredictable; so all you can do is head out to explore and see what you see. If a geyser suddenly goes off next to you, you'll have a wonderful thrill.

## Norris Geyser Basin & Museum

Looking down on the basin from the museum, you see far across a great, white wasteland spouting of steam, a truly hellish vista of land that seems entirely hostile to life. This view from above gives Norris the best first impression of any of the road-accessible geyser basins, and it has one of the park's most consistent geysers as well. **Echinus Geyser** goes off roughly hourly, and you can get close to its billowing torrents of highly acidic water. Lots of other interesting geysers and thermal features are here, too, including the world's tallest geyser, the annoyingly inconsistent **Steamboat**

**Geyser.** It shot more than 300 feet in the air in May 2000 after being quiet for 8 years, and was seen by only two people. It has erupted as frequently as 23 times in a summer and as infrequently as once in 50 years. Pick up the 25¢ trail guide, which covers a couple of miles of paths through the gurgling, rumbling basin floor.

The **Norris Geyser Basin Museum** (☎ 307/344-2812) occupies two rooms in a log building above the basin. Interesting graphic placards explain how the geothermal features work and will hold your attention for up to half an hour. A roving ranger answers questions.

## PLACES FOR LEARNING
## In the Park

Most of the museums in the park are at the visitor centers described above under "When You Arrive" (p. 318). The **Norris Geyser Basin Museum** is described above.

**Museum of the National Park Ranger, Norris.** At the Norris Campground. ☎ 307/ 344-7353. Free admission. Summer daily 9am–6pm; fall daily 9am–5pm. Closed mid-Sept to mid-May.

This is a charming, relaxing museum of great interest to children. The displays tell the history of the Park Service and how early rangers lived, with uniforms and mock-ups of rooms. The changes in the parks are an interesting window on the changes in society. Best of all, the museum occupies a beautiful old log building by a creek where retired rangers spin yarns about the old days to anyone who asks.

## In West Yellowstone

This tourist town isn't worth sacrificing time in the park to visit, but these sites are of interest if you are in the area.

**Yellowstone Hisoric Center.** Yellowstone Ave. and Canyon St., West Yellowstone. ☎ 406/ 646-1100. www.yellowstonehistoriccenter.org. Admission $7 adults, $5 ages 3–12, $20 per family. Summer daily 9am–9pm; fall daily 9am–7pm. Closed Oct to May 15.

When he was 8 years old, Teddy Roosevelt started a museum to keep birds' nests, bones, and interesting rocks he found. He called it the Roosevelt Museum of Natural History. Each of his brothers and sisters had a museum job. One was in charge of seashells, another was responsible for bugs, and another wrote down what they decided in their meetings. Teddy's job was naturalist. His favorite thing was to go on trips to the country to look for plants, animals, and birds and to write about them in his journal. He carefully drew pictures of the animals he found and described what he saw them do, labeling each one with common and scientific names he found in books. When his family went on trips to Europe or Africa, down to the seashore or up to the mountains, he would add to his collections and his notes.

Teddy came from a wealthy family. When he was born, in 1858, there were no laws that said children had to go to school, so he studied and read at home, played with his brothers and sisters, and explored and wrote about nature. It was a happy family and they did everything together; but Teddy was spoiled compared to most children. He got just about anything he wanted. When he decided to make a zoo at the family's country home, he hired the other kids in the neighborhood to catch mice and turtles instead of doing it himself. He kept the turtles in the family's clothes washing tub until one of the family's servants complained and he had to move them.

It wasn't that Teddy was lazy. He was a skinny little boy and always seemed to be sick. When he did meet children outside his family, they often picked on him because he was so small. Teddy's worst problem was asthma, a sickness that causes attacks that make it hard to breathe. Children who have asthma today can take medicine that makes the attacks go away quickly, but when Teddy was a boy, those medicines hadn't been invented yet. Doctors told people to do awful things to cure it. Teddy had to smoke cigars, drink strong black coffee, and take medicines that made him throw up. His father would take him on carriage rides in the middle of the night to try to get better air. If they were on vacation, the whole family would pick up and move to a different hotel or different town to try to find a place where Teddy wouldn't have asthma attacks. They often changed their plans, but nothing worked very well to stop the attacks.

Teddy's father wanted to take him out West for a trip. Teddy loved reading adventure books about the Wild West — which was still pretty wild in those days — and he desperately wanted to go. He was about 11 years old at the time. But after some bad asthma attacks, Teddy's father decided they couldn't take such a rough trip with such a sick, weak boy. He sat Teddy down with his mother and said, "Theodore, you have the mind, but you have not the body, and without the help of the body the mind cannot go as far as it should. You must make your body." Teddy understood

This brand-new museum in West Yellowstone's old railroad depot had yet to open at this writing. Started by a community group seeking to preserve the group of buildings surrounding the 1908 railroad link to West Yellowstone, it should include stage coach and rail cars, wildlife displays, and information on town history.

**Grizzly Discovery Center.** Canyon St., West Yellowstone. ☎ **406/646-7001.** www.grizzly discoveryctr.com. Admission $7.95 adults, $3.50 children under 16, free for children under 5. Year-round daily 8am–dusk.

You're not likely to see grizzlies or wolves in the park, but you can see them here in a nicely landscaped area, like a tiny zoo. The staff did a good job of holding the kids' interest while telling them about the animals and their rescue. A small museum area also is well pitched for kids. The huge gift shop helps support the not-for-profit operation.

**Yellowstone IMAX Theater.** 101 Canyon St., West Yellowstone. ☎ **406/646-4100.** Admission $7.50 adults, $5.50 children 3–11, free for children under 3. Summer daily 9am–9pm; winter daily noon–9pm; showings hourly on the hour.

what his father was saying, and that summer he began working out at a gym many hours a day. Soon, his father installed a gym in the house, with punching bags and gymnastics equipment. Teddy worked hard every day, building his muscles and stamina. He spent time outdoors and got involved in sports. It took a long time, but it worked. Teddy never got rid of his asthma completely, but he became a strong athlete. When he was older, he owned a ranch and was a hero in the cavalry, the part of the Army that rode horses in those days.

Being fit and healthy meant Teddy could do the things he wanted to do outdoors: horseback riding, hunting, camping, exploring new places. He studied animals all his life and went to wild places all over the world, having adventures even more exciting than the ones he had read about in books as a child. He went to Yellowstone and worked in favor of laws to stop hunting in the park and to keep it from being ruined by businesses. In 1901, he became president of the United States. He loved being president and used the opportunity to have fun and to save natural places in parks and forests. And he kept exercising, traveling, and hunting. He even fought boxing champions at the White House.

The public liked President Teddy Roosevelt because he spoke his mind and did funny and interesting things. Even back then, everything the president did was in the news. In 1902, for example, he went bear hunting in Mississippi. The hunters' dogs drove a scraggly little bear out of the woods. The bear killed one of the dogs, and the hunting guides caught it and tied it up, then brought Roosevelt so that he could shoot it. But he looked at the bear, tied up in front of him, and refused to kill it. He was the kind of hunter who believes the animal has to have a fair chance, and he wouldn't shoot a helpless bear that had no way to escape. A cartoonist in the Washington Post drew a cartoon of Roosevelt refusing to kill the bear. A man named Morris Michtom, who owned a toy shop in Brooklyn, New York, saw that cartoon and had the idea of making a stuffed bear and naming it after the president. His wife sewed the first "Teddy Bear." It was an immediate hit.

Teddy Roosevelt was the greatest president in American history for conserving habitat for wildlife. He started the National Forest Service and set aside 5 national parks, 51 wildlife refuges, and 18 national monuments, including the Grand Canyon and the area that started Olympic National Park. In all, he preserved 150 million acres of land from going out of government ownership. That's an area almost as large as the state of Texas. If he hadn't been so interested in nature as a boy, and if he hadn't worked so hard to become fit and healthy, none of that might have happened.

Like IMAX theaters that have cropped up outside several of the Western parks, this facility shows a movie about Yellowstone on a huge screen. The film is mostly scenery and wildlife, but also tells about early park history and the area's geology and the workings of geysers. It's well done and entertaining to children, but expensive for less than an hour. The lobby contains fast-food outlets.

# ACTIVITIES
## Backpacking

Yellowstone is a one of the best parks for backpacking, for many reasons. It's huge, with plenty of room for everyone. The backcountry permit system is understandable and well managed, and permits are easy to get. You can take long hikes in spectacular places, making destinations of backcountry geysers and seeing lots of bison, elk, and other wildlife. But you don't have to go far to have a backcountry wilderness experience — some beautiful campsites are just a couple miles off the road. A family with school-age children without prior backcountry experience can handle it with careful planning to avoid excessive packs or long days. You just need to be self-sufficient and to follow carefully the Park Service's bear avoidance rules, which you'll receive in detail when you get your backcountry permit. Gathering dead wood is permitted in most areas of the park, but fires should be kept in rings at established campsites. Of course, you also need a camp stove.

Details on the backcountry system are explained under "Backcountry Camping Permits" in chapter 1; more hiking information appears below. Check out the **Yellowstone Institute,** under "Programs" (p. 329), for a guided option. Another choice is a guided stock trip, with a horse or llama carrying your stuff, covered under "Horseback Riding" (p. 328).

## Biking & Mountain Biking

Family biking at Yellowstone is quite limited, but there are some opportunities. Hiking trails and boardwalks are off-limits to bikes, and the park's main roads are too narrow and busy to be safe with kids. It's also not feasible for most families to come for the 3-week season without traffic, in the spring after the snow is gone but before the cars are allowed in on the 3rd Friday in April. During that period, snow conditions permitting, the roads between the west entrance and Mammoth and from Norris to Canyon are open only to bikes and other nonmotorized transportation. Call ☎ **307/ 344-2109** for current conditions.

Bikes are not for rent in the park, but there are a few mountain-biking routes if you bring your own. **Fountain Flat Drive** is a 5-mile route from Midway Geyser, just north of Old Faithful. **Bunsen Peak Road,** just south of Mammoth Hot Springs, is a very challenging 10-mile ride, one way, with many steep grades, and no vehicles allowed. The 8-mile **Blacktail Plateau Drive,** just west of Roosevelt Lodge, is a fun, hilly ride. All of these are one-way rides that require you to double back to your car.

## Boating

Most boating at Yellowstone starts from **Bridge Bay Marina,** on the northwest corner of the lake, not the most interesting area for paddling with its straight, steep shores topped by a highway. The less-than-thrilling tour-boat ride is covered under "Yellowstone Lake & West Thumb" (p. 321). Yellowstone National Park Lodges (see "Yellowstone Address Book," p. 301) operates the marina, catering mostly to anglers (see "Fishing," below). But you can also use their service to get to backcountry lakeside campsites in the southern part of the lake, places you otherwise couldn't reach with young or nonbackpacking members of your group. The marina offers shuttle service, and you can take a rented canoe along to provide mobility at the site. For the ride they charge $55 an hour with a 4-hour minimum. You should reserve well ahead for this service; they take reservations starting January 2. You'll also need a backcountry camping permit (see p. 17). Canoes at the marina rent for $35 a day, but it's too far from Bridge Bay for most families to paddle directly to a campsite, and they don't want you to take the canoe out of the area on your car. The marina also rents rowboats and skiffs with outboard motors, but these are really just for anglers, since you are not allowed to land them except at the dock.

If you bring your own canoe or kayak or rent one in Grand Teton National Park or Jackson (see "Canoeing, Kayaking & Boating," in chapter 15), you can explore Lewis Lake and Shoshone Lake, launching from the Lewis Lake Campground near the south entrance. These are true wilderness waters, very beautiful, and with interesting shoreline. The water is cold, however, and to be safe you need to stay near shore, wear life jackets, and bring warm clothing in dry bags that you can put on if you get wet. Also, plan your paddling in the morning because stormy winds can whip up the lakes in the afternoon.

Boats brought from outside the park require a boating permit from the park service. Permits cost $5 for 7 days for nonmotorized vessels, such as rowboats, canoes, and kayaks, and $10 for a week for motorized vessels. Permits are sold at the south entrance, Lewis Lake Campground, Grant Village Visitor Center, Bridge Bay Ranger Station, and Lake Ranger Station; at Canyon and Mammoth visitor centers you can buy permits only for boats without motors. Grand Teton National Park boat permits are honored at Yellowstone.

## Fishing

Thanks to the growth aided by hot water from below, trout in Yellowstone streams can grow as much as four times faster than in cold mountain streams in similar areas without geothermal activity. Catch-and-release regulations have helped keep fishing exceptionally good. The trout can get quite a workout, being caught as many as 10 times a season. On some streams, only fly-fishing is permitted.

Regulations, permits, and gear for sale or rent are available at the Hamilton Stores (see "For Handy Reference," p. 319), and you can get permits and guidance at a visitor center or ranger station. A Park Service fishing permit good for 10 days is $10, free for children 12 to 15 years old; children 11 and under don't need a permit but must be supervised by an adult. You don't need a state fishing license within the park. Yellowstone National Park Lodges (see "Yellowstone Address Book," p. 301) offers guided fishing from Bridge Bay Marina, on Yellowstone Lake, for $55 to $72 an hour for a boat that holds up to six people, with a 2-hour minimum; reserve well ahead. You can rent your own boat, too. A rowboat is $30 a day, and a boat with an outboard is $30 an hour; reservations are not accepted. Fishing on the lake opens in mid-June, elsewhere in the park around Memorial Day, and lasts well into the fall. You can also arrange remote wilderness fishing expeditions with the stock outfitters mentioned under "Horseback Riding" (p. 328).

## PRACTICALITIES: MOTIVATING A RELUCTANT HIKER

Julia, at 5, sometimes didn't see the point of hiking farther down the trail when the flowers were pretty right here. Occasionally, she would flop down and say she was tired when I knew she had miles left in her: That summer her personal best was up over 4 miles a hike. What I learned was that her weariness wasn't physical, it was mental. She was bored. So when she started to drag, I started asking her questions. How would she spend her birthday, still many months away? That got her talking, planning the theme, the colors, the cake, the guest list — she would chatter on endlessly, her feet flying over the trail. She invented another favorite subject herself. Copying my didactic monologues about the natural history of the park, she began telling us about her imaginary animals, tigercats, which often hid in the bushes along the trail. A question about tigercats, about their food or their babies, would elicit miles of explanation. Now, whenever I think of the wide, bright plains of northern Yellowstone, I hear the musical chirp of Julia's voice and I smile.

## Hiking

I love hiking, but even if I didn't I would hike away from the roads at Yellowstone. That's how you get away from the crowds. After a mile or so, a bubble seems to pop, and you find you're out under the sky, alone in a world that seems brighter and more real because it belongs to your eyes only. The small part of the universe where everything is controlled by people is left behind, and the beauty of Yellowstone seems brand new.

More than 1,000 miles of trails cross the park, so it isn't hard to find your own place. To help choose a good day hike, get one of the free handouts the Park Service produces on each park area; some of the information is consolidated as well on their *Dayhike Sampler* brochure. Trail guide books and maps are covered under "Reading Up" (p. 308). Some great family trails include these: At Mammoth, the Beaver Ponds Loop, an easy 5-mile route from Liberty Cap, at the springs, leading to a beaver pond (go in the evening or early morning to see the beaver); at Madison, the half-mile Harlequin Lake trail, with good bird-watching; Tower Fall and Mt. Washburn trails (see "Tower Fall," p. 321); and the Clear Lake/Ribbon Lake trails (see "Grand Canyon of the Yellowstone," p. 321).

## Horseback Riding

Yosemite National Park Lodges (see "Yellowstone Address Book," p. 301) operates stables for trail rides at Roosevelt Lodge, Mammoth Hot Springs, and Canyon Village. The rolling grassland of the Northern Range at Roosevelt is the best setting for a ride, a scene out of your fantasies of the West. It's the only site with the option of stagecoach rides (really they're large carts) for the very young and a fun cookout and sing-along every evening. The kids really enjoyed it. Don't expect anything intimate, however, because the rides often amount to long parades of riders. One-hour rides are $23.50. Two-hour rides are $35, but are not offered at Mammoth. Children must be at least age 8 and 4 feet tall; up to 11 they have to go with someone at least 16 years old on another horse. Call ahead to reserve and be sure to arrive early for the ride to sign the paperwork. The Roosevelt stagecoach rides are $6.75 adults, $5.50 ages 2 to 11. The cookout adds around $15 per person to the cost of each ride.

For more serious riders, dozens of outfitters offer half-day, all-day, and overnight backcountry rides and pack trips with horses or llamas. Typically, outfitters will guide you into remote country on horseback, providing the animals, meals, and gear for around $150 to $300 per person, per day. They usually have minimum age and experience levels for guests. You can go with just your family, or join a group. Guided fishing on backcountry streams

is a specialty of many of the operators. It seems like a perfect way to the wilderness for families who enjoy horses. All the licensed operators, with links to many, are listed on the park's website, at www.nps.gov/yell/planvisit/services/stockout.htm. One long-established outfitter that covers the whole park is **Yellowstone Mountain Guides,** P.O. Box 3006, Bozeman, MT 59772-3006 (☎ **406/388-0148;** www.yellowstone-guides.com).

## Rafting

Rafting isn't permitted in the park itself, but several companies offer raft rides outside. They run on the Yellowstone River from Gardiner, where it flows north out of the park, and on the Gallatin and Madison rivers, from the western side near West Yellowstone or Big Sky, Montana. You can choose half- or full-day rides on wild or calm water. The **Yellowstone Raft Company** has offices in Gardiner (☎ **406/848-7777;** www.yellowstoneraft.com) and Big Sky (☎ **406/995-4613**). It offers trips on all three rivers, kayak instruction, and guided float fishing. The website has good trip descriptions. They take children as young as age 6. Prices for half days range from $31 to $39 for adults, about $10 less for children 12 and under; full days, which include lunch, are $66 to $92 for adults, $46 to $76 for kids.

## Swimming

We had a wonderful afternoon playing in the river at Madison Campground, where the water is partly warmed by the geothermal water flowing down the Firehole River. The Firehole itself has popular swimming holes with limited parking on Firehole Canyon Drive, which runs one way from just south of Madison. River currents can be dangerous, especially for kids, and there are no lifeguards; so be careful and, if in doubt, check with a ranger. Swimming in hot springs can be deadly; don't even think about it.

## Winter Sports & Sightseeing

Yellowstone is the best national park for winter sports. Snow is reliably deep in the winter season in areas above 7,000 feet, which includes all the park except the Northern Range. And in winter the scenery is better. White brings sharper contrasts and cleaner shapes. The geysers and other thermal features seem exaggerated in the cold, and they create strange microclimates of plant and animal life, attracting wildlife with warmth and the absence of snow. Equally important for visitors, the park is well developed for cross-country skiing, snowshoeing, and sightseeing.

The winter season, when hotels, visitor centers, and other businesses are open, begins in late December and lasts until the 2nd week of March. Most activities revolve around **Old Faithful Snow Lodge** and **Mammoth Hot Springs Hotel,** which remain open for the season (see "Where to Spend the Night," p. 310). Mammoth, at a lower elevation, doesn't get heavy snow, and you can drive there year-round. Old Faithful is the more romantic choice, snowed in all winter and reachable only by snow coach (a small bus on caterpillar tracks). Yellowstone National Park Resorts (see "Yellowstone Address Book," p. 301) runs the snow coach to Old Faithful daily from West Yellowstone, Mammoth, and Flagg Ranch Resort, outside the south gate. The fares average $45 one way, $22 for children 2 to 11. Commentary and a chance to stretch your legs are included on the ride, which lasts up to 4 hours. Day tours also run from Old Faithful and Mammoth to the Grand Canyon of the Yellowstone, a cross-country skiing destination with spectacular views of the canyon. Shorter sightseeing tours go to other areas. Mammoth also has an outdoor skating rink and inexpensive skate rentals and hot tubs. The visitor centers at the two main areas are the only ones open in the winter season. Warming huts, many with snacks, operate at spots all over the park, which are listed in the newspaper. Nature trails remain open, too.

### NOTE: NO MORE SNOW MACHINES

In 2000, the Park Service announced the decision to phase out snowmobiling at Yellowstone and Grand Teton National Parks. Officials said the machines produced too much pollution and noise, disturbing wildlife and degrading the park for other visitors. The decision erased one of the most popular activities at the park and came as a huge blow to West Yellowstone, a town that had built a winter economy based on snowmobiling. Assuming President Bush's administration or current litigation doesn't change the rule, the number of machines will be capped in the winter of 2001–02, cut 50% in 2002–03, and gone entirely in 2003–04. Contact Yellowstone National Park Lodges (see "Yellowstone Address Book," p. 301) to reserve one of those last rides.

**Nordic skiing** is the main activity at the park. Some 170 miles of groomed trails originate from Old Faithful, Mammoth, and Tower Fall and go everywhere in the park, along snow-bound roads and into the backcountry. Free shuttles carry guests at Mammoth Hot Springs, an area of relatively little snow, to a higher-elevation skiing area. Vans and snow coaches go from there to other areas, for a fee, generally under $12 for adults, half price for children. Old Faithful guests can ski from the Old Faithful Snow Lodge or take a snow coach farther afield and ski back. The concessionaire operates ski-rental shops at Old Faithful and Mammoth; packages rent for $14.25 a day or $35 for 3 days. They offer private and group lessons, and guided tours and private guides too. Snowshoes rent for $11 a day. See "Cold Weather Preparations," in chapter 1, for what to wear.

## PROGRAMS
## Children's Programs

The visitor centers sell $2 **Junior Ranger** newspapers for ages 5 to 7 and for ages 8 to

12. After completing the workbook questions, doing outdoor activities, attending ranger programs, and turning in the newspapers with various signatures, kids get a patch. Take a good look at the newspaper before getting into this because it's likely to take quite a bit of your and your child's time and may be difficult if you don't cover a large portion of the park. You'll also need quiet time to do writing activities; if you can't finish while at the park, it's okay to do some of it on the way home and mail in the worksheets for your patch. The winter program costs $3, and you can check out snowshoes, hand lenses, and thermometers from the visitor centers to do some of the neat science activities.

## Family & Adult Programs

The park newspaper lists ranger programs all over the park, mostly near the most popular natural features. They start every hour or two all day during the height of the summer season. The programs are walks and lectures, not activities or lessons, and are primarily aimed at adults. In the evening during the summer, campfire talks and slide shows are offered every night at many of the campgrounds and some other sites; the exact list of locations depends on annual park service budgets.

### THE YELLOWSTONE INSTITUTE

The institute offers intensive programs in natural history, outdoors skills, art, history, photography, and many other subjects, using Yellowstone as the classroom all seasons of the year. The catalog of choices is truly impressive. Groups are small and leaders are experts in their fields, with college credit available for some of the 1- to 5-day sessions. Most classes are intended for adults, although families with mature teens can check on particular offerings. There are also family sessions that include children as young as 7, and backpacking trips for teens. Prices are typically around $60 a day. The institute is at Buffalo Ranch, in Lamar Valley in the northeast part of the park, near Cooke City. About half of the classes happen there. The institute is sponsored by the **Yellowstone Association** (see "Yellowstone Address Book," p. 301). The catalog is released in January, and popular courses fill fast.

# WHERE TO EAT

## IN THE PARK

Due to the distances in the park, I've arranged dining information in this chapter by area, starting from Mammoth and working around the park clockwise.

**Reservations** make a meal at the formal hotel restaurants something to look forward to all year. At this writing, they began accepting them in January, and evenings were booking up in April. You need to reserve your table when you set up the rest of your trip; you can always cancel later. Less formal places don't accept reservations.

**The children's menu** is the same at all the more formal dining rooms, with breakfast $1.75 to $3, and lunch and dinner $3 to $4.25. It's the bland food most kids like: burgers, grilled cheese, pb&j, chicken or fish strips, or spaghetti with tomato sauce.

The **Hamilton Stores** have old-fashioned soda fountains and grills at several sites, which often are the most convenient and fun places to eat. They are all open roughly 8am to 9pm. Besides those mentioned at the villages below, small fountains with limited menus are located at Tower Fall and Fishing Bridge.

## MAMMOTH HOT SPRINGS

The **Terrace Grill** is a fast-food outlet, similar to a McDonald's in food, price, and furniture, without the brand names. It is open 7am to 9pm in the high season, shorter hours off-season.

**Mammoth Hot Springs Dining Room. ☎ 307/ 344-5314.** Breakfast $3.50–$7, lunch and dinner $6–$14.25. Summer daily 7am–9pm, shorter hours off-season.

I especially like this restaurant. Families get to enjoy the airy Art Deco dining room and tablecloths without all the formality and expense of the other big hotel restaurants. You don't need reservations and the food is good but not ostentatious. Most entrees are served for lunch or dinner, including both a list of burgers and items such as brie chicken, vegetarian stir-fry, and trout.

## ROOSEVELT LODGE

The western trail ride cookout is covered under "Horseback Riding" (p. 328).

**Roosevelt Lodge.** No phone. Reservations not accepted. Breakfast $3.75–$6.50, lunch $4.50–$7.75, dinner $6.50–$18.25. Daily 7–10:30am, 11:30am–3pm, and 5–9pm. Closed Sept–May.

The casual dining room is part of the lobby in the historic main lodge, like a big ranch house. The menu leans to steaks, chili, barbecue, and other cowboy fare, but everything you expect in a usual hotel cafe also is there. It's a good place for a sit-down meal with kids.

## CANYON

Canyon is too busy and too hectic for my taste. It's a huge facility, built in the 1950s and apparently little changed since then. Certain details, like the star-shaped fluorescent-tube chandeliers, are so out they're back in and back out again. The place reminded me of a

big student center. It operates June through mid-September.

There are four places to eat, serving more than 5,000 meals a day. In the Hamilton Store, there is an **old-fashioned fountain,** with a grill serving burgers. In the restaurant building, a **picnic shop** has a couple of tables and takeout for the picnic tables outside. They serve sandwiches, wraps, salads, and rotisserie chicken ($3.50–$9) and are open 11am to 9:30pm, closing at 5pm in September. Next door the cafeteria serves hordes of diners in a setting that was dark and noisy when I stopped in. Breakfast tops out in price at $3.50 for an omelet, lunch is around $5, and dinner runs $6 to $11. There are stations for pasta and for American food. Hours are daily 6:30 to 10:00am, 11:30am to 2:30pm, and 5 to 10pm.

**Canyon Lodge Dining Room. ☎ 307/ 242-3999.** No reservations accepted. Breakfast $3.75–$6.75, lunch $6–$7.75, dinner $8–$15.50. Daily 7–10:30am, 11:30am–2:30pm, and 5–10pm.

This is an old-fashioned western steak house, with a menu of ribeye, New York strip, prime rib, top sirloin, and chicken fried steak to match the authentic 1950s decor.

## LAKE VILLAGE

The village has a fountain serving cold sandwiches and ice cream at the Hamilton Store, in an interesting and even strange building between the lodge and hotel. You can also buy sandwiches made to order from a deli in the big yellow hotel building, 10:30am to 9:30pm.

The main dining choice for families is the cafeteria at Lake Lodge, a huge log building with a rustic, historic feel. Breakfast is traditional and inexpensive. For lunch, two stations operate, for fajita wraps or for hot meals such as pot roast or lasagna ($4–$8). For dinner, a prime-rib station replaces the wrap station ($4–$13). Hours are 6:30 to 10am, 11:30am to 2:30pm, and 4:30 to 9:30pm.

**Lake Yellowstone Hotel.** ☎ **307/242-3899.** Breakfast $4–$7, lunch $5–$8.25, dinner $13–$23. 6:30–10am, 11:30am–2:30pm, and 5–10pm. Dinner reservations required.

I hesitate to rave, because I know that the staff of seasonal restaurants often changes every year, but the dinner we had here was so extraordinary I just can't help it. I had sautéed boneless breast of duck with a balsamic vinegar and artichoke heart sauce; the flavor emphasized what's best about duck, and its disadvantages seemed to disappear. Barbara's fusilli with gorgonzola, roasted crimini mushrooms, and pine nuts blew us both away with its strong but perfectly balanced flavors and textures, becoming a new standard we use to compare such dishes (she says it's the best food she's ever had). Light pours into the large dining room, with very high ceilings, and over the wood floors and restored 1920s details. The service was perfect. Our children behaved themselves, thank God, because we would have felt quite out of place if they hadn't.

## GRANT VILLAGE

There are three restaurants. The Village Grill is in the Hamilton Store. Furnished like a fast-food restaurant, it has quick table service for a menu of sandwiches, burgers, soup, and a salad bar ($3.50–$6.75; breakfast $3.75–$6). Kids' meals are served on a Frisbee, which we made good use of later. All in all, it's hard to do better for a hassle-free lunch.

The Lake House is quite casual, too, serving pizza ($9–$11) and a pasta bar ($5 kids, $10 adults) for dinner in a dining room that sits on the lake at a defunct marina. Breakfast is continental or a buffet that costs $4.25 children, $6.50 adults. Hours are 7 to10:30am, closed lunch, and 5:30 to 9pm.

**Grant Village.** ☎ **307/242-3499.** Breakfast $4–$7, lunch $5–$7.75, dinner $6.75–$18.25. 6:30–10am, 11:30am–2:30pm, and 5:30–10pm. Dinner reservations required.

This place most resembles the typical American mid-range hotel restaurant. The dining room occupies a modern building with big windows and a high vaulted ceiling and far fewer tables than the park's big, old restaurants. The atmosphere is dim and subdued. The breakfast and lunch menus are traditional, the dinner menu slightly more adventurous, but specializing mostly in beef and trout.

## OLD FAITHFUL

There are seven places to eat in the Old Faithful area, not counting all the espresso carts, ice cream stands, and such. The Hamilton Stores have two choices: a historic fountain and a pizza place. Yellowstone National Park Lodges has two fast-food outlets: The Pony Express at Old Faithful Inn (10:30am–7:30pm) and the Geyser Grill at the Old Faithful Snow Lodge (7am–9pm), serving burgers and sandwiches for lunch and dinner and, at the Geyser Grill, breakfast items under $3, such as English-muffin egg sandwiches.

The dining room at the cafeteria at the Old Faithful Lodge is memorable, with its construction of huge timbers and stone and the immense windows of many panes looking out on the famous geyser. The choices for lunch or dinner are many, including heavy hot dishes such as meatloaf or lasagna, and sandwiches, trout, burgers, or barbecue ($4–$8) with prime rib added in the evening ($11–$13). I enjoyed eating there much more than I expected. Hours are 11am to 9pm.

**Obsidian Room (at the Snow Lodge).** No reservations. ☎ **307/545-4900.** Breakfast $4–$6.50, lunch $6–$11.50, dinner $6–$16.25. 6:30–10am and 11:30am–10pm.

Like the cafe restaurant in any modern high-end hotel, this dining room serves a varied menu in a setting of polished casualness. There are a few trendy choices, but the menu leans heavily on fancy burgers and the like. Housed in the gorgeous new hotel, it is the most modern in the park.

**Old Faithful Inn Dining Room.** ☎ 307/
**545-4999.** Dinner reservations required. Breakfast
$4–$7, lunch $5–$7.75, dinner $8.75–$20.
6:30–10am, 11:30am–2:30pm, and 5–10pm.

The restaurant at the inn appears more formal
than it is. The staffers wear uniforms, but their
behavior is loose and congenial, with something of a sense of controlled crisis as they rush
to serve the huge dining room. The cuisine is
mainly traditional, with specialties of prime
rib, pork chops, or the park's ubiquitous trout,
here sautéed and topped with pecans and
lemon butter. Our meals were satisfactory but
unmemorable. Children need to be on good
behavior, but the noise and activity will cover
most sins. Lunch is casual, and includes a
western buffet.

## OUTSIDE THE PARK

Fast food and western diners are not hard to
find in the towns around the park, especially
West Yellowstone, which has been invaded by
fast-food chains. I've mentioned a couple of
restaurants with the hotels where they are
housed ("Where to Spend the Night," p. 310).
Our favorite was the **Firehole Grill,** which
had exceptional barbecue and friendly, effi-
cient service. It has since moved to 603
Highway 20 in West Yellowstone (☎ **406/
646-4948**), but if the food and attitude
remain the same, it will still be a great place.

# Grand Teton National Park

The Teton Range is a shock the first time you see it. The gray-rock mountains seem impossibly steep and sharp. They stand so tall that you have to take a good look just to get used to how big they are. It's not only that the Tetons are tall; what makes them so awesome is the way they stand up like a wall from the flat ground on their eastern side. Most mountains have a ramp of foothills in front of them, and usually you have to be a lot farther away to see a whole mountain — that's how the Tetons are on the west side. But on the Tetons' east side, you can get close to something very big without being on it. From the valley floor to the top of Grand Teton, a distance of about 3 miles, the elevation rises 7,000 feet, or more than a mile, straight up. The mountains fill the sky.

It takes a little longer to appreciate the flat land that you stand on when you look up at the mountains, but the flat is more important for animals and for the families traveling to the park. Not much can live up on those rocky mountain peaks in the snow and cold. The valley, called Jackson Hole (*hole* is a word for valley), is a special place, a perfect habitat for elk, moose, and many other animals. The wall of mountains protects the valley from the worst of the snowy weather. As you drive into Jackson Hole, you can sense the way this land is protected, as if it's in the palm of a great hand, and the Tetons are the fingers. As you hike, camp, ride, swim, or canoe, the mountains are always there to the west, inspiring you and enclosing the big sky. As you climb up into the mountains, you can see how the rich life of the lowlands slips away, and you can feel the thin, cool air of that higher world. When you return, the lowlands seem even more inviting.

Yellowstone is like a three-ring circus, with geysers and canyons and mountain lakes. Grand Teton, on the other hand, is a single grand opera stage. The main show is the Teton Range and Jackson Hole. There's as much or more to do in the outdoors, but not as much sightseeing to keep you on the run, and that gives the park a more relaxed feel. The town of Jackson (often called Jackson Hole) is a fun and bustling ski resort with good restaurants.

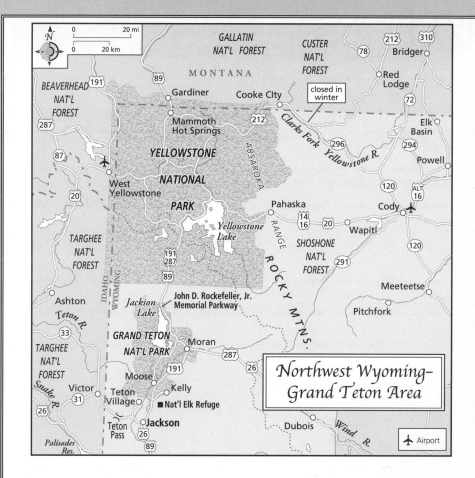

Northwest Wyoming–
Grand Teton Area

## BEST THINGS TO DO

- Hike around the ponds of Jackson Hole to see moose, bison, trumpeter swans, white pelicans, and lovely views.
- Ride the aerial tram to the top of Rendezvous Mountain to start a high-elevation hike with sweeping views and cool, thin air.

- Canoe String and Leigh lakes or Jackson Lake, and dive in for a swim.
- Camp in the backcountry by canoe or by backpacking.

See "Activities" (p. 353).

## HISTORY: ROCKEFELLER TO THE RESCUE!

If you had enough money to buy anything, you might find there were things you wanted that money couldn't buy. Being rich doesn't make people think of you as a good person or remember you after you die. A rich person ends up the same as a poor one. When I think of people I want to be like or who did things that made my life better, I don't often think of rich people. I think of leaders who helped create freedom and justice, or spiritual leaders who taught people how to live right.

But John D. Rockefeller, Jr., one of the richest men who ever lived, found a way to use his money to make something that will live on and make future generations grateful. He was born with the money because his father started the world's largest oil companies. The son's great achievement was the way he spent the money. He bought up land for some of America's greatest national parks, including Grand Teton, Acadia, and Great Smoky Mountain national parks (all of which are in this book), and many others.

The first superintendent of Yellowstone National Park, Horace Albright, started Grand Teton National Park. Albright was a young man from California who loved spending time in the mountains. He was one of the first members of the new National Park Service when it took over the parks from the Army in 1916. The first time Albright saw Jackson Hole and the Tetons, he wanted to add them to Yellowstone. But times had changed since Yellowstone became a park in 1872, when settlers had barely touched the Rockies. Now there were people living on the flat lands of Jackson Hole, and they had worked hard to build ranches there. Jackson Lake had been dammed in 1906, raising its level to help water farms. Later the Park Service fought off plans to dam Jenny Lake and other beautiful waterways. Locals wanted to make their living on this land, not have it made into a park. The representatives they elected to Congress stopped the park from happening for many years.

One group in the valley, however, thought it could make money from a park. People had built dude ranches in Jackson Hole where visitors could come to ride horses and enjoy the beauty of the area. They thought that if the mountains were protected in a park, their businesses could be more successful. Albright got together with this group, and together they worked to persuade their neighbors and Congressmen to support the park. But the local residents wanted only the mountains in the park, not the valley. The Teton Range never could have been developed into farms and towns, whether or not it was a park — it is too steep and rugged. Because no one else had a use for the mountains other than looking at them, most people could agree to put them into a park. In 1929, after Albright's original park idea was cut down to just the mountains and six lakes at their base, Congress passed the law that created Grand Teton National Park.

But Albright didn't give up. In 1924, John D. Rockefeller, Jr., brought his family to visit Yellowstone. Albright set up a special tour for the Rockefellers and made friends with them. He knew that Rockefeller had helped create Acadia National Park in Maine, but he didn't ask for help for Grand Teton right away. Two years later, however, when the Rockefellers came back, Albright drove them to Jackson Hole. They picnicked on the hill next to where Jackson Lake Lodge is today and saw five moose. The spot is one of the grandest and most beautiful you will ever see, and they had a wonderful day. The next day, they drove farther and saw how human development was spreading into some of Jackson Hole's prettiest areas. Because only the mountains and lakes were in the park, the valley had been left open for businesses. Even in the 1920s, the areas of unplanned roadside tourist development were ugly. The Rockefellers were horrified, and it wasn't long before they agreed with Albright's plan — they would buy the property in the valley and give it to the government to expand Grand Teton National Park.

If you're going to buy a whole valley, you have to be very careful about how you do it. As soon as people know that one of the richest men in the world wants to buy their land, they will probably raise the price. In a place like Jackson Hole, where many people opposed expanding the park, buying the land would be even more difficult. So Rockefeller and Albright decided to buy the land secretly. Rockefeller set up a company that hired people to buy land without telling them why, or who was paying the bills. The buyers just got a list of what property to buy and the money to do it. At the same time, Albright worked secretly in Washington, D.C., to keep more government-owned land in Jackson Hole from being made into private homesteads or otherwise given away. The project worked. Soon, all the land in Jackson Hole that Albright wanted

for the park was controlled by Rockefeller or the federal government.

When people in Wyoming found out, they were furious about being fooled. They felt their valley and their ability to make a living had been stolen. They accused the pro-park group of breaking the law, and a scandal broke out, with investigations and hearings. Albright resigned to take a better-paying job, and no one found evidence he'd done anything wrong.

Rockefeller had hoped to give the land to the park fairly quickly, but the local residents wouldn't give up. Their representatives in Congress stopped the Park Service from accepting the land for years. In 1942, after working on the project for 15 years, Rockefeller wrote a letter to the president saying he would give up on the whole thing if something wasn't done. The next year, President Franklin Roosevelt made Jackson Hole a national monument. A national monument is an area like a park; but it's usually smaller, and the president has the power to create it without Congress. The Congressmen who had stopped the park before were so angry that they passed a bill to do away with the monument and take away the president's power to create monuments. Roosevelt vetoed the bill, and the monument survived.

Over the next years, the feelings of people in Jackson started to change. After World War II ended, more tourists started coming to the area to see Grand Teton. Finally, in 1950, the residents stopped fighting. Congress passed a bill to add the national monument to the old Grand Teton National Park, creating the size and shape the park is today. To settle the disagreement over the park, the ranchers who were already using park land to graze their cattle were allowed to stay for as long as they and their children were alive. In the eastern part of the park, you can still see those ranchers' houses and animals. Today, pretty much everyone thinks the park was a good idea. A few ranchers may be left, but most jobs and businesses in the area depend on the visitors who

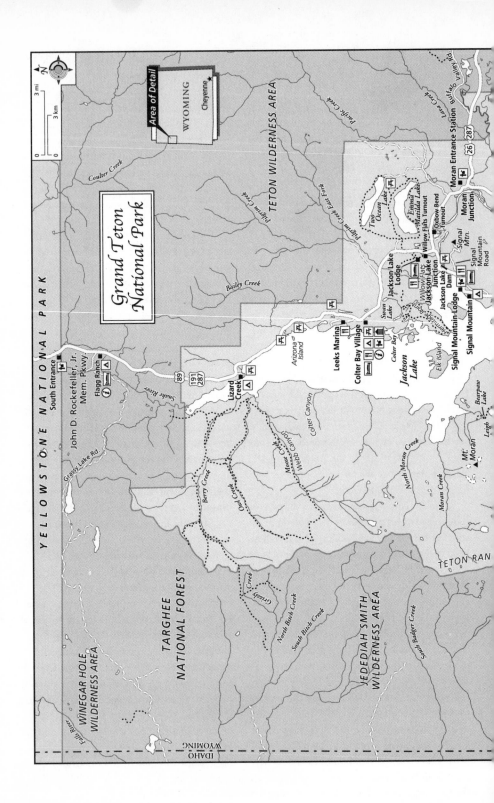

Grand Teton National Park

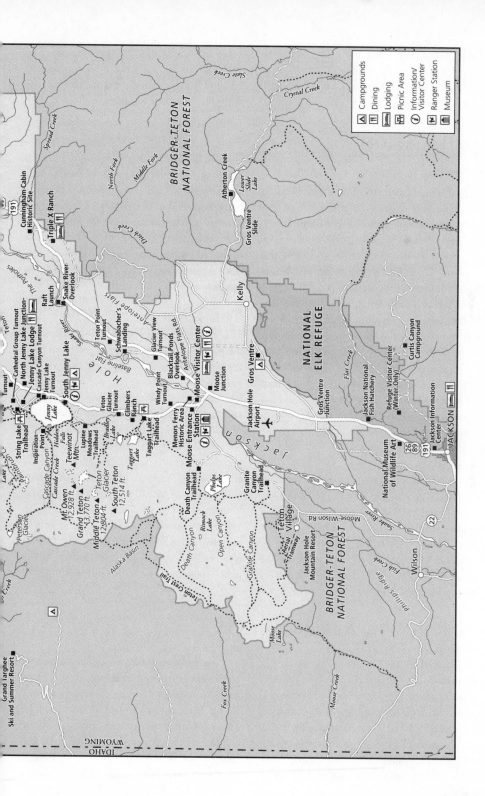

BRIDGER-TETON
NATIONAL FOREST

State Creek

Crystal Creek

North Fork

Middle Fork

Spread Creek

Ditch Creek

Atherton Creek

Lower
Slide
Lake

Gros Ventre
Slide

Kelly

Cunningham Cabin
Historic Site

(191)

Triple X Ranch

Snake River
Overlook

The Potholes

Raft
Launch

Teton River

Antelope Flats

Teton Point
Turnout

Schwabacher's
Landing

Glacier View
Turnout

Antelope Flats Rd.

Blacktail Ponds
Overlook

Moose Visitor Center

Moose
Junction

Gros Ventre

NATIONAL

ELK REFUGE

Flat Creek

Curtis Canyon
Campground

Jackson National
Fish Hatchery

Refuge Visitor Center
(Winter Only)

National Museum
of Wildlife Art

Jackson Information
Center

JACKSON

Gros Ventre
Junction

Jackson Hole
Airport

JACKSON

Cathedral Group Turnout
North Jenny Lake Junction
Jenny Lake Lodge
Cascade Canyon Turnout
Jenny Lake
Turnout

South Jenny Lake

Baseline Flat

Teton
Glacier
Turnout

Climbers
Ranch

Windy Point
Turnout

Menors Ferry
Historic Area

Moose Entrance
Station

HOLE

Inspiration
Point

String Lake
Trailhead

Jenny
Lake

Cascade Canyon Trail

Hidden
Falls

Cascade Creek

Teewinot
Mtn.

Lupine
Meadows

Teton
Glacier

Bradley
Lake

Taggart Lake
Trailhead

Taggart
Lake

Death Canyon
Trailhead

Phelps
Lake

Granite
Canyon
Trailhead

Teton
Village

Aerial
Tramway

Jackson Hole
Mountain Resort

Moose-Wilson Rd.

Snake River

Fish Creek

Phillips Ridge

(22)

Wilson

(26)
(89)
(191)

Peterson
Glacier

Mt. Owen
12,928 ft.

Grand Teton
13,770 ft.

Middle Teton
12,804 ft.

South Teton
12,514 ft.

Alaska Basin

Teton Crest Trail

Death Canyon

Open Canyon

Rimrock
Lake

Granite Canyon

Moose
Lake

BRIDGER-TETON
NATIONAL FOREST

Fox Creek

Moose Creek

Grand Targhee
Ski and Summer Resort

IDAHO
WYOMING

Campgrounds
Dining
Lodging
Picnic Area
Information/
Visitor Center
Ranger Station
Museum

come to the park. They bring in a lot more money than ranching ever could.

Rockefeller and Albright lived to see their plan succeed. Rockefeller, who loved building things, personally took charge of constructing the beautiful Jackson Lake Lodge in his old age. And his family held onto one ranch in the valley for their own vacations.

# ORIENTATION

## THE PARK

Grand Teton National Park is about 45 miles long and half as wide. It reaches from the south entrance of Yellowstone National Park and the John D. Rockefeller, Jr., Parkway, at the north, to the town of **Jackson** and the National Elk Refuge at the south. The **Teton Range** towers along the western side of the park. **Jackson Lake** sits in the mountains' lap in the northern part of the park. Most boating, camping, and lodgings are on the eastern shore of the lake. Most hiking trails up into the mountains start south of Jackson Lake, near **Jenny Lake.** The **Snake River** starts from the southeast corner of Jackson Lake and runs south through the flat valley called **Jackson Hole** and into a canyon south of Jackson.

## THE ROADS

A two-lane U.S. highway runs the length of the park. It's numbered 89 and 191 all the way along, from Yellowstone to Jackson, but it's known locally as **Highway 89.** A highway from the east, **U.S. 26/287,** meets 89 at a "T" at Moran Junction, halfway up the park. The **Teton Park Road** runs from just north of Moran Junction along the base of the Teton Range to the small lakes and trailheads, ending back on 89 at Moose Junction, near the south end of the park. Entrance stations are located so that you can drive 89 through the park from Moran Junction to Jackson without paying an entrance fee. You do have to pay to drive the park road or to go north from Moran Junction toward Yellowstone.

## THE TOWNS

The expensive ski-resort town of **Jackson** is the gateway to the park and a good way into the whole region. It's completely touristy, but nevertheless has managed to keep some charm and uniqueness. **Teton Village** is a ski-resort area west of Jackson, where the aerial tram climbs the mountains and there are some restaurants, lodgings, and campgrounds. To get there from Jackson, you turn off West Broadway on Route 22, cross the Snake River, and then drive north on Highway 390, also known as the Moose-Wilson Road. Past Teton Village north to Moose, this road is rough, narrow, and winding, but very pretty. **Moose** is a developed area at the southern end of the park, where the main visitor center is.

# MAKING THE ARRANGEMENTS

## WHEN TO GO

The busy season at Grand Teton is in July and August, when temperatures are warmest — perfect, in fact. Snow slowly disappears from the mountains and is gone completely in late July or early August. Thunderstorms sweep through the mountains many afternoons. Nights can be chilly. Popular trails and campgrounds are busy.

June and September are quieter. Daytime weather is still comfortable, but nights can be cold. Mountain trails are still snowy in June. By late May, snow clears out of Jackson Hole. That's where campgrounds are and where families spend most of their time. Ice on the lakes is gone in mid-May.

Almost everything in the park shuts down from October 15 to May 15. The main winter

| | AVG. HIGH (°F) | AVG. LOW (°F) | SNOWFALL (IN.) |
|---|---|---|---|
| Nov.–Mar. | 26–39 | 1–14 | 16 |
| April | 49 | 22 | 9 |
| May | 61 | 31 | 3 |
| June | 71 | 41 | 0 |
| July–August | 79–80 | 40–41 | 0 |
| September | 69 | 32 | 1 |
| October | 56 | 23 | 4 |

*Elevation approximately 6,400 feet.*

activities are downhill skiing at the resorts in Jackson and wildlife viewing at the National Elk Refuge.

## HOW MUCH TIME TO SPEND

To get out on the trails, lake, and river, you need at least 3 days, but you could spend a week without getting bored if you enjoy the outdoors. If you're interested only in sightseeing, you can see the mountains just by driving through the park on your way to Yellowstone.

## HOW FAR TO PLAN AHEAD

Telephone reservations for accommodations in the park become available in October for the following summer, but written requests are accepted earlier. The best rooms fill by February but April is not too late to act; the rougher cabins at Colter Bay last the longest. Activities can be reserved starting in the early spring, but reservations aren't always needed before you arrive unless there's something you want to be sure to do. Campgrounds in the park, except the RV park at Colter Bay, do not accept reservations. See "Camping," below, for information on the daily scramble for sites, and to find out about the system to reserve permits to camp in the backcountry.

## READING UP

You can get most of these books and maps at visitor centers, online, or by mail order from **Grand Teton Natural History Association, ☎ 307/739-3606;** www.grandtetonpark.org. **Hiking:** *Great Trails for Family Hiking: The Tetons,* by Jerry Painter (Pruett Publishing, www.gorp.com/pruett/), a father of five, is exceptionally detailed, well thought out, and even fun to read. **Maps:** The *Trails Illustrated* topographic map is the most detailed and complete map of the whole park; it costs $9.95. Some of the best day-hike areas are covered in detailed color maps and field guides that cost only a few dollars each, a good buy if you are taking the aerial tram to Rendezvous Mountain, or hiking Colter Bay or Cascade Canyon. **History:** *Crucible for Conservation: The Struggle for Grand Teton National Park,* by Robert W. Righter (Grand Teton Natural History Association), is a detailed, scholarly, but clearly written account for adults.

## GETTING THERE
### By Car

See the "Getting There" section on Yellowstone (p. 309) for approaches from that direction. If you're coming from the west or south, take I-15 to Idaho Falls and then drive over the back of the Tetons to Jackson via U.S. Highway 26 and state roads 31, 33, and 22 (the way is well marked). From the east, U.S. 26/287 leads to the park from across Wyoming, splitting from I-80 or I-25 on the other side of the state.

## By Air

Jackson has the area's major airport, served by jet from Chicago and Dallas by **American** (☎ 800/443-7300), from Salt Lake City by **Sky West** (☎ 800/453-9417), and from Denver by **United Express** (☎ 800/241-6522). It has eight car-rental agencies, including **Alamo** (☎ 800/462-5266 or 307/733-0671), **Budget** (☎ 800/533-6100 or 307/733-2206), and **Thrifty** (☎ 800/699-1025 or 307/739-9300). You can also rent an RV in Jackson from **Cruise America's** outlet, Eagle Rent-a-Car (☎ **800-327-7799** or 307/739-9999). See "Practicalities: The RV Advantage," in chapter 8, "Layers upon Layers," for advice. If you want to shop around for airfare or car rentals, try Idaho Falls or Salt Lake City.

## WHAT TO PACK

The advice on Yellowstone, in chapter 14, "Yellowstone National Park," is good for Grand Teton too. Be prepared for cool nights and afternoon thunderstorms. Remember to bring good hiking shoes or boots; mountain hiking often covers steep, rugged trails. Do bring your swimming suits for the delicious lakes.

# WHERE TO SPEND THE NIGHT

## CAMPING
### Park Service Campgrounds

Except the Colter Bay RV park, Grand Teton National Park campgrounds do not take reservations. Visitor centers and entrance booths post or will report which campgrounds are full as the day progresses. You have to get up early and participate in a stressful process to get a site in one of the more popular campgrounds in the high season, but two larger campgrounds usually have sites as late as early afternoon. The spectacular Jenny Lake tent campground fills at dawn before people leave and has a 7-day limit (all others have 14-day limits). Signal Mountain goes soon after Jenny Lake. I've listed fill-up times below as a guide; but of course, these vary during the week and by season.

Here's the routine (I can't call it a system) for getting a site in one of the popular campgrounds. Arrive at the campground as early as possible; I got to Jenny Lake at 7 one morning and didn't get a site. Pick up a registration envelope at the entrance and drive around the campground. Each site has a post with a registration slip on it, upon which is written the date of departure of the current occupant. If you find a site with that day's date, stop and ask the people if they are in fact leaving. If the answer is yes, post your own registration marker and leave a member of your party to wave others past, then scurry back to the entrance and register and pay your fee. If you find an unoccupied site, make sure it has no registration paper or other sign of being taken, then leave your own paper plus a lawn chair, an "OCCUPIED" sign, or one of your offspring, while you go register.

Clearly, you can't manage this early-morning registration on the day you arrive at the park, so you will have to stay in town or at one of the less popular campgrounds your first night and move the next morning if you want one of these coveted sites.

All campgrounds but the RV park charge $12 per night, and all campgrounds have flush toilets.

**Colter Bay.** At Colter Bay Village, north of Jackson Lake Junction. 310 sites; tents or RVs. Showers, laundry, dump station. Fills around noon. Closed Oct–May.

Despite its size, this campground is well designed to give good privacy to the sites, set among trees and boulders. Sites don't have lake views. Tenters should ask for a loop where RV generators are not allowed. Tent sites have gravel pads, which does a lot to keep you dry in a storm. The park's primary family-oriented facilities serve the campground, including restaurants, showers, laundry, visitor center, museum, and store. A swimming beach on Jackson Lake is nearby, as are the wonderful family trails at Swan Lake and Heron Pond (see "Hiking," p. 354).

**Colter Bay RV Park.** At Colter Bay Village. $34–$36 per site in summer, $22–$24 in spring and fall. 113 sites; RVs only. Full hookups; showers, laundry. Closed Oct–May.

This RV park is well wooded with pines and sits near the store and other facilities. Sites have picnic tables, but fires and tents are not allowed. Make reservations well ahead with the Grand Teton Lodge Company (see "Grand Teton Address Book," p. 336).

**Gros Ventre.** Near the south end of the park, between the entrance and Kelly. 360 sites; tents or RVs. Dump station. Fills in the afternoon. Closed mid-Oct to May.

This large campground is the last to fill because it's on the east side of Jackson Hole, distant from the lakes, mountains, and visitor facilities. It's a wonderful campground, with loops of well-separated sites along the Gros Ventre River, among cottonwoods, grass, and sagebrush. Here you should find quiet and space.

**Jenny Lake.** At South Jenny Lake. 49 sites; tents only. Fills early morning. Closed Oct–May.

Lucky campers who arrive early (see tips for getting a site above) get sites in this spectacular campground, one of the most desirable in any of the national parks. Tents nestle on large, private sites among small pines and little grassy hills at the base of the Tetons. Even the bathrooms fit in. The park's most popular trails and loveliest canoeing and swimming waters are nearby.

**Lizard Creek.** At the north end of the park on Hwy. 89. 60 sites; tents or RVs. Fills early afternoon. Closed Sept to mid-June.

The campground is on Jackson Lake, among thick pines at the northern end of the park. There are many walk-in sites, with wonderful privacy, and even some with lake frontage. A pizzeria is at the marina up the road (p. 358), but mostly this area of the park is quiet and undeveloped.

**Signal Mountain.** On the park road near Jackson Lake Junction. 86 sites; tents or RVs. Store, dump station. Fills mid-morning. Closed Oct–May.

Some campsites overlook Jackson Lake from a steep hill while others hide among the pines. The views are excellent and the campground is not too large. We enjoyed swimming from the small beach. The campground is well-used, and some sites have been receiving much-needed restoration. Signal Mountain Lodge, with its store, marina, and restaurant, is nearby.

## Backcountry Permits

To camp on the hiking trails or lakes outside campgrounds, you need a free backcountry permit. (See "Backpacking," p. 353 and "Canoeing, Kayaking & Boating" p. 353, for advice on trips.) Campsites and camping zones are shown on a map distributed free by the Park Service. To get a copy, write to the address at the beginning of the chapter, call the backcountry office (☎ **307/739-3309**), or download it from the Web at www.nps.gov/ grte/sitepub/freepubs.htm. You'll also need a topographic map and a trail guide to plan your hiking itinerary; see "Reading Up" (p. 341) for recommendations.

Only 30% of the permits are given out by reservation, so plenty are available for walk-in applicants at the Moose and Colter Bay visitor centers 24 hours before the trip begins (be there when the center opens at 8am to get your choice). To be certain of a particular site, or to make sure you match your itinerary to your group's abilities, a reservation is a good idea. Reservations for the summer are taken from January 1 to May 15 by mail, by fax (☎ 307/739-3438), or in person. Sites are allotted according to whose request gets there first, so a mad rush of faxes comes in on New Year's Day, clogging the machine so that requests are lost. Sending your request later might be more effective. No-shows are released at 10am on the day of the trip.

## Forest Service Campgrounds

Campgrounds in the Bridger-Teton and Caribou-Targhee national forests are helpfully marked on the official Grand Teton National Park map. Those that accept reservations are noted below. Reserve through the Forest Service's national system, described in chapter 1, "Planning Your Trip." All have vault toilets and piped drinking water. For more information, contact the national forests directly (see "Grand Teton Address Book," p. 336), or stop at the visitor center in Jackson, which is staffed by forest rangers.

### BRIDGER-TETON NATIONAL FOREST

These campgrounds are east of the park or Elk Refuge.

**Atherton Creek.** On Lower Slide Lake about 6 miles up Gros Ventre Road. $10 per site. Reservations accepted for an additional fee. 13 sites; tents or RVs. Closed Nov–May.

This campground faces the landslide-created lake from a steep hillside with aspen and spruce trees and much open ground. There are a dock for swimming and a place to launch canoes and boats. The Gros Ventre Slide nature trail is just down the lake (see p. 352). The road is narrow and unpaved, with some steep drop-offs, making the campground isolated and quiet. Four and 5 miles farther on the same road, the **Red Hills** and **Crystal Creek campgrounds** are even more remote. Camping at these primitive, tent-only campgrounds costs $8 per site and reservations are not taken. They have 11 sites total and are closed November to May.

**Curtis Canyon.** 8 miles from Jackson over dirt roads; follow Broadway out of town past Elk Refuge, then follow signs. $10 per site. Reservations accepted for an additional fee. 12 sites; tents or RVs. Closed mid-Sept to May.

This inner canyon campground is in an alpine setting above the elk refuge.

**Hatchet.** About 8 miles east of Moran Junction entrance station, Hwy. 26/287. $10 per site. No reservations. 9 sites; tents or RVs. Closed Oct–May.

This is a shady campground with good scenery near the highway to the park.

### TARGHEE NATIONAL FOREST

The forest, administered jointly with Caribou National Forest, is west of the park, mostly in Idaho.

**Teton Canyon.** 12 miles east of Driggs, ID. $8 per site. Reservations accepted for an additional fee. 19 sites; tents or RVs. Closed mid-Sept to mid-May.

This out-of-the way campground is a back door to the Teton Range trails most used for backpacking trips and trail rides.

**Mike Harris.** Rte. 22 west of Jackson. $8 per site. No reservations. 11 sites; tents or RVs. Closed mid-Sept to mid-May.

Secluded among small pines, the campground is rich in berry bushes.

**Trail Creek.** Rte. 22 west, 3 miles west of Mike Harris. $8 per site. No reservations. 11 sites; tents or RVs. Closed Sept–May.

Among the spruces right next to the creek and mountain road, the campground suffers from car noise.

## Commercial Campgrounds

With the great public campgrounds in the area, there's little reason for tenters to camp outside the park or national forests, but if you bring an RV and Colter Bay RV Park is full, here are two choices near the park. **Jackson/Teton Village KOA** (☎ 800/KOA-9043 or 307/733-5354), open from May to mid-October, is just south of the ski area and aerial tram west of Jackson, on Highway 390. It's a pleasant spot of shady willows. Full-hookup sites are $40 for two, $5.50 for each additional person; they take Visa, MasterCard, and American Express. **Grand Teton Park RV Resort** (☎ 800/563-6469 or 307/543-3483; www.yellowstonerv.com), open all year, is on the dry land 6 miles east of the Moran Junction entrance station on Highway 26/287. A full-hookup site is $37.50 for two, $4 for each additional child 4 to 17, $5 for each additional adult. They take major credit cards.

## HOTELS & CABINS
## In the Park

Reservations for lodgings in the park require deposits of 1 to 3 nights' advance payment, and cancellation carries a fee. Check before you reserve.

### GRAND TETON LODGE COMPANY

The main concessionaire at the park is the **Grand Teton Lodge Company** (see "Grand Teton Address Book," p. 336). I've covered two of their three facilities; the luxurious Jenny Lake Lodge is not suitable for most families. Rooms lack TVs or cooking facilities.

Guests at any of the properties can use the pool at Jackson Lake Lodge. Children 11 and under stay free, unless you need a rollaway bed. The company accepts Visa, MasterCard, and American Express, but requires deposits by check or money order.

**Colter Bay Village.** 166 cabins, 9 with shared bathroom; 66 tent cabins. $125 2-room cabin with bathroom for up to 4 people. $68–$102 double cabin with bathroom; $8.50 per extra person over age 11. $33 double with shared bathroom. Tent cabins $33 double; $4 per extra person. Cabins closed Oct–May; tent cabins closed Sept–May.

These are the park's main family accommodations, at the center of lakeside activities. The metal-roofed cabins are authentic, rough-hewn log structures, with dark linoleum floors and rag throw rugs. Many were brought here from original sites where they were built by settlers. Unlike older cabins at Yellowstone, they've been kept in prime condition. They're spacious and each time I've visited I have found them remarkably clean and fresh. There are many types, from simple single rooms to places as large as a house. All prices seemed a decent bargain, especially for large families who normally need two units. Like real log cabins, they tend to be dark, and the bathrooms have only shower stalls, no tubs. Also, with the old wiring, there are no air-conditioners or fans, but the thick pine forest keeps it shady.

The tent cabins are fun, but more than halfway to camping, and rather close together for that. They consist of concrete slabs with log walls and canvas roofs. Small wood stoves and cots are inside and barbecues are out front. The units are closely spaced. Everyone in the tent cabins uses a shared bathhouse and showers cost extra.

Restaurants are covered under "Where to Eat" (p. 357).

**Jackson Lake Lodge.** 385 units. Main lodge $99 double, $180 with view; cottages $120–$210 double; suites $385–$550 double; $9 per extra person over age 11. Closed mid-Oct to mid-May.

Fires need fuel, heat, and oxygen. The trick to getting a fire started is getting the wood (fuel) to its ignition temperature (heat) with enough flow of air (oxygen) that it can burn.

If you're camping in a campground, buy your wood. We've learned to grab the first bundle we see on sale when we approach a park. Some parks allow wood gathering, but near campgrounds there's rarely any to be found that's any good. Starting a fire with wet or green wood is almost impossible. The moisture smothers flames and keeps the wood too cold to burn. Bring newspaper and fire starters to get the fire going. Fire starters, small lumps of pressed sawdust treated with wax, are better than paper because they burn brightly for several minutes. A box of a dozen costs a few dollars. Use the newspaper to start the fire starter.

If you're camping in the backcountry and fires are permitted, look for dead wood that has had a chance to dry for at least a year. Look under a tree canopy or on a snag that's off the ground, for example. Anything wet, rotten, or recently alive won't work. You'll need a hatchet, and having a saw too makes it much easier. I bring paper to get the fire started when backpacking, but birch bark, dry grass, or tiny spruce twigs will work with a lot more effort. Trying to light a fire in the backcountry in the rain or in a very damp area usually isn't worth the trouble. In an emergency it's better to rely on your camp stove than to struggle with getting a fire started.

In the backcountry or the campground, a lighter is the best source of flame, but have waterproof matches stored in a couple of places just in case. Available at any sporting-goods store, these matches are treated with wax so that they will still light if they get damp.

Next, you need kindling. Before wood will burn, it has to reach its ignition temperature, which is roughly 650°F for dry wood in good conditions. To get a big piece of wood that hot, you need a strong fire. That's what the kindling is for. Gathering kindling is a great job for kids. Any thin, dry

---

Rockefeller built this hotel himself, near the spot on Picnic Tree Hill where he first fell in love with the Tetons. Some criticize the concrete building for not fitting the traditional national park mold, but I think its straight lines and airy space are perfect for the setting. They frame the overwhelming view from the main lobby sitting room. The immaculate rooms are just as good, elegantly decorated in light Western decor. For families, the best are cottage rooms with patios that open onto the grass and the moose-filled willow flats. Somehow, these units manage to be tasteful, luxurious, and vacation-casual all at the same time. In the evening climb the hill for an unforgettable sunset view, likely decorated with moose in the foreground. The lifeguard-protected outdoor pool is large and splendid, with a baby pool. The hotel's several dining choices are covered under "Where To Eat" (p. 357).

### OTHER LODGINGS INSIDE THE PARK

The **Flagg Ranch Resort** is on the John D. Rockefeller, Jr., Parkway north of the park (see chapter 14).

**Dornan's in Moose Spur Ranch Log Cabins.** At Moose Junction (P.O. Box 39), Moose, WY 83012. ☎ **307/733-2522.** Fax 307/739-9098. www.dornans.com. 12 cabins. High season $140–$210; low season $100–$150. AE, MC, V.

These are large, well-appointed log cabins on the Snake River near the south end of the park, below the Dornan's complex of stores, eateries, and outdoors outfitters. Rustic-style furniture sits on wood floors between log walls. Each has a living room and kitchen with one or two bedrooms; they sleep four to six.

stick or twig will do. But also prepare with some good stuff — thin pieces you split off one of the dry logs you bought, using your hatchet.

Finally, you need air. We build fires by making a house: A medium-sized stick is the ridgepole, propped up between rocks or larger logs. The paper or fire starter goes underneath, and the kindling forms the rafters. There are other good ways to do it, including the classic Boy Scout teepee shape, but the important thing to remember is that the kindling will burn only if there's a free channel for air coming from underneath and leaving on top. But not too much air. If the kindling is too far apart, the air coming through the gaps will cool the pieces to below their ignition point before the fire can spread.

The fire starts. Don't add big logs right away. Have a range of sizes, adding slightly larger pieces one at a time. As your fire grows, it will put off enough energy to heat larger logs to their ignition point. Each log that you add should enlarge the house, keeping the air flow open but the fire compact so that each burning log adds to the heat of the others around it. If you have any wet or green wood, wait to use it until the fire is roaring; then, the fire's heat will dry the wood so it can burn.

Cooking over a campfire works best after it has burned down to coals, just like a barbecue grill at home. The yellow flame that comes off a fire is made of burning particles of carbon and other material from the hot wood. If you put a pot or other cool object in the flame, the carbon particles that touch it cool to below their ignition point and stick as black soot rather than burning. After a fire burns down to coals, with hot blue flame or no visible flame at all, it's perfect for cooking or roasting marshmallows.

Of course, a camp stove is more practical and useful, but not nearly as much fun. I've covered that subject in chapter 22, "Olympic National Park."

**Signal Mountain Lodge.** South of Jackson Lake Junction on park Rd. (P.O. Box 50), Moran, WY 83013. ☎ **307/543-2831.** Fax 307/543-2569. www.foreverresorts.com. 78 cabins. $92–$216 cabin for up to 6 people. AE, DISC, MC, V. Closed mid-Oct to mid-May.

This is the classic lakeside family resort, with the significant advantages of friendly, professional management and a location in the heart of the park, with trails and boating from the grounds. The accommodations range from simple cabins to a couple of houses with cooking facilities, but most are on the more modest end of the price range. Some are charming old log cabins with stone fireplaces. Lakefront units have porches or decks over the water. All have telephones, but the only TV is in the common room. Some have only showers, not tubs. Reserve 6 months ahead. Rent canoes and boats or book their guided fishing and

scenic raft floats. We enjoyed swimming, but many find it too cold. There's a coin-op laundry too. The restaurant is covered under "Where to Eat" (p. 357).

## A DUDE RANCH
The original way to visit the area was to spend a week or two at a dude ranch such as the **Triangle X Ranch** (☎ **307/733-2183;** www. trianglex.com), which has been serving guests since 1926. It's a working ranch, within the park on the east side of Jackson Hole, with a comfortable but authentically rough atmosphere for guests, who come for weeklong stays in log cabins starting at over $1,000 per person. I ran into a Dad who had been coming back 19 straight years — his children refuse to go anywhere else. Kids break off each day for their own supervised activities (mostly riding,

of course) and even have their own dining room back at the lodge.

### IN JACKSON

Shop around with the help of the chamber of commerce (see "Grand Teton Address Book," p. 336), which has links to many lodgings at www.jacksonholechamber.com.

**Best Western The Lodge at Jackson Hole.** 80 S. Scott Lane (P.O. Box 7478), Jackson, WY 83002. ☎ **800/458-3866** or 307/739-9703. Fax 307/739-9168. www.lodgeatjh.com. 154 units. High season $159–$219 double; low season $99–$149 double; children 14 and under stay free in parents' room. AE, DISC, MC, V. Rate includes full breakfast.

This well-crafted luxury hotel with a stone-and-log front has large, fresh rooms with microwaves and many other extras. The decoration is warm and dark; and the rooms feel solid, so you don't worry about bothering the neighbors. Carved wooden bears are all over the place, peeking out of unexpected places where Julia delighted in finding them. The pool is cool, too, with doors that can make it indoor or outdoor. Rates include breakfast and appetizers, served from a buffet in a dining room off the lobby. The neighborhood, an area with supermarkets and car dealerships, doesn't match the posh hotel.

**Hitching Post Lodge.** 460 E. Broadway (P.O. Box 4397), Jackson, WY 83001. ☎ **307/733-2606.** Fax 307/733-8221. www.hitchingpostlodge.com. 33 units. High season $78–$189 double to quad; low season $38–$89; $5 each additional person. MC, V.

Charming little cabins dating from the 1930s are just off the sidewalk in the downtown walking area. The older "authentic" cabins are a bargain. Although old-fashioned, with their log walls and painted paneling, I found them clean and spacious, with refrigerators and microwaves. A unit with two queen-sized beds rents for $92. The newer deluxe cabins are comfortable duplex homes, each with a large sitting room, a full kitchenette and two bedrooms. A small pool and grassy play area are outside. A continental breakfast is included in peak season.

**The Virginian Lodge.** 750 W. Broadway (P.O. Box 1052), Jackson, WY 83001. ☎ **800/262-4999** or 307/733-2792. Fax 307/733-4063. virginian-lodge.com. 170 units. High season $95 double, $102–$185 suite; low season $45 double, $46–$85 suite; $7 per extra person, children under 12 free. AE, DISC, MC, V.

The hotel's brown, suburban-ranch–style exterior is so out-of-date it's now retro, but the prices are right and the large, grassy courtyard, with its large pool, will keep the kids active — some were playing touch football there when I last visited. The rooms have paneling and some have been used hard; but they were clean on my inspection and many were large and had good configurations for families. Some have microwaves, coffeemakers, and small refrigerators. There are a restaurant, a laundry, and an RV park on-site.

# WHEN YOU ARRIVE

## ENTRANCE FEES

The $20 entrance fee covers both Grand Teton and Yellowstone national parks; it's good for 1 week in both. The fee isn't collected for the highway from Moran Junction to Jackson and the land east of the Snake River, including Gros Ventre campground, but you do have to pay to get into most of the best part of the park.

## VISITOR CENTERS
### Park Service

**Moose Visitor Center.** Near Moose Junction, at the south end of the park. ☎ **307/739-3399,** TDD 307/739-3400. June–Aug daily 8am–7pm; Sept–May daily 8am–5pm.

**Emergencies** ☎ **911** works anywhere in the area. To reach **park dispatch,** call ☎ **307/ 739-3300.** The **Grand Teton Medical Clinic** (☎ **307/543-2514,** or 307/733-8002 after hours) operates during the business day from mid-May to mid-October, near Jackson Lake Lodge at the park's midpoint. **St. John's Hospital** (☎ **307/733-3636**) is at 625 E. Broadway St. in Jackson.

**Stores** Within the park, general stores are at Colter Bay Village and Dornan's in Moose. Convenience stores are at South Jenny Lake and Signal Mountain Lodge. There are large supermarkets in Jackson.

**Banks** ATMs are located at Jackson Lake Lodge, the Colter Bay Village store, and Dornan's in Moose. **Jackson State Bank** (☎ **307/739-3790**) is on Town Square in Jackson, at 112 Center St.

**Post Offices** There are post offices in the park at Moose and Moran Junction. In Jackson, the post office is at 220 W. Pearl St., near Town Square.

**Gear Sales & Rental** Some camping and fishing supplies are available at the general stores. **Dornan's** (☎ **307/733-3307** or 307/733-3699), at Moose Junction, sells fishing, camping, and climbing equipment, and rents bikes, canoes, and kayaks. Car carriers for any of the equipment are included in the rental price. For more on renting boats and canoes, see "Canoeing, Kayaking & Boating" (p. 353). In Jackson, **Gart Sports** (☎ **307/733-4449**), at 450 W. Broadway, and **Jack Dennis Outdoor Store** (☎ **307/733-3270**), at 50 E. Broadway, are full sporting-goods stores.

This main visitor center has displays about the park's natural history, frequent films, and useful postings and information for hikers. The bookstore is large.

**Colter Bay Visitor Center.** ½ mile west of Colter Bay Junction on U.S. 89/191/287, near the north end of the park. ☎ **307/739-3594,** TDD 307/ 739-3544. June–Aug daily 8am–8pm; spring and fall daily 8am–5pm. Closed Oct to mid-May.

In the park's main northern activity hub, this visitor center bustles with people asking questions and buying books before heading out on the many nearby activities. Inside, the Colter Bay Indian Arts Museum contains a rich collection of Native American art and other objects from all over the country presented in a visually interesting if subdued space. Many of these objects are surprisingly fresh and finely made, but a lack of context reduces the time they will hold children's interest. Native American residents sometimes put on demonstrations and sell crafts.

**Jenny Lake Visitor Center.** Grand Teton Park Rd. at Jenny Lake. Daily 8am–7pm. Closed late Sept to May.

This information station, with maps and geology displays, is in a small wooden building on the edge of Jenny Lake. The center serves as the most popular starting point for hikes into the mountains and is a good place to stop for trail conditions, advice, maps, and the like.

## Commercial Centers

**Jackson Hole and Greater Yellowstone Visitor Center.** 532 N. Cache St. Summer daily 8am–7pm; winter daily 8am–5pm.

This large facility at the north edge of Jackson overlooks the elk refuge — there are telescopes set up to watch the elk — and dispenses information for the local chamber of commerce and all the land agencies in the area, including the national park and national forests. Besides the rangers and other helpers, the center contains wildlife exhibits and a bookstore.

## Getting Around
### By Car

Driving is the only practical way for a family to get around the park. Distances aren't great, but you can eat up a lot of time driving unless you plan your visit to avoid splitting up your day in park areas.

### By Bike

Adult bicyclists tour the park on the shoulders of the highways, but I wouldn't feel safe doing that with kids. Bikes are not allowed off-road. Mountain-biking options are under "Activities" (p. 353).

## Keeping Safe & Healthy

Take a look at "Dealing with Hazards," in chapter 1, for sections on dangerous wildlife, elevation, hypothermia, and lightning, all of which are risks here. Be especially well prepared for mountain hikes. Try to start as early in the morning as possible to avoid afternoon thunderstorms. They can bring lightning and damp, chilly conditions that can lead to hypothermia. Bring warm clothing you can wear in layers — it is cool in the mountains even on warm days down below.

# Enjoying the Park

## Natural Places
### Jackson Lake

The lake sits at the foot of the Tetons in the foreground of a view so dramatic that it seems unreal at first. Sometimes the water reflects the mountains. At other times, afternoon winds turn it silver. The mountains helped make this lake and the other, smaller lakes to the south. The water fills in low spots left behind by glaciers that once cascaded down from the peaks. Once, all the rock and dust that is the flat ground of Jackson Hole was up above. Water — both liquid and frozen — chipped and wore away at the mountains and spread out the broken and powdered rock into a flat valley. Where the last of many glaciers stopped, they left rowlike piles of ground-up rock marking their greatest size, the way a bathtub ring marks how high your bath water came. These low ridges are called moraines. One formed the natural dam that holds back the south end of Jackson Lake. (See "How Glaciers Work," in chapter 13, "The Nature of High Places.")

In 1906, before the area was a park, the government built a dam of its own at the lake's outlet, the start of the Snake River. The human-made dam raised the lake and kept the water level from going up and down, the way

it used to when spring melt filled the lake and warm summer days drained it. This more even flow of water made the Snake River, which comes from the lake, more useful for farmers downstream in Idaho. People who wanted to preserve the area wish the dam had never been built. The park road crosses the dam just south of Moran Junction. The river below is a prime spot to see white pelicans that are feeding on trout; human anglers also congregate below the dam.

Enjoy the shores of Jackson Lake. On the east side, at Colter Bay Village or Signal Mountain Lodge, you can swim and toss pebbles in the water while watching the view change. Southward from Colter Bay, the **Heron Pond** and **Swan Lake trails,** and other level trails of various lengths, trace the lake's edge and then circle wetlands full of waterfowl, including trumpeter swans — easy family loop hikes with the reward of incredible views. The sight of the Tetons across Heron Pond is so perfect it is hard to believe even when you see it. Use the map mentioned under "Reading Up" (p. 341) to figure your route, which can be as long or as short as the combination of paths you choose.

Start a paddle by canoe from the marina at Colter Bay to explore the tiny islands there and, in Half Moon Bay, just south, sheltered waters with lots of folds to feed the young imagination. You can see deep into the clear water. Backcountry campsites are within easy paddles of the marinas at Colter Bay or Signal Mountain Lodge, allowing families who can't hike far to get out on their own. Catch dinner from the lake. More accomplished paddlers can head out to Elk Island or to other island sites across the lake (see "Backcountry Camping Permits," p. 343). If you're not up to handling your own boat, tour boats take guests to sit-down meals out on the lake. The concessionaire offers guided fishing too, or you can rent a boat to fish. Details on all those choices are under "Activities" (p. 353).

## Jenny Lake & Cascade Canyon

A glacier once flowed down Cascade Canyon, giving it a U-shaped bottom, and plowed into Jackson Hole, digging the dip that's now filled with Jenny Lake. The rounded eastern shore was once the glacier's face. The path up Cascade Canyon is gradual, scenic, and rich in wildlife after a short, initial steep section to the Inspiration Point overlook. Easy trails into the Tetons are few, so this is a very popular route, and quite crowded in summer. The lake is circled by paths and the eastern shore has a visitor center, a campground, and other facilities — a pretty spot, but frequently crowded.

I set out for a hike into Cascade Canyon at dawn and had it mostly to myself, following the 2-mile path around the lake to the canyon trailhead, a pretty walk over level terrain. Early morning is the best time for wildlife, and I saw a black bear, bighorn sheep, and moose, as well as birds and small animals. Then, on the way back, I was suddenly surrounded by hundreds of people and the trail was as crowded as a busy city sidewalk. The boat had started running. The Jenny Lake launch runs back and forth from near the visitor center, at the south end of the lake, to the Cascade Canyon trailhead, subtracting those 2 miles off each end of the hike. It seems like a good idea for families, because it extends your range into the mountains, but I don't enjoy a hike with so many other people; to me, it spoils the experience. The **Teton Boating** launches (☎ **307/733-2703,** summer only) run every 20 minutes from 8am to 6pm June through September. The round-trip fare is $5 adults, $3.50 ages 7 to 12, free 6 and under; one way (if you hike early and use it to come back) is $4 and $3. They also rent skiffs with outboard motors for $12 an hour.

## String Lake & Leigh Lake

Our best day ever at Grand Teton was spent hiking along the shore of String Lake and Leigh Lake, the sun off the water splashing through the trees, the immense mountains above us showing through the same gaps. The afternoon was hot, so as we got warm we jumped into the lake (we wore our swimsuits under our clothes). String Lake is shallow and as narrow as a river, so the sun warms the water; we swam to a boulder and dried on the warm rock. Leigh Lake is large and bright and the water colder; it is far enough from the crowded trailhead to get away from other people. Eight backcountry campsites are along its shore, easily reached by canoe; a 250-yard portage connects the two lakes. Trails loop String Lake, run north past Leigh Lake to Jackson Lake or up Paintbrush Canyon, or south to Jenny Lake; you can devise a route that matches your abilities. Take Teton Park Road to the North Jenny Lake Junction, then the Jenny Lake Loop Road to the String Lake picnic area; the trailhead and canoe-launch beach are there.

## The Tetons

The abrupt way the mountains rise, as improbable as a crayon drawing, rips through habitat zones of elevation that usually change more gradually. In a few miles on a steep hike into the Tetons you pass from the open, arid range of Jackson Hole, through the pines, across the green tundra and flowers of the alpine zone, and into barren high country where only scattered pinpricks of color grow among fields of misty gray stone. Up here snow lasts too long to allow plant life to reclaim the ancient rock. Hot summer never arrives. There are a few living things here — brave little pikas, lichens, and miraculous little flowers, for example — but I get a ghostly feeling of standing in an eternal, lifeless realm.

From below, the Teton Range looks so rugged that it's hard to imagine how people climb them. Getting to the top requires equipment and training, but families with fit school-age children can get far enough to find out what the alpine habitat is like, and to see dizzying views from high above. Most trails start in the southwest area of the park, from Jenny Lake south to the Teton Village ski area. The Cascade Canyon hike is described above under "Jenny Lake & Cascade Canyon"; other hikes and the aerial tram are described below under "Hiking" (p. 354).

## Jackson Hole & the Snake River

The valley in front of the Tetons stretches out, amazingly flat. From up in the mountains it looks like a map: the lakes nearest, then low moraine ridges where trees grow, across the Snake River, over broad sagebrush flatlands to the far mountains. Fine soil in some spots holds enough water for trees to grow in the valley, but across most of it fragments of rock rubbed off the mountains by glaciers make up the ground. There the water from rain and snowmelt quickly sinks in, so only plants adapted to the high desert can grow. Bison and pronghorn like that habitat, and you can sometimes see them along the roads on the east side of the valley, in the Antelope Flats area. Along the river, cottonwoods stand above a tangle of willows, perfect moose food. The slow part near Jackson Lake Junction, called Oxbow Bend, is the place to see moose and other mammals and waterfowl such as white pelicans, and a superb spot to launch a canoe in gentle water.

Before towns like Jackson blocked the valley, elk used Jackson Hole as a corridor,

migrating from Yellowstone each fall on the way to lower land where they could spend the winter. After the town arrived, the herds stopped here and starved because there wasn't enough winter food. The **National Elk Refuge,** at the south end of Jackson Hole (www.nationalelkrefuge.fws.gov), was set aside well before the rest of the park to help save the elk. Each winter, the U.S. Fish and Wildlife Service feeds hay to more than 7,000 elk that group there. Rangers from the service answer questions at the Jackson Hole and Greater Yellowstone Visitor Center at 532 N. Cache St. in Jackson (see p. 349), and in winter you can join sleigh rides over the refuge from the National Museum of Wildlife Art (see "Wildlife Watching," p. 356). Other hikes, bike rides, horseback riding, canoeing, and river floats are covered below in "Activities," below.

## Gros Ventre Slide

In 1925, in the valley where the Gros Ventre River flows down into Jackson Hole, a piece of a mountain tumbled and made a dam. A brand-new lake filled on top of the roads and ranch land that had been there. In 1927, the top of the dam broke, sending a flash flood into the valley below, killing six people. Today much of the natural dam remains, and you can walk on the slide along a nature trail where plants have yet to cover the jagged rock and dead trees that fell that day. The tops of more dead trees still stick through the surface of Upper Slide Lake. The lake and slide are in Bridger-Teton National Forest, on the east side of the park; driving north from Kelly, turn right into the mountains on narrow, unpaved Gros Ventre Road. Campgrounds in the area are covered on p. 344.

## PLACES FOR LEARNING
## Menor's Ferry Historic Site

Less than a mile north of the Moose Visitor Center on the park road, a spur leads to this early homestead and Snake River ferry, an important crossing until a bridge was built in 1927 (you also can park at the Dornan's complex and take the restored ferry across). It's well worth a stop. Follow the free park-service guide from building to building, getting a feeling for self-sufficient life here before the automobile. With luck, you'll find the general store open with a clerk in costume (hours vary, normally summer daily 9am–4:30pm). Buy a candy stick from a jar, just as children did a century ago, and see how simple a store was back then. You can also see a display of carriages and ride on the restored ferry, pulled across the river with ropes. Don't miss Maude Noble's Cabin, site of an important early meeting to create the park, which now holds a fascinating display of historic photographs. Nearby, take a look at an old log church, the Chapel of the Transfiguration.

## Cunningham Homestead

South of Moran Junction on U.S. 89, this early homestead ranch with just a single cabin still standing takes a lot of imagination to picture. My children were enthralled, however, by the modern irrigation ditches that cross the property.

**National Museum of Wildlife Art.** On U.S. 89, just north of Jackson. ☎ **307/733-5771.** www.wildlifeart.org. Admission $6 adults, $5 students, free for children 4 and under; families $14. Summer daily 8am–5pm; spring and fall Mon–Sat 9am–5pm, Sun 1–5pm; winter daily 9am–5pm.

Families should not miss this stunning museum. The award-winning sandstone building melds into the cliffs above the Elk Refuge. Inside, galleries contain an arrestingly displayed collection of wildlife art in various styles, from a masterpiece Haida totem pole to hyperrealistic images of big game. The kids' area is lots of fun and adds to displays about how art is made and about animals throughout. There are also a cafe for light meals, an auditorium for films, and a schedule of programs. In the winter, sleigh rides through the Elk Refuge start here (p. 352).

## ACTIVITIES
## Backpacking

Grand Teton is known for challenging and spectacular backpacking trips and has some that strong family hikers can handle, too. Trips wind through the rugged canyons of the Tetons, along backcountry camping zones where you can choose your own campsite on the tundra. After you're up there, the network of trails offers lots of choices for side trips. The Park Service's free "Backcountry Camping" map covers 10 routes ranging from 17 to 38 miles (download from www.nps.gov/grte/sitepub/freepubs.htm); you will also need a detailed topographic map (see "Reading Up," p. 341). Most of these hikes are for fit adults and teenagers who have already tested their abilities before climbing into this steep, high-elevation setting, where the air is thin and the weather cold. Those are the famous hikes. Grand Teton also has several opportunities for families with younger children to spend time camping on their own away from people at the foot of the mountains along and north of Leigh Lake (see "String Lake & Leigh Lake," p. 351). Get a backcountry permit through the system described on p. 343.

## Canoeing, Kayaking & Boating

Exploring the lakes and their islands in a canoe is my idea of fun. Even better, get a backcountry campsite and spend 2 or 3 nights out alone on an island, like the kids in the *Swallows and Amazons,* by Arthur Ransome. Paddling in Jackson, String, and Leigh lakes, and in Oxbow Bend of the Snake River, is covered above under "Natural Places" (p. 350). If your children are too young for canoeing — meaning you can't trust them not to tip it over — you can rent a motorized skiff or rowboat on Jackson Lake. Rent by the hour from **Colter Bay Marina (☎ 307/543-2811)** or **Signal Mountain Lodge (☎ 307/543-2831).** An aluminum canoe goes for $9 an hour or $60 a day; motorboats go for $18 to $50 an hour, or $105 to $225 a day. Signal Mountain rents rowboats for the same price as canoes. For longer rentals, you can get better equipment at a lower rate by renting away from the water and carrying the canoe on your car. **Dornan's** at Moose (☎ **307/733-3307** or 307/733-3699; see "For Handy Reference," p. 349) rents canoes for $30 a day. Serious paddlers should contact **Rendezvous River Sports/Jackson Hole Kayak and Canoe School** (☎ **907/733-2471,** www.jhkayak school.com), at 1035 W. Broadway in Jackson, a paddle sports specialty store. Either outlet provides the car carrier with the rental.

If you bring your own craft, get a permit to take it out on the park's lakes or rivers (rental boats should already have permits). Buy the permit from one of the Park Service visitor centers, $5 for nonmotorized craft, $10 for motorboats, good for 7 days in both Grand Teton and Yellowstone national parks.

Lake water at Grand Teton is swimmable in late summer, but it is cold and you must be cautious about falling in accidentally. Always wear life jackets and have dry, warm clothing along. Plan trips in the morning to avoid afternoon winds and thunderstorms, which can rough up the water and bring the threat of lightning strikes.

## Fishing

The park is known for trout fishing. The Snake River cutthroat is native. In the lakes, you can fish for lake and brown trout and whitefish. The Park Service manages the fishery for the wildlife that use it, encouraging catch-and-release for anglers, but you can keep fish taken from certain waters. Carefully check regulations and license information from the visitor centers, or download it from www.nps. gov/grte/sitepub/freepubs.htm. Fishing tackle, required Wyoming licenses, and advice are available at **Dornan's** at Moose (☎ **307/ 733-3307** or 307/733-3699), at some general stores, and at businesses in Jackson. Guided fly-fishing and lake fishing are offered by the **Grand Teton Lodge Company** (☎ **800/ 628-9988** or 307/543-2811).

## Hiking
### EASIER TRAILS

I've described most of my favorite level-ground hikes above under "Natural Places." The String and Leigh Lake trails offer lovely scenery and swimming (p. 351). At the Gros Ventre slide you can hike over the debris from a natural catastrophe (p. 352). Inspiration Point and Cascade Canyon, the easiest walk into the mountains, is the park's most popular hike (see "Jenny Lake & Cascade Canyon," p. 351). The Heron and Swan Lake trails at Colter Bay (see "Jackson Lake," p. 350) have the superb views and great waterfowl viewing. Similar wildlife-watching walks, with fewer people, go to Christian Pond, Emma Matilda, and Two Oceans lakes from the east side of the road near Jackson Lake Lodge; as you hike farther, you see fewer people.

### HIKES FROM THE AERIAL TRAM

There are plenty of hikes into the Tetons, but if you or your children can't handle a steep 5-mile climb — and many can't, at least enjoyably — you can still get into the high country by taking the aerial tram in Teton Village. Built to serve the extremely challenging Rendezvous Mountain ski area, the tram rises from the resort west of Jackson to an elevation of 10,450 feet, well above the tree line, with stunning views of the surrounding mountaintops and down into Jackson Hole. The ride itself is fun, and you can start some wonderful hikes from here, losing elevation rather than gaining. The easiest one-way trek leads straight down the ski mountain (you pay full fare just to go up, but if you hike up and ride down only, it's free). Other routes cover a lot of ground in the Tetons, and you can even use the tram as the start of an overnight (get the special map, covered under "Reading Up," p. 341). With younger children, rambling around the mountaintop will be enough. The rock and tundra seem limitless. The tram is expensive — $15 for adults, $5 for children 6 to 17, free for 5 and under — so plan your day to make the most of it. Go early to avoid thunderstorms and to allow plenty of time for hiking. Bring warm clothes, food, and lots of water. The Corbet's Cabin snack bar is near the upper tram station. The tram runs July to Labor Day 9am to 7pm, closing at 5pm late May through June and in September. Call ☎ 888/DEEP-SNO or 307/733-2292 for information. To get there, take Highway 22 west from Broadway in Jackson, then turn right on 390; it's 12 miles from Jackson.

### HARDER HIKES

School-age children of tested ability or fit teenagers will enjoy climbing up into the Tetons. Be prepared for a steep, long hike with proper foot gear, clothing, water, snacks, and so on. Also, check at the Moose or Jenny Lake visitor centers for trail conditions. Snow and ice last in the high mountain valleys through June, or even later. South of Jenny Lake, from the Lupine Meadows Parking Area, the **Surprise Lake Trail** is a scenic but very steep climb, rising 3,000 feet over 4½ miles, one way. The destination is a small lake in a glacier-carved crater amid the bare, broken rock of the high country. Without going that far, you can enjoy the views and turn back after 3 miles. The **Death Canyon Trail** offers good views at various levels, so you don't feel driven to go farther than you have energy for; the trailhead is down the Moose-Wilson Road, west from the Moose Visitor Center.

## Horseback Riding

This is horse country, and many operators offer trail rides and pack trips in the region. Check with the tourist authorities in Jackson, listed at the beginning of this chapter, for referrals outside the park. Within the park, **Grand Teton Lodge Company** (☎ 800/628-9988 or 307/543-2811) offers rides and cookouts from Colter Bay or Jackson Lake Lodge. Rides range from 1½ to 2½ hours and cost $25 to $35 per person. Children must be at least 8 years old and 4 feet tall. Younger children can go on the breakfast and dinner ride cookout in a wagon. The cookouts take 3

or 4 hours and aren't offered on Mondays. Call before your vacation to reserve if it is a priority. For a riding vacation, see the dude ranch listed under "Where to Spend the Night" (p. 342).

## Mountain Biking

Trails in the park are closed to bikes; but dirt roads are open and some national forest lands around the park permit bikes on trails. In the park, **Snake River Road,** off the park road just south of Signal Mountain Road, is a scenic, 14-mile dirt road. The **Shadow Mountain area,** just outside the east border of the park in Bridger-Teton National Forest, has many trails of varying difficulty.

Dornan's at Moose (☎ **307/733-3307** or 307/733-3699) rents adults' and kids' basic mountain bikes and bike trailers, and high-performance models, for $24 to $35 a day.

## Rafting

Snake River rafting is famous, but the legendary rapids are outside the park, south of Jackson. Floats within the park are gentle, mostly for looking at the scenery and listening to the guide's commentary about the passing riverbanks. Such outings always depend on the guide's knowledge and people skills, and ours, unfortunately, was untrained in natural history and irritating over the long tour. Floats cover one of two stretches of river: a slower upper stretch which may be more scenic and a somewhat faster run from Schwabacher Road to Menor's Ferry; ask which you will be on. It typically takes 3 to 5 hours to cover 10 miles of water. We went with **Grand Teton Lodge Company** (☎ **800/628-9988** or 307/543-2811), which runs many outings each day, including lunch and dinner floats, and charges $38 to $50 for adults, $19 to $34 for children 6 to 11. Kids under 6 are not allowed. Check with the visitor center for many other operators.

Rough white-water rafting takes place outside the park, south of Jackson, in the Snake River Canyon along Highway 89. A lot of operators offer these floats, but **Sands' Wild Water River Trips** (☎ **800/358-8184** or 307/733-4410; www.sandswhitewater.com) has the singular claim of having taken President Clinton, Chelsea, and the Secret Service through the rapids on a 1995 vacation. A 3½-hour whitewater outing over 8 miles of river costs $35 for adults, $30 for ages 12 and under.

## Tour-Boat Rides

If you don't want to rent your own boat or canoe, you can get out on Jackson Lake in a comfortable, classy little tour boat operated by the **Grand Teton Lodge Company** (☎ **307/543-2811**). The outing includes breakfast or dinner on Elk Island at a cookout with picnic tables. The trips are sedate fun and do give you some time to look around on your own on the island. They don't often see wildlife. The breakfast cruise is $26 for adults, $14 for children 3 through 11; the dinner cruise is $45 for adults, $25 for children. A scenic cruise without food or landings is $14 for adults, $7 for children.

## Wildlife Watching

It isn't necessary to seek wildlife at Grand Teton. If you spend a few days hiking and canoeing, you will have encounters. I've mentioned some animals you can expect to find in different habitats in **"Natural Places"** in the sections on Jackson Lake (p. 350) and Jackson Hole and the Snake River (p. 352), and under **"Hiking"** (p. 354). The willow flats, a big marsh between the river and Colter Bay, is one of the park's richest wildlife habitats. Especially at dawn and dusk, a walk out the back of the Jackson Lake Lodge and up Lunch Tree Hill offers sweeping views of the flats, where you can often see moose munching on the willows. Hiking farther from the lodge, toward Hermitage Point, you pass beaver dams where waterfowl and other animals gather. The Teton Science School offers various guided Wildlife Expeditions all year, described below.

In the winter, more than 7,000 elk converge on the National Elk Refuge, right next to the town of Jackson (see "Jackson Hole & the Snake River," p. 352). They're easy enough to see, but to get a closer look on a fun outing, join one of the sleigh rides from the National Museum of Wildlife Art (p. 353). The rides operate 10am to 4pm mid-December through March and cost $12 for adults, $8 for ages 6 to 12, free for 5 and under. Reservations are not accepted.

# PROGRAMS
## Park Service
### CHILDREN'S PROGRAMS

The **Young Naturalist Program** at Grand Teton is similar to the Junior Ranger programs at other parks. A four-page newspaper workbook is pitched to grade-school children and makes good use of the park to teach about nature — it's not just busy work. First and second graders will likely need help. After completing the workbook, attending two ranger programs, and paying $1, kids can get a patch at any visitor center.

### FAMILY & ADULT PROGRAMS

The Park Service offers a full schedule of ranger-led programs, including talks, walks, vehicle caravans to see wildlife, demonstrations of Native American culture, and tours of the Indian Arts Museum at the Colter Bay Visitor Center. Some programs require reservations. There are also campfire talks and slide shows. Check the park newspaper, or pick up a weekly calendar at a visitor center.

## Summer Camps

**Teton Science School.** East side of Jackson Hole, north of Kelly (P.O. Box 68), Kelly, WY 83011. ☎ **307/733-4765**. www.tetonscience.org.

Based for the past 30 years on a former dude ranch, this well-regarded summer natural-history school offers programs for children and adults. Children in grades 3 through 6 can attend 5-day day camps for $180; they fill in April, so apply well ahead. Residential sessions for junior- and senior-high school students last 2 to 5 weeks. Adult courses lasting 1 to 4 days cover a catalog of topics based in the park. The school also offers wildlife-viewing safaris in specially customized open-topped vehicles, led by biologists. Sunrise and sunset programs cost $85 for adults, $45 for children 5 to 12; children under 5 are not allowed. Other safaris last as long as a week. Check the catalog on the website.

# Fun Outside the Park

The world-famous downhill skiing in Jackson is outside our scope, but I have to mention a couple of fun things to do there in summer. The **Alpine Slide** at the Snow King Mountain (☎ 307/733-7680; www.snowking.com) was a highlight of our children's summer. It's a sort of summertime luge run, with two tracks that descend 2,500 feet down the mountain. Riders ascend on a chairlift and come down each on his or her own sled, controlling speed with a break on a lever. It was so much fun I kept expecting a grown-up to tell us to cut it out. The slide is open 10am to 9pm daily, and single rides costs $8 for ages 13 and up, $4.75 for ages 6 to 12, and $1 for under 6 (riding with a parent). There are discounts for multi-ride passes; might as well bite the bullet, because you won't be able to do it only once. **The Jackson Teton County Recreation Center** (☎ 307/739-9025), at 155 E. Gill Ave., has lots of facilities, including a large pool with a 180-foot water slide, a toddlers' pool, and a hot tub. They're open Monday through Friday 6am to 9pm, Saturday noon to 9pm, Sunday noon to 7pm. Admission is $6 adults, $3.50 children.

# Where to Eat

## In the Park
## Colter Bay Village

There are two family restaurants at Colter Bay, as well as the store, where you can buy good sandwiches for a picnic. The **Chuckwagon Restaurant** is in a large, windowed dining room with many booths and corny western decor, which is hot on a warm day. The service was quick when we visited, starting with a family bowl of salad to share. Our meals from the menu of steak and pasta were satisfying, if uninspired. The children's menu is exceptional. Lunch is $5 to $6.75, dinner $7.25 to $16.25, with most entrees around $10. It is open daily in season 7:30 to 10am, 11:30am to 2pm, and 5:30 to 9pm. Next door, the **John Colter Café Court** is a noisy but pleasant cafeteria serving deli items, pizza, and rotisserie chicken. Prices are quite reasonable, all under $6 except for the $13 whole chickens. It is open 6:30am to 10pm.

## Jackson Lake Lodge

The lodge has four places to eat. The **Mural Room** is a gorgeous formal restaurant with dinner entrees around $20, but unless someone is babysitting for you, I doubt you'll see the inside except at the breakfast buffet, which costs $10 and is served 7 to 9:30am. (Even then the atmosphere was a bit stiff for our crew.) The **Pioneer Grill,** next door, is a lot more fun, with its popular huckleberry pancakes for breakfast, onion rings on a skewer, and soda fountain. All seating is around a chrome lunch counter, a retro treasure that's unfortunately not practical for large families or when it's crowded and hard to find seats together. Full meals are under $10, and there is a long children's menu. It is open 6am to 10pm. You can also eat a light breakfast in the **Blue Heron Coffee House,** a quiet corner off the lobby, 6 to 10am. The **Pool Grill** serves sandwiches, burgers, and pizza during the day, and an all-you-can-eat western barbecue for dinner. The food is unmemorable, but the ultra-relaxed setting by the pool is pleasant. It costs $15.

## Signal Mountain Lodge

We really liked this small, casual restaurant overlooking Jackson Lake. The food was more interesting than that at most family restaurants, but most important for us, dining with three kids, the restaurant was professionally run — the food came quickly and the staff was friendly and handled our special requests smoothly. Breakfast is $5 to $6.50; lunch choices are generally $6 to $8 and also are available at dinner, when they add a few entrees under $12. The restaurant is open in summer 7am to 10pm, closing an hour earlier in spring and fall.

## Leek's Marina Pizzeria

Near the north end of the park, this is a popular place for a pizza, sandwich, salad, or beer overlooking the lake. It's a quieter spot than Colter Bay. The restaurant is open in season Monday through Thursday 11am to 9pm, Friday through Sunday to 10pm.

## In Jackson

### LOW-STRESS MEALS

In Jackson, you can get most kinds of familiar fast food, including Denny's, Domino's Pizza, Kentucky Fried Chicken, McDonald's, Pizza Hut, Subway, and Taco Bell. For something with a bit more atmosphere, try **Jedediah's** (☎ **307/733-5671**), at 135 E. Broadway, near the town square. Dining rooms are in the small, rough rooms of an old house and on a sunny patio. The atmosphere is noisy and festive, the service casual to a fault, the menu a step above that of the typical diner. Most items are under $7 and the children's selections under $4. They're open 7am to 2pm year-round, 5 to 9pm summer only.

### BEST-BEHAVIOR MEALS

**Calico Italian Restaurant and Bar.** On Hwy. 390 to Teton Village. ☎ **307/733-2460.** Dinner main courses $9–$18. Daily 5–10pm.

For grown-ups, there are sophisticated northern Italian food, rich risotto, great oyster chowder, and grilled items. For the kids, there's good pizza, a children's menu under $2.50, and a huge lawn where they can play with balls, games, and toys while the food is being prepared. Parents watch from the porch or through big windows and French doors while sipping cocktails and microbrews. The airy dining room has high ceilings and stained glass, and the decor mixes trendy Italian style and casual Western touches. Unfortunately, the place is so popular that service suffers.

# CHAPTER 16

# Rocky Mountain National Park

The tops of the Rocky Mountains are an edge. At the top, you're at the tip of North America, above the whole continent. You're higher than almost all the people, plants, and animals, above everything but air and space. Rocky Mountain National Park contains a lot of special places, but none more memorable than these high edges of the earth. Even visitors who don't want to get far from their cars can experience the thin, cool air and pure light on Trail Ridge Road. Those with more spirit can use the road as a way to a kind of place that's usually out of reach of all but the sturdiest climbers, and begin their journey from there.

The park is shaped like a saddle on the back of the Rockies' Front Range. On either side, the land rises through different life zones of plants and animals, each step of elevation providing just the right temperature and moisture for its own community of plants and animals. The park begins in big ponderosa pines, just above the level of the sagebrush range. Higher, Engelmann spruce and alpine fir grow, then shrivel as you rise and timberline approaches. At the top, the mountains' backs stretch away from the trees, granite barely clothed by the thin alpine tundra. Less than a dozen miles farther, you're over the spine, back down into the trees on the other side. Everywhere in the park, the elevation is written all around you in the kinds of trees, animals, flowers, and ponds you see — if you know how to read nature's handwriting.

Parts of the park are quite crowded in the summer, but without much effort you can leave the most popular trails and go off on your own. The park has some beautiful campgrounds and exceptional educational offerings too.

## BEST THINGS TO DO

- Take a hike. Trails range from easy walks on the shore of a mountain lake to a famous climb to the top of 14,255-foot Longs Peak.
- Ride a horse or bicycle through the park.
- See elk, bighorn, and moose in their natural habitats.

**Rocky Mountain National Park.** Estes Park, CO 80517-8397. ☎ **970/586-1206.** TDD 970/586-1319. www.nps.gov/romo.

**Rocky Mountain Nature Association** (for maps, books, and seminars). Rocky Mountain National Park, Estes Park, CO 80517. ☎ **800/816-7662** or 970/586-0108. www.rmna.org.

**Arapaho and Roosevelt National Forests.** Forest Service Information Center, 1311 S. College Ave., Fort Collins, CO 80524. ☎ **970/498-2770.** TTY 970/498-2707. www.fs.fed.us/arnf.

**Estes Park Chamber Resort Association.** 500 Big Thompson Ave., Estes Park, CO 80517. ☎ **800/443-7837** or 970/586-4431. www.estesparkresort.com.

**Grand Lake Area Chamber of Commerce.** P.O. Box 57, Grand Lake, CO 80447. ☎ **800/531-1019** or 970/627-8007. www.grandlakechamber.com.

Another useful travel website: Estes Park Welcome Center at www.estes-park.com.

- Backpack in the high country, connecting campsites as close as a mile or two.

- Join one of the exceptional educational programs.

See "Activities" (p. 375).

# HISTORY: ESTES, MILLS & MUIR

The crest of the Rockies never was a place where people lived. In the summer, Native Americans hunted on the alpine tundra, but they generally made their homes in warmer, lower lands. The same was true of white settlers. The Rockies were a barrier to overcome on the way west, not a place to build farms and ranches. Trappers, explorers, and gold prospectors came through and named some of the mountains, but the first people to settle in the area were the family of Joel Estes, who built a ranch in Estes Park in 1860. (Around here, a **park** is a warm, open valley.)

Estes didn't stay long — ranching, even in Estes Park (at 7,500 ft. elevation), was too cold and wintry. But the valley the family had pioneered soon became a center of activity for people coming to see and climb the mountains, and to hunt. Estes Park was special because you could reach it by following not-too-steep river valleys from the east, as you still do on highways 34 and 36. It's like a stair-

case landing on steps into the mountains. The town of Estes Park has developed and spread since the earliest days, but it's still mainly a base for recreation in the surrounding Rockies.

Enos Mills arrived in the area in 1884 at the age of 14 and went to work as a guide on Longs Peak. Later, he built an inn near the mountain, and over his life he climbed Longs Peak almost 300 times. But a trip he made to San Francisco in 1889 turned out to be more important for the history of the park. Mills was looking at a plant growing on sand dunes where Golden Gate Park is today when a gentleman in his 50s approached and struck up a conversation. It was John Muir, the great nature writer who helped protect Yosemite National Park and many other parks. (For more on Muir, see "John Muir & Wilderness Values," in chapter 17, "Rock, Life & Change.") Muir and Mills hit it off. They visited Muir's ranch and hiked on Mount

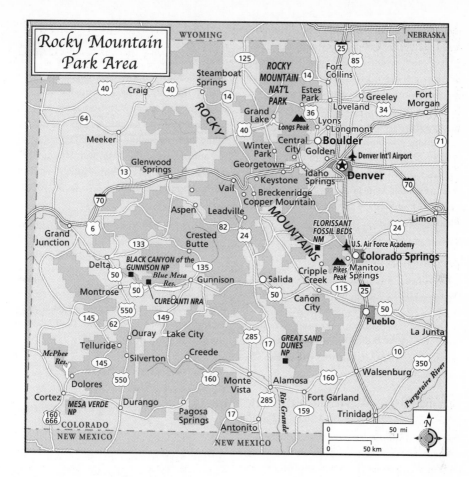

Tamalpais together, and when Mills went back home to Colorado, they wrote to each other.

Mills decided to model his life on Muir's. In the summer, he guided visitors up Longs Peak and ran his inn. In the winter he wrote and traveled to tell people about the beauty of the area and the need to protect it. He wanted to put a huge area of the Rockies into a park, from Longs Peak most of the way across Colorado to Pikes Peak. In 1913, when Muir lost his greatest battle, to stop the damming of the Hetch Hetchy River in Yosemite National Park, Mills wrote to encourage him with the news that the loss would make him work harder. "As you well know, it is the work you have done that has encouraged me . . . in the big work that I am planning to do," he wrote. In 1915, Congress created Rocky Mountain

National Park. It's not the huge park Mills had originally wanted, but he still is deservedly called the father of the park.

The park has changed a lot since those days. Hunters had wiped out the elk by the time the park was set aside. The Park Service handled the problem by bringing in 49 elk from Yellowstone National Park and killing off the animals that prey on them — gray wolves and grizzly bears. Today, the park needs the wolves and bears again because there are too many elk for the area of habitat that's left for them. Hunters keep the numbers down by killing elk that wander outside the park.

Another change came with the construction of roads. In 1932, the Park Service built Trail Ridge Road to connect Estes Park and Grand Lake, on opposite sides of the park, and to provide access to the high country. Building a road at over 12,000 feet elevation was a difficult project, and the road is unique in giving car travelers the ability to see this kind of mountaintop terrain. But it's also safe to say that today the Park Service would never build such a road, across such pristine scenery. The government also built a tunnel under the park, another project that would probably not be approved today. It brings water from Grand Lake and the man-made reservoirs nearby across the Continental Divide to the drier east side of the Rockies.

Today, the park's biggest problem is too many people. It's a relatively small park and roads and hiking trails can get crowded in the summer. More important, animals that use the park in the summer need winter habitats lower down the mountain, but those areas weren't all set aside for preservation. Development of roads and towns has slowly taken away land the animals need. Elk even wander among the streets of Estes Park in the winter — it's their normal winter habitat.

# ORIENTATION

Rocky Mountain National Park is a rectangle roughly 16 miles wide (east-west) and 25 miles long (north-south). It's only 65 miles from Denver, making it a popular weekend destination. It's quieter during the week. The park has four main areas.

## ESTES PARK & MORAINE PARK

Most of the campgrounds and visitor facilities and the most popular trails are on the east side of the park, around Estes Park and on roads that punch partway into the park from there. Moraine Park is another valley just inside the national park, the site of a museum, campground, trails, and stables. The main roads to Estes Park are U.S. highways 34 and 36, which loop around and connect in the front part of the park. Estes Park is a thriving tourist town with every service you might need.

## THE HIGH COUNTRY

The central, alpine area of the park is the famous highlight. It's reached by 48-mile Trail Ridge Road (Highway 34), which crosses the whole park, from Estes Park on the east to Grand Lake on the west. The road closes for the winter from mid-October to May.

## THE WESTERN SIDE & GRAND LAKE

The western side of the park, near the little resort town of Grand Lake, is quite different from the east. The mountainsides here are thickly wooded with fir, spruce, and pine. Below are the lakes and swampy moose habitat. The west side gets more snow, has colder winters, and is less used by people, in part because of its greater distance from Denver.

## LONGS PEAK & WILD BASIN

The southeast area of the park contains the path to Longs Peak and other mountain trails. This less-used area, including the secluded Wild Basin, is reached from several points along Route 7, which runs along the national park boundary south of Estes Park.

# MAKING THE ARRANGEMENTS

## WHEN TO GO

The 3 summer months are all busy, but July and August are the prime tourist season.

Daytime temperatures are comfortable to cool at elevations in the park. Thunderstorms routinely come in the afternoon through

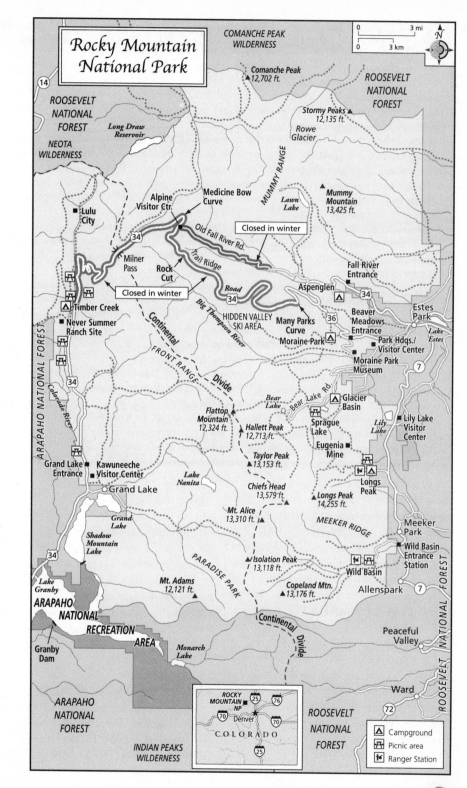

**Rocky Mountain National Park**

COMANCHE PEAK
WILDERNESS

0 — 3 mi
0 — 3 km

N

Comanche Peak
▲12,702 ft.

ROOSEVELT
NATIONAL
FOREST

ROOSEVELT
NATIONAL
FOREST

Stormy Peaks ▲
12,135 ft.

Rowe
Glacier

NEOTA
WILDERNESS

Long Draw
Reservoir

MUMMY RANGE

Mummy
Mountain
13,425 ft.

Lulu
City

Alpine
Visitor Ctr.

Medicine Bow
Curve

Lawn
Lake

Old Fall River Rd.

Closed in winter

34

Milner
Pass

Trail Ridge

Rock
Cut

Closed in winter

Road

34

Fall River
Entrance

Aspenglen

Fall River
Entrance

34

Timber Creek

Big Thompson River

HIDDEN VALLEY
SKI AREA

Many Parks
Curve

36

Beaver
Meadows
Entrance

Estes
Park

Continental

Never Summer
Ranch Site

FRONT RANGE

Moraine Park

Park Hdqs./
Visitor Center

Lake
Estes

34

Divide

Moraine Park
Museum

Colorado River

ARAPAHO NATIONAL FOREST

Bear
Lake

Bear Lake Rd.

Glacier
Basin

7

Flattop
Mountain
12,324 ft.

Hallett Peak
12,713 ft.

Sprague
Lake

Lily
Lake

Lily Lake
Visitor
Center

Grand Lake
Entrance

Kawuneeche
Visitor Center

Lake
Nanita

Taylor Peak
▲13,153 ft.

Eugenia
Mine

Longs
Peak

Grand Lake

Chiefs Head
13,579 ft.

Longs Peak
▲14,255 ft.

Grand
Lake

Mt. Alice
13,310 ft. ▲

MEEKER RIDGE

Meeker
Park

Shadow
Mountain
Lake

PARADISE PARK

Isolation Peak
▲13,118 ft.

Wild Basin

Wild Basin
Entrance
Station

34

Lake
Granby

Mt. Adams
12,121 ft. ▲

Copeland Mtn.
▲13,176 ft.

Allenspark

7

ARAPAHO
NATIONAL
RECREATION
AREA

Monarch
Lake

Continental
Divide

Peaceful
Valley

ROOSEVELT NATIONAL FOREST

Granby
Dam

ARAPAHO
NATIONAL
FOREST

ROCKY
MOUNTAIN
NP

25

76

Denver

70

70

COLORADO

25

ROOSEVELT
NATIONAL
FOREST

Ward

72

INDIAN PEAKS
WILDERNESS

▲ Campground
⊞ Picnic area
⛺ Ranger Station

## EXPERIMENT: MAKING AN ALTIMETER

Airplane pilots and mountaineers find out how high they are with a device called an altimeter, which measures air pressure. At higher elevations, less of the atmosphere is pressing down, so if you know the air pressure, you know how high you are. (This is explained in "Elevation & Air Pressure," in chapter 13, "The Nature of High Places.") You can make your own altimeter that really works and see how it changes as you drive or climb into the Rockies.

The simplest version of an altimeter is a party balloon that you blow up and measure. As you go higher, the balloon gets bigger. The amount of air inside the balloon isn't changing — the balloon is sealed, so air can't get in or out. But as you rise, the pressure of the air outside the balloon is weaker; that means each molecule of air is taking up more space. The wall of the balloon is flexible, so the air inside falls to the same pressure as outside. As the molecules of air in the balloon take more space, the balloon has to stretch to fit them all.

A balloon isn't such a good altimeter, however, for several reasons. One reason is that you need some math to figure out how the size of the balloon relates to how high you are. Another is that blown-up balloons are not very convenient to carry around. But we've figured a way around both of those problems with this party-balloon altimeter.

Our invention is to put the inflated balloon underwater in a baby bottle. As the balloon gets bigger, the water rises higher on the measuring lines on the side of the bottle. Between altitude readings, you can screw the cap on the bottle for safekeeping. If you don't have a baby, bottles are inexpensive and available in any grocery store. I think any clear, tall, narrow container without a neck should work, but we haven't been able to find a commonly available one in which it is possible to blow up the balloon and not have it float up to the top of the water.

Step one is to blow up the balloon inside the baby bottle. Theoretically, a sealed zip-top bag with a little air in it would also work, but it is too hard to get the bag into the bottle and have it stay underwater (if you can sacrifice the container, you could glue the bag down with super glue). The balloon should fill the bottle half or two-thirds of the way up. Tie it off and push it to the bottom with the blunt end of a pencil or the handle of a spoon. Now add a measured amount of water that's enough to cover the balloon, and get rid of any air bubbles underneath.

mid-September, so early starts are always necessary for outdoor activities. In June, snow lingers in the high country, although Trail Ridge Road usually opens in late May. Old Fall River Road, an unpaved alternate route into the mountains, often doesn't open until July 4. September may be the best time to visit — crowds are smaller and the weather is still comfortable.

Lower-elevation trails on the east side of the park stay open to hikers most of the winter. Snow closes the high country roads in October. January and February are the favored months for winter sports, when there's a thick snowpack that hasn't yet gotten wet or mushy.

## HOW MUCH TIME TO SPEND

Most visitors to Rocky Mountain National Park just drive through for the view. The park doesn't have a lot of varied activities or sightseeing destinations to keep you busy, although you could spend a day or two that way. It's mostly a park for relaxation and hiking. With the perfect summer temperatures, spectacular scenery, and choice of trails, you could easily spend a week exploring, getting in shape, and forgetting your problems.

## HOW FAR TO PLAN AHEAD

Often a couple of weeks or a month of advance planning is enough for rooms in Estes Park, even for summer. For the best selection, call 3 months ahead. For campground sites at

By looking at the marks on the side of the bottle, you can tell how much space the balloon takes up. For example, we blew up a balloon in a baby bottle and then added 100 milliliters (ml) of water. The water came up to the 225ml mark on the side of the bottle. We figured that 225ml total minus the 100ml of water added meant we had 125ml of air in the balloon. (You can use milliliters or ounces.)

As you go to higher elevations, the balloon will get bigger, and the water level in the bottle will rise. (The water doesn't change in size — it's just to help measure.) A rise of 1,000 feet means the air pressure lessens by roughly 4% (4/100), so for each 1,000 feet you go up, the balloon will get 4% larger. Figure out 4% of the size of your balloon. In our case, the balloon was 125ml. By calculating 4% of that, we learned that 1,000 feet elevation would make the balloon grow by 5ml (125 × .04 = 5). When we went up 1,000 feet, the water would rise from the 225ml mark to the 230 mark. Every 1,000 feet higher and the water would rise another 5ml; 2,000 feet was 235, 3,000 feet 240, and so on. For convenient measurements, you can mark the bottle in advance where each 1,000 feet will come.

If you don't want to figure out the 4% 1,000-foot marks, you can also make it work by going to two places of known elevation and marking how high the water comes. For example, mark the water level in the bottle at the elevation where you are, then use a topographic map to find a point 1,000 feet higher and mark the water level again there. If the two marks are 1cm apart on the bottle, then you know that every 1cm change in the water level equals about 1,000 feet, and you can use a ruler to mark 1,000-foot lines all the way up the bottle. (This will work only if the bottle has fairly straight sides.)

We made the altimeter in about 20 minutes and had a lot of fun with it. Of course, party balloons slowly lose air and water can spill; so you may need to refigure your measurements. Also, changing weather (barometric pressure) and changing temperature will alter your readings: both affect air pressure, which is what the device measures.

Moraine and Glacier campgrounds, reserve as soon as possible, using the national reservation system outlined in chapter 1, "Planning Your Trip."

## READING UP

The best source for books on the park is the **Rocky Mountain Nature Association** (Rocky Mountain National Park, Estes Park, CO 80517), which operates the visitor center bookstores and sells online or by mail order (☎ **800/816-7662** or 970/586-0108; www.rmna.org/bookstore). **Hiking:** *Hiking Rocky Mountain National Park*, by local experts Kent and Donna Dannen (The Globe Pequot Press; www.globe-pequot.com), is exhaustive, clearly written, and easy to use.

**Maps:** National Geographic's Trails Illustrated topographic map covers the park in adequate details and contains the backcountry campsite numbers.

## GETTING THERE
### By Car

Several interstate highways converge near Denver, which is only 65 miles from the park on **U.S. 36. Interstate 25** is 30 miles east of the park by way of Highway 34. The west entrance is connected to **Highway 40,** which goes due west or joins I-70.

### By Air

Fly into **Denver International Airport** and rent a car there from any national rental agency. **United** (☎ **800/241-6522**) has a hub

## WEATHER CHART: ESTES PARK & GRAND LAKE

| | | AVG. HIGH (°F) | AVG. LOW (°F) | PRECIP. (IN.) | SNOW DEPTH (IN.) |
|---|---|---|---|---|---|
| **Jan.–Feb.** | Estes Park | 40 | 17 | 0.4 | 1 |
| | Grand Lake | 33 | 3.1 | 1.6 | 22 |
| **Mar.–Apr.** | Estes Park | 49 | 24 | 1.1 | 0.5 |
| | Grand Lake | 45 | 15 | 1.7 | 18.5 |
| **May–June** | Estes Park | 68 | 38 | 1.9 | 0 |
| | Grand Lake | 65 | 30 | 1.8 | 0.5 |
| **July–Aug.** | Estes Park | 77 | 45 | 2.1 | 0 |
| | Grand Lake | 75 | 37 | 2.2 | 0 |
| **Sept.–Oct.** | Estes Park | 65 | 34 | 1.0 | 0 |
| | Grand Lake | 62 | 26 | 1.5 | 3.5 |
| **Nov.–Dec.** | Estes Park | 43 | 20 | 0.5 | 0.5 |
| | Grand Lake | 36 | 8 | 1.5 | 7 |

in Denver, and many major airlines have daily service, including **Delta** (☎ **800/221-1212**) and **Northwest** (☎ **800/225-2525**).

## WHAT TO PACK
### Clothing

Most of the park is above 8,000 feet, and it reaches upward to over 14,000 feet. Air temperature is 3° to 5°F lower for each 1,000 feet you rise, so it's about 20°F cooler at the Alpine Visitor Center than it is in Estes Park. It's also consistently windy up there. You'll need layers of clothing that allow you to strip down on a hot hike and then warm up and protect yourself from a chilly wind or rain squall. Winter visits require heavy winter clothing and breathable, synthetic clothing for skiing or snowshoeing. (See "Cold Weather Preparations," in chapter 1.)

### Gear

Summertime campers won't require any special gear, as long as you have an extra layer for cold nights. Be sure to bring sun hats, sunblock, and high-quality sunglasses for time spent at high elevations. At 10,000 feet, you have one-third less atmosphere above you to protect you from the ultraviolet wavelengths of the sun than you do at sea level. Use only quality UV sunglasses; cheap children's sunglasses can cause eye damage by dilating the eyes but not screening out ultraviolet light. You'll also need good boots or hiking shoes — even for the kids — to keep your feet in shape over several days. If you have a toddler, bring a quality backpack carrier — strollers aren't practical here.

## WHERE TO SPEND THE NIGHT

### CAMPING
#### Park Service Campgrounds

Rocky Mountain is a great park for camping. The campgrounds are beautiful and woodsy,

but town is never more than half an hour away. There are five campgrounds in the park. Two, Moraine and Glacier Basin, are reserved through the national reservation system described in chapter 1. Make your reservations as soon as you can for the summer season to make sure you get a site.

The three campgrounds where reservations aren't taken fill every night, and sites are especially difficult to get on weekends. Arrive early in the morning, when people are leaving, to have a good chance for a site.

The maximum stay in summer is 7 days, except for Longs Peak, where the limit is 3 days. Winter camping is limited to 14 days. All campgrounds except Longs Peak have evening campfire programs in the summer.

**Aspenglen.** On Hwy. 34, just inside the Fall River entrance. $16 per site. 54 sites; tents or RVs. Flush toilets; ice and firewood for sale. Closed Oct–Apr.

The campground is in a steep river valley, with sites not so far apart as at Moraine, but pleasingly arranged on the slope. Tent platforms have gravel pads to help you keep dry.

**Glacier Basin.** On Bear Lake Rd. $16 per site. Reservations accepted. 150 sites; tents or RVs. Flush toilets, dump station; ice and firewood for sale. Closed Sept–May.

This campground is about halfway up the Bear Lake Road, across from the shuttle-bus stop that can take you down to Moraine Park or up to trailheads. The area is thickly wooded with pines.

**Longs Peak.** 1 mile off Rte. 7, south of Lily Lake. $16 per site in summer; $10 per site when water is turned off (late Sept to Memorial Day). 26 sites; tents only. Flush or vault toilets; ice and firewood for sale.

This campground, at 9,400 feet elevation, is intended as a base for hikers planning to climb Longs Peak (see p. 374). It's a low-key campground among thick, small pines, with gravel tent pads. Stays are limited to 3 days in summer.

**Moraine Park.** Near Estes Park off Hwy. 36. $16 per site in summer; $10 per site when water is turned off (late Sept to mid-May). Reservations accepted. 247 sites; tents or RVs. Flush or vault toilets, dump station; ice and firewood for sale.

This campground sits among little hills, granite boulders, small pines, and meadow grass. It was ingeniously designed to tuck sites away from each other, so some feel like the backcountry. Elk wander around the edges at times; you can hike right from the campground, and the stables and museum are close by. A shuttle bus comes by regularly in the summer.

**Timber Creek.** Trail Ridge Rd., Kawuneeche Valley. $16 per site in summer; $10 per site when water is turned off (late Sept to Memorial Day). 100 sites; tents or RVs. Flush or vault toilets, dump stations; firewood for sale.

Towering pines block the light but offer little privacy between the sites at this flat campground near the highway. It fills later than others, but you should still be there by noon in summer.

## Backcountry Permits

Rocky has more than 120 backcountry campsites, spaced closely along the hiking trails. Some are only a mile or two from the trailheads, making backpacking for families practical even if you can't cover much ground in a day.

The first step to getting a permit for backcountry camping is to buy a map and trail guide (see "Reading Up," p. 365) and figure out where you want to go. The sites are also marked on the *Rocky Mountain Backcountry Camping Guide* distributed free by the Park Service. Reservations open March 1 for the whole summer, by mail or in person at the Headquarters Backcountry Office or the Kawuneeche Visitor Center. You can reserve by phone (☎ 970/586-1242; TDD 970/586-1319) from March 1 to May 15 and again beginning October 1 for the remainder of that calendar year, but between those times you can reserve only by mail or in person. Besides the obvious, like your name and address, you'll need to specify the campsites you want and the exact dates, and pay a $15 fee. The first sites to go are those in the areas of Glacier Gorge and Andrews Creek.

You often can get sites, especially out of the peak season, without reserving, just by showing up at the office or visitor center, but I wouldn't count on it. No sites are held back specifically for walk-ins. See "Backpacking" (p. 375) for more details on setting up a trek.

## Forest Service Campgrounds

Arapaho and Roosevelt national forests, which are managed jointly, surround the park with a larger area of backcountry, much of it wilderness, and many campgrounds. Forest Service campgrounds handy to the park's entrances are marked on the park map, and I've provided basic information here on each. All six can be reserved through the national system described in chapter 1, which carries an extra fee beyond the camping fee noted below. All have drinking water and vault toilets, unless otherwise noted.

### East Side

These campgrounds are in the **Boulder Ranger District** (☎ 303/444-6600). All are usually open from mid-May to mid- or late October.

**Olive Ridge.** Hwy. 7 near Wild Basin. $12 per site. 56 sites; tents or RVs.

This large campground is the closest to the east entrances of the park.

**Peaceful Valley.** On Hwy. 72 off Hwy. 7 southeast of park. $12 per site. 17 sites; tents or RVs.

This campground has access to fishing and hiking trails.

**Camp Dick.** 1 mile west from Peaceful Valley on an unpaved road, southeast of park. $12 per site. 41 sites; tents or RVs.

This campground has access to fishing and hiking trails.

### West Side

These campgrounds are around the reservoirs southwest of the park, in the Arapaho National Recreation Area, which, in addition to camping fees, charges day-use fees per vehicle of $5 for 1 day, $10 for 3 days, and $15 for 7 days. They are oriented toward fishing and boating. All are open to tents and RVs. For information, call the **Sulphur Ranger District** (☎ 970/887-4100).

**Arapaho Bay.** Southern end, Lake Granby, Arapaho Bay Rd., off Hwy. 34. $12 per site. 84 sites. Vault toilets. Open Memorial Day to Labor Day.

**Green Ridge.** Southern side, Shadow Mountain Lake, on Hwy. 34. $12 per site. 77 sites. Flush toilets, dump station. Open May–Oct.

**Stillwater.** Western side, Lake Granby, on Hwy. 34. $12 per site, $20 with electricity. 127 sites. Showers, flush toilets, electric hookups, dump station. Open year-round.

## Commercial Campgrounds

There are plenty of good campgrounds in Estes Park and a few in Grand Lake. Making reservations is a good idea in the summer. Besides those listed below, I can recommend **Blue Arrow RV Park and Campground** (☎ 800/582-5342 or 970/586-5342), just outside the Beaver Meadows entrance. The **KOA Kampground** (☎ 800/562-1887 or 970/586-2888) is on Highway 34 as you enter town.

**Mary's Lake Campground.** Mary's Lake Rd., 3 miles south of Estes Park (P.O. Box 2514), Estes Park, CO 80517. ☎ **800/445-6279** or 970/586-4411. Full hookups $28 for 2 people, tents $21 for 2 people; $3 per extra person over age 5. 150 sites. Swimming pool, playground, basketball, laundry, fishing, store.

Situated on 60 acres at the edge of a small lake just outside town, this campground has a real Rocky Mountain feel. RVs park together, while tents have more woodsy places to set up among pine trees and rock outcroppings, not much different from a national park campground.

**National Park Resort Camping and Cabins.** 3501 Fall River Rd. (Hwy. 34), Estes Park, CO 80517. ☎ **970/586-4563.** Full hookups $27–$30 for 2 people, tents $23–$25 for 2 people; $3 per extra person over age 2. 92 sites. Laundry, store, horseback riding.

The campground is right on the edge of the park in the steep valley of the Fall River, among ponderosa pines. Many sites have views or back onto the woods and the park.

**Winding River Resort.** From Trail Ridge Rd. (Hwy. 34), just north of Kawuneeche Visitor Center, turn on County Rd. 491 (P.O. Box 629), Grand Lake, CO 80447. ☎ **800/282-5121** (reservations) or 970/627-3215. Full hookups $22–$24 for 2 people, tent sites $20 for 2 people; $3 per extra person over age 4. 150 sites. Store, laundry, petting farm, playground, horseback riding.

Back in the woods by itself a few miles from Grand Lake, this campground is abuzz with activities: hay rides, ice-cream socials, chuckwagon breakfasts (a sort of Western picnic), and the like.

## HOTELS

There are no lodgings inside the park, but you'll find lots of family-oriented motels and cabins in Estes Park and Grand Lake. A good room in the summer in Estes Park costs about $100 a night, and a nice cabin big enough for a family is about $125 a night. Lodging in Grand Lake costs a bit less. All rates below are for the high season, late June through August; rates drop around 25% in the off-season.

# Estes Park

**The Baldpate Inn.** 4900 S. Hwy. 7 (P.O. Box 4445), Estes Park, CO 80517. ☎ **970/586-6151.** www.baldpateinn.com. 12 rms (4 with bathroom), 3 cabins. $80–$100 double, $140 cabins; $15 per extra adult, $10 per extra child. DISC, MC, V. Closed Nov–Apr.

This is an extraordinary place in many ways. Just down the road from the Lily Lake Visitor Center, it looks like a tree house from the outside. It was built of native timber in 1917. I was charmed by the rooms and the service provided by members of the family that runs the inn. Beds have quilts handmade by the mother. There are no phones or TVs. Rates include an elaborate breakfast from the restaurant downstairs, which is one of the area's most popular and renowned. It's so popular, in fact, that dinner reservations are essential, despite a menu that includes only soup, salad, bread, and muffins. (Dinners are served from Memorial Day to September. Hours are 11:30am to 8pm daily, and the meal is $10.75 for adults and $8.25 for children under 10.)

All that leaves out the most extraordinary thing: a collection of 20,000 keys, started in 1923 at Clarence Darrow's suggestion. It contains many fascinating and historic keys in a room from a locksmith's fevered nightmare. It's worth the trip by itself.

**Big Thompson Timberlane Lodge.** 740 Moraine Ave. (P.O. Box 387), Estes Park, CO 80517. ☎ **800/898-4373** or 970/586-3137. Fax 970/586-3719. www.bigthompsontimberlane lodge.com. 58 units. TV TEL. $99–$335. Rates are per unit regardless of number of guests. AE, DISC, MC, V.

A well-landscaped compound right along the Big Thompson River contains a great array of choices of family accommodations and activities. The lodgings, well off the highway, include white-walled motel suites, cottages with pine paneling, and log homes that sleep up to 10 people. All have refrigerators and either a stove or a microwave. About half have showers, not tubs. Outside, there are a heated pool, a separate toddler pool and adults-only hot tub, picnic areas with barbecue grills, and the stream, stocked with trout. Indoors you'll find another large whirlpool, a self-serve laundry, and toys, games, and books for the kids. They want families here, and work to make them comfortable.

**Glacier Lodge.** Hwy. 66 south of park entrance (P.O. Box 2656), Estes Park, CO 80517. ☎ **800/523-3920** or 970/586-4401. www.glacierlodge.com. 28 rms and cabins. $125–$160 cabins for 4. 4-day minimum stay in summer. DISC, MC, V. Closed Nov–Apr.

This is a place where you can really stretch out and relax. Cabins sit on a grassy compound across the Big Thompson River from the road. There are a swimming pool, playground, sport court, riding stable, and lots of other recreation facilities. Most cabins have cooking facilities and fireplaces, and the resort also offers cookouts and occasional evening activities for children. Rooms do not have phones.

Along the same road, several other attractive cabin lodgings sit by the river. Many charge lower rates and don't have a 4-day minimum, but they don't offer Glacier Lodge's extras. **Rockmount Cottages** (☎ **970/586-4168**), next door to Glacier Lodge, has trim log cabins and lots of flowers; two-bedroom cottages are $115 to $135 a night.

**Stanley Hotel.** 333 Wonderview Ave. (P.O. Box 1767), Estes Park, CO 80517. ☎ **800/976-1377** or 970/586-3371. Fax 970/586-3673. www.estes-park.com/stanleyhotel/. 135 units. $159–$209 double, $269–$299 suites. $10 each additional adult, under age 18 free. AE, DISC, MC, V.

This grand white clapboard hotel overlooking the town aims to maintain the style established in 1909 by its builder, F. O. Stanley (inventor of the Stanley Steamer car). A recent remodeling has spruced up this historic property, although it remains a little threadbare in places. With its formal feeling, the Stanley isn't for all families, but the history and scale make it fun. The hotel occasionally offers concerts and other events that recall a gracious old-time

style of travel. There are a huge outdoor pool and tennis courts, plus two restaurants.

## Grand Lake

Besides the choices below, **Lemmon Lodge** (☎ **970/627-3314** in summer; 970/725-3511 in winter; www.lemmonlodge.com) is an attractive, old-fashioned cabin resort on 5 acres at the edge of town, right on the lake. Cabins, which sleep from 2 to 12 people, range from $70 to $325 per night.

**Grand Lake Lodge.** Off Trail Ridge Rd. just inside the park boundary (P.O. Box 569), Grand Lake, CO 80447. ☎ **970/627-3967.** Fax 970/627-9495. www.grandlakelodge.com. 56 cabins. $70–$160 cabins for 2–6 people. 2- or 3-night minimum stay. AE, DISC, MC, V. Closed mid-Sept to May.

Bordering the national park and overlooking Grand Lake from a mountainside, these comfortable, old-fashioned cabins have covered porches, about a quarter of them screened in; all but the two-person units have kitchenettes. Built in 1921 and run by the same family since 1953, the resort feels like a step back in time. It has a pool, a playground, riding stables, and many other forms of recreation, but no phones or TVs.

The restaurant at the lodge is exceptional for its quality and character. The night I visited, the maitre d' was hugging everyone in sight while discreetly managing a crisis involving a bridegroom's shoes. He represented one of three generations of the James family working the room. The grill along the wall flared and voices boomed off the high log rafters, with elk heads looking down proudly. Couples sat over candles on the porch, gazing down on the lake. The service was perfect, and the cuisine memorable: A recent menu included elk medallions with cranberry sauce. The staff knows how to keep children happy, too. It's well worth a stop. Lunches range from $5.95 to $8.25, dinner entrees from $13 to $21. Make reservations for dinner.

**Western Riviera Motel.** 419 Garfield Ave. (P.O. Box 1286), Grand Lake, CO 80447. ☎ **970/627-3580.** Fax 970/627-3320. 15 units. $90–$110 per unit, sleeping from 1 to 6. AE, MC, V.

This is a trim little motel right across the street from Grand Lake, where there's a beach, playground, and boat rental.

# WHEN YOU ARRIVE

## ENTRANCE FEES

The entrance fee is $15 per vehicle, per week. National passes apply (see chapter 1).

## VISITOR CENTERS
## Park Service

**Beaver Meadows Visitor Center.** On Hwy. 36, at the Beaver Meadows Entrance, in Estes Park. ☎ **970/586-1206.** Summer daily 8am–9pm; off-season daily 8am–5pm.

The small main visitor center, made of stone and steel, hums with activity. People collect information, make backcountry camping reservations, and watch an orientation film.

**Alpine Visitor Center.** On Trail Ridge Rd., 23 miles from headquarters. No phone. Daily 9am–5pm. Closed mid-Oct to Memorial Day.

The location, at 12,000 feet, rather than the building draws throngs of people, giddy in the thin air, to this visitor center. It contains exhibits on alpine ecology and has a viewing area where you're likely to see elk. There are also a huge gift store and a snack bar. From the parking lot, a short path climbs to a knob where car passengers can get a sense of walking in the mountains.

**Kawuneeche Visitor Center.** Near Grand Lake Entrance Station, Trail Ridge Rd. (U.S. 34). ☎ **970/627-3471.** Summer daily 8am–6pm; off-season daily 8am–4:30pm.

This attractive building with a patio crossed by a creek has displays on what to do in the park on the western side of the Front Range, and how nature here differs from nature on the eastern side. You can get backcountry permits here, too.

**Fall River Visitor Center.** On U.S. 34, just east of the Fall River entrance, in Estes Park. No phone. Daily 8am–8pm. Closed Oct–May.

Opened in the summer of 2000, this center looks like a mountain lodge on the outside. Inside are exhibits on park wildlife, including full-size bronzes of elk and other animals, an activity room for children, an information desk, and a bookstore. The attached **Rocky Mountain Gateway** (☎ **970/577-0043**) offers snacks and sandwiches from a cafeteria, as well as somewhat pricey souvenirs and clothing.

**Lily Lake Visitor Center.** Rte. 7, south of Estes Park. Daily 9am–4:30pm. Closed Sept–May.

This small visitor center is across the road from a pretty little lake that's circled by a half-mile stroller- and wheelchair-accessible path. There are displays and handouts on recreation in the park and in the adjacent national forests.

## Commercial Visitor Centers

**Estes Park Chamber Resort Association Visitor Information Center.** 500 Big Thompson Ave. (Hwy. 34, just before split of bypass and business routes). ☎ **800/443-7837** or 970/586-4431. Summer Mon–Sat 8am–8pm, Sun 10am–5pm; winter Mon–Sat 8am–5pm, Sun 10am–4pm.

This is a useful little visitor center, where you can pick up information, see menus from most of the town's restaurants, and locate lodgings — you describe what you want, and the staff finds you a room. Across a footbridge is a small playground.

**Grand Lake Area Chamber of Commerce Visitor Center.** Rte. 34, Grand Lake. ☎ **800/531-1019** or 970/627-3372. Daily 9am–5pm in summer, reduced hours in winter.

Pick up business and recreation information for the west side here.

**Emergencies** Dial ☎ **911** in an emergency. The park's emergency office is at ☎ **970/586-1399.** The **Estes Park Medical Center** (☎ **970/586-2317**) is at 555 Prospect Ave.

**Stores** Large supermarkets in Estes Park include a Safeway in a shopping center on Highway 34 across from the visitor center. There are smaller stores in Grand Lake.

**Banks** A **Key Bank** branch in Estes Park is across Highway 34 from the town visitor center. ATMs are all around town.

**Post Office** At 215 W. Riverside Dr. in Estes Park.

**Gear Sales & Rental** **Estes Park Mountain Shop,** 358 E. Elkhorn Ave., Estes Park (☎ **800/ 504-6642** or 970/586-6548; www.estesparkmountainshop.com), rents camping equipment, skis, and snowshoes, and sells outdoors gear and clothing. It has an indoor climbing gym and offers climbing classes and trips. Fishing gear is available to rent or buy at **Scot's Sporting Goods,** on Moraine Avenue (Highway 36) in Estes Park (☎ **970/586-2877**). You can rent mountain bikes and snowshoes from **Colorado Bicycling Adventures,** 184 E. Elkhorn Ave., Estes Park (☎ **970/ 586-4241;** www.coloradobicycling.com).

## GETTING AROUND
## By Car

The park is easy to navigate using the map rangers hand out at the gate. The park is small enough that you can camp or stay in one place as a base and go to the opposite side for a day hike. But plan your activities all on one side during a day, or you may eat up a lot of time driving back and forth.

Pick up a free map of Estes Park at the town visitor center, 500 Big Thompson Ave. Walk whenever you can in town — traffic can be slow, and the streets are confusing at first.

## By Shuttle

A free shuttle bus runs from the Moraine Park Campground to the Cub Lake trailhead. It goes up Bear Lake Road to various points, including the Glacier Basin Campground. You can transfer to another shuttle, to Bear Lake. The bus stops at all the trailheads along the way, allowing hikers to plan routes that loop back to the road and get a lift back to the car. Check the park newspaper for times and season of operation when you visit. In the busy summer period, the shuttles often run every 15 minutes.

## KEEPING SAFE & HEALTHY

Besides the specific advice here, see "Dealing with Hazards," in chapter 1, for information about bears and other dangerous wildlife, giardia, hypothermia, and sunburn.

## Elevation

Most people never go to elevations as high as those found along Trail Ridge Road except in airplanes (which are pressurized to the equivalent of about 5,000 ft.). The air up here is much thinner, and it takes time for your body to adjust, especially if you're exerting yourself. You may feel dizzy or lightheaded, or have headaches, a fast heartbeat, or nausea. If you push yourself too hard, it could be dangerous. Children may feel it first and become sluggish — check on kids being carried in backpacks to make sure they're alert.

To reduce the effects of elevation, start your vacation with hikes at lower elevations and work your way up to more strenuous expeditions higher in the mountains. Also, drink lots of water. The only cure for altitude sickness is to return to lower elevation. You should feel better quickly. Also, make sure children and adults have protection from the sun at high altitudes, where ultraviolet radiation is much stronger. See "What to Pack" (p. 366).

## Lightning

Lightning is a special concern at Rocky Mountain. Thunderstorms come almost every afternoon in the summer, and alpine terrain above the tree line is a dangerous place to be when they do. You may be the tallest thing around. Plan your hikes so that you're back in the trees by afternoon, and review "Dealing with Hazards," in chapter 1, so that you know what to do if you're in an exposed area when lightning comes.

## Ticks

Hikers should tuck in their pant legs and use insect repellent on the outside of clothes to keep ticks off. Check everyone after a hike, and remove any ticks you find completely with a pair of tweezers. Ticks in this area cause Colorado Tick Fever and Rocky Mountain Spotted Fever, not Lyme disease.

# Enjoying the Park

## Natural Places
### Trail Ridge & the Mummy Range

The road that crosses the park follows a natural ramp up into the mountains, Trail Ridge, which Native Americans used to cross the Rockies thousands of years ago. **Trail Ridge Road** crosses alpine tundra above tree line for 11 miles, giving unique access to a huge swath of mountaintops and high-elevation terrain for hikers and walkers. The Park Service gives away a brochure with commentary for each of the pull-outs.

On the other side of a steep mountain valley, unpaved **Old Fall River Road** winds up into the mountains to the same point, near the Alpine Visitor Center. It opens alpine and wooded terrain in the Mummy Range to hikers.

On each side, you can learn how plants survive in the wind and cold. It's almost always very windy up here, and the thin, cool air is dry. Any branches that stick out quickly dry out and die. The same drying-out process happens to you — a good reason to bring and drink lots of water and wear clothing that protects you from the wind. Trees that get a start in a protected spot behind a rock grow gnarled and short as the wind carves them back, in a manner similar to the way salt spray shapes trees and bushes at the seashore. Tundra plants survive by growing very slowly — so they don't need much food or energy — and staying low, out of the wind. Try lying down on the tundra to feel how the wind calms a few inches from the ground. Because the tundra grows so slowly, it's important not to harm it. Trampled tundra plants can take 100 years to return. Close to the road, you must stay on trails; farther out on the mountainside, when trails give out, you can walk on the tundra, but avoid going in single file. If the weather is good, there's no reason not to wander out on a heathery mountainside. Venturing farther, as you climb, even the tundra gives out, and you can walk across broken granite that no plant has yet pioneered.

There are several trails to hike in the area. From Trail Ridge Road, the **Old Ute Trail** follows the original ridge route 6 miles down to Beaver Meadows, across each life zone. Unless you have a vehicle at either end, you'll want to hike partway and double back. From the top, you can go about 2 miles before the steep elevation loss begins that would be hard to climb back up. The **Tundra Communities Nature Trail** is near the road's high point and is accessible to strollers and wheelchairs. More trails start at **Milner Pass,** on the Continental Divide. From Old Fall River Road, you can reach trail-less alpine hiking and a series of easy, high-altitude mountains to climb at the **Chapin Pass Trailhead.** Be sure to take a topographic map and check the weather before hiking off trails above tree line. For more on hiking, maps, and guides, see "Hiking" (p. 377) and "Reading Up" (p. 365).

## MORAINE PARK & HORSESHOE PARK

The park areas of the Front Range are valleys protected from extreme weather by the mountains. The meadows and gentle terrain make a safe home for wildlife in the winter. These two parks, just inside Rocky Mountain near Estes Park, were beds for glaciers. Looking at a topographic map, you can see where a glacier pushed down the path of the Big Thompson River, which now flows in Forest Canyon, and plowed out a flat area in Moraine Park. The rock that the glacier took from the mountains piled up around its sides and front in hills called moraines that still surround the valley. Horseshoe Park, site of Aspenglen Campground, lay under the front of a glacier that came down the valley where Fall River is now.

Besides being great campgrounds, these parks are places to hike on relatively level trails where you're likely to see a lot of birds and animals. You also can join trail rides at Moraine Park. In the summer, a free shuttle bus runs to the Cub Lake and Fern Lake trailheads in Moraine Park, allowing different loop hikes that end with a ride back to the car.

## BEAR LAKE ROAD AREA

Bear Lake Road runs from Moraine Park about 9 miles and 1,500 vertical feet upward into an area of steep, craggy mountainsides and small, round reflecting lakes. An extraordinary network of trails connects to the road at spots all along the route, including at a stable at Sprague Lake. There are flat, half-mile loops suitable for toddlers, and more ambitious hikes that climb right up to the Continental Divide. At Glacier Basin, a campground and a parking lot are on the route of a shuttle bus that drops off and picks up hikers

along the road. This eases parking problems and allows you to plan longer hikes, perhaps downhill all the way, that don't require you to double back.

At the top, near the round mirror of Bear Lake, a ranger answers questions at a kiosk and helps hikers figure out which route is best for them. The Park Service's free trail map of the area shows the web of trails, with mileage and difficulty ratings. The biggest drawback of the area is that it is the park's most crowded, especially on weekends.

## LONGS PEAK

Hikers climb the highest mountain in the park thousands of times a summer. Most traverse an 8-mile-long trail that gains almost 5,000 feet. Sixteen miles with 10,000 feet in total elevation change is a hard day for the strongest hikers, so Longs Peak should come only after you have proved yourselves on other all-day hikes at high altitude. About half of the trail is above tree line, so to be out of areas exposed to lightning by afternoon, you have to start before dawn. The hike begins at a tents-only campground and ranger station on Route 7 on the southeast side of the park. It ends on the granite slab of the peak, at 14,255 feet, a significant and memorable accomplishment. The tallest mountain in the lower 48 states is Mt. Whitney, in the Sierra Nevada, which is only 240 feet higher.

## WILD BASIN

In the extreme southeast of the park, this area is reached by a dirt road, which holds down the number of people who use the trails. The basin is surrounded by high peaks, with trails that trace among them to high-elevation lakes. It's a good area for a backpacking trip, with lots of backcountry campsites. Most of the hikes are fairly challenging.

## THE WEST SIDE & COLORADO RIVER

Trail Ridge Road drops down into the Kawuneeche Valley, facing the Never Summer Mountains, about 5 miles south of the valley's head. It runs due south about a dozen miles to Grand Lake. During the last ice age, a glacier made this valley, its face molding the dip where the lake settled in. The Colorado River starts at the head of the valley, building from its wetland bottoms and coursing south among the towering trees. It flows freely for about 20 miles from the Continental Divide, then leaves the national park and almost immediately gets caught by a series of dams. The Colorado will be waylaid many times more before an intermittent trickle makes it to the Gulf of California.

Here in the Rockies, the river is born wild from the clouds that hit the west side of the Front Range and drop their rain and snow (see "Making Clouds & Rain," in chapter 13). This moisture affects the valley's habitat in many ways. The forest of spruce and fir is darker than the pine woods on the drier, east side of the park. The willows and other swamp-loving brush make food for moose, which don't live on the east side. The deep snow attracts skiers and provides the water that fills lakes for boaters and waters the American west. Grand Lake is a natural lake next to the park, and two man-made lakes lie just south and west. The west side attracts far fewer visitors than the east, but has many miles of backpacking trails that climb the back side of the park and the Never Summer Mountains.

## PLACES FOR LEARNING

**Moraine Park Museum.** On Bear Lake Rd. No phone. Free admission. Daily 9am–5pm. Closed mid-Oct to mid-Apr.

This museum explains the creation of the landscape. It covers geology, glaciers, thunderstorms, and other forces in a creative, engaging way that will interest visitors at every level. In one of many interactive exhibits, a glacier really moves, showing how it works. Downstairs is a good little bookstore with a kids' section and gifts.

**Historic Never Summer Ranch.** Trail Ridge Rd., just south of Timber Creek Campground. No phone. Free admission. Daily 10am–4:30pm. Closed Sept to mid-June.

A half-mile off the road, the restored buildings of an old ranch have been kept open for inspection. Volunteer guides dressed in period costume answer questions, and there's a brochure that describes self-guided walks.

## ACTIVITIES
## Backpacking

Camping out in the backcountry allows you to get away from the busy day hiking trailheads and into your own wild area where you can be alone. You don't have to be able to hike far in — the backcountry campsites at Rocky are plentiful and often less than a mile apart. Beginners can reserve sites near the trailhead. You'll get used to hauling all your stuff out into the woods, and learn what it's like to lie down to sleep with your family with no other human being in earshot. And a piece of empty countryside is an excellent playground. If your family can hike 5 miles a day with a pack, you can experience the park's more remote trails. Strong hikers can cover the park's longest trails in a few days.

Grizzly bears are gone from the park, but you do need to prepare for black bears and for smaller mammals like porcupines that can smell food that's left out and go after it in bags and packs. Learn how to avoid attracting animals by reading "Dangerous Wildlife," in chapter 1, and from the backcountry guidance the Park Service offers. Bring plenty of rope to hang food and garbage from a high tree branch. Campfires are not allowed in most of the backcountry, and then only in metal fire grates at a few sites. Trail guides and maps are covered in "Reading Up" (p. 365). Also see "Backcountry Permits" (p. 367).

## Climbing

These high, granite peaks challenge with some famous climbs. Beginners and families can get started in the sport easily at the park, where at

On a cold, dry winter day when the sun is shining toward you, you may see flashes of light in the powder snow. It seems magical, as if a billion tiny diamonds are hidden in the whiteness. The next day, or even an hour later, the flashes may be gone — a light wind may disturb the powder, or a little warm air could erase the sparkles. Snowflakes are always changing, even after they fall.

On a warm, dry summer day when you're hiking in the mountains, you may see flashes of light in the gray granite bedrock. (You'll find lots of granite at Rocky Mountain, Yosemite, Sequoia/Kings Canyon, and Acadia national parks.) The light may change and the flashes disappear in a moment, but if you were to come back in 1,000 years with the sun at the same angle, you could probably see that same flash again. Granite is one of the hardest and longest-lasting rocks, and the granite you see today could have been around since before the first animals lived on our planet.

Snow sparkles last a moment, and granite sparkles last practically forever, but both happen for the same reason. The sparkle comes from one of the basic ways that nature works. Most solid material fits together along straight lines that meet in squares, hexagons, and other geometric shapes called **crystals.** Most of the time the crystals are too small to see, but in granite and snow, a flat side of a crystal is sometimes large enough to catch the sunlight like a mirror and flash at you.

All matter can be solid, liquid, or gas. We're most used to water in these three forms: ice, liquid water, and the vapor from boiling or evaporating water. A molecule of water is made of two hydrogen atoms and one oxygen atom (that's why it's called $H_2O$). Because of the way the atoms are made, each molecule is like a tiny magnet, with a positive electric charge on one side and a negative charge on the other. When the water is vapor, the molecules fly around too fast for the magnets to pay attention to each other. When the water cools, the molecules slow down, and when they bump into each other, the positive end on one sticks to the negative end of another. After that happens enough times, you have a drop of water. That's how water condenses from vapor into liquid. Now, take away more energy, slowing down the molecules more — chill the water, in other words — and the molecules get even closer together and can fit together more strongly. They organize into six-sided crystals, in which their electric poles lock together best, and the water freezes.

least two reputable schools cater to family travelers who want to climb. **Estes Park Mountain Shop,** 358 E. Elkhorn Ave., Estes Park (☎ 800/504-6642 or 970/586-6548; www.estesparkmountainshop.com), offers lessons and indoor and outdoor climbing, even for younger children; see "Summer Camps" (p. 380) for more information. The park concessionaire for guided climbing and instruction is the famous **Colorado Mountain School,** P.O. Box 1846, Estes Park, CO 80517 (☎ 888/CMS-7783 or 970/586-5758; www.cmschool.com).

## Fishing

Trout fishing is allowed in some of the park's lakes and streams with a Colorado fishing license. High-altitude lakes often can't support

fish, and the Park Service no longer allows stocking of non-native species. Lists of places where fish may be found are available with regulations from the Park Service. The rules differ from state regulations, so read them carefully. The many places to fish outside the park include Estes Lake and Grand Lake.

**Scot's Sporting Goods,** on Moraine Avenue (Highway 36) in Estes Park (☎ 970/586-2877), is run by a friendly couple who love fly-fishing and offer lessons and guided trips. They also sell and rent fishing packages and other gear. A fishing license costs $5.25 for a day, $18.25 for 5 days; children under 16 don't need one.

Kids may also enjoy fishing in a commercial fishing pond on Moraine Avenue in Estes Park, where there's no chance of not catching

Making crystals is like packing a suitcase. The faster you do it, the less organized it is. In the case of the molecules in crystals, slower packing means they have time to get lined up the right way and snap into place by the millions, until you can see the pattern without a microscope. Ice crystals can grow big and complicated — delicate snowflakes, for example, or frost on a window. And even after it's ice, water still changes. Ice can evaporate or pick up water vapor from the air. Snowflakes change shape as the powder turns into crusty hard snow. If snowflakes fall on a glacier, they may press together into rock-hard ice that can help bulldoze mountains. When the conditions are just right, big ice crystals can form in powdery snow. They catch the sun and sparkle.

Granite comes from below the earth, not above, but the way it works is basically the same. The hard granite on the surface is like ice on top of a big pool of hot, liquid rock that makes up the earth below. Below the surface, this liquid rock is called **magma,** and when it comes out in the air it's called **lava.** If magma has a lot of a mineral called silica in it, it becomes granite when it freezes into rock. If it comes out as lava, it cools quickly into rhyolite, a kind of rock common at Yellowstone National Park. The crystals in those rocks are too small to see because they cooled so fast that they didn't have time to fit together in orderly patterns. If the rock cools even faster, you get obsidian, which is black glass — it has no crystals at all. Scientists call obsidian a very thick liquid, not a solid, because — as in window glass — the molecules aren't organized.

Granite is made of the same kind of magma as obsidian and rhyolite, but it never came to the surface when it was liquid. The magma cooled far under the earth, very slowly, in blobs called **plutons,** which could be many miles wide. Square crystals of light quartz and feldspar had time to grow. The longer it took the rock to cool, the larger the grains became. The molecules snapped together strongly, so the granite is hard and lasts a long time. After it hardened, ice and water wore away the rock around it, leaving mountains of granite. Some of the crystals are large enough to catch the sun and sparkle.

So both snow and granite sparkle because, deep down, everything is made the same way.

---

a fish. **Trout Haven** (☎ 970/586-5525) fills their little pond with trout, gives you the gear, helps you use it, and maybe even cooks the fish for lunch, if you like. They charge 60¢ an inch (about $6 to $7 a fish), not including cooking. Is it really fishing? Maybe not, but small children won't care.

## Hiking

Rocky Mountain National Park is one of the nation's greatest places for day hiking. On any summer day, you can hike in mountain meadows, in marshy river bottoms, in forests of pine or fir, around alpine lakes, or above tree line among the rocks and tundra at the top of the Rockies. There are hikes for every level of age and fitness. The Park Service has built flat, paved nature trails around three lakes (Bear, Sprague, and Lily) that are accessible from the road. Most families will be able to handle the somewhat more challenging trails that loop in ever-greater distances from Bear Lake and Moraine Park, or short doubling-back nature walks and trail segments in every one of the park's ecosystems. When you work up to a tougher hike, there are plenty of those too. They include the unique opportunity to walk self-directed across the alpine tundra, or to climb a high-altitude peak without special equipment or training.

I've covered specific trails above under "Natural Places" (p. 373). The park has many more than I can mention, and often the most important thing is to find a trail that isn't too crowded. One way to do this is to start from one of the main trailhead areas and choose a route after you get the lay of the land, simply hiking as far as you wish and turning back. This is a reasonable approach for **Bear Lake Road, Moraine** or **Horseshoe Park, Wild Basin,** and the **Kawuneeche Valley.** Along **Trail Ridge Road** you can find open tundra to break out on your own; just be sure not to trample the tundra near the road.

I enjoy hiking most when I have a good topographic map and detailed trail guide, such as those mentioned under "Reading Up" (p. 365). Without buying a book or map, you can get help choosing a trail from a Park Service handout that lists five dozen routes with length, elevation gain, and difficulty level. Another sheet lists day hikes you can make in the winter. With the free park map to find the trailhead, those handouts are all you need for most hikes.

## Horseback Riding

Unlike the standard 1-hour circles at many national parks, the trail-ride concessionaire at Rocky offers rides as long as all day, going a considerable distance over the eastern half of the park. You also can book pack trips. The **Hi Country Stables Corp.** has stables at Moraine Park (☎ 970/586-2327; www.hicountry stables.com) and on Sprague Lake (☎ 970/586-3244), near Glacier Basin Campground on Bear Lake Road. Rides leave beginning at 8am and at various times during the day, and last from 2 to 8 hours. A 2-hour ride costs $35; all day is $80. Children as young as 6 can ride their own horse, and younger children can ride with a parent.

## Mountain Biking

Roads in the park are open to mountain biking, and on the national forest lands outside the park you can ride on trails. **Colorado Bicycling Adventures,** 184 E. Elkhorn Ave., Estes Park (☎ 970/586-4241; www.colorado bicycling.com), rents bikes and offers guided mountain-biking rides. It's the only agency permitted to do so in the park or in Roosevelt National Forest. A couple of these trips coast

downhill much of the way and are geared to families. They cost about $70 for adults, $50 for children under 12. The company will also give you a map and advice on where to ride if you rent.

## Rafting

There's no rafting in the park, but various operators take floats to the west and north of the park, on the Cache La Poudre and Colorado rivers. Various lengths and levels of roughness are available for kids as young as 7. Two companies based in Fort Collins are **Rocky Mountain Adventures** (☎ 800/858-6808 or 970/586-6191; www.shoprma.com) and **Wanderlust Whitewater Rafting** (☎ 800/745-7238 or 970/484-1219; www.awanderlustadventure.com).

## Wildlife Watching

You'll likely see animals if you spend much time hiking in the park. You can wildlife watch from the car too. If you do, stay in the car, because moving or approaching the animals will frighten them, ruin the viewing for everyone, and possibly endanger your family. Bring binoculars or a long camera lens.

The best places are open meadows and alpine areas where you can see a long way. In the spring and early summer, bighorn sheep go to **Horseshoe Park** to lick minerals that they can get from certain spots (the park service sometimes posts a crossing guard for them). Later, they spend time on **Specimen Mountain,** reachable on the **Crater Trail,** which starts at the Milner Pass pull-out. (The trail is closed from May to mid-July for lambing season.) Moose like the swamps and ponds of the **Kawuneeche Valley,** on the west side. Elk and mule deer show up commonly in the meadows in places like **Moraine Park** in the fall, and you can pick out elk on the tundra on drives on **Trail Ridge Road.** In the fall, elk congregate for mating in these eastern parks, and even in the town of Estes Park. They are most active early and late in the day. Ask a ranger about the best places to go during the season you visit. For kids, it may be more fun to concentrate on the animals you can easily find in your campground and on your hikes. They can figure out what the animals are and watch their behavior, rather than spending a lot of time trying to see a specific species of big game.

## Winter Sports

On the east side of the park, where snow is scarce, people mostly use snowshoes for spring hiking to see wildlife and to explore higher-elevation trails while the snow lingers. There are no groomed ski trails, but you can rent backcountry skis and snowshoes and get advice at **Estes Park Mountain Shop,** 358 E. Elkhorn Ave., Estes Park (☎ 800/504-6642 or 970/586-6548; www.estesparkmountain shop.com).

The west side of the park gets good, deep snow late December through February. Here you can explore the spectacular hiking trails in white on cross-country skis and snowshoes. Rangers lead ski and snowshoe outings from the **Kawuneeche Visitor Center** (see p. 371). Snowshoes and cross-country skis are available for rent in Grand Lake at **Never Summer Mountain Products,** 919 Grand Ave. (☎ 970/627-3642), open daily 9am to 5pm. Rental cost is $12 for a 24-hour period for both cross-country skis and snowshoes. The National Park Service recently outlawed snowmobiling within the park except for one trail from the Kawuneeche Visitor Center into adjacent **Arapaho National Forest,** but riding remains a popular activity in the national forests. Check with their ranger office or the Grand Lake Area Chamber of Commerce (see "Rocky Mountain Address Book," p. 360).

## PROGRAMS
## Children's Programs

The **Junior Ranger** program is one of the best in the park system. The kid-sized 26-page Junior Ranger Log Book is free at the visitor centers. After finishing it, attending a ranger program, talking to people, handing out

## PLACES FOR RELAXED PLAY & PICNICS

The meadows and tundra-covered mountain-sides of Rocky Mountain National Park are wonderful playgrounds, where kids can romp and experience a special freedom. A playground with equipment is located near the visitor center in Estes Park, and there's lots more to do at Estes Lake, described below in "Fun Beyond the Natural Wonders." Numerous picnic areas are marked on the park map.

stickers about not feeding animals, and collecting 10 pieces of trash, children get a plastic badge that looks like the ones real rangers wear. Rangers make a big deal with the award, announcing it over the public address system. The material is fun and well thought out and doesn't require parents to drive all over the park, as some programs do. There's even a field guide where kids can check off plants, animals, and birds they see. Children 6 to 11 or so should enjoy the activities; the younger kids will need help reading the booklet.

The weekly schedule of ranger programs published in the park newspaper usually includes several activities specifically for children ages 6 to 12. Rangers teach about insects, birds, fire, and other natural history topics with stories, puppets, games, and the like. Generally, parents have to chaperone their kids.

The **Rocky Mountain Nature Association** offers more in-depth programs for children as young as 6 or as old as 18. Most are half-day outings, cost only $15, and don't require prior reservations. Participants do arts and crafts, learn about nature, or learn about Native American ways. A few more demanding programs, for teens, last all day and do need advance registration. Get information and even sign up online on their website (www.rmna.org); other contact information is under "For Handy Reference" (p. 372).

## Family & Adult Programs

During the summer, the park offers more than 150 ranger programs each week on a great range of nature, history, and outdoors topics, including many guided hikes. Evening programs take place at the Beaver Meadows Visitor Center, Kawuneeche Visitor Center, and all the campgrounds except Longs Peak. A schedule is published in the park newspaper.

In addition to its children's programs, mentioned in the previous section, the **Rocky Mountain Nature Association** offers an extensive program of seminars and outings aimed primarily at adults but also accessible, in some cases, to teens and families. They cover natural history, art, outdoor skills, and other topics, and last from a half day to a week. On summer weekends, there are many choices, and even a few in later fall and early spring. Check the catalog and register online at www.rmna.org, or use the contact information in "For Handy Reference" (p. 372).

## Summer Camps

There are a couple of day-camp options near the park. The **YMCA of the Rockies** owns a large conference center and family resort on the east side of the park. It offers a day camp for children from potty-trained 3-year-olds through high-school age, with an amazing variety of outdoor activities. A 1-day session is $20. You have to reserve by midwinter, or get a cancellation, because the sessions book up. You need to be a member of the Y somewhere to participate. Check availability online at www.ymcarockies.com, or contact **Estes Park Center,** YMCA of the Rockies, Estes Park, CO 80511-2550 (☎ **970/586-3341,** ext. 1280).

**Estes Park Mountain Shop,** 358 E. Elkhorn Ave., Estes Park (☎ **800/504-6642** or 970/586-6548; www.estesparkmountain shop.com), also offers fun day programs for children as young as 8. One outing rides the aerial tram from Estes Park up to a mountain site that is a base for hiking and climbing. Generally, reservations are not needed.

# FUN BEYOND THE NATURAL WONDERS

## ESTES PARK

The town of Estes Park was born to serve tourists, and it takes that job seriously to this day. **Elkhorn Avenue,** also known as U.S. Highway 34 Business, is home to a cute pedestrian-oriented row of businesses, just scruffy enough to avoid seeming like plastic tourist stuff. Besides the restaurants and shops, there are little museums, arcades, and other attractions that amuse children. Beyond this core, the town consists mostly of car-oriented strip development, where you'll find plenty of kid activities: minigolf and go-carts, the fishing pond described under "Fishing" (p. 376), a water slide, and so on. They're empty calories compared to the national park, but you can't eat granola for every meal. The **Estes**

**Park Ride-A-Kart Family Amusement Park and Cascade Creek Mini-Golf,** at Highway 34 just west of Mall Road as you enter town (☎ **970/586-6495**), is the ultimate in this kind of thing. It has bumper boats, a tiny train, 36 holes of minigolf, and more. Also check out the strip on **Moraine Avenue** near the Beaver Meadows entrance to the park.

You can rent canoes, paddleboats, and fishing boats on Estes Lake from a little marina operated by the **Estes Valley Recreation and Park District** (☎ **970/586-2011;** www.estes valleyrecreation.com). It also rents bikes and has a wading area, picnic area, and kids' play area. A **public swimming pool** is south of the lake at Brodie Avenue and Community Drive.

## GRAND LAKE

People visit Grand Lake and the reservoirs nearby for boating, fishing, and recreation around the lakes. Boats are for rent in town, and there's a lake beach along the town, although the water is quite cold.

# WHERE TO EAT

## LOW-STRESS MEALS
### Fast Food

Estes Park has plenty of franchise fast food. Some of the chains in town include **Dairy Queen, Kentucky Fried Chicken/Taco Bell, Subway, and McDonald's,** all of which you can easily see along the main highways as you pass through town.

### Diners

In Estes Park or Grand Lake it's easy to find cafes serving burgers and fries where your coffee cup is never allowed to sit empty.

In Estes Park, **Big Horn Restaurant,** 401 W. Elkhorn Ave. (☎ **970/586-2792**), is a justly popular Western cafe — nothing fancy, but hearty breakfasts, fast service, and dinners from $7 to $15. **Molly B,** 200 Moraine Ave. (☎ **970/586-2766**), seems like just another somewhat grubby version of the same thing, but it turns out to be much more. The thoughtful and varied dishes include many vegetarian options. It's open all day in summer, for breakfast and lunch only the rest of the year. Dinners are $8 to $17.

In Grand Lake, **Marie's Grand Lake Cafe,** 928 Grand Ave. (☎ **970/627-9475**), is packed at breakfast. It serves inexpensive diner meals all day.

### Pizza & Tacos

**Bob and Tony's Pizza,** 124 W. Elkhorn Ave. (☎ **970/586-2044**), has perfected an atmosphere that kids will enjoy. A brick wall in the dining room has graffiti on it, and a back room has a pool table, foosball, and video games. Order at a counter and eat in or carry out. They're open daily 11am to 10pm in summer, shorter hours the rest of the year.

**Grumpy Gringo,** 1560 Big Thompson Ave. (☎ **970/586-7705;** www.grumpygringo. com), with its private booths, plants, and decoration, might strike you as too fancy a place, but in fact the service and atmosphere are casual and the prices low, with a children's menu. Choose from a good selection of burritos, enchiladas, fajitas, and other Mexican standards, plus burgers and sandwiches. It is open 11am to 10pm in summer, slightly less in winter.

### Best-Behavior Meals

For details on two favorite restaurants in the area, at the **Baldpate Inn** and **Grand Lake Lodge,** see "Where to Spend the Night" (p. 366). Here's another choice:

**Dunraven Inn,** 2470 Colo. 66, Estes Park (☎ **970/586-6409**). Main courses $7–$32. Sun–Thurs 5–10pm, Fri–Sat 5–11pm. Shorter hours in winter.

This is a place where parents can enjoy scampi, veal parmigiana, or the house specialty, a charbroiled steak in a sauce of peppers, black olives, mushrooms, and tomatoes. It will be a fairly elegant evening, but there are a kids' menu and fanciful decoration, including various images of the *Mona Lisa,* one with a mustache. Reservations are highly recommended.

# The Sierra Nevada

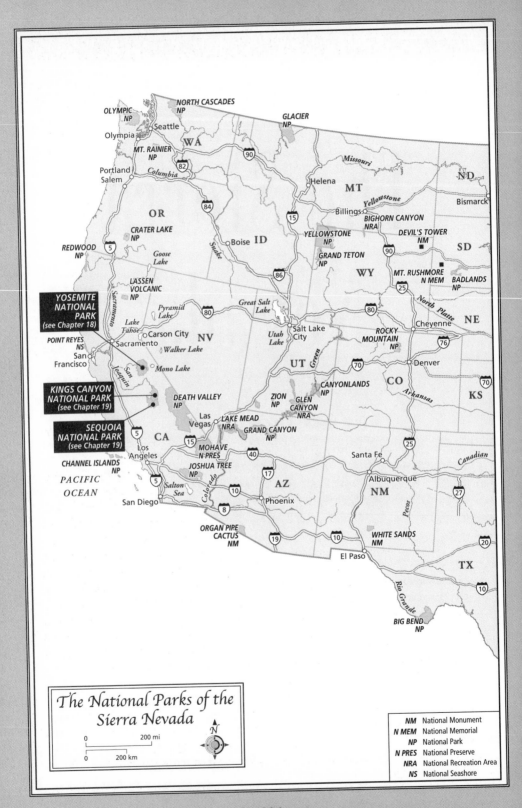

OLYMPIC
NP

NORTH CASCADES
NP

GLACIER
NP

Seattle

Olympia

WA

MT. RAINIER
NP

Portland
Salem

*Columbia*

84

82

90

*Missouri*

Helena

MT

*Yellowstone*

Billings

Bismarck

ND

OR

CRATER LAKE
NP

*Snake*

Boise

ID

15

YELLOWSTONE
NP

BIGHORN CANYON
NRA

DEVIL'S TOWER
NM

SD

REDWOOD
NP

*Goose
Lake*

5

GRAND TETON
NP

90

MT. RUSHMORE
N MEM

BADLANDS
NP

LASSEN
VOLCANIC
NP

*Pyramid
Lake*

*Great Salt
Lake*

WY

25

*North Platte*

NE

YOSEMITE
NATIONAL
PARK
(see Chapter 18)

*Lake
Tahoe*

*Sacramento*

Carson City

NV

80

Salt Lake
City

*Utah
Lake*

ROCKY
MOUNTAIN
NP

Cheyenne

76

80

POINT REYES
NS

San
Francisco

Sacramento

Walker Lake

*San
Joaquin*

Mono Lake

UT

*Green*

70

Denver

CO

*Arkansas*

70

KS

KINGS CANYON
NATIONAL PARK
(see Chapter 19)

DEATH VALLEY
NP

ZION
NP

CANYONLANDS
NP

GLEN
CANYON
NRA

SEQUOIA
NATIONAL PARK
(see Chapter 19)

5

CA

Los
Angeles

15

Las
Vegas

LAKE MEAD
NRA

GRAND CANYON
NP

Santa Fe

25

*Canadian*

CHANNEL ISLANDS
NP

PACIFIC
OCEAN

5

MOHAVE
N PRES

JOSHUA TREE
NP

40

Albuquerque

NM

27

San Diego

*Salton
Sea*

*Colorado*

10

AZ

17

Phoenix

*Pecos*

ORGAN PIPE
CACTUS
NM

8

19

10

WHITE SANDS
NM

El Paso

20

TX

*Rio Grande*

BIG BEND
NP

10

The National Parks of the
Sierra Nevada

N

0         200 mi

0      200 km

| | |
|---|---|
| NM | National Monument |
| N MEM | National Memorial |
| NP | National Park |
| N PRES | National Preserve |
| NRA | National Recreation Area |
| NS | National Seashore |

# CHAPTER 17

# Rock, Life & Change

The round shapes of the granite bedrock dip at the edge of Lower Cathedral Lake and continue under the clear water without a break. The lake, it seems, is nothing more than a bowl of stone where the clean water of melting snow collects for the summer. Solid peaks of gleaming granite circle the lake like the rounded tips of the earth's white bones. Lying with eyes closed on the sun-warmed rock at the lake's edge, you can feel the strength of the mountains beneath you. The air is cool and silent here, above 9,000 feet elevation, and as fresh as a new idea. Days on these bare granite places feel clean and pure. In 100 centuries since the end of the Ice Age, the glacier-polished stone has barely chipped. Only a few scraps of soil have gathered in the cracks. At the top of the Sierra Nevada, these 80-million-year-old rocks are still new. You continue hiking after the break, and the rocks seem to pass some of their power to your legs, which carry you effortlessly over the trail.

Another scene from the Sierra Nevada: a dark, damp place. The odor of earth is rising, but the sky is missing. Above, the vertical lines of huge tree trunks keep going up until they meet in green branches so high you can't make out the details. This is a grove of giant sequoias. The trees are so large that a single trunk, hollowed out, is bigger than most people's living rooms. The trees have fallen and grown hollow over time, and people have lived in them. There was even a hotel in one tree, early on. These are some of the earth's oldest and largest living things, as old as 3,000 years and as large as 30 feet across and 300 feet tall. These are ancient places, the last left from before the mountains were built, when such giants grew across the West. Voices die out in the grove. The wood and earth seem to soak up the sound. Then people stop talking. Nothing you can say seems important around these great things, growing since before most of our history was written down.

## THE PARKS

*Sierra Nevada* means "snowy mountain range" in Spanish. The mountains were named (not very creatively) by a Spanish missionary who saw them from across California in 1776. The range is 400 miles long, filling much of eastern California. On the west, the mountains rise steeply from the huge, flat farming region of the Central Valley. On the east, they're even steeper, rising like a wall from the Great Basin Desert.

## Yosemite National Park

The park, east of San Francisco roughly in the middle of the Sierra, is best known for Yosemite Valley, an amazing canyon where waterfalls drop thousands of feet from granite walls. The valley is a small part of the park, however, and is overrun with people. You'll want to spend most of your time hiking in the spectacular high-country areas and in the mountainside forests that aren't nearly as crowded.

## Sequoia & Kings Canyon National Parks

These connected and jointly managed parks in the southern Sierra are not as crowded as Yosemite, but otherwise they have much in

---

### A NOTE ON THE NAME "SIERRA NEVADA"

In Spanish, *sierra* means "a rocky mountain range," and *nevada* means "snowy." A simple nickname, but there's a trick to it. With some mountains, like the Rocky Mountains, the short name is the plural of the long name — "the Rockies." But you wouldn't call a mountain range "the ranges" for short, so the short name for the Sierra Nevada is "the Sierra," not "the Sierras."

---

common with it. **Sequoia** is famous for its huge groves of the big trees, and also has wonderful hiking and camping areas, swimming, high-country trails, cave exploring, and other qualities that have nothing to do with giant sequoias. **Kings Canyon** centers on the magnificent canyon of the Kings River. Its granite walls tower over the desert-like floor of the canyon like the cliffs of Yosemite Valley, but few people visit.

# NATURAL HISTORY & TIME

A week's vacation can seem to last half your life when you're a kid. Each day you see vivid new things you'll always remember. In 1 day you hike a rocky canyon trail, swim in a river, explore a cave, eat in camp, and sit by the fire telling ghost stories. By the time you get into your sleeping bag, the morning seems like days ago. By the time the family car pulls into your driveway at the end of the trip, you hardly recognize your house — nothing is exactly the way you remember it. How long ago it seems you left those rooms and smelled the odor of home! But, of course, it isn't the house that's changed. You have. Next winter, when you return to a routine of going to school every day, a week will pass as quickly as a day did while you were on vacation. It will seem that everything always stays the same. As

you grow older, time seems to go by faster and faster. When you have children, years start to fly by as fast as months and weeks did when you were young. Then your week in the mountains seems too brief, not like the endless adventure of discovery it was as a child. The old people I have known have told me that their childhood memories were the sharpest and most colorful. Those vivid moments last a lifetime.

As poorly as we understand time in our own lives, it's just about impossible to understand the time nature takes to do things. One way to try is to compare these big spans of time to the stages of a human life. If a giant sequoia were planted at the same time as a person were born, the tree would be as far along in its life as a toddler just learning to talk when the person died as an old great-grandparent. But in the life of the Sierra Nevada mountains, the oldest sequoia only lives as long as a week-old newborn. And in the life of the earth, the Sierra's age is the same as a 2-month-old baby. All of the 10,000 years of human history fit into the span of a few generations of trees in a sequoia grove, or about an hour and a half in the life of the earth.

We are babies in this landscape, but we can do something amazing. We can use our minds and the evidence around us to look down into those deep wells of time and see what was going on millions of years before the first human child was born. The old trees and long-lasting rocks of the Sierra help show the story.

## THE SIGNS OF CHANGE

Here's a puzzle: High in the Sierra, there are big areas of white granite without a thing growing on them. Even where soil does cover the rocks, it's a thin layer, and only certain kinds of trees and plants can grow. In these same mountains, lower down, groves of the biggest trees in the world grow, as they have for thousands of years, in deep, moist soil. Elsewhere, light green grasses wave in damp meadows, and tall ponderosa and sugar pines tower on the mountainsides. Why are these places so different? And while we're wondering, how did the mountains get those strange, rounded shapes, anyway?

Geologists, who study rocks, and biologists, who study living things, start with what's in front of them now to figure out how it got that way long ago. The forests and mountains are still changing, and they probably changed the same way in the past. For example, lakes are slowly turning into meadows, and meadows into forests. Even if we can't live long enough to see one lake become a meadow, we can study enough different lakes at different stages of change to figure out how it happens.

Rivers carry stuff called **sediment** into lakes — soil, sand, plant parts, and anything

else that happens to be caught in the flow of the river. When the flowing river meets the still lake, the water slows down and the sediment in the water falls to the bottom. You can usually see the pile of sediment as a shallow spot near the incoming river or even a small delta of dry land around its mouth. Slowly, that shallow spot gets larger until the lake is full of sediment and turns into a swampy meadow. In some meadows in Yosemite's high country, the ground is still so damp that only grasses and marsh plants will grow there. Those areas are not done changing from lakes to meadows. In other meadows, grasses growing over many seasons have died and rotted into soil, making more solid ground, and trees are slowly filling in from the edges.

In each lake on its way to becoming a forest, the process went step-by-step. After you look at enough different places at the different steps, you can compare them and be pretty sure what each one was like in the past, at an earlier step. How far back can you look? The lake basins were gouged out by glaciers, which, as we know from other evidence, melted about 10,000 years ago. Some lakes, like Lower Cathedral Lake, have barely started to fill with soil. Others are now forests of big trees.

## CHANGING CLIMATES

Heat from the inside of the earth builds up mountains, and weather powered by sun slowly tears them down. At the moment, the earth is winning here — the Sierra still is growing, some say at a rate of about 15 inches each century. Each winter, moist air from the Pacific runs into these mountains and dumps some 30 feet of snow on their tops (for an explanation of mountain weather, see "Natural History: Making Great Mountains & Weather," in chapter 13, "The Nature of High Places"). Then as the snow melts, it waters plants that wear down the mountains and feeds rivers like the Kings River that carve through canyons, down into the rocks.

The weather in the Sierra seems pretty predictable. In the summer it's dry and sunny, with rain coming mostly from thunderstorms. In the winter, snow falls. Over the course of a person's life, the seasons always seem to change the same way, and you start to think of that pattern as endless. But there's a lot of evidence that the Sierra has been much colder than it is now. The marks of glacier ice that once pushed through Yosemite Valley come up 4,000 feet on the valley walls, almost to the top of Half Dome. (See "Experiment: Finding Glacier Tracks," in chapter 18, "Yosemite National Park," to see for yourself where glaciers went.) In Alaska and a few places high in the Sierra, we can still see glaciers at work. They're made of deep snow that never melts over the summer. Over years it packs down into ice and slowly oozes over the mountains. For these mountains to be nearly covered by glaciers, as the rocks certainly tell us they were, the weather must have been colder than it is now.

We don't notice climate changes because they're much longer than our lives, but the weather is always getting warmer and colder. Now it's slowly warming, melting ice from the North Pole and Antarctica and raising the seas. Geologists drilling very old ice in Greenland and Antarctica have found evidence of many past ice ages coming about every 20,000 years, when glaciers spread over much of the world and then melted away again (see "Waves of Glaciation," in chapter 2, "Moving Water, Moving Land").

The last ice age melted back about 10,000 years ago. The time we live in now, without many glaciers, is called an **interglacial period,** because it is like other times between ice ages ("inter" means between). The ice drills and other evidence show that our interglacial period is unusual, however, for having a stable climate pattern. At other times over the past 100,000 years, the earth has gone through sudden changes to great ocean currents and air movements, causing large changes in the weather. People first learned to grow food, and civilization began, about 10,000 years ago, the same time our warm, steady climate began. It makes sense if the weather helped.

Certainly, life was harder before. In the Sierra, glaciers slid down over the mountains and along the valleys many times during the repeated ice ages. Glaciers flatten every living thing in their path, including forests; scrape off all the soil; and grind down through the granite bedrock itself to make amazingly steep, broad valleys, like Yosemite Valley.

## EROSION & SOIL CREATION

Glaciers can cut through rock like a scoop through ice cream. When they melt, all that's left behind is the bare rock, and the pieces that were broken off. Plants and trees need more than rock to grow on — they need soil. Breaking down rocks to soil is called **weathering.** Here's how it works.

Granite in the Sierra is strong and doesn't weather easily, but it has wide, straight cracks between big blocks, and smaller cracks that you can barely see. Cracks are the starting point. Water seeps down into these cracks and freezes. Water takes up more space when it freezes, so it pushes the sides of the crack apart. After many winters, the rock splits. If the rock is on the edge of a mountain, it falls, and the mountain gets a steep cliff where the crack was. That's called **mechanical weathering.** During the warmer months, liquid water can widen the cracks, too. When water mixes with carbon dioxide in the air or with soil lying on top of the granite, it can combine to make chemicals that attack the rock, such as weak carbonic acid. The acid seeps into tiny cracks and chemically changes light-colored feldspar grains in the rock, loosening their hold on the other grains. That's called **chemical weathering.** As the feldspar grains weaken, they also grow larger, forcing apart the cracks in the rock and allowing in more acid. That's a combination of chemical and mechanical weathering. Along Generals Highway in

Sequoia National Park, there are places where the glaciers didn't take away the soil. The acidic water dripped down from the soil into the granite underneath for a very long time. When the road builders came through, the granite was so weak from chemical and mechanical weathering that they could dig through it with a power shovel instead of blasting with dynamite.

After chemical and mechanical weathering have made a large crack in the granite, the crack fills with dust and soil blowing in the wind, and tough little plants start to grow. The California fuchsia (see "The Little Field Guide," p. 392) is one of the first, but sometimes small trees like the Jeffrey pine can make it in these narrow places, too. Their roots grow down into the crack and may help push it apart, and they hold the soil in place. The soil holds moisture against the rock so that it can continue weathering and widening. Over many generations, the plants and trees in the crack die and rot into soil, like rotting leaves or the compost pile in your backyard. The soil slowly covers the rock. Grasses and other plants take root and hold the spreading soil in place, helping it continue to spread. Hiking in the high country, you can see many cracks with plants in them at each stage. When the soil is deep enough, bushes and trees can begin to grow, starting a forest. Falling needles and leaves constantly add to the soil, and dead trees rot on the ground, giving new seedlings a place to plant their roots.

Making soil takes a long time in the Sierra. The rock is hard, the weather is dry, and the winters are long. Where you see bare fields of stone, soil making has hardly started after 10,000 years. These are high places where the granite doesn't have many cracks. In other places, thin layers of poor soil support small pines and dry grasses amid boulders and rock outcroppings. In the place of glacial lakes, rivers have washed soil together from the mountains, making meadows or even forests. Farther down the mountains, warmer weather and longer summers allow more time for plants to grow. With more growth, there's more material to rot, and more soil is made. With more soil on top, the rock underneath breaks down faster, too. Sequoias grow well in this new, sandy soil, with its little fragments of rock crystals mixed in, and they survive only in groves on the western slope of the Sierra (see "Sequoias," p. 391).

## MAKING THE SIERRA

How did the granite, with its cracks, get there in the first place? Geologists have figured that out, too, but you have to go much further back in time. This rock began 210 million years ago, and most of what you see in the parks is 80 to 100 million years old. Dinosaurs were walking the earth when, 6 miles below a sea floor, big blobs of melted rock were pushing up and slowly cooling and hardening into granite. (For an explanation of how granite hardens and its crystalline structure, see "Read Aloud: Why Both Snow & Granite Sparkle," in chapter 16, "Rocky Mountain National Park.")

Mountains rose up from the sea and were worn down to nothing by the weather over many millions of years. Slowly, 6 or 7 miles of rock wore away until the granite came out into the air. About 10 million years ago — just yesterday in the history of the earth — the Sierra we know today started to rise, most scientists believe. It happened along a fault, or crack, in the earth's surface, on the east side of the range. The Teton Range, in Grand Teton National Park, grew the same way (see "Making the Tetons," in chapter 13). Like a door in the earth, the entire block of land where the mountains now stand split from the block to the east. The mountains tilted up and the desert tilted down, giving the east side an incredibly steep, rocky slope almost 3 miles high. On the western side of the mountains, the rise from California's Central Valley is much less sharp, like a ramp, or the back of the door. Most of the work happened in the past 2½ million years and is still going on.

All that pushing cracked most of the granite into big square blocks. If you look closely at a piece of granite, you'll see that it's made of dark and white grains, or crystals, that have flat sides and squarish edges. When big pieces break, they split along those lines in cracks called **joints.** Weathering gets started along the joints as the rock wears down into soil. In some places, joints make the rock look like a checkerboard and trees grow in them in tidy lines.

In other places, without joints, the rock cracked in another interesting way that gave it a rounded shape. As we have learned, this granite hardened 6 miles down in huge blobs. Six miles of rock weighs a lot, and it squished the hard granite underneath. When the covering rock wore away, the pressure of all that weight was gone, and the granite sprang back the way your bed bounces up when you get off of it. But granite is much harder than a bed; it can't bend without breaking. Where the granite had checkerboard cracks, the parts moved separately. But where held together in huge, unbroken pieces, it puffed up to its new size by breaking along ball-shaped lines into layers, like an onion. Imagine a solid ball growing larger. The outermost surface of the ball has to grow the most while the center hardly changes at all. But in an unbending material like rock, the layers can't move differently without splitting apart.

The final step came when weathering wore away the outer layers of granite, shaping the rocks into domes. This shaping is called **exfoliation,** a word that means "peeling" — in this case, the layers of rock that peel off. Half Dome, above Yosemite Valley, is an example of both exfoliation (on the rounded side) and joint cracking (on the cliff side). The glaciers that came down the valley, almost reaching the top of Half Dome, helped by polishing the shapes and dragging away all the rock that had fallen off as the mountain weathered into its funny shape.

## CAVES

When the hot granite blobs flowed underground, they destroyed most of the rock that had been there before, but not all of it. Walls of older rock were left between some of the bubbles. On the west side of Sequoia and Kings Canyon National Parks, some of this older rock was marble. It started out at the bottom of an ocean some 200 million years ago, when seashells and other calcium fell to the sea floor and slowly were pressed into limestone. Later, buried deep under the ground, the limestone was cooked and pressed until it turned into marble.

The calcium in marble dissolves in water, especially if the water has some acid in it. Rainwater that passed through the evergreen needles rotting on the forest floor picked up acid. About 60 million years ago, all the ingredients were in place for the acidic water to carve caves out of the marble. The water seeped down into the rocks. When it met a layer of something that it couldn't flow through, it cut a channel by dissolving the marble. Later, when the mountains rose, those channels were raised out of the water and became cave passages.

In Crystal Cave, in Sequoia National Park, and Boyden Cave, in Sequoia National Forest, you can see some of the miles of weird corridors made by water flowing through the marble millions of years ago. Where water has continued to drip down, the dissolved calcium has made stalactites and thin soda straws, like icicles of rock. They continue to grow, slowly dripping in the dark, and adding, at most, 1 or 2 inches in a century. Although they're solid rock, they're as thin and delicate as threads. A public tour of the cave follows a half-mile loop of the 3 miles in Crystal Cave. Although Boyden Cave is similar, the tour is shorter and there are fewer rock formations; however, it is much easier to get to (see "Crystal Cave & Boyden Cave," in chapter 19, "Sequoia & Kings Canyon National Parks"). Crystal Cave

## READ ALOUD: COUNTING TREE RINGS

In the spring, when there's lots of sunlight and water, trees grow quickly. The rest of the year, they grow slower. Fast growth makes soft, light-colored wood. Slow growth makes harder, darker wood. Through the seasons, as the tree thickens its trunk, it adds a layer of light wood each spring, followed by a dark one through the summer, fall, and winter. When the tree is cut down, the layers look like rings. You can count them from the center to the edge, one spring at a time, to find out how old the tree is.

Counting tree rings works with any kind of wood except wood from the tropics, where all the seasons are the same. Count the rings in your campfire wood to find out how long it took to grow, or count the rings in the boards in the picnic table. You might not be able to tell how old the whole tree was, because you probably won't have all the rings from the center to outer bark, but you can tell how many years it took to grow that one piece of wood. You also can figure out what part of the tree a board came from. If it has a complete circle of rings, you know it came from the center of the tree. If the rings make only part of a circle, figure out how big that circle would have to be to go all the way around. The imaginary circle you make is the size of the tree where your board came from, and the center of the imaginary circle is the tree's center.

If you have a lot of patience, you can count the rings of fallen or cut giant sequoias. Many sequoia stumps are at Big Stump, Converse Basin, and Princess Campground, near Grant Grove in Kings Canyon National Park. The greatest number of rings anyone has counted in a fallen sequoia is 3,200. The oldest trees of all are bristlecone pines — small trees that grow in the eastern Sierra in Inyo National Forest, near Bishop, east of Kings Canyon National Park. Scientists have drilled into their living trunks and taken out cores with 4,600 rings.

Scientists use tree rings to learn a lot more than the age of a tree. They can also find out what the weather was like long ago. In a dry or cold year, a tree can't add much wood, so the tree ring is thin. In good growing years, a tree adds thick rings. Sometimes other events mark a tree and show up in the rings. A fire that scorched the bark but didn't kill the tree can appear as a dark patch in the rings. Recently, scientists studying tree rings in the Southeast U.S. found that the years that the first English colonists landed at Roanoke Island and Jamestown, about 400 years ago (see "History & Culture: First Encounters," in chapter 2) were years of terrible drought. Before, everyone had thought that the colonists were just bad farmers.

With the giant sequoias, you can go much further back, to before the first white man set foot in America, before the English language was first spoken, before Jesus was born, back all the way to when Moses led the Jews out of Egypt. What was the weather like in the Sierra that summer? You can find out from the tree rings. It was probably pretty much the way it is now. In the time it takes for the mountains to change, 3,200 years just isn't very long.

---

is only one of about 200 that have been discovered in the park. Who knows how many more are left, undiscovered, places that have never been touched by light.

## SEQUOIAS

Back when the caves were getting started, 50 million years ago, trees like the sequoia covered much of North America. Only the sequoia and the giant redwood of the California coast are left from that family of huge trees, and they hold on in only a few special places. The big trees need a lot of water, and over time their forests became drier and cooler. Many species became extinct. By the time of North American ice ages, the sequoia grew only in the Sierra. About a third of those that survived were cut by loggers before the remaining trees were protected (see "History & Culture: Changing Values," p. 395).

Sequoias grow in many places if they're planted, but they need a lot of luck to get planted in the wild. The seeds grow into young trees only with help of chickarees (a kind of squirrel) to get the cones open, and they sprout only on loose open soil, which is available only when there has been a recent fire or when park rangers have removed the needles and other material from the forest floor. To make it through the first year, the seedling needs constant moisture, and to survive its first 150 years it needs an opening without much competition from other kinds of trees. All these things happen in these groves, but the groves haven't gotten any larger in many centuries.

Sequoias live so long — up to 3,000 years — because they have defenses against the things that kill most trees. Fire can scorch a sequoia tree and even hollow it out, but as long as some of the outer layer of the tree stays alive, it keeps growing and adding wood. The bark, 2 feet thick on a big tree, contains an acid called **tannin** that wards off insects and fungi that would kill other trees. After a sequoia falls, it might not rot for hundreds of years, because tannin is a preservative. In fact, sequoias usually don't die unless they fall over from having their roots undermined by water or something like that.

Sequoias get so large because they live so long and grow so fast. A sequoia can add an inch a year to its trunk. The biggest one, the General Sherman tree, is more than 270 feet tall and 36 feet thick. The wood's no good for building, but if it were, this one tree has enough wood to build 40 five-bedroom houses, with another house's worth of wood added every 40 years.

But who would build a house out of a 3,000-year-old tree? No wooden house will ever last 3,000 years.

## THE LITTLE FIELD GUIDE

### MAMMALS & REPTILES

Besides the creatures listed here, see the jack rabbit, mule deer, coyote, and rattlesnake (p. 189); bighorn sheep (p. 286), and pika (p. 288).

Black Bear

### Black Bear

Growing to 5 or 6 feet, black bears are common in the Sierra. Major problems have resulted from humans living in black bear country. Careless campers and picnickers have allowed bears to get their food and garbage, and now many bears are so used to thinking of humans as sources of food that they walk right through busy campgrounds and rip open cars (see "Read Aloud: How to Save a Bear," in chapter 18, "Yosemite National Park"). Blackies normally eat berries, nuts, and plants, with an occasional squirrel thrown in. You might be able to tell a black bear from the larger brown or grizzly bear (no longer found in California) by size or color. The sure signs are that the grizzly has a raised hump over the shoulders and its nose sticks out from its face, while a black bear's back and neck slope fairly evenly and its nose and face form a smooth profile.

### Bobcat

Bobcats are common in the foothills and lower Sierra, but you're very lucky if you see one. They hunt rabbits, squirrels, and other animals, often at night, hiding under logs in

Bobcat

rocky areas to sleep. If you hear a blood-curdling howl at night, it could be a bobcat. They're about as large as a middle-sized dog, growing to 2½ feet long.

## Sierra Nevada Golden-Mantled Ground Squirrel

These brave little guys will come right into campsites to raid the picnic basket. They have small tails and black-and-white stripes on the side of the body. They look like chipmunks but are larger (the body is about 6 in. long) and don't have stripes on their heads as chipmunks do.

## BIRDS

In addition to the birds listed here, you might see some described in other chapters, such as the raven and western bluebird (p. 190), mountain chickadee, golden eagle, and hairy woodpecker (p. 289).

Steller's Jay

## Steller's Jay

This striking blue and black bird has a large black crest — it's the only Western jay with a crest. Steller's jays live in Sierra pine forests and often visit campgrounds to pick up crumbs. They also live in the Rockies, the Pacific Northwest, and coastal Alaska. The name was given by the naturalist Georg Steller, who helped discover Alaska in 1741.

## White-Headed Woodpecker

Common in the Yosemite Valley, these 9-inch-long birds are black except for white heads and wing patches; they're the only woodpeckers in the Sierra with white heads. They can blend in and be hard to spot until they take flight. They feed by peeling scales of bark off trees, not by hammering them like other woodpeckers.

## TREES & PLANTS

In addition to the flora here, also refer to the ponderosa pine (p. 191), lodgepole pine, Indian paintbrush, and lupine (p. 290).

## California Black Oak

This is the common oak of the Yosemite Valley, also found elsewhere in the Sierra. It grows acorns that were the main food of the southern Miwok, the Native Americans who lived in the area. You can recognize this oak by its large leaves with deep notches, which are dark green on top and light green and hairy underneath.

## California Fuchsia

This shrubby plant has reddish-orange, tube-shaped flowers that all face in the same direction. They bloom in August or later, after other plants are done. Hummingbirds use the blossoms in their fall migrations. The California Fuchsia is one of the first plants to pioneer cracks in the Sierra's granite; you'll find them at elevations of 5,000 to 6,500 feet.

## Columbine

You can recognize the Sierra's two species of columbine by their delicate 2-inch flowers, which may bloom at any time during the summer, depending on the elevation. The Coville's, or Alpine, Columbine grows in

Columbine

rocky places in the high mountains and has cream-colored blossoms. The Crimson Columbine is gorgeous, with many red flowers, and prefers lower-elevation places with seeping water.

Giant Sequoia

## Giant Sequoia

The big ones are pretty easy to recognize — just look for a tree the size of a 30-story building. You'll find them only in the protected groves in the national parks and on neighboring lands on the west side of the southern Sierra. Small sequoias are shaped like a cone, with branches that come straight out from the trunk. Only when they grow old do they develop the shape of giant broccoli plants, with long, bare trunks, the first branch 100 feet or more from the ground. The sequoia was named for the Cherokee man who first put his tribe's language in writing. He lived in the Appalachian Mountains of the Southeastern U.S. (see "Becoming Assimilated," in chapter 6, "Bringing Back the Past"; also see "Sequoias," p. 391, for more on the trees).

## Mountain Misery

This short, green shrub covers the ground in some open places or in the mixed forests below 6,000 feet, especially in Kings Canyon. The leaves are sticky and grab onto your shoes and pant legs. To me, they smell like cooked artichokes. Shepherds named the plant for the misery of having to pick it off their animals, but the plants don't hurt you.

Poison Oak

## Poison Oak

This vacation-ruining plant, the Western version of poison ivy, has sap that 9 out of 10 people are highly allergic to. Reactions range from a nasty, itchy rash to rare, life-threatening windpipe constriction. Poison oak grows mainly below elevations of 5,000 feet as a vine or in a thicket. Look for leaves in groups of three. Avoid it by wearing long pants and not touching any remotely suspect plant. Clothing can carry the potent sap for up to a year if not washed. Ordinary hand soap won't wash the sap off your skin; you need rubbing alcohol or soap strong enough to wash off tree sap. See "Dealing with Hazards," in chapter 1, "Planning Your Trip," for tips on treatment.

## Sugar Pine

If you find a pinecone that's more than a foot long, it came from a sugar pine (cones from the white pine can grow 6 in. to 1 ft.). Sugar pine trees grow in the forest of big trees on the western slope of the Sierra and farther north in California and Oregon. The largest of the pines, sugar pines commonly grow 150 feet tall and 5 feet across and can be much larger.

There are lots of other pines in the Sierra, and if you have a detailed field guide, telling them apart can be an interesting puzzle. For children, it may be enough just to learn it's a pine, without knowing the variety.

Sugar Pine

# HISTORY & CULTURE: CHANGING VALUES

It's easy to understand what most animals want. Each needs food, water, shelter, and, when it grows up, to find a mate and have babies. A woodpecker wants those simple things, and so does a deer, and they always have. The way animals change the world around them — the environment in a national park or anywhere else — is just their way of getting what they want. A woodpecker pokes holes in trees to find insects to eat; a deer grazes on plants. They don't decide whether they're taking too much. If there are too many of a species like deer, they'll eat until they destroy their own habitat and they starve. As long as they can keep eating, drinking, seeking shelter, and having babies, every generation acts just the same.

It's a lot harder to understand what people want. We need food, water, shelter, and families, too, but we also want much more. Exactly what we want is different for each of us and changes as time passes. A girl might want a new bike so badly she can hardly stand it, while her father feels the same way about a sports car. Most of us want money, because it can buy us things like that. But most of us also have other things that are worth more to us than money — for example, our families and friends, our country, and our religious beliefs. These most important wants are called **values.**

All of us have our own values, whether or not we think about them. You show your values every time you decide to recycle a soda can or help a friend. Our families have values, too. We share them through our rules, the way we treat each other, and how we spend our time

and money together — our values of love, caring, and respect. Parents might teach their children about the value of family by going on vacation together rather than staying home and buying a new TV. Our whole culture (all people together) has shared values, too. Like a family, we show our cultural values through our laws, the way we treat each other, and how we use what we have — our money and our land.

Many people think the national parks show one of the best parts of our shared values. In these special places, we've put the value of beauty and wilderness above the good things we could get from using the land for logging, farming, and mining. We need the wood, food, and metal the land could give us, just as a woodpecker needs the insects under the tree bark, but somehow we decided that leaving these places alone was more important. Other animals could never decide not to use something they need. They don't have values. It wasn't easy for the people who set aside the parks, either.

## OLD VALUES & NEW

Our values about nature have changed amazingly fast. Nothing I know of shows this better than the giant sequoias. Walking among them at Giant Forest in Sequoia National Park, I thought of the thousands of years they had stood in that cool, shadowy forest. How many people had lived their lives, died, and been forgotten while these trees kept growing? And how irreplaceable they were — only a few groves left out of great forests of giants that stood before the first person was born. A tiny seed planted today wouldn't grow as big as the largest sequoias until the year 5000 — and who knows who would be around to see it? I felt deep respect and a need to protect these ancient treasures. When I thought of them being cut down, I thought I'd cry.

Later that day, I saw the pictures at the Grant Grove Visitor Center of men logging these trees 100 years ago. I already knew that about a third of the sequoias had been cut (in the national forests around Grant Grove, you can still see the huge stumps), but it had never crossed my mind that the people who did it were proud of themselves. To bring down such a large tree, a lumberjack had to be very good at his job. The trees were hundreds of feet tall, and the wood was brittle and broke easily. To bring a sequoia down in one piece, the lumberjacks would have to find a way to cushion the fall. Just cutting through a 30-foot-thick tree was difficult. In the pictures of men with fallen giants, the pride glows from their faces. They look as if they think of themselves as heroes for making something useful of the trees.

Most sequoia wood was used for fence posts, stakes to hold up grapevines, and similar purposes on the farms of the San Joaquin Valley. The wood was too brittle for building. The lumber company that cut the most sequoias didn't even make money on it and went broke in the end, because moving the wood down from the mountains was so expensive. But the companies certainly thought what they were doing was right, and they took a lot of pictures to show their accomplishments. One photograph shows a crowd of loggers standing on the upturned cut edge of a sequoia.

When I saw those pictures, I simply couldn't imagine how those men felt. How could they be proud of destroying something so old, grand, and beautiful just to make fence posts? The funny thing is, I think the lumberjacks would be just as surprised to know we think of them today as villains instead of heroes. But back when those pictures were taken, the oddballs were the people who wanted to save the trees — the people who share our values today — not the lumberjacks.

That change in our culture's values about nature happened quickly. It took less than 100 years. And it didn't happen by accident. People who loved nature convinced other people that it was worth saving. Much of that work, the development of its greatest leader, and some of the most dramatic events in the history of conservation happened here in the Sierra.

## PIONEER VALUES

White Americans came to California in 1849 in a great rush for gold in the foothills of the Sierra Nevada west and north of Yosemite. The United States had just added California to its territory. The previous rulers, the Mexicans and the Spanish, hadn't explored the Sierra. When American pioneers arrived here in the 1850s, the Native Americans they found were getting their food pretty much the same way they had for hundreds of years before whites came. They fed themselves by hunting and fishing, and by collecting nuts, mushrooms, fruit, and other wild foods. In the summer, some villages moved to the mountain valleys, like Yosemite Valley. In the winter, they moved down to warmer homes in the foothills.

The values of the tribes in the southern Sierra and the pioneers who came to settle California could hardly have been more different. Like other Native Americans, the Indians here saw themselves as a part of nature. Their myths and spiritual beliefs related them to the animals, plants, and places around them. Shamans, or spiritual leaders, put them in touch with the spirits of animals and helped cure problems in the everyday world.

For us today, nature is something to study, visit, or just ignore. But if you lived in the

Sierra, depending completely on the cycles of the seasons to provide what you needed to survive, you might feel differently. Imagine having food to eat only if you followed ancient traditions telling you how to gather and store acorns for the winter. If you knew of no other way of life, you probably would think of yourself as a part of nature. If you believed that you had a spirit, you would probably assume that the animals did, too. The Native Americans of the southern Sierra certainly changed their environment — for example, they set wildfires to clear trees so that the animals they hunted would have more food. But how they used the land did not change. Their way of life was **sustainable.** That means they didn't use up or destroy the land, water, plants, or animals so that future generations also would have the things necessary for life.

If you think of nature as being like a river, the Native Americans were like fish. The pioneers, on the other hand, were engineers diverting the water and building dams. The pioneers placed no value on nature for itself, but saw it as a bank of wealth to draw from. They wanted gold from the hills, lumber from the forests, range to graze animals, and fields to grow crops. The West seemed like an unlimited frontier with enough resources for everyone to take whatever they wanted and still have plenty left over. The first rush of people came hoping to strike it rich finding gold. Most of them didn't, but they could still build farms, lumber mills, and ranches. They ended up richer than they could have been back in the Eastern U.S., where land was harder to get. Within a few years, pioneers were pushing their way up into the Sierra and settling on the Native Americans' land, cutting trees for lumber and using the meadows for grazing sheep. There was some fighting, but the tribes had no chance. Their way of life was wiped out within 50 years of the settlers' arrival, their people killed by new diseases, and their land taken.

## VISITORS' VALUES

Even the earliest explorers and pioneers were impressed by the beauty of some of the Sierra's most amazing places, especially the Yosemite Valley. Artists and photographers started going there in the 1850s to show the world the wonder of the place. In 1864, President Lincoln signed a proclamation giving the valley and the Mariposa Grove of sequoias to the state of California to be preserved for visitors to enjoy. But even when it was a park, people at the time didn't see the value in leaving the land the way it was if it could be made better for visitors. The value of the park was the enjoyment people could get out of it, whether or not it was kept natural.

An example is the drying out of the Yosemite Valley. The valley was mostly a big, swampy meadow when visitors started coming. At the end of the Ice Age, a glacier left a dam called a moraine along the end of the valley, making a lake. Over thousands of years, the lake filled with soil. All over the Sierra, these glacial lakes became meadows and then slowly dried out until trees could grow and the meadows could become forests (see "The Signs of Change," p. 387). When whites arrived, the Yosemite Valley meadows were still only partway through the long process of becoming dry land. The openings allowed great views of the cliffs; but the ground was too wet for the visitors' tastes, and there were too many mosquitoes. In 1879, park managers blew up part of the natural dam and drained the water from the meadows. That sped up the next step, the growth of forest on the land. The meadows shrank, cutting off the views of the cliffs. Less than half the open meadowland is left today, and the Park Service has to clear trees and shrubs to keep that from filling in.

## JOHN MUIR & WILDERNESS VALUES

Today it's a safe bet that the Park Service would never blow up a natural dam like the one in Yosemite Valley. Many people helped increase the value we put on nature, and hardly anyone was more important than John Muir. As a child he loved nature, sketching and studying on his father's farm in Wisconsin. As a young man, after a career as an inventor, he decided to spend his life in the outdoors, studying natural places and writing. In 1868, he arrived in the Yosemite Valley, and the next year he moved to the Sierra, working jobs like building tourist cottages, herding sheep, and running a sawmill.

Muir spent the next 10 years hiking in the Sierra, carefully observing nature and writing about what he saw in his journals. He explored hundreds of miles of the Sierra that few people had seen before, studying the rocks to learn how glaciers shaped the mountains and writing down details about the flowers, birds, animals, and trees. On one trip he found and named Giant Forest, in what became Sequoia National Park. He walked until late that evening "through the deep shadowy aisles, wholly dissolved in the strange beauty, as if new arrived from the other world." On the way, he also saw loggers cutting the giant sequoias near Grant Grove — the lumberjacks who were so proud of themselves in the pictures — and he was disgusted. Soon after, he decided to spend the rest of his life working to save the Sierra's natural places.

Muir's main weapons in fighting for the mountains were his writing, his ability to make friends, and his persuasiveness when he talked about the park and showed it to powerful people. The time he spent to really learn about the place helped him speak convincingly. Although some of his ideas later proved to be wrong, he had the main thing right. He saw that nature is a single whole system that works only when all its parts are in place. The plants, animals, land, and water all depend on each other. He said that saving the wilderness meant more than setting aside a few of the spectacular places. The rivers, forests, and meadows needed to be protected, too, to keep all the parts together that depended on each other.

Muir had seen how the Yosemite Valley was being ruined by careless visitors with horses trampling everything. The mountain meadows had been scraped bare of their flowers and grass by too many livestock grazing. And irreplaceable forests were being destroyed by loggers and other developers who cared only about making money, not what they left behind. Muir wrote about the need to save the land for people, but he also believed that nature should be protected for itself, whether or not it would help people. "Wilderness is a necessity," Muir wrote. "Mountain parks and reservations are useful not only as fountains of timber and irrigating rivers, but as fountains for life."

Muir's lectures and writings helped to persuade the U.S. government to create Yosemite and Sequoia national parks in 1890. Along the way, Muir became world famous. He befriended President Teddy Roosevelt and many other powerful people, whom he influenced to help conserve nature (see "Read Aloud: Teddy Roosevelt Toughens Up," in chapter 14, "Yellowstone National Park"). Muir inspired others who did work like his, including Enos Mills, who set out to create Rocky Mountain National Park after meeting Muir (see chapter 16). Muir founded the Sierra Club, still one of the largest conservation groups. It helped stop the damming of the Grand Canyon in the 1960s and helped push through a law that set aside a third of Alaska as national parks and other conservation lands in 1980. Muir lost some big battles, too. He couldn't stop the damming of the Hetch Hetchy valley in Yosemite National Park. It has 2,000-foot-high granite walls and crashing waterfalls, and it was partly flooded to be a reservoir for San Francisco.

## PARK VALUES TODAY

In history books, John Muir ended up being the hero. Some people admire him and study his writings as if he were a religious prophet. No one thinks that way of the loggers and the builders of the Hetch Hetchy Reservoir. Once they were the heroes, but now, if we think of them at all, we're more likely to shake our heads and wish they had had never come here. Our values today, at least when it comes to national parks, are closer to John Muir's values than to the loggers' values. Now the National Park Service makes decisions carefully. It takes years to consider any change in a park, produces studies that fill huge books, and lets everyone have their say. After a decision is made, the Park Service spends many more years to carry it out. Through this careful planning, the Park Service has come up with a philosophy: The most important thing about the parks is not how we use them today, but preserving them for the future by keeping them as close as possible to the way they were before white people arrived.

In the parks, you can see these new values on the land. The Park Service is taking away projects it once paid to build. At Yosemite, the Park Service plans to get rid of some of the bridges, campgrounds, and buildings in Yosemite Valley to reduce the signs of people. It plans to demolish one and maybe two graceful old stone bridges built by an earlier generation of conservationists. At one time, the Park Service hoped to stop cars from coming into the valley at all, but it had to drop that idea and settle for reducing the number of cars with parking lots outside the valley (see "History: Fight for the Valley," in chapter 18). In Sequoia National Park, Giant Forest used to be full of vacation cottages, hotels, restaurants, and even a dance hall. That's all gone, and the market has been made into a museum (see "Giant Forest," in chapter 19, "Sequoia & Kings Canyon National Park"). The low-key, noncommercial feeling of the park is new. Not everything can be restored, though. There's no way to bring back the Native American way of life, for example. But we can be sure there will be no more sequoias cut down or Hetch Hetchy reservoirs built in national parks.

Outside the parks, however, our values about how we use the earth haven't changed nearly as much. For the past 30 years, our country has tried to improve the environment, and we've made some progress with cleaner air and water (see "Read Aloud: Dirty Air & Nature," chapter 19). But we still use natural resources — land, water, fuel, and so on — as if there's a limitless supply, not sustainably. There is a limit to what we can use. We know that, because we know that the earth is only so large. Our cities and towns are spreading and taking up more and more wildlife habitat. The last of our old-growth forests are being cut, in the U.S. and in other countries. Our wilderness areas are still being drilled for oil and gas, and threatened with oil spills. We need the resources (land for buildings, wood for paper, oil and gas for our cars and heat), so we can't just say, "Stop!" But we have to say stop sometimes. And we might have to learn to use less. We might have to give up things we want. After all, unlike other animals, we have the ability to hold other values higher than just taking whatever we want at the moment.

# EXPLORING THE REGION

If you're coming to the area from elsewhere in the country, one option is to fly into the San Francisco Bay Area, Los Angeles, or other places where you can enjoy a few days of city activities. Linking the park areas is easy enough by a half-day drive down from the mountains to Fresno and then up to the other park. But unless you have more than a week, there's no point in visiting both areas, which have similar qualities. At each you'll find great hiking and camping, spectacular scenery, big trees, and rocky high country. Yosemite is more crowded and developed, with reservations needed far ahead. It has easy access to the high country. Sequoia and Kings Canyon are quieter, with a low-key feeling, plentiful campsites, and fewer hotel rooms.

# Yosemite National Park

You can't avoid being impressed by Yosemite Valley. On the valley floor, you might get caught up in the everyday world of buses and campgrounds, but then a patch of light will catch your eye, way up at the top of your field of vision where all you expect to see is blue sky. And it will suddenly impress you again: That's solid rock up there, catching the light straight above you. Just to see the granite cliffs, you have to tip your head back, so the wonder of it keeps surprising you whenever your attention settles back to the earth. This is one of the world's unique places, where you can stand at the foot of a waterfall that's nearly a half mile high. Unfortunately, being unique, it's also terribly popular and fills with people in the summer. Sometimes seeing the cliffs up above is a special relief because it takes your eyes away from the uncomfortable crowd you're standing in.

What most people haven't discovered, or don't care to know, is that Yosemite Valley is only a small part of Yosemite National Park. If you dislike crowds, as we do, spend just a day in the valley to see the sights, then head out to the other 1,169 square miles of the park. In the Wawona area, the Hetch Hetchy valley, or the high country of the Tuolumne Meadows, you can hike all day and see only a few other people. One memorable day we hiked a couple of miles to a mountain lake, found we had it to ourselves, and took a deliciously cool swim in our underwear. These were some of the most beautiful and spiritually refreshing places I'd ever visited. I had the feeling we'd left the city behind in Yosemite Valley and now we were visiting the real national park. No one should miss Yosemite Valley, but the park is big enough to do much more, and to do it without being in a crowd.

## BEST THINGS TO DO
- Hike over the bedrock high country to see unbelievable scenery.
- Play in the streams of Yosemite Valley or Wawona.
- See the high waterfalls and cliffs of Yosemite Valley and the giant sequoias of the Merced Grove.

### Park & Forest Information

**Yosemite National Park.** P.O. Box 577, Yosemite, CA 95389. ☎ **209/372-0200.** TTY 209/372-4726. www.nps.gov/yose.

**The Yosemite Association** (for books, maps, and educational programs). P.O. Box 230, El Portal, CA 95318. ☎ **209/379-2648.** Fax 209/379-2486. www.yosemite.org.

**Yosemite Concession Services (YCS).** 5410 E. Home Ave., Fresno, CA 93727. Lodging and general information ☎ **559/252-4848;** TTY 559/255-8345; fax 559/456-0542. Tour desk ☎ **559/372-1240.** www.yosemitepark.com.

**Stanislaus National Forest.** 19777 Greenley Rd., Sonora, CA 95370. ☎ **209/532-3671.** www.r5.fs.fed.us/stanislaus.

**Sierra National Forest.** 1600 Tollhouse Rd., Clovis, CA 93611-0532. ☎ **559/297-0706.** www.r5.fs.fed.us/sierra.

**Inyo National Forest,** Mono Basin Scenic Area. P.O. Box 429, Lee Vining, CA 93541. ☎ **760/647-3044.** www.r5.fs.fed.us/inyo.

### Regional Traveler Information

**Yosemite Area Regional Traveler Services** (inter-agency transportation service). 369 W. 18th St., Merced, CA 95340. ☎ **209/723-3153.** www.yosemite.com.

**Mariposa County Visitors Bureau.** P.O. Box 967, Mariposa, CA 95338. ☎ **888/554-9012** (for recorded messages) or 209/966-7081. www.homeofyosemite.com.

**Yosemite Sierra Visitors Bureau.** 4063 Hwy. 41, Oakhurst, CA 93644. ☎ **559/683-4636.** www.yosemite-sierra.org.

**Tuolumne County Visitors Bureau.** P.O. Box 4020, Sonora, CA 95370. ☎ **800/446-1333** or 209/533-4420. www.TheGreatUnfenced.com.

**Mono Lake Committee.** P.O. Box 29, Lee Vining, CA 93541. ☎ **760/647-6595.** www.monolake.org.

---

• Carry your tent and get into the backcountry in the cool, spectacular mountains.

• Try cross-country skiing or snowshoeing in the winter.

See "Activities" (p. 429).

# HISTORY: FIGHT FOR THE VALLEY

The southern Miwok Indians called Yosemite Valley *Awahni,* which means "big mouth" in their language. The band who lived there in the summers were the *Awahnichi,* or "people of Awahni." In the winter some moved down the Merced River into the warmer foothills. They ate mainly acorns from the black oak, which they made into mush and bread, and also deer, trout, mushrooms, and other wild foods. The Spanish met the native people of

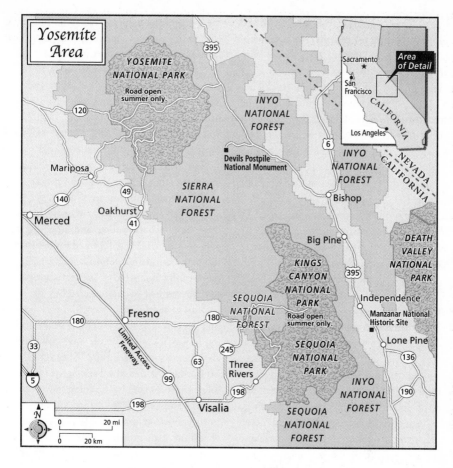

the Sierra in the 1780s, and within a few decades many of the Southern Miwok and other mountain tribes were dead from diseases brought by the newcomers. They lacked natural resistance (see "The Great Epidemics," in chapter 2, "Moving Water, Moving Land"). The surviving Awahnichi left Awahni and lived with other tribes. Years later, Tenaya, the son of an Awahnichi chief and a Mono woman, gathered some of the former Awahnichi and members of other tribes and returned to the valley.

Tenaya had the misfortune of leading his people when their tribe was defeated and broken up. Soon after the great gold rush of 1849, whites began taking over the area, killing natives and grazing cattle on their mountain land. The cattle ate the precious acorns. The

Awahnichi reacted to the threat to their traditional food source by hunting the livestock and raiding the whites' stores, killing some ranchers and storekeepers. Whites in the area formed an army, the Mariposa battalion, to force the Indians out of Awahni, which they called Yosemite Valley, in 1851. They moved Tenaya and his people to a reservation near Fresno, but the Awahnichi kept returning to their valley. In 1852, they killed two gold prospectors who came into the valley, and the U.S. Army killed five Indians in return. Tenaya led his people out of Awahni for the last time, to live near Mono Lake, but the next year he was killed in an argument and his band broke up.

The Southern Miwok and other tribes of the Sierra had to take on white ways to survive. They worked for ranchers, danced and made baskets for tourists, ate new foods, and lived in new houses. When John Muir arrived, he wrote that the Indians were dirty people; in fact, the opposite was true. They bathed often, more than the white settlers who forced them from their land. But they wore dirt on their faces when they were in mourning, and they had a lot to mourn when Muir met them.

Some of the soldiers who invaded Yosemite Valley in 1851 recognized it as a special place. They were probably even more impressed by the cliffs and waterfalls than we are when we first visit, because they didn't know what to expect. The Native Americans had cleverly spread the word that their valley was a horrible place, so whites hadn't bothered to go there. After the Awahnichi were forced out, several artists and photographers came to Yosemite. Their works spread all over the United States, and Yosemite became famous for its beauty. John Muir was recovering from an injury in 1867 when he saw a folder of pictures of Yosemite and decided he would go there. Other visitors came, too, and hotels were built in the valley and on the horse and stagecoach trails along the way, including one at the historic site at Wawona. In 1864, the Congress and President Lincoln gave Yosemite Valley and the Mariposa Grove of sequoias to the state of California, with the promise that it would be used only for the enjoyment of the public. It was the first time in the United States that nature was preserved.

But the original state park was badly managed and too small. The forests and meadows around Yosemite Valley continued to be damaged by logging and too much livestock grazing, and the valley was turned over to tourism businesses that commercialized it and plowed up the wildflowers for crops and grazing. John Muir and other conservationists wanted a park that would include areas around Yosemite Valley as well. In 1889, Muir met the editor of an important national magazine, the *Century*, and showed him his concerns about the damage to the high country in Tuolumne Meadows. The editor published an article Muir wrote calling for a national park to protect the area around Yosemite Valley. In 1890, Congress quickly passed a law setting aside the park, before the sheep and lumber businesses had a chance to react and fight it. In 1906, Yosemite Valley and other areas the state owned were added to the national park.

The history of the park since then has been about the changing goals of the people running it. First there was an effort to get park land under control, getting rid of the herds of sheep in the backcountry and stopping logging companies that still owned timber within the park boundaries. John D. Rockefeller, Jr., the wealthy donor to many national parks, contributed half of the funds to buy the trees back from the loggers. Next, the park had to find a way to deal with ever more visitors coming to see Yosemite. People have complained about crowding in Yosemite Valley since John Muir's day. At first the Park Service tried to solve the problem by building more roads, hotels, campgrounds, trails, and visitor centers to accommodate more people. As the number of visitors kept growing, however, it became clear that more facilities didn't solve the problem. No one could enjoy nature in such a crowd. At times, Yosemite Valley became a busy and dangerous city.

Finally, the Park Service recognized that saving Yosemite meant protecting it from visitors, too. In 1997, a huge flood on the Merced River swept through Yosemite Valley, washing away some campgrounds and hotel buildings. It was an opportunity to begin restoring the valley closer to the way nature made it. After 3 years of planning and discussion, the Park Service decided not to rebuild the washed-out campgrounds and to rebuild hotel rooms in ways that would do a better job of fitting into the area. The biggest changes in this new plan will happen along the river, where a bridge, camping, and hotel rooms will be removed and the land returned to its natural state. Trails, parking lots, and roads will be moved;

the stables will be removed; and new buses that produce less pollution will carry visitors around the valley.

The changes will be expensive and take a long time (a more ambitious plan approved in 1980 never did come to pass). But some lovers of the park think the Park Service didn't go nearly far enough. For example, while the new plan reduces lodgings and campsites by more than 200 units, more than 1,400 units will remain. And the dream of getting rid of cars from the valley, written into the park plan in 1980, will not happen — instead, parking lots in the valley will be reduced and new parking lots will be built outside the park with shuttles to carry some visitors in. Park Service officials feel they went as far as they could in their new plan while still serving the numbers of people who want to see the valley, but nothing they plan to do will reduce those numbers.

My own feeling is that the valley simply is too small for all the people who want to see it. While removing some buildings and roads will help, the wilderness feeling I most value from the National Parks can't be brought back that way. Yosemite Valley is still worth seeing as a great monument to nature's strength, but a visit also is a constant reminder of how people are changing the world with our growing numbers and wealth. Like a rising tide, we're filling places like this. Unless we start holding people out, the only hope for a natural experience is to climb to higher ground the crowds haven't found yet.

# ORIENTATION

## THE PARK

Yosemite National Park is an oval roughly 45 miles long and 30 miles wide. The long part lies north-south, the direction of the 400-mile-long Sierra Nevada range. The mountains rise gradually on the wooded western side to over 13,000 feet before dropping abruptly to the desert on the east. Here are the main areas.

## Yosemite Valley

The center of activities and services is Yosemite Valley, a 3,000-foot-deep crack in the side of the Sierra in the southwest part of the park. This is the place with the high waterfalls that most people think of when they hear the word *Yosemite* — that's why it's crowded. Besides hiking, biking, rafting, and swimming, there are museums, shops, large hotels, and the tourist facilities of Yosemite Village and Curry Village.

## The High Country

At Yosemite, you can drive to wonderful hiking trails and views of amazing bare granite peaks and canyons high on the back of the Sierra. On the east side of the park, on Tioga Road, the **Tuolumne Meadows** is the park's developed visitor destination in the high country. On the west side, the road to **Glacier Point**, above Yosemite Valley, leads to trails and a high-country campground as well.

## The West Side

**Wawona,** at the southern tip of the park near the Mariposa Grove of sequoias, is a historic visitor area, with hotels and services. North from Yosemite Valley, forest campgrounds and trails are scattered throughout the west side of the park. At the north, the primitive **Hetch Hetchy** area is beautiful and little used.

## THE ROADS

The park's roads have various names and segments, but the pattern is simple. A twisting north-south road, which has different names in different sections, runs along the western edge. It connects three entrances from Wawona, past Yosemite Valley and the entrance there (a section called Wawona Road), north to the Big Oak Flat entrance (Big Oak Flat Road), where Evergreen Road

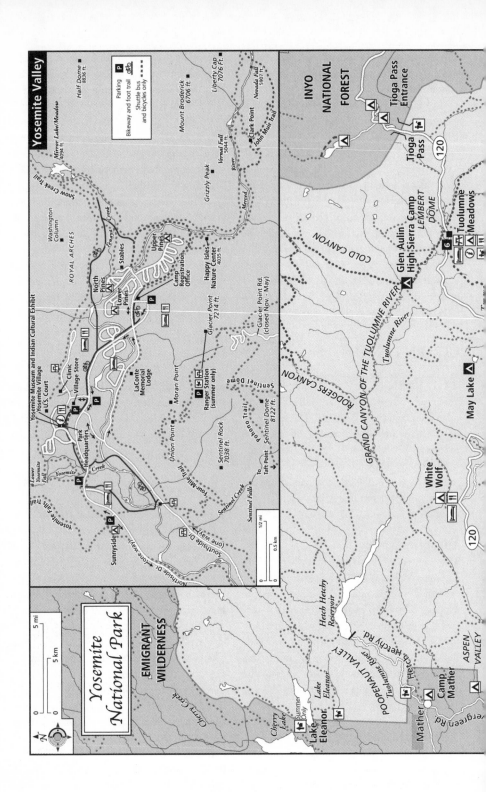

## Yosemite Valley

- Parking **P**
- Bikeway and foot trail 🚲
- Shuttle bus and bicycles only

**Half Dome** 8836 ft.

Mirror Lake/Meadow 4094 ft.

Mount Broderick 6706 ft.

Liberty Cap 7076 ft.

Nevada Fall 5907 ft.

Clark Point

Vernal Fall 5044 ft.

Grizzly Peak

Merced River

Snow Creek Trail

Washington Column

ROYAL ARCHES

Tenaya Creek

Stables

North Pines

Lower Pines

Upper Pines

Camp Registration Office

Happy Isles Nature Center 4035 ft.

Yosemite Museum and Indian Cultural Exhibit

Yosemite Village

U.S. Court

Clinic

Village Store

LaConte Memorial Lodge

Moran Point

Ranger Station (summer only)

Sentinel Dome 8122 ft.

Glacier Point 7214 ft.

Glacier Point Rd. (closed Nov - May)

Park Headquarters

Union Point

Sentinel Rock 7038 ft.

Pohono Trail

John Muir Trail

Four-Mile Trail

Yosemite Creek

Lower Yosemite Fall

Sentinel Creek

Sentinel Falls

To Taft Point

Sunnyside

Yosemite Falls Trail

Northside Dr. (one way)

Southside Dr. (one way)

0   1/2 mi
0   0.5 km

### Yosemite National Park

EMIGRANT WILDERNESS

0   5 mi
0   5 km

INYO NATIONAL FOREST

Tioga Pass Entrance

Tioga Pass

Glen Aulin High Sierra Camp

LEMBERT DOME

Tuolumne Meadows

COLD CANYON

GRAND CANYON OF THE TUOLUMNE RIVER

Tuolumne River

RODGERS CANYON

May Lake

White Wolf

Hetch Hetchy Reservoir

POOPENAUT VALLEY

Tuolumne River

Hetch Hetchy Rd.

Cherry Creek

Cherry Lake

Lake Eleanor

Lake Eleanor

Summer Only

Mather

Camp Mather

ASPEN VALLEY

Evergreen Rd.

120

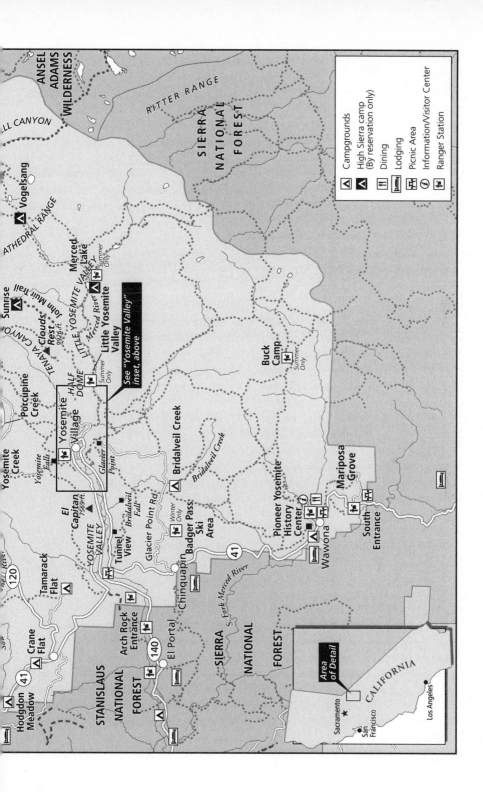

and then narrow Hetch Hetchy Road run farther north to the reservoir. The Glacier Point Road leads into the high country above Yosemite Valley from the Wawona Road.

The 39-mile **Tioga Road** (Highway 120) runs east-west from Crane Flat, north of Yosemite Valley, to the eastern entrance to the park and then down the steep mountainside to Lee Vining and the Mono Lake area. Open only in the summer and fall, its eastern half through the park's bare granite high country is one of the world's most spectacular drives.

## The Gateway Towns

There are no sizable towns near the park. Small gateway communities are at **El Portal,** from the Arch Rock entrance, close to Yosemite Valley; at **Fish Camp,** outside the Wawona entrance at the south end of the park; and at **Lee Vining,** on the east side near the Tioga Pass entrance. Farther afield, **Mariposa** is beyond El Portal, and **Oakhurst** is beyond Fish Camp, and **Sonora** is beyond the north entrance.

# Making the Arrangements

## When to Go

The 3 months of summer vacation from school are the busiest at Yosemite; but it gets busy in May and crowds at popular spots last well into September. The dry summer weather pattern brings clear skies and little rain, except occasional afternoon thunderstorms. In the foothills and lower on the mountains, including Yosemite Valley (4,000 ft.), it can be quite warm in midsummer (see the weather chart below). Temperatures are 10 to 15 degrees cooler in Tuolumne Meadows, perfect weather for hiking. The high country is snowbound through May, and Tioga Road opens only around the end of the month or in early June, with dry hiking postponed until July. Avoid summer weekends if you can, especially around holidays. But expect crowds in Yosemite Valley at any time during the summer, and make your reservations way ahead.

Good weather usually lasts through September and part of October. From December to March, winter sports gear up, including cross-country and downhill skiing, snowshoeing, and ice skating. Spring break isn't the best time for Yosemite because of the lingering snow and mud.

## How Much Time to Spend

Yosemite is not a place to pass through quickly. Just getting to the park and around on its twisting roads takes a long time. No one should miss seeing Yosemite Valley, but I wouldn't want to spend my whole visit there, either, because of all the people. A minimal trip would spend 1 or 2 days in the valley and 2 or 3 in one of the other areas, relaxing and hiking. A week would be ideal.

## How Far to Plan Ahead

Reservations are extremely tight May through September, especially if you want to stay in Yosemite Valley. Campground reservations during the peak book up as soon as they become available, 5 months ahead (the national reservation system is explained in chapter 1, "Planning Your Trip"). Some campgrounds don't take reservations (see p. 412), but you should arrive early to grab one of those sites. Reserving backcountry camping permits is covered on p. 417.

Rooms at Yosemite should be the first thing you plan so that you can take what's available and then work out the rest of your arrangements around those dates. Hotel reservations open 366 days before the stay, and to be assured of a room with a private bathroom, you need to call or reserve online the minute your date becomes available (see "Where to Spend the Night," p. 412, for details on how to use the system). You have a better chance of reserving tent cabins closer to your date, often just a few weeks out. You might be able to upgrade after you arrive. With a reservation

## WEATHER CHART: YOSEMITE VALLEY

| | AVG. HIGH (°F) | AVG. LOW (°F) | PRECIP. (IN./MONTH) |
|---|---|---|---|
| **ELEVATION 4,000 FEET** | | | |
| Nov.–Mar. | 48–59 | 26–31 | 5.6 |
| April | 65 | 35 | 3 |
| May | 73 | 42 | 1.3 |
| June | 82 | 48 | .7 |
| July–Aug. | 90 | 53 | .3 |
| September | 87 | 47 | .9 |
| October | 74 | 39 | 2.1 |

system that books up so early, cancellations are frequent (check on the cancellation policy when you reserve, because there are stiff penalties for late cancellations). Often you can get a room 30, 15, or 7 days before the date, when blocks of rooms are released, or on the day of the stay, if someone chooses not to stay over. On the day of the stay, call or visit the hotel desk at 10am to get on a waiting list.

## READING UP

The **Yosemite Association** (☎ 209/379-2648; www.yosemite.org) carries a large library of books and maps you can order online, by phone, or at visitor centers, including all of these. **Trail Guides and Maps:** Day hikers need no more than the map and guide publications sold for $2.50 by the Yosemite Association. They're available for Yosemite Valley, Tuolumne Meadows and the Wawona areas, and their environs. Backpackers and hikers who want to know more and use more obscure trails should buy Jeffrey P. Schaffer's encyclopedic *Yosemite National Park: A Natural History Guide to Yosemite and Its Trails* (Wilderness Press), which covers every route in detail, and includes a plastic topographic map.

## GETTING THERE
### By Car

**From the west,** the drive from the San Francisco Bay area is 5 hours on interstates 580 and 205 and Route 120. Beware of a sign that tries to send you through Modesto, instead taking I-205 toward Stockton, exiting onto I-5 north, and traveling north on I-5 for just 1 mile before exiting onto 120, which goes east all the way to the park.

**From the south,** take Highway 99, exiting either in Fresno to take Route 41 to the southern, Wawona entrance, or in Merced to take 140 to the Arch Rock entrance, near Yosemite Valley. It's about 7 hours from Los Angeles.

**From the east,** the most direct route to the park, open only in the summer and fall, is the Tioga Road, Route 120. It connects to north-south U.S. 395 near Lee Vining, which eventually connects to the major east-west routes.

### By Air

The closest city with a significant airport is Fresno, 60 miles south of the park's south (Wawona) entrance. Fresno's airport is served by about 10 major and commuter carriers, including **United** (☎ 800/241-6522; www.ual.com) and **Northwest** (☎ 800/225-2525;

Yosemite's huge glaciers have been gone for more than 10,000 years, but their tracks remain. You can see the signs all over the hard granite of the Sierra if you know what to look for — the polish, scratches, and chatter marks; huge rocks moved far across the landscape; U-shaped valleys; and long, skinny piles of rubble.

You can see the evidence of glaciers at many national parks and seashores that are now far from large glaciers. They include Yosemite, Sequoia, Yellowstone, Grand Teton, Rocky Mountain, Acadia, and Cape Cod. How did glacier marks get there? The only explanation is an ice age that happened long ago, when glaciers must have covered most of North America. By looking closely, we can see how the force of the moving, sliding ice shaped much of the land we now call the United States and Canada. (More complete explanations of glaciers are under "Changing Climates," in chapter 17, "Rock, Life & Change," and "How Glaciers Work," in chapter 13, "The Nature of High Places.")

In the 1830s, Louis Agassiz, a scientist, first had the idea that glaciers shaped the mountains in his country, Switzerland. He developed a theory, totally new and outrageous at the time, that the country had been covered with thousands of feet of moving ice. Then he carefully gathered the evidence to prove it, finding the same signs on the rocks and land that you can find yourself. Finally, others began to believe, too, but exactly where the glaciers were and what they did is something geologists still study and argue about.

Here are some of the signs you can look for on your hikes and drives — the same signs Agassiz first recognized. Develop your own theories about how glaciers came through the landscape, and then find the evidence to prove it.

**Polish:** On exposed granite bedrock, look for places where the normally rough rock is smooth and shiny. Often, the smoothness will be in patches, surrounded by rough dents in the rock where some of the granite has since worn away. Imagine moving ice thick and heavy enough to cut through this rock and leave this polished surface. Examples are all over Yosemite, especially on domes around Tuolumne Meadows.

**Grooves & Chatter Marks:** The same kind of rock outcropping where you might find glacial polish is a good place to look for grooves and chatter marks. When a stone gets stuck under a sliding glacier, it can cut a line in the bedrock below. Notice how these grooves all point the same way — that's the direction in which the glacier was going. Chatter marks happen where a rock moving with the glacier gouged out a line of small dips. Instead of scratching steadily, it built up pressure and then suddenly jerked forward. They're rarer than grooves, but quite obvious when you find them.

**Erratics:** Some of the best pieces of glacier evidence that Agassiz and his colleagues found were big boulders in places where they didn't belong. A glacial erratic might turn up in the middle of a

---

www.nwa.com). Most major car-rental agencies are represented there, including **Budget** (☎ 800/527-0700 or 559/253-4000) and **Avis** (☎ 800/331-1212 or 559/454-5029, ext. 0).

To shop around for prices or spend time in a more interesting gateway, try the San Francisco, San Jose, or Oakland airports and visit the Bay Area before Yosemite.

## WHAT TO PACK
## Clothing

The dry summers at Yosemite can bring cool mornings in the high country and hot afternoons down in the valley. On visits in July and September, we spent most of our time in shorts and wore sweatshirts and sweaters in the evening and the first hours after waking up. Waterproof clothing and layers of warm synthetic underwear and wool are safety

field or on top of another piece of rock of a completely different type. By finding rock just like the out-of-place boulder (often miles away), you can figure out where it came from. How else could a huge boulder move so far except in a glacier? An erratic along Tioga Road is near Tenaya Lake.

**Nunataks, Domes & Cirques:** Some dome-shaped mountains, like Lembert Dome in Tuolumne Meadow, got their rounded shape from glaciers moving over them. In many places in the Sierra, you can find spots where hard granite is in wavy forms left by a flowing glacier. But be careful, because many domes, including Half Dome in Yosemite Valley, were made by a process called exfoliation, which has nothing to do with glaciers (see "Making the Sierra," in chapter 17). Right near a dome, and a bit higher, another mountaintop might be pointy and jagged. Maybe it was sticking up from the top of glaciers that were flowing over the lower mountains, rounding them down. Mountain peaks sticking above glaciers are called nunataks. Another common glacier-made form is a cirque, a bowl-shaped valley or amphitheater on the side of a mountain. It's where a glacier started. With cirques on two or three sides, very pointy mountains stick up in the middle. Mt. Conness, visible from the trail to Gaylor Lakes from the Tioga Pass entrance, is an example of a peak surrounded by cirques.

**Moraines:** The rock carried away by glaciers has to go somewhere. Like huge conveyor belts, glaciers carry the fine rock dust, pebbles, and boulders they scrape from the mountains down into the valleys, leaving the stuff in lines at the front and side edges of the ice. These line-shaped mounds are called moraines. They can be large hills or small berms. Often, they dam up a lake or river in front of the glacier, which later will become a flat meadow, as in Yosemite Valley. You can still see that moraine on the left as you drive out of the Valley, past El Capitan but before Valley View. Geologists use moraines to figure out the shape and order of the glaciers that moved through an area.

**U-Shaped Valleys:** When a river runs through a valley, it wears away rock in the riverbed and along the banks, carving deeper in a narrow line. The sides might fall in and be washed away, widening the top of the valley, but the bottom of the valley stays narrow. In a sandbox, you could copy the way a river works by digging with a narrow stick. A glacier carves rock, too, but it's much wider, filling the valley from rim to rim. Its scraping is like digging in a sandbox with a wide board. Valleys and canyons shaped like a V were probably made by rivers. Valleys with flat bottoms and steeper walls, shaped like a U, were probably made by glaciers. Yosemite is the most famous glacial valley. It was started by a river, then widened and deepened by glaciers. You can look at any valley and make an educated guess from its shape whether a river or glacier made it. Your educated guess is your hypothesis. If you can find other glacier tracks in the valley, your hypothesis might be confirmed.

precautions for backpacking or longer hikes in the high country, where snow could show up even in the summer. In mid-May 1904, John Muir and President Teddy Roosevelt slept under the stars at Glacier Point and woke to find 4 inches of snow on their sleeping bags! Cold, wet weather is common in the spring and fall. See "Cold Weather Preparations," in chapter 1.

Bring swimsuits for hotel pools, streams, and mountain lakes. If you stay at one of the historic hotels, you'll need nice shirts and pants to eat in the formal dining rooms; at the stuffy Ahwahnee, coats and ties are required in the dining room in the evening.

## Gear

Summer-weight gear is adequate on most nights, but in the high country an extra layer is a good idea, such as an extra bag or synthetic long underwear, in case you get hit by unusually cold weather. In the spring and fall, you might need heavier sleeping bags. Mosquito repellent and good tent screens are often a necessity. If you're driving from home, consider bringing your own bikes for the paved trails in Yosemite Valley, because the rentals are expensive and mostly of low quality.

# WHERE TO SPEND THE NIGHT

## CAMPING
## Park Service Campgrounds

There are 14 campgrounds in the park, including one run by the park concessionaire. The four car-camping areas in Yosemite Valley are the most popular; book your summer dates as soon as they become available on the national reservation system (see chapter 1). Sites are easier to come by outside the valley, and first-come, first-served campgrounds are available (as noted below); but you still must reserve well ahead or arrive early in the day to get a site. On weekends, it might not be possible to get a site, but during the week there are a few campgrounds with better availability, which I've noted below. A couple of campgrounds, at Hetch Hetchy Reservoir and along Tioga Road, are only for hikers with backcountry permits and aren't listed here.

We wouldn't have missed camping at Yosemite, but the campgrounds were the worst-maintained we found in the many parks we visited. Many are poorly laid out and barren of ground cover. Showers are hard to come by, and bathrooms are often below normal standards, many even lacking lighting. The Park Service plans to redesign and rehabilitate the Yosemite Valley campgrounds, but that will take several years. It can't come too soon. They're as crowded as RV parks and feel as natural as parking lots.

The park allows firewood gathering outside Yosemite Valley and below 9,600 feet elevation as long as you don't cut live or standing wood and don't use a chain saw. The result seems to be woods near campgrounds unnaturally denuded by people aggressively attacking with saws and hatchets. Buying firewood is a better bet, both environmentally and so that you can build a good fire. In Yosemite Valley, to improve air quality, campfires are limited to 5 to 10pm. They cannot be started with pine needles or cones, which smoke; you must use newspaper or fire starter instead.

Human-dependent black bears are a major problem at Yosemite. Listen to the instructions you're given. All food and anything like soap that has an odor should be stored in the metal cabinets at the campsites when you're not actively using them. Latch the cabinet. On more than one night we have listened from our tent as a bear worked at the latches. Don't bring oversized coolers that won't fit into the cabinets; the cabinets vary in size, but generally are at least 17×17 inches in height and width. Bears rip open many hundreds of cars every summer to get food left in the trunk or passenger compartment. Don't even leave untidy papers in the car that a bear might mistake for food wrappers. For more on bears, see "Read Aloud: How to Save a Bear" (p. 418) and "Dangerous Wildlife," in chapter 1.

### YOSEMITE VALLEY

The 2000 Yosemite Valley Plan calls for the campgrounds to be rehabilitated and reconfigured with new walk-in sites and more natural surroundings. The total number of campsites will actually go up by 25, while many sites near the Merced River will be removed. It's hard for me to imagine how they will manage all that, because the campgrounds already are extremely tight in the land they've got; but the work certainly is needed. The Park Service hopes to complete some of this by 2003, but at this writing did not have funding and expected some of it to take longer. I expect my descriptions here will be accurate for several years at least.

All the valley campgrounds have flush toilets. A dump station is at Upper Pines. The three "Pines" drive-in campgrounds adjoin each other near Curry Village, where you can shower, do laundry, buy groceries, swim in the pool, and rent bikes and rafts. They're open to tents or RVs. The Housekeeping Camp is a half mile west and has laundry facilities. The shuttle bus can take you to Yosemite Village.

**Upper Pines.** $18 per site. Reservations always required. 238 sites; tents or RVs. Open year-round.

This is the valley's big campground, and under the park's new plan it will grow, adding 45 more natural walk-in sites for people who agree not to bring their cars. Any improvement is welcome. The campground as currently configured is unappealing, with small sites crammed in with no screening other than the thick smoke and no ground cover other than pine needles. I've never felt claustrophobic while camping before. The huge size makes bikes handy and strollers essential for little ones, because you could have a significant walk just to get to the shuttle stop.

**Lower Pines.** $18 per site. Reservations always required. 60 sites; tents or RVs. Closed Nov–Feb.

Across the street from Upper Pines, this campground has the same poor design and other disadvantages, but it is smaller and has some river frontage, making it the more attractive choice.

**North Pines.** $18 per site. Reservations always required. 85 sites; tents or RVs. Closed Nov–Mar.

This riverside campground will be removed under the new park plan to reclaim the natural vegetation. Until then (it could take 5 years), its waterside sites provide more room and a more natural setting than the nearby Upper Pines, but otherwise it is the same.

**Housekeeping Camp.** ☎ **209/372-8337,** or 209/252-4848 for reservations. $48 per site for up to 4 people; $4.75 per extra person over age 12. 264 units; tents provided. Flush toilets, showers, laundry. Closed mid-Oct to mid-Apr.

Don't stay here unless you're desperate. The grim units resemble cells, with bare cinderblock walls, and were dirty and ill-maintained when I visited. The roof is canvas and the beds are metal cots with plastic-covered mattresses. You rent linens separately at the office, where you can also get a camp stove to cook on the picnic table at your unit. Showers, toilets, and a huge coin-op laundry are in a central bathhouse, where soap and towels are provided. The park plan calls for removal of all but 100 units to restore the river zone; they'll be little missed, because the place was deserted when I visited in mid-September.

**Camp 4** (also known as Sunnyside Walk-In). North side of Yosemite Valley. $5 per person. No reservations. 35 sites; tents only. Open year-round.

Populated by young rock climbers with beards or ponytails, this crowded encampment offers an idea of what a Civil War bivouac would look like if the soldiers had just been on an REI shopping spree. Sites are simply rectangular patches of ground, and they are allocated like hostel dorms, with more tents added until each site contains six people. To get a place, you should be in line early in the morning. Plans are to expand the campground.

## THE WESTERN SIDE

These campgrounds are reached by the roads of the western side of the park, with its tall forests of ponderosa pines and firs. These sites are easier to get into than the Yosemite Valley campgrounds, but securing your spot should still be your priority. Make reservations where possible (noted in the listings below). Lines often form in the morning for first-come, first-served sites.

**Bridal Veil Creek.** Glacier Point Rd., 7.6 miles from Hwy. 41. $12 per site. No reservations. 110 sites; tents or RVs. Closed Sept–May.

Set at 7,200 feet elevation, well off Glacier Point Road, the campground is cooler, quieter, and more natural than those in Yosemite Valley, which lies to the north. Trailheads for excellent hikes are here and elsewhere along the road, many with stupendous views into the valley. Small pines separate the sites and there are ample unspoiled lands nearby for exploration and play. Arrive early to get a site.

**Crane Flat.** On Hwy. 120, north of Yosemite Valley. $18 per site. Reservations required. 166 sites; tents or RVs. Closed Oct–May.

Sites are on a gentle hillside among large, shady evergreens and massive rock outcroppings. There's a peaceful feeling. The location, near the Merced and Tuolumne sequoia groves, is 17 miles from Yosemite Valley and near the store and gas station at the western end of the Tioga Road. The elevation of 6,191 feet puts the weather in between that of the valley and the high country.

**Hodgdon Meadow.** On Hwy. 120, just south of the Big Oak Flat entrance. $18 per site during reservation period, $12 otherwise. Reservations accepted for May–Sept. 105 sites; tents or RVs. Open year-round.

The sites are on a hillside among huge pine trees. They tend to be small, but you can wander into the woods that are open and free of undergrowth. The elevation of 4,872 feet is relatively warm, like Yosemite Valley, which is 25 miles away. Since few popular attractions are near, reservations are relatively easy to get; in midweek, you might even land a site without reserving.

**Wawona.** On Hwy. 41 near the south park entrance. $18 per site during reservation period, $12 otherwise. Reservations accepted for May–Sept. 93 sites; tents or RVs. Open year-round.

This low-elevation campground, at 4,000 feet, is among my favorites at Yosemite. Sites are strung on terraces along the bank of the south fork of the Merced River among oak, pine, and cedar trees. Water conditions permitting, there are plenty of swimming holes near campsites, and a great family float ends here (see "Rafting," p. 430). The best sites are in loop B, sites 31 through 44; loop C (45–99) is also attractive, but more tightly spaced. The area's attractions include the Mariposa Grove,

the Pioneer Yosemite History Center, and the steam railroad; a grocery store and restaurants are also on hand.

## ON TIOGA ROAD

These five campgrounds are along Tioga Road (Highway 120 East), which rises to almost 10,000 feet over the top of the Sierra. The road closes in the winter and doesn't reopen until late May or early June. Snow and mud may linger through June. Mosquito repellent is indispensable in July at all these campgrounds. They are the easiest to get into without a reservation, but they do fill up on summer weekends. Bring good lights, because they generally lack electricity in the bathrooms. I've arranged the campgrounds by distance from the western, Crane Flat end of the road.

**Tamarack Flat.** Take Tioga Rd. 3 miles from Crane Flat and turn right on the 3-mile access road. $8 per site. No reservations. 52 sites; access road not passable for large RVs or trailers. Pit toilets; no tap water. Closed mid-Sept to June.

This place is for those who enjoy natural, primitive campgrounds where you can camp in a private site, well separated from your neighbors by thick trees and rock outcroppings, but where you also must gather and treat your own water and use a crude, aged outhouse. Three miles from the Tioga Road on a very slow and nearly disintegrated winding way — the remains of the old stagecoach route that continues as a hiking trail into Yosemite Valley — the campground is halfway to being backcountry, far from electricity or road noise. Chances are better of finding a site here than at most other places. Boil or use filter treatment on the water you get from Tamarack Creek before you drink it.

**White Wolf.** On Tioga Rd., 14½ miles from Crane Flat. $12 per site. No reservations. 87 sites; tents or RVs. Flush toilets. Closed mid-Sept to June.

This campground is at an elevation of 8,000 feet near White Wolf Lodge and trailheads for Harden or Lukens lakes, or longer backpacking trips into the Hetch Hetchy area and

Grand Canyon of the Tuolumne River. The campsites sit among pines and rock outcroppings, which offer some screening missing with the lack of ground cover. By arriving early, you may be able to get an outer-loop site with plenty of space. Limited showers and meals are available at the lodge see "High-Country Camps (Tent Cabins)" (p. 417).

**Yosemite Creek.** Take Tioga Rd. 15 miles east from Crane Flat; then, turn right on Old Tioga Rd. and drive 5 miles. $8 per site. No reservations. 75 sites; access road not suitable for large RVs or trailers. Pit toilets, no tap water. Closed mid-Sept to June.

This is a very secluded, primitive campground that puts you well away from the road and at the trailhead for some great hiking and backpacking, including the 13-mile trail down into Yosemite Valley at the falls. Treat the water you draw from the creek.

**Porcupine Flat.** Tioga Rd., 24 miles from Crane Flat. $8 per site. No reservations. 52 sites. RVs not allowed in some sites; pit toilets, no tap water. Closed mid-Sept to June.

Sites are broadly separated among pines in this primitive campground, just off the Tioga Road at 8,100 feet. It meets some of the same trails as the Yosemite Creek Campground, which is just a couple of miles away on foot. Treat water you gather.

**Tuolumne Meadows.** On Tioga Rd., 37 miles from Crane Flat. $18 per site. Half reservations, half same-day check-in. 304 sites; tents or RVs. Flush toilets. Closed Oct–June.

This huge campground with small hills is close to Tuolumne Meadows and many supremely lovely hikes. You can use the shuttle, there are campfire programs, groceries are available, and horseback riding and showers of sorts are nearby (see the box below). The thin mountain air, at 8,600 feet, is cool and dry. However, on our last visit the campground was in bad shape, its roads falling apart and bathrooms poorly maintained. Make reservations or arrive early, especially on weekends.

# Forest Service Campgrounds

Yosemite is surrounded by Stanislaus, Sierra, and Inyo national forests (see "Yosemite Address Book," p. 402). Each park has campgrounds near the park entrance, some of them as attractive as the park campgrounds and almost as likely to fill on summer evenings. There are also places for dispersed camping, or setting up your tent anywhere you choose; check at a ranger station.

## INYO NATIONAL FOREST

These campgrounds lie to the east of the park, where the Tioga Road descends steeply from the Sierra to the strange Mono Lake basin, an amazing piece of topography. Despite the elevation of 9,500 feet or more, the mountains' rain shadow makes the area around the campgrounds an arid zone. All are closed mid-October through May and none takes reservations. Many more campgrounds are a little farther afield, as well as trails and a lot of interesting sites around Mono Lake. Get area information from the Mono Lake center listed under "Visitor Centers" (p. 421).

**Tioga Lake.** On Hwy. 120, 1 mile outside park. $11 per site. 13 sites; tents only. Running water.

Some of the campsites sit by the lake, but none has much shade or privacy. The other two campgrounds are preferable.

**Junction.** On Hwy. 120, 2 miles outside park. $6 per site. 13 sites; tents or RVs. No running water; treat water from stream.

About half of the campsites lie among protruding bedrock with shady evergreen trees, a very pleasant setting. The junction in the name is for a road that leads up to Saddlebag Lake and other campgrounds there.

**Ellery Lake.** On Hwy. 120, 2 miles outside park. $11 per site. 12 sites; tents or RVs. Running water.

Across the road from Junction, this lakeside campground is paved and trim, with brush effectively screening the sites.

Bathrooms in the large, heavily used campgrounds can get grungy and lack hot water. Sometimes portable toilets are set up outside to deal with all the people. The park's primitive campgrounds don't have running water, and the streams that run by can dry up late in the season. Bring as much water along as you can. Water you gather from streams must be treated with a filter or by boiling before drinking. Learn how to do that under "Gear," in chapter 1.

In Yosemite Valley, the showers at the pool at Curry Village are open to the public 24 hours a day all year. You have to wait at popular times. Showers at the Housekeeping Camp also are open to the public, operating in season 7am to 10pm; the large coin laundry there operates all year 8am to 10pm. Showers cost $2 per person at all the showers in the park, and at Curry Village you can borrow a towel. Pay an attendant or at the front desk. The new Yosemite Valley Plan calls for showers at the campgrounds, as well.

Outside the valley, it might be easier to stay dirty and rinse off when you take a swim. There are no public showers at Wawona. Showers are available at White Wolf and Tuolumne Meadows lodges, on Tioga Road, but in each case they are available for campers only after the guests are done, in the midafternoon, so you waste the best part of the day. Also, at each site there are only a few stalls for many people, and the water is on a pushbutton arrangement that makes washing difficult, especially with kids. Consider camping several days and then spending a night in a real hotel (not a tent-cabin lodge) to clean up before returning to camping.

## SIERRA NATIONAL FOREST

**Summerdale.** On Hwy. 41, 1 mile south of the south entrance station, near Wawona. $14 per site. No reservations. 30 sites; tents or RVs. Vault toilets, running water. Closed Sept–May.

Just outside the park near Mariposa Grove and the steam railroad, this is one of the area's loveliest campgrounds. Quietly nestled in a valley far below the highway, the broadly separated campsites sit under large deciduous shade trees around a meadow. Campers swim in the creek. The outhouses are lighted.

## STANISLAUS NATIONAL FOREST

These campgrounds are near the park's north entrances, at Big Oak Flat and Hetch Hetchy.

**Diamond O.** On Evergreen Rd., 6 miles north of the Big Oak Flat entrance. $13 per site. 38 sites; tents and small RVs. Vault toilets, running water. Closed Dec to late Apr.

Below the narrow, winding road to Hetch Hetchy, the well-built campground occupies a shady hillside of pines. It's a place of peaceful beauty and repose. The Middle Fork of the Tuolumne River flows by, a popular fishing spot. Some sites have good privacy, and the campground is disabled accessible. Elevation is 4,400 feet.

**Sweetwater.** On Hwy. 120, 10 miles from park entrance. $11 per site. 13 sites; tents or small RVs. Vault toilets, running water. Closed Dec–Mar.

**Lost Claim.** On Hwy. 120, 13 miles from park entrance. $9 per site. 10 sites; tents or RVs. Vault toilets, hand-pumped water. Closed Oct–Apr.

**The Pines.** On Hwy. 120, 16 miles from park entrance. $10 per site. 12 sites; tents or small RVs. Vault toilets. Closed Dec–Apr.

On the way east on Highway 120 to the Big Oak Flat entrance, these three small campgrounds are all at an elevation of around 3,000 feet in the often hot foothills. Sweetwater is the most appealing, with large sites on a single loop under big pine trees. The Pines is near the Groveland ranger station; sites there are rather exposed in a dry, pine-oak plant community.

## Commercial Campgrounds

If you're looking for an RV park with full hookups, the closest is the small **Indian Flat RV Park** in El Portal (☎ **209/379-2339**), 6 miles outside the park on Route 140. Others are sprinkled around the area. Ask for referrals at the visitor centers listed below.

## High-Country Camps (Tent Cabins)

The concessionaire, **Yosemite Concession Services** (see "Yosemite Address Book, p. 402), operates two lodges of tent cabins along Tioga Road and five backcountry camps during the summer only. Contact YCS directly for reservations; the numbers listed below are for the front desks. Cribs are not available. Dining at each lodge is described under "Where to Eat" (p. 434).

**Tuolumne Meadows Lodge.** Near the east park entrance on Tioga Rd. (Hwy. 120). ☎ **209/372-8413**. 69 tents. $56 double; $8 per extra person over age 12, $4 for 12 and under. Closed mid-Sept to mid-June.

The tents provide minimal shelter, just canvas over a concrete slab, with metal cots and a wood stove, and the shared bathhouse is undersized and inhospitable; but I'm told dates in August can book up within 5 minutes of becoming available, a year before. That's because of the location. A fork of the Tuolumne River roars over granite boulders out back, and some of the park's best trails leave from the grounds. About 20 tents are saved for guests starting a week's circuit of the High Sierra Camps, described below.

**White Wolf Lodge.** On Tioga Rd. (Hwy. 120), 14½ miles from Crane Flat junction. ☎ **209/372-8416**. 4 cabins with private bathroom, 24 tents. $71 double with bathroom, tents $52 double; $8 per extra person over age 12, $4 for 12 and under. Closed mid-Sept to mid-June.

The lodge consists of a group of tents and cabins among the trees behind a small bathhouse and a permanent main building, which contains the dining room and the tiny store. The

only attraction, certainly a good one, is the trails nearby, including the route to the High Sierra Camps (see below).

**High Sierra Camps.** On the High Sierra Loop Trail. High Sierra Camp desk (information and applications) ☎ **559/253-5674**. 204 cots in 5 camps. $100 adults ages 13 and up; $65 children ages 7–12; rates are per person per night and include breakfast and dinner. No children under age 7. Closed mid-Sept to June.

These five camps allow you to hike a 50-mile loop through the Sierra's most beautiful high country without carrying a tent, a sleeping bag, a stove, or food. You can do the hikes with a ranger, or go on horseback, or go on your own. Each night hikers sleep in male and female dorms, eat in a tent dining room, and can take a hot shower. I climbed to the Sunrise Camp and was impressed by how welcoming and well built it seemed, with a solar-energy system and a shower building that put to shame those found at the lodges on the road. Unfortunately, an experience of such quality must be rationed. Reservations for the following summer are awarded by lottery from applications received from October 15 to November 30. Sometimes you can get late reservations at the Merced Lake Camp, and cancellations after May 1 are awarded to those who call the desk. It's also possible to reserve meals through the lottery for independent backpacking trips.

## Backcountry Permits

Unlike other parks, Yosemite doesn't have camping zones or backcountry sites, but you need a free wilderness permit from the Park Service to camp in the backcountry. Permits are rationed according to the trailhead where you'll enter the backcountry. Once in, you can camp anywhere you want in open areas, as long as it's at least 1 mile from the road, or 4 miles from a developed area (Yosemite Valley, Tuolumne Meadows, Wawona, Hetch Hetchy, or Glacier Point). This is a good, flexible system.

# READ ALOUD: HOW TO SAVE A BEAR

Kate McCurdy has a tough job. She is a wildlife biologist at Yosemite National Park, a person who has devoted her career to animals, but part of her job is to help decide which black bears should be killed. She hates to do it; but when bears get too used to finding their food in garbage cans and car trunks, they can be dangerous and there is no alternative. The rest of her time, she works to keep bears wild.

Bears are smart animals. In the wild they learn how to scratch ants out of a rotted log for dinner, how to dig up a yellow-jacket hive, and how to find acorns around an oak tree. When they discover that people can be a source of food, they learn to recognize coolers and fast-food wrappers, too. Some bears at Yosemite know how to open cars like soda pop cans, inserting their claws in the crack above the door and peeling it down. If the bear doesn't find what it is looking for in the passenger compartment, it may dig through the back seat to get anything stored in the trunk. Bears even learn which cars they like best to rip into, with minivans and Honda and Toyota sedans big favorites. Sometimes, when a bear finds a lot of food in a certain model and color of car, it hits similar vehicles for the next few nights, looking for more.

In 1998, bears were breaking into cars every night. That year there were 1,540 bear incidents in the park causing $650,000 in damage. The National Park Service decided to try harder. Rangers installed larger food storage cabinets in the campgrounds, they made the rounds more often to inform campers about proper food storage, and they started chasing off bears at night — really scaring them so that they would not come back. People needed to learn how to keep food away from bears, and bears needed to learn not to expect food from people.

The same good brains that helped the bears learn bad habits seem to have helped them learn to stay away from the campgrounds, too. "I've never worked with an animal with more ability to learn," McCurdy said. Bear incidents and damage dropped by more than half the very next summer. Since the rangers started their new efforts, no new bears have come into the campgrounds, although some of the same old problem bears still come back.

The new way of doing things is a lot more work for the park rangers, but McCurdy said it's well worth it if they don't have to kill so many bears. Keeping food in the lockers is not much work for campers, but we can have the same good feeling that we are saving the bears, too.

---

Of 100 trails, only about 5 usually fill their quotas; they're best reserved ahead. They include Half Dome (which books up as soon as it becomes available), Cathedral Lakes, and the Tuolumne Meadows to Glen Aulin trail. Reservations open 24 weeks before the start of the trip and close 2 days before. You can find detailed information at www.nps.gov/yose/wilderness. To reserve, go online (www.yosemitesecure.org/wildpermit/), call ☎ 209/372-0740, or write to **Wilderness Permits,** P.O. Box 545, Yosemite, CA 95389. If you write, first call or go online to find out what information to send. The reservation fee is $5 per person on the trip, payable by major credit card or by check to the Yosemite Association.

At least 40% of each trail's quota of permits is available for walk-ins beginning the day before the trip starts. These permits, along with the reserved permits, are given out at five offices: the **Wilderness Center** in Yosemite Valley, open summer 7:30am to 7pm; the **Tuolumne Meadows Wilderness Center,** summer 7am to 7pm; the information centers at **Big Oak Flat** and **Wawona** (listed under "Visitor Centers," p. 421); and the **Hetch Hetchy** entrance station, open winter 10am to 4pm, longer hours summer, with permit information posted at all times. Lots of trailhead permits will be available when you arrive even without a reservation, but get there early the day before your hike to have the best choice. You'll have to listen to an orientation before going out to get important information about bears, safety, and protecting the wilderness. Be prepared to keep your food in bear-resistant canisters, which you can rent for $3 when you get to the park.

See "Backpacking" (p. 429) for more advice, including suggestions on where to go.

# HOTELS
## Yosemite Valley

These three lodging facilities are operated by **Yosemite Concession Services** (see "Yosemite Address Book, p. 402), known around the park as YCS. All three are open year-round. A fourth, Housekeeping Camp, is listed under "Camping" (p. 412). Use the central YCS number for reservations; the phone numbers below are for the hotels' front desks. YCS accepts the following credit cards: American Express, Carte Blanche, Discover, Japan Credit Bank, MasterCard, and Visa. See "How Far to Plan Ahead" (p. 408) for tips on reserving rooms. If YCS doesn't have a room available when you call, the staff will try to book you into one of a few places the company represents outside the park.

Rates listed here are for the high season. Modest off-season discounts apply. Kids 12 and under stay free with their parents except where noted, and cribs are available except in the tent cabins. Unless otherwise noted, none of the accommodations has TVs or phones. You can park at the hotel when you arrive; leave your car there and get around on the shuttle or a bicycle.

Hotel restaurants are under "Where to Eat" (p. 434).

**The Ahwahnee.** In Yosemite Village. ☎ 209/372-1407. 123 units. $306 double; $20 per extra person over age 12. Open year-round.

Built in 1926 to serve wealthy park visitors and fully restored in 1997, the hotel has a grandeur approaching the absurd, like a Cecil B. DeMille stage set for an emperor's mountain lodge. Stop in to see the incredible common rooms, museums of past opulence full of fabulous Native American art, spectacular stained glass and ceilings, and fireplaces big enough to walk around in. Of course, the rooms are posh, too, decorated with Mission furniture and lots of fabric, and supplied with TVs, phones, refrigerators, bathrobes, and all you would expect from an upscale hotel. The hotel has its own pool, off-limits to the riffraff from the other lodgings. The tennis courts will be removed under the new Valley plan, perhaps a nod to how out of place all this now seems.

**Curry Village.** On the south side of Yosemite Valley. ☎ **209/372-8333.** 18 rms, 118 cabins with private bathroom, 80 cabins without bathroom, 422 tent cabins. $103 double room, $10 per extra person over 12; $75 double cabin with bathroom, $8 per extra person; $57 double cabin without bathroom, $7 per extra person; $48 double tent cabin, $8 per extra person over 12, $4 under 12. Some units open year-round.

This place is a city of tents and cabins, with kids running around happily and screaming in the pool. It reminds me of a summer camp, including the central bathhouses. The majority of the units are tent cabins, which consist of wood-framed canvas tents on wooden platforms with lights but without electric outlets and all but 65 without heat. About 140 of these will be removed under the new Valley plan because of danger of falling rock from the cliffs above. The advantages of staying at Curry Village are the low rates, relatively easy availability, and ultracasual atmosphere. The disadvantages: a crowded, institutional feel with a constant rush of people and lines, and spartan lodgings.

**Yosemite Lodge.** On the north side of the valley west of Yosemite Village. ☎ **209/372-1274.** 245 units. $103–$130 double room; $10–$12 per extra person over age 12. Open year-round.

This is the park's one big hotel with standard American rooms (with phones). It has been a focus of rehabilitation plans since some of the buildings disappeared in the 1997 flood. The plan calls for rebuilding the hotel with more economy lodgings in new buildings that fit in better with the park setting; at this writing, the park hadn't decided when that will happen. In the meantime, you will find comfortable, out-of-date rooms in two classes, either with a single double bed or with two beds and a patio. Rooms lack air-conditioning, bathrooms are quite small, and common areas are worn and unimpressive, but they're still the best choice for most people who want a normal hotel room in the valley. The complex contains a choice of restaurants (p. 434), the valley's main tour desk, a large outdoor pool, and an amphitheater where evening ranger programs are held.

## Wawona to Oakhurst

Other than Yosemite Valley, only Wawona has real hotel rooms within the park. You'll find many more good choices just outside the south park entrance, in Fish Camp, and down the road in Oakhurst. The area has the Mariposa Grove of giant sequoias, the Pioneer Yosemite History Center, and the steam railroad. Fish Camp is a wide place in Highway 41. Oakhurst, 15 miles downhill from there, is a highway community in the warm foothills. Establishments are listed here by distance from the park. Hotel restaurants are described under "Where to Eat" (p. 434).

**Wawona Hotel.** On Hwy. 41 in Wawona, near the south park entrance. Policies and reservations covered under "Yosemite Valley" (p. 419). ☎ **209/375-6556.** 104 units, 50 with bathroom. $137 double with bathroom, $96 without bathroom; $14 per extra person over age 12.

These big wooden buildings — the oldest date back to 1879 — preserve the feeling as well as the look of early vacation travel. They have wooden recliners on broad verandas and big lawns, inviting a slower pace. The rooms have antique or period furniture, such as marble-topped dressers, and the bathrooms have claw-foot tubs. Some of the discomforts have

been preserved, too, because the rooms tend to be small and lack air-conditioning or other modern features. There's an outdoor pool, tennis courts, and a nine-hole golf course.

**Tenaya Lodge.** 1122 Hwy. 41 (P.O. Box 159), Fish Camp, CA 93623. ☎ **800/635-5807** or 559/683-6555. Fax 559/683-6147. www.tenayalodge. com. 242 units. $279 double; $15 per extra adult, children under 18 stay free. Discounts and packages available. AE, CB, DISC, JCB, MC, V.

Set on 35 acres back in the trees just 2 miles outside the park, this luxurious resort is everything a family could want in park lodgings. Besides offering large, sumptuous rooms decorated in a Native American motif and containing every upscale amenity, the resort makes a point of its family activities, including horseback rides to the nearby Mariposa Grove and an evening kids' camp for ages 5 to 12 that sets parents free for 4 hours. Large indoor and outdoor pools, a playground, and an arcade are on-site. Reserved 60 days ahead for the high season.

**Best Western Yosemite Gateway.** 40530 Hwy. 41, Oakhurst, CA 93644. ☎ **800/938-4774** or 559/683-2378. Fax 559/683-3813. www.hotels west.com/yos. 122 units. $86–$99 double, $8 each additional person over age 12, free 12 and under.

In a series of nine buildings on a meticulously landscaped hillside, the comfortable rooms are an excellent value, with handy features such as microwaves, coffeemakers, and refrigerators. One building holds two-bedroom family suites, which rent for $139 for up to six people in the high season. Some have kitchenettes, too. The children will enjoy the lawns, garden paths, a good playground, and beautiful indoor and outdoor pools. By staying here you save money and get a better room than in the park; but you add a half-hour drive from the south entrance and the area is hot and not scenic.

## El Portal

A few businesses stand along the road just outside the park downstream from Yosemite Valley on the Merced River, near the Arch

Rock entrance. Two large hotels here under one family's ownership offer good standard rooms and have pools. Each stands in the Merced's rocky canyon at a hot, treeless elevation of about 2,000 feet. The riverside **Yosemite View Lodge** (☎ 209/379-2681) is the newer and better appointed of the two, with kitchenette rooms at $119 and family suites at $179. **Cedar Lodge** (☎ 209/379-2612) has many family suites and even one huge unit with its own private swimming pool. Rooms start at $99 double in summer. Reserve either hotel at ☎ 800/321-5261 or www.yosemite-motels.com.

## East of the Park

Route 120, the Tioga Road, plunges within 10 miles from Tioga Pass, just below 10,000 feet, to the desert around Mono Lake and the little community of Lee Vining. There's a charming, historic lodge with well-kept cabins just outside the park boundary at 9,600 feet, the

**Tioga Pass Resort** (no phone; messages at ☎ 209/372-4471 or www.tiogapassresort. com). Unfortunately, reservations are all booked up on January 1, 2 years ahead, but you can sometimes grab a last-minute cancellation. There are several nice-looking motels in Lee Vining; the Mono Lake Committee Information Center offers referrals (see p. 422).

## Near Hetch Hetchy

Well off the beaten track, **Evergreen Lodge** (☎ 800/935-6343 or 209/379-2606; www.evergreenlodge.com) offers nice, old-fashioned family cabins under the shade of towering pines, for $85 to $105 a night, including a continental breakfast in the lodge restaurant. It's on the narrow, twisting Evergreen Road just outside the Hetch Hetchy entrance. Guests can join trail rides or use the pools and tennis courts across the road at Camp Mather, a facility owned by the city of San Francisco.

# WHEN YOU ARRIVE

## ENTRANCE FEES

The park entrance fee of $20 per vehicle is collected at each entrance and is good for 7 days. National passes are accepted (see "Passes & Fees," in chapter 1).

## VISITOR CENTERS
### In the Park

Hours at the visitor centers change with annual budgets, and what I've listed may change. Museums in the park are under "Places for Learning" (p. 428).

**Yosemite Valley Visitor Center.** In Yosemite Village. No phone. Summer daily 8am–7pm; spring and fall daily 8am–4:30pm; winter daily 9am–4:30pm. Open year-round.

The park's main visitor center has a slide show, a busy information desk, a bookstore, and a room of exhibits. The Wilderness Center just down the street handles backcountry permits

and might be a quieter place during the day to ask about hiking and the outdoors.

**Big Oak Flat.** At the park entrance on Hwy. 120. ☎ 209/375-1899. Daily 9am–5pm. Closed mid-Oct to Mar and Mon–Tues early in the season.

Stop here, near the northern end of the park roads, for questions, maps, and backcountry permits.

**Tuolumne Visitor Center.** At the east end of Tioga Rd. ☎ 209/372-0263. Summer daily 8am–7pm; low season daily 9am–5pm. Closed Oct–May.

This visitor center has a modest set of displays on park history and nature, an information desk, and a bookstore.

**Hills Studio.** On the grounds of Wawona Hotel. ☎ 209/375-9531. Summer daily 8:30am–5pm; low season daily 9am–4:30pm. Closed mid-Oct to Apr.

This new center was planned to replace the old Wawona Information Station (on Chilnualna Falls Rd., off Hwy. 41), but it hadn't happened yet at this writing. The historic building by the hotel parking lot is a place to inquire about the shuttle to the Mariposa Grove, which leaves near here, as well as pick up maps and get backcountry permits.

## In the Gateway Communities

Contact information for each of these organizations is under "Yosemite Address Book" (p. 402).

### FROM THE NORTH OR WEST, VIA HIGHWAY 120

**Tuolumne County Visitors Bureau.** 542 W. Stockton Rd., Sonora.

This route to the park is largely undeveloped. Sonora lies about 10 miles north of Route 120 on Route 41.

**Groveland Ranger District.** 24525 Old Hwy. 120, Groveland. ☎ 209/962-7825.

This office is on your route from the west, about 6 miles east of Groveland, with information on camping and recreation in Stanislaus National Forest.

### FROM THE WEST, HIGHWAY 140

**Mariposa County Visitors Bureau.** 5158 Hwy. 140, Mariposa.

Mariposa is the last decent-size town on the route to the Arch Rock entrance. The staff will help you find lodgings that meet your specifications.

### FROM THE SOUTH, HIGHWAY 41

**Yosemite Sierra Visitors Bureau.** 40637 Hwy. 41, Oakhurst.

This nonprofit bureau is the last information stop outside the Wawona entrance.

### FROM THE EAST, HIGHWAYS 395 & 120

**Mono Basin National Forest Scenic Area Visitor Center.** Hwy. 395 just north of Lee Vining. Daily 9am–5:30pm.

Plan to spend an hour at this center if you're in the neighborhood. It contains a fascinating museum on the weird desert lake, which has no outlet except evaporation, and its interesting ecology. A desk and bookstore provide information on the surrounding campgrounds and wilderness.

**Mono Lake Committee Information Center.** Hwy. 395 in Lee Vining.

The committee is a unique organization. It helped save Mono Lake, which was shrinking, and continues to teach and advocate for it, but also offers visitor information, a bookstore, public Web access, and an interesting shop.

## GETTING AROUND In Yosemite Valley

### BY CAR

Avoid driving in the Valley, because it's aggravating and too many cars degrade the experience for everyone. The 2000 Valley plan should improve the situation, but it is unlikely to happen before 2004. Here's the old and the new. Old: As you drive into the valley, stop at the pull-outs for meadow walks and to see Bridal Veil Falls; then, park at the day-use parking area near Yosemite Village (arrive early to find a space), or park at your hotel or campsite and go from there by shuttle bus or bike. New: Use the day-use parking at Yosemite Village as currently allowed, or park outside the Valley at now only-imagined new lots and ride the shuttle in.

### BY BUS

The free **shuttle bus** comes every 10 minutes during peak times and every 20 minutes in the spring and fall. The system is simple and much easier than driving. The bus stops are numbered and buses run in a loop from lower to higher numbers. Maps are posted everywhere and are given away free in the park newspaper when you enter the park. The bus is without windows in summer, and the ride can be a fun time to meet other families.

A comprehensive list of park services appears inside the back page of the park newspaper.

**Emergencies**   Call ☎ **911,** inside or outside the park. The park's 24-hour dispatch number in Yosemite Valley is ☎ **209/372-0214. Yosemite Medical Clinic** (☎ **209/372-4637**) is in Yosemite Village on the way toward the Ahwahnee Hotel. It has 24-hour emergency care, 8am to 9pm drop-in hours, and a limited pharmacy.

**Stores**   A good-size grocery store, the **Village Store,** operates year-round in Yosemite Village. Other, smaller year-round groceries are at Curry Village, and at Wawona next to the Pioneer History Center. In the summer, stores also operate at Crane Flat, at the west end of Tioga Road, and at Tuolumne Meadows, in a tent on its eastern end. And there's a small summer store at the Housekeeping Camp in Yosemite Valley.

**Banks**   There's no bank in the park, but a Bank of America ATM is just south of the **Village Store** in Yosemite Village, and local banks have ATMs at Yosemite Lodge, in the Curry Village gift shop, and in the Wawona store. Outside the park, **County Bank** is on Highway 140 in Mariposa.

**Post Offices**   In Yosemite Valley, post offices are located in the village near the visitor center, in Yosemite Lodge (to be removed), and at Curry Village in the summer. Wawona has a post office near the store. When Tioga Road is open in the summer and fall, a post office operates at Tuolumne Meadows.

**Gear Sales & Rental**   The Mountain Shop (☎ 209/372-8396) in Curry Village is a well-stocked outdoor store for backpacking as well as climbing equipment. Yosemite Mountaineering School (☎ 209/372-8322) is located there and at Tuolumne Meadows in the summer, and it rents back-packing and climbing gear, as well as offering programs described under "Backpacking" (p. 429) and "Climbing" (p. 430). You can get basic camping supplies at all the stores in the park. Ski and snowshoe rentals are covered under "Winter Sports" (p. 431), rafts under "Rafting" (p. 430), and bikes under "By Bike," above.

---

Two-hour narrated **tours** of Yosemite Valley in open-topped vehicles leave every half hour from Yosemite Village and the hotels. They cost $20 for adults, $15 for children.

Buses for tours or to shuttle hikers to Glacier Point and elsewhere are covered under "Outside the Valley" (p. 423).

### By Bike

If your group is fit, the best transportation option in the valley is bicycles. Paved bike trails, separate from traffic, weave through the upper valley, and there are bike racks anywhere you might want to stop. Bring your own if you can. If not, bikes are for rent at **Yosemite Lodge** (☎ 209/372-1208) and **Curry Village** (☎ 209/372-8319). Rates are $5.25 an hour

or $20 a day for one-speeds with pedal breaks; children's sizes cost the same. These are beat-up, heavy old bikes. Six-speeds with trailers go for $10.50 an hour or $33 a day, and jogging strollers cost $5 an hour or $14 a day. Both locations are open daily from 8am to 6pm in the high season, 10am to 5pm off-season. Biking on hiking trails is forbidden. Mountain biking, and any family biking outside the valley, isn't a good option at the park.

## Outside the Valley
### By Car

The practical way for families to get to and around most of the park is in a car. Allow at least double the time you normally would, not including stops. Even without traffic you can't travel fast on these winding mountain roads, and there usually is lots of slow traffic. Also, be prepared for carsick kids, if that's a concern in your family, especially when driving north and south along the west side of the park.

An excellent booklet, *Yosemite Road Guide*, is published by the Yosemite Association and sold in the visitor centers for $3.50. Short essays are keyed to roadside mileposts in the park and on the approaches. However, we never got to read these at the park, because I was driving and Barbara refused to look away from the spectacular scenery to read it aloud.

In the winter, you must carry chains, which can be required in slick conditions. For current road conditions call ☎ 209/372-0200.

### BY BUS

A **free shuttle bus** runs up and down Tioga Road in the summer, connecting Tenaya Lake to Tioga Pass and the points between. This is handy for hiking, because it allows you to hike between different trailheads and get a lift back to your car or the campground. The shuttle from Wawona to Mariposa Grove is explained under "Sequoia Groves" (p. 426).

Paid shuttles and tours also serve much of the park. All are operated by the concessionaire, YCS, and can be reserved at hotel activity desks or by calling (see "Yosemite Address Book," p. 402). Shuttle buses carry hikers back and forth from Yosemite Valley, allowing one-way day hikes or backpacking into or out of the Valley. The **Glacier Point Hikers' Bus** travels 3,214 feet upward (see "Glacier Point," p. 426) so that you can hike 4.8 miles back down. The bus runs three times a day from Yosemite Lodge and costs $10.50 for adults, $5.50 for children. Reserve a day ahead with YCS, the concessionaire. The tour bus (see below) has the same one-way fare, with commentary and a longer ride. To hike one way between the Tioga Road and Yosemite Valley, or for other hikes with starting and ending points along the road, the **Tuolumne Meadows Hiker's Bus** runs daily in July and August, leaving Yosemite Lodge at 9:30am

and Tuolumne Meadows at 5:30pm. The round-trip fare is $22 for adults, $11 for children; one-way fares depend on where you get off. Finally, YCS **guided bus tours** go from the valley to Glacier Point and Mariposa Grove. I expect most children would get bored. The tours cost $28.50 to $53 for adults.

## KEEPING SAFE & HEALTHY

About 10 or 20 visitors die at Yosemite each year. The Park Service launches far more search-and-rescue operations here than at other mountain parks, even accounting for the larger number of visitors. Rangers blame the tendency of visitors used to the urban world to underrate the dangers of the cliff's vertical landscape, fast rivers, and high elevation. In the wilderness, only you control your safety. Besides the points below, read up on these safety topics covered under "Dealing with Hazards," in chapter 1: elevation, giardia, hypothermia, lightning, Lyme disease, motion sickness, and snake bites.

## Black Bears

The bears of Yosemite are so used to humans that encounters are common. They've never killed anyone, but because the meeting can be scary, know what to do in advance. Backpackers should use bear-resistant canisters. Read the Park Service material or "Dangerous Wildlife," in chapter 1. Also see "Read Aloud: How to Save a Bear" (p. 418).

## Drowning

Keep a close eye on kids playing in or near streams and lakes. If in doubt, don't swim. Moving water is more powerful than it looks and can have dangerous vertical eddies. Swim only from sandy banks — not rocks, which can be slippery and difficult to climb.

## Falls

There are many places where a careless person can fall to his or her death. Don't expect guardrails. Many fatalities are young males engaging in risky recreation. Young children are usually smart enough to hold hands and stay safe in high places, but keep an eye on your teenagers. If they want to scale rocks, sign them up for rock-climbing classes with a professional (see "Climbing," p. 430).

# Enjoying the Park

## Natural Places
## Yosemite Valley

As you enter Yosemite Valley, the mountains seem to open like a curtain onto one of the world's main attractions. It's not something you can be prepared for. The granite walls of the valley soar up to 3,000 feet, more than a half mile, where the sun treats their bold shapes differently than the shadows in the ordinary world below. Waterfalls tumble from the top, disintegrating into showers of mist and spray during the long free fall. As you stand below in the sun, the cool water touches your cheek like a caress.

Yosemite Valley started as a crack in the granite that the Merced River slowly carved into a V-shaped canyon about 2,400 feet deep (measuring from the top of El Capitan). Then a series of glaciers plowed through. The big one was about 1 million years ago, when a glacier filled the valley with so much ice that only the tip of El Capitan stuck out. We know it went that high because it left boulders behind called glacial erratics, up on the rim (see "Experiment: Finding Glacier Tracks," p. 410). That glacier ground out the valley something like 2,000 feet deeper and about a mile wide, straightening out the crooked river canyon and making the sides smoother and steeper. Later, at least two more glaciers came through, but they didn't get nearly as high on the sidewalls. If they had, they would have worn away the huge spires and cracks on the valley sides that help make it so beautiful. Each glacier left behind broken rock in the bottom of the valley. The last glacier, at its largest about 20,000 years ago, went only as far as Bridalveil Meadow, and it built a line-shaped hill across the valley called a **moraine.** It worked as a dam to hold back a lake that filled the valley. That lake slowly filled with dirt carried down from the mountains, leaving the flat meadow and forest now on the valley floor. This dirt layer is about 1,000 feet deep, lying above the true rock floor that the glacier carved out. Downstream, the Merced still runs through a V-shaped valley as it leaves the park, because the glaciers didn't make it down that far.

There's a lot for a family to do in Yosemite Valley, including fun stuff like floating down the Merced in a little raft, biking the paved trails, or hiking trailheads and other sites, seeing the museums, and hiking to the spectacular waterfalls. But it's not a wilderness experience, or even, much of the time, a natural experience. The valley is a city, or at least a town. It has thousands of visitors and the workers to serve them, stores, health facilities, churches, and everything else a town has, all squeezed into the 7- by 1-mile valley floor. Yosemite Village is a busy pedestrian mall served by frequent and often-crowded buses. On the short trail to Lower Yosemite Falls one summer day, I was so surrounded by people I felt claustrophobic, unable to get far enough away not to smell others' perfume and cologne. That trail is being rebuilt and the parking lot removed, but the people will still be there. Steeper trails are less crowded once you get beyond the level that weeds out hikers in poor physical shape, including the wonderful Mist Trail and John Muir Trail to Nevada Falls from Happy Isles, with its unfolding series of waterfalls, and the Upper Yosemite Falls Trail, from Camp 4. But the steepness that weeds out couch potatoes also eliminates most kids younger than about age 10. (Consider the trails on Glacier Point Road, in the next section.)

For many families, the solution is to take advantage of the fun here and accept all the other people. Just plan to find your solitude elsewhere. The families I saw floating and splashing in Merced River had the right idea. They were using Yosemite Valley as the world's most beautiful playground, knowing that playgrounds are crowded. (See "Places for Learning" and "Activities," below, for what to do in the valley.)

The map on the back of the park newspaper, the *Yosemite Guide,* is handy for understanding the layout of the valley, the walking and bike paths, and the order of the bus stops. You can get it when you enter the park, or download it from www.nps.gov/yose/yguide. htm. Our valley map (p. 406) is useful, too, but the big changes are underway with uncertain timing. The inexpensive guide listed in "Reading Up" (p. 409) is all you'll need for hiking.

## Glacier Point

This is a mind-blowing overlook directly above Yosemite Valley's Curry Village. Standing at the railing, you are at the top of a 3,200-foot vertical cliff, able to see almost straight down. It's a short, paved walk from the large parking lots to the overlooks. From different spots you can see in different directions across much of the park. Rangers wander through the crowd to answer questions and offer talks, which you can find out about in the park newspaper. A snack stand is open 10am to 5pm during the summer, but go earlier than that to avoid the crowds.

After you get a load of the view, use Glacier Point Road to get off into high country away from most other people on some terrific family hikes. The road is 16 miles long, splitting from the Wawona Road south of Yosemite Valley, and is closed beyond the Badger Pass Ski Area (see "Winter Sports," p. 431) during the winter. From the point itself, two paths lead down to the valley. Hiking both ways would be well beyond most families' abilities, but you can take a shuttle bus one way (see

"By Bus," p. 422). The Four Mile Trail takes you right down into the valley, a walk that should take 3 hours or less. For a longer and even more interesting hike, with three incredible waterfalls, take the Panorama Trail and John Muir Trail via Nevada Falls, a downhill hike of 8.5 miles. These are busy trails. At mile 13.2 of the Glacier Point Road, some great short hikes may be less crowded (still, get there early) and offer little ones the chance to climb one of Yosemite's granite domes. Sentinel Dome is 1.1 miles from the trailhead, an easy climb with incredible views. At 8,122 feet, it is the highest viewpoint into the valley other than Half Dome. Taft Point, 1.1 miles the other way from the trailhead, has weird and scary cracks, as well as cliff-overhang views. The hike itself isn't threatening, but hold hands near the end. You can link both into a 4.5-mile loop by using a 2.3-mile section of the Pohono Trail from Sentinel Dome to the midpoint of the Taft Point Trail. (From the Sentinel Dome end it is confusing: Follow the sign to Glacier Point, turning left or west at the T).

## Sequoia Groves

About 500 giant sequoias grow in **Mariposa Grove,** the park's largest, near the south entrance. These huge, ancient trees are among the world's greatest natural wonders. You can't help but be impressed by the 2,700-year-old Grizzly Giant, with its immense base, or the amazing length of the fallen monarch. The grove's most famous tree, the Wawona Tunnel Tree, with a 30-foot vehicle tunnel cut in 1881, died of the wound, falling in 1969, but there are other trees you can walk under, including the bizarre Clothespin Tree, with its natural tunnel.

The grove covers a large area and the big trees are separated more widely than at the groves in Sequoia and Kings canyon national parks (covered in the next chapter). This more sparse character, combined with the land's steepness, forces visitors to decide how to see the Mariposa Grove. The popular way is to ride an open-air tram pulled by a tractor over a road up to the Upper Grove area, site of the thickest stands of trees and the Tunnel Tree. There it stops for a look at the tiny, dark Galen Clark Museum and a chance to get out and hike back down, skipping the last half of the tour. The tram leaves every 20 minutes in the summer for a 1-hour ride and costs $10.50 for adults, $5.50 for children 5 to 12, free for those 4 and under, with a maximum family fare of $25. It's appealing to get a ride up the hill, but the forest seemed diminished by the corny narration and the crowded cart. A guy sitting next to me said, "That tree don't look so big," an impossible reaction for someone walking through this grove. Instead, I recommend picking up the 50¢ guide brochure and hiking up the hill as far as you can; a 2.5-mile round-trip, with little elevation gain, will take you to the Fallen Monarch, Grizzly Giant, California Tunnel Tree (still standing) and the Clothespin Tree. The museum is 2.1 miles from the trailhead, one way, and the top of the grove is 3 miles.

Parking is a problem at the grove. The lots at the trailhead fill quickly (again, starting early helps). When they do, you have to take a shuttle, which stops at the park's south entrance, where the small lot fills fast, and at the Wawona Store. That's inconvenient, since Wawona is several slow miles away and you have to wait for the bus both ways. The solution is to plan plenty of time for your visit; half a day would be reasonable.

Two other, smaller groups of sequoias, **Tuolumne** and **Merced groves,** are along Big Oak Flat Road, north of Yosemite Valley. Tuolumne has 25 trees and Merced even fewer. You have to walk into both groves, so they're more peaceful than Mariposa Grove. To get to Tuolumne Grove, you park near Crane Flat and walk 1 mile on an old road that meets a half-mile nature trail. Merced Grove, a little farther north, is 1½ miles off the road; if you make the hike, you might have it to yourself.

# Tuolumne Meadows & Tioga Road

Tioga Road rises into the mountains and crosses the top of the Sierra. From the west, you come up through towering pines and then break out on solid granite highlands shaped like the billowing folds of a windswept flag. The biggest views start around Olmsted Point, where Tenaya Canyon falls away to Yosemite Valley. The road is chipped from granite. A lake fills a bowl of solid rock. A cliff juts up at random, without a tree to give a sense of how high it is — then you see rock climbers on it, the size of ants, and you know it's very big. At Tenaya Lake, canoeists and swimmers splash around. At Tuolumne, the meadows spread broad and green, decorated by bright points of wildflowers and surrounded by towering white mounds of granite domes. Then, after the pass, the mountains drop abruptly to a desert basin and Mono Lake.

The air is cool and fresh along Tioga Road, which crests at an elevation of 9,900 feet, and there's more room to spread out away from crowds than in Yosemite Valley. The area isn't rich in sightseeing, but it is a great place to camp, take easy or challenging day hikes or go backpacking, swim in cold water, and perhaps join a horseback ride. A free shuttle runs back and forth on Tioga Road to link trailheads, so you can plan a hike with different starting and ending points (see "By Bus," p. 422). The area doesn't open until snow clears from the road, around late May or early June. Mosquitoes are intense though July.

**Soda Springs** is a flat, 1-mile hike that anyone can manage starting near the Tuolumne Meadows campground. Naturally carbonated water bubbles up in the meadows in tiny ponds. Another great family day hike is the climb to **Dog Lake.** We had a picnic and a swim from the point that sticks out into the lake. The trail behind **Lembert Dome** is the less steep of two routes; the other trailhead is near Tuolomene Meadows Lodge, and you can connect the two with the shuttle. Just the loop with the lake is 2.6 miles. If you climb to the top of the dome, the total is 4.2 miles — an easy half day with two great destinations. From White Wolf Lodge, the Harden or Lukens lakes trails are good, easy day hikes, each around 5 miles, round-trip. Many of my favorite hikes in the area are more challenging, however, rising up into the bare, rounded granite mountains to strange, rock-rimmed lakes. Teens and strong 10-year-old hikers can manage the steep, 8-mile round-trip hikes to Lower Cathedral Lake, on the John Muir Trail from Tuolumne Meadow, or Sunrise Lakes, starting from the west end of Tenaya Lake. If you can spend a couple of nights, these and other trails link for spectacular backpacking trips. A string of five High Sierra Camps offers dormitory beds in tent cabins for hikers (see "Where to Spend the Night," p. 412). Or, if you don't win the lottery for a bed, you can get a permit to camp nearby, use the outhouse and bear lockers, use piped water at some, and perhaps buy a meal in camp.

## Hetch Hetchy

The Hetch Hetchy area at the north of the park is an easy and little-used way into the wilderness. This canyon on the Tuolumne River is most famous for the conservation fight over the O'Shaughnessy Dam, which was approved by Congress in 1913 over the objections of John Muir and still gathers drinking water for San Francisco. But even with the reservoir, the valley remains a grand area with good hiking and great views. As with Yosemite Valley, and on a similar scale, river erosion started digging Hetch Hetchy and glaciation followed to straighten out the valley, deepen it, and widen it. Unlike in Yosemite Valley, however, glaciers here continued to come right to the top of the canyon during each ice age, grinding the sides to the end of the last glacial period, 10,000 years ago. The result is that Hetch Hetchy's walls are relatively smooth, without the cracks and spires that give Yosemite some of its character. It's a good place to find glacier tracks such as polish and

chatter marks (see "Experiment: Finding Glacier Tracks," p. 410).

The roads coming here are narrow, winding, and scenic. Exit the main part of the park at Big Oak Flats and drive 7.4 miles north through a thick, dark forest on Evergreen Road, then reenter the Hetch Hetchy entrance and take Hetch Hetchy Road 9.1 miles to the dam. The views into Poopenaut Valley are dizzying, and remote trails climb and descend from the road. The best family hike leads across the dam, through a tunnel, and 2.5 miles to Wapama Falls, which tumbles 1,000 feet down the canyon walls. It's an easy, mostly level trail though rocky, arid terrain under 4,000 feet, and can be warm. Many other trails lead from here for steeper hikes or backpacking expeditions. The campground at the dam is for backpackers with permits only. Other than the bathroom and pay phone, there are no services.

## PLACES FOR LEARNING
### Yosemite Valley

**Yosemite Museum and Indian Village of Ahwahnee.** Next to the visitor center in Yosemite Village. No phone. Museum: Summer daily 8am–4:30pm; fall–spring daily 9am–4:30pm; closed for lunch. Indian Village: Always open.

Ongoing talks and native craft demonstrations are the great attractions of this little museum. Our son was fascinated. The small gallery displays a collection of southern Miwok and Paiute artifacts. Outside, a nature trail recreates the tribes' buildings and shows their ways. Families shouldn't miss it. Sometimes demonstrations take place there; other times, you can follow the self-guided path with a booklet. Another gallery, open 10am to 4pm in the summer (except during the noon–1pm lunch hour) and sporadically the rest of the year, shows a collection of art on the valley or revolving exhibits.

**Nature Center at Happy Isles.** In the upper valley. Summer daily 9am–5pm; spring and fall daily 10am–4:30pm; closed for lunch. Closed Oct to mid-May. Hours and seasons vary, so check at the visitor center.

This one-room nature center has up-to-date exhibits on the park's plants and animals and on bear avoidance. Younger children may enjoy the animal dioramas, but it's not a hands-on place. The wooded streamside trails welcome a few minutes' ramble.

**LeConte Memorial.** ☎ **209/372-4542.** Wed–Sun 10am–4pm. Closed Sept–Apr.

The Sierra Club runs a library, a children's corner, and education programs (listed in the park newspaper) from this former visitor center.

**Ansel Adams Gallery.** Next to the main visitor center. ☎ **209/372-4413.** www.adamsgallery.com. Summer daily 9am–6pm; fall–spring daily 9am–5pm.

Adams' black-and-white photographs of Yosemite helped to popularly define the area and made him one of our best-known photographers. His family still runs the shop, which sells his prints and those of other photographers, as well as inexpensive gifts and cards.

## Wawona

**Pioneer Yosemite History Center.** On Hwy. 41, Wawona. No phone. Open-air displays always open. Check park newspaper for hours of demonstrations and coach rides.

Kids enjoy this little village of old cabins and other buildings brought from all over the park, the covered bridge, and the collection of antique carriages. In July and August, Wednesday through Sunday (check the park newspaper), volunteers dress in costume and play the roles of historic park figures. We talked with a blacksmith hammering away at a horseshoe. You can take a short stagecoach ride at times, too ($3 adults, $2 children 3–12). At other times, pick up the guide booklet to find your way around; it's not nearly as interesting without people in it.

## ACTIVITIES
## Backpacking

Yosemite has more than 800 miles of trails, including many that are mostly above tree line, crossing the granite bedrock of the high Sierra. Besides the beauty, I enjoy the way this alien terrain helps peel away the world of people on an overnight. Also, by spending the night out, you can explore longer trails and get away from the day hikers. You may start to meet others so rarely that you're eager to see them and compare your adventures. The high country is cool in the summer, and the weather is usually fine (of course, you must still prepare for bad weather). Other advantages of backpacking here include a simple backcountry permit system (see "Backcountry Permits," p. 417) and ample support provided by the park and concessionaire, which ranges from equipment rental (see "For Handy Reference" p. 423) to facilities in the backcountry. The five High Sierra Camps have dorms and showers for hiker guests, and backpackers can eat there by prior arrangement and camp nearby to use outhouses, bear boxes, and, at some, running water (See "High Sierra Camps," p. 417).

The disadvantages of a backpacking trip at Yosemite depend on your group's abilities. These trails tend to be steep, and at high elevations that can be tough, especially if your pack is heavy. I've seen miserable backpackers huffing and puffing up the trails with huge loads (overpacking is the most common beginner's mistake). There are easier places to take your kids on a first backpacking expedition. The other big factors in planning are the season and elevation. The high country isn't free from snow until July, and mosquitoes last through the month. Lower-elevation trips, including some around Hetch Hetchy, are open earlier, but those areas get hot in midsummer. If you're up for a week or more on the trail, there are few better opportunities in the country than the **John Muir Trail,** running from Yosemite Valley through Tuolumne Meadows and 211 miles down the Sierra to Mount Whitney, in Sequoia National Park, or the **Pacific Crest Trail,** which runs from Mexico to Canada.

You'll need to start planning at home. Maps and trail guides are covered under "Reading Up" (p. 409). Although you can camp anywhere off the roads, you'll want to find out where good sites are. Also prepare by learning black bear avoidance techniques and planning to fit all your food, soap, or anything else with a strong odor in a bear-resistant canister, for rent at the park. The park provides copious advice (or see "Dangerous Wildlife," in chapter 1).

You can also backpack at Yosemite with a guided group, offered by **Yosemite Mountaineering School** (see "Climbing," below). Make a reservation, but the school will take drop-ins if there's room. Planned excursions range from a short-distance learning-to-backpack trip to 4-day excursions with mountain climbing on the way. With a group of three or more, you can set up a custom trip for a little more than the cost of joining one of the regular hikes. They cost about $125 per person per day and include all meals and camping equipment. **Yosemite field seminars** also offers educational backpacking trips (see "Programs," below).

## Climbing

Yosemite's solid and spectacular granite cliffs are the most popular places to rock climb in the United States. **Yosemite Mountaineering School** has taught climbing here since 1969 and sells climbing equipment and sells and rents camping equipment. Daily beginning classes take students up 60 feet after they learn the necessary skills. Kids as young as 14 are accepted, and the fee is around $70 (more if fewer than 3 sign up). Advanced classes are available, too. The school is based in Tuolumne Meadows (☎ **209/372-8435**) from June to September and year-round in Curry Village in Yosemite Valley (☎ **209/ 372-8344;** www.yosemitemountaineering. com).

## Hiking

There are a few other things to do at Yosemite, but they're mainly garnish to the main meal, hiking. You have to walk in the high country and through the sequoia groves to really get what the place is about — the textures of rocks and plants, the smell of the clean high country and the dusky forest, the way the sun feels on your cheek at the end of a long, tough climb. Just driving to overlooks doesn't do it. Bring your hiking shoes and try to do a trail every day.

I've covered some favorite trails in each of the sections under "Natural Places," which begins on p. 425. Of course, there are many other choices. Use a book such as the one I've recommended under "Reading Up" (p. 409), or buy the inexpensive map guides to the three main park areas published by the Yosemite Association, which include trail maps and descriptions, and lots of other interesting information.

## Horseback Riding

Stables operated by the park concessionaire in **Yosemite Valley** (☎ **209/372-8348**), at **Tuolumne Meadows Lodge** ☎ **209/372-8427**), and at **Wawona** (☎ **209/372-6502**) offer guided trail rides daily in the summer and private pack trips. The park plans eventually to remove the stables in the Valley. Two-hour rides are $37.50 per person, 4-hour rides are $51.25, and all-day rides are $74.75. Children must be at least 7 years old and 44 inches tall, and riders must be less than 225 pounds. To reserve rides, call the stables, contact a hotel activity desk, or use Yosemite Concession Services' main contact information, listed under "Yosemite Address Book" (p. 402).

## Rafting

River floating at Yosemite mostly is for fun and splashing around, not thrills. The easiest and busiest spot for a float is the Merced River as it flows through Yosemite Valley. The river can be ferocious during spring melt, and late in the summer water gets scarce; but in June and July it's generally gentle enough for family play with inflatables. You can use an air mattress or inner tube, slowly floating under the branches of spreading trees and past swimming beaches. To save the riverbanks, try to get in and out at sandy or gravel spots. Floating is allowed between 10am and 6pm from Stoneman Bridge to Sentinel Beach (the picnic and swimming area below Sentinel Dome). The concessionaire rents small rafts at Curry Village (☎ 209/372-8341) from 10am to 4pm that you can paddle yourself 3 miles downstream. They cost $12.50 for adults, $10.50 for children 12 and under, per person. A shuttle picks up rafters and brings them back. It makes its last run at 6pm.

There's an even better place outside the valley, where you might be the only family floating all day. In the Wawona area, you can float 3 miles down the Merced's south fork from Swinging Bridge, above the history center on Forest Drive, down to the Wawona Campground, passing through the pines and under the covered bridge. Use whatever you like — raft, tube, air mattress, or canoe — but you'll have to bring it along because there are no rentals or shuttle. Stop at the campground, because below, the water gets too rough.

## Swimming

The cold, pure water flowing from the Sierra is irresistible on a hot hike. A plunge into a mountain lake is a shock to the system that brings me back to life when I'm tired. Once you strip down and dive in, you want to do it again every time you see inviting water, but that happens far too often. Hikers can swim all over the park wherever they find safe and inviting water. Avoid swift or powerfully moving water, test cautiously before your kids jump in, and don't swim if you're unsure. And, as the Park Service warns, don't dive and don't swim above waterfalls — obvious advice, but people have died that way. Also, Hetch

Hetchy Reservoir and Lake Eleanor are off-limits for swimming. The most popular stream for swimming is the **Merced River** as it passes through Yosemite Valley. There are plenty of spots to get in; just find a sandy place where you won't slip on rocks or damage the bank.

In the valley, large outdoor pools are open to the public at **Yosemite Lodge** and **Curry Village** daily in the summer. Hours vary. The fee for nonguests is $2 adults, $1.50 children.

## Winter Sports

The high country is inaccessible to vehicles in the winter; but you can get there on skis, and roads are plowed in the western areas and up Glacier Point Road as high as the Badger Pass ski area. The landscape is more beautiful in the snow, when the coating of white puts colors in stark contrast. You can still tour the sequoia groves and many trails on skis or snowshoes, and you have an improved chance of seeing mule deer and other animals that remain active in the winter. The skiing season is December through March, if snow allows. There's downhill skiing at the Badger Pass ski area (7,000 ft.), and cross-country trails go higher from there on Glacier Point Road, which is groomed for skiing all the way to Glacier Point. Snow is unpredictable in

---

### PLACES FOR RELAXED PLAY & PICNICS

There are limitless places for relaxed play at Yosemite, but there's no public playground equipment in or near the park. There are a couple of picnic areas at swimming spots along the Merced River in Yosemite Valley and one near the Ahwahnee Hotel. In Wawona, picnic grounds are at the Pioneer Yosemite History Center, near the campground, and in Mariposa Grove. Several picnic areas are along the Tioga Road, with especially appealing spots near Tenaya Lake.

Yosemite Valley — it can be useable in January, February, and possibly March. Wawona is at the same elevation, and Mariposa Grove is a little higher. There are plenty of rooms available in Yosemite Valley in the winter, with discount skiing packages offered.

## Downhill Skiing

Partway up Glacier Point Road, the **Badger Pass ski area** has been in operation since 1935. Most experienced skiers will find the area less than challenging, on the level of a community ski slope rather than a destination resort, but for beginners it's great. There are four lifts and a rope tow, with 85% of the hill rated beginner or intermediate. The vertical drop is 800 feet. The area offers instruction for skiing and snowboarding, a structured kids' program that takes them off your hands all day for lessons and play, and babysitting for potty-trained children ages 3 to 9. Weekend all-day lift tickets are $28 for adults and $16 for children; ski packages rent for $20 for adults and $15 for kids, and snowboard packages are $30.

## Cross-Country Skiing & Snowshoeing

Yosemite's cross-country and backcountry skiing is truly exceptional: plenty of snow, lots of groomed trail, varied terrain, and fabulous views. Some 40km (25 miles) of groomed tracks start at Badger Pass, including a 17km (10.5-mile) skating or diagonal-stride track that leads up to Glacier Point and the incredible views there. There are no trail fees.

There are 90 miles of marked trails from Badger Pass that aren't groomed by machines, and the backcountry is open to exploration without limit. Backcountry camping permits are issued at the Badger Pass Ranger Station. There are two ski huts for overnights. The Ostrander Ski Hut costs $20 from the Yosemite Association (see "Yosemite Address Book," p. 402). The Tuolumne Ski Hut is open to the first comer; call the **Tuolumne Ranger Station** at **209/372-0450** to see if it is open. Also call the nearest ranger station for avalanche conditions before heading out.

**Yosemite Cross-Country Ski School** (☎ **209/372-8444**), operated by the concessionaire, teaches all techniques and ability levels, as well as telemark skiing, and rents touring, skate, and telemark skies. Their backcountry trips include introductory overnights to the ski hut at Glacier Point, cross-park camping expeditions, and custom trips.

## Snowshoeing

The ski school at Badger Pass rents snowshoes too, for $14.25 a day. Modern snowshoes are easy to use even for beginners and give you great freedom in the backcountry, where you can hike all alone on trails that are jammed with people in the summer. Two-hour ranger-led snowshoe outings go daily from Badger Pass in the season. There's a $3 fee, and snowshoes are provided.

## Skating

An outdoor rink at Curry Village in Yosemite Valley (☎ **209/372-8341**) is open all winter. Admission is $5 for adults, $4.50 for children for each of four daily sessions. You can rent skates for $2.

# PROGRAMS
## Children's Programs

The Park Service, Sierra Club, Yosemite Institute, and Yosemite Concession Services all offer programs for kids, which are listed together with the other family and adult programs in the park newspaper and start from many different sites.

The park's **Junior Ranger program** takes two forms. In the summer, children can join a 2-hour ranger-led session for ages 8 to 13. At the end, participants receive a badge. Generally, parents have to go along. The other way for your children to earn a badge is by completing a booklet that costs $3.50 at visitor centers, attending a ranger program such as a campfire, picking up trash, and handing in the work at a visitor center. The booklets, published by the Yosemite Association, are for ages 3 to 6, the *Little Cub Handbook*, or ages 7 to 13, the *Junior Ranger Handbook*. These are excellent educational materials, spiral bound, printed on stiff paper and amusingly illustrated, with activities that help children use their own senses to deepen their appreciation of the park, not the typical busy work you would want to do only on a rainy day. Pick up a copy for your children even if you don't intend to work toward a badge.

## Family & Adult Programs

### PARK SERVICE

Check the park newspaper for the schedule of programs at each park area offered by a variety of organizations. Park rangers lead activities at Yosemite Valley, Wawona, Mariposa Grove, Crane Flat, Big Oak Flat, White Wolf, and Tuolumne Meadows. Campfire programs take place nightly at many campgrounds. Many of the offerings are guided hikes that take much of the day and include casual natural history commentary. In Yosemite Valley, painting classes take place most days on an informal basis at the Art Activity Center near the Village Store; you just show up and join the group. Photography sessions happen most days of the week, too. Because some programs have size limits, when you arrive take a look at the park newspaper to decide what you might want to do, and sign up at the visitor center.

### YOSEMITE THEATER

Live dramatic and musical performances take place every night of the summer at the visitor center auditoriums. They're staged by professionals and sponsored by the Park Service and the Yosemite Association. Tickets cost less than a night at the movies. Shows last 60 to 90 minutes. Past performances have included music about the park and the environment — great for kids — and one-man shows on the life and thoughts of John Muir. Times are listed in the park newspaper.

### YOSEMITE FIELD SEMINARS

The **Yosemite Association,** P.O. Box 230, El Portal, CA 95318 (☎ **209/379-2648;** www.yosemite.org), offers dozens of hikes, natural history lessons, art and writing workshops, and backpacking trips that use the park as a classroom. The sessions, which last 1 to 8 days, are offered February through October. Only a few sessions are intended for families, but teens can join others with their parents when appropriate — call and ask. A typical 3-day session is $150.

# FUN OUTSIDE THE PARK

Yosemite Mountain Sugar Pine Railroad (☎ 559/683-7273; **www.ymsprr.com**) runs a steam-powered excursion train around a 4-mile loop south of the park from April to October. A self-propelled Jenny Car — an enclosed, gas-powered vehicle historically used by railroad and logging workers — takes tours when the steam engine isn't fired up. The noise, steam, and fire of the locomotive are a thrill, even if the route of the narrow-gauge line through the pines isn't spectacular. The operation re-creates a logging train that operated here from 1908 to 1924. The station is at 56001 Highway 41 in Fish Camp, just outside the park's south entrance near Wawona, with a little museum, shops, and places to picnic. Tickets are $12 for adults, $6 for children 3 to 12 on the 1-hour steam-train ride, and $8 and $4 on the 30-minute Jenny Car tour. Train seating is not covered, so wait for a sunny day.

# WHERE TO EAT

## IN YOSEMITE VALLEY
### Low-Stress Meals

The **Pavilion Buffet cafeteria at Curry Village** feeds families by the thousands, which helps explain the bland, institutional food. The interior is dark but was not too noisy when I visited. The setup of the place gets you in and out quickly: You pay by the person when you enter, then pick whatever food you choose. Breakfast is 7 to 10am and costs $9 adults, $5 ages 5 to 12, $3 under 5; dinner is 5:30 to 8pm and $12, $7.50, and $4, respectively. It is open April through October. The **Pizza Deck** next door, open in the same season on evening weekdays, or from noon on weekends, is very popular but lacks indoor seating. A summer-only hamburger stand carries the usual fast-food choices.

The noisy cafeteria at Yosemite Lodge was converted to a year-round food court in 2001, after I visited, to serve pizza, pasta, burgers, and salads. Hours were undecided at this writing. The lodge also has a less hectic mid-range choice, the Garden Terrace, which serves breakfast and dinner from a buffet. Dinner is $8.25 for adults, $5.50 for kids 5 to 12, and $1.50 for those under 5.

The outdoor mall of Yosemite Village has several quick food choices. Degnan's Deli is open year-round, selling sandwiches and fast food to eat on the picnic tables outside; the Village Grill sells fast-food fare mid-April through October; and The Loft offers pizza and pasta summer only. At least one of the three is always open 8am to 6pm.

### ON TIOGA ROAD

The Tuolumne Meadows Grill, a snack bar in a tent, is located at the store on Tioga Road, serving burgers, hot dogs, and breakfast 8am to 6pm in the summer. Otherwise the only eateries are **White Wolf Lodge** (☎ 209/372-8416) and **Tuolumne Lodge** (☎ 209/372-8413), which serve dinner to nonguests

only by reservation, the same day only. Guests can reserve farther out. You may be able to get breakfast with a wait at either. Tuolumne's tent dining room has long tables on a painted concrete floor and metal stacking chairs. Breakfast, 7 to 9am, is $4 to $7. The dinner menu starts at $9 for a hamburger and goes up to $18. White Wolf serves simple food, but its small dining room makes a table hard to get. Breakfast hours are 7:30 to 9:30am. Facilities in the high country are open mid-June through mid-September.

### AT WAWONA

Your best bet for a simple family meal is to drive 2 miles from the south park entrance to the Tenaya Lodge (see p. 420), which has a deli, a grill serving burgers and pizza, and a casual fine-dining restaurant. The restaurant at the Wawona Hotel is described below.

## Best-Behavior Meals

Each of the park's three hotels has a formal dining room. YCS seems to find good chefs, and the meals I've had have ranged from quite good to brilliant; but only well-behaved older children and teens (and not all adults) will have the patience required. They're open year-round, except Wawona, which is open mid-March though November and some winter weekends.

The **Ahwahnee Dining Room** (☎ 209/372-1489), in the famous Yosemite Valley luxury hotel, is certainly something to look at, with its high vaulted ceilings and tall windows, but many families would not be comfortable there. The evening dress code requires jackets and ties for men and dresses or pantsuits for women, and the atmosphere remains stiff and proper at other, casual-dress meals. Breakfast is served 7 to 10:30am, lunch 11:30am to 3pm, and dinner 5:30 to 9pm; lunch is $10 to $14.50, dinner entrees $19 to $30. A four-item children's menu is $5.75 to $8.75.

The **Mountain Room** restaurant at Yosemite Lodge (☎ 209/372-1274) is far more relaxed yet maintains a pleasingly opulent feel, with large windows looking out on the cliffs and falls above. My meal was flawless: a smoked trout appetizer, salad with a spicy vinaigrette dressing, and a main course of grilled, boneless lamb chop with mint-flavored pesto. Even off-season, however, each course came slowly, a pace far beyond the patience of most children and many adults. Main courses are $15 to $20; the children's menu is $7. Reservations are advisable. Hours are 5:30 to 8:30pm.

I like the dining room at the **Wawona Hotel** (☎ 209/375-1425), with its old-fashioned wood floors, high ceilings, tall windows, and tablecloths. The food was extraordinary on my last visit, particularly a creamy chowder I had, velvety and subtly flavored, which will forever change what I expect from that dish. The setting suggests formality, but each time we've dined there, the service has been professional enough to put us all at ease, even the children. The fatal flaw is that they don't accept reservations for dinner (except parties of eight or more), and no family can wait as long as may be necessary, over 90 minutes at times. Lunch is $3 to $8, dinner $7 to $22; the children's menu is $3.75 to $6.75. Hours are breakfast 7:30 to 10am, lunch 11:30am to 2pm, and dinner 5:30 to 9pm. They put on an outdoor barbecue Saturdays from 5 to 7pm.

# CHAPTER 19

# Sequoia & Kings Canyon National Parks

I remember many moments from our visits to these sister parks. Walking among the giant sequoias in awe. Families playing in the granite pools of the Marble Fork of the Kaweah River at the Lodgepole Campground. Climbing from the Mineral King area to upper Monarch Lake, 10,700 feet high, cooling in the frigid water, and then drying in the sun on the warm bedrock. Sharing the amazement of the forms of Crystal Cave with my son. His memorable afternoon in a ranger-led program just for kids. Entering the hidden sanctum of Kings Canyon. Walking in a meadow there, thousands of feet below the tops of pale cliffs. Most of all, I remember feeling that this was the way a national park was meant to be. National parks were never meant to be places to worry about crowds, reservations, regulations, and how to find a leftover piece of wilderness no one else has taken. At Sequoia and Kings Canyon nothing is crowded and no one seems to be worrying about anything. They became two of our favorite parks.

Sequoia and Kings Canyon are officially two national parks; but they're connected and managed together, so there's no real reason for them to be separate. Sequoia contains most of the world's largest giant sequoias, including huge groves where you can hike and camp without seeing another person. With a little effort, you can also explore the park's vast backcountry of granite mountains. Kings Canyon National Park contains more sequoias, and one of the nation's deepest and most impressive canyons. Roads reach only the tiniest sliver of the park, leaving immense backcountry for long hiking or horse-packing trips. Neither park has many hotel rooms, and RVs have trouble on many of the narrow roads; mostly, families tent in the many superb campgrounds, where finding a site is never much of a problem. Surrounding and in between the parks, Sierra and Inyo national forests take in many more miles of wild land with roads to get to remote places and recreation facilities that offer some unique ways to have fun together.

## BEST THINGS TO DO

- Walk in Giant Forest to see the world's biggest tree and many others giants.
- Hike along the rushing Kings River in a canyon meadow or up into the granite high country.
- Tour Crystal or Boyden Cave to see weird rock formations and branching passages and to experience total darkness.
- Swim in delicious river pools where Native Americans bathed in the foothills near the Ash Mountain entrance.
- Plan a backpacking or horse-packing trip into true mountain wilderness of amazing beauty.

See "Activities" (p. 460).

## HISTORY: A MESSY DEMOCRACY

It has been said that only God can make a national park, and it's true that no one knows how to create natural wonders like the giant sequoias and the cliffs of Kings Canyon, only how to destroy them. It does take a law passed by the U.S. Congress and signed by the President to draw boundaries on a map around those places and call them a national park, protecting the land forever. And even doing that isn't easy. Most parks had at least some people against them, and for some parks, it took many years to get Congress to agree — 84 years in the case of Kings Canyon. Long after the job is done, when visitors love a park, it can be hard to imagine why anyone would

want it any other way. Few people remember the fierce disagreements. But the truth is that the real reasons some parks were created didn't have much to do with the reasons we love them.

The story of Sequoia and Kings Canyon shows the weird way we make national parks. Sequoia National Park was born in the mind of a young newspaper editor, George Stewart of the *Visalia Delta*. He saw the giant sequoias being logged in the mountains east of town in the 1870s and thought they should be saved. He wrote in his newspaper about the waste of the ancient trees and persuaded his neighbors, farmers in the San Joaquin Valley, to tell their

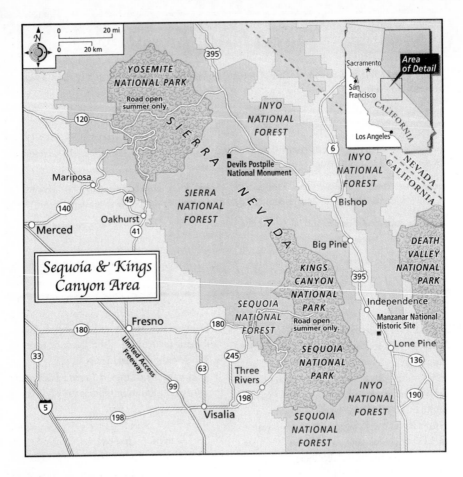

representatives in Congress about it, too. The farmers thought the loggers up in the mountains should be stopped, but their main reason was not the beauty of the trees. They believed logging and grazing sheep in the Sierra made the water run off faster during the spring snowmelt, so that none was left for their farms in the late summer.

Under the laws of that time, the government gave away land or sold it for next to nothing for people to cut down the trees and make lumber for building or to make paper. While Stewart tried to convince people there should be a park, loggers took large areas of the forest to cut down for the wood. One group called the Kaweah Colony received the area of Giant Forest and started to build a road to the sequoias so that they would have a way

of removing the trees they cut down. By the time Stewart got a member of Congress to introduce a bill to set aside the park (the first step to making a law), all that was left available was a small area in the south. Everything else had been given away for logging. The bill made it through Congress very quickly, in only 2 months. President Benjamin Harrison signed it on September 25, 1890.

But at the same time something else was happening that Stewart knew nothing about. Congress had been working on a bill for Yosemite National Park. Just before it came up for a vote in the House of Representatives, a Congressman presented a different version of the bill, with a changed list of the lands to be included in the park. The members of the House didn't know what they were voting on, because they had no written copy of the new bill. It passed anyway. When people sorted it out later, they realized that Congress had made Yosemite five times larger than they had originally planned. Sequoia National Park, which had been created less than a month earlier, was also expanded by more than five times and now included Giant Forest. Grant Grove was protected in brand-new General Grant National Park.

To this day, no one knows exactly what happened. There's no record of who came up with the new boundaries, and even the original papers disappeared. Someone made a secret agreement to create these huge parks, but who did it and why? Historians studying the story believe that the most likely explanation is that the Southern Pacific Railroad was responsible. It owned large logging businesses in other parts of California. If customers bought wood from the sequoia groves instead, it might hurt the railroad's wood business. The new park boundaries stopped that from happening. When Congress made Sequoia National Park so much bigger, it took most of the large sequoia trees away from the loggers, including the Kaweah Colony. It's likely one of the railroad's people slipped a friendly Congressman the boundaries for the larger parks just before the vote.

However it happened, we can be glad Giant Forest was saved, but George Stewart was unhappy about the sneaky way the park grew. He thought the Kaweah Colony was treated unfairly. They had followed the government's rules to get Giant Forest and their new road was almost done, but they were forced off the land and arrested for cutting trees in the new national park.

Kings Canyon National Park took much, much longer, but its story also is strange. John Muir got it started. After helping start Yosemite National Park (see "John Muir & Wilderness Values," in chapter 17, "Rock, Life & Change," and "History: Fight for the Valley," in chapter 18, "Yosemite National Park"), he wrote an article about Kings Canyon in 1891. He called the canyon "a grander valley of the same kind" as Yosemite and included a map of the area he thought should be set aside. His important friends in Washington, D.C., got to work, and within 2 years, President Harrison placed Kings Canyon and almost all the rest of southern and central Sierra Nevada in new forest reserves, which we now call national forests.

At the time, most people thought a national forest was the same as a national park, but it turned out the two were quite different. The U.S. Forest Service protected the national forests from being sold, but allowed people to use them for logging, grazing, hunting, or building dams. The National Park Service, on the other hand, has only two uses for the national parks. It preserves the land naturally for future generations, and it allows visitors to come and enjoy it. For many years, the Park Service asked to take more of the Sierra Nevada into Sequoia National Park, but the Forest Service didn't want to give up its land. Even though the agencies were part of the same government, they spent a lot of time fighting and spreading nasty rumors about each other. In 1926, the Park Service won some National Forest land when Congress expanded Sequoia National Park to take in the mountain area in the east of the park, but that land wasn't very useful for the national forests anyway because it was remote and didn't have many trees.

The fight for Kings Canyon was much harder. The Park Service wanted to protect the canyon John Muir had said was even better than Yosemite Valley (I think he was exaggerating, but it is very beautiful). Many other people wanted to build a dam there to hold back the Kings River in a big lake, something they could do only in a national forest, not in a national park. The city of Los Angeles wanted the dam for drinking water, the electric power companies wanted it for power, and the farmers of the San Joaquin Valley wanted it so that they could water their crops. Like children fighting over a toy, they battled back

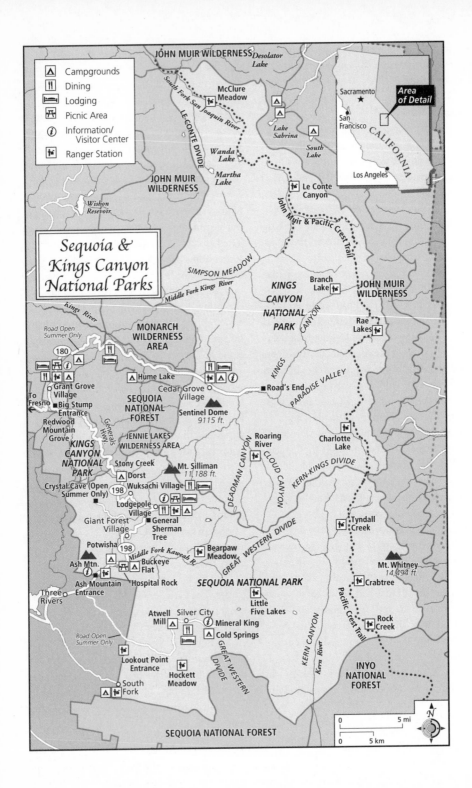

Sequoia & Kings Canyon National Parks

and forth. And, as often happens with children who can't share, no one got any of it. The dam wasn't built as their disagreement went on, year after year and then decade after decade.

In 1939, Congress discussed creating Kings Canyon National Park, including the whole area of the park today except the canyon itself. Representative Alfred Elliot, who was against the park, tried to stop it by making people believe that the main supporter of the new park was dishonest. Elliot wrote a fake letter to park supporter Representative Bud Gearhart and put $100 in the envelope. Then Eliot started privately passing around copies of the forged letter. But Gearhart heard about what Elliot was doing and he did something very clever. Instead of complaining about what Elliot was doing, he secretly investigated what had really happened but said nothing. Then, as the Congress got ready to vote on the park, Gearhart stood up on the floor of the House of Representatives and laid out all the evidence, uncovering Elliot's nasty doings. The other Congressmen and the crowd watching from the gallery roared with applause for Gearhart. Then Elliot got up to speak, but he couldn't think of anything sensible to say back, and he was jeered and laughed at. When the vote came up, the park bill passed, creating Kings Canyon National Park.

But the new park left out the most important part, the Cedar Grove area of Kings Canyon itself. It was added only in 1965, long after the people who originally asked for it had died. For most of that time, the supporters of building the dam had done the park supporters' job for them by fighting over who would get to use the water from the dam they hadn't built yet. By the 1960s, most people no longer believed in putting such a unique and beautiful place underwater, regardless of who would use the water. So Congress finally added the canyon to the park. The farmers were able to build other dams lower down the river, which took care of their need for water. L.A. got its water from other projects. And we all get the park.

In 2000, President Clinton set aside more land with a proclamation that created Giant Sequoia National Monument from part of Sequoia National Forest. It's an area not that much smaller than Sequoia National Park itself, taking in the entire gap between Sequoia and Kings Canyon national parks, including the recreational area at Hume Lake, a lot of land around Grant Grove, and a huge area south of Sequoia National Park. The new monument is like a park but is managed by the Forest Service. Its main use is preservation. Adding the two parks and the monument together, the idea started by that one Visalia newspaper editor has preserved a stretch of the Sierra about 100 miles long.

# ORIENTATION

## THE PARKS

Sequoia and Kings Canyon national parks take in much of the southern Sierra Nevada. The rest is in Sequoia, Sierra, and Inyo national forests, which surround the parks. The two national parks are connected and operate as one. Roads reach only a small part of each park, on the west side.

**Sequoia National Park** is the southern park. Its main visitor facilities are near and just to the north of the Lodgepole Visitor Center, midway along Generals Highway through the park. Giant Forest, Crystal Cave, and the warm, dry foothills area are to the south on the highway.

**Kings Canyon National Park** is the northern park. Most visitor facilities are in Grant Grove Village, a pocket to the west of the main part of the park on Highway 180, which continues east through part of Sequoia

National Forest and into 3,000-foot-deep Kings Canyon. The small developed area here is called Cedar Grove.

## THE ROADS

No road crosses the Sierra Nevada in these parks, or anywhere close by. The east side of the parks is all remote backcountry (see "Getting Around," p. 453, for how to get there).

**GENERALS HIGHWAY** The main thoroughfare in Sequoia National Park, the 46-mile Generals Highway, is among the nation's most scenic and memorable drives, leading from Grant Grove south through part of Sequoia National Forest and then along the park's western side. South of Lodgepole, the road weaves among the huge trees of Giant Forest — sometimes even splitting in half to go around them — then descends steeply with fabulous views to the south, Ash Mountain entrance in the foothills. This part of the road is as wiggly as a wet strand of spaghetti and perpetually under construction. A vehicle over 19 feet long is physically unable to stay in its own lane on some of the curves, and it's unwise to take trailers or RVs over 22 feet. Those who are susceptible can count on carsickness.

**KINGS CANYON HIGHWAY** This road, an extension of Highway 180, passes over steep, dry terrain that will take your breath away. It's quite different from the luxurious forest of the roads in Sequoia. Entering the canyon, the highway runs along the bank of the Kings River until it reaches the tiny lodge and store and large campgrounds at Cedar Grove, 28 miles from Grant Grove. The road is closed in the winter.

**BACKCOUNTRY ROADS** Various dirt roads or narrow paved roads pierce a little way into the parks or approach their edges in places. These all are difficult routes tough or impossible to navigate for RVs. **Mineral King Road** is an incredibly twisty, narrow, and partly unpaved road leading up into the mountains in the southwest part of the park; you pay for the great destination with a really exhausting ride. The **Hume Lake Road** (County Road 13S09) runs from Kings Highway 6 miles east of Grant Grove to General's Highway, 5 miles south of Grant Grove, with many winding curves through the trees. Several other minor backroads are covered in the sections about their destinations.

## THE GATEWAY TOWNS

The only town right at the park is Three Rivers, a small tourist-oriented settlement along Highway 198 at the south entrance. The nearest major centers are the flatland cities of Visalia, about 30 miles from the south entrance, and Fresno, more than 50 miles from the north entrance.

# MAKING THE ARRANGEMENTS

## WHEN TO GO

While below the parks the San Joaquin Valley burns in a furnace of summer heat, Giant Forest and Grant Grove, at elevations of 6,500 feet and above, are almost 20°F cooler. Cedar Grove, on the floor of Kings Canyon, is between those levels in elevation and can be desert-like. Crowding isn't a big problem even in the summer, but weekends are the busiest times. Fall is fine, too, and the park is largely deserted.

When snow comes, Kings Canyon Highway and Mineral King Road close, and Generals Highway between Grant Grove and Lodgepole can be closed for days or even weeks after a storm. Trails are marked for cross-country skiing and snowshoeing among the sequoias. For spring break, most of the

## WEATHER CHART: SEQUOIA NATIONAL PARK

| | LODGEPOLE, ELEVATION 6,750 FEET | | | ASH MOUNTAIN, ELEVATION 1,690 FEET | | |
|---|---|---|---|---|---|---|
| | AVG. HIGH (°F) | AVG. LOW (°F) | PRECIP. (TOTAL IN.) | AVG. HIGH (°F) | AVG. LOW (°F) | PRECIP. (TOTAL IN.) |
| Dec.–Feb. | 39 | 16 | 25.6 | 57 | 37 | 13.2 |
| March | 44 | 21 | 7.5 | 64 | 42 | 4.3 |
| April | 49 | 25 | 3.1 | 71 | 46 | 2.5 |
| May | 57 | 32 | 1.3 | 79 | 53 | 1 |
| June | 67 | 38 | .7 | 90 | 61 | .4 |
| July | 75 | 44 | .5 | 98 | 68 | .1 |
| August | 75 | 43 | .3 | 97 | 67 | .1 |
| September | 68 | 38 | 1.5 | 91 | 61 | .5 |
| October | 58 | 30 | 1.8 | 81 | 53 | 1 |
| November | 46 | 22 | 4.6 | 67 | 43 | 2.9 |

park remains snowed in, although campgrounds and trails in the foothills area are open. In heavy snow years, snow remains at the elevation of the sequoias and main campgrounds through Memorial Day.

## HOW MUCH TIME TO SPEND

Most people just drive on Generals Highway, take a look at the sequoia trees, and drive out the same day. That's like bicycling through a museum. If you enjoy the outdoors, you can spend your whole vacation at these parks. A week would be well spent hiking and relaxing in the area. In the front area of Sequoia National Park, a short visit would take 2 or 3 days and include the sequoias, Crystal Cave, hiking, and maybe river swimming. Spend at least a full day at Kings Canyon; several days would be better. The Mineral King area demands a couple of days to justify the arduous drive.

## HOW FAR TO PLAN AHEAD

Most people visit these parks on the weekends, with far fewer visiting during the week. If you

plan your visit for Sunday through Thursday, you'll find it easier to get reservations and avoid crowds at popular sites such as the caves. Hotel rooms and cabins should be reserved 2 or 3 months out for the summer; but you can reserve as early as you like, and if you don't reserve until later, you still have a good chance of getting a room.

Only two campgrounds, Lodgepole and Dorst, have sites on the national reservation system (see chapter 1, "Planning Your Trip"); call as soon as you make your plans, but sites don't all book up right away. Those campgrounds are full all summer. There are many other campgrounds in the park and in the nearby national forests that don't take reservations. Sites are abundant on weekdays, and you can get a site on weekends by arriving early in the day. Cedar Grove and national forest campgrounds are the last to fill up.

## READING UP

**Sequoia Natural History Association** (☎ 559/565-3759; www.sequoiahistory.org) carries a large selection of books and maps in visitor centers and a mail-order catalog. The books are listed online too, but at this writing ordering was not automated.

**Hiking:** The association publishes a *Map & Guide* for each park area, including trail descriptions and fine-scale topographic maps. They cost $2 each and are all most visitors will need for day hikes or short overnights, covering Grants Grove, Cedar Grove, Lodgepole, Giant Forest, and Mineral King. For more detailed descriptions, get Steve Sorensen's *Day Hiking Sequoia* (Sequoia Natural History Association, $13), which covers 50 hikes, including suggestions on where to fish, swim, and explore history. Sorensen has children, and his book gives special attention to hikes that kids will enjoy. Sadly, a companion volume on Kings Canyon National Park is out of print. **Maps:** If you want to go beyond the maps mentioned above, several topographic trail maps covering the whole park are printed on plastic. I think the best is from Tom Harrison Cartography, sold for $9 (☎ **800/265-9090** or 415/456-7940; www.tomharrisonmaps.com). Contact them directly for their more detailed maps of areas within the park. You can order finer-scale USGS topographic maps from SNHA, too. **History:** *Challenge of the Big Trees,* by Lary M. Dilsaver and William C. Tweed (Sequoia Natural History Association), is an authoritative but readable account for adults.

## GETTING THERE
### By Car
The parks are 300 miles from San Francisco and 240 miles from L.A. From either city, use north-south I-5 and/or Highway 99 to get to Visalia, for Sequoia National Park, or to Fresno, for Kings Canyon National Park. From Fresno, **Highway 180** leads to the north (Big Stump) entrance, at Grant Grove. Use this route if you have a large RV or trailer. From Visalia, **Highway 198** leads to Three Rivers and the Ash Mountain entrance, near the Foothills Visitor Center. Large RVs should avoid that route unless they park outside and

bring along a car for going on, because the Generals Highway leading into the park isn't suitable for vehicles over 22 feet.

There's no route to the east side of the Sierra for many hours' drive north or south. No road even touches the parks on the east, but you can get close on routes into Inyo National Forest from **Highway 395,** the north-south route that runs on the east side of the Sierra. See "Getting Around" (p. 453) for more on that area.

### By Air
Fresno is the major airport in the region. See "By Air" under "Getting There," in chapter 18 (p. 409), for information on carriers and car-rental agencies there.

## WHAT TO PACK
### Clothing
In the summer, you'll spend most of your time in shorts and T-shirts. Summer rains come mostly in afternoon thunderstorms. Be prepared for cool mornings, but generally the climate is perfect. Bring your swimsuits for playing in streams. Bring a layer of warm wool or synthetic clothing for backpacking the high country. There's little need for clothes more formal than you wear camping. In the cold months, be ready for heavy snow and temperatures around freezing at the elevation of the sequoias (see "Cold Weather Preparations," in chapter 1).

Temperatures depend on elevation. In summer the foothills area, at around 2,000 feet, is scorching. Grant Grove, Giant Forest, and other main visitor sites along the Generals Highway are at around 6,500 feet, and about 20°F cooler, just about perfect in the summer. Cedar Grove, in Kings Canyon is, 4,600 feet, and Mineral King, in Sequoia, is about 8,000, with corresponding temperature differences.

### Gear
Lightweight gear will handle all but exceptionally cold nights at the elevation of Lodgepole Campground during the normal

camping months of the summer and fall; for cold nights, prepare with an extra layer. Backpackers heading for the high country could encounter freezing temperatures at night even in the summer. Strollers can navigate some sequoia grove trails, but using a backpack to carry your baby or toddler gives you far more freedom.

# WHERE TO SPEND THE NIGHT

## CAMPING

These parks are heaven for tent campers, who have far more choices and flexibility than do those who stay in hotels or come in an RV (RVs can't go everywhere; see "By RV," p. 453). The campgrounds here are some of the best designed and maintained in the national park system.

Two Park Service and several Forest Service campgrounds take reservations through their national systems, each described under "Camping & Hotel Reservations," in chapter 1, "Planning Your Trip"). Even without a reservation, sites are easy to come by at many first-come, first-served park and national forest campgrounds. Some Forest Service campgrounds are equivalent to the park campgrounds even in location, because they lie in gaps between sections of the parks, while others lie along the remote eastern edge of the park. I've listed the two agencies' campgrounds together, grouping the campgrounds by location.

Black bears invade campgrounds every night, often tearing cars open looking for food. Use the steel cabinet at your campsite to store food you're not eating, and latch it, because bears do try the latches. Also, don't bring a huge cooler because it may not fit in the cabinet. Sizes vary, with the smaller units 17 inches high, 16 inches deep, and 47 inches long. Firewood gathering is permitted, but buying your wood is easier and more environmentally sound. Gather only wood that's both dead and down. RV generators are allowed 9am to 9pm only.

## Generals Highway

These five campgrounds are on Generals Highway between the Ash Mountain and Grant Grove entrances, arranged by their distance from the south, Ash Mountain entrance.

**Potwisha.** On Generals Hwy., 4 miles from the Ash Mountain entrance, Sequoia National Park. No reservations. $14 per site. 42 sites; tents or RVs. Flush toilets, dump station, pay phone. Open year-round.

At 2,100 feet, the low elevation of this campground makes it hot in the summer and comfortable in the winter. The ground cover is desert-like and there's not much shade or screening to sites; but the sites are large, many with a pull-through arrangement for RVs. The Kaweah River runs along the campground, with spots for river play down an embankment. The Potwisha Indians used this area for its year-round warmth and rivers. The Potwisha Pictograph Loop goes from near the campground dump station to the pictographs and one of the swimming holes in the Kaweah where the Potwisha bathed every morning.

**Buckeye Flat.** ½ mile off Generals Hwy., about 6 miles from the Ash Mountain entrance, Sequoia National Park. $14 per site. No reservations. 28 sites; tents only. Flush toilets. Closed Oct to mid-May.

I love this campground! Accessible only to tenters because of the narrow half-mile access road, it is on a peaceful and shady hillside among a variety of deciduous trees. Sites are large and have great privacy among boulders and rock outcroppings. Best of all, a lovely swimming hole in Paradise Creek is a short walk from your site, down the bank between sites 17 and 18. A trail leads up the creek to more swimming spots. At an elevation of 2,800 feet, this campground is hot in the summer.

**Lodgepole.** On Generals Hwy. just north of Giant Forest, Sequoia National Park. $16 per site. Reservations accepted. 214 sites; tents or RVs. Flush toilets, showers, laundry, dump station, store. Open year-round.

Strung along the banks of the Marble Fork of the Kaweah River at an elevation of 6,750 feet, Lodgepole is the kind of campground that could be the center of your whole vacation. It combines a beautiful place to camp and proximity to family-oriented facilities at Lodgepole Village, including a good visitor center, showers, laundry, store, snack bar, and shuttle stop for rides to Giant Forest. The children's Walter Fry Nature Center is in the middle of the campground, offering excellent ranger programs. Getting the right site is important. Sites 1 to 22, nearest the visitor center, are small and lack ground cover, and are reserved for RVs; sites 36 to 60 and 151 to 214, for tents or RVs, lie on each side of the river; and sites 69 to 150, in upper Lodgepole, are for tents only, near where the river tumbles over granite shelves and boulders. Campers play in the river, horseback riding and sequoias are just down the road, and several hiking trails leave from here (see "Lodgepole & Wolverton," p. 457).

**Dorst.** On Generals Hwy. 8 miles NW of Lodgepole, Sequoia National Park. $16 per site. Reservations accepted. 204 sites; tents or RVs. Flush toilets, dump station, pay phone. Closed Sept to mid-May.

This is a nicely developed campground, nestled among pine and fir trees that screen the many sites. A meadow borders the campground, and a branch of Dorst Creek flows by at 6,800 feet elevation. Three excellent day hikes start from the campground. It's 2 miles (one way) to the remote sequoias of Muir Grove, 2½ miles to Lost Grove, and 3¼ miles to the spectacular views from the top of Little Baldy (cut off 1½ miles by starting from Generals Highway). There's a place to play a half mile up the Cabin Creek Trail in Dorst Creek, when the water isn't too high.

**Stony Creek (Upper and Lower).** On Generals Hwy., 10 miles SE of Grant Grove, Sequoia National Forest. $16 per site upper campground, $8 lower. Reservations taken for an additional fee. 68 sites; tents or RVs. Flush toilets at lower campground, portable toilets at upper; showers, laundry, pay phone nearby. Closed Oct to Memorial Day.

Conveniently located just outside Sequoia between the two parks, these campgrounds on either side of the highway are near the Stony Creek Lodge, with its restaurant, laundry, and public showers (see p. 450). The lower campground is attractive and well wooded, with sites far apart, the creek running by, and rock outcroppings shaping the land. The upper part is dusty and undeveloped. Elevation is 6,400 feet. The Lost Grove of sequoias is just inside the park, about 1 mile away.

## Grant Grove
**Azalea.** 113 sites. Open year-round.
**Crystal Springs.** 62 sites. Closed Oct to mid-May.
**Sunset.** 200 sites. Closed mid-Sept to late May.

These three campgrounds are all within walking distance of Grant Grove Village, 3 miles from the north (Big Stump) park entrance. They have flush toilets and are near the village's showers, store, restaurant, visitor center, and horseback riding. Each campground charges $14 per site and permits tents or RVs. The elevation is 6,500 feet, within shadowy, needle-carpeted forest. Year-round Azalea is right next to the sequoia grove itself on a bolder-strewn hill with pine, fir, and cedar. Sites inside the loops are barren and exposed, but some sites on the outer edge of loops are large and more interesting. Crystal Springs looked the most appealing of the three to me. Ground cover has not been trampled as much, and the setting on a rocky hill makes many good campsites. Sunset is large and largely flat, with little screening.

## Hume Lake
In the woods east of Grant Grove, Sequoia National Forest contains a rich recreation area

around Hume Lake. Developed facilities are described under "Hume Lake Christian Camps" (p. 451). Campgrounds are along the narrow and twisting country road 13S01, which runs 15 miles from Kings Highway at Princess Campground, 6 miles northeast of Grant Grove, to Generals Highway, a few miles south of Grant Grove. I've described campgrounds in north-to-south order on that road. All are between 5,000 and 6,000 feet elevation. Princess and Hume Lake campgrounds accept reservations. Several other, primitive Forest Service campgrounds are in the national forest. Get information from Sequoia National Forest's **Hume Lake Ranger District** (☎ **559/338-2251**) on Highway 180 near Dunlap.

**Princess.** Hwy. 180 and Road 13S01, 6 miles from Grant Grove, Sequoia National Forest. $12 per site. Reservations taken for an additional fee. 87 sites; tents or RVs. Pit toilets, running water, dump station. Closed Labor Day to Memorial Day.

The meadow campground occupies space among large boulders and the huge stumps of giant sequoias, which were logged a century ago when they were as much as 2,500 years old. The sites are large and well separated, along three paved loops.

**Hume Lake.** On Hume Lake, 3 miles from Hwy. 180, Sequoia National Forest. $16 per site. Reservations taken for additional fee. 75 sites; tents or RVs. Flush toilets. Closed Oct to Memorial Day.

This is a well-developed campground on the hillside over the north side of the fishing lake. Sites are broadly separated among pine and cedar trees, but dusty due to the trampling of long use. A nearby road leads down to the water for swimming or boating.

**Manzanita RV Park.** At Hume Lake Christian Camps. ☎ **559/335-2000**, ext. 287 summer, 559/251-6043 winter. $20 per site up to 2 people, $3 each additional person. MC, V. 7 sites. No tents.

This RV park is part of the Hume Lake Christian camp described on p. 451. It has the closest full hookup sites to the park; but it has no public bathrooms, showers, tables, or other amenities, and no tents or fires of any kind are allowed. Guests do have access to the camp's exceptional facilities.

**Landslide.** South of Hume Lake, 6 miles from Hwy. 180, Sequoia National Forest. $10 per site. 6 sites. Pit toilets, running water. Closed Labor Day to Memorial Day.

The campground is small, rough, and remote, but lovely, with just a few huge sites on a hill among pines and cedars.

**Tenmile.** South of Hume Lake, 8 miles from Hwy. 180, Sequoia National Forest. Free. 10 sites. Pit toilets, running water. Closed Labor Day to Memorial Day.

This primitive campground, along Tenmile Creek, shady and dusty, is like the backcountry.

## At Cedar Grove

**Sentinel.** 82 sites; tents or RVs. Closed Nov–Apr.
**Canyon View.** 37 sites; tents only. Open only when needed.
**Moraine.** 120 sites; tents or RVs. Open only when needed.
**Sheep Creek.** 111 sites; tents or RVs. Open only when needed.

These four campgrounds in Cedar Grove, at the bottom of Kings Canyon 28 miles from Grant Grove, sit in a row along the south side of the Kings River. At 4,600 feet, the air is warm and dry in the summer, with some desert plants and others from the mountains. Away from the river, the cedars, oaks, and ponderosa pines have open ground between them; the green grows thicker as you get closer to the water.

Sentinel is the only campground that's open all season. It has the tiny visitor center, pay phones, and the campfire amphitheater. Canyon View is a smaller, less-manicured campground where tenters can get away from RVs. Moraine, the largest of the four, often doesn't open because the sites aren't needed. Each campground has flush toilets and water, and there is a dump station. The nearby Cedar

Grove Lodge (see p. 451) has a fast-food restaurant and store, and there are showers and a laundry for campers. The camping fee is $14.

## Mineral King & South Fork

These three primitive Park Service campgrounds are in the remote southwestern area of Sequoia National Park, where toilsome roads hold down the number of visitors. RVs and trailers should not attempt Mineral King Road or South Fork Drive. The Mineral King area and road are covered on p. 459. None of these campgrounds takes reservations.

**Atwell Mill.** On Mineral King Rd., 20 miles from Hwy. 198. $8 per night. 21 sites; tents only. Pit toilets, showers nearby. Closed Nov to Memorial Day, water off Oct 1.

If you're used to the usual busy, trampled campground, the lush grass and ferns among large pine, fir, and cedar are refreshing. Sites are large and screened by a small hill. One-hundred-year-old sequoia stumps are scattered around, the remains of the mill of the campground's name. The Silver City Lodge is nearby (see p. 451), where you can shower and get a meal. The campground is rough and primitive, however, with pit toilets. Two lightly used trails reach secluded sequoia groves.

**Cold Springs.** On Mineral King Rd., 25 miles from Hwy. 198. $8 per site. 40 sites; tents only. Pit toilets, pay phone. Closed Nov to Memorial Day, water off Oct 1.

The campground sits by the East Fork of the Kaweah River under huge, shady conifers. Sites are far from each other on rugged ground. At 7,500 feet, the rocky high country above Mineral King Valley is near at hand from this highest campground in the park. It's a great starting point for spectacular high Sierra backpacking or rides with the pack-station operator (see "Horseback Riding & Stock Packing," p. 461).

**South Fork.** On South Fork Dr., 13 miles from the Hwy. 198 intersection in Three Rivers. $8 per site May–Oct, free in winter. 13 sites; tents or RVs, but road not recommended for RVs. Pit toilets, no drinking water. Open year-round.

The campground is at the edge of the park at 3,600 feet, at the end of a partly unpaved road that branches from the highway outside the park. The Park Service does not charge an entrance fee on this route. The main feature is the Ladybug Trail, good in the spring while the high country is still under snow. Boil or treat water from the South Fork of the Kaweah River for drinking or cooking.

## On the East Side of the Parks

These campgrounds are off Highway 395, the north-south route along the eastern side of the Sierra. For backpackers heading to wilderness trips in the remote eastern area of the parks, this information on the campgrounds in **Inyo National Forest** (☎ 760/873-2400; www.r5.fs.fed.us/inyo) might be useful. Family travelers visiting the parks' main areas should not consider these campgrounds, which are many hours from where you want to be.

At **Whitney Portal,** 13 miles west of Highway 395 at Lone Pine, a substantial campground sits at the starting point to climb Mt. Whitney. Farther north, the 9,200-foot-high **Onion Valley Campground** is 13 miles west of Independence near the trailhead over **Kearsarge Pass,** a backpacking route that runs due west into Kings Canyon. On the same road 6 miles west of Independence, **Gray's Meadow Campground** is on a stocked trout stream. Sites at all three campgrounds can be reserved through the national system (see "Camping & Hotel Reservations," in chapter 1) or obtained on arrival.

Continuing north on 395, Big Pine is the turn for campgrounds in high, narrow canyons up Big Pine Canyon Road, just outside the John Muir Wilderness. **Upper Sage Flat** and **Big Pine Creek** take reservations. Several other campgrounds near the wilderness are reached from Bishop, on Route 168.

## Backcountry Camping

To camp outside a campground in the back-country, which accounts for more than 90% of the parks, you need a permit from the Park Service or Forest Service. The nearest ranger station issues a certain number of permits for each trailhead, ranging from 15 to 30 people per trailhead in the park to more than 70 for some Forest Service trailheads. The Park Service takes reservations by mail or fax (☎ 559/565-4239) from March 1 until 21 days before the start of your hike. It holds back about a quarter of the permits for people who ask for them on arrival, starting at 1pm the day before the hike at the ranger station for the trailhead you want to use. After 9am on the day of the hike, rangers give away permits that haven't been picked up by people with reservations. Most trails don't fill the quota most days, but the popular trails do. Long weekends are the busiest. At quiet times, when some ranger stations close, you just fill out a permit form and leave it in a box.

To start, get a good topographic map, a trail guide (see "Reading Up," p. 443), and the Park Service's *Backcountry Basics* newspaper. You can order Park Service publications through a voice-mail system (☎ 559/565-3341). If you have specific questions, including those on the availability of particular trailheads, call the **backcountry office** at ☎ 559/565-3708. You can reserve only in writing. After selecting your route and an alternative, send in your request, which requires a complete itinerary and other information explained in *Backcountry Basics* or on the park's website (www.nps.gov/seki/bcinfo.htm). Include the $10 reservation fee, payable by Visa or MasterCard if by fax; if using the mail, you can also pay by check. There's no fee if you don't make a reservation.

Many trails cross Park Service and Forest Service land; you need only one permit, from the agency where your hike begins. The Forest Service system differs from the Park Service system in some respects, but its list of trailheads and ranger station addresses is included in *Backcountry Basics*. See "Sequoia-Kings Canyon Address Book" (p. 437) for national forest contact information. For more on backpacking and wilderness travel with pack and saddle animals, see "Backpacking" (p. 460).

## FOR RVs

If you need full RV hookups, try **Lemon Cove/Sequoia Campground,** in Lemon Cove, 13 miles west of Three Rivers on Highway 198 (☎ 559/597-2346), which has a pool and laundry.

## HOTELS & CABINS

The main lodgings at Sequoia and Kings Canyon have been rebuilt from the ground up in recent years. You have a choice of a brand-new luxury hotel or a run-down but oddly quaint old cabin. Each park has lodgings run by a concessionaire, but private and national forest land intermix with park land and have lodging options just as good or better. I've addressed the choices geographically. All rates are for the high season; off-season rates drop as much as 40%.

## On Generals Highway

These lodgings are along the main road that connects the two parks and runs through a section of Sequoia National Forest. They are arranged north to south.

**Grant Grove Village and John Muir Lodge.** 3 miles inside north park entrance (5755 E. Kings Canyon Rd., #101, Fresno, CA 93727). ☎ 559/335-5500. www.sequoia-kingscanyon.com. 30 lodge rooms, 53 cabins, 9 with bathroom. Lodge $128 double, cabin $88–$93 double with bathroom, $38–$55 without bathroom; $10 each additional person 13 and older, free 12 and under. AE, DC, MC, V. Some rooms open year-round.

The wood-sided Muir lodge fits in well on a hill above the village facilities. It is just a few years old and has comfortable rooms in autumn colors with rustic-style furniture. The rooms have telephones and coffeemakers but bathrooms are small. Some of the cabins and their shared bathhouse are shockingly dilapidated. The slow pace of renovation is a complicated story of the relationship of the Park Service to its hotel operators. However, if you're looking for a rough outdoors experience, they do have some charm, with primitive dwellings not much different from those pioneers would have lived in. About half of the units are tents; the other half consist of shed-like cabins of bare boards with flashlights for light. Some of these have been remodeled, but even they were poor in quality when I last visited.

**Montecito-Sequoia Lodge.** South of Grant Grove, Sequoia National Forest (2225 Grant Rd., Suite 1, Los Altos, CA 94024). ☎ **800/227-9900** or 650/967-8612; 559/565-3388 at the lodge. www.montecitosequoia.com. 32 rooms with bathroom, 13 cabins with shared bathhouse. Weeklong summer family camp $660–$845 per person; spring/fall lodging $55–$79 double, $35–$55 each additional person; winter $99–$129 double, $49–$109 each additional person. Meals and activities included. AE, DISC, MC, V.

This is a special place. In the summer, it is a combination children's summer camp and adult resort. Families visit together for week-long sessions, but the children go off to structured, supervised activities during the day — including archery, art, crafts, canoeing, fencing, naturalist walks, horse and pony rides, riflery, sailing, swimming, tennis, water-skiing, and more. A single day's choices fill a page. Meanwhile, the parents do whatever they want outdoors in the park, joining in resort activities or just sitting around the pool. At mealtimes and in the evening, the families come together again. In the winter, the resort grooms 80km (50 miles) of cross-country ski trails for skate or diagonal stride, rated beginner to expert, and rising to the top of an 8,500-foot mountain. There is a rope tow with a 350-foot drop for sledding and skiing. They teach all skiing styles, including telemark for getting into the backcountry, and you can leave your kids in activities while you ski. At this elevation they get 20 feet of snow a year.

There's a philosophy behind all this, and I don't think profit is the top motivation: The rates are very reasonable for an all-included vacation. The lodge is old and not fancy, but enjoys a lovely setting in woods with its own large pond. Meals are buffet style. Accommodations are in rustic cabins using a shared bathhouse or in strictly utilitarian but well-kept rooms in various buildings without phones or TVs. A typical unit has a living room, a kids' room with four bunks, and a master bedroom. You're not expected to spend much time there, but you'll be perfectly comfortable. Reserve 6 months ahead for camp.

**Stony Creek Lodge.** On Generals Hwy., 10 miles south of Grant Grove (5755 E. Kings Canyon Rd., #101, Fresno, CA 93727). ☎ **559/335-5500.** www.sequoia-kingscanyon.com. 11 units. $96 double, $10 each additional person 13 and older, free 12 and under. AE, DC, MC, V. Closed Oct–May.

This small roadside lodge just north of Sequoia National Park has a store and restaurant downstairs (see p. 464) and a hall of small rooms upstairs. They were clean on my visit but quite drab and out-of-date, without phones or TVs. It's just a place to sleep.

**Wuksachi Lodge.** Just north of Lodgepole. P.O. Box 89, Sequoia National Park, CA 93262. ☎ **888/252-5757** or 559/253-2199. www.visitsequoia.com. 102 units. $130–$185 double, $10 each additional person age 13 and over, 12 and under free. Crib or extra bed $11. AE, DC, DISC, MC, V.

This new lodge shows how classic rustic park architecture can be updated into a modern hotel. The hillside buildings are solid as rock, with cedar and granite exteriors, and the rooms were built with top-quality materials and craftsmanship — room doors are solid wood, and the large bathrooms have the finest countertops. The large rooms have high ceilings and are decorated with Mission-style furniture. They have telephones and coffeemakers. The lodge building, however, is a long walk (the staff uses golf carts), and there are no elevators. You'll drive to most activities, because the lodge stands off on its own; but in the winter a network of 28 miles of diagonal stride ski trails meets the hotel, and the inexpensive winter rates include equipment use. The restaurant is listed under "Where to Eat" (p. 464).

## Off the Beaten Track

**Cedar Grove Lodge.** On Hwy. 180, 32 miles from Grant Grove (5755 E. Kings Canyon Rd., #101, Fresno, CA 93727). ☎ 559/565-4040. www.sequoia-kingscanyon.com. 21 units. $90 double, $10 each additional person 13 and older, free 12 and under. AE, DC, MC, V. Closed Oct–Apr.

The location on the floor of Kings Canyon is what makes these rooms precious — they're the only ones. The accommodations consist of dated but comfortable standard rooms with two queen beds, off a central hallway above the grocery store and snack bar, in a somewhat rumbly plywood structure. On one end, the hallway ends in a pleasant upper deck where guests sit and look out over the Kings River. The small bathrooms have shower stalls, not tubs. While rooms are air-conditioned, they lack telephones or TVs. Unless you book one of the three kitchenette units, which rent for the same price, you will have to eat at the snack bar, described on p. 464. Also, don't stay here if you have trouble with stairs.

**Hume Lake Christian Camps.** 64144 Hume Lake Rd., Hume, CA 93628. ☎ 559/335-2000 summer, 559/251-6043 winter. Fax 559/335-2523 summer, 559/251-4003 winter. www.humelake.org. 32 hotel rooms. $105 double, $23 additional person 12 and up, $19 ages 7–11, $16 ages 2–6. Rates include choice of 2 meals daily. MC, V.

This nondenominational Christian conference center is an incredible vacation value for families, who can use the rooms and facilities in summer like a hotel, regardless of their interest in the Christian programming. A person uncomfortable with religious messages might be uncomfortable here, however, because the camp's ministry through conferences of hundreds of people all year — couples, teens, and families — is its true purpose. Camps for various ages are offered in summer. (Schedules are on the website.) The facilities on the lovely 360-acre site are too many to list here, but include the lakefront, with boats and canoes to rent; bikes for rent for the country roads; skis and skates in the winter; a large outdoor pool; and so on. The hotel rooms are huge and immaculate, with plenty of room for a family with a crib, and have attractive details and historic photos of the camp. The already-low rate includes two buffet meals a day of your choice at the on-site Pine Tree Inn restaurant. A store and gas station are on-site, too.

**Silver City Lodge.** On Mineral King Rd. (P.O. Box 56), Three Rivers, CA 93271. ☎ 559/561-3223 summer, 805/528-2730 winter. Fax 805/528-8039. www.silvercityresort.com. 14 units. Cabins $70–$150, chalets $200–$250. Closed Oct–May.

On the road to the remote Mineral King Valley, the same family has offered lodgings, meals, and famous pie since the 1930s. It's a place to come for a while and decompress in the cool mountain air, far from traffic or travel but near great high-country trails; getting here is too hard to justify less than a couple of nights at least. They have a playground too. The nine cabins are cute and cozy, ranging from a rustic unit with kerosene light and bare wood walls and floor to one with a full kitchen, two bedrooms, and a big wood stove. They share a bathhouse. Three larger chalets are modern three-bedroom houses with cedar siding and stone foundations and full bathrooms. They have electricity and Internet access, but no phones. Book the chalets at least 3 months ahead; the cabins are easier to reserve.

## In the Backcountry

**Bearpaw Meadow High Sierra Camp.** 11½ miles east of Giant Forest. ☎ 888/252-5757. 6 2-bed tents. $150 per person for 2, $75 for 3rd person in tent (without bed); rates include meals. Closed mid-Sept to mid-June.

The camp, operated by Delaware North Park Services (see "Sequoia-Kings Canyon Address Book," p. 437), gives those lucky enough to

# PARK CAMPING BASICS: TOILETS, SHOWERS & LAUNDRY

The campground bathrooms at Sequoia and Kings Canyon are typical of national parks and forests. We found that some were better kept up than those at other parks, perhaps because of lighter use. They have only cold water. Public showers are more plentiful here than at other parks.

The showers at **Lodgepole,** open May to October, operate with quarters and cost 75¢. There aren't enough, though, so you might have to wait at popular times. The year-round coin-op laundry is large and stays open, like the showers, daily 8am to 8pm. The showers might be closed for cleaning at midday. At Grant Grove, campers can use the grungy showers only during the inconvenient hours of 11am to 4pm, when the cabin guests aren't using them. They cost $3.

Showers at **Cedar Grove** are dedicated to the campers. They cost $3; use of a towel is $1. In the summer, the showers are open all day and into the evening, but closed during the middle of the day on weekdays. The laundry is open daily from 8am to 6pm.

Other showers for campers are in the Mineral King area at **Silver City Lodge** near the Atwell Mill Campground, and in Sequoia National Forest at **Stony Creek Lodge** on Generals Highway near Stony Creek Campground (9am–5pm daily, $3 per person).

get reservations the chance to hike into the mountainous backcountry without having to carry gear — a bed and an excellent hot meal are waiting. The camp is at the intersection of several trails at 7,500 feet elevation. Tents are set up for two, but a third person can sleep on the floor. Reservations become available January 2 for the whole summer and are quickly filled; however, there is a 60-day cancellation policy, so if you call exactly 60 days before the date you want, you have a chance of getting it.

**Pear Lake Ski Hut.** 6 miles from Wolverton Meadow. Contact Sequoia Natural History Association (see "Sequoia-Kings Canyon Address Book," p. 437). $15 per person.

The hut is a destination for a winter backcountry trip, a cabin where everyone packs in together after skiing to the site at 9,200 feet elevation. It's a steep route for experienced skiers, and you must be prepared for winter backcountry travel; the SNHA website (www.sequoiahistory.org) has a checklist.

## In Three Rivers

The small town of Three Rivers, along Highway 198 outside the parks' south (Ash Mountain) entrance, has groceries, family restaurants, and hotels. The highway is known as Sierra Drive in town. This is a hot, arid area, below the Sierra forests. Besides the place I've described below, here are two other family hotels with swimming pools and in-room refrigerators: **Holiday Inn Express Three Rivers,** 40820 Sierra Dr. (☎ 800/HOLIDAY or 559/561-9000; www.basshotels.com/holiday-inn), and **Buckeye Tree Lodge,** 46000 Sierra Dr. (☎ 559/561-5900 www.buckeyetree.com).

**Best Western Holiday Lodge,** 40106 Sierra Dr. (P.O. Box 129), Three Rivers, CA 93271. ☎ 888/523-9909 or 559/561-4119. Fax 559/561-3427. www.bestwesterncalifornia.com. 54 units. $87–$97 double, $4 each additional person over age 12, free 12 and under. AE, DISC, MC, V.

This is a nicely landscaped motel with a shady picnic area, swing set, basketball hoop, pool, and path to the nearby Kaweah River. Large, newer rooms are worth the extra $10, with patios and fireplaces, big TVs, microwaves, and other amenities. The older rooms also were clean and comfortable. A small guest laundry is on-site, and the rate includes a continental breakfast.

# When You Arrive

## Entrance Fees

Sequoia and Kings Canyon national parks are one park in all but name. Rangers collect a fee of $10 per vehicle when you enter, good for 7 days in either park. National passes cover the fee (see "Passes & Fees," in chapter 1, for details). If you're also headed to Yosemite, where the fee is $20, you'll be more than halfway to paying for the $50 National Park Pass to all the parks.

## Visitor Centers
### Park Service

**Grant Grove.** On Hwy. 180, near the Big Stump entrance in Grant Grove Village. ☎ **559/565-4307.** Summer daily 8am–5pm; winter daily 9am–4:30pm.

This visitor center exhibits on the giant sequoias were installed in 1963, but we found them interesting anyway. The photographs of the loggers felling the grand trees are memorable. A 24-foot round room is the size of a sequoia trunk, with a tiny sequoia seed displayed in the middle of it. A 10-minute slide show gives an overview of Grant Grove, and there's a desk for questions and a bookstore.

**Lodgepole.** On Generals Hwy., just north of Giant Forest. ☎ **559/565-3782.** Summer daily 9am–6pm; winter Fri–Tues 9am–4:30pm.

You could spend more than an hour in this visitor center's excellent museum on park nature. A wall mural explaining the food web is fascinating. There's also a slide program on natural history and an extensive bookstore. Buy tickets for Crystal Cave here. The Lodgepole store, showers, and other facilities are nearby.

**Cedar Grove.** Near the end of Hwy. 180, in Kings Canyon. Daily 9am–5pm. Closed Nov to mid-Apr.

This is a small log cabin where you can ask questions and buy maps.

**Foothills.** At the south end of Generals Hwy., just inside the Ash Mountain entrance. ☎ **559/565-3341.** Summer daily 8am–5pm; winter daily 8am–4:30pm.

Stop here as you enter the park or on the way out of the park to Mineral King to ask questions, buy maps and Crystal Cave tickets, and look at a modest collection of exhibits.

## Forest Service

Approaching the north end of the park on Highway 180, you can pick up National Forest Service information at Sequoia National Forest's **Hume Lake Ranger District** (☎ **559/338-2251**), near Dunlap. It's open weekdays from 8am to 4:30pm.

## Getting Around
### By Car

The twisting roads, especially the south half of Generals Highway, cause carsickness and make for slow driving. Allow an hour from the south entrance to Lodgepole, another hour to Grant Grove, and an hour from Grant Grove to Cedar Grove. Allow 2 hours to cover the 24 miles of Mineral King Road. Several roads are closed in the winter. After November snows, Kings Canyon Highway (Hwy. 180) is closed until late April, and Mineral King Road is closed until late May. Generals Highway north of Lodgepole closes in heavy winter snows and can be blocked for days or even weeks. Other, minor roads also remain closed in the winter.

### By RV

This is not a great park for RVs. There are few places to hook up your rig near the park, and several key roads are not recommended or are just plain unsafe for large vehicles. The Park Service recommends RVs over 22 feet stay off Generals Highway (Hwy. 198) from Lodgepole to the south entrance, and very large RVs or trailers are prohibited on most

**Emergencies**   Dial ☎ **911** from anywhere in the park. The main park number (☎ **559/565-3341**) connects to park dispatch 24 hours a day. First aid is available at the visitor centers. The nearest **hospital** is at 215 Crispi Ave. in Exeter (☎ **559/592-2151**), down Highway 198 most of the way to Visalia from the south (Ash Mountain) entrance.

**Stores**   Small grocery stores with food, camping supplies, and other necessities are run by park concessionaires at Lodgepole, Grant Grove, and Cedar Grove. Hours are daily from 8am to 8pm in the summer, and from 9am to 5pm the rest of the year; the Cedar Grove store, however, is closed during the winter. Convenience stores are located at Silver City Lodge on the Mineral King Road and at the Hume Lake Christian Camps.

**Banks**   An ATM is in the lobby of the lodge in Grant Grove. Bank of the Sierra on the main drag in Three Rivers also has an ATM.

**Post Office**   Grant Grove Village and Lodgepole Village each have postal stations.

**Gear Sales & Rental**   The camping supplies at the park stores offer the only gear for sale. The closest sporting-goods stores are in Visalia and Fresno. You can rent bikes, boats, skis, and skates at Hume Lake Christian Camps (p. 451), and skis and snowshoes are for rent at the Montecito-Sequoia Lodge (p. 450) and Lodgepole Market.

park roads; they simply won't fit. Narrow roads closed entirely to RVs large or small include Mineral King Road and the road to Crystal Cave.

## In Any Vehicle

**Gasoline:** No gas is for sale in the park proper, but there are gas stations at Hume Lake Christian Camps (p. 451), at Silver City Lodge on Mineral King Road (p. 451), and at Kings Canyon Lodge on Highway 180 on the way to Cedar Grove. Silver City and Kings Canyon lodges both use old-fashioned pumps that measure the fuel in a glass cylinder, museum pieces in action.

**Driving to the East Side:** You can't drive from the west to the east side of the parks directly, and unless you have a very good reason to go, the trip probably isn't worth it. Without delays, the trip from the midpoint on the west side to the midpoint on the east side takes 6 hours. The year-round route takes you south to Bakersfield, east on Highway 178, then north on Highway 395. The other way is to go north and cross the mountains on

Yosemite's Tioga Road (open in the summer only), and then go south on 395. Or you could hike it. That takes about a week.

## By Shuttle Bus

A shuttle runs in July and August from Lodgepole Village and Wuksachi Lodge to the Giant Forest area. It's free and allows you to ride one way and hike back on a great network of trails.

## KEEPING SAFE & HEALTHY

Besides the special warnings below, Sequoia and Kings Canyon have risks associated with black bears, dehydration, elevation, giardia, lightning, poison oak, and snakebites. I've covered those in chapter 1 under "Dealing with Hazards" (p. 26).

## Carsickness

The twisting Generals Highway or Mineral King Road could upset the strongest stomach. Leave plenty of time for this route so that you can stop and get some air. Make sure those who are susceptible can see outside and get fresh air. Avoid greasy foods. We've had good luck with children's Dramamine (advice on its use is under "Seasickness & Motion Sickness," in chapter 1).

## Drowning

This is the most common cause of death in the park. Swimming in the rivers is fun, but it's easy to misjudge the power of moving water, which can appear still on the surface. Once you're in, it can be difficult to get out on slippery rocks. Children playing near streams can fall in and disappear. Accidents happen quickly. Your good judgment is your safeguard. If in doubt, swim only where others are swimming or talk to a ranger. Never, ever dive in.

# ENJOYING THE PARKS

## NATURAL PLACES
### Grant Grove

A mile from the visitor center, the compact Grant Grove is a good place to see your first sequoias on entering the park. A paved loop trail less than a half mile in length has stops keyed to a guide that costs $1 at the visitor center.

The **General Grant** tree is the third largest in the world and is the national Christmas tree and a national shrine. It's 40 feet across at the base but relatively young among the biggest sequoias, at 1,800 to 2,000 years old. This and many other sequoias got their names from Civil War heroes, because that war was still fresh in the memories of explorers who came here in the 1870s. In more than a century since, the trees haven't changed much, but the names have come to seem strange — not big enough for these big trees.

Another highlight of Grant Grove is a hollow fallen tree you can walk through. It was once used as a stable, cabin, and even a hotel, although not one I think I would recommend. The north loop, in a less-visited area of the grove, adds 1 unpaved mile to the walk.

### Near Grant Grove

The park and national forest around Grant Grove contain some incredible and rarely visited places, open secrets that most visitors fly right by.

My favorite area here is peaceful, awesome **Redwood Canyon,** the largest surviving sequoia grove. It's a little tricky to find. Drive 5 miles south from Grant Grove on Generals Highway to a sign pointing left that reads HUME LAKE/QUAIL FLAT; turn right instead of left, on the unmarked dirt road, descending among immense trees 1.9 miles to the Redwood Canyon Trailhead. Here a network of trails descends into the grove, with loops of up to 10 miles (pick up a map at the Grant Grove Visitor Center). Gigantic trees fill the land and there are few other people; you get the opportunity to feel an ant-sized part of the forest, not just a tourist. With a backcountry permit (see p. 449) you can spend the night among the big trees.

A great family hike is to be had on the **Park Ridge Trail,** a mountaintop with great views that you can hike without much elevation gain because your car does the climbing to the trailhead. Take the road marked Panoramic Point behind Grant Grove Village and drive 2.3 steep, twisty miles to the parking lot. The trail follows the ridge with views on both sides (smog permitting) 2.5 miles to a fire lookout.

**Hume Lake,** part of the new Giant Sequoia National Monument, lies in national forest land behind Grant Grove. It is a woodsy recreation area, with lake swimming, boating and fishing, and many miles of dirt forest roads for biking. Climbing those roads to the east leads to the top of the mountains above Kings Canyon, beautiful high country with trails leading down into the park. Explore! To get there, take the roads to Hume Lake and Quail Flat 5 miles south of Grant Grove on the Generals Highway; or take the Kings

From highway pull-outs and mountaintops looking into San Joaquin Valley, on the west side of the Sierra Nevada, a cloud often fills in the lowlands like water in a lake. That dirty haze is called **smog,** and it does a lot worse than mess up the view. Smog has a chemical in it called **ozone** that hurts trees and our lungs. Scientists can tell which trees have been damaged by ozone when they find brown spots on them. About 40% of the ponderosa and Jeffrey pines in Sequoia and Kings Canyon national parks have the spots. Experiments show that if the ozone pollution gets much worse, young sequoias could be hurt, too.

Ozone is good in the upper atmosphere, near space, where a thin layer of it protects the earth from some of the sun's burning ultraviolet light. But ozone isn't natural near the earth, where we breathe it. Down here, it is made by people.

When we burn fuel in our cars, trucks, factories, and power plants, we take in air, use it, change it, and then put it back out through the tailpipe or smokestack. Oxygen and nitrogen, the two most common elements in air, combine during burning into **nitrogen dioxide** ($NO_2$), made of molecules with 2 atoms of oxygen and 1 of nitrogen. In 1 or 2 days of hot, sunny weather, ultraviolet light from the sun helps the nitrogen dioxide hook up with another oxygen atom from the air and lose the nitrogen atom. That leaves molecules with 3 oxygen atoms ($O_3$). Normal oxygen that we breathe, and that supports life on earth, has 2 atoms in each molecule ($O_2$). Add a third atom to the molecule and you have deadly poisonous ozone.

Along the coast of California, people in cities burn a lot of fuel in cars, trucks, and buildings. The nitrogen dioxide they make floats east in the normal winds to the hot, sunny San Joaquin Valley. With lots of sunlight and warm temperatures, the valley is a perfect place for turning nitrogen dioxide into ozone. The ozone made in the valley keeps floating east until it runs into the Sierra Nevada and builds up, waiting for a strong wind to blow it away. The amount of ozone in the air on the west side of Sequoia and Kings Canyon national parks commonly exceeds government health limits. The smog often is worse than that in L.A.

The trees have been hurt most in areas near the valley: Grant Grove, Giant Forest, and Ash Mountain. The ozone hurts their ability to use sunlight to make food, which is called **photosynthesis** (it is explained in chapter 22, "Olympic National Park"). The trees don't die from ozone pollution, but because it makes them weaker they might die from insects or disease. In laboratory experiments, scientists have tried growing sequoias in a chamber with lots of ozone. They found that if ozone levels rise 50% from what they are now, the sequoias will have trouble with photosynthesis too.

Highway 6 miles to the Princess Highway and turn toward the lake there.

## Giant Forest

The biggest sequoias grow in Giant Forest, including **General Sherman,** the world's largest tree. But it's not just the size of the biggest tree that makes the grove special. The place feels like it is a towering cathedral of trees. Even the air feels ancient.

The 2-mile-long **Congress Trail** weaves through the forest. It's the most inspiring paved nature trail we've ever walked. Buy the inexpensive guide booklet first. Strollers do fine. A web of other, unpaved trails weaves deeper through the forest. Handy, inexpensive trail guides are for sale at the visitor center, so you can connect loops for a hike of any length. If you're camping at Lodgepole, you can ride the free shuttle in the summer to trailheads in Giant Forest and hike back.

On the south side of the forest, a narrow paved road leads 3 miles through the trees past several curious sites on the way to **Moro Rock** and **Crescent Meadow.** A climb up the rock is not to be missed. It's a barren granite dome

California has done more than any other state to require cars to put out less pollution, but the problems caused by burning fuel go way beyond California. All burning of fuel puts out carbon dioxide, even your campfire or your body burning the fuel of your food. Fuel burns by hooking up carbon in the fuel with oxygen in the air. Adding 1 carbon atom and 2 oxygen atoms makes **carbon dioxide** ($CO_2$). In the past 100 years, people have done a lot of burning — in factories, power plants, cars, furnaces, everywhere — and there's more and more carbon dioxide in the atmosphere. That doesn't hurt us directly. We make carbon dioxide when we breathe, and plants and trees need it. But in the atmosphere, carbon dioxide acts like a roof over the earth, keeping heat from the sun from bouncing off into space. It's called a **greenhouse gas**, because it acts like the glass roof on a greenhouse. Most scientists believe that more carbon dioxide in the atmosphere means a hotter earth, the way a greenhouse gets hotter on a sunny day.

The earth was already warming before humans lit so many fires. The oceans have been coming higher on the land since the last Ice Age as water in huge glaciers melted. What will happen if we speed that up? Scientists disagree. We just don't know enough about how the earth works. But it seems sensible to expect that the seas will rise faster and weather in most places will change. In 50 years, places close to the beach now might be underwater. Places where plants grow now may become deserts while other places become wetter. Ocean currents that influence storms and seasonal climate may change, bringing cold, stormy weather to areas that are warm and mild now. In the mountains, life zones may move, with plants and animals that like warm weather growing at higher elevation as the high country warms. Trees and plants that like cooler weather or need a rare kind of habitat might disappear. The giant sequoia groves already survive only in small areas where they have certain temperatures, soil, moisture, fires, fairly flat ground, and animals to open their cones. If the climate changes in the next century (a brief time in the life of the sequoia), some of these conditions that allow sequoias to survive might change their groves.

World leaders have begun to talk about limiting how much carbon dioxide the people of the earth put into the atmosphere. It's difficult, because to live the way we do, we need our cars and factories. We'd like to be able to draw borders around the national parks to make them safe, and then go on living however we like back home. We're beginning to realize that we can't. We're learning that what we do every day affects all living things in ways we can't predict or control.

---

with a quarter-mile staircase tracing dizzying drops on each side. If the weather is clear, the view from the top is mind-blowing. Drive to the end of the road for the trailhead at Crescent Meadow. Sequoia walks are different here because the meadows contribute light, flowers, and wildlife. At least do the 1.6-mile **Crescent Meadow/Log Meadow Loop,** with the goal of seeing Tharp's Log, a home in a fallen tree made by the area's first white settler. Kids love it.

The Crescent Meadow trailhead also is the starting point for the High Sierra Trail, a back-packing route all the way across the range, or a good day-hiking route that rises gently into the mountains with good views.

## Lodgepole & Wolverton

The Lodgepole campground and visitor center lie in the glacier-carved Tokopah Valley, along the Marble Fork of the Kaweah River. The lodgepole pines in the valley are the last before the tree line and the open granite of the High Sierra. An easy 1.7-mile trail along the river leads to that terrain before coming to a dead end at the head of the valley and **Tokopah**

**Falls.** Along the way, water pours over round granite shelves and boulders, making inviting pools for a swim on a hot day; check at the visitor center to find out whether water levels are safe for swimming.

Many other trails, horseback riding, and skiing start from **Wolverton Road,** which branches a bit over 1 mile south on Generals Highway. The **Alta** and **Lakes trails** lead from Wolverton into the spectacular high country.

## Crystal Cave & Boyden Cave

**Crystal Cave** was carved from marble by Cascade Creek, part of which still flows through a smooth-shaped stone trough on the floor of the passages. Millions of years of dripping water formed thin strands of rock that look like sticky melted cheese stretched apart from a sandwich. In other places, the rock makes daggers, fins, and narrow holes that lead into darkness, and a big gallery where the floor drops away into a chasm (See "Caves," in chapter 17). A ranger-led 50-minute tour travels a half mile of the 3-mile cave from mid-May to early September, between 11am and 4pm daily. You have to buy tickets in advance at the Lodgepole or Foothills visitor center; they're not available at the cave, because the ticket system meters the number of cars at the small lot. Buy your tickets early on weekends; they're $6 for adults, $3 for kids 6 to 12. You can't buy a ticket within 90 minutes of your tour's start. With tickets in hand, drive Generals Highway to a dirt road about 14 miles from the Foothills Visitor Center, and then go 7 miles on that narrow, winding route. RVs and vehicles over 20 feet are not allowed. After parking, present your ticket at a booth and descend a steep quarter-mile trail past the lovely Cascade Falls. Going from Lodgepole to the cave's mouth takes 45 minutes' driving time and 15 minutes' walking time. By the time you get to the cave mouth, you're hot, and the cool dampness inside the mountain feels good — but bring a sweater to avoid a chill in the 48°F underground cave. The hike back up the hill to the parking lot is tiring on a hot day, and some people were having trouble on the day we were there.

**Boyden Cave** also has a neat tour. The rock formations aren't as many or as bizarre as Crystal Cave and the tour is shorter; but Boyden is a lot easier to get to and is plenty long and impressive enough to give you that spooky cave feeling. You also have a good chance of seeing bats. The 45-minute tour covers 750 feet of a 1,000-foot cave in the wall of Kings Canyon in Sequoia National Forest on the way to Cedar Grove. There's a short but steep climb to the mouth from the parking lot and ticket booth by the Kings River. For summer weekends, it's wise to call ahead and reserve a spot on a tour (☎ **209/736-2708; www.caverntours.com**). Tours operate from 10am to 5pm daily May through October and cost $6.50 for adults and $3.25 for children 3 to 13.

## Kings Canyon & Cedar Grove

In 1891 John Muir wrote that Kings Canyon was similar to Yosemite Valley but grander. I'm not sure, but I do think Kings Canyon is a better place to visit. The similarity comes from the way the canyons were made. In each, a river cut a narrow valley; then, a glacier followed, steepened the walls, and flattened the bottom. In each, you can stand in a green meadow by a river and look straight up at cliffs of granite 3,000 feet high. But Kings Canyon is wilder. Partly, that's because the rock is cracked instead of rounded, the river faster, and the journey into the canyon more of an adventure, passing through a narrow gorge of marble. But mostly, King Canyon is wilder because it is not clogged with people. There are only 21 hotel rooms here, and day-trippers usually don't bother with a drive of about an hour one way from Grant Grove. There are plenty of campsites, plus river fishing and swimming, and wonderful hikes where you see few other people.

The **Zumwalt Meadow Trail,** near the end of the road beyond Cedar Grove, is a flat 1-mile loop that crosses the river and then circles the meadow, where you can see the contrast of the powerful cliffs above and delicate ferns and flowers below. The meadow was a glacial lake that has slowly filled (see "The Signs of Change," in chapter 17). It's a lovely hike, easy enough for anyone in the family. There's a sandy spot just over the footbridge where people swim, but check with a ranger on the safety of the river level.

For a more challenging outing, the **Paradise Valley Trail** is a gorgeous, mostly shady hike to scenic Mist Falls, at 4 miles, or 6 miles to Paradise Valley itself, a beautifully pastoral mountain valley. The trail begins at the end of the road and is flat or rises only gradually until you approach the falls, when it gets quite steep the rest of the way to Paradise Valley. After the 2-mile mark, you branch to the left to follow the South Fork of the Kings River as it tumbles over rounded granite down the canyon. There are several appealing spots to play in the water, conditions permitting. Beware of slippery rocks, however, especially walking near the falls, where there are some dangerous spots. On the way back, hike on the south side of the Kings River on the Sentinel Trail.

From near Cedar Grove Village, the **Hotel Creek Trail** climbs steeply through arid terrain to pine forest on the north side of the canyon, looking back down into the canyon with impressive views. Once you make that stiff climb, you can return on the Lewis Creek Trail to make a 7-mile loop. Start early, because it's hot. The **Don Cecil Trail** takes you up the canyon side on the south, with a spur to the top of 8,500-foot Lookout Peak; only strong hikers should try to go all the way. Or have a horse do the work. Trail rides and backcountry trips are available from a stable listed under "Horseback Riding & Stock Packing" (p. 461).

## Mineral King Valley

By starting at this rocky, 7,500-foot-elevation valley, you can quickly hike into the Sierra's open high country on an extraordinary network of lightly used trails. The routes tend to be steep, but they lead to amazing places, with grand views every time you turn around. I'll never forget an overnight to the Monarch Lakes, a steep 4.5 miles to a pair of lakes sitting above 10,000 feet in the lap of sheer, rocky peaks. It seemed primeval. Short of the road's end, there are several good forest hikes, too, including hikes to remote sequoia groves from the Atwell Mill area. But don't zip up here for a day hike. Unless you are camping at Atwell Creek or Cold Springs campground (p. 448) or have a cabin at Silver City Lodge (p. 4451, reserve this area for backpacking or horse trips (there's a pack station at the end of the road; see p. 461). The drive and the hikes are too long and the elevation is too high to try to do much in 1 day.

The remoteness and quiet that make the area so appealing owe to the difficulty of getting there. The ludicrously windy Mineral King Road leads 24 miles from Three Rivers, about 1 mile outside the park. Over much of its length it snakes back and forth so sharply you can do less than 10 miles an hour and is wide enough only for one car. RVs can't use the road. Cars have to creep along, and even then you will need to stop to prevent motion sickness. The road is closed due to snow from early November to Memorial Day.

## Mt. Whitney

At 14,495 feet, Mt. Whitney is the highest peak in the United States outside Alaska. It's on the east side of the park, and you can't see it from the west side where visitors normally go. To get from the west to the east takes more than 5 hours of driving (see "Getting Around," p. 453). From mid-July to early October, climbing Mt. Whitney requires no technical skills, but the elevation and 7,000-foot gain over a 10.7-mile trail, one way, are beyond the ability of all but the strongest hikers, especially those who aren't used to the elevation. Also, you need a permit even for a day hike in the Mt. Whitney Zone; permits are given by lottery, and applications are accepted only in the month of February. Details are online at www.r5.fs.fed.us/inyo/vvc/mtwhtny/, or call the **Interagency Visitor Center** at (☎ **760/876-6222**). There are many other beautiful climbs in the park without red tape or travel hassles; check at the visitor centers.

## PLACES FOR LEARNING

The new **Giant Forest Museum,** on Generals Highway in Giant Forest, was unfinished at this writing, but should be in place for the 2002 season. It will teach about the giant trees that surround it. Hours had not yet been set. The museum occupies an old market in a park village that used to stand here among the sequoias, the other buildings of which the park service wisely decided to demolish to bring back the trees' natural setting.

The **Walter Fry Nature Center,** in the Lodgepole Campground, is a simple but engaging children's natural history museum, with hands-on displays that could keep a curious kid's attention for more than an hour. The center is the base for a children's program that's as good as any we encountered at the parks we visited; check there to find out what your kids can get involved in. The center is open in July and August, daily from 10am to 5pm.

The visitor centers are described on p. 453.

## ACTIVITIES
## Backpacking

No road crosses the Sierra Nevada from Yosemite to Bakersfield. That's one measure of how remote this country is. Including the wilderness areas in the national forests, a 150-mile-long section of the Sierra is largely without human mark, one of the biggest such areas in the U.S. outside Alaska. Ninety percent of the national park land is accessible only by foot — yours or a horse's. There are 800 miles of trails in the parks, more in the surrounding national forests, and significant areas without trails to be explored on side hikes or orienteering treks.

But to get into the wilderness, you don't have to attempt a weeklong journey across the mountains or climb the highest peaks. You also can enjoy the parks, and really get to know your family, by hiking 4 or 5 miles to a mountain lake and camping there for a couple of days, exploring the area on day hikes or just playing in the mountains. With areas like Redwood Canyon to explore (p. 455), you don't need to choose a very tough route, so there's no need for beginners to shy away from giving it a try. Books and maps for planning a trek are listed under "Reading Up" (p. 443).

Backpackers need to learn about avoiding black bear, especially how to store food. Some backcountry campsites have bear-proof metal cabinets; otherwise, you need to use a bear-resistant canister. Read "Dangerous Wildlife," in chapter 1, and ask for details when you get your backcountry permit.

Another option is to join a guided hike (see "Field Seminars," p. 464), or to travel guided on horseback or with pack animals to carry your gear (see "Horseback Riding & Stock Packing," p. 461).

## Fishing

Lots of people fish for trout with spinning or fly-fishing gear all over the parks; almost everywhere is open. However, complicated state fishing regulations apply in the park and should be studied. You can get regulation information, limited tackle, and licenses at the Lodgepole, Grant Grove, and Cedar Grove stores. Anyone age 16 or older needs a California license. Fishing gear is not available for rent anywhere in the parks, so bring your own. Steve Sorensen's *Day Hiking Sequoia* (see "Reading Up," p. 443) contains advice on where to fish, and rangers will give you ideas, too. Some popular areas suitable for kids are the **Kings River** in Cedar Grove, the **Kaweah River** along the Tokopah Falls Trail near Lodgepole, and **Dorst Creek.** Harder-to-reach spots will have bigger and more numerous fish.

# Hiking

These parks have as many great day hikes as anywhere we have visited, with wonderful destinations and not too many other people. On many routes, welcoming stream pools beckon for a cooling splash. Even many of the sequoia grove trails are lightly used, although highlights in Grant Grove and Giant Forest are liable to be crowded on weekends. There are two main kinds of hikes at the parks. The easier routes explore the forests, meadows, river valleys, and sequoia groves of the western Sierra's wooded, midlevel elevations or follow creeks in the hot foothills. More challenging routes climb up into the high country. High Sierra terrain of granite bedrock and long views isn't gained without a climb at Sequoia and Kings Canyon.

Almost anywhere you find yourself, good hikes are nearby. I've listed some favorites with each area covered under "Natural Places" (p. 455), and with the descriptions of the Atwell Mill, Buckeye Flat, Dorst, Lodgepole, and Potwisha campgrounds. Get maps and trail details from the publications listed under "Reading Up" (p. 443); for most visitors, the $2 *Map & Trail Guide* for each park is absolutely essential.

# Horseback Riding & Stock Packing

Pack stations are located at four places in the parks. Each is a little different; I've described them below. You can take a short beginner's ride or a long trip into the wilderness. Day trips range from 1 hour to all day and travel through level terrain or climb to high overlooks. Overnight trips penetrate the backcountry. The outfitters provide the food and gear and cook for you, or you can bring your own and get a discount. They'll even pack you out to a backcountry location and leave you, and then come back and get you at a prearranged time. Few parks are better suited to seeing wilderness this way. Reserve backcountry trips as far ahead as possible — some dates

book up 1 year in advance. Day trips might not require reservations, but call ahead anyway.

# Kings Canyon National Park

At **Grant Grove Stables,** rides leave from near the lodge and go through the forest. A 1-hour ride is $12; the longest ride, 2 hours, costs $30. Beginners and kids as young as 5 are okay.

**Cedar Grove Pack Station** offers short hourly rides to the river, longer rides that climb to overlooks and higher forest terrain, and overnight trips. The 1-hour ride is $20, all day costs $80, and there are choices in between. All overnights are customized and cost around $120 per person per day, with food and gear included.

Call either stable at ☎ **559/565-3464** in the summer, ☎ **559/337-1273** in the winter to reserve; written correspondence should be addressed to P.O. Box 295, Three Rivers, CA 93271.

# Sequoia National Park

Wolverton Pack Station, 2 miles from the Lodgepole area, offers day trips and overnights. A 2-hour ride is $40; all day, $75. Rides go as far as the high country at Pear Lake or 11½ miles to the High Sierra Camp at Bear Paw Meadow. Riders must be at least 8 years old.

With close access to the high country, **Mineral King Pack Station** specializes in overnights and backcountry fishing trips, and can travel all the way to Mt. Whitney. It offers a variety of trips, depending on how much work you want to do and whether you walk or ride. Prices start at $75 per day per animal, plus $125 per day for the packer and horse that accompany your group. Children must be at least 10 years old, and riders must weigh less than 215 pounds.

These two pack stations can be reached at P.O. Box 63, Sequoia National Park, CA 93262-0063 (☎ **559/565-3039**) in the summer; or at 3287 N. Palo Verde Blvd., Lake

# EXPERIMENT: MAPPING RIVER EDDIES

Rivers are fascinating to watch. The water all goes the same place, but it moves through the riverbed in complicated patterns, around rocks and snags, over ledges, and into slower pools and backwaters. Here's an experiment that helps you make a map of patterns in the river that you can't see. Grown-ups should do it with kids so that they don't fall into the water and drown. Almost any river will do, but one with some shallow water where you can safely wade works best.

Eddies are places in a river where the water flows in a circle or spiral, such that at some point the water is flowing upstream. They're places where fish can rest from swimming against the current and where lots of floating sticks and bugs get caught up. An eddy sometimes happens where the river suddenly gets wider or runs into a boulder or log — anywhere the flow of water has to circle to fill in a place that is out of the direct current. You usually can't see an eddy directly, but you can see how it affects things that are floating on the water. That's how this experiment maps eddies.

You'll need a piece of paper and a pencil or pen. Scout the river edge for a place you think might have an eddy — a small bay or somewhere that the water is suddenly calmer. Draw a detailed map of the immediate area, just a few feet up and down the stream and as far out as you can safely reach. You'll need to make it detailed and accurate enough that you can judge easily where something in the river belongs on your map. You could try measuring with a stick or a piece of string.

Now find something that floats to drop in the water: pieces of a cone from a tree, pine needles, pieces of leaves, or something like that. It needs to be small and light. Drop the first one into the river at a spot near the upstream end of your map, as far out into the stream as you can safely reach. Watch its course carefully, and place a line on the map showing where it went. Now drop another item a little closer to shore and mark its course on the map. Keep up the process until you have lines showing where the current flows on every part of your map.

If you end up with any circles or curlicues, you've found an eddy. Even if you don't, you have a map of the current in that part of the river. It's fun to predict where each current line will go before you drop the next leaf or pine needle in the water. Does the current starting in each spot always go to the same place? Do small differences in where you start always mean small differences in where you end up? Do the current lines ever cross? Why do you think the water slows down or circles when it goes into an eddy or wide spot? Can you figure out how the water gets into the eddy and how it gets out again?

---

Havasu City, AZ 86404 (☎ 520/855-5885) in the winter.

## Swimming

On a hot hike, a dip in a chilly mountain stream is a dose of paradise. Children don't seem to worry so much about how cold the water is. Grown-ups may not stay in for long, but still get a clean, rejuvenated feeling from a quick splash. Mountain lakes tend to be extremely cold, suitable only for in-and-out shock therapy for hot, sweaty bodies. Beware of hypothermia if the weather is anything but warm and still. Other safety information is covered under "Drowning" (p. 455); take it

seriously, for these waters take lives every summer.

The best river swimming holes are in the foothills, near the south end of the Generals Highway. Just inside the park, before the Ash Mountain entrance, the **Indian Head Swimming Hole** is a quarter-mile off the road. A one-eighth-mile trail leads to **Hospital Rock Swimming Hole** from the picnic area of the same name on Generals Highway. Other good spots are located at the Potwisha and Buckeye Flat campgrounds (p. 445). Some of these spots, with clear, glassy water overhung by tree branches, are lovely and wonderfully peaceful, a small slice of the Eden the

Potwisha Indians must have enjoyed in these mountains. Fewer pool-sized swimming holes occur at the higher elevations; but there are spots to splash in the water in the Kaweah River near Lodgepole and on hikes from Kings Canyon, and Hume Lake has good swimming, covered above under "Natural Places" (p. 455). Other possibilities show up on hikes, but be careful.

## Winter Sports

With many roads and facilities closed by snow, the parks receive far fewer visitors in the winter. But those who do come have the chance to see the giant trees on a sharply contrasting background of white, and there are some superb cross-country ski trails and snowshoeing opportunities. Experienced Backcountry skiers will find few better places for adventures. There's even a hut for overnight stays at Pear Lake (see p. 452). Snow conditions for skiing and snowshoeing at the elevation of Grant Grove and Giant Forest usually last from January to March. In the foothills, snow doesn't stick, and hiking continues all year. At this writing there were few groomed trails within park boundaries, but the Lodgepole market rents snowshoes and skis for touring and backcountry trekking. Skis also are for rent at Grant Grove. The best ski trails are found in Sequoia National Forest, at Montecito-Sequoia Lodge, which has an extensive network groomed for diagonal stride and skating, a rope tow, rentals, and lessons for all levels and styles, including backcountry skiing (see p. 450). Sledding areas are at Wolverton, Big Stump (near the north entrance), and Azalea Campground, near Grant Grove.

## PROGRAMS
### Children's Programs

The rangers at the **Walter Fry Nature Center,** in the Lodgepole Campground, run summer sessions that children enjoy and learn from. A ranger also leads a daily **Kids' Walk** for children ages 5 to 8, without other grown-ups along. Our son loved it. The time is listed in the park newspaper, the *Sequoia Bark.* Sign up in advance at the center to avoid having too many kids show up. Outside the center, a **campfire program** just for kids takes place on summer afternoons.

The **Junior Ranger program** at Sequoia is simple and nicely pitched at the right age levels. The Jay Award is for children 5 to 8; it uses a booklet with activities that don't require much reading. The Raven Award gets into more complex natural-history topics and involves more writing. In addition to the workbooks, kids collect trash and attend at least two programs or go on a nature walk; it's not difficult to do in a day. The best part is getting the award, a patch. Go to a campfire program 20 minutes before it starts so that the ranger can check the child's work. When the program begins, each patch winner is called in front of the whole audience to receive the patch and get a round of applause. Pick up the booklet for $2.33 at the visitor center or nature center.

## Family & Adult Programs & Camps

Besides these options, Montecito-Sequoia Lodge (p. 450) and Hume Lake Christian Camps (p. 451) offer some great family choices with structured activities and camps.

### PARK SERVICE

Ranger walks and talks change often. Current offerings are listed on bulletin boards at campgrounds and visitor centers. Generally, they're casual — you just show up at the time and place.

**Campfire programs** happen every night in the summer at Lodgepole, Dorst, Sunset (at Grant Grove), and Sentinel (at Cedar Grove) campgrounds, and less frequently at Potwisha Campground, Mineral King, and Silver City Lodge. The programs usually involve an outdoor slide show and lecture and, depending on the ranger, some singing or other fun.

A campsite or the woods are the perfect playground, but adults should check for poison oak. Most picnic areas are marked on the park map you'll receive when you arrive. The picnic areas that aren't shown are at the **Foothills** and **Lodgepole visitor centers, Big Stump,** and **Mineral King.** In Sequoia National Forest, picnic at **Stony Creek,** which is on Generals Highway between Lodgepole and Grant Grove, or **Grizzly Falls,** just outside the park near Cedar Grove.

## FIELD SEMINARS

Sequoia Natural History Association offers sessions with highly qualified leaders — professors, researchers, teachers, and outdoors experts — teaching natural history and outdoor skills. Most sessions are 1 to 3 days long, and many include group camping. Generally, they're aimed at adults, although teens would enjoy some of the offerings; call and ask before signing up. Some sessions may be especially for families, but the lineup changes annually. Prices range from $10 to $50 for a 1-day session, up to $500 for a weeklong winter mountaineering trek. For program information, contact the association (see "Sequoia-Kings Canyon Address Book," p. 437).

# WHERE TO EAT

## LOW-STRESS MEALS

**Grant Grove Village** has a good, old-fashioned family restaurant that looks as if it hasn't changed in 30 years. There are a lunch counter, a buffet, and big platters heaped with food. Service is friendly and familiar, like that at a truck stop. The servers know how to treat children, although the portions are too large for little ones. Lunch is $5 to $7, dinner $8 to $16. It is open year-round, summer 7am to 8pm, winter 7am to 7pm.

**Cedar Grove's** only restaurant is a snack bar with a menu beefed up to serve the lodge guests, with items such as New York steak, trout, or pasta. You order at the counter, sit on fast-food–style benches, and eat off paper plates. Dinner main courses range up to $16, but most of the menu is in the snack-bar range. It is open during the season 7am to 8pm.

A snack bar and deli are located at Lodgepole, with patio seating, open daily 8am to 8pm in summer. The price range is $3.25 to $9.

The restaurant at **Stony Creek Lodge** serves pizza, pasta, and sandwiches in a family-dining atmosphere. Main courses are $5 to $12 for lunch or dinner, served noon to 8pm summer only.

Up Mineral King Road, I enjoyed a good meal and lots of iced tea on the deck at **Silver City Lodge** after a tough hike. The simple food is well done and service is friendly, with burgers $4 to $6.50, dinners around $9, and kids' items such as pb&j or grilled cheese $2. They're justly famous for their pies. Open hours in season are Thursday through Monday from 7am to 8:30pm, Tuesday and Wednesday for coffee and pie only.

## BEST-BEHAVIOR MEALS

The restaurant at Wuksachi Lodge occupies a room with a high ceiling, big windows, and a large fireplace — despite being brand new, it looks historic. Reservations are required for dinner, but you don't need to spend a lot, because the lunch menu is served in the evening too. Main courses at lunch are $6 to $7.75, dinner up to $22. Breakfast is served 7:30am to 9:30am, lunch 11:30am to 2pm, and dinner 4:30 to 8:30pm.

# The West Coast

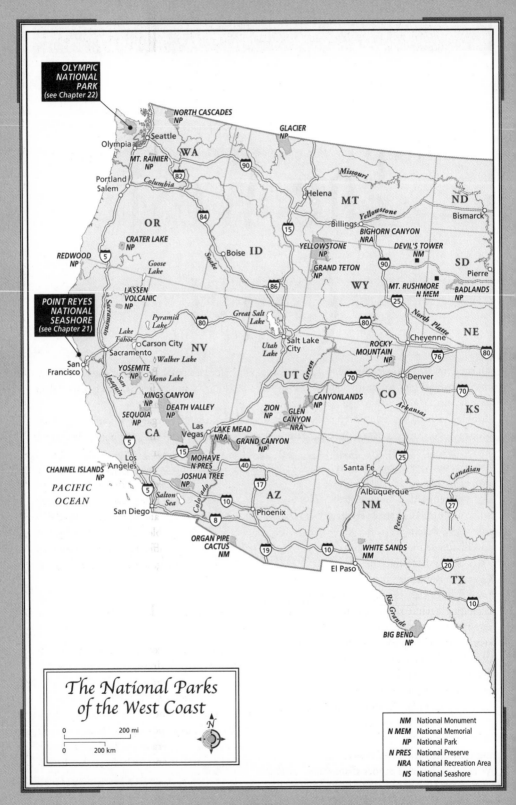

NORTH CASCADES
NP

GLACIER
NP

Seattle

Olympia

MT. RAINIER
NP

WA

Portland
Salem

Columbia

*Missouri*

Helena

MT

ND

*Yellowstone*

Billings

Bismarck

BIGHORN CANYON
NRA

DEVIL'S TOWER
NM

CRATER LAKE
NP

Boise

ID

REDWOOD
NP

*Goose
Lake*

*Snake*

YELLOWSTONE
NP

GRAND TETON
NP

WY

MT. RUSHMORE
N MEM

SD

Pierre

LASSEN
VOLCANIC
NP

*Pyramid
Lake*

*Great Salt
Lake*

BADLANDS
NP

*North Platte*

NE

*Lake
Tahoe*

Carson City

NV

Sacramento

*Walker Lake*

*Utah
Lake*

Salt Lake
City

ROCKY
MOUNTAIN
NP

Cheyenne

San
Francisco

YOSEMITE
NP

*Mono Lake*

*Green*

UT

CO

Denver

KS

KINGS CANYON
NP

DEATH VALLEY
NP

ZION
NP

GLEN
CANYON
NRA

CANYONLANDS
NP

*Arkansas*

SEQUOIA
NP

CA

Las
Vegas

LAKE MEAD
NRA

GRAND CANYON
NP

Los
Angeles

MOHAVE
N-PRES

Santa Fe

*Canadian*

CHANNEL ISLANDS
NP

PACIFIC
OCEAN

JOSHUA TREE
NP

*Salton
Sea*

Albuquerque

NM

*Pecos*

San Diego

*Colorado*

AZ

Phoenix

ORGAN PIPE
CACTUS
NM

WHITE SANDS
NM

El Paso

TX

*Rio Grande*

BIG BEND
NP

*Sacramento*

*San
Joaquin*

# The National Parks
of the West Coast

0        200 mi

0        200 km

N

| | |
|---|---|
| NM | National Monument |
| N MEM | National Memorial |
| NP | National Park |
| N PRES | National Preserve |
| NRA | National Recreation Area |
| NS | National Seashore |

# Ecology: Fitting It Together

In the Hoh Rain Forest, life seems to swim in the air around you, entering your lungs with each breath. Mosses hang from tree branches, drinking it in. They don't need to touch the ground because the air itself brings them all the water and nutrition they need. Drowsy light spreads evenly over soft green shapes, filtering down through trees so tall that it seems as if the sky is missing. All is glowing green. There's no sense of time. The moss below looks so thick that if you were to lie down you might sink in and disappear into an enchanted dream.

A few miles west, on the coast of the Olympic Peninsula, breakers roar ashore in parallel lines starting far out in the mist and exploding against rocky sea stacks that stand away from shore like castle turrets. The spray swirls into the air and joins the mist. The colors are different from those in the forest — grays, blues, and a colder green — but the moist, salty air carries the same feeling of magical, abundant life. Down the coast, it goes on. At Point Reyes, the waves pound ferociously on shores of rock or white sand, and the blowing mist blurs the line between land and sea. Windy beaches and moors share the wildness

of the open ocean. Back from the shore, redwoods thrive in the fog, reaching higher than any other trees on earth.

Nature is a smorgasbord here on the West Coast, with different, dramatic ecosystems within a half-hour drive of each other. Stunning places are easy to find and be alone in, along the shoreline and in forests and coastal grassland. There's lots to do and learn in sand, tide pools, and rain forest. Travel distances are manageable and cities close by, but these parks don't suffer much from crowding; with some planning, it doesn't have to be an issue.

## POINT REYES NATIONAL SEASHORE

San Franciscans keep this place mostly to themselves. People drive an hour from the city for weekends in the romantic B&Bs of idyllic west Marin County, but during the week the place is deserted. The national seashore is a triangular peninsula poking out from the coast just north of San Francisco, with many miles of lonely beaches and high, foggy headlands.

Landward, superb sea-kayaking waters and protected forest lands are rich with bird and marine life. Adjoining public lands harbor forests of giant redwoods and miles of hiking trails. The weather is mild all year, making Point Reyes good for a visit most of the time.

## OLYMPIC NATIONAL PARK

Located on the diverse area known as Olympic Peninsula, west of Puget Sound and Seattle, the park is a collection of exceptional places: along the coast, a strip of wild shoreline; on the west side of the Olympic Mountains, rainforest valleys of huge trees; up in the mountains, snowy alpine terrain and a glacier; in various places, lovely lakes, backpacking trails, and hot springs. There's plenty to do and more than you can see in a typical vacation. The weather, though wet, is mild over a long season.

# NATURAL HISTORY: THE SYSTEMS OF LIFE

The miracles of nature go far beyond the wonder and beauty of certain places. An even deeper miracle is that by studying these places we can understand how they work and learn the rules nature uses to fill them with life. What seems accidental at first — a certain tree or animal living in a certain place, for example — turns out to fit into an amazing system in which each living thing has a job. Look deeper and you find that places that look completely different, with distinct kinds of plants, land, and weather, work by the same rules, even if all the parts in the system are different. It's as if a playwright wrote a script and sent it out to all the theater groups in the world. In one place the part of the hero might be played by a fat old man and in another by a tall young woman, but what they do is always the same. The script nature wrote never ends, and we never can understand exactly how it goes; but scientists have gotten down the characters and the basic story — the system of how nature's parts work together. They call their study **ecology.**

Around Point Reyes and the Olympic Peninsula, you can see many natural places almost side by side that look completely different. A rocky seashore tide pool couldn't look less like a grove of giant trees; the plants and animals that live in each look nothing alike. Each place has its own community of living things, all supporting or taking from each other, but not many plants or creatures can survive in both. At first it seems the only thing they have in common is that each place feels full of life and energy. In fact, these communities work in much the same way, by the rules of ecology that seem to work everywhere.

## THE ENERGY SOURCE

The first thing virtually all living things have in common is that they get their energy from the sun. Energy is what makes you go. When you start feeling hungry and run-down around lunchtime, you might get the energy you need by eating a roast-beef sandwich. The bread was made from wheat that got energy from the sun. The beef came from cattle that ate plants that got their energy from the sun. When you eat the sandwich, your body uses the energy stored in the beef and bread to make it through the afternoon. You're running on the sunlight that grew the wheat and the cattle's food. Energy stored in gasoline makes your car go, and it came from the sun, too. Long ago, plants in the sea got energy from the sun. They died and slowly got buried deep in the earth, and with enough time and pressure they turned into oil. Much later, a company drilled the oil and refined it into gas. Your car runs on million-year-old sunlight.

Plants catch and store the sun's energy with **photosynthesis,** the most important process to life on earth. I've explained it in more detail under "Read Aloud: Photosynthesis," in chapter 22, "Olympic National Park." Plants are like factories. They take in water and gas in the air called carbon dioxide, and with energy from sunlight they turn it into oxygen and sugar. (The plant also makes the sugar into many other compounds, which I'll call sugar for simplicity.) Sugar is fuel for plants and animals — energy from the sun stored in a solid, usable form. Photosynthesis can catch and use up to a third of the sun's energy that hits a plant. Later, that energy can be released quickly or slowly. Fires use it up fast, when they burn; compost piles or rotting leaves on the forest floor use it slowly, as they decompose into soil. You can feel the heat in a compost pile as it rots: That heat originally came from the sun.

Rain forests and redwood groves are very good at catching and storing the sun's energy and turning it into wood and other plant life. That's because they have plenty of water, mild temperatures, and a storehouse of energy and nutrients to grow on in the soil, which is made of dead plants and trees from the past and minerals from the earth that plants need. The oceans grow more than 80% of the earth's plant matter, most of it in plants too small to see without a microscope, called **phytoplankton.** They float around like soup near the surface of the world's oceans, taking in water, carbon dioxide, and sunlight, making oxygen and sugar, and then being eaten by other creatures. (I am calling algae plants for simplicity.)

## THE FOOD WEB

In the ocean, tiny animals eat phytoplankton, and larger animals eat the tiny animals. An animal that eats another is called a **predator;** the animal that is eaten is called **prey.** On a rocky shore with tide pools, mussels and barnacles eat plankton they filter out of the water, and sea stars eat the mussels. That's called a **food chain.**

But it's always more complicated than that, because most animals eat more than one kind of food. Dog whelks, a type of snail, eat mussels and barnacles, and sea stars eat the dog whelks as well as mussels. A seagull or sea otter may eat a sea star, dog whelk, or mussel. When a food chain gets tangled that way, we call it a

**food web,** because if you draw a picture of who eats whom, the lines between the animals look like a web. Offshore, small fish eat plankton, larger fish eat the small fish, seals and sea lions eat the large fish, and killer whales eat the seals and sea lions. Onshore, caterpillars eat plants, small birds eat caterpillars, and owls and hawks eat small birds. Rabbits eat plants, and foxes eat rabbits. Some creatures feed on living things, and others feed on dead plants and animals. For example, a dead killer whale is eaten by bacteria, crabs, and fish; those small animals are eaten by larger fish, which are eaten by seals, and eventually another killer whale eats the seal. The energy originally caught from the sun by the tiny phytoplankton keeps working its way around.

Whether you're talking about the ocean or the rain forest, food webs have certain rules that always hold true. One rule is that all energy has to start with plants, which get it from the sun. Another rule is that with each step up in the food chain, the predators get stronger, faster, and fiercer — owls, for example, are scarier than robins. And at each step, most of the energy is lost. A plant stores only some of the energy coming from the sun; it uses the rest to live, or just loses it. A rabbit nibbling on the plant stores only some of that energy. Some is lost, and the rabbit uses more to live, storing only a little in its body. When a fox eats the rabbit, it can't use all the energy stored in the rabbit, either. Generally, only one-tenth of the energy at each level is passed on to the next higher level.

As each level of the food chain loses more energy, it can support fewer animals. If a rabbit needed an acre of woods to find its food, and a fox needed to eat 100 rabbits a year, then only one fox could survive on each 100 acres of land without running short of food (these are made-up numbers). Animals at the very top of the food web need huge areas to support them — 100 square miles for a mountain lion, for example. All of Point Reyes is big enough for only a single pair of mountain lions. For the same reasons, food webs can usually have no more than five steps of predators up from the plants. Nothing eats killer whales, owls, hawks, mountain lions, and the like — there aren't enough of them to support a group of even more ferocious predators.

## ECOSYSTEMS

Food webs can fit together in ways that help the plants or animals that are being eaten, too.

Sea otters like to live in kelp forests, places near shore where seaweed called kelp grows up from the bottom. They tie kelp around their feet to anchor themselves in rough weather. Kelp is a plant that gets energy from the sun through photosynthesis, and kelp forests make a home for fish, and seals and birds come to eat the fish. Sea urchins — little animals that look like pin cushions (a picture is on p. 474) — eat kelp, and sea otters love to eat sea urchins.

You might not guess that the otters keep this ecosystem together, but remove the otters and the whole thing falls apart. In the 1800s, American and Russian hunters killed almost all the otters on the West Coast for their pelts. Laws stopped sea-otter hunting in 1911. Since then, otters have returned to some places on the coast, but not many have come back to Point Reyes. One reason is that when the otters were killed, no one was left to eat the urchins, and without a limit on the numbers of urchins, the urchins ate the kelp forests until nothing was left. That hurt the fish, seals, and birds that also used the kelp forest. It hurt the urchins too, because they had no kelp left to eat. Without kelp forests to live in, the otters probably won't come back. With less kelp growing off Point Reyes, there's less energy caught from the sun, and fewer fish, seals, and birds. The whole environment is less productive without the otters — it captures less energy and produces less life.

When you look at the environment that way, you're talking about an **ecosystem.** Ecologists study the way the plants and animals in an ecosystem work together as if the whole thing were one big machine. They measure how much energy the ecosystem takes in, where the energy goes, how much life and what kinds of life grow in the ecosystem, how the place and weather affect the living things, and the inner workings that fit the whole thing together.

An ecosystem isn't easy to draw a line around because animals and ocean waters don't stay put, but at these national parks there are some clear examples. The rocky shoreline is one ecosystem, the salt marshes of Point Reyes are another, and so are the forests of the coastal mountains. A seagull might pick up a snail from the shore and drop it in the forest, but most of the time the plants and animals in each ecosystem stay mostly with each other.

## ECOSYSTEM INPUTS

Ecologists have learned to predict how nature will act — how many trees and plants will grow and how many baby animals will be born — using computer programs with numbers that stand for plants and animals. If the rules of nature they've figured out are right, then the same program works for different ecosystems, wherever they are found.

Each ecosystem has differences that give the computer different information. They include the amount of rain and sunlight, the shape of the land, the nutrients in the water, the richness of the soil, and the temperature and extremes of the seasons. On the Pacific coast, currents that change during the year bring changing temperatures of seawater and different flows of water with more or less food. Birds, whales, and fish migrate up and down the coast to find what they need; plants and animals that can't move have to be able to handle the changes. In the winter, storms smash against the coast, and many animals leave. Only tough plants and animals can live on the rocky shores where the waves pound. In the protected salt marshes and bays, many more kinds of creatures and grasses do well in gentle, still water. They produce much more life, but those plants and animals wouldn't make it where the stormy waves roll.

Dampness floats off the Pacific Ocean in weather that moves east from sea to land. At Point Reyes, the amount of annual rainfall doubles 10 miles east of the coast, where hills reach up to catch the clouds. Near the coast, fog whistles across broad, hilly prairie, watered by about 20 inches of rain a year that falls mostly in the winter. Grazing elk and fires set by the Coast Miwok people kept this land open long ago; since white settlers arrived and removed the Miwok and elk, cattle have cropped the grass. Farther east, where a hill bunches up, 40 inches of rain falls. Douglas firs grow where the soil is good; the top-heavy Bishop pines grow where there's a bit less rain and the soil is not as rich. Across the highway the coastal mountains rise higher, and the additional rain and fog allow giant coast redwoods to grow for thousands of years, over 300 feet high.

The Olympic Peninsula has the same pattern of differences in rainfall, only more extreme. On the coast, 80 inches of rain falls a year, and in the mountains over 200 inches. After the clouds are drained in the mountains, they pass to the east side of the peninsula, where only 20 inches of rain falls in a year. On the coast, Sitka spruces grow. Back in the protected valleys on the west side of the mountains, these trees are as large as tall buildings, and western hemlocks tower with them. Even when it's not raining here in the rain forest, the air is damp, and life and growth are so rich and thick that in places you can't see anything that isn't alive. Where the giant trees have fallen, lines of seedlings sprout up from their rotting trunks. Higher into the mountains, the air gets cooler; smaller mountain trees grow that can handle winter and deep loads of snow.

## NATURAL COMMUNITIES

The forest helps decide what animals live within it. In the rain forests of huge old trees on the Olympic Peninsula, fungus grows among the tree roots, helping the trees gather water and nutrients from the soil and protecting them from disease and insects. The trees pay back the debt by passing energy from their photosynthesis to the fungus. Underground, the fungus passes some of that energy to new trees on the forest floor that don't get much light for their own photosynthesis, helping them get started. Flying squirrels like eating this fungus. Most of the time, the squirrels swoop around in the branches of the tree top canopy to stay safe from owls, but when fungus is available, they dig around on the forest floor. That's when the spotted owl has its best shot at a favorite food — flying squirrels. Spotted owls fly in between the big trees, staying away from the great horned owls that would like to eat them. Large great horned owls have trouble flying in tight spaces. So spotted owls can live only here, where the big old trees offer protection from a predator (the great horned owl), and fungus grows to feed their prey (the flying squirrel).

But ecosystems change. On the Olympic Peninsula outside the national park, people have changed the rain-forest system by cutting down the old trees and planting new ones like crops in a field. As you drive through Olympic National Forest, you can easily recognize these places when you see the smaller trees, all the same age, that grow much closer together than trees in the old forest. Studies show what's pretty clear by just looking at these new forests: Without the different sizes and ages of trees, fewer kinds of animals and plants can live there. For example, the spotted owl, with its special needs for flying space and food, would have a hard time finding a home there. As people have cut down old-growth forests in the Northwest for wood, farms, and towns, the spotted owl has come under threat of extinction. Now many areas of old-growth rain forest in the Northwest can't be cut; the law says the spotted owl's home must be protected so that it won't disappear. Spotted owls also live in the old coast redwood forests, including Muir Woods.

Change comes naturally in ecosystems, too. When patterns of wind change far out over the ocean, a warm-water current called

El Niño comes to the West Coast, bringing a lot of rain to California and even bigger changes in the ocean. Normal currents stir up the bottom, bringing to the surface nutrients that plankton need in order to grow. El Niño's flow doesn't do that and is too warm for good plankton growth. El Niño means less plankton, and that means less food for the small fish and animals that are the food for birds and larger fish and sea animals. If birds that feed on small fish can't find enough food to stay healthy, they may miss an entire year of having chicks. The common murre, a black sea bird that looks a bit like a penguin, flies low above the waves to catch fish. At one time, millions of common murres lived in huge colonies on rocky islands along the West Coast up into Alaska and Kenai Fjords National Park. But oil spills kill murres by the thousands, and El Niño makes it hard for them to bounce back.

## COMPETITION

When an ecosystem changes and plants and animals die, there are almost always other plants and animals around to take advantage of the energy and land that's left. Every living thing does its best to spread over more space and have more young, taking more of the energy in the ecosystem and giving its own kind a better chance to survive. That's called **competition.**

Different species have different ways of winning in competition. On the West Coast, mussels and barnacles compete for room on rocky shores where they can attach themselves and catch plankton from the passing water. Both animals are eaten when they're small by snails called dog whelks and limpets, but the snails can't handle a large, grown-up mussel. Lower on the shore, sea stars do eat large mussels, but sea stars can't stay out of the water for long; so on the upper part of the shore, where the tide goes out every day, the large mussels are safe from sea stars. That means that mussels that get big are the best competitors in this ecosystem on the upper shore; they might be eaten occasionally by a bird or otter, but

they're safe from the predators that get rid of their competitors, the barnacles. So why isn't the upper shore covered with mussels? One reason is that logs floating in the ocean smash against the shore, destroying some of the shells in thick colonies of mussels. Once that gap is opened, waves can break more big mussels against the rocks. Once an area of rock is cleared, small mussels and barnacles have to compete for space again while being eaten by limpets and whelks.

In a forest, trees may be cleared from the land by fire, flood, storm, disease, or a glacier, just as the mussels are cleared from rocks by floating logs. The first plants to come back on the cleared land are species that start lots of seeds and grow fast, but they may not be the best competitors in the long run. Annual grasses, weeds, and shrubs come right after a fire. Bishop pines, common at Point Reyes, and Douglas firs, found at Point Reyes and Olympic National Park, open their cones and plant seedlings after a fire, so they may be the first trees to return. They push out the shrubs and grasses as they get larger by spreading their roots to suck up the water and casting shadows over the ground. If no fire comes to renew the forest, Bishop pines could die of old age in about 80 years, and some other kind of tree may grow in their place. In the Northwest rain forests, a Douglas fir could live 1,000 years and grow hundreds of feet tall, but eventually western hemlock will take over the land. Small Douglas firs can't grow in the shade cast by the hemlocks. In the deep, old-growth rain forest, Sitka spruce and western hemlock are the best competitors. Eventually, the competition there evens out. At that point, no species in the forest is able to beat out any other for more energy or room, so they all continue to grow in the same space year after year.

As soon as the forest is cleared, the process begins again: The fastest species fill in an open area, then the most competitive species slowly take over. This is called **plant succession.** In the Hoh Rainforest in Olympic National Park, an ancient, unchanging forest stands on a high place above the Hoh River. Nearer the river, where floods happen more often, a younger forest still is changing, with species competing for space in an earlier step in succession. Only in places where disasters are rare do the forests have time to make it to the final stage of development, as in these protected rain-forest valleys or the coastal valleys where the redwoods grow near Point Reyes. In most places, fires and floods come too often, returning the competition to step one. In 1995, for example, a fire burned a large chunk of Point Reyes National Seashore and 45 homes, from Mount Vision south to the shore. Since both of the main kinds of trees on Point Reyes spread best after a fire, we can guess that fires come here fairly often, before plant succession can move on to whatever would be the next stage of development. But just to the east, in the damp, foggy valleys, redwood trees have won the competition; there, you'll find giants that have grown for 2,000 years.

## The Little Field Guide

### Mammals & Marine Life
Besides those discussed below, the following can also show up in this region: barnacle ,harbor seal, hermit crab (p. 46); humpback whale and moon snail (p. 47); sea star or star fish (p. 48); gray fox and white-tailed deer (p. 144); coyote, jack rabbit, and mule deer (p. 189); mountain lion (p. 288); and bobcat (p. 392).

### California Mussel
Dark blue, brown, and black California mussels make up one of the most common species on the northern West Coast. They hang onto rocks by threads in thick colonies. When the tide covers them, they filter plankton from the water. When the tide goes out, they close their two-part shells for protection from the drying air, and they wait. Blue mussels, also common, are the commercially harvested species you find in restaurants. Both kinds are good to eat. However, mussels concentrate pollution and other poisons, so it's dangerous to gather them without local knowledge.

Gray Whale

### Gray Whale
In the spring, these animals, which weigh up to 80,000 pounds, pass close to shore on their migration from winter calving grounds off western Mexico to summer feeding grounds off western Alaska. They return in late fall and winter. They don't have fins on their backs. To feed, they dive down and sift food out of the gunk from the bottom through the comb-shaped baleen in their mouths. Watching from shore is popular at Point Reyes (see "Whale Watching," in chapter 21, "Point Reyes National Seashore") and the Olympic Peninsula (see "Whale & Wildlife Watching," in chapter 22, "Olympic National Park").

Killer Whale
(or Orca)

### Killer Whale (or Orca)
These whales either travel in organized family groups called pods, feeding mostly on salmon and other fish, or are loners, prowling for prey that could include sea lions, or even humpback or gray whales. On the water you'll

usually see only the whales' shiny black back and long dorsal fin. When the whale sounds (dives), the flukes of the tail appear. Like people swimming, orcas turn head down when they want to go deeper. Orcas grow up to 30 feet long.

## Limpet

Limpets are common in West Coast tide pools. Their shells are shaped like Chinese hats. There are many varieties, some large enough to be used as human food or decorations for Native American costumes. Most limpets eat algae, but they also can consume tiny mussels and barnacles that have just attached to rocks.

Sea Anemone

## Sea Anemone

These are among the most fun and bizarre animals to find in a tide pool. They look like huge flowers with thick stalks, but the flower petals are really sticky tentacles that grab and poison fish or other small animals that come too close. Any gentle contact will make an anemone quickly close up, leaving it looking like a rock. Sea anemones come in many varieties, in different sizes and colors.

Sea Lion

## Sea Lion

Groups of sea lions have certain rocks called haul-outs where they rest together and rookeries where they mate and give birth. Like whales, otters, and seals, they're mammals and have to hold their breath to dive deep for the fish they catch. They are larger than seals and feed on salmon and other fish that people also eat, so commercial fishing can reduce their food supply and lower how many can live in an area.

Sea Otter

## Sea Otter

Shiny otters float on their backs in groups called rafts, tying kelp around their legs to stay in place. Otters use their tummies as tables for food or to carry their babies. Unlike other marine mammals, they don't have a layer of fat to keep them warm. Instead, otters rely on their fur, which is the finest and most thickly spaced fur of any animal, and on their bodies' ability to produce heat from the huge amounts of food they eat. Otter like clams, crabs, and sea urchins, which they pick off the bottom of the ocean during long dives when they hold their breath.

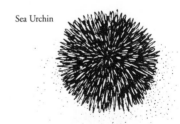

Sea Urchin

## Sea Urchin

These animals have spines that stick out like pins from a pin cushion. The spines protect the urchin and allow it to move, like a centipede's legs. They fall off when the urchin dies, leaving a delicate, beautifully etched shell. Kelp is a favorite food, although they eat almost anything, and sea otters are an important predator. Many kinds of urchins are common and interesting to find in tide pools; some have eggs that are eaten as sushi.

## Tule Elk & Roosevelt Elk

Tule elk like the open, grassy lands on Point Reyes. Commercial hunts killed them off during the gold rush in the 1850s, but they were brought back in the 1970s and now are easy to find in a reserve on Tomales Point, at the north end of Point Reyes. Roosevelt elk, also rare, are the largest elk. They prefer the forests of Olympic National Park, where I've seen them in the Hoh and Quinault rain forests. Both kinds of elk make a big difference in their ecosystems. Tule elk helped keep Point Reyes' grasslands from turning into bushes and forest. Roosevelt elk, which like to eat hemlock sprouts but not Sitka spruce, may help keep hemlocks from taking over the rain forest.

## BIRDS

Besides the birds listed here, you may see some described in other chapters, such as the osprey, herring gull, sanderling, and great blue heron (p. 48), ruffed grouse (p. 145), raven (p. 190), hairy woodpecker (p. 288), and Steller's jay (p. 393).

Belted Kingfisher

## Belted Kingfisher

Found by lakes, streams, and wetlands all over the United States, including Olema Marsh at Point Reyes, the kingfisher is about the size of a pigeon. It has a blue-gray crest and a long, sharp bill for catching fish.

## Common Loon

These large, striking birds with sharply contrasting black-and-white coloring have an unforgettable, mournful cry that is symbolic of America's outdoors. In the summer, they nest on northern lakes. They spend the winter fishing in coastal waters all over the United States.

## Common Murre

The size and shape of a football, these birds don't look as if they'd be able to fly, but they do. Their little wings flap like crazy as they skim over the waves. Murres live in huge colonies on rocky islands, making them very vulnerable to oil spills and El Niño weather changes. Each female has only one egg a year. They depend on having a lot of birds together on the rocks for protection, so recovery from die-offs is slow.

Great Horned Owl

## Great Horned Owl

This big owl, found all over North America south of the Arctic, is a fierce hunter at the top of the food chain. It preys on rabbits, ducks, and even other owls, including the endangered spotted owl of the old-growth forest in the Pacific Northwest. The owl's powerful flight, hypnotic eyes, and "hoo-hoo-hoo hooooo" call give shivers even to some people.

Pelican

hills along the foggy coast and are common at Point Reyes, where the odd shape adds to the beauty of sunset over grassy ridges.

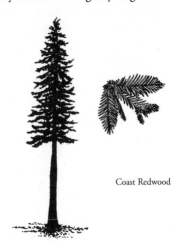

Coast Redwood

## Pelican

The enormous brown pelican, common at Point Reyes, is striking and instantly recognizable. Pelicans fly over the coast, diving into the water to catch fish in their huge beaks. Their wingspan is over 7 feet. The white pelican, pictured here, is rarer in this area and even bigger, although it is easy to find at Grand Teton National Park. It feeds by herding fish between a group of birds.

## TREES & PLANTS

In addition to the flora here, also refer to the quaking aspen, lodgepole pine, Indian paintbrush, and lupine (p. 290); columbine (p. 393); and poison oak (p. 394).

## Coast Redwood

The world's tallest trees are also among the most beautiful. They create spaces like cathedrals in groves at places like Muir Woods and Samuel P. Taylor State Park, both near Point Reyes (chapter 21). The tallest redwood is 368 feet tall, at Redwood National Park. It takes 500 years for a redwood to grow up, and the oldest are 2,000 years old. Of the huge redwoods that stood when whites arrived on the West Coast, less than 5% remain standing — yet, incredibly, loggers only recently stopped cutting the old growth. The wood resists rot and is good for decks and siding.

Bishop Pine

Douglas Fir

## Bishop Pine

You can recognize these pines by the long trunk that leads to a round blob of branches and needles at the top — it's a sort of Dr. Seuss tree. Bishop pines grow only on the low

## Douglas Fir

The needles of the Douglas fir are softer than those of the Sitka spruce, and thinner and less orderly than the western hemlock's. Douglas firs grow huge in coastal forests — over 200 feet tall, and 1,000 years old — but plant seedlings only after a fire. Their range is from Point Reyes to British Columbia; a smaller subspecies grows in the Rocky Mountains. This tree provides much of our lumber and many Christmas trees too.

## Douglas Iris

Common at Point Reyes on the coast, this lily has a large, delicate flower like a flag atop a plant, which can be a couple of feet tall. The flowers can have a broad range of colors but are deep purple to pale lavender at Point Reyes. They bloom beginning in late February or March.

Sitka Spruce

## Sitka Spruce

This grand tree towers with the western hemlock in the old-growth stands of the coastal rain forest from Washington north, often growing to 160 feet tall, and sometimes over 200 feet. It is used for lumber. You can tell Sitka spruce from western hemlock by its sharp needles, stiff branches, and pointy top (the hemlock's top bends over and its needles are soft).

Trillium

## Trillium

These little white lilies grow in the open forests and rain forest of the Olympic Peninsula. They may turn up at Point Reyes, and are common in the Muir Woods. They're also called "wake-robins" because they show up in the early spring at about the time that robins arrive.

## Western Hemlock

These are thick, dark green trees with soft, blunt, juicy needles that grow in two rows on droopy branches and tops. They like damp soil below the mountains from northern California to south-central Alaska — the temperate rain forest — where they're the final tree in forest succession (see p. 472). You can tell the western hemlock from other common rain-forest trees by the top, which droops instead of sticking straight up.

## Western Red Cedar

These trees commonly grow up to 8 feet thick in the damp coastal forests; the largest western red cedar has a trunk over 20 feet thick. An amazing huge cedar grows just off U.S. 101 south of Beach 6 at Olympic National Park marked by a sign that says BIG CEDAR. Northwest Indians used red cedar to build lodges and to carve canoes, boxes, and helmets. They wove the stringy bark into rope, blankets, and cloaks. The wood doesn't rot, and today it's used for shingles, decks, boats, and the like. The scaly branches droop and have a strong cedar smell.

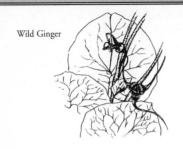

Wild Ginger

## Wild Ginger

These deep forest plants grow at Olympic National Park and Point Reyes. The strange, three-pointed flowers of purple-brown are hidden under heart-shaped leaves. Wild ginger is a creeping plant that blooms in spring and early summer. Pioneers used the roots and stems for ginger.

# HISTORY & CULTURE: HUMAN ECOLOGY

Life must have been sweet for the Native Americans living on the West Coast. The weather was mild and food was plentiful. Unlike some other American Indians, who struggled in deserts, mountains, or the arctic just to survive, residents of the Pacific coast had no need to plant crops or keep domesticated animals to get by. People had to work hard, but they also had a lot of time for art and religion. The first Europeans to land on Point Reyes, Sir Francis Drake and Spanish sailors who wrecked there in 1595, were impressed by the Coast Miwok's happiness and the richness of their land. (For more on Drake's voyage, see "Read Aloud: Sir Francis Drake," in chapter 21.) The people were strong, and many were even fat. They wore jewelry of shells and feathers, capes, headdresses, and other signs of wealth, but in the area's mild weather didn't wear clothes except for the women's grass or animal-skin skirts. The Native Americans of the Olympic Peninsula were even richer, and their magnificent art is still valued all over the world for its beauty and meaning.

An ecologist would look at these people and point out that their wealth and success came from being at the top of the food web in productive ecosystems (these concepts are explained in the first half of the chapter). Ecologists study people the same way as they do other animals, using the same rules they have learned about natural ecosystems to understand human beings too. Many other people disagree with that idea. They say God made people different from animals. Certainly, humans are different from most animals — humans are able to plan how we change the environment. But the Native Americans might have been more on the side of the ecologists.

## PART OF NATURE

The Coast Miwok and Northwest Indians, and most Native Americans and people around the world living off the land, thought of plants, animals, and land as being more than something just to use or enjoy. They relied on the natural world around them and knew that they survived only as a part of it. When a Coast Miwok cut part of a tree, he would leave something in return — something valuable — and thank the tree. The people's stories and their religious ceremonies talked about animals as having spirits with great powers. According to one story, Coyote created the dry land and the Miwok people. Northwest native peoples believed that in an old time animals and people were one, and then their spirits were put into different forms: human beings, whales, birds, even mountains, rocks, and glaciers. Those animals and places were equal to people. To use them, people carefully followed religious traditions to show their respect and ask for help and guidance.

If you relied on the turning of the seasons and gifts of the sea and forests for your life, you'd probably feel more a part of nature, too. The Makah of Ozette, on the tip of the Olympic Peninsula, were whaling people.

They set out on the sea in cedar canoes to hunt whales with harpoons tipped with sharpened shells. It was risky work, and the whale had a good chance of killing the hunters. They paddled out, got close enough to a whale to spear it, and then followed as the whale pulled a float made of a blown-up seal skin until it tired out. The reward was great. A whale could feed a village for a long time, and the captain who brought one home was a hero for his people — as important as our most famous basketball players and movie stars are to us. Naturally, the whalers and their families spent a lot of time praying and preparing spiritually for such a big and dangerous event. After commercial whaling nearly wiped out the whales, the Makah had to give up their hunt, but they have revived their whaling tradition, taking their first whale in almost 80 years in May 1999.

The Northwest Indians lived in wooden longhouses on the coast in the winter, usually with everyone in the village in just a couple of houses. In the summer, they went to fishing and hunting camps. They caught salmon, hunted deer and elk, picked berries, and gathered shellfish. Each village had different traditions, depending on the best ways to get food from their lands. They dried many foods, saving them to eat over the winter, when they also would tell stories and carve cedar artwork. The highest class of people — like kings and princes — used the best fishing and gathering places and owned slaves they won from other villages in war. The Coast Miwok lived in small villages of wooden huts within an hour's walk of the shore, staying in the same place year-round. They gathered acorns, hunted, fished, and collected shellfish. To improve the elk hunting, they probably burned the grass on Point Reyes so that the coastal prairie wouldn't be taken over by bushes and trees that the elk couldn't eat. A family might own a particular oak tree where they gathered nuts, but they didn't plant crops.

We don't know exactly how many Native Americans lived along the West Coast, but it was a lot fewer than the number of people who live there now. Ecologists would say the number of Native Americans was limited by their ecosystem, just as only so many bears and mountain lions can live in an area. People were the most successful competitors among the animals on the coast, but their spread was limited by the food the environment around them could produce.

## THE EUROPEAN WAY

Scientists believe that all people are related, all descendants of ancestors forgotten long ago who hunted and gathered food in Africa. Many thousands of years ago, as the numbers of those first people grew, they spread to new lands. New generations in new places grew up to look and behave in new ways, eventually forgetting all about the people and places left behind many generations ago. People became different races and tribes and, later, different nations. Today, when wars and other conflicts break out, those small differences often seem more important than the common ancestry that makes us alike.

Most scientists believe that the first people in North or South America arrived from northeastern Asia during the last Ice Age, although we can't be sure if they walked or paddled their way. So much of the ocean was frozen 15,000 years ago that the water level was much lower than it is today, allowing land to connect Alaska to Siberia. The Asians may have traveled along that shoreline in animal-skin boats. After the glaciers melted, around 10,000 years ago, the Native Americans developed cultures that lasted thousands of years. Each people learned ways of living on the land and getting food in their own area, passing down traditions of great skill in harvesting the plants and animals found there.

As the Native Americans were creating their cultures, on the other side of the world the so-called Western civilization grew up without the two knowing about each other. In Africa, Europe, and Asia, using horses and oxen, farmers learned to produce more food and support more children. Eventually they built cities, invented writing and reading, and founded kingdoms capable of building big ships to cross the ocean. People who live in cities don't have to worry about nature so much — someone else raises the food and they can go out and buy it whenever they want. A family didn't have to think about how many acorns a certain oak tree would grow that year, as the Coast Miwok did. Western religious beliefs were as different as their ways. They told of mankind being created by God, not by animals, and said that God told them to rule over the animal kingdom.

Western civilization made humans an amazingly competitive animal. Like a fast-growing plant in a new place, people spread and increased their numbers quickly. In North America, these newly arriving people did many of the things ecologists would predict a strong new predator at the top of the food web would do. They got rid of competing predators, like grizzly bears and wolves. They built farms and settlements on land the Native Americans had used for their own hunting, gathering, or farming. The newcomers were farmers, hunters, and gatherers too, but on a much bigger scale than the Indians. They hunted whales and sea otters from big ships instead of canoes. Without any limit on their ability to kill those animals, they nearly wiped out the prey, including otters, some kinds of whales, and other marine mammals. Commercial hunters came to Point Reyes and killed all the elk. Ranchers took over the land for cattle, planting grasses that grew faster than the native kinds. In the late 1800s, egg companies in San Francisco collected the eggs of common murres for peoples' breakfasts. Murres lay only one egg a year, so the 25 million eggs taken for food nearly did away with the birds.

Of course, it makes no sense for a species to drive its prey to extinction. If some prey animals survive, they may breed and provide more food for the predator later. But ecology tells us that it does happen. An animal's first job is to survive; if a wolf needs meat, he will kill the last deer so he can live. Most of the time, however, when a predator is close to wiping out its prey, finding the last few animals becomes too difficult, and the predator either starves or switches to different prey. Either way, without the prey, the number of predators has to go down, and that lets the prey make a comeback.

Native Americans may have overhunted some animals to extinction. Archaeologists disagree on exactly what happened, but many species of large land animals disappeared at the time the Native Americans began hunting, around 11,000 years ago, including American camels, beavers as large as bears, and hairy elephants called woolly mammoths. A kind of duck that couldn't fly was probably killed off by Pacific coast natives around 4,000 years ago. But the slaughter of birds and animals by settlers who came to California after the 1849 gold rush was far greater than anything that had happened before. With a selfish drive beyond that of the wolf or other predators who kill only to eat, hunters killed as much as they could for the money they would make or to get rid of wild animals that were a nuisance. Their guns also made them much better hunters than any other predators, and when the prey was gone, they didn't starve — they just moved on to a new line of work.

## NEW LIMITS

In the late 1800s, people began to see that the slaughter of American wildlife had to stop or soon nothing would be left. The number of people on the land was many times what nature could support from hunting and gathering. New inventions changed things, too. Instead of using whale oil in lamps, people began to burn kerosene, which is made from crude oil that comes out of the ground. Taking energy from under the ground helped the ecosystem support a lot more people in many other ways too. Before they started burning coal, people in Europe had burned all their trees for heat. Electricity allowed energy to be sent long distances. Engines running on gasoline let people get around without feeding hay to a horse. Each change allowed the earth to hold more people, as we came to rely less on the energy we could take from the ecosystem growing today and more on the fuel left in the ground by plants that grew long ago.

But new technology can't change the laws of ecology: We still take our energy from the sun, and there is only so much of it to go around. The oil we use for fuel comes from ocean plants that gathered it from sunlight millions of years ago. Since we started using oil about 150 years ago, about half of the supply is gone (although the exact amount isn't known). And burning the fuel releases the carbon dioxide stored within it millions of years ago when it was alive. That added carbon dioxide is changing the earth's atmosphere and may slowly change the weather, sea level, and ocean currents (for more on global warming, see "Read Aloud: Dirty Air & Nature," in chapter 19, "Sequoia & Kings Canyon National Parks").

We stopped hunting and taking eggs from the seabirds on the West Coast, but spills from ships carrying oil have killed thousands of birds at a time. The oil makes their feathers bunch together so that they can't hold out the cold water, and it poisons the birds and their prey. It takes a long time for a colony of birds like common murres to replace the birds that are killed in an oil spill; sometimes, another spill hits as soon as they do. Overfishing hurts birds, too, by taking away their food. Puffins used to live on the rocks at Point Reyes, but few are left because their favorite food, sardines, was fished out in the 1940s. Many wild birds were hurt by a poison called DDT that farmers used to spray on their fields to get rid of insects. Birds ate the poison, making the shells on their eggs so thin that they would break before hatching. Pelicans have made a comeback since DDT was banned in the 1960s. The last California condor was seen flying over Point Reyes in the 1950s, and now none are left in the wild. These huge birds,

with wingspans of over 9 feet, fed on dead whales, elk, and other large mammals that mostly are gone now.

How we use land changes the environment, too. Like hemlock trees in the rain forest that take over the best growing areas by casting deep shadows on other trees, people take over resources that weaker animals were using. The hemlocks, for example, have a lot of cellulose, which is good for making cellophane, yarn, and plastic. We use old-growth trees for that and plant new ones in their place. But some animals in the forest that were already using the giant trees can't live in the newly planted forests. The most famous of these creatures is the spotted owl, which lives in the old-growth forests of the Olympic Peninsula and in the California redwoods, but there's a whole food web of creatures that need the old growth. The spotted owl was in danger of extinction when the government stopped most logging in the Northwest's old-growth forests.

Another example is the silver salmon (or coho), which spawned by the thousands in the rivers of Marin County, around Point Reyes, during the Coast Miwok's time. The people held ceremonies and celebrations when the fish returned from the ocean in the fall. To lay their eggs, or spawn, salmon need streams with gravel bottoms and moving water. Today, most West Coast streams are used by people for water instead. They hold dams that block the fish and that slow the flow of water so that dirt settles in the spaces between the pebbles of gravel. Some salmon are left in Tomales Bay, behind Point Reyes, but not many compared to the number there once were.

## HOW WE LIVE TODAY

Many of Olympic National Park's streams still have salmon runs. The return of the salmon each year has always been important in the life of the Northwest's native peoples and the forest. Salmon are born in streams, then go out to swim in the ocean for 2 to 5 years, eating smaller fish and fattening up. Near the end of their lives, they come back to the stream where they were born to spawn, and then die on the bank. The dead fish are a great gift of food and nutrients to the forest ecosystem and for birds, animals, insects, and reptiles that eat their flesh.

For the fish to use the streams, the environment around them has to be protected. Big trees on the shore shade the water so that it doesn't get too warm for salmon, and their roots catch dirt, keeping it from washing into the stream and possibly filling in the spawning gravel. There are fewer fish now than there once were on the Olympic Peninsula, but compared to most places outside Alaska or Canada, there are many more streams that still have salmon runs. The Elwha River was the peninsula's richest, with big runs of all five species of Pacific salmon, until two dams were built to produce electricity, in 1911 and 1926. The salmon runs were destroyed, with only a few fish coming back each year. Then, in 1976, Native Americans who had relied on the salmon asked for the dams to be removed. Almost 20 years later the government, the owners of the dams, and the people who use the electricity finally agreed. In 2000, the government took over the dams and plans to take them down in 2004 after new equipment is installed to keep the local water supply clean. The electricity isn't a big deal — the dams provided only one-third of the power used by one of the pulp mills in Port Angeles. But if the salmon come back, it will be a big deal to the Native Americans, fishermen visiting the park, and the animals that eat dead salmon along the river banks. It will be a case of our species going against the ecological rules,

giving up energy and resources for a weaker species.

We do many things that don't give our species an advantage in competition — things we just want to do. Most of us think about things other than survival. The United States is such a rich country that we can afford to set aside valuable natural resources like forests and seashores in national parks. We can hike into these areas to see beautiful places and try to get a feeling for nature. Our tents and sleeping bags are nylon, our raincoats are Gore-tex, our backpacks are made of tough synthetic fabric and aluminum, and we have camp stoves that can cook a meal before you could gather the wood for a fire. Imagine how envious a Coast Miwok of 400 years ago would feel to see a family camping that way. He could never hope for the comfort and ease we get when we're backpacking, and that's when we're roughing it.

But we also can't have what he had. We can't fish, hunt, and gather our food in these woods — there are too many of us. Some parks can barely fit the visitors who want to go there just to see the place. If we all took enough clams, salmon, and berries to feed us during our visit, the parks would soon be stripped bare. Instead, we can stay in the woods only a short time, limited by our Park Service permits and the food we carry on our backs. Imagine if, on the last night of a backpacking trip at Point Reyes, you saw a Coast Miwok family of 400 years ago. You might feel as envious as they would, seeing them feasting on scallops, salmon, or venison around a shared fire, enjoying a peaceful life as a part of this beautiful, bountiful place.

# CHAPTER 21

# Point Reyes National Seashore

The mist flew over Drakes Beach like a river in the sky, then cleared and let the warm sun beam down on us through the wind. We watched as slashing plumes of dry, windblown sand painted and textured the dark, wet sand by the shore. Above us, the beach had cut pale bluffs straight across softly rolling grassy hills. No wonder Sir Francis Drake thought it looked like the cliffs of Dover and named the place New Albion, after his home. We gathered shells and built sand-castle cities, huddling together and shouting to be heard over the roaring surf and warm wind. Our daughter, Julia, age 2 at the time, dictated her spelling of her brother Robin's name as I wrote it in the sand with a toe: J-J-7-8-D. Back at the visitor-center snack bar, we lunched on oysters and corn that a guy was barbecuing on the deck and realized that in a morning of walking miles on a beach in July, we hadn't met another person.

We were constantly surprised by natural beauty at Point Reyes, on both tiny and grand scales. As we drove down Sir Francis Drake Road in the fog, a perfect little view of the raging gray sea popped into the dip between a pair of grassy hills. "That looks like it should be on a postcard," Robin said. On another journey, we stumbled on a large herd of elk out on a windy ridge top with ocean on each side. The drive is only 20 miles from one side of the park to the other, but in that distance the land transforms from a placid, warm seaside area of woods, calm swimming beaches, and charming little towns into a windblown wild of grassy hills and ponds out of *King Lear,* William Shakespeare's play about a mad king. At the end, the road reaches the high, rocky headland above the Point Reyes Lighthouse. In the fog, we could only imagine the drop-offs hidden below us. Then, while descending a long, ridgeline staircase to the lighthouse, we stepped out of the mist and suddenly could see the water far below — much farther than we'd imagined. Here, in season, you can gaze down with binoculars at murres and elephant seals on the rocks far below, and the whales passing out to sea.

It's a natural paradise, but Point Reyes is mostly unknown outside the San Francisco

Bay Area. People from the city, less than an hour away, come up for the weekend, but I doubt the place ever feels crowded; during the week, even in peak season, you're often alone. The two excellent campgrounds near the national seashore have vacant sites except on the weekends. Perhaps most remarkable of all, the people who live here appreciate what they have and have kept the area from growing into a tawdry tourist trap. Their strict community planning has made the towns of western Marin County lovely and worth visiting. There are no franchises, ugly signs, or strip development; instead, you'll find lots of pottery shops, memorable restaurants, seaside pastures dotted with grazing cows, and old boats silhouetted in the sunset.

## BEST THINGS TO DO

- Take advantage of solitude at the beach for long, misty walks and sandcastle building.
- Explore tide pools for strange, unfamiliar creatures.
- Mountain-bike through the pine forest or on trails across the seaside prairie.
- Go sea kayaking in protected Tomales Bay or Drakes Estero.
- Bird-watch and visit a bird research center.
- Hike through the towering coastal redwoods, and take short backpacking trips through the shoreside pine and fir forest.

See "Activities" (p. 500).

## HISTORY: HOLDING BACK THE CITY

The most unusual event in the history of Point Reyes and the area around it is what didn't happen. It wasn't spoiled. And that wasn't easy.

Point Reyes National Seashore and Golden Gate National Recreation Area are the largest national parks near a big city, by far. Where most cities would have built big suburbs of

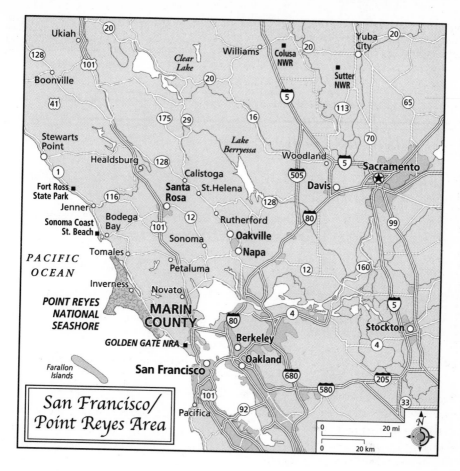

San Francisco/
Point Reyes Area

expensive houses, condominiums, shopping malls, and offices, San Francisco has these parks, with miles of lonely shoreline, prairie, and forest — a real wild country. The communities neighboring the parks are more attractive than the towns outside other national parks, including parks out in the middle of nowhere. There are no chain restaurants or hotels, no ugly signs, no tourist junk. It's as if the clock stopped before all that was invented. If it weren't too late for so many places, Point Reyes could be a lesson in how to protect the towns around national parks.

Sir Francis Drake was the first European to land on Point Reyes, in 1579; he left little other than his name. A Spanish ship carrying treasure from the Philippines to Mexico landed at Point Reyes in 1595. Most of the crew

had gotten off to look around when a storm came and blew the ship onto the shore, where it broke up and sank. The 70 surviving sailors made it to Mexico in a small boat. One of them came back in 1603 and named the point for the religious holiday when he arrived, the Day of the Three Kings. English speakers later shortened the name, *Punto de los Reyes,* to Point Reyes.

The Coast Miwok were certainly surprised and impressed to see these visitors. They had never encountered anything like the white men's ships and tools, and they may have thought the explorers were ghosts from beyond the western horizon, the land of the dead in their beliefs. They made jewelry of the broken china from the wrecked ship, which later was found by archaeologists in the

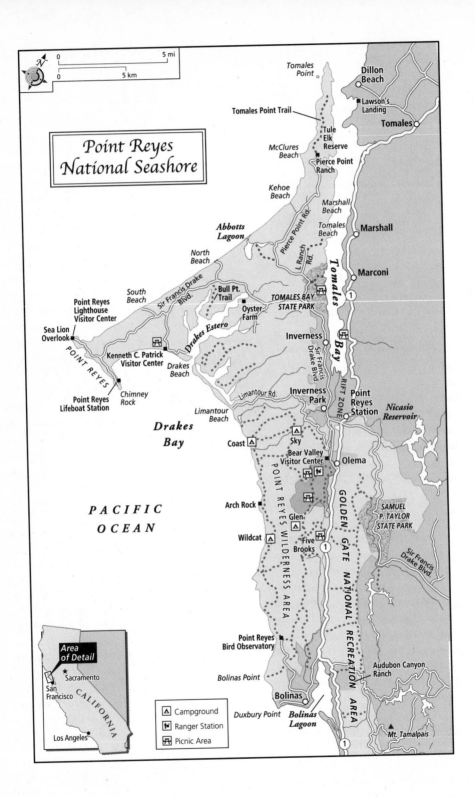

Point Reyes National Seashore

remains of their villages. Every so often, someone finds a piece of the ship's 400-year-old porcelain on the beach, but historians believe that the sailors probably took their valuables with them. Europeans only started to move into the area 200 years later, after Spanish missions were built around San Francisco Bay. The Spanish wanted to convert Native Americans to European ways; instead, 90% of the Coast Miwok died of new diseases and malnutrition.

After the United States took over California in 1846, the Shafter family from Vermont took ownership of Point Reyes. To produce butter for the San Francisco market, they set up a series of ranches, named in order from A to Z (as they still are). To get there, you took a schooner to Drakes Estero, or a stagecoach that went across the county to San Rafael twice a week. James Shafter thought a railroad would make more sense, and he put his money into a line from Sausalito to Point Reyes Station. It was finished in 1875, but the railroad lost money. Shafter and his descendants worked and sold off property to repay the money he lost on the railroad for the next 60 years, until all the land had been sold, just before World War II.

Not much had changed in the area. Ranchers still grazed cattle on the Point Reyes Peninsula and the grasslands east of Tomales Bay. There were small, historic hotels in Olema and businesses in Point Reyes Station that served the farmers. But when the war ended, developers started looking at western Marin County as the next natural extension for San Francisco. The opportunities for building subdivisions and vacation resorts were obvious: The land was beautiful, unspoiled, and, with the completion of the Golden Gate Bridge in 1937, a short drive from San Francisco. Local people had set aside some land in small parks, and the National Park Service studied buying the whole peninsula. It calculated the cost in 1935 as $45 an acre. But developers opposed the park because they saw a chance to make money building on

the land. The price rose fast as they cut trees, built houses, and sold lots. The ranchers were also against the new park because they wanted to keep ranching.

The Park Service got the ranchers' support by agreeing to let them stay and rent their land back from the park. Today, the Park Service still extends those ranch leases every 5 years because it believes that the ranches still belong on Point Reyes. With the ranchers' support, in 1962 Congress passed and President Kennedy signed a law creating the national seashore. It gave the Park Service money to buy the land — enough money to pay about $230 an acre. But that wasn't nearly enough. The value of coastal California land was shooting up, and once owners knew that the government had to buy their property for the new park, they held out for top dollar. Point Reyes National Seashore wasn't completed until 1972, at a cost of about $1,100 an acre. Today, of course, coastal land is worth much more.

The time it took to protect Point Reyes gave people in Marin County a chance to see the mistakes that were made in other national park communities around the country. Originally, officials had planned a freeway to Point Reyes Station, with major roads through the national seashore to carry visitors. But around the time the park was finished, in the early 1970s, people realized that car-centered development had made a mess in national parks and suburban communities across the country. It brought traffic jams, pollution, and ugly roadside business areas, and ruined the natural experience that people came to the parks to enjoy. Today the Park Service is trying to get cars out of some parks, and communities all over the United States are spending money to build streets that look like the historic walking districts they once destroyed by building freeways and malls.

In 1972, the local government in west Marin dropped the idea of the freeway and rezoned the land to stop development. It passed laws saying property couldn't be cut up into pieces smaller than 60 acres, too large for anything but ranching. In 1980, environmentalists and ranchers started a group to protect farmland from rising costs. The group would pay the ranchers for agreeing that their land could be used only for ranching, not development. That protected half as much land again as the national seashore. Local laws also stopped roadside franchise businesses and ugly signs. The area looks today much as it did 50 years ago, before the junk-food era. The towns are quiet and charming, the roads are narrow and lined with natural trees and pastures, the views are wide and sweeping.

The town of Bolinas, at the south end of the national seashore, carried the fight against the outside world even farther — it didn't want tourists at all. Local people tore down the sign pointing the way to the community along Route 1. The highway department replaced it more than 30 times, but it was always torn down in the dead of night, with the support of the local people. Finally, the highway department gave up. Go to Bolinas anyway; park and walk around on the narrow streets (directions are below under "Orientation"). It's a uniquely attractive town, with a main street that fades away into a beach.

There's a bad part to all this protection. With the restrictions on dividing up land, the price of housing has gone up to the point that only people who are financially well-off can afford to move there. There are few minority people in the communities, and some people complain of a snobbish attitude. For families, there aren't many inexpensive hotel rooms. Restaurants are mostly sit-down places with menus. But I'd happily put up with such inconveniences at every national park to have their surroundings as pretty as Point Reyes.

# ORIENTATION

## THE PARKS

Pick up a free map at the Bear Valley Visitor Center, just inside the national seashore near Olema (take Bear Valley Road west from Route 1).

### Point Reyes National Seashore

The national seashore takes in land west of the coastal highway, Route 1, a short drive north of the Golden Gate Bridge. It's a roughly triangular peninsula about 27 miles wide at the base that sticks 12 miles out into the Pacific. The Olema Valley and long, narrow Tomales Bay separate the peninsula from the mainland; the San Andreas Fault and Route 1 run along this line. The eastern, wooded half of the peninsula is along Inverness Ridge, which runs in the same direction as the fault. To the west, the woods give way to bushes, pastures, and large marshy estuaries that reach like fingers through the area. Many miles of sandy beaches run along the south and west sides of the peninsula, while the southern area, reached through Bolinas, has rocky beaches. The sea is warm enough for swimming only in enclosed waters, including Tomales Bay and Bolinas Lagoon.

### Golden Gate National Recreation Area & Muir Woods

The recreation area extends from the east side of Point Reyes to San Francisco along Route 1. The northern, undeveloped portion is managed by the national seashore and is a good place for mountain biking, meadow hiking, and enjoying ocean beaches below great cliffs. The recreation area also includes sites in San Francisco that fall outside our scope.

Muir Woods National Monument, a valley redwood grove, is in the recreation area just north of the Golden Gate Bridge off Route 1. Hiking trails radiate from there across Mount Tamalpais, but the main activity is following the short nature trail to see the trees.

## Samuel P. Taylor State Park

Seven miles up Sir Francis Drake Boulevard from Olema, the state park protects a valley grove of coast redwoods, with mountain hiking trails and a picnic and camping area among the huge trees.

## THE TOWNS

These are the towns in or adjacent to the national seashore.

## Inverness

This village faces Tomales Bay, on Sir Francis Drake Boulevard a few miles within the national seashore from Olema or Point Reyes Station. There are a motel, bed-and-breakfasts, a small store, and a couple of restaurants.

## Point Reyes Station

The seashore's largest town is small and pleasant — even the grocery store is aesthetically pleasing. The town lies about 2 miles north of Olema on Route 1, near a shortcut to the national seashore.

## Olema

A small group of historic clapboard hotels and look-alikes stand along Route 1 just outside the main park entrance, with a couple of restaurants and the area's main campground.

## Bolinas

Bolinas is a charming collection of vacation homes and old-time businesses. Residents make a tradition of tearing down the sign pointing to the town, but finding it is easy enough. Take the first road west from Route 1 north of Bolinas Lagoon or south of Olema. The turn is just north of Milepost 16. This is also the way to the Point Reyes Bird Observatory field station and the Palomarin shoreline.

## The Roads

Only twisting, two-lane country roads give Pt. Reyes access. The main road outside the park is north-south **Route 1,** the cliffside coastal highway. **Sir Francis Drake Boulevard** crosses east-west from San Rafael, on Route 101 along San Francisco Bay, to Olema and Route 1, where the two merge briefly going north before Sir Francis Drake continues west into the national seashore and out to the lighthouse at the headlands. **Pierce Point Road** branches from Sir Francis Drake to the north of the park. **Bear Valley** and **Limantour roads** lead from Olema to the visitor center and central part of the park. **Mesa Road** runs from Bolinas to the southern tip of the park.

# MAKING THE ARRANGEMENTS

## WHEN TO GO

Summer is the busiest season at the national seashore and the neighboring sites; but only weekends pose any problem, and we didn't encounter bothersome crowds even on Independence Day. During the week you can have many areas to yourself. I've covered the seasons for whales below, under "Whale Watching" (p. 502).

The temperature always stays in a narrow, comfortable range year-round, but Point Reyes is the foggiest, windiest spot on the West Coast. The seasons here are of rain, wind, fog, and dry weather, basically corresponding to winter, spring, summer and fall. The pattern is controlled by three alternating sets of ocean currents. The winter rainy season usually lasts from November to March; rain at this time comes mostly during ferocious ocean storms in December and January, with many pleasant days between storms. Little rain falls from April through October, but fog takes its place. Strong winds start in the spring, causing ocean waters to turn over so that cold water surfaces near the shore. As damp ocean air passes from an offshore area of warm water to this cold-water area, thick fog forms and blows over the shore. April and May are the windiest months.

The fog builds up to July, the driest and foggiest month of the year, and lasts into September.

But on any particular summer day, the weather varies drastically on each side of Inverness Ridge, which forms a dam against the fog. To the east you could have a warm, sunny picnic and swim on Tomales Bay, while a few miles to the west you would encounter cool, whipping mist. The hour of the day matters, too. As the fog moves eastward over the warm land, it evaporates back into vapor and leaves clear skies. As the day progresses and the land heats up, the line of fog moves out toward the shore. The fog gives the seashore mysterious beauty and keeps the weather cool. It also leaves as much water on plants in a year as 12 inches of rain.

In the fall, starting in late August or September, the winds and upwelling ocean currents die down. The fog leaves and more long, sunny dry spells set in. It's a sort of annual Indian summer.

## How Much Time to Spend

Most people come to Point Reyes from the San Francisco area for weekends or day trips to watch the whales or walk on the beach, but you can easily spend a week here without getting bored. If you really want to relax, rent a house for 2 weeks.

## How Far to Plan Ahead

There aren't many rooms at Point Reyes, but weekends and holidays are the only times that getting reservations is a real problem. For those periods, book as far ahead as possible. Midweek rentals are not hard to get, although the farther you plan ahead the better your selection will be. Olema Ranch Campground may have empty sites midweek even during the summer season, but weekends have to be reserved far in advance.

## Reading Up

**Trail Guides:** Dorothy Whitnah's *Point Reyes* (Wilderness Press, www.wildernesspress.com) is a sprightly and well-informed trail guide,

which also covers area history, the roads, beaches, and other outdoor attractions. **Maps:** An excellent trail map, printed on plastic, is published by **Tom Harrison Cartography** (☎ 800/265-9090 or 415/456-7940; www.tomharrisonmaps.com). **Natural History and Culture:** *The Natural History of the Point Reyes Peninsula,* by Jules G. Evens (Point Reyes National Seashore Association), is an authoritative, adult-level compendium. *The Coast Miwok Indians of the Point Reyes Area,* by Sylvia Barker Thalman, is a short, illustrated survey of their culture and history. Both are published by the Point Reyes Nature Association.

## Getting There
### By Car

**From San Francisco,** the fastest route is **U.S. 101** north across the Golden Gate Bridge to Larkspur, then across to the west side of Marin County on **Sir Francis Drake Boulevard.** From the south, the 101 exit can be confusing: Take the exit for I-580, the Richmond-San Rafael Bridge, but then veer left from the ramp, to the west. Avoid rush hour, when it all clogs up. **From the north,** leave 101 in Novato, going west on San Marin Drive 2 miles to a right onto Novato Boulevard, then 6 miles to a left onto Point Reyes-Petaluma Road, which will take you to Route 1 at Point Reyes Station. **From the east,** you can exit I-580 onto Sir Francis Drake before hitting 101. **Route 1** is the most scenic route from the north or south, and you should take it at least one way just for the experience (unless your kids get carsick).

### By Air

The closest airport is in San Francisco, just south of the city. It's served by all major carriers and car-rental agencies. If you want to shop for ticket or car prices, check the San Jose and Oakland airports.

## What to Pack
### Clothing

For summer visits, you can count on little or no rain, but you will need warm sweaters and

| | AVG. HIGH (°F) | AVG. LOW (°F) | AVG. PRECIP. (IN.) |
|---|---|---|---|
| Dec.–Jan. | 55 | 39 | 20 |
| February | 61 | 42 | 8 |
| March | 65 | 43 | 6.5 |
| April | 70 | 44 | 2.8 |
| May | 75 | 47 | 1 |
| June–Sept. | 82 | 51 | 1 |
| October | 75 | 48 | 2.6 |
| November | 64 | 44 | 6.8 |

windbreakers with hoods for days in strong, foggy winds on the outer beaches. In early spring and late fall, rain is more frequent, and in midwinter you'll need good rain gear for occasional drenching storms. Uncomfortable heat or freezing cold are unknown, but in an hour you might change from shorts and T-shirts to sweaters, jackets, and long pants. Bring some tidy clothes for elegant places you're likely to go — restaurants, B&Bs, and the like. Ties and dresses aren't needed.

## Gear

Bring binoculars; the marine mammals you see at Point Reyes will be far off, and bird-watching is one of the best activities here. Summer-weight camping gear will be sufficient with warm clothes, but be ready for wind. Beach toys and other frivolous items aren't as readily available here as at other beach areas, so pick up what you need in one of the towns you pass through on the way.

# WHERE TO SPEND THE NIGHT

## CAMPING

Besides these campgrounds, the Park Service can give you a list of others up to 60 miles away. See "Tomales Bay State Park" (p. 498) for another camping option. Overnight trips to Tomales Point are covered under "Sea Kayaking" (p. 501).

You can camp among the dunes near Dillon Beach at **Lawson's Landing** (☎ 707/ 878-2443; www.lawsonslanding.com) about 20 miles from the national seashore by road but just across Tomales Bay from the park's Tomales Point. They rent boats, too (see "Fishing," p. 500). They charge $14 for camping and accept Visa or MasterCard. Reservations are not taken by phone, and it can fill on holiday weekends. This a lovely, iso-

lated seaside spot; but there are no designated sites and at present some areas have only portable toilets. Inland, there's a 270-site **KOA campground** near Petaluma, 25 miles from the national seashore, at the Penngrove exit on Highway 101 (☎ **800/KOA-1233** or 707/ 763-1492).

**Olema Ranch Campground.** 10155 Hwy. 1 (P.O. Box 175), Olema, CA 94950. ☎ **415/663-8001.** Fax 415/663-8832. www.olemaranch.com. Full hookups $28, tent sites $20; $3 per extra person over age 5. AE, DISC, MC, V. 200 sites; tents or RVs. Hot showers, Laundromat, store, post office, organized activities.

This large, grassy campground under tall pines is a center of activities for the national seashore. It takes the place of the car-camping campgrounds you would find at most other national parks. They even have children's story programs in the amphitheater. It's comfortable and well run, with water faucets even at the large tent sites. On busy weekends the lack of screening between sites creates a sort of communal feeling. Reserve well ahead for those times; sites are in less demand on weekdays. Bike rentals are on-site, and the Bear Valley Visitor Center is about a mile away.

**Samuel P. Taylor State Park.** Sir Francis Drake Hwy., 7 miles from the Olema entrance to the national seashore, P.O. Box 251, Lagunitas, CA 94938. ☎ **800/444-7275** or 415/488-9897. http://cal-parks.ca.gov. $12 per site; reservations taken for $7.50 surcharge. 61 sites; tents or small RVs. Flush toilets, hot showers, dump station.

Ten minutes from the national seashore, this campground is among towering coast redwoods on a steep hillside. It's shady, quiet, and private. There could hardly be a prettier place to camp. Reservations become available 7 months ahead.

Samuel P. Taylor was a gold-rush entrepreneur who started a paper recycling mill and gunpowder factory here, as well as one of the nation's first recreational campgrounds. The park, which takes in almost 3,000 acres along Lagunitas or Papermill Creek, offers many activities. You can watch silver salmon spawning in the creek, hike a network of short trails shown on a free park guide map, or ride the paved 3-mile bike trail through the trees. Even if you're not camping, you can use the beautiful picnic ground under the redwoods for the $2 day-use fee.

## Backcountry Camping

There are four backcountry campgrounds in the national seashore, reachable only by hiking, biking, or horseback riding. You need a backcountry permit to use them, reserved up to 3 months ahead to the day with a credit card by phone or fax. They take calls at ☎ 415/663-8054 Monday through Friday between 9am and 2pm (the staff does answer the phone at other times, but doesn't take

reservations then). The fax number is 415/663-1597; download the fax form at www.nps.gov/pore/recreation/camping/campfax.htm. The phones are busy when the weekend permits for 3 months later become available, and they go fast. The only way to jump ahead is to go to the desk in person on a weekend, when the phone system isn't open. For dates other than weekends, it's not so hard to get a site, but make a reservation as early as you can anyway. The permit costs $10 per night and must be picked up at the **Bear Valley Visitor Center** before you start your hike.

The backcountry campgrounds occupy the sites of former ranches. They have running water and pit toilets, and each site has a picnic table and charcoal grill. You may need to treat the water; ask a ranger (water treatment is covered under "Gear" in chapter 1, "Planning Your Trip." All but Glen allow pack animals and have group sites, which makes Glen quieter than the others. (See "Horseback Riding," p. 501, for the address of the horse concession.)

**Coast.** On shore, east of Limantour Rd. 12 sites.

This campground is on a grassy, brushy bluff near the end of sandy Limantour Beach and tide pools at Sculptured Beach. The shortest hiking route is only 1.8 miles from the Laguna Trailhead off Limantour Road. An easy bike route runs 2.8 miles from the Point Reyes Hostel on Limantour Road.

**Glen.** West of Five Brooks Stables. 12 sites.

This is a quiet, remote campground, without group sites or pack animals. It's also the least spectacular, located in a forest clearing. The hike to the campground on the Bear Valley Trail is 4½ miles.

**Sky.** On the west side of Mt. Wittenberg, near Bear Valley Visitor Center. 12 sites.

The partly wooded sites here have great views to the ocean from 1,025 feet elevation. The easiest way to reach the campground by foot or bike is 1.7 miles down an old road from the Sky Trailhead on Limantour Road, but there are many other choices of routes.

**Wildcat.** On the coast north of Palomarin. 2 family sites, 3 group sites.

Mostly for groups, the campground is 5½ miles from the Palomarin Trailhead.

# HOTELS & BED-AND-BREAKFASTS

The planning that has kept west Marin County attractive has also led to a shortage of rooms for families. Compounding the problem, many of the area's bed-and-breakfasts cater to romantic weekends and often shun families. I've listed four choices that do accept families, and you can reach more small inns through the booking agencies listed below under "Cottages." Consider renting a cottage; you often don't have to stay a full week to do so (see below). If you come up empty, there are lots of hotels in San Rafael, Novato, Sausalito, and other towns along U.S. 101, within 45 minutes of the national seashore. Contact the **Marin County Convention and Visitors Bureau** (☎ 415/499-5000; www. visitmarin.org) for a referral in that area.

**Golden Hinde Inn and Marina.** 12938 Sir Francis Drake Hwy. (P.O. Box 295), Inverness, CA 94937. ☎ 415/669-1389. Fax 415/669-1128. www.goldenhindeinn.com. 35 units. $75–$114 double, $119–$129 suite; $10 per extra person age 13 or older. AE, MC, V.

This is a reasonably priced family motel, quite a rarity in the area. It sits on the shore of Tomales Bay with a little bit of a beach, just inside the national seashore. The better rooms overlook the water with 1960s decor (even lava lamps), vaulted ceilings, and kitchenettes. They're light and pleasant, and there are about a dozen. Most of the other rooms are simply faded roadside motel rooms, without much to recommend or condemn them. There's a small pool where you can swim when the mist peels back. A sea-kayak rental (see "Activities," p. 500) and restaurant (see "Where to Eat," p. 503) are at the motel.

**Holly Tree Inn and Cottages.** 3 Silverhills Rd., Inverness Park (P.O. Box 642), Point Reyes Station, CA 94956. ☎ 415/663-1554. Fax 415/663-

8566. www.hollytreeinn.com. 4 rms, 3 cottages. $145–$175 double; $15 per extra person, child or adult. AE, MC, V.

In a quiet, dreamy 20-acre canyon near Tomales Bay in the park, a creek and paths weave through lush plantings around the elegant yet comfortable clapboard inn. Even more remarkable, it caters to families in two of the rooms and the cottages, one of which is on pilings over Tomales Bay. The Balogh family raised their own kids here and didn't want to exclude others. Among the many charming touches, a set of blocks are models of the buildings in Point Reyes Station. Some rooms have only shower stalls, not tubs, and all lack TVs and telephones.

**Inverness Valley Inn.** 13275 Sir Francis Drake Blvd. (P.O. Box 428), Inverness, CA 94937. ☎ 800/416-0405 or 415/669-7250. invernessvalleyinn. com. 10 units. $130 double weekends, $115 weekdays; $20 each additional child or adult. AE, MC, V.

This, the closest lodging to the beaches, also may be the best for families. Situated on a natural 15-acre site with two tennis courts, a pool and hot tub, and plenty of room to run, it consists of a series of small buildings with patios that open onto the lawn. Some of the light, fresh rooms have high vaulted ceilings, kitchenettes, and grills. They're decorated with hardwood, tile, and bold fabrics.

**Motel Inverness.** 12718 Sir Francis Drake Hwy. (P.O. Box 1108), Inverness, CA 94937. ☎ 415/669-1081. 7 units. $99–$175 double; $10 per extra person over age 6. AE, MC, V.

This is a motel that feels like a B&B, where the smallish rooms have skylights and sumptuous decoration of bright patterns and wicker. A large common room overlooking the water brings guests together with a fireplace, large TV, and pool table. Rooms lack telephones. The Inverness location puts you near the park.

**Point Reyes Seashore Lodge.** 10021 Coastal Hwy. 1 (P.O. Box 39), Olema, CA 94950. ☎ 415/663-9000. Fax 415/663-9030. www.pointreyes seashore.com. 21 rms, 1 cottage. $125–$180 double, $215–$235 suite, $295–$325 cottage; $25 per extra person age 12 and over, $5 per extra child. AE, DISC, MC, V.

This is a dramatic and luxurious modern building, thoughtfully designed and landscaped to fit in with the local style so that it looks historic. The management aims at couples; but rooms are large and some have beds for families. There are phones in the rooms, but no TVs. The Bear Valley Visitor Center is nearby.

## COTTAGES
If you can stay long enough to make it worthwhile, a cottage is the way to go at Point Reyes. Unlike the policy at many tourist destinations, it isn't necessary to take a place for a whole week. Two- or 3-day minimums are common, especially over weekends. Prices range from about $125 a night to more than $300; they're no more than comparable inn lodgings, but you save by not having to eat at restaurants. Location is an issue. Many rentals are quite distant from the national seashore, so get as close as you can to limit your daily drive.

A booking agency can help you find the right place. **Point Reyes Lodging,** P.O. Box 878, Point Reyes Station, CA 94956 (☎ 800/539-1872 or 415/663-1872; www.ptreyes.com), is a collaboration of various cottages and small inns. They can fax you a current vacancy listing, or you can navigate to the individual establishments through the website. **West Marin Network,** P.O. Box 834, Point Reyes Station, CA 94956 (☎ 415/663-9543), has a storefront office in Point Reyes Station, where owner Bobbi Stumpf also runs the chamber of commerce. She represents many B&Bs and cottages and knows the area well. Contact real-estate agents offering vacation rentals through the chambers of commerce (see "Point Reyes Address Book," p. 484) or www.coastaltraveler.com.

Here are two good places. **Fairwinds Farm,** P.O. Box 581, Inverness, CA 94937 (☎ 415/663-9454; www.fairwindsfarminverness.com), has a large cottage with a hot tub on 5 acres of deep woods atop Inverness Ridge; animals wander around and there is a playhouse for the kids. **The Country House** (☎ 415/663-1627; www.ptreyescountry house.com) has three bedrooms and an apple orchard right in Point Reyes Station.

At Dillon Beach, at the north end of Tomales Bay, about 20 miles from the park area (allow an hour), you can rent a cottage near where **Lawson's Landing** offers clamming, pier fishing, and small-boat rentals (see "Camping," p. 491, and "Fishing," p. 500). Dillon Beach Property Management (☎ 800/447-3767 or 707/878-2204; www.dillon beach.com) has a range of about two dozen choices.

# WHEN YOU ARRIVE

## ENTRANCE FEES
There are no fees to enter the national seashore. Admission to the Muir Woods National Monument is $2 per person 17 and older. Day-use fees at both Samuel P. Taylor and Tomales Bay state parks are $2.

## REGULATIONS

Mountain bikes and horses are allowed on many Point Reyes trails, but dogs are outlawed in most places. The beaches where dogs are allowed are marked on the Park Service map. Check the park newspaper or ask at the visitor center for more dog rules.

An improperly extinguished campfire burned 45 houses and one-sixth of the park in 1995. Permits are now required for all fires, except charcoal contained in a grill and carried out afterward. Beach fire permits are free at the visitor center.

## VISITOR CENTERS
## Park Service

**Bear Valley Visitor Center.** On Bear Valley Rd. near the park entrance in Olema. ☎ **415/663-1092.** Mon–Fri 9am–5pm, Sat–Sun and holidays 8am–5pm.

This is a first-rate visitor center in a large barn building. Exhibits explain the seashore's habitat areas and the wildlife that lives there. There are also a slide show, a good selection of books, and rangers to answer questions. See the working seismograph that measures the shaking of the ground on the San Andreas Fault, which is a short walk away. Nature trails on the fault, to a Coast Miwok village and a stable, are described below under "Places for Learning" (p. 499).

**Ken Patrick Visitor Center.** At Drakes Beach. ☎ **415/669-1250.** Summer Fri–Tues 10am–5pm; Sept–May Sat–Sun and holidays 10am–5pm.

This visitor center is in a sort of beach house with a cafe (see "Natural Places," below). There are many fun things to look at, including a large saltwater aquarium, whale bones, fossils, old charts, and displays on weather, navigation, and other subjects. The ranger may be willing to show you stuff in the aquarium. Ken Patrick was a ranger killed in the line of duty by deer poachers in 1972 on Mount Vision.

**Lighthouse Visitor Center.** Point Reyes Headlands, at the end of Sir Francis Drake Hwy. ☎ **415/669-1534.** Thurs–Mon 10am–5pm.

This small visitor center has interesting displays on whales, birds, and shipping. It stands at the top of the 308 steps down to the lighthouse itself, described below under "Natural Places" (p. 496).

## Commercial Visitor Centers

In Point Reyes Station, a storefront visitor center run by the West Marin Chamber of Commerce is on Route 1 at Mesa Road. It offers lodging referrals and other local information (☎ **415/663-9232;** www.pointreyes. org). On the San Francisco Bay side of the county, stop in at the Marin County Convention and Visitors Bureau, at 1013 Larkspur Landing Circle, Larkspur, CA 94939, right off Sir Francis Drake Boulevard east from the U.S. 101 exit, near the bay ferry terminal. They keep a room-availability board for the larger area (☎ **415/499-5000;** www. visitmarin.org).

## GETTING AROUND
## By Car

Your car will get you almost anywhere in the national seashore and the surrounding natural areas, but some places are short on parking. During peak winter whale-watching weekends, you may have to park at Drakes Beach and take a $3.50 shuttle (free for kids 12 and under) up to the headlands, where the parking lot is small. Bolinas also has little room for cars, so park and walk.

The biggest problem for families is that kids often get carsick on the area's roads. Route 1, the Sir Francis Drake Boulevard, and the other roads within the park all are narrow and twisty. Friends of ours were more or less pinned down in their cottage because their son kept getting sick. If this is a concern, get lodgings within the national seashore to reduce driving time, and try children's chewable Dramamine.

## By Bike

Most of the roads are too narrow and heavily traveled for family biking, but there are side roads and trails where you can go; see "Mountain Biking" (p. 501).

## KEEPING SAFE & HEALTHY

The national seashore's outer beaches aren't suitable for swimming. The water is cold (around 55°F), and the surf and currents are ferocious. When big surf is coming in, you should be careful just walking on the west-facing beaches because surprisingly large waves called sneakers can swoosh up the beach and pull you in. Drakes Beach is more protected for sea kayakers and surfers, but if you get in trouble, you're on your own. See "Swimming" (p. 502) for safer places to go in the water. Also, stay back from bluff edges, which give way easily.

In addition, be sure to read up on Lyme disease and poison oak, which is very common in these woods, in "Dealing with Hazards," in chapter 1. A picture of poison oak is on p. 394. Also beware of stinging nettle, which is painful on bare skin. Learn to identify these plants from the samples at the Bear Valley Visitor Center.

## ENJOYING THE PARK

### NATURAL PLACES
### Point Reyes Headlands

Sir Francis Drake Boulevard rises past ranches and pastures to its end on a T-shaped ridge over the sea, 21 miles from the Bear Valley Visitor Center. To the right, the road comes to a small parking lot, where you can park and walk about a quarter mile atop the cliffs to the **Lighthouse Visitor Center** (see "Visitor Centers," p. 495). This part of the point is like the prow of a ship pointing straight out into the Pacific. When the fog breaks — rarely in the summer — you can look down on elephant seals, sea lions, and common murres on the rocks 600 feet below. During whale migrations, this is the place to watch them swimming up the coast. A row of windswept cypress trees planted long ago by the lighthouse keepers catches moisture from the fog and drips constantly; there are no other trees. A rain-catching basin once provided water for the lighthouse. The buildings are fascinating, and some are still occupied by Park Service workers.

From the buildings and visitor center, 308 steps lead down the cliff to the iron **Point Reyes Lighthouse,** bolted onto the side of the cliff. It was placed low to get it out of some of the fog — this is the foggiest spot on the West Coast. The platforms along the way are good rest stops and places to perch for wildlife watching. The stairs close at 4:30pm and are closed Tuesday and Wednesday and whenever the winds are over 40 m.p.h. The lighthouse is well worth a visit, but not for people afraid of heights.

On the other side of the point is the spectacular mile-long walk to **Chimney Rock,** and the way down to the restored **lifesaving station** that faces Drakes Bay. This is also a good tide-pooling area (see p. 502).

### The Beaches

The outer sandy beaches, **North and South Beach,** are accessible from Sir Francis Drake Boulevard. They're all part of vast Point Reyes Beach, a wild place where summer fog and wind roar off the sea and the full force of the Pacific's great swells smash on sand. The dune-backed beach extends many miles farther than most people will walk — it's a lonely wilderness. The waters are too rough and cold, and the currents too fast, for swimming or wading.

Farther north, on Pierce Point Road — which branches from Sir Francis Drake Boulevard just past Inverness — are a series of shores at the end of interesting walks. The drive itself is spectacular, following the rounded ridge top with sweeping ocean views on each side and herds of elk wandering about. **McClures Beach,** at the end of the road and

⁴/₁₀ mile down a steep bluff trail, is framed on each end by sharp buttresses of rock. A keyhole opens to the next beach to the south when the tide is out. These are fine tide-pooling grounds, but don't climb high on rocks or tempt the water. **Kehoe Beach** is a broader beach backed by dunes; the .6-mile walk to it passes through rolling meadows. **Abbotts Lagoon** is yet another kind of shoreline, where a barrier sandbar protects rich sea-bird habitat. The smooth water gives way to the ferocious open ocean when you complete the walk to the deserted, driftwood-strewn outer beach, about 1.5 miles from the trailhead one way.

**Drakes Beach** faces south and is more protected and easier to get to, but it's still many miles long and often foggy and deserted. The milder seas and currents allow some careful wading and sea kayaking. The water is too cold for swimming. Turn near the end of Sir Francis Drake Boulevard. There are plenty of parking and an interesting visitor center (see p. 495) with a friendly, inexpensive little place to eat. **Drakes Beach Cafe** (☎ **415/669-1297**) has tables behind big windows or on a deck overlooking the beach. The fresh, local seafood fits perfectly — we enjoyed the barbecued oysters — and the menu, ranging from $3.40 to $9, includes good burgers too. They're open 10am to 6pm daily June to September and take no credit cards.

**Palomarin Beach** is a rocky place at the end of dirt Mesa Road. Head north from Bolinas, beyond the fascinating bird observatory (p. 499). This little-used area of the park has excellent bird-watching and tide pooling and several remote hiking trails. The walk to the beach is a steep third of a mile.

## The Estuaries & Coastal Prairie

Behind Point Reyes's sandy shores, unique tidal estuaries reach among the low, grassy hills in the heart of the peninsula. The shallow water of Drakes Estero runs miles up narrow bays rich in salt marsh life and visited by hordes of birds. You can see the area by sea kayak or by hiking along trails that cross the softly rolling grassy hills. Reach these trails, all marked on park maps, from Sir Francis Drake Boulevard at the Bull Point or Estero parking lots, or on Limantour Road, which splits from Bear Valley Road near Point Reyes Station. The **Estero Trail** has a base of crushed rock that makes it accessible to wheelchairs partway.

## The Forests

A pine and fir forest runs along Inverness Ridge on most of the east side of the national seashore. Most of the hiking, biking, and horseback trails weave through the deep woods and forest meadows to the sea in the southern part of the park, from the Bear Valley Visitor Center south. The trip to remote, roadless points along the shore through the forest — a beautiful journey — is only 4 miles by foot or mountain bike from the visitor center. This higher area of the park is less often foggy than the west side, but is still often misty and cool.

## Tomales Point

The northern point of the national seashore, between Tomales Bay and the Pacific Ocean, is a remote area of unreal beauty. Tule elk range over a treeless coastal prairie that extends from shore to shore all along the long, narrow point. Wherever you find yourself on this round ridge, your eye is overwhelmed with Godlike vision — you just can't believe how much you can see. Pierce Point Road ends just beyond the historic ranch site (p. 499) at a trailhead for a 4.7-mile path to the end of the point. It's also possible to explore the area by sea kayak on Tomales Bay, obtaining a permit to camp out along the shore (see "Sea Kayaking," p. 501).

## Tomales Bay State Park

This state park, which lies within the national seashore on the western shore of Tomales Bay, surrounds delightful **Heart's Desire Beach.** The water is clean, warm, shallow, and gentle enough for swimming, or wading for little children. The narrow passage of Tomales Bay allows the sun to warm the water, and Inverness Ridge holds back the wind and fog. There are changing rooms, bathrooms, and free cold showers. This is a great place for a picnic, and sea kayakers launch here, too. Trails lead through the woods to other pocket beaches along the shore; pick up a 50¢ map from the ranger station. A first-come, first-served hike- or bike-in campground has six sites that cost $3 per person. The day-use fee, for both campers and day visitors, is $2 per vehicle.

The park is on Pierce Point Road (Star Route) north of Inverness. It's open daily from 8am to 5pm. Call ☎ **415/669-1140** for more information.

## Just Outside the National Seashore: Muir Woods National Monument

This canyon grove of coast redwoods lies within a half-hour drive of San Francisco. Every day, crowds from the city flood along the paths as if touring the galleries of a museum. But if Muir Woods is a tree museum, it is probably the most impressive museum you'll ever see.

Unlike 19 out of 20 coast redwoods standing when whites arrived on the West Coast, these trees didn't get cut down, a fact we owe to one man — William Kent — who saved the grove and started protecting the parkland on surrounding Mount Tamalpais that became Golden Gate National Recreation Area and Mount Tamalpais State Park. Kent was simply so impressed with the trees that, although he could hardly afford it, he bought Redwood Canyon to keep them from being logged. Then he gave the land to the government as a national monument to save it from being flooded by a dam. President Teddy Roosevelt wanted to name the monument for Kent, but Kent insisted that it be named for naturalist John Muir. (See chapter 12, "Bryce Canyon National Park," for more on Roosevelt, and chapter 17, "Rock, Life & Change," for more on Muir.) Oddly enough, Kent later was elected to Congress and voted in favor of building the Hetch Hetchy Dam in Yosemite National Park, which broke Muir's heart.

Coast redwoods, by far the world's tallest trees, are related to the giant sequoias, shorter trees that are much bigger because of their thick trunks. Both kinds of trees need a special habitat. The coast redwoods grow only in the

Pacific fog belt, with its mild temperatures and moist air. Like the wood of sequoias, their wood has a lot of an acid called tannin, which stops rot and wards off insects that kill other trees. Coast redwoods can live through fires too, as long as the tree isn't completely destroyed. Redwoods live for more than 2,000 years; in fact, there's no end to how long they can live if they aren't knocked down, burned up, or cut. (More on the coast redwood can be found in chapter 20, "Ecology: Fitting It Together"; the giant sequoia is covered in chapter 17, "Rock, Life & Change.")

Muir Woods is off Route 1, just north of the Golden Gate Bridge. It's open daily from 8am to sunset. Go early to avoid some of the throngs and parking problems, but even crowds can't spoil the wonder of this place. Using the excellent Park Service trail-guide map, follow the mile-long, self-guided nature trail through the heart of the biggest trees along clear Redwood Creek. Rangers offer talks often during the day on the trail or in the visitor center. Many other less-used trails radiate from here for longer hikes, also shown on the nature trail map. A snack-bar restaurant serves simple meals near the entrance. For more information, contact **Muir Woods National Monument** (☎ 415/388-2595; www.nps.gov/muwo).

Two other places to see coast redwoods are near the national seashore: Samuel P. Taylor State Park (see "Camping," p. 491) and Audubon Canyon Ranch (see "Bird-Watching," p. 500).

## PLACES FOR LEARNING
**Point Reyes Bird Observatory Field Station.** On Mesa Rd., north from Bolinas (4990 Shoreline Hwy. 1, Stinson Beach, CA 92970-9701). ☎ **415/868-1221.** www.prbo.org. May–Nov Tues–Sun 7am–5pm, banding 7am–noon; Dec–Apr Wed and Sat–Sun only.

We stumbled upon this small wooden building by a dirt road on our way to go tide pooling at Palomarin. We walked into the banding lab, where a biologist was measuring and banding a wren. She explained her work and held the bird's tiny chest to our ears so that we could hear its fast-beating heart. A volunteer brought in a chickadee from the nets. After study, my son Robin, then age 5, tossed it from his hands back into the air. Never had science felt so intimate. We wouldn't have missed this visit for anything. The nonprofit observatory studies and protects birds in the national seashore and the huge bird colonies on the Farallon Islands. The staff leads occasional bird walks for visitors and welcomes volunteers at the observatory, where there's also a one-room museum.

**Pierce Point Ranch.** At the north end of Pierce Point Rd. ☎ **415/669-1534.** Open daylight hours.

Urban children especially will enjoy seeing how ranch families lived self-contained on remote Tomales Point, with their animals, schoolhouse, and a large barn (it's the only building you can enter). The ranch operated for 100 years starting in 1858. Tomales Point is covered on p. 498.

## At Bear Valley
These three sites all are next to the Bear Valley Visitor Center, on Bear Valley Road near the park entrance in Olema.

### COAST MIWOK CULTURAL EXHIBIT
A half-mile nature trail from the visitor center passes through a replica of a Coast Miwok village called Kule Loklo. Nestled among oak trees where the Native Americans would have gathered acorns, it's quite rough and realistic. You can go in the buildings and imagine what it was like to live there. The path is a bit rough for strollers.

### EARTHQUAKE TRAIL
The San Andreas Fault is visible on this half-mile trail from the Bear Valley Visitor Center. It is paved and easy for strollers, and marked with explanatory signs. This was the epicenter of the quake of 1906, and you can see where

the fault slipped 16 feet along a broken fence line. The fault is quite clear on a map of Point Reyes, too, running along a straight line that includes Bolinas Lagoon and Tomales Bay. West of the fault, the point is riding northwest past the rest of California as it is pulled along by the Pacific tectonic plate. Also check out the seismograph in the visitor center.

## MORGAN HORSE RANCH

Rangers use Morgan's to patrol the park and sometimes offer demonstrations at the ranch behind the visitor center. At other times, you can look at the old farm machinery, tack room, and stables on your own. The ranch is open daily from 9am to 4:30pm; for more information, call ☎ 415/663-1763.

## ACTIVITIES
## Backpacking

Beginning family backpackers could find few better places to start than Point Reyes. The trails are not long, and they lead to gorgeous places. The backcountry campgrounds have running water, picnic tables, fire grates, and animal-proof food storage lockers. You can reach two of them after less than 2 miles of flat hiking, and you can link campsites together for a multiple-day trip of easy stages of up to 4 nights. Be prepared for wind with your equipment and your kids: A flapping tent can be noisy and scary for them. The reservation system and sites are covered on p. 492, maps and trail guides under "Reading Up" (p. 490).

## Bird-Watching

The thickets, forest, estuaries, and ocean shores of Point Reyes offer habitats to an extraordinary variety and abundance of birds — more, experts say, than any other area of the same size in North America. More than 470 species have been counted, although many of those are rare wanderers who found their way here by chance. Besides the different kinds of habitat, birds like Point Reyes for its predictable, mild climate and its place on the coast, between north and south. This is a

breeding ground for both the common murre of the northern oceans and the south's brown pelican. Bird-watchers should bring binoculars and field guides, but you encounter spectacular creatures such as pelicans and egrets without really trying.

If you take bird-watching seriously, check with the local experts on where to go in season. There are plenty to ask at the visitor centers, at the bird observatory (p. 499), or at the **Audubon Canyon Ranch** (☎ 415/868-9244; www.egret.org), a 1,000-acre preserve facing Bolinas Lagoon on Route 1 just south of the national seashore. Breathtaking snowy egrets and great blue herons (p. 48) nest in the coast redwoods here, swooping down to the lagoon to gather food for their young. During the nesting season, mid-March to mid-July, the preserve is open to the public free of charge weekends 10am to 4pm and Tuesday through Friday 2 to 4pm by appointment.

## Fishing

You can fish from the shore in much of the national seashore, in some streams, and in freshwater at reservoirs in the hills east of Route 1. The staff at the **Bear Valley Visitor Center,** on Sir Francis Drake Boulevard near the park entrance in Olema, offers advice on where and how. The **Building Supply (☎ 415/663-1737)** in Point Reyes Station sells fishing gear. At Dillon Beach, at the northern end of the east side of Tomales Bay, you can dig clams, fish from a wharf, get gear, or rent a rowboat or motorized skiff from **Lawson's Landing (☎ 707/878-2443;** www.lawsonslanding.com). Get information before your trip from the **California Department of Fish and Game,** P.O. Box 47, Yountville, CA 94599 (☎ 707/944-5500; www.dfg.ca.gov). A 2-day nonresident license is $10.75. Children under 16 don't need a license.

## Hiking

Point Reyes has many miles of trails through forest, coastal prairie, and shrub thickets full of birds. Starting from the visitor center of the same name, the easy **Bear Valley Trail,** which is also an excellent mountain-biking route, leads through forest 4.4 miles to the shore. The first 3 miles go over an old dirt road, and 1.6 miles down the way, at Divide Meadow, there's a picnic area with a bathroom. The trail also joins many of the park's less-used trails, which you can use to make loop hikes and wander off by yourself. At the end you come to Arch Rock, where Coast Creek (which you've been following) flows through a natural opening before going into the ocean. Millers Point, named for the congressman who helped start the park (he was buried nearby), has views across the sweep of Drakes Bay. Also start at the visitor center for the 5-mile **Mount Wittenberg Loop,** a 1,300-foot climb with views of the shore and Olema Valley.

Limantour Road meets many trails for hikes over the wooded mountains, in the bushy hills, or on the grasslands around the estuaries. Using a trail map, you can choose a loop or destination of almost any length. The **Coast-Laguna Loop** is a fairly flat 5 miles with terrific bird-watching and ocean views. Many less-used trails in the scrub and grass of the coastal bluffs lead from Mesa Road, north of Bolinas.

I've mentioned several other hikes under "Natural Places," including the spectacular Tomales Point hike and several family hikes to and along the beaches. Nature walks at the Bear Valley Visitor Center are described on p. 499. Maps and trail guides are covered under "Reading Up" (p. 490). You can also pick out a trail and get a usable map free from the visitor center.

## Horseback Riding

Many of the park's trails are open to riders. **Five Brooks Ranch,** about 3 miles south of Olema on Route 1 (☎ 415/663-1570; www. fivebrooks.com), offers rides through the forests of the eastern side of the park. An all-day ride makes it to Wildcat Beach, where you can ride through the foam. Rides of 1, 2, 3, and 6 hours cost $30, $50, $80, and $150,

respectively. Children as young as 6 may go on the 1-hour rides, but riders must be over 8 for the longer ones. Call at least a day ahead for the short rides, further ahead if you want to go all day or to set up a private ride with your own route and time. Write to P.O. Box 99, Olema, CA 94950, for information.

## Mountain Biking

Point Reyes is one of the best national parks for mountain biking. Many trails are open to bikes, and businesses nearby serve bikers. The Tom Harrison Cartography map (see "Reading Up," p. 490) indicates which trails are open to mountain bikes. A Park Service handout lists five routes of various difficulty levels, ranging from 5.6 to 15 miles. For families with children, the **Bear Valley Trail** may be the best route. It leads from the visitor center to a bike rack a mile from the sea, and you can walk the rest of the way to Arch Rock. Bikes are for rent at **Olema Ranch Campground** (☎ 415/663-8001) on Route 1 and **Building Supply** (☎ 415/663-1737) in Point Reyes Station. At around $25 a day to rent, bringing them from home on your car makes sense.

## Sea Kayaking

There are few better places for a first sea-kayaking excursion than warm, gentle Tomales Bay, where you may see pelicans, snowy egrets, and harbor seals. Kayakers can camp on remote Tomales Point. A paddle through the rich, shallow waters of Drakes Estero is what sea kayaks were made for. Sea kayaking is fun for kids — and safe as long as you can count on them to take it seriously. The child sits in the front seat as you paddle in the back. **Blue Waters Kayaking,** at the Golden Hinde Inn on Tomales Bay (☎ **888/865-9288** or 415/669-2600; www.bwkayak.com), offers a variety of guided paddles, including 3-hour beginner outings on weekend mornings ($49 adults, half price ages 13 and under). Get their schedule of other paddles before your trip, because they hit each destination in the park — Drakes Estero, for example — only once a month. They also do classes and overnight trips along the shore of Tomales Point and, for kids ages 12 to 16, a 5-day kayaking day camp. They rent closed-deck sea kayaks only to those who have completed a course; anyone can rent a sit-on-top kayak — a plastic boat with no openings — regardless of experience. Rates start at $25 for 2 hours in a single, $35 in a double.

## Swimming

The ocean water breaking on the outer beaches is rough and frigid all year. South-facing Drakes Beach may be calm enough for wading, but for children it's better to go to the beaches on Tomales Bay (see "Tomales Bay State Park," p. 498). People also swim from the beach in Bolinas; one warm afternoon we saw languid teens wading across the lagoon while beached seals complacently watched them.

## Tide Pooling

There's as much as an 8-foot difference between high and low tides at Point Reyes, leaving a strip where the sea floor turns into the beach for part of the day. Where the shore has a rocky shelf in that intertidal zone, water is left behind in tide pools where you can see ocean life carrying on at your fingertips. Children love tide pooling, because you can see wildlife up close, touch it, and understand what the creatures are doing — they don't run away. To learn more, see "Natural History: The Systems of Life," in chapter 20; "The Intertidal Zone," in chapter 2; and "Experiment: Tide Pool Plant or Animal?" in chapter 3. Tide-pool creatures are described in the "The Little Field Guide" in chapters 2 and 20, although you may want a field guide in color to figure it all out.

Some preparation is needed for tide pooling. You need footwear that offers good traction and that you can get wet. A change of socks and other clothes makes sense. A hand lens and a bucket help you get a good look at the creatures. Before going, check the tides with a ranger or get a copy of the tide book distributed at the visitor centers (be sure to apply the time correction for your location). You want to be on the beach at least an hour before low tide and leave before the tide has risen higher than it was when you arrived. Negative numbers on the chart represent the lowest tides; the lower the tide, the more you'll see. Be sensitive; avoid stepping on creatures and crushing them, be gentle when you pick anything up, and put both living things and rock back where you found them.

The area's best tide-pooling spots include **Chimney Rock** near the lifesaving station (see "Natural History: The Cycles of the Sea" in chapter 2, "Moving Water, Moving Land") and **McClures Beach** on Pierce Point Road (p. 496). The largest tide-pool area is Duxbury Reef, at Agate Beach County Park in Bolinas; from Mesa Road, turn left on Outlook Road, then right on Elm, and follow it to the end. **Sculptured Beach** also is a good spot, a 2-mile walk south from Limantour Beach.

## Whale Watching

Nearly all the gray whales in the world swim close to Point Reyes on their annual migrations, drawing the park's biggest crowds of the year to watch them from the high headlands at the tip of the point. Grays spend the midwinter months off Mexico in warm seas where they give birth but find little to eat, swimming north to the food-rich waters of the Gulf of Alaska for the warmer months. The migration south passes Point Reyes in December or January, with the peak of up to 100 whales a day seen around the first of the year. The northern migration comes in two groups. Males and adult females pass by in February or March; mothers with calves, in April or May. It's thought that they swim close to shore to avoid killer whales. All you have to do to see them is find a place on the headland and peer out with binoculars. On weekends, you may have to park down below and take a shuttle.

Boats go out to see the whales off Point Reyes from San Francisco. **Oceanic Society Expeditions,** Fort Mason Center, Building E, San Francisco, CA 94123-1394 (☎ 800/326-7491 or 415/474-3385; www.oceanic-society. org), a nonprofit organization involved with important conservation work, offers all-day gray whale cruises ($50 per person) led by experts during the winter and spring. In the summer and fall, the cruises ($65) visit the Farallon Islands for bird-watching and to see blue and humpback whales far offshore. Call for the schedule, and reserve ahead. Children under 10 aren't allowed, and because the boat goes into the open ocean, it's wise to be prepared for seasickness. The society also has a hotline (☎ **415/474-3385**) with information on current marine-life sightings.

## PROGRAMS

The national seashore runs a few ranger programs on weekends starting from the Bear Valley Visitor Center, the lighthouse, or other sites. Check the park newspaper or website (www.nps.gov/pore) for dates and times of a changing menu of programs, which could include the typical talks and nature walks or a tide-pool excursion or work party — habitat restoration, for example.

**Point Reyes Field Seminars,** sponsored by the National Seashore Association, offers programs through the year, including many half-day outings geared specifically for families. These trips cover tide pooling, birding, geology, and other topics, and generally cost under $30 for a child-parent pair. The catalog, listed on the website at www.ptreyes.org, has even more programs for adults (an instructor may admit a mature teen) covering many areas of natural history, art, or photography. Most are 1-day seminars under $70. Reserve well in advance. The website is the easiest way to get information and a registration form, but you can also get a catalog or register by phone at ☎ **415/663-1200** Monday through Friday between 10am and 5pm. Direct postal mail to the association through the park's address.

# FUN BEYOND THE NATURAL WONDERS

Our family loves the **Bay Area Discovery Museum** (☎ **415/331-2129**), a campus of hands-on science exhibits, play areas, and arts-and-crafts activities aimed at children from ages 1 to 10 at the foot of the Golden Gate Bridge on the Marin Country side. You can make a day full of playful discoveries. We built paper boats for the water play area, watched bees swooping into a hive down a runway, and watched the workings of a clear toilet, among many other things. The museum is in Fort Baker, part of Golden Gate National Recreation Area, at the last exit on U.S. 101 before the bridge; take the exit to Alexander Avenue and follow signs for the fort. Admission is $7 for adults or children, free for those under age 1. It's open Tuesday through Thursday 9am to 4pm, Friday to Sunday 10am to 5pm, and closed Monday. Avoid crowded weekends. The snack bar serves light meals.

# WHERE TO EAT

## LOW-STRESS MEALS

Local zoning laws prohibit franchise restaurants in the area, but you can find a sandwich or fast food at a few places. I mentioned the pleasant cafe at Drakes Beach on p. 497. You can get picnic supplies at the market on Route 1 in Point Reyes Station, and the Inverness Store also has a deli with seating. It is open 9am to 7pm.

**Bovine Bakery,** a local favorite on Route 1 in Point Reyes Station (☎ **415/663-9420**), sells fresh baked goods, coffee, and tea, and serves pizza until 6pm. They don't take credit cards.

**Café Reyes** (☎ 415/663-9493), on Route 1 in Point Reyes, hits a perfect chord by combining adult food and atmosphere with a relaxed, kid-friendly attitude. In an old-fashioned garage with cement walls and a high tin ceiling — but ingeniously remodeled to resemble a cantina — you'll find blocks and letter tiles stored near the boosters and child seats. The mostly Mexican cuisine, ordered at the counter, is generally quite good — spicy and exotic for the adults, appropriately bland for the kids. All items are under $10, with most $7. They have a fine selection of local beers. Hours are daily noon to 9pm. They don't take credit cards.

We also enjoyed the **Gray Whale**, on Sir Francis Drake Boulevard in Inverness (☎ 415/669-1244), an excellent little pizzeria. The menu isn't long, with pizzas, salads, sandwiches, and pasta, but the food is classy — a shrimp and pesto pizza, for example, or a masterpiece vegetarian made with pesto and seven other toppings. Meals are generally less than $7 for lunch or dinner. You order at the counter and sit outdoors or in a dining room with a rough-edged, seaside feel. In summer they're open Monday through Friday 11am to 9pm, Saturday and Sunday 8:30am to 9pm; winter hours are slightly shorter.

## BEST-BEHAVIOR MEALS

**Barnaby's by the Bay.** In the Golden Hinde Inn, 12938 Sir Francis Drake Hwy., Inverness. ☎ 415/669-1114. Lunch or dinner $5–$23. Thurs–Tues noon–8pm.

The restaurant in the Golden Hinde Inn faces Tomales Bay with big windows. It's a traditional seafood place, with an authentic, well-scuffed feel. Our meals were prepared simply and well, but the kids' portions were too large — feed them off your own plate. If you don't like fish, smoked ribs or roasted chicken are your only choices.

## PLACES FOR RELAXED PLAY & PICNICS

There are many places to play here — the beaches, the grasslands, and the area around the visitor center, for example. A **public playground** with a picnic table is north of Point Reyes Station on Route 1, just before the elementary school. Picnic areas at **Bear Valley Visitor Center, Drakes Beach, Tomales Bay State Park**, and **Divide Meadow** on the Bear Valley Trail are marked on the Park Service map. At **Samuel P. Taylor State Park** (p. 492) a lovely picnic ground sits among shady coast redwoods; there's a $2 day-use fee.

**Olema Farm House.** 10005 Hwy. 1, Olema. ☎ 415/663-1264. www.olemafarmhouse.com. Breakfast $4–$12, lunch $6.25–$9.25, dinner $12.25–$23. Breakfast menu Sat–Sun 8am–1pm; lunch menu daily 11am–4pm; dinner menu Sun–Thurs 5–9pm, Fri–Sat 5–10pm.

This restaurant is in a historic building right in the village. The bar dominates the front; other tables fit in a small dining room or on a pleasant shaded deck with benches out back. The dinner menu runs to traditional continental cuisine, with entrees such as cioppino, roasted pork loin, or chicken marsala under $16.50, but you can also get an inexpensive burger or fish-and-chips. Barbecued oysters are a specialty for lunch or dinner. The kids' menu is under $6.

**Station House Cafe.** Main St., Point Reyes Station. ☎ 415/663-1515. www.stationhouse cafe.com. Reservations accepted. Breakfast $4–$8, lunch $5.50–$13, dinner $7.50–$17. Mon–Thurs 8am–10pm, Fri–Sat 8am–11pm.

This is a place not to miss if you're at Point Reyes for a couple of days. The cuisine is creative and varied, with lots of local seafood plus something for everyone in the family. The outdoor garden dining area is lovely for lunch or an early dinner. The indoor dining room has festive pub decor where children's loud voices are unlikely to bother anyone. There's music on the weekends.

# CHAPTER 22

# Olympic National Park

The last hook of land at the northwest corner of the state of Washington is a rich, mysterious kingdom of forest. On the outer coast, waves roar in from the vast sea in row after row of breakers, seething against rocks and sea stacks that stand away from the shore like the teeth of the continent. The sea's moisture blows ashore in ragged mists and overstuffed clouds that soon spill out clattering drops of rain. The hypnotic dampness clings to tall, dark evergreens, with branches and trunks that drip with moss and sprout ferns.

The rain forest is like a place under a spell that makes everything grow, life piling upon life in deep, pillowy layers. Your hair feels damp, as if ferns could sprout from between its roots at any moment. Rivers rush through, carrying back to the sea water that had fallen as snow on the mountain tundra. Salmon use watery passages into the forest to swim up from the ocean. They pass over clean gravel in clear creeks and into silver-surfaced lakes, drawing the forest's animals to feed on their rich flesh, fattened at sea. Only a few people are there to see; mostly, the forest is silent and unbroken by voices.

The people of the Northwest have these places largely to themselves. Visitors come out to the peninsula from Seattle when the weekend forecast promises sun, but the great masses of people who fill many parks in the summer haven't found their way to Olympic National Park. A single two-lane loop highway leads into this large rural maritime and logging region. The little towns are only partway through the switch from muscular logging communities to softer-edged tourism towns. Campgrounds are everywhere, on park, national forest, state, and county lands. Old wooden lodges are tucked up in the rain-forest valleys, along lakes edged with timber and standing out on the coastal bluffs above raging, misty seawater.

The park is huge, and the other public lands around it make it seem much bigger. Rather than a single, simple highway through the park, roads wind up valleys and out to points on the coast in many branches — a good match for the infinite, branching variety of nature here. The deep heart of the park can be reached only on the long backpacking trails. There's no way to take it all in. Instead, relax and enjoy being part of a living system much larger than you are.

## BEST THINGS TO DO

- Hike a rain-forest trail, seeing the moss and ferns and feeling the enveloping dampness, or an alpine path with sweeping views.
- Play on the rocky outer beaches, searching at low tide for weird little sea animals.
- Swim at Sol Duc Hot Springs or one of the lakes.
- Plan a backpacking trip to get deep into the park away from other people.

See "Activities" (p. 526).

## HISTORY: LOGS OR TREES?

Driving along Highway 101 between the park's coastal strip and its main area of mountains, you pass through forests in different stages of growth. A hill that's stripped bare of trees comes after a dense forest of medium-sized trees growing close together. Next comes land that was clear-cut 10 years ago and replanted with Douglas firs, which have grown as large as Christmas trees. The logging companies often post signs giving the years the trees were harvested, replanted, thinned, and harvested again, in cycles of 60 to 90 years. Even a child can see the differences between these tree farms and the old-growth forests in the national park. There, huge and small trees grow together in patches of shadow and light, and the forest seems never to change — it takes many human lifetimes for the trees there to grow old and die.

These patches of ancient forest and replanted trees tell the story of the Olympic Peninsula. When you drive from a patch of little trees to a stand of huge ones, you're seeing the results of a century of disagreement over how to use this land — whether to save the big trees or make them into products for people to use. So far, the results have come out about half and half.

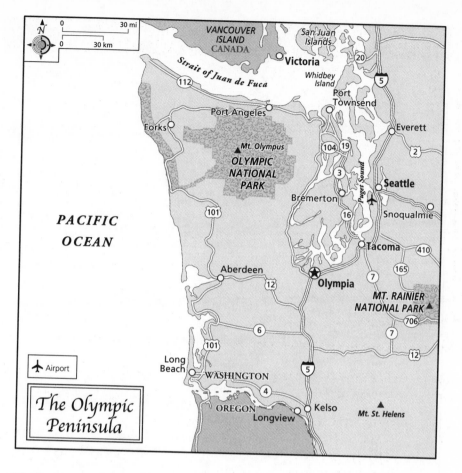

The first people of the Olympic Peninsula used wood, as all the Native Americans of the Pacific Northwest did. They chopped down western red cedar to split into planks for clan houses and to carve into art and useful items. They carved huge logs of red cedar into long oceangoing canoes. Other woods they used for bows, spears, harpoons, or bowls; they knew what kind of tree was best for each. But the Natives didn't clear-cut old forests (which means cutting down all the trees). There weren't that many people, and they were using the trees only for their needs. The loggers who came later were selling wood to the whole world.

White Americans started settling on the peninsula in the 1850s. Like the natives, they settled around the coast. The middle, where the mountains hold glaciers and thick rain

forests, was left blank on maps long after most of the connected part of the United States was explored and settled. The area was too rugged to get across; even today, there are no roads across the middle of the peninsula, only around the edges. In 1889 and 1890, a group sponsored by the *Seattle Press* took 6 months to make the trip from Port Angeles, on the north, to Aberdeen, on the southwest side. A group of scientific explorers crossed going the other way in 1890. They found the big trees of the rain forest and knew right away that loggers would want them.

When they returned, the leaders of the trip set to work to protect the land they had explored. Judge James Wickersham, a member of the expedition, wrote to Major John Wesley Powell, the head of the U.S. Geographic Survey, asking that this land be set aside before

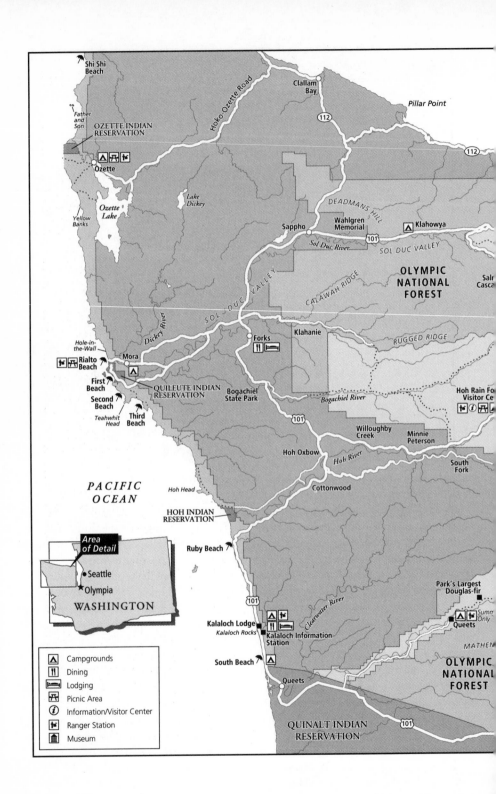

**Legend:**

- ▲ Campgrounds
- 🍴 Dining
- 🛏 Lodging
- ⛱ Picnic Area
- ⓘ Information/Visitor Center
- 👤 Ranger Station
- 🏛 Museum

508  **Olympic National Park**

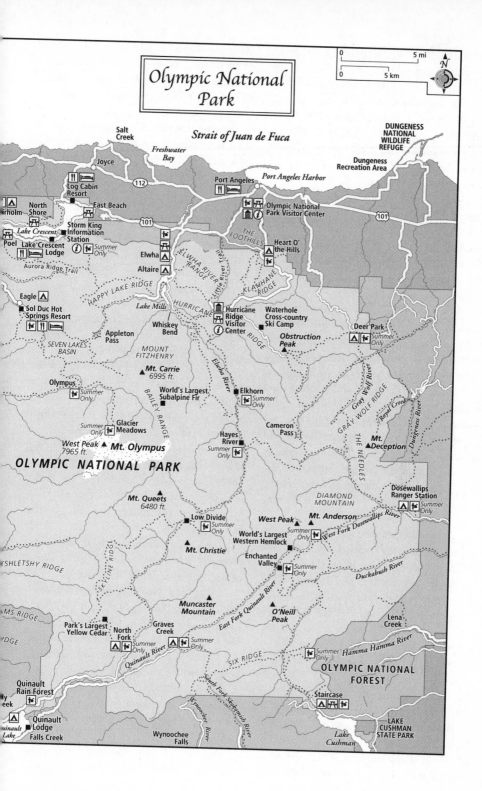

Olympic National Park

the entire West was stripped of old trees. Powell had explored the Grand Canyon and much of the Southwest; Wickersham later went on to Alaska, where he explored and helped set aside Denali National Park. In 1897, President Grover Cleveland set aside 2.2 million acres on the peninsula in a forest reserve, including all the land from the mountains to the western coast.

From that day until the present, logging companies and conservationists have fought over how much of that forest reserve should be saved in old growth and how much used for timber harvest. Soon after the forest reserve was set aside, logging interests tried to get land out of it. They complained to the government in Washington, D.C., that the western lowlands in the reserve should be used for farming, not forests. They weren't telling the truth — the area had forests of huge trees, and the forest soil and constant rain made it useless for farming. But they won, and within 3 years of the reserve's being made, one-third of the land was taken out of the reserve and put into private ownership by farmers. People did apply for farm homesteads, but many quickly sold the land to the lumber companies. The companies cut down the old-growth trees and started the tree farms we see in the western area of the peninsula today.

The first land set aside for preservation was protected to save the Roosevelt elk. The largest wild herd lives on the peninsula. These are the largest elk, and members of Elks clubs across the country wanted their teeth for souvenirs; to get the teeth, commercial hunters slaughtered thousands of elk, leaving the meat to rot. In 1909, President Theodore Roosevelt — after whom the elk were named — set aside a national monument on the Olympic Peninsula to help save the elk from extinction. The monument took in rain-forest valleys in the mountains, including about two-thirds of the land that's now in the national park. But those lines didn't last long, either. People in favor of more logging persuaded President Woodrow Wilson to take away about a third of the national monument just 6 years later.

In the 1930s, conservationists mounted their strongest push to protect the trees, and Congress began discussing a new national park on the peninsula. The fight continued for some time, until President Franklin Roosevelt took the problem into his own hands. He went to the Olympic Peninsula in 1937 and met the local people in Port Angeles who wanted the park. He told the two sides that he agreed there should be a park, and that the park should be larger than many logging supporters wanted. In 1938, Congress passed the law that set aside the park, which was a little bit larger than the original national monument.

Battles over the park's boundaries continued for decades more. Today, Olympic National Park totals 914,890 acres. It is a bit less than half of President Cleveland's forest reserve, but almost twice the size of President Wilson's national monument.

The park we visit today, and the sharp lines between areas of ancient forest and areas of young, all-the-same trees, are like a recording of the decisions made over the past 100 years. Today, disagreements are settled about the land in the national park, but they go on in many other places here in the Pacific Northwest and around the world. Conservationists think more land needs to be protected to provide areas of habitat large enough for some kinds of wildlife (see "The Food Web" and "Natural Communities," both in chapter 20, "Ecology: Fitting It Together"). Loggers and businesspeople, on the other hand, say they should be able to keep using the forests to produce wood and paper that people need and so that people in their towns will have jobs. In recent years, the conservationists have been winning in the Northwest, and fewer old trees than ever are available for cutting.

On the Olympic Peninsula, towns are changing with the changes in how the land is used. Port Angeles still has mills that use trees from the peninsula, but the townspeople also have spruced up their downtown area a lot in recent years to make it more attractive to visitors coming to see the national park. More and more people get their jobs from businesses for visitors. Those visitors come to see the old trees still standing. In the long run, the ancient forests may be worth more alive than dead.

# ORIENTATION

## THE PARK
The park has three main parts. Roads lead around the rim of the park to connect them.

## The Eastern Mountains
Starting from park headquarters, in Port Angeles, at the park's northeast corner, a road leads up into the alpine section of the park at **Hurricane Ridge.** It's popular for skiing and sledding in the winter and for views and mountain walks in the summer. Just west of town, a road following the Elwha River leads up to trails that rise from big trees into the mountains. From the southeast, dirt roads lead through the national forest to remote backpacking trails.

## The Western Forests
Along the west side of the Olympic Mountains, roads lead up a series of lushly forested river valleys. I'll describe them from north to south. The **Sol Duc Valley** has a lodge and hot springs; the **Hoh Rainforest** is in the next valley, of the same name, and has a visitor center and campground; the **Queets Rainforest** is a less visited area reached by a long unpaved road; and the **Quinault** is at the park's southeast corner, where a historic lodge sits by a large lake. **Crescent Lake,** which also has a lodge, lies on lowlands on the north side of the park, surrounded by big trees, between the Elwha and Sol Duc rivers.

## The Coastal Strip
The park protects a long, narrow coastal strip on the western edge of the Olympic Peninsula facing the open Pacific Ocean. This is a land of enormous surf, rocks and sand, tide pools, and long backpacking beach walks. It's separated from the rest of the park by a strip of Olympic National Forest and state and private timberlands 12 to 25 miles wide. **Kalaloch Lodge** is at the south end of the coastal strip.

## THE TOWNS
Except for the lodges and towns, the area is rural, with many miles of undeveloped forest highways and occasional country stores.

## Port Angeles
Port Angeles is the commercial center for the park region. It's a typical western town, with a few streets of businesses in old downtown buildings and a larger highway area of fast-food outlets and parking lots. It's a good place to start your visit, seeing a few sites and stocking up before heading into the park. The main park visitor center and the road to Hurricane Ridge are just above the town.

## Forks
On the western side of the peninsula, in the logging district between the mountain and seashore areas of the park, Forks is a rural logging community along Highway 101. The only sizable town in that part of the park, it has a few motels.

## THE ROADS
The main road is **U.S. Highway 101,** a two-lane loop that circles the entire peninsula, from Aberdeen to Olympia. All other roads into the park branch from U.S. 101 at one point or another.

# MAKING THE ARRANGEMENTS

## WHEN TO GO

Anytime you visit the Olympic rain forests, you've got a good chance of getting wet. The driest (and most popular) months are July and August, when there's a 20% to 30% chance of rain on an average day. June is next driest, followed by May and September, then April, when the chance of rain is more than 50/50 on an average day. From October to March, as much rain falls here in a month as many places get in a year. December and January are the wettest months — a typical day has a 70% chance of rain.

Olympic is never crowded the way some other national parks are, but there are some shortages on weekends in the July and August high season. Sometimes the parking lots in the Hoh Rainforest fill, and cars are held back until someone leaves; the same can happen at Hurricane Ridge in the winter. On our last visit, in late July, we encountered little crowding and found lots of empty campsites. Lodge reservations for the high months have to be made many months ahead. Many facilities close in the winter, but the weather remains mild. If you can stand the rain, you can have the park to yourself.

## HOW MUCH TIME TO SPEND

The quick, drive-through approach to visiting national parks won't work well at Olympic. It's too big and varied, and to see much you have to take long spur roads and get out of the car. For a long vacation, however, there are few better places. The park has many interesting destinations that reward time and exploration, with lots of campgrounds and lodges you can link in a slow tour from point to point. Many people come for a weekend from Seattle to visit just one area of the park. If you want to see each of the park's ecosystems, the coast, rain forest, and mountains, you need 4 days to a week; 2 weeks will give time to relax and really explore.

## HOW FAR TO PLAN AHEAD

If you intend to camp, no advance planning is needed. Park Service campgrounds don't take reservations, and usually they all fill only on sunny summer weekends. At busy times, you need to arrive early in the day, but if you miss out on your first choice, there are many public campgrounds near the park.

Motel rooms in the towns should be reserved ahead for the summer high season, but chances of finding one are good. The lodges in the park fill much earlier. July and August can be booked up by March, with less lead time required for other times. Reservation rules vary at each, but it's wise to call as soon as you know your plans.

## READING UP

The **Northwest Interpretive Association** (☎ 360/452-4501, ext. 239; www.nps.gov/olym/nwia.htm) sells a good selection of books and maps in park visitor centers and by mail order; at this writing, they listed products online but did not accept orders that way. **Maps:** The plastic *Trails Illustrated* topographic trail map covers the park in adequate detail on two sides of a single sheet, and costs $10. **Hiking:** Robert L. Wood's *Olympic Mountains Trail Guide: National Park and Forest* (The Mountaineers Books) covers every trail in the region. **Nature:** Tim McNulty's *Olympic National Park: A Natural History Guide* (Houghton Mifflin) is engaging, well researched, and comprehensive.

## GETTING THERE
### By Car or Ferry

To **Port Angeles** from Seattle's Sea-Tac Airport or other mainland points north or east, you can choose the fun way or the fast way. The fast way is to take **Interstate 5** to Tacoma, crossing the Tacoma Narrows Bridge and taking Route 16 north through Bremerton to Route 3. Then cross the Hood Canal Bridge on Route 104, and meet

|  | AVG. HIGH (°F) | AVG. LOW (°F) | PRECIP. (IN. IN TOTAL PERIOD) |
|---|---|---|---|
| **Nov.–Feb.** | | | |
| Quinault | 46 | 35 | 78 |
| Port Angeles | 47 | 35 | 15 |
| **March–April** | | | |
| Quinault | 55 | 37 | 24 |
| Port Angeles | 53 | 38 | 3 |
| **May–June** | | | |
| Quinault | 67 | 46 | 15 |
| Port Angeles | 63 | 46 | 2 |
| **July–August** | | | |
| Quinault | 74 | 52 | 6 |
| Port Angeles | 68 | 51 | 1 |
| **Sept.–Oct.** | | | |
| Quinault | 65 | 47 | 20 |
| Port Angeles | 62 | 47 | 4 |

Highway 101 about 40 miles east of Port Angeles. The fun way is to take a **ferry** across Puget Sound, from Seattle's Pier 52 at 801 Alaskan Way to Bainbridge Island. From there drive north to the Hood Canal Bridge. The ferry is slower because of the wait to get on board, which recent budget cuts will not improve, but you can spend that time exploring the touristy waterfront. The ferry itself is large and comfortable, and the views of the city and boats are great. Without boarding delays (which can be a couple of hours) the trip from Sea-Tac to Port Angeles takes 2½ to 3 hours by road or ferry. For more ferry information, contact **Washington State Ferry** (☎ 206/464-6400; www.wsdot.wa.gov/ferries). A Washington State Ferry also connects Victoria Island to Seattle.

If you're going to the **southwest part of the park,** including Lake Quinault or Kalaloch Lodge, from either north or south, or going anywhere in the park from the south, take I-5 to Olympia. To go north, join U.S.

101 there to Port Angeles. To go west, take four-lane highways 8 and 12 to Aberdeen, and join the other end of the 101 loop north from there. From Olympia, either Quinault or Port Angeles is 2 hours away. If you're already on coastal 101 going north, you just keep going north.

A **Black Ball Transport ferry** (☎ 360/ 457-4491; www.northolympic.com/coho) runs most of the year from Victoria, British Columbia, to Port Angeles, making it possible to loop across Victoria Island and return by the Washington ferry mentioned above to Seattle.

## By Air
Seattle-Tacoma Airport, known as Sea-Tac, is served by all major airlines and car-rental firms. You can save a 3-hour drive by flying from Sea-Tac to Fairchild International Airport, in Port Angeles, on **Horizon Air** (☎ 800/547-9308; www.horizonair.com) for around $120. **Budget** (☎ 800/527-0700 or

360/452-4774; www.budget.com) rents cars in Port Angeles.

## WHAT TO PACK

The weather in the Olympic Peninsula varies from dry to soggy within a few miles, although the temperature stays pretty much the same wherever you are at the same elevation, mild year-round near sea level and cool or snowy up above. As you can see from "Weather Chart: Quinault & Port Angeles," above, Quinault Ranger Station, in the rain forest on the west side of the park, gets almost 6 times the rainfall of Port Angeles, on the east side. The moisture coming off the ocean causes the difference in rainfall. Clouds drop about 80 inches of rain a year on the coast, 140 on the rain-forest valleys on the west side of the mountains, more than 200 inches (that's more than 16 ft.) of water in rain and snow on the mountaintops, and as little as 10 inches a year on the eastern side of the mountains, in Sequim. It's all because of the way the mountains force air rising across their western slopes to cool, condensing the moisture into rain. On the far side, the air drops down again, warms up, and can hold much more water without rain. These ideas are explained under

"Making Clouds & Rain," in chapter 13, "The Nature of High Places."

## Clothing

Bring raincoats that will keep you dry so that you can keep hiking and seeing the park when rain is falling. You'll also need warm sweaters for the damp chill. Don't forget warm-weather clothes and swimsuits too — it won't rain all the time, especially in the summer. Trails can be muddy, so you may need extra socks and pants. Pack two pairs of shoes, one to keep clean and one you can get dirty on the trail. You won't need formal clothing in the best restaurant in the area, but you may need something better than camping clothes. In the winter or spring, bring winter clothes for skiing or sledding at Hurricane Ridge.

## Gear

Make sure your tent is waterproof. Bring plastic tarps and cord, or buy them when you arrive, to shelter your picnic table and keep your tent dry. Unless you hike to high elevations, you won't encounter severe cold. A camp stove is a necessity because any wood you find will be wet and difficult to burn. For watching whales and other wildlife on the coast, bring good binoculars.

# WHERE TO SPEND THE NIGHT

## CAMPING

The northern Olympic Peninsula has an extraordinary number of campgrounds, run by the Park Service, the Forest Service, the state of Washington, and the counties. Most of them are memorable places to camp, in mossy forests, on riverbanks, on lakeshores, and by the sea. The map on p. 507 or the park map shows each, and is a better guide to finding them than written directions I can give. I've listed campgrounds by area, with the name of the agency that runs each after the name. Generally, sites cannot be reserved but are plentiful during the week, although some

campgrounds fill in the morning on weekends in July and August.

Olympic National Park has 17 campgrounds. The Park Service advises that they're not appropriate for trailers longer than 21 feet, and some have shorter limits. The Park Service doesn't establish precise seasons of operation, although I've given the general rule for each below. All open in May, but even those that remain open all winter may not have water turned on. If you're visiting outside the summer months, call to find out which campgrounds are open and have water. If the water is off, there's usually no fee. Four campgrounds have RV dump stations, as noted below; the fee is $3.

Firewood collection is permitted in most places where it isn't for sale, but the wood you find in this wet climate is difficult to burn.

Campfire ranger programs take place in the summer at Heart O' the Hills, Lake Crescent, Sol Duc, Hoh, Mora, and Kalaloch campgrounds. Check the *Bugler* park newspaper for days and times; topics are posted on campground bulletin boards.

## North Side

**Altaire.** Olympic National Park. Up Elwha River Rd., about a mile beyond the Elwha Campground, west of Port Angeles. $10 per site. 30 sites; tents or RVs. Flush toilets. Closed winter.

This campground, similar to Elwha, is near the dam and ranger station. Many trails start near here.

**Elwha.** Olympic National Park. About 3 miles up Elwha River Rd., just west of Port Angeles. $10 per site. 41 sites; tents or RVs. Flush toilets. No water in winter. Open year-round.

This is a pretty spot, on the floor of the narrow Elwha Valley. The campground is shaded by moss-covered trees that branch high above the ground, but there's no screen between the sites. A picnic shelter has a stone fireplace. Many trails start near here.

**Fairholm.** Olympic National Park. On Hwy. 101, west end of Lake Crescent. $10 per site. 88 sites; tents or RVs. Flush toilets, dump station, store, restaurant. Closed winter.

On a ferny slope above the west end of the lake, this pleasant campground is a center of activities. The lake has a boat ramp and swimming area, and up on the road there are a restaurant and store. A nature trail circles through the woods.

**Heart O' the Hills.** Olympic National Park. About 5 miles up Hurricane Ridge Rd. $10 per site. 105 sites; tents or RVs. Flush toilets. Open year-round.

Just inside the pay station on the way to Hurricane Ridge, this campground is the most convenient to Port Angeles, but it has a deep-forest feeling, among tall red cedars, hemlocks, and big boulders on hilly ground. Our site, like many on the outside of the loops, faded into the mossy woods and massive trees in the back and was visually blocked almost completely on the other sides, so we felt like we were camping alone in the deep woods. The lovely Heart O' the Hills Trail extends 2 miles from the east side of the campground among ferns and immense trees. It's an easy family hike.

**Salt Creek.** Clallam County Parks Department. Off Rte. 112 west of Port Angeles (3506 Camp Hayden Rd). ☎ 360/928-3441. www.clallam.net/park. $10 per site. 90 sites; tents or RVs. Flush toilets, showers, dump station. Open year-round. Gates close at dusk.

This wonderful 196-acre park, around a World War II defensive site on the Strait of Juan de Fuca, includes a prime tide-pooling shore, fishing, trails, a playground, and lots of open lawn for play. Many sites nestle in the trees along the bluff over the water.

## West Side Forests

**Bogachiel.** Washington State Park. On Hwy. 101, south of Forks. ☎ 360/374-6351. $13 per site, $19 with water and electricity. 42 sites; tents or RVs. Flush toilets, showers. Open year-round.

This attractive little campground on the Bogachiel River seemed well maintained and comfortable and has coin-op showers.

**Graves Creek.** Olympic National Park. Up South Shore Rd. in the Quinault Rainforest. $10 per site. 30 sites; tents or RVs. Flush toilets. No water in winter. Open year-round.

This isolated campground is set deep in the rain forest along a dirt road. There are a mile-long nature trail among the trees and a trailhead to backpack up to the Enchanted Valley, one of the park's most beautiful trips.

**Hoh.** Olympic National Park. Near the Hoh Rainforest Visitor Center. $10 per site. 88 sites; tents or RVs. Flush toilets, dump station. Open year-round.

Although the big, mossy trees of the rain forest are nearby, this campground is on open ground among smaller trees near the Hoh River, which rushes right by some sites. It's pleasant but doesn't have the deep forest feel of some others.

If you can't get in here, a series of primitive state Department of Natural Resources campgrounds lie along the road on the way in, where you'll also find some handy stores (see "For Handy Reference," p. 522).

**July Creek.** Olympic National Park. North Shore Rd., Quinault Lake. $10 per site. 29 sites; tents only. Flush toilets. No water in winter. Open year-round.

This is one of my favorite campgrounds, set among huge trees on the steep shore of the lake. There's a creek running through, and there are private sites where you can swim right from your tent. Campers park near the road and carry their gear in a few hundred feet.

**Klahowya.** Olympic National Forest. On Hwy. 101, west of Lake Crescent. $8–$12 per site. 55 sites; tents or RVs up to 30 ft. Flush toilets and vault toilets. Closed winter.

This is a lovely, shady campground by the highway. Some sites are private, in dense forest, while others front the Sol Duc River. There's a nature trail too. Electricity is sometimes available at two sites, for $10 extra.

**North Fork.** Olympic National Park. Up North Shore Rd. in the Quinault Rainforest. No fee. 7 sites; tents only. Carry in water. Open year-round.

This primitive campground lies in mossy trees. It's close to the start of backpacking trails and near the end of a long dirt road.

**Queets.** Olympic National Park. More than 10 miles off Hwy. 101 in the Queets Rainforest. $8 per site. 20 sites; tents or RVs under 15 ft. No running water   ...en year-round.

...ive campground, more than 10 ...mpy dirt road from Highway ...tart of trails up the Queets ...k are often seen here.

**Sol Duc.** Olympic National Park. Sol Duc Hot Springs Rd. $12 per site. 82 sites; tents or RVs. Flush toilets, dump station. Closed winter.

This may be the park's best vacation campground. It lies near the end of the spur road into the valley, just below a short trail to the misty Sol Duc Falls and the steep but beautiful Deer Lake Trail to the high-country lake. Just down the road in the downstream direction are the warm and hot pools, restaurant, RV park, and store at Sol Duc Hot Springs Resort. Pool fees and facilities are covered on p. 519. The campground itself is long and narrow, giving many sites their own place in the woods above the river.

**Willaby and Falls Creek.** Olympic National Forest. South Shore Rd., Quinault Lake. $14 per site drive-in, $11 walk-in. 22 and 31 sites; tents or RVs up to 27 ft. Flush toilets. Closed winter.

These campgrounds, about a mile apart on the south side of the lake, perch among large trees where you can swim right from the campground. Anglers get trout and Dolly Varden char. The beautiful lodge, a network of trails, and a store are nearby.

# Western Coast

**Kalaloch.** Olympic National Park. On Hwy. 101, north of Kalaloch Lodge. $12 per site. 175 sites; tents or RVs. Flush toilets, dump station. Open year-round.

Two lines of sites sit on a strip of windblown grass and small twisted trees between the highway and the steep bluff overlooking the beach. Sites are well screened, and many have dramatic views. The store and restaurants at Kalaloch Lodge are nearby.

**Mora.** Olympic National Park. On Mora Rd., west of Forks. $10 per site. 94 sites; tents or RVs. Flush toilets, dump station. Open year-round.

More than a mile from Rialto Beach on a quiet, paved road, this campground is among tall, shady trees near the Quillayute River. A store with crude showers is a couple miles away.

**Ozette.** Olympic National Park. In Ozette, on the Hoko-Ozette Rd. $10 per site. 13 sites; tents or RVs. Flush toilets. Open year-round.

The area on the north shore of large Ozette Lake is a long drive from the rest of the park but has a lot to offer, including a remote beach that's a 3-mile walk along a board trail through the woods. The **Lost Resort** (☎ 360/963-2899; www.northolympic.com/lostresort) has a store, deli, and campground about a half mile up the road.

**South Beach.** Olympic National Park. On Hwy. 101 at the south end of park. $8 per site. 50 sites; tents or RVs. Flush toilets, no drinking water. Closed winter.

This campground, resembling a parking lot, is unappealing for tenting, but it may be the thing if you are traveling in an RV, because there are good views from atop the open coastal bluff at the south end of the park's shoreline strip. The water isn't potable, but there are flush toilets.

## East Side

This less-visited area of the park is reached by roads through the Olympic National Forest and doesn't connect easily to the rest of the park. Besides various national forest and state park campgrounds, there are three national park campgrounds: **Staircase,** $10 per site, 59 sites, RV accessible, with flush toilets; **Dosewallips,** $10 per site, 30 sites, tents only, with flush toilets; and **Deer Park,** $8 per site, 14 sites, tents only, with pit toilets.

## RV Parks

Within the park, RV parks are at Sol Duc Hot Springs Resort and Log Cabin Resort (p. 519). Many more RV parks are in and around Port Angeles. They include **Arney's Dam RV Park,** near the Elwha River at 47 Lower Dam Rd. (☎ 360/452-7054, northolympic.com/arneys), a wooded park with 39 full-hookup sites for $20 per night and 2 acres of tent sites. They have a small store, laundry, and coin-operated showers, and prefer not to take credit cards. The **Port Angeles KOA,** 7 miles east of town on Highway 101 at 80 O'Brien Rd. (☎ 800/562-7558 or 360/457-5916; www.koa.com), has 112 sites, charging $29 for full hookups, including cable TV. In addition to all the usual amenities, it has a swimming pool, sauna and hot tub, and mini-golf course.

## Backcountry Camping Permits

You need a backcountry permit to camp overnight on trails and beaches outside the campgrounds. They're easy to get, and permits are limited only on certain hikes from Memorial Day to Labor Day. At any other time, and on most trails all the time, you can be certain of getting a permit at a ranger station or the **Wilderness Information Center** (☎ 360/565-3101), behind the visitor center in Port Angeles. Their highly informative website is at (www.nps.gov/olym/wic.htm). Some trails have self-registration where you fill out a form at the trailhead and mail in the money. Permits cost $5 each, plus $2 per person per night.

The reservation system is simple. Call the Wilderness Information Center beginning 30 days before the starting date of the hike, then pick up your permit and pay for it when you arrive. During the summer, the following trails have quotas limiting the number of permits that are given: **Ozette Loop, Grand and Badger valleys, Lake Constance, Flapjack Lakes, Hoh River,** and **Sol Duc.** There are no reservations on Hoh and Sol Duc. You walk in and apply for the permit when you arrive. Reservations are optional on all the other quota hikes except Ozette. Half of the permits are given by reservation and half are held for walk-ins. For Ozette, you have to make a reservation, even for the same day, before going to the Ozette area.

Proper food storage is important because of black bear and, on the coast, raccoons. Bear-resistant canisters rent for $3 at the Wilderness Information Center and some ranger stations (see "Dangerous Wildlife," in chapter 1, "Planning Your Trip"). At many sites, you can

In Port Angeles, there are public rest rooms on the city pier near the end of Lincoln Street, in The Landing Mall behind the Chamber of Commerce Visitor Center, and at the park visitor center. In the park, campgrounds, visitor centers, and lodges have the closest bathrooms.

hang your food from wires put there for the purpose (bring plenty of rope), but rope hanging from branches is no longer effective.

You don't need a backcountry permit in the national forest, but you do need a pass to park at the trailheads, which costs $3 per day. They're sold at all Forest Service offices and some businesses.

In Port Angeles, you can shower at the **William Shore Memorial Pool** on Fifth Street (☎ **360/417-4595**), where admission for open swimming is less than $2.50 adults, $2 children. **Spic 'N' Span Laundromat** is at 1105 E. Front St.

At Quinault Lake, coin-operated showers and laundry machines are in a building next to the post office, on South Shore Road across from the Rain Forest Resort east of the lodge.

In Forks, the large Red Carpet Laundry is on the corner of Fernhill Road and Forks Avenue, and public showers are at Bagby's Town Motel, on Forks Avenue at the south end of town.

Away from towns, public showers are at Salt Creek and Bogachiel campgrounds, listed above. At Sol Duc Hot Springs Resort you can shower at certain hours even without paying to use the hot springs (see p. 519).

## HOTELS
### In the Park

Each of these places is run by a different park concessionaire. Except for special suites and the like, they generally do not have telephones, TVs, or air-conditioning. Taxes as high as 15% apply to the rates listed.

**Kalaloch Lodge.** 157151 Hwy. 101, Forks, WA 98331. ☎ **360/962-2271.** 64 rms and cabins. $120–$225 double; $10 per extra person age 5 and older. AE, DISC, MC, V.

The lodge, sided with weathered shingles, and its cabins stand at the edge of the bluff over the beach, where frothy surf constantly pounds. Erosion threatens the lodge with destruction and closed its outdoor dining, but at this writing no date was set for demolition or relocation. Motel rooms are nearby in a wooded area. From atop the grassy, blufftop grounds, it's a short walk down to the beach; you even receive a tide table when you check in. The cabins are best for families. Many are recently remodeled and have kitchenettes and wood stoves or built-in fireplaces supplied with wood daily. You have to bring your own utensils. Many have incredible views. The cabins book as much as a year ahead, and by 6 months out you should have your place at this most attractive place to stay in the park. Motel and lodge rooms are available later; they're nice, too, but notable mostly for the fantastic location. A convenience store is in the parking lot.

**Dining:** The lodge restaurants serve three meals a day. You can get usual diner food for breakfast or lunch, and in the evening choose that sort of meal inexpensively, or order from a brief fine-dining menu which includes salmon, halibut, steaks, and pasta.

**Lake Crescent Lodge.** 416 Lake Crescent Rd., Port Angeles, WA 98363-8672. ☎ **360/928-3211.** www.olypen.com/lakecrescentlodge. 37 rms, 17 cottages. $102–$118 double, $102–$142 cottage for 2; $11.50 per extra person regardless of age. AE, DISC, MC, V. Closed Nov–Apr.

Here Franklin Roosevelt laid down the law to his staff and said there would be an Olympic National Park; looking out on the lake under big trees, you can see why. The best cabins were built for his 1937 visit. Stone fireplaces, warm wood floors, plank paneling, and

Adirondack chairs by the lake add to their historic atmosphere; worn 1970s-style furniture undercuts it. The lodge building is a grand three-story gray shingle building with dormers and a relaxing veranda. Most of the inexpensive, shared bathroom accommodations in this building are too small for families (prices listed are only for larger rooms). Other rooms occupy simpler cottages or motel buildings that seem transported from the 1950s. We found all of them out-of-date in style, but exceptionally clean and well kept. Cabins book up a year to 6 months out. Rowboats rent for $12 a half day, and good trails are nearby.

**Dining:** Stop to enjoy the historic atmosphere without all the planning required for an overnight stay. The dining room is airy and echoes with a wood floor. The adult lunch menu is short but sufficient, and there is a good children's menu. In the evening, they specialize in seafood.

**Log Cabin Resort.** 3183 E. Beach Rd., Port Angeles, WA 98363. ☎ **360/928-3325.** www. logcabinresort.net. 4 rms, 24 cabins. $96 double, $49–$115 cabin for 2; $11 per extra person age 6 and older. Full hookup RV sites $26. Closed Nov–Feb. DISC, MC, V.

This is the working man's version of the Lake Crescent Lodge, facing the lake from the northeast corner. Families stretch out and have fun on the grass and lake beach without worrying about bothering anyone and use barbecues that are all over the place. There are five categories of accommodations. At the top of the range are the lodge rooms and six-person chalets, which have lakefront patios and everything you would want from an old-fashioned lake resort. The rustic cabins, on the other hand, are little changed from the 1920s, and the camping log cabins are like frontier shelter. A boathouse rents rowboats, canoes, pedal boats, and kayaks. There's also a store on-site.

**Dining:** The restaurant also is a down-market alternative to the Lake Crescent Lodge. Only breakfast and dinner are served in the main dining room, a family place with a steak-seafood menu. Midday meals come from a small snack bar.

**Sol Duc Hot Springs Resort.** Sol Duc Rd., off Hwy. 101 south of Lake Crescent (P.O. Box 2169), Port Angeles, WA 98363-0283. ☎ **360/327-3583.** Fax 360/327-3593. www.northolympic. com/solduc. 32 cabins. $104–$125 cabin for 2; $15 per extra person over age 3; pool pass included. RV sites $16 (does not include pool pass). Closed late-Sept to mid-May except weekends; closed weekends Nov–Mar. AE, DISC, MC, V.

The hot-springs pools are the centerpiece of this resort at the head of a long valley. There are a big pool for swimming under the branches of big trees, two hot pools for soaking, and a toddler pool. Every member of our diverse family easily found hours of amusement one long afternoon. The modern cabins are clean and serviceable, but surprisingly spare and unadorned. The more expensive duplex units have cooking facilities. Outside, there's plenty of grass for play, and the river. Lodging rates include a pool pass; if you're not staying over, you can use the pools for $10 adults, $7.50 ages 4 to 12, $3 ages 1 to 3. Nonguest campers can use the locker rooms and showers just to wash up for $3, 9 to 10am and the last hour of the day (8–9pm in high season). The RV park has only electric and water hookups, but there's a dump station.

**Dining:** The dining room is undersized for the resort and service can lag for breakfast or dinner; but when our meals arrived they were better than we expected. In the evening the menu included local seafood well prepared; the children enjoyed their selections, including a teddy bear pancake for breakfast. There's a deli where you can order lunch.

## Quinault Lake

**Lake Quinault Lodge.** South Shore Rd. (P.O. Box 7), Quinault, WA 98575-0007. ☎ **360/288-2900.** Fax 360/288-2901. www.visitlakequinault. com. 92 units. $100–$135 double; $10 per extra person 6 and older. AE, MC, V.

If you were making a movie, you'd choose this place for the historic Northwest resort. The big, graceful central building, roofed and sided with cedar and trimmed in white, is surrounded by old evergreens and the lake. The rooms, in various buildings, are uneven in quality, but some are quite large and welcoming. All I saw were acceptable. There are a game room and a swimming pool in a rather dark chamber. An excellent set of easy hikes through the national forest begins just across the road.

**Dining:** The lobby and **Roosevelt Room** restaurant are grand and comfortable, open three meals a day. The evening menu isn't long, but everyone should find something to order from the choices of salmon, halibut, and other regional items. Sandwiches for lunch are around $7, dinner entrees $15 to $20.

**Lake Quinault Resort.** 314 North Shore Rd., Amanda Park, WA 98526. ☎ **800/650-2362** or 360/288-2362. www.lakequinault.com. 9 units. $109–$139 double; $10 per extra person (no charge for infants). AE, DISC, MC, V.

A couple took a run-down lakefront motel and turned it into a showplace, with a broad lawn that runs down to the water from a deck with planters and wooden lawn chairs. It feels more like a bed-and-breakfast than the resort of the name, however, and you may not be able to relax with children for fear they'll mess up the Martha Stewart decoration. Several large rooms or suites are suitable for families with cooking facilities. All rooms have satellite TV, but no telephones.

## Port Angeles

**Red Lion Hotel Port Angeles.** 221 N. Lincoln St., Port Angeles, WA 98362. ☎ **800-RED-LION** reservations or 360/452-9215. Fax 360/452-4734. www.redlion.com. 187 units. $109–$139 double, $10 each additional adult; children under 18 free in parents' room. AE, DISC, MC, V.

For a family on a park tour, this is the place to stay in Port Angeles. Besides offering big rooms with upscale amenities right on the water, they make a point enhancing park visits, with ranger-led evening campfires on the beach outside, bike and sea-kayak rentals, and other activities. The location is prime, near the ferry dock, waterfront park, tide-pool aquarium (p. 529), and cool little playground, and within walking distance to downtown restaurants. A swimming pool and hot tub are next to the parking lot. Everything was perfect on our visit, and we hated to leave.

**Portside Inn.** 1510 E. Front St., Port Angeles, WA 98362. ☎ **877/438-8588** or 360/452-4015. www.portsideinn.net. 109 units. $80 double, $140 suite, children under 18 free. AE, DISC, MC, V.

On the edge of town, near Burger King, the Super 8, and other businesses along a commercial strip, this three-story stucco building contains excellent budget motel rooms. All have queen-sized beds, coffee machines, and hair dryers, and suites are large and well suited for families. There are a Laundromat and a small pool.

## Forks

**The Forks Motel.** On Hwy. 101 (P.O. Box 510), Forks, WA 98331. ☎ **800/544-3416** or 360/374-6243. Fax 360/374-6760. www.forksmotel.com. 73 units. $54–$75 double; $5 per extra person over age 12. AE, DC, DISC, MC, V.

The attractive rooms at this family-operated motel offer good value, but vary widely in size and amenities. All were very clean and well maintained when I visited, with up-to-date bathrooms even in the economy units. The eight kitchen suites, each with three queen-sized beds, rent for only $87 a night. A smallish pool is surrounded by a fence in a landscaped parking lot courtyard. There's also a good coin-op laundry.

# WHEN YOU ARRIVE

## ENTRANCE FEES

The park entrance fee is $10 per vehicle and is good for a week. It isn't collected on every road into the park, and in the winter it's hardly collected at all, although you always have to pay to enter Hurricane Ridge or the Hoh Rainforest. In the summer, fee stations also operate at Elwha, Sol Duc, and Staircase. Fees are not collected along the coast, at the Quinault Rainforest, and in other areas on small roads. National passes cover the fees (see "Passes & Fees," in chapter 1). A $1 parking fee applies at Ozette, on the western coast. The Forest Service charges trailhead parking fees, covered in the next section.

## VISITOR CENTERS
## National Park & Forest

Besides the visitor center listed below, there are two summer-only information stations where you can ask questions. **Storm King Information Station** (☎ 360/928-3380) is near Lake Crescent Lodge on the south shore of the lake, along Highway 101. **Kalaloch Information Station** (☎ 360/962-2283) is near the Kalaloch Lodge on the western shore, as Highway 101 leaves the park.

East of the park, the **Hood Canal Information Station** (☎ 360/877-5255) is north of Shelton as you approach from the direction of Seattle. It is open year-round.

Hours for each of these centers vary annually depending on park budgets.

**Olympic National Park Visitor Center.** 3002 Mt. Angeles Rd., Port Angeles (1½ miles up from town, on the way to Hurricane Ridge). ☎ 360/565-3130. Summer daily 8:30am–5:30pm; winter daily 9am–4pm.

This is the main center, where you can buy books and maps, get backcountry permits, and learn about the park's natural history. Pick up copies of exceptionally interesting natural trail guides for areas you will visit; they cost only 50¢ each. A small museum explains the biology of different park areas, and a terrific little discovery room for kids has bones, hides, puzzles, and the like. There are two trails here, the short, wheelchair-accessible **Living Forest Trail,** and the very lovely **Peabody Creek Trail.** Families should not miss this trail of less than a mile, which descends steeply from the west side of the parking among huge trees to a pair of bridges on the creek. It's a perfect introduction to the kind of beauty you come to the park for.

**Hoh Rainforest Visitor Center.** Upper Hoh Rd., Hoh Rainforest, east of Forks. ☎ **360/374-6925.** Hours vary, usually daily 9am–6pm.

The good little museum, though somewhat aged, explains the rain forest and identifies trees and plants. The area's amazing rain records are posted. Ranger programs start here, and the rangers post trail conditions for longer hikes.

**Hurricane Ridge Visitor Center.** On Hurricane Ridge, south of Port Angeles. Hours vary, generally open daily in summer, Fri–Sun winter.

This simple visitor center was scheduled for remodeling; it is in the same warm-up building as the snack bar and ski rental.

**National Park Service and U.S. Forest Service Visitor Center.** On Hwy. 101, Forks. ☎ **360/374-7566.** Hours vary, generally daily in summer, Mon–Fri winter.

The bus center in Forks houses rangers offering advice, handouts, and Forest Service permits.

## Commercial Centers

**Port Angeles Visitors Center.** 121 E. Railroad Ave. ☎ **360/452-2363.** Summer daily 7am–10pm; low season Mon–Fri 10am–4pm.

Near the ferry dock in Port Angeles, this center offers brochures on businesses all over the area and is staffed by volunteers who answer questions.

# FOR HANDY REFERENCE

**Emergencies**  Dial ☎ **911** in emergencies. Park Service dispatchers often can be reached during the day at ☎ **360/565-3120.** Ranger stations can help in an emergency, too, and they're never far from where you are; each is shown on the park map. The **Olympic Medical Center** (☎ **360/417-7000**) is at 939 Caroline St. in Port Angeles.

**Stores**  A **Safeway** supermarket is at the corner of Lincoln and Fourth streets in Port Angeles. It has a deli, and a Subway sandwich shop is across the street. In Forks, a large **Thriftway** grocery store is on Highway 101, connected to **Ace Hardware,** which has lots of outdoors supplies. Little country stores are all over the park, including at Fairholm on Crescent Lake, on the road to the Hoh Rainforest, at Kalaloch Lodge, and near Quinault Lodge on the south side of Quinault Lake.

**Banks**  The **Bank of America** at the corner of Laurel and Front streets in Port Angeles has an ATM, as do many businesses.

**Post Office**  Each little town around the peninsula has a post office. In Port Angeles, it's at 424 E. First St.

**Gear Sales & Rental**  Port Angeles has lots of places to buy outdoors equipment. Here are three just on Front Street: **Brown's Outdoor Store,** at 112 Front St. (☎ **360/457-4150**), is an excellent backpacking, camping-gear, and outdoor-clothing store; **Olympic Mountaineering,** at 140 Front St. (☎ **360/452-0240;** www.olymtn.com), specializes in backpacking and climbing and offers classes and tours; and **Sound Bikes & Kayaks,** 120 Front St. (☎ **360/457-1240;** www.soundbikeskayaks.com), rents bikes and sea kayaks. You can find limited supplies all over the park, including at **Ace Hardware,** next to the Thriftway grocery store on U.S. 101 in Forks. **Peak 6 Adventure Store,** at 4883 Upper Hoh Rd. (☎ **360/374-5254**), 5 miles from U.S. 101 on the way to the Hoh Rainforest, is an exceptional boutique outdoor store and outfitter.

---

**Forks Chamber of Commerce Visitor Center.** On Hwy. 101, at the south end of Forks. ☎ **360/374-2531.** Daily 10am–4pm.

The center is next to the town's Timber Museum.

## GETTING AROUND

The park is large, and the roads rarely go in a straight line between two points. From Sol Duc Hot Springs to the Hoh Rainforest, for example, is about 8 miles as the crow flies, 23 miles on foot, and 72 miles by car. From Port Angeles to Quinault is 128 miles of often slow driving on two-lane Highway 101. It's difficult to use a single base to see the whole park. If you have time, stay in two or three places; if your visit is short, concentrate on one part of the park and see more areas the next time you come.

## KEEPING SAFE & HEALTHY

The dampness brings a risk of hypothermia at any time of year; see "Dealing with Hazards," in chapter 1.

## Surf & Logs

The waves on the ocean beaches of the Olympic Peninsula can be incredibly powerful, picking up huge tree trunks that have washed down the rivers and smashing them repeatedly against the rocks and sand. People on the shore have been crushed by logs. Be careful climbing among the driftwood logs that pile up on the beach, which can easily shift.

## Tides

At low tide in many places on the coast, you can walk around rocky headlands that are partly underwater when the tide comes in.

Don't get trapped by the incoming tide. Hike these routes only when the tide is going out, and take paths over the top whenever you can.

Tide tables are available from the visitor centers and at many stores.

# ENJOYING THE PARK

## NATURAL PLACES
### The Western Coast

You can smell the salt spray before you get to the ocean. When you break through the last line of trees, you can see why. From the beach to the horizon, the white froth of surf is tearing the water's streaked gray surface to pieces, flinging saltwater into a powerful wind. The waves farthest from shore melt into the distance and the thick, damp air out among tiny, rocky islands sticking up from the waves, called sea stacks. On the beach, the last gasp of each wave spends itself rattling pebbles and throwing seaweed, logs, floats, shells, and puffy froth onto the beach. It's not a stormy day, but you can imagine what storms must be like here from looking at the sand, pebbles, and huge trees that storm waves have left above the beach, and even back in an eroding forest.

The violence of the sea here makes life in the tide pools and the summer visits of marine mammals along the shore even more impressive. When the tide is out, the brutal surf pulls back and leaves shelves of rock where tiny animals carry on in temporary ponds of clear, cool seawater. Ranger walks explore the tide pools daily in the summer at **Rialto Beach** and **Beach Number Four,** north of Kalaloch, but you don't need an expert to study the strange and sturdy plants and animals that have adapted to live here (see "Tide Pooling" and "Whale & Wildlife Watching," p. 529).

There are four parts to the park's more than 60 miles of coastline. The Park Service gives out a handy map and guide on two sides of a legal-sized piece of paper. The easiest section of beach to get to, and the least isolated, is the southern portion where Highway 101 runs along the bluff. Access trails descend steeply to the beach from small parking lots every few miles. Even on a crowded day at a spot like Ruby Beach, a short walk puts you on your own; we spent a memorable afternoon there building sandcastles, running from waves, and looking at little creatures. The only campgrounds and lodgings right on the sea are on this section, at Kalaloch and South Beach (see "Where to Spend the Night," p. 514), but overnight beach hiking isn't allowed here. Roads go all the way to the beach only at Rialto Beach and La Push, west of Forks on Route 110.

The rest of this coastline may be the most remote in the nation outside Alaska. The access points at Ozette, the Makah Indian Reservation, and the mouth of the Hoh River, near Oil City Road, require visitors to hike at least part of the way to get to the shoreline. The **Ozette Loop** leaves from the ranger station, follows a boardwalk trail to the beach at Cape Alava, runs along the beach to Sand Point, and returns on a trail to the ranger station. It's the most popular overnight route on the beach, and you have to reserve your permit before going to the ranger station (see p. 517). The 23-mile section from Ozette to Rialto Beach is a good, challenging backpack route.

The easiest access for families is to backpack north from **Rialto Beach,** where you can park, camp when you get tired at least a mile up the beach, and hike back the same way. Good tide pools are at the Hole-in-the-Wall Rock, a little over a mile from the parking lot. There are no quotas or reservations for that hike. Camping in the trees above the beach, you can hear the waves' constant roar and, at night, see the vague shapes of towering sea stacks against dark, swirling mists. Except for occasional scrambles over the steep, muddy trails that go over points you can't walk around, the hike is easy. These headland trails are marked with orange and black targets. The other remote coast sections, north of Ozette and from the Hoh to La Push, have more rugged beaches, trickier stream crossings, and longer and more challenging headland trails. Time your movements to avoid high tide. Tide tables are posted at trailheads, and you can get tide charts from the visitor centers.

## The Northern Coast

The national park doesn't include shoreline along the Strait of Juan de Fuca, but I would be remiss not to mention the pretty places to get down to the sea on that coast. Since it isn't exposed to waves from across the Pacific, the northern side of the Peninsula is better for marine recreation, and sea-kayaking tours go there. **Freshwater Bay County Park,** at the end of Freshwater Bay Road off Route 112, is a gentle shore, the site of kayaking tours, and a great place to find crabs, sea birds, and other creatures that prefer a muddy, low-energy environment. It is open May 15 to September 15 and has a boat ramp, a picnic area, and toilets. **Salt Creek County Park,** site of a terrific campground (p. 515), has rougher, rockier shores appealing for exploration at low tide.

## The Rain Forests

The western region of the Olympic Peninsula gets enough rain to be called rain forest, but it's in the valleys between the paws of the mountains that the moisture gets thick enough to grow strange, enchanted groves of giant trees. The ¾-mile **Hall of Mosses Nature Trail** in the Hoh Rainforest is an exquisite and dramatic example accessible to even young children. The hike is well worth it even when crowded to see and learn from vivid examples of rain-forest life that you will see again on longer, more secluded hikes. This area averages 150 inches of rain a year. Pointy sword ferns grow from the trunks of big, healthy trees. Big leaf maples stand like skeletons for communities of moss, with leaves breaking free from just the tips of their branches. The club moss hangs down from these trees in big green globs. It's an epiphyte, a kind of plant that doesn't need to touch the ground because it takes the nutrients and water for growth straight from the air. Even on sunny days, the air here is full of tiny drops of water holding even tinier dots of dirt — that's why each breath you take tastes so rich.

On the forest floor, you can see how the rain forest recycles life. When a big tree falls and its trunk begins to rot, new trees sprout there. The raised log gives the seedlings minerals they need and, by being off the ground, warmth and protection from competing plants. As the new trees grow, their roots eventually reach around the nursery tree down into the soil. In 100 years, the dead tree will rot away completely while the new trees continue to grow, seeming to stand on legs over the opening where the old log used to be. You can see nurse logs at each stage of decay in the Hoh and learn to recognize them anywhere you see them in the forest. Wherever trees are in a line, a nurse tree probably lay long ago.

The mile-long **Spruce Trail** shows a younger rain forest, closer to the Hoh River, where floods and storms have cleared out the trees from time to time. A 17.5-mile trail goes up the valley to the Blue Glacier, with long connecting trails to other areas of the park.

The other west-side rain-forest valleys you can reach by road are the **Queets and Quinault valleys.** Each has its own character. A long gravel road leads up the Queets River to a quiet campground and trailhead. You'll have it much to yourself. The Quinault Rainforest is easier for visitors, but still less crowded than the Hoh. Long Quinault Lake has park on the north side, with a campground, a ranger station, and nature trails through huge trees, and national forest on the south side, with a historic lodge and a network of trails. Farther up the valley, longer park trails branch off into the forests and mountains. Roosevelt elk are common in the Hoh,

Queets, and Quinault valleys, especially in places with low trees and brush to nibble on.

## Sol Duc Valley

Facing north instead of west, the Sol Duc valley doesn't catch enough moisture to be called a rain forest, but it's among the park's best places for a family to visit. A road leads south into the valley from U.S. 101 just west of Lake Crescent, tracing the salmon-rich Sol Duc River. At Salmon Cascades you can see silver (or coho) salmon leap upstream to their spawning grounds in August and later in the fall; other times, the Cascades are a pleasant stop on an easy walk. At the head of the valley, the river pours over a misty waterfall, and the 3.5-mile **Deer Lake Trail** leads up to the high country, one of the park's shortest routes above tree line. The Sol Duc Hot Springs are a great family swimming place; the lodge and campground there are covered on p. 519 and p. 516, respectively.

## Lake Crescent

This placid lake, surrounded by big evergreens, is on the north side of the park, west of Port Angeles on Highway 101, which goes around the south side. It makes a good center of a park visit because you can swim, fish, and paddle in the lake, yet some very inviting family hikes or bike rides are nearby. (Fishing at this writing was catch-and-release only.)

There are three main visitor areas on the lake. The best developed is on a point on the south side, site of the Lake Crescent Lodge (p. 518), where you can rent rowboats by the hour, of the Olympic Park Institute (p. 530), and of the picnic ground and boat ramp at the Storm King Information Station. From the station, the mile-long **Marymere Falls Trail** crosses under the highway and then passes through huge trees in green, mossy light, over a pair of log bridges, and up a few stairs and switchbacks to where Falls Creek pours on rock through a grove of tall trees. It's an easy family hike; if you want more of a challenge, a steep hike up Mount Storm King branches

off. The second area is the Log Cabin Resort (p. 519), on the northeast edge of the lake, which has a swimming beach and a more extensive boat-rental operation. The third area is at the west end of the lake, site of the Fairholm Campground (p. 515), which has a swimming beach and a nearby store and restaurant. Down a quiet road from here, the **Spruce Railroad Trail** runs around the north side of the lake to near the Log Cabin Resort. Made from the abandoned roadbed of a rail line built during World War I to haul out strong, light Sitka spruce for airplanes, it's a broad, level trail bordered by ferns, thickly shaded, with glimpses of the lake flashing through. Rare in the parks, mountain biking is permitted on this trail, as well as hiking.

## The Elwha River

The Elwha River runs through a narrow valley above the highway, just west of Port Angeles, into deep forest. The **Geyser Valley Loop Hike** is a mostly flat 5-mile route that starts at the end of the narrow, unpaved road that forks left from the pavement just beyond the ranger station. It's a good family day hike past abandoned cabins of early settlers, with views of the river canyon.

## Hurricane Ridge

A steep, spectacular drive 15 miles from Port Angeles leads to this area at the tree line, where subalpine forest bounds broad meadows. In the summer, the trails lead past wildflowers and sweeping views over the mountains of the peninsula, and offer a good chance to see alpine wildlife. Paved nature trails show off some of the best views near the visitor center, but summer crowds can be thick enough to spoil the experience. The paved 1.5-mile Hurricane Hill Trail, from the picnic area at the very end of the road, gets somewhat lighter use. More rugged trails lead to other, less crowded heights, but you may not feel comfortable with younger children on the steep drop-offs. Perhaps the best alternatives for longer hikes are to descend by trails to a lower

All the world's plants, trees, and seaweed, in the forests, in deserts, or floating in the ocean, from the tallest redwood to the tiniest spec of pond scum that you can see only with a microscope — all work the same way. They all use photosynthesis to catch the energy in sunlight and turn it into a solid form. Only plants and algae (which are like plants of the sea) can make light into food, but all animals need that food to live. Plants feed us, and they make the oxygen we breathe. Without photosynthesis, there would be no life on Earth.

Almost everything around us is made of atoms of a few basic elements, like oxygen, carbon, and hydrogen. They stick together to make molecules, like water or sugar. To glue atoms together into some kinds of molecules, you have to add energy, such as heat from the sun. When those molecules come apart again, dividing into atoms or smaller molecules, the energy that went into sticking them together comes out again. A corn plant, for example, takes the energy of the sun to make the sugar molecules in an ear of sweet corn. When you eat the ear of corn, your body breaks those molecules apart to get the energy back out — that's the energy that lets you live and grow. The same thing happens when a tree stores the sun's energy in its wood, which is made of sugar and other molecules that the tree makes from sugar. A fire burns the wood the way your body burns the corn, breaking up the molecules and releasing the energy the sunlight put in to make them. In a wood fire, it comes out as heat and light.

For photosynthesis to happen, plants need light, water, and a gas in the air called carbon dioxide. Carbon dioxide molecules are made of carbon and oxygen. Water is a molecule made of hydrogen and oxygen. Chemists use letters and numbers to stand for these atomic elements because they make it easier to understand how the molecules break apart or add together. (This may be easier to understand if you write it out on a piece of paper.) Hydrogen is H, oxygen is O, and carbon is C. Water is $H_2O$, or two atoms of hydrogen and one of oxygen. Carbon dioxide is $CO_2$, or one carbon and two oxygen. Adding up the atoms, water and carbon dioxide have one C, two H, and three O atoms between them. That's almost the same as sugar, which is $CH_2O$, or one C, two H and one O

---

point on the road or into the Elwah Valley, but for such one-way hikes you need transportation at the other end. In the winter, Hurricane Ridge is a small skiing area with a rope tow, and good for sledding (see p. 525); it is open and the road plowed of snow only Friday through Sunday. There are a visitor center and a snack bar.

## PLACES FOR LEARNING

With our enthusiasm for tide pooling, we greatly enjoyed the **Arthur D. Feiro Marine Biology Laboratory,** at the waterfront at the north end of Lincoln Street in Port Angeles (☎ **360/417-6254;** www.olypen.com/feiro-lab). It's just one room, but they have several touch tanks containing tide-pool specimens of prodigious size and a few aquariums of local marine life. Volunteers engage kids, letting

them touch creatures you may not be lucky enough to find in the wild. They're open Memorial Day to mid-September Tuesday through Sunday, 10am to 6pm, and off-season Saturday and Sunday noon to 4pm. Admission is $2.50 adults, $1 ages 6 to 12.

## ACTIVITIES
### Backpacking

Trails cross the Olympics from each of the valleys around the mountains' edges, offering an extraordinary choice of long-haul backpacking trips. You can rise from rain forest to alpine terrain and big blue glaciers and descend on the other side back down to the forest. I put on my pack and hiked on the coast. When I woke up in the night, I could hear the roar of the waves smashing against sea stacks; outside, the driftwood logs glowed like bones in the dim mist.

atom. Two O atoms are left over. With the energy of the sun, the water and carbon dioxide do add together, and make sugar with a two-atom oxygen molecule left over. That oxygen molecule, which is the same as the oxygen we breathe, floats off the plant back into the air.

To get the energy back out of the sugar, you need to turn it into water and carbon dioxide again. To do that, you have to add an oxygen molecule to replace the one that floated off the plant. That's why you breathe. Your lungs draw in oxygen ($O_2$), and your body puts it together with sugar ($CH_2O$), to release the energy in the sugar. That makes water ($H_2O$) and carbon dioxide ($CO_2$), which you breathe out again. Fire works the same way: It takes in oxygen, and it puts out carbon dioxide. The carbon dioxide from your breath or your campfire floats around until it runs into a plant that makes it into oxygen and sugar again.

All the plants and animals on Earth are passing oxygen, carbon dioxide, and water back and forth. At the rate that living things on Earth use oxygen, it would run out in a few thousand years if plants didn't keep making it. The carbon dioxide would run out even quicker — in a few hundred years — if animals, plants, and fires weren't burning sugar and breaking it up into carbon dioxide and water. Through this carbon cycle, all living things on earth are related and working together. Animals make carbon dioxide for plants, and plants make oxygen for animals.

Look around you and see if you can find things made by photosynthesis. Sugar is only the first step in plants. They turn sugar and soil into many other materials, including starch and fiber. Wood and all the things we make it into — paper, cardboard, fabric — come from photosynthesis, and so does the cotton in your clothes. Photosynthesis made the plants that sank to the bottom of the ocean and got pressed together into coal and oil. We use coal and oil for gasoline and to make plastic and the nylon in your clothing and carpets. Your food comes from photosynthesis, even the meat — it has the energy an animal got from eating a plant, and the plant got that energy from photosynthesis. And you — you're made of the food you eat and the air you breathe. Plants used photosynthesis to put together the water, carbon dioxide, and sunlight to make you.

The challenges of backpacking here are the dampness and the long, rugged routes. Rain and fog can test your gear and patience, and fires are just about impossible to light. Most trails cover large distances, and it's easy to overestimate what your family can manage. On the other hand, you don't have to go far to find a campsite. You will need a permit and gear to store your food against black bear and, on the coast, raccoons; see "Backcountry Camping Permits" (p. 517). Trail maps and guide books are covered under "Reading Up" (p. 512).

If you choose to do a multiple-day hike using different trailheads and have only one car, a backpacker trailhead shuttle is available from **Olympic Tours & Charters** (☎ **866-764-3946** or 360/452-3858; www.tourtheolympics.com).

## Fishing

Salmon and trout fishing are a major draw to the Olympic Peninsula. Knowing when and where the fish are running is critical to success. Moreover, the regulations are complex and state and park regulations overlap on the same lands. You can get all the regulations from the park or its website (under "Search" enter "Olympic and fishing"). There are lots of guides and places to get gear in the area; ask for referrals at the town visitor centers (see "Olympic Address Book," p. 506).

## Hiking

The trails and beaches of Olympic National Park offer solitude and stirring beauty, and you can't really appreciate the park without walking some of them. I've mentioned some favorites in the Hoh Rainforest, in the Sol

Duc and Elwha valleys, at Lake Crescent and Hurricane Ridge, and along the western and northern shores, under "Natural Places" (p. 523), and in the descriptions of the Heart O' the Hills and Graves Creek campgrounds (p. 515), and at the Olympic National Park Visitor Center in Port Angeles (p. 521). But I've only scratched the surface. Great hikes lead from every park area, almost anywhere you find yourself, many starting at the ends of remote dirt roads and other out-of-the-way places on the way to real wilderness.

The Park Service hands out informative lists and descriptions of dozens of trails all over the park. See "Reading Up" (p. 512) for resources with more detail. One drawback to consider in planning your route is that there are few day-hike loops except the easy nature trails. Most trails are long, requiring you to hike a few miles and then double back. Set a realistic goal. Trails in the rain forest can be muddy, so prepare with extra shoes, socks, and pants, as well as rain gear.

## PLACES FOR RELAXED PLAY & PICNICS

Most picnic areas are marked on the park map. Four picnic grounds are around **Lake Crescent,** including one at the Storm King Information Station. Picnic tables are at the main park visitor center in Port Angeles, Hurricane Ridge, Elwha Campground, Ozette and Rialto beaches, and the Hoh Rainforest Visitor Center, among other places.

You can play almost anywhere in the park where there are lawns, beaches, and forests. Playgrounds with equipment in Port Angeles are on the waterfront at the end of **Lincoln Street,** and on the way to the park visitor center in a large park on **Race Street** between First and Second streets. Public rest rooms are near both playgrounds. In Forks, a large playground in **Tillicum Park** is at the north end of town on Highway 101.

## Mountain Biking

In the park, Spruce Railroad Trail around the north side of Crescent Lake (see "Lake Crescent," p. 525) is open to biking. Olympic National Forest has more mountain-bike trails. Bikes are for rent by **Sound Bikes & Kayaks,** 120 E. Front St., Port Angeles (☎ **360/457-1240;** www.soundbikeskayaks.com).

## Rafting

Concessionaires offer rafting on the Elwha and Hoh rivers, both fairly gentle floats with mild white water and forest scenery. Children can go along. **Olympic Raft and Kayak, 123 Lake Aldwell Rd.,** Port Angeles (☎ **888/452-1443** or 360/452-1443; www.raftandkayak.com), has daily summer trips on each river for $49 per person, $39 for children under 12.

## Sea Kayaking

The park's coastal waters are too rough for sea kayaking, but guided outings do go to lakes in the park and the more protected ocean waters of the Strait of Juan de Fuca, where you have a good chance of seeing sea birds, sea lions, and other marine mammals. **Olympic Raft and Kayak** (see "Rafting," above) offers several daily trips in the summer to Freshwater Bay (see "The Northern Coast," p. 524), just west of Port Angeles, and on Crescent Lake and the dam-filled Lake Aldwell, on the Elwha River. The trips last 2 to 4 hours, and cost $42 to $99 per person. They also rent kayaks and canoes.

## Swimming

We enjoyed splashing around in Lake Crescent at the Log Cabin Resort, and you can also swim at Lake Crescent Lodge, East Beach Picnic Area, and Fairholm Campground. There are no lifeguards. The water wasn't warm in mid-July, but it was refreshing and fun. Swimming in **Ozette Lake** and **Quinault Lake** is informal, from docks or a place you choose on the shore.

## Tide Pooling

The western coastal strip has shores of sand, pebbles, cobbles, boulders, and bedrock. For tide pooling, the easiest places are bedrock shelves that extend out flat near the low-tide line, where water collects in little ponds. These shelves can occur on any kind of shoreline, but they're most frequent near rock headlands. Muddy shores without much wave energy are good, too, such as Freshwater Bay (see "The Northern Coast," p. 524). Generally, you can find good tide pooling at **Beach Four,** north of Kalaloch on Highway 101, and at **Rialto Beach,** west of Forks, where rangers lead daily low-tide walks. Times are listed in the park newspaper, the *Bugler*. But you don't need someone to show you the way, and many other places are also promising; the fun of tide pooling is relaxed exploration and discovery. Ask at a visitor center for directions and consult a tide chart — the lower the tide, the more you'll see. Go out at least an hour before low tide and see what you find. A hand lens and field guide add another level of fascination. Inexpensive tide-pool identification booklets are available at visitor centers.

Turn over rocks to see what's under them, pick up mobile creatures with shells, and catch tiny fish in a bucket; but put them all back exactly where they were. Be gentle. Don't step on plants or animals if you can help it, don't pry or force anything, and try to preserve every life. Protect your own life too: Know what time the tide will change, and keep an eye on your watch so that it doesn't sneak up on you. Don't walk on slippery rocks over water, and keep your children nearby.

## Whale & Wildlife Watching

High places along the coast are the best spots to watch migrating whales and to see sea lions, seals, and sea otters that come to the ocean shore in the summer to feed. The visitor centers have a newsprint guide to the Olympic Coast National Marine Sanctuary, an ocean area that protects the waters off the park's coastline and a bit north and south. Gray whales pass by the peninsula on their way north from Mexico to Alaska starting in March and April, and go back in the winter. With patience and binoculars, you can see them from high places all along the coast, including **Kalaloch,** the parking lots on Highway 101 above **Beach Four** and **Beach Six,** and **Cape Flattery,** at the tip of the peninsula in the Makah Indian Reservation.

Other marine mammals use the shore in the spring, summer, and fall. Seeing them is never a sure thing, and you may need a spotting scope to get a good look. Harbor seals show up all along the shore. Seeing sea lions and sea otters may require a hike that's beyond the range of young children, and if your goal is to see them and you don't — a significant possibility — disappointment will follow. It's better to just take the hike and count the sightings as a bonus. **Cape Alava,** a 3.3-mile hike from the Ozette Ranger Station, looks out on islands where sea lions haul out and where sea otters show up in the floating kelp beds. Both also may be seen off **Cape Flattery.** The beach south from **Third Beach,** off La Push Road, may have sea lions and seals. Sea otters could also be in the kelp off **Cape Johnson,** about 3.7 miles north of Rialto Beach, which is accessible by beach at low tide.

## Winter Sports: Skiing, Snowshoeing & Sledding

Most places you can get to by road in Olympic National Park receive little snow, but Hurricane Ridge gets more than 30 feet a year. Ski season lasts from late December to March. A local club operates a couple of rope tows and a Poma lift on a small ski area, only about 70 acres with a vertical rise of 665 feet. A full-day pass is $15; call ☎ 360/417-4555 for information. There are also more than 20 miles of ungroomed cross-country ski routes, most of them hilly, and some good for Telemark skiing. Rangers lead snowshoe walks in the winter, and there's an area for sledding. A desk in the bottom floor of the visitor center rents gear at reasonable prices. Snowstorms and other factors permitting, the area is open on weekends in the winter; on weekdays, a gate generally blocks the road well below the area of heavy snow except Friday through Sunday 9am to 4pm. Call the recording at ☎ 360/565-3131 to check on conditions.

## PROGRAMS
### Children's Programs
The Northwest Interpretive Association produces a meaningful workbook of nature activities for kids. Children who finish the workbook, attend a ranger-led program, and go for a hike earn a **Junior Ranger** badge. The booklet costs $1 at the visitor centers, and children as young as 5 will be able to do it, with help. Don't get into it unless you have time to devote. If children are going to learn the answers to the questions in the booklet on their own, a visit of at least a couple days is required.

### Family & Adult Programs
Ranger programs take place at many sites around the park, including Heart O' the Hills

campground, Hurricane Ridge, Lake Crescent, the Hoh Rainforest Visitor Center, Rialto Beach, and Kalaloch. The Forest Service offers programs at the Lake Quinault Lodge. Times and topics for park programs are listed in the park newspaper, the *Bugler*. Occasionally, programs target families with children; more often, the walks and talks are for adults, but are open and enjoyable to children. See "Camping" (p. 514) for which campgrounds have evening campfire programs.

Consider spending a few days of your trip learning intensively about the park. The **Olympic Park Institute,** 111 Barnes Point Rd., Port Angeles, WA 98363 (☎ 360/928-3720; www.yni.org/opi), offers seminars from May to mid-October, with many choices in July and August, including several for families with children. Most programs last a full weekend. A typical tide-pool session was $165 adults, $105 children, including 2 nights and six meals at the institute's campus on Lake Crescent. Reserve well ahead. The catalog is on the website.

# WHERE TO EAT

## PORT ANGELES
### Low-Stress Meals
Port Angeles has many various fast-food franchises, mostly found on the east side of town along Highway 101. Some healthier and more memorable places are downtown. **Bonny's Bakery** (☎ 360/457-3585), in an old brick firehouse at 215 S. Lincoln St., serves hearty sandwiches and soups as well as treats. You can eat in a light dining room or at picnic tables outside. It's open Monday through Friday 7:30am to 4pm, Saturday 8am to 3pm. **La Casita** (☎ 360/452-2289), at 203 E. Front St., is a small, friendly family restaurant in a storefront right downtown, with large portions of good food inexpensively priced. A big dinner costs $6.50 to $14.50, with most items

under $10. Year-round hours are at least Monday through Saturday 11am to 9pm, Sunday noon to 9pm, but they stay open until 10 or 11pm in summer.

### Best-Behavior Meals
**Bella Italia.** 117-B E. First St., Port Angeles. ☎ 360/457-5442. www.northolympic.com/bella. Dinner $8–$20. Sun–Thurs 4–9pm, Fri–Sat 4–10pm.

This surprisingly sophisticated southern Italian restaurant hides in the basement of a health-food store. The dining room is charming and intimate, and the service highly professional. The cuisine shows signs of successful experimentation using fresh local seafood in traditional themes — Dungeness crab or smoked salmon ravioli, for example. The proprietor, Neil Conklin, emerges from the kitchen periodically to strike up conversations with guests. The "bambini" menu is exceptional, too.

**Chesnut Cottage Restaurant.** 929 E. Front St., Port Angeles. ☎ **360/452-8344.** Breakfast $5.50–$8.75, lunch $6.50–$10. Daily 7am–3pm.

Great for breakfast, this place makes a point of serving families well, but it's as far from the typical diner as can be, with elaborate country and Victorian decor in a custom-made brick building with high ceilings. Considering the fancy surroundings, prices are quite low for the rich meals. Kids' menu items are cute, fun, and inexpensive.

## IN THE PARK

Away from Port Angeles, the best places to eat are at the park hotels; otherwise, it's greasy-spoon fare.